American Government

POWER AND PURPOSE
2010 ELECTION UPDATE

BRIEF ELEVENTH EDITION
2010 ELECTION UPDATE

American Government

POWER AND PURPOSE

Theodore J. Lowi
CORNELL UNIVERSITY

Benjamin Ginsberg
THE JOHNS HOPKINS UNIVERSITY

Kenneth A. Shepsle
HARVARD UNIVERSITY

Stephen Ansolabehere
HARVARD UNIVERSITY

W. W. NORTON & COMPANY
NEW YORK • LONDON

W. W. Norton & Company has been independent since its founding in 1923, when William Warder Norton and Mary D. Herter Norton first published lectures delivered at the People's Institute, the adult education division of New York City's Cooper Union. The firm soon expanded its program beyond the Institute, publishing books by celebrated academics from America and abroad. By mid-century, the two major pillars of Norton's publishing program—trade books and college texts—were firmly established. In the 1950s, the Norton family transferred control of the company to its employees, and today—with a staff of four hundred and a comparable number of trade, college, and professional titles published each year—W. W. Norton & Company stands as the largest and oldest publishing house owned wholly by its employees.

Illustrations: p. 164, Library of Congress; p. 440, The Granger Collection, NY.
Editor: Ann Shin
Assistant editor: Jake Schindel
Project editor: Kate Feighery
Design director: Rubina Yeh
Production manager: Christine D'Antonio
E-media editor: Dan Jost
Manuscript editor: Barbara Curialle
Graphic artist: John McAusland
Composition: TexTech, Inc.
Manufacturing: Worldcolor, Taunton

ISBN 978-0-393-11821-6 (pbk.)

W. W. Norton & Company, Inc.,
500 Fifth Avenue, New York, N.Y. 10110
www.wwnorton.com

W. W. Norton & Company Ltd.,
Castle House, 75/76 Wells Street, London W1T 3QT
1 2 3 4 5 6 7 8 9 0

Contents

7 The Executive Branch   187

8 The Federal Courts 218

PART 3 DEMOCRATIC POLITICS

9 Public Opinion and the Media 252

APPENDIX

Preface

This book was written for faculty and students who are looking for a little more than just "nuts and bolts" and who are drawn to an analytical perspective—but who also prefer a brief format text. No fact about American government is intrinsically difficult to grasp, and in an open society such as ours, facts abound. The philosophy of a free and open media in the United States makes information about the government readily available. The advent of the Internet and new communication technologies have further expanded the opportunity to learn about our government. The ubiquity of information in our society is a great virtue. Common knowledge about the government gives our society a vocabulary that is widely shared, and enables us to communicate effectively with each other about politics. But it is also important to reach beyond that common vocabulary and develop a more sophisticated understanding of politics and government. The sheer quantity of facts in our society overwhelms us at times. In a 24/7 news cycle it can be hard to pick out what stories are important and to stay focused on them. The single most important task of the teacher of political science is to confront popular ideas and to choose from among them the small number of really significant concepts that help us make better sense of the world. This book aims to help instructors and students accomplish this task.

This Brief Eleventh Edition represents a major revision of the text. Those who have used the book in the past know that we have always emphasized the role of American political institutions. We have not strayed from this emphasis. In this new edition, we have both sharpened our analytical focus and made it more teachable. We have explained the ways in which institutions mediate the expression and impact of popular preferences on governmental action. In every chapter we encourage students to think critically and analytically about how well the institutions discussed in that chapter serve the goals of a democratic society.

Though our approach remains institutional, Part 3 of the book has been thoroughly revised to provide a more current and integrated treatment of mass political behavior. Chapter 9 (Public Opinion and the Media) has been rewritten to present an up-to-date account of what motivates people's political preferences—and to set up a more unified discussion of political behavior in the chapters that follow. The chapter includes new sections on how today's media—including new media—influence public opinion, and on the debate over how polarized America really is. Chapter 10 on elections has also been rewritten for this new edition. It highlights how the design of our electoral institutions and laws affects the ways in which citizens' preferences are (or are not) reflected in government. The new section on how voters decide takes full account of recent research, providing a more nuanced perspective on voter knowledge in particular. Similarly, the other chapters in Part 3, on parties and interest groups, have been deeply revised.

The 2008 elections and the Obama presidency represent a dramatic change in our politics. The Obama and McCain campaigns of 2008 inspired a new generation of voters; they brought many new voters to politics and many older but discouraged voters back in. Turnout hit its highest point since the 1964 election. Shifts in public opinion about the government since 2004 have altered the political terrain in the United States, and the changed communication environment in the country has eroded traditional media, especially print media. The 2006 and 2008 elections altered control of Congress, from a Republican majority to a Democratic majority sufficiently large to prevent a partisan filibuster in the Senate. Throughout this Eleventh Edition, particular attention has been given to these changes.

Other major changes and key features of this Eleventh Edition include:

- **"Analyzing the Evidence"** units in every chapter take a closer look at how political scientists analyze data (both quantitative and qualitative) to understand some political phenomenon discussed in the chapter. These two-page spreads use strong graphics to help students see how we know what we know about a specific topic. A new primer on "Analyzing the Evidence" has been added to Chapter 1, to offer the student guidance on how to understand a graph, table, or chart, and how to use data to draw conclusions.

- **"Core of the Analysis"** outlines at the start of each chapter preview the main points of the chapter.

- Within the chapter, **"In Brief"** boxes summarize fundamental material and have proven invaluable to students in preparing for exams, according to reviewers.

- **Key terms** are defined in the adjacent margin, as well as in the glossary.

ACKNOWLEDGMENTS

Our students at Cornell, Johns Hopkins, and Harvard have been an essential factor in the writing of this book. They have been our most immediate intellectual community, a hospitable one indeed. Another part of our community, perhaps a large suburb, is the discipline of political science itself. Our debt to the scholarship of our colleagues is scientifically measurable, probably to several decimal points, in the footnotes and Further Readings sections of each chapter. Despite many complaints that the field is too scientific or not scientific enough, political science is alive and well in the United States. It is an aspect of democracy itself, and it has grown and changed in response to the developments in government and politics that we have chronicled in our book.

We are pleased to acknowledge our debt to the many colleagues who had a direct and active role in criticism and preparation of the manuscript. In drafting previous editions, we relied heavily on the thoughtful reviews we received from David Canon, University of Wisconsin; Russell Hanson, Indiana, University; William Keech, University of North Carolina; Donald Kettl, University of Wisconsin; Anne Khademian, University of Wisconsin; William McLauchlan, Purdue University; J. Roger Baker, Wittenburg University; James Lennertz, Lafayette College; Allan McBride, Grambling State University; Joseph Peek Jr., Georgia State University; Douglas Costain, University of Colorado; Robert Hoffert, Colorado State University; David Marcum, University of Wyoming; Mark Silverstein, Boston University; and Norman Thomas, University of Cincinnati. The following reviewers provided feedback that guided our revisions for this tenth edition: Andrew Battista, East Tennessee State University; Timothy Boylan, Winthrop University; Terri Fine, University of Central Florida; Samuel Hoff, Delaware State University; Marilyn Hoskin, University of New Hampshire; Richard Johnson, Oklahoma City University; Mark Joslyn, University of Kansas-Lawrence; Stephanie Slocum-Schaffer, Shepherd University; Katy Stenger, Gustavus Adolphus College; and Robert Watson, Florida Atlantic University.

For their advice on the Eleventh Edition, we thank Scott Ainsworth, University of Georgia; Bethany Albertson, University of Washington; Brian Arbour, John Jay College; James Battista, University at Buffalo, State University of New York; Lawrence Becker, California State University, Northridge; Damon Cann, Utah State University; Jamie Carson, University of Georgia; Suzanne Chod, Pennsylvania State University; Michael Crespin, University of Georgia; Ryan Emenaker, College of the Redwoods; Kevin Esterling, University of California—Riverside; Brad Gomez, Florida State University; Sanford Gordon, New York University; Christian Grose, Vanderbilt University; James Hanley, Adrian College; Ryan Hurl, University of Toronto; Josh Kaplan, University of Notre Dame; Wendy Martinek, Binghamton University; Will Miller, Southeast Missouri State University; Evan Parker-Stephen, Texas A&M University; Melody Rose, Portland State University; Eric Schickler, University of California—Berkeley; John Sides, George Washington University; Lynn Vavreck, University of California—Los Angeles.

An important contribution to the Eleventh Edition was made by the authors of the "Analyzing the Evidence" units. Jamie Carson of the University of Georgia authored the "Analyzing the Evidence" spreads for Chapters 2, 3, 5, 6, 7, 8, and 10. Andrea Campbell of MIT contributed the "Analyzing the Evidence" section for Chapter 9. And Kevin Esterling of the University of California—Riverside revised the section in Chapter 11. We thank the three of them for their excellent contributions to the book.

This Election Update Edition includes two substantial new sections, one on the first two years of the Obama presidency and one on the 2010 elections. For their extensive help in developing these new sections, we wish to thank Joseph Williams and Eitan Hersh.

Perhaps above all, we wish to thank those who kept the production and all the loose ends of the book coherent and in focus. Ann Shin has been an extremely talented editor, continuing to offer numerous suggestions for each new edition. Jake Schindel helped keep track of the many details. Kathleen Feighery has been a superb project editor, following the great tradition of her predecessors. Christine D'Antonio has been an efficient production manager.

We are more than happy, however, to absolve all these contributors from any flaws, errors, and misjudgments that will inevitably be discovered. From that standpoint, a book ought to try to be perfect. But substantively we have not tried to write a flawless book; we have not tried to write a book to please everyone. We have again tried to write an effective book, a book that cannot be taken lightly. Our goal was to restore politics as a subject matter of vigorous and enjoyable discourse, recapturing it from the bondage of the thirty-second sound bite and the thirty-page technical briefing. Every person can be knowledgeable because everything about politics is accessible. One does not have to be a television anchor to profit from political events. One does not have to be a philosopher to argue about the requisites of democracy, a lawyer to dispute constitutional interpretations, an economist to debate a public policy. We would be very proud if our book contributes in a small way to the restoration of the ancient art of political controversy.

Theodore J. Lowi
Benjamin Ginsberg
Kenneth A. Shepsle
Stephen Ansolabehere

American Government

POWER AND PURPOSE
2010 ELECTION UPDATE

Introduction: Making Sense of Government and Politics

1

HOW DOES AMERICAN GOVERNMENT WORK?

American government and politics are extraordinarily complex. The United States has many levels of government: federal, state, county, city and town—to say nothing of a host of special and regional authorities. Each of these governments operates under its own rules and statutory authority and is related to the others in complex ways. Each level of government, moreover, consists of an array of departments, agencies, offices, and bureaus undertaking a variety of sometimes overlapping tasks. Sometimes this complexity gets in the way of effective governance, as in the case of governmental response to emergencies. America's federal, state, and local public safety agencies seldom share information and frequently use incompatible communications equipment, so they are often not even able to speak to one another. For example, on September 11, 2001, New York City's police and fire departments could not effectively coordinate their responses to the terrorist attack on the World Trade Center because their communications systems were not linked.

The complexity of America's government is no accident. Complexity was one element of the Founders' grand constitutional design. The framers of the Constitution hoped that an elaborate division of power among institutions and between the states and the federal government would allow a variety of competing groups, forces, interests, and ideas to have a voice in public affairs—while preventing any single group or coalition from monopolizing power. One set of interests might be active and powerful in some states, other forces would be influential in the national legislature, and still other groups might prevail in the executive branch. The overall pattern would disperse power and opportunity, allowing many groups to achieve at least some of their political goals. In this way, America's political tradition associates complexity with liberty and political opportunity.

But although America's institutional complexity may create many avenues and possibilities for political action, this complexity also places a considerable burden on citizens who might wish to achieve something through political participation. They may not easily discern where particular policies are actually made, who the influential decision makers are, and what forms of political participation are most likely to be effective. This is one of the paradoxes of political life: In a dictatorship, lines of political authority may be simple, but opportunities to influence the use of power are few; in America, political opportunities are plentiful, but how they should be used is far from obvious. Indeed, precisely because America's institutional and political arrangements are so complex, many Americans are mystified by government. As we shall see in Chapter 9, most Americans have difficulty making sense of even the basic features of the Constitution.

If America's government seems complex, its politics can be utterly bewildering. Like the nation's governmental structure, its political processes have numerous components. For most Americans, the focal point of U.S. politics is the electoral process. As we will see in Chapter 10, tens of millions of Americans participate in a host of national, state, and local elections in which they listen to thousands of candidates debate what may seem to be a perplexing array of issues. Candidates fill the air with promises, charges, and countercharges, while an army of pundits and journalists, which we will discuss in Chapter 9, adds its own clamor to the din.

Politics, however, does not end on Election Day. Indeed, given the growing tendency of losers to challenge election results in the courts, even elections do not end on Election Day. Long after the voters have spoken, political struggles continue in the Congress, the executive branch, and the courts and embroil political parties, interest groups, and the mass media. In some instances, the participants in political struggles and their goals seem fairly obvious. For example, it is no secret that business groups and upper-income wage earners strongly support programs of tax reduction; farmers support maintenance of agricultural price supports; labor unions oppose "outsourcing" of production. Each of these forces has created or joined organized groups to advance its cause. We will examine some of these groups in Chapter 12.

In other instances, though, the participants in political struggles and their goals are not so clear. Sometimes corporate groups hide behind environmental causes to promote economic interests surreptitiously. Sometimes groups claiming to want to help the poor and downtrodden seek only to help themselves. And to make matters worse, many of the government's policies are made behind closed doors, away from the light of publicity. Ordinary citizens can hardly be blamed for failing to understand bureaucratic rule making and other obscure techniques of government.

MAKING SENSE OF GOVERNMENT AND POLITICS

Can we find order in the apparent chaos of politics? The answer is that we can, and that is precisely the purpose of our text. It should be noted before we begin that "finding order in the apparent chaos of politics" is precisely what political scientists do. The discipline of political science, and especially the study of American politics, is devoted to identifying patterns and regularities in all the noise and maneuvering of everyday political life. This is motivated by two fundamental questions: What do we observe? And why?

The first question makes clear that political science is an *empirical* enterprise. By this we mean that it is ultimately interested in identifying facts and patterns that are true in the world around us. What do voters decide when they enter the polling booth? What strategies and tactics do candidates employ to capture votes? What decisions do legislators make about how to vote on bills? What groups organize and put pressure on the institutions of government? How do the media report politics? What tools are available to the president to get what he wants in dealing with Congress (legislative-executive relations)? How have courts intervened in regulating political life? And how do they come to the decisions they have made (judicial politics)? These and many other questions have been explored by political science in an effort to ascertain what is true about the political world, and will be taken up in more detail in later chapters.

The second question is fundamental to any science. We not only would like to know *that* something is true about the world. We also want to know *why* it is true. Knowing why something is true requires us to create in our minds a theory of how the world works. In this way we not only describe politics, we *analyze* it. One of the most important purposes of this book is to provide concepts and tools to help readers critically analyze what they observe in politics and government. In this chapter, we shall offer a number of concepts that we hope will clarify why American government works the way it does. We will conclude with a brief guide to analyzing evidence related to the ways these concepts play out in the American political system.

Forms of Government

Government is the term generally used to describe the formal political arrangements by which a land and its people are ruled. Government is composed of institutions and processes that rulers establish to strengthen and perpetuate their power or control over a territory and its inhabitants. A government may be as simple as a

autocracy A form of government in which a single individual—a monarch or dictator—rules.

oligarchy A form of government in which a small group—landowners, military officers, or wealthy merchants—controls most of the governing decisions.

democracy A system of rule that permits citizens to play a significant part in the governmental process, usually through the election of key public officials.

constitutional government A system of rule in which formal and effective limits are placed on the powers of the government.

authoritarian government A system of rule in which the government recognizes no formal limits but may, nevertheless, be restrained by the power of other social institutions.

totalitarian government A system of rule in which the government recognizes no formal limits on its power and seeks to absorb or eliminate other social institutions that might challenge it.

coercion Forcing a person to do something by threats or pressure.

tribal council that meets occasionally to advise the chief, or as complex as our own vast establishment with its forms, rules, governmental bodies, and bureaucracies. Governments vary in their structure, in their size, and in the way they operate. Two questions are of special importance in determining how governments differ from one another: Who governs? How much government control is permitted?

In some nations, political authority is vested in a single individual. This is called **autocracy**. When a small group of landowners, military officers, or wealthy merchants control most of the governing decisions, that government is an **oligarchy**. If many people participate, and if the populace is deemed to have some influence over the leaders' actions, that government is tending toward **democracy**.

Governments also vary considerably in how they govern. In the United States and a small number of other nations, governments are severely limited by law as to what they are permitted to control (substantive limits), as well as how they go about it (procedural limits). Governments that are so limited are called **constitutional**, or liberal, governments. In other nations, including many in Europe, South America, Asia, and Africa, political and social institutions that the government is unable to control—such as an organized church, organized business groups, or organized labor unions—may help keep the government in check, but the law imposes few real limits. Such governments are called **authoritarian**. In a third group of nations, including the Soviet Union under Joseph Stalin, governments not only are free of legal limits but seek to eliminate those organized social groupings or institutions that might challenge or limit their authority. Because these governments typically attempt to dominate every sphere of political, economic, and social life, they are called **totalitarian**.

Foundations of Government

Whatever their makeup, governments historically have included two basic components: a means of coercion, such as an army or police force, and a means of collecting revenue. Some governments, including many in the less developed nations today, have consisted of little more than an army and a tax-collecting agency. Other governments, especially those in the developed nations such as the United States, attempt to provide services as well as to collect taxes in order to secure popular consent for control. For some, power is an end in itself. For most, power is necessary to maintain public order.

The Means of Coercion. Government must have the powers to get people to obey its laws and punish them if they do not. **Coercion** takes many forms, and each year millions of Americans are subject to one form of government coercion or another. One aspect of coercion is conscription, whereby the government requires certain involuntary services of citizens. The best-known example of conscription is military conscription, which is called "the draft." Although there has been no draft since 1974, there were drafts during the Civil War, World War I, World War II, the postwar period, and the wars in Korea and Vietnam. With these drafts, the American government compelled millions of men to serve in the armed forces; one-half million of these soldiers made the ultimate contribution by giving their lives in their nation's service. If the need arose, military conscription would probably be reinstituted.

Power in Constitutional, Authoritarian, and Totalitarian Governments

Constitutional Governments

Scope: power prescribed by a constitution.

Limits: society can challenge government when it oversteps constitutional boundaries.

Examples: United States, France, Japan.

Authoritarian Governments

Scope: answer only to a small number of powerful groups.

Limits: recognize few obligations to limit actions, whether or not such obligations exist.

Examples: Spain from the 1930s to the 1970s (under General Francisco Franco) and Russia today.

Totalitarian Governments

Scope: government encompasses all important social institutions.

Limits: rivals for power are not tolerated.

Examples: Germany's Third Reich in the 1930s and 1940s (under Adolf Hitler), the Soviet Union from the 1930s through the 1950s (under Joseph Stalin), and North Korea today.

Eighteen-year-old men are required to register today, just in case. American citizens can also, by law, be compelled to serve on juries; to appear before legal tribunals when summoned; to file a great variety of official reports, including income tax returns; and to attend school or to send their children to school. Government also has the power to punish those who do not obey its laws.

The Means of Collecting Revenue.　Each year American governments on every level collect enormous sums from their citizens to support their institutions and programs. Taxation has grown steadily over the years. In 2009, the national government alone collected $1 trillion in individual income taxes, $262 billion in corporate income taxes, $774 billion in social insurance taxes, $82 billion in excise, estate, and gift taxes, and another $67 billion in customs duties. The grand total amounted to more than $2 trillion, or almost $6,500 from every living soul in the United States. But not everyone benefits equally from programs paid for by their tax dollars. One of the perennial issues in American politics is the distribution of tax burdens versus the distribution of program benefits. Every group would like more of the benefits while passing more of the burdens of taxation on to others.

Why Is Government Necessary?

As we have just seen, control is the basis for government. But what forms of government control are justifiable? To answer this question, we begin by examining the ways in which government makes it possible for people to live together.

To Maintain Order. Human beings usually do not venture out of their caves (or the modern counterpart) unless there is a reasonable probability that they can return safely. But for people to live together peacefully, law and order are required, the institutionalization of which is called government. From the standpoint of this definition, the primary purpose of government is to maintain order. But order can come about only by controlling a territory and its people. This may sound like a threat to freedom until you ponder the absence of government, or anarchy—the absence of rule. According to Thomas Hobbes (1558–1679), the author of *Leviathan*, anarchy is even worse than the potential tyranny of government because anarchy, or life outside "the state," is characterized by "continual fear, and danger of violent death . . . [where life is] solitary, poor, nasty, brutish and short."[1] Governmental power can be a threat to freedom, yet we need government to maintain order so that we can enjoy our freedom.

To Protect Property. After safety of persons comes security of a person's labor, which we call property, or private property. Protection of property is almost universally recognized as a justifiable function of government. John Locke (1632–1704), the worthy successor to Hobbes, was the first to assert clearly that whatever we have removed from nature and also mixed our labor with is considered our property. But even Locke recognized that although the right to own what we have produced by our own labor is absolute, it means nothing if someone with greater power than ours decides to take it or trespass on it.

So something we call our own is ours only as long as the laws against trespass improve the probability that we can enjoy it, use it, consume it, trade it, or sell it. In reality, then, property can be defined as all the laws against trespass that permit us not only to call something our own but also to make sure that our claim sticks. In other words, property—that is, private property—is virtually meaningless without a government of laws and policies that makes trespass prohibitive.

To Provide Public Goods. David Hume (1711–76), another worthy successor to Hobbes, observed that although two neighbors may agree voluntarily to cooperate in draining a swampy meadow, the more neighbors there are, the more difficult it will be to cooperate to get the task done. A few neighbors might clear the swamp because they understand the benefits each of them will receive. But as you expand the number of neighbors who benefit from clearing the swamp, many neighbors will realize that all of them can get the same benefit if only a few clear the swamp and the rest do nothing. This is called **free riding**. A **public** (or collective) **good** is, therfore, a benefit that neighors or members of a group cannot be kept from enjoying once any individual or a small minority of members have provided the benefit for themselves. The clearing of the swamp is one example; national defense is another. National defense is one of the most important public goods—especially when the nation is threatened by war or terrorism. Without government's coercive powers

free riding Enjoying the benefits of some good or action while letting others bear the costs.

public good A good that (1) may be enjoyed by anyone if it is provided and (2) may not be denied to anyone once it has been provided.

---

[1] Thomas Hobbes, *Leviathan, or The Matter, Forme, and Power of a Common Wealth, Ecclesiasticall and Civil* (1651; repr., New York: Macmillan, 1947), p. 82.

through a policy (backed by taxation) to build a bridge, produce an army, or provide a swamp-free meadow, "legal tender," or uniform standards of weights and measures, there is no incentive—in fact, very often there is a disincentive—for even the richest, most concerned members to provide the benefit.[2]

Influencing the Government: Politics

In its broadest sense, the term *politics* refers to conflicts over the character, membership, and policies of any organizations to which people belong. As Harold Lasswell, a famous political scientist, once put it, politics is the struggle over "who gets what, when, how."[3] Although politics is a phenomenon that can be found in any organization, our concern in this book is narrower. Here, **politics** will refer only to conflicts and struggles over the leadership, structure, and policies of governments. The goal of politics, as we define it, is to have a share or a say in the composition of the government's leadership, how the government is organized, and what its policies are going to be. Having such a share is called power or influence. Most people are eager to have some "say" in matters affecting them; witness the willingness of so many individuals over the past two centuries to risk their lives for voting rights and representation. In recent years, of course, Americans have become more skeptical about their actual "say" in government, and many do not bother to vote. This skepticism, however, does not mean that Americans no longer want to have a share in the governmental process. Rather, many Americans doubt the capacity of the political system to provide them with influence.

As we shall see throughout this book, not only does politics influence government, but the character and actions of government also influence a nation's politics. The rules and procedures established by political institutions influence what forms political activity may take. We define **institutions** as the rules and procedures that guide political behavior. The institutions of a constitutional government such as that of the United States are designed to gain popular consent by opening channels for political expression.

politics The conflicts and struggles over the leadership, structure, and policies of government.

institutions The rules and procedures that guide political behavior.

FROM COERCION TO CONSENT

Americans have the good fortune to live in a constitutional democracy, with legal limits on what government can do and how it does it. Such democracies were unheard of before the modern era. Prior to the eighteenth and nineteenth centuries, governments seldom sought—and rarely received—the support of their ordinary

---

[2] The most instructive treatment of the phenomenon of public goods and the free rider is Mancur Olson, Jr., *The Logic of Collective Action: Public Goods and the Theory of Groups* (1965; repr., Cambridge, Mass.: Harvard University Press, 1971), pp. 33–43, esp. n. 53.

[3] Harold Lasswell, *Politics: Who Gets What, When, How* (New York: Meridian Books, 1958).

subjects. But beginning in the seventeenth century, in a handful of Western nations, two important changes began to take place in the character and conduct of government. First, governments began to acknowledge formal limits on their power. Second, a small number of governments began to provide the ordinary citizen with a formal voice in public affairs through the vote.

Limiting Government.   The key force behind the imposition of limits on government power, beginning in seventeenth-century Europe, was a new social class, the "bourgeoisie." *Bourgeois* is French for "freeman of the city," or *bourg*. Being part of the bourgeoisie later became associated with being "middle class" and with being in commerce or industry. In order to gain a share of control of government—to join the kings, monarchs, and gentry who had dominated governments for centuries—the bourgeoisie sought to change existing institutions—especially parliaments—into instruments of real political participation. Parliaments had existed for hundreds of years, controlling from the top and not allowing influence from below. The bourgeoisie embraced parliaments as the means by which they could wield their greater numbers and growing economic advantage against their aristocratic rivals.

Although motivated primarily by self-interest, the bourgeoisie advanced many of the principles that became the central underpinnings of individual freedom for *all* citizens—freedom of speech, of assembly, and of conscience, and freedom from arbitrary search and seizure. It is important to note here that the bourgeoisie generally did not favor democracy as such. They were advocates of electoral and representative institutions, but they favored property requirements and other restrictions so as to limit participation to the middle classes. Yet, once the right to engage in politics was established, it was difficult to limit it just to the bourgeoisie. We will see time after time that principles first stated to justify a selfish interest can take on a life of their own, extending beyond those for whom the principles were designed.

The Expansion of Democratic Politics.   Along with limits on government came an expansion of democratic government. Three factors explain why rulers were forced to give ordinary citizens a greater voice in public affairs: internal conflict, external threat, and the promotion of national unity and development.

First, during the eighteenth and nineteenth centuries, every nation was faced with intense conflict among the landed gentry, the bourgeoisie, lower-middle-class shopkeepers and artisans, the urban working class, and farmers. Many governments came to the conclusion that if they did not deal with basic class conflicts in some constructive way, disorder and revolution would result. One of the best ways of dealing with such conflict was to extend the rights of political participation, especially voting, to each new group as it grew more powerful.

Another form of internal threat is social disorder. Thanks to the Industrial Revolution, societies had become much more interdependent and therefore much more vulnerable to disorder. As that occurred, and as more people moved from rural areas to cities, disorder had to be managed, and one important approach to that management was to give the masses a bigger stake in the system itself. As one supporter of electoral reform put it, the alternative to voting was "the spoliation of property and the dissolution of social order."[4] In the modern world, social disorder helped to compel East European regimes and the republics of the former Soviet Union to take steps toward democratic reform.

The second factor that helped expand democratic government was external threat. The main external threat to governments' power is the existence of other nation-states. During the past three centuries, more and more tribes and nations—people tied together by a common culture and language—have formed into separate principalities, or **nation-states**, in order to defend their populations more effectively. But as more nation-states formed, the more likely it was that external conflicts would arise. War and preparation for war became constant rather than intermittent facts of national life, and the size and expense of military forces increased dramatically with the size of the nation-state and the size and number of its adversaries.

The cost of defense forced rulers to seek popular support to maintain military power. It was easier to raise huge permanent armies of citizen-soldiers and induce them to fight more vigorously and to make greater sacrifices if they were imbued with enthusiasm for cause and country. The expansion of participation and representation in government were key tactics used by the European regimes to raise that enthusiasm and support.

The third factor often associated with the expansion of democratic politics was the promotion of national unity and development. In some instances, governments seek to subvert local or regional loyalties by linking citizens directly to the central government via the ballot box. America's Founders saw direct popular election of members of the House of Representatives as a means through which the new federal government could compete with the states for popular allegiance.

nation-state
A political entity consisting of a people with some common cultural experience (nation), who also share a common political authority (state), recognized by other sovereignties (nation-states).

The Great Transformation: Tying Democracy to Strong Government

The expansion of democratic politics had two historic consequences. First, democracies opened up the possibility that citizens might use government for their own benefit rather than simply watching it being used for the benefit of others. This consequence is widely understood. But the second is not so well understood: Once citizens perceived that governments could operate in response to their demands, they became increasingly willing to support the expansion of government. The public's belief in its capacity to control the government's action is only one of the many factors responsible for the growth of government. But at the very least, this linkage of democracy and strong government set into motion a wave of governmental growth in the West that began in the middle of the nineteenth century and has continued to the present day.

---

[4] Quoted in John Cannon, *Parliamentary Reform, 1640–1832* (Cambridge: Cambridge University Press, 1973), p. 216.

DOES AMERICAN DEMOCRACY WORK?

The growth of democracy in the United States has led to wider participation, which in turn has fulfilled the democratic ideals of popular sovereignty and majority rule. Thus, democratization creates the possibility that citizens can use government for their own benefit. But what are the trade-offs involved in democracy? Are there unintended consequences of too much democracy?[5] The answers to these questions are complex. Despite over two hundred years of development, American democracy has still not worked out the inconsistencies and contradictions woven in its very fiber by the framers of the Constitution. Similarly, despite all that political scientists and political historians know about American government and politics, puzzles and anomalies reflecting the contradictions within American democracy remain for which we don't have fully satisfactory answers. We conclude this chapter by examining three of them.

Delegating Authority in a Representative Democracy

For over two centuries, we have expanded popular sovereignty to the point where a citizen, from the time he or she is roughly the age of a college freshman to the time that final breath is taken, can engage in political activity at various levels of government. Yet citizens often find it convenient to delegate many of these activities, sometimes (as when we don't pay attention, or vote, or even register to vote) conceding the field entirely to highly motivated individuals and groups. Ours is a **representative democracy** for very pragmatic reasons. Most citizens have lives to live and private concerns to attend to, and, therefore, acquiesce in an arrangement enabling them to economize on the effort they must devote to their own governance.

We think of our political representatives as our agents, whom we "hire" to act on our behalf. In this relationship, citizens are the principals—those with the authority—who delegate some of their authority to politicians. This **principal-agent relationship** means that citizens don't always get what they want, despite popular sovereignty, because, inadvertently or not, they allow agents to pursue their own self-interest or to be influenced unduly by those who care more or who have more at stake. Thus, popular sovereignty is qualified (some would say undermined) by our willingness to off-load governance responsibilities onto professional agents.

The Trade-off between Freedom and Order

If the imperfect fit between popular sovereignty and delegation of governance to a "political class" constitutes one anomaly, a second involves the trade-off between

representative democracy A system of government that provides the populace with the opportunity to make the government responsive to its views through the selection of representatives who, in turn, play a significant role in governmental decision making.

principal-agent relationship The relationship between a principal and his or her agent; this relationship may be affected by the fact that each is motivated by self-interest.

---

[5] For a review and analysis of the detrimental consequences of the "opening up" of American democracy since the 1960s, see Morris P. Fiorina, "Parties, Participation, and Representation in America: Old Theories Face New Realities," in *Political Science: State of the Discipline,* Ira Katznelson and Helen V. Milner, eds. (New York: Norton, 2002). For a more general and provocative analysis of the detrimental effects of too much democracy, see Fareed Zakaria, *The Future of Freedom: Illiberal Democracy at Home and Abroad* (New York: Norton, 2003).

liberty and coercion. We have taken pains to suggest that governments are necessary to maintain order, to protect property, and to provide public goods. All these activities require a degree of coercion. Laws, regulations, and rulings constrain behavior and restrict the uses of property. Taxes include claims on labor income, on gains in the value of capital, and on the transmission of estates from one generation to another. In short, all of these things constitute limits on liberty. The anomaly here is that liberty is one of the very purposes for which such coercion is necessary in the first place. So a pinch of coercion is one of the ingredients in the stew of liberty. But where to draw the line? And even if we had an answer to this question, there is another: How can we arrange our political life to ensure just the right amount of coercion and no more? As the history of experiments in democratic self-government reveals, coercion is a slippery slope. Especially after the events of September 11, 2001, it is clear that a strong desire for public goods such as security from terrorism lulls us into accepting extensive limitations on citizens' liberties.

The Instability of Majority Rule

A third anomaly involves the multitude of purposes pursued by different citizens. It is not always easy to add them up into a collective choice without doing damage to the interest of some. As we shall see in subsequent chapters, majority rule, especially as manifested in the real institutions of constitutional democracies, is vulnerable to the powers of agenda setters, veto players, financial fat cats, and group leaders (political bosses, union heads, corporate CEOs, religious leaders). All democracies struggle with the fact that outcomes, because they entail disproportionate influence by some, are not always fair. In our American democracy, we put a great deal of faith in frequent elections, checks and balances among government institutions, and multiple levels of government. But again we may ask where to draw the line: Elections how frequent? How powerful the checks? How many governmental levels? At what point is something broken enough to need fixing? American political history is filled with instances of decisions, followed by reactions, followed by a revisiting of those decisions, followed by further reactions. The disproportionate influence of some would appear inescapable, despite our efforts to control it. We revisit decisions. We reform institutions. We alter political practices. But still perfection eludes us.

In all these puzzles and anomalies, normative principles sometimes clash. Popular sovereignty, individual liberty, delegation, and multiple purposes constitute the circle that cannot quite be squared. We noted earlier that making sense of the apparent chaos, puzzles, and contradictions in politics is the goal of political science. Whether they are trying to understand the puzzles we have just discussed or any of the countless other phenomena we observe in American politics, political scientists try to develop theories that can be tested using empirical evidence. The "Analyzing the Evidence" unit at the end of this chapter describes some of the ways that political scientists analyze and attempt to better understand the patterns and events that shape our political system. With these concepts and tools for analysis in hand, we turn in Chapter 2 to the Founding and the Constitution.

How Do Political Scientists Know What They Know?

The basic concepts introduced in this chapter provide a foundation for understanding and explaining the facts of political life. There are two things, however, that we need to appreciate before proceeding—things that political scientists regularly do in their analysis of politics. The first we have already mentioned earlier in this chapter. In order to make analytical arguments about politics, we need to define the key concepts that help us develop theories about why things happen the way that they do. Second, we need to understand how political scientists uncover facts about politics and what tools they use to analyze and interpret these facts. What data are relevant to an argument about politics? Where can we find such data? How do we learn things from these data? How do we test arguments about the data?

In each of the empirical chapters to follow, you will find an "Analyzing the Evidence" box, highlighting arguments and evidence on some of the subjects of that chapter. In this first "Analyzing the Evidence" section, however, we provide a more methodological discussion. Here we introduce some simple ways in which political scientists examine arguments about politics—ways in which political scientists know what they know. This is no more than a basic primer on how political scientists work with political data, but we believe you will find it helpful in assessing arguments and evidence in succeeding chapters.

Consider just a few arguments about American politics:

1. Most Americans have strong psychological attachments to parties, and they vote in line with their party attachments.

2. Members of Congress seek reelection, and they will vote for laws that majorities in their constituencies would also support.

3. The chief executive of a government—the president, governor, or mayor—is the most powerful person in that government, and on important policy questions will win more often than any other politician.

How should we think critically about such claims? What is the reasoning that sustains a claim, and what is the evidence to support it? What are alternative explanations? Throughout this book we will present some of the most important facts about American political behavior and government and discuss how they help us understand the motivations of individuals and the nature of politics.

Consider one of the most basic questions about voting. In elections, Americans face two main alternatives in the form of the two major political parties—the Democratic Party and the Republican

Party. Each party promises to pursue distinctive economic policies. Since at least the 1930s, the Democratic Party has favored economic policies that redistribute income to poorer segments of society; Republicans, on the other hand, favor lower taxes and little or no redistribution. Such policies, if enacted into law, have real consequences for people's livelihoods. If those are the choices, it makes perfect sense to vote according to your economic self interest: Choose the party that maximizes your income.

This is quite a compelling argument. Indeed, many economists take it as axiomatic that people vote to maximize their personal income or economic self-interest. On reflection, however, we see that other factors also affect election outcomes and voting, including personal qualities of candidates, important noneconomic issues, and even the force of habit. These other factors suggest alternative explanations, including the possibility that people try to choose the ablest individuals to serve in office, that people vote according to beliefs or ideologies or issues that bear little relation to their income, and that people vote in line with psychological attachments to parties that they developed in childhood.

The criterion for a good argument is how well it helps us understand reality. Is it consistent with past experience? Does it do a good job of predicting events, such as current legislative outcomes or a future election? How well does it fit current circumstances or repeated observations over time? Familiarity with some basic concepts and tools will help us grapple with these issues.

What are Data? The first step in any systematic study is to define terms. Often, research begins with a puzzling or sensational event. For example, elections are exciting events, and we want to understand many facets of them. Perhaps the central question about elections for political scientists is, Why do people vote the way they do? There is, in this example, a behavior that we generally want to explain, *vote choice*. We represent this general construct mathematically as a variable. A variable defines all possible outcomes that might have occurred and assigns them a unique label or value. Vote choice, for instance, may take four possible values or outcomes: Vote for the Democratic candidate, vote for the Republican candidate, vote for another party or candidate, or don't vote.[1]

The second step is to measure the behavior of interest. This stage requires the collection of data. Observation of a small set of events can be quite enlightening. We might, for instance, conduct in-depth interviews with a dozen or so people about how they decided to vote. However, we usually require more evidence to support a given claim; a small number of people might not be sufficiently representative.

Censuses and random sample surveys are staples of social science data collection. With a *census* we observe all individuals in the population at a given moment. Every ten years, the United States conducts a comprehensive enumeration of all people living in the country. The U.S. Constitution requires a decennial census for the purposes of

VOTES CAST FOR PRESIDENT, 2008

Source: Federal Election Commission, www.fec.gov (accessed 7/6/09).

[1]We could complicate our analysis by expanding the number of potential descriptions of vote choice. For example, vote for Democratic presidential candidate and Democratic congressional candidate, Democratic presidential candidate and Republican congressional candidate, and so on. The set of categories or values that our variable can take on is an important decision the researcher must make.

apportionment of seats in the U.S. House. Today, the census provides unique and comprehensive view of the American population, including information on families, education levels, income, race and ethnicity, commuting, housing, and employment.[2] An election is a census of sorts, because it is a comprehensive count of all votes cast in a given election. Likewise, the set of all roll-call votes cast by members of Congress in a given session is also a census.

A *survey*, on the other hand, consists of a study of a relatively small subset of individuals. We call this subset a sample. One of the most important social science research projects of the second half of the twentieth century is the American National Election Studies, or ANES for short. The ANES is a national survey that has been conducted during every presidential election and most midterm congressional elections since 1948 to gauge how people voted and to understand why. Today, many important surveys examine American society and politics, including the General Social Survey, the Current Population Survey, and the American Community Survey (all by the Census Bureau), and exit polls conducted by national news organizations.[3] Most of the information used by public policy makers, businesses, and academic researchers— including estimates of unemployment and inflation, television and radio ratings, and most demographic characteristics of the population (used to distribute federal funds)—are measured using surveys.

Summarizing Data. Communicating the information in a census or survey requires tools for summarizing data. The summary of data proceeds in two steps. First, we compute the frequency with which each value of a variable occurs. Frequency may be either the number of times that a specific behavior or value of a variable occurs or the percent of the observations in which it occurs. Second, we construct a graph or statistic that summarizes the frequencies of all values of the variable.

The *distribution* of a variable expresses the frequencies of the values of a variable. That chart distribution may be represented graphically with a bar chart (also called a histogram) or a pie chart. It may also be represented by a statistical table. On its horizontal axis, a *bar chart* displays all possible values of a variable; the heights of the bars equal the frequency or percent of cases observed for each value. In the 2008 U.S. presidential election, 38% of the people did not vote, 28% of the people voted for Republican John McCain, 33% of the people voted for Democrat Barack Obama, and 1% of the people voted for third-party candidates. The frequencies sum to 100 percent. It is common to restrict the analysis to voters only, in which case McCain won 45.7% of the votes cast and Obama won 52.9% of the votes cast, with the remaining votes scattered across other candidates. The bar chart on page 13 shows the histogram of the presidential vote in the 2008 election.

A *statistical table* displays the values of the variable along the left-hand side of the table and the frequencies to the right.

The distribution of income in the United States offers a somewhat different example. The U.S. Census offers many different definitions of income, so we must settle on one: household income before taxes and transfers. This variable takes a range of values from the smallest household income to the

VOTES CAST FOR PRESIDENT, 2008	
John McCain	28%
Barack Obama	33%
Other candidates	1%
Did not vote	38%

Source: Federal Election Commission, www.fec.gov (accessed 7/6/09).

[2] www.census.gov
[3] All of these resources are publicly available. We encourage you to consult them on the Web or at the library.

largest household income, and then reports frequencies by categories. Category 1 is "less than $10,000"; category 2 is "$10,000 to $14,999"; category 3 is "$15,000 to $24,999"; and so forth up to the top category, which is "over $200,000." All possible income levels are covered in this classification, and the categories can be ordered from lowest to highest. The histogram below presents the distribution of incomes in the U.S. population in 2007.

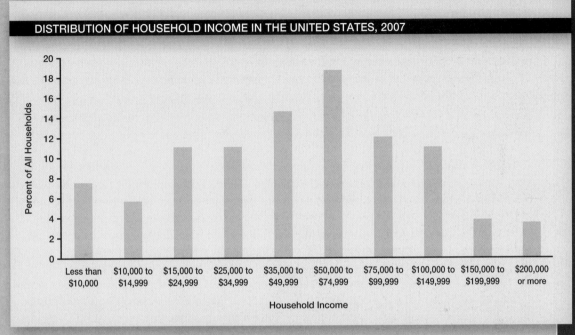

DISTRIBUTION OF HOUSEHOLD INCOME IN THE UNITED STATES, 2007

Source: U.S. Census Bureau, www.census.gov (accessed 7/6/09).

Variables such as income can be characterized with statistics, such as the median or mean. In this example, the *median* is the value of household income such that half of all households have income below that value and half have income above it. Fifty percent of all cases have income above the median value, and fifty percent have income below it; thus, the median is also called the fiftieth percentile. The median household income in the United States in 2007 was $50,233. We can see this in the histogram by beginning with the lowest value and adding up the percentages associated with each successive value until the cumulated percentage equals 50 percent. The *mean*, or average, equals the sum of each household's income (or personal income of all people in the United States) divided by the number of households. Personal income totaled approximately $11.6 trillion in 2007, and there are 117 million households. So, in the United States in 2007, the average household income was $99,800.

Why do the mean and median differ? When we calculate the median, every household is equal. We merely count the percent above and below a certain income level. The mean value weights households according to their incomes; consequently, a household with $200,000 income contributes 10 times as much to the calculation of the mean as a household with $20,000. If there were only small differences in income among households, the mean would be very close to the median. The difference between the median and the mean thus provides a measure of inequality.

The median is particularly important in thinking about voting. In an election involving two parties or candidates, it takes at least 50 percent of the votes to win. In a legislature, any bill must receive at least half of the votes of those present in order to pass. Suppose a piece of legislation directly affects people's incomes by taxing those with income above a certain level, say $75,000, and transferring that income to people who make less than that amount. Suppose also that people only care about their personal income when thinking about this bill. We may use the distribution of incomes to calculate directly what percent of people will support the bill and what percent of people will oppose it. If we use the data on the preceding page, we find that approximately one-quarter of households have income higher than $75,000, and three-quarters have income less than $75,000. If people voted only on the basis of their income—their economic self-interest—then 23 percent would oppose the tax bill and 77 percent would support it. In such a setting we can see that democracy would inevitably tax the rich.

Testing Arguments Using Data. The argument that democracy will tend to redistribute income depends on an important assumption—that people vote their economic self-interest. Is that assumption correct? Political science involves entertaining propositions, such as the claim that people vote their economic self-interest, and then testing those ideas using quantitative and other sorts of data.

Testing a claim or argument requires making comparisons: Compare the predictions from a given argument or proposition with data relevant to that idea. Usually, such conjectures take the form of a hypothesis that there is a strong relationship between two variables, such as income and the vote. To test for such a relationship, we examine how the distribution of one variable (called the dependent variable, in this case the vote) depends on the values of another variable (the independent variable). The difference in the outcome across values for the independent variable is called an *effect*.

In the case of income and vote choice, we want to know how much voting decisions depend on individuals' income levels. Compare two types of people—those who live in high-income households (income above $120,000) and those who live in low-income households (income below $15,000). Do these two types of people differ in the frequency with which they support policies that lead to greater income redistribution, and parties and candidates that favor such policies? As stated earlier, in the United States today, the Republican Party generally favors lower income taxes and less income redistribution, and the Democratic Party favors higher income taxes and more income redistribution. We therefore want to know if those in high-income households vote Republican at a much higher rate than those in low-income households. The difference in voting behavior between these two groups is the *effect* of income on the vote.

Tables offer a convenient way to display the relationship between two variables. As we saw earlier, a table presents all possible combinations of the values of two variables in a rectangular array. The top of the array corresponds to one of the variables and is divided into

VOTE BY LEVEL OF INCOME IN 2008 NATIONAL EXIT POLLS

Income (% of people)	Obama	McCain	Other
Under $15,000 (6%)	73%	25%	2%
$15,000–30,000 (12%)	60%	37%	3%
$30,000–50,000 (19%)	55%	43%	2%
$50,000–75,000 (21%)	48%	49%	3%
$75,000–100,000 (15%)	51%	48%	1%
$100,000–150,000 (14%)	48%	51%	1%
$150,000–200,000 (6%)	48%	50%	2%
$200,000 or More (6%)	52%	46%	2%

Source: www.cnn.com/ELECTION/2008/results/polls/USP00p1 (accessed 5/21/09).

columns, one for each of the values of the variable. The left side of the array corresponds to the other variable and is divided into rows, one for each value of this variable. Each cell, then, corresponds to a unique pair of values of the two variables (the intersection of a given row and a given column). In our example the variables are income and vote choice. The first cell corresponds to survey respondents who voted for Obama and who are from families with income below $15,000. The cells in the table on page 16 correspond to the percent of people in each income group who chose Obama, McCain, or someone else.

To see whether the income gap in voting is indeed large, we can use the data in this table to examine the actual voting behavior of different sorts of individuals. The national exit polls in 2008 reveal that 73 percent of voters with income less than $15,000 chose Barack Obama (and approximately 25 percent John McCain). In contrast, 52 percent of those with income over $200,000 chose Barack Obama (and only about 46 percent John McCain). The difference in the support for Obama across these two income groups is 21 percentage points (73–52). This large difference reveals that income is associated with vote choice, but it is not absolutely determinative. In particular, no income group voted overwhelmingly Republican in this election.

Consider an alternative argument, offered by the political scientists Angus Campbell, Philip Converse, Warren Miller, and Donald Stokes in *The American Voter*. People have a psychological attachment to party from which they rarely deviate. This argument suggests that those who identify personally with one of the parties vote almost entirely along party lines. The following table shows that is true; the effect of party identity is much larger than the effect of income. Knowing someone's party identity provides a strong indicator of how he or she will likely vote.

VOTE BY PARTY IDENTIFICATION IN 2008 NATIONAL EXIT POLLS			
	Obama	McCain	Other
Democrat (39%)	89%	10%	1%
Republican (32%)	9%	90%	1%
Independent (29%)	52%	44%	4%

Source: www.cnn.com/ELECTION/2008/results/polls/USP00p1 (accessed 5/21/09).

As we explore many alternative arguments about vote choice, we can make many different comparisons—Democrats versus Republicans, men versus women, college graduates versus high school graduates, and so forth. In each case, we begin by making a table of the frequencies and compute the percentages within each group that voted Democratic or Republican. Our goal is to find which, if any of these potential explanations, best accounts for the variation in voting. Throughout this book, we will consider other outcomes beside voter behavior, such as members' of Congress support for different types of legislation and the percent of times that the executive succeeds in passing legislation—in each case, what we know about these phenomena in American politic is informed by an analytical approach to evidence.

FOR FURTHER READING

Crenson, Matthew A., and Benjamin Ginsberg. *Downsizing Democracy*. Baltimore: Johns Hopkins University Press, 2002.

Downs, Anthony. *An Economic Theory of Democracy*. New York: Harper, 1957.

Dunn, John. *Democracy: A History*. New York: Atlantic Monthly Press, 2006.

Dworkin, Ronald. *Is Democracy Possible Here?* Princeton, N.J.: Princeton University Press, 2006.

Esman, Milton. *Government Works*. Ithaca, N.Y.: Cornell University Press, 2000.

Finer, S.E. *The History of Government*. New York: Oxford University Press, 1999.

Ginsberg, Benjamin. *The American Lie: Government By the People and Other Political Fables*. Boulder, Colo.: Paradigm, 2007.

Hartz, Louis. *The Liberal Tradition in America*. New York: Harcourt, 1955.

Higgs, Robert. *Neither Liberty Nor Safety: Fear, Ideology and the Growth of Government*. New York: Independent Institute Press, 2007.

Huntington, Samuel P. *Who Are We? The Challenges to America's National Identity*. New York: Simon & Schuster, 2004.

reader selection ○ Kiewiet, D. Roderick, and Matthew McCubbins. *The Logic of Delegation*. Chicago: University of Chicago Press, 1991.

Lupia, Arthur, and Mathew D. McCubbins. *The Democratic Dilemma: Can Citizens Learn What They Need to Know?* New York: Cambridge University Press, 1998.

reader selection ○ Olson, Mancur, Jr. *The Logic of Collective Action: Public Goods and the Theory of Groups*. 1965. Reprinted with new preface and appendix. Cambridge, Mass.: Harvard University Press, 1971.

Shepsle, Kenneth A., and Mark S. Bonchek. *Analyzing Politics: Rationality, Behavior, and Institutions*. New York: Norton, 1997.

Skocpol, Theda. *Diminished Democracy*. Tulsa: University of Oklahoma Press, 2004.

Tilly, Charles. *Democracy*. New York: Cambridge University Press, 2007.

Tocqueville, Alexis de. *Democracy in America*. Isaac Kramnick, ed. New York: Norton, 2007; orig. published 1835.

Wolfe, Alan. *Does American Democracy Still Work?* New Haven, Conn.: Yale University Press, 2006.

 Additional study and review materials are available online at wwnorton.com/studyspace/

The Founding and the Constitution

2

The story of America's Founding and the Constitution is generally presented as something both inevitable and glorious: It was inevitable that the American colonies would break away from England to establish their own country successfully; and it was glorious in that it established the best of all possible forms of government under a new Constitution, which was easily adopted and quickly embraced, even by its critics. In reality, though, America's successful breakaway from England was by no means assured, and the Constitution that we revere today as one of the most brilliant creations of any nation was in fact highly controversial. Moreover, its ratification and durability were often in doubt. George Washington, the man venerated as the father of the country and the person chosen to preside over the Constitutional Convention of 1787, thought the document produced that hot summer in Philadelphia would probably last no more than twenty years, at which time leaders would have to convene again to come up with something new.

That Washington's prediction proved wrong is, indeed, a testament to the enduring strength of the Constitution. Nonetheless the Constitution was not carved in stone. It was a product of political bargaining and compromise, formed very much in the same way political decisions are made today. As this chapter will show, the Constitution reflects political self-interest and high principle, too. It also defines the relationship between American citizens and their government. To understand the character of the American Founding and the meaning of the American Constitution, it is essential to look beyond the myths and rhetoric and explore the conflicting interests and forces at work during the revolutionary and constitutional periods. Thus, we will first assess the political backdrop of the American Revolution, and then we will examine the Constitution that ultimately emerged as the basis for America's government.

- The framers of the Constitution, although guided by underlying values, also had conflicting goals and interests.
- These conflicting interests were settled through the rules and procedures—the institutions—set forth in the Constitution.
- The Constitution not only provides a framework for government but also often guides the policy process—even to this day.

THE FIRST FOUNDING: INTERESTS AND CONFLICTS

Competing ideals and principles often reflect competing interests, and so it was in Revolutionary America. The American Revolution and the American Constitution were outgrowths of a struggle among economic and political forces within the colonies. Five sectors of society had interests that were important in colonial politics: (1) the New England merchants; (2) the southern planters; (3) the "royalists"—holders of royal lands, offices, and patents (licenses to engage in a profession or business activity); (4) shopkeepers, artisans, and laborers; and (5) small farmers. Throughout the eighteenth century, these groups were in conflict over issues of taxation, trade, and commerce. For the most part, however, the southern planters, the New England merchants, and the royal office and patent holders—groups that together made up the colonial elite—were able to maintain a political alliance that held in check the more radical forces representing shopkeepers, laborers, and small farmers. After 1750, however, British tax and trade policies split the colonial elite, permitting radical forces to expand their political influence and setting into motion a chain of events that culminated in the American Revolution.[1]

Political Strife and the Radicalizing of the Colonists

The political strife within the colonies was the background for the events of 1773–74. In 1773, the British government granted the politically powerful East India Company a monopoly on the export of tea from Britain, eliminating a lucrative form of trade for colonial merchants. Together with their southern allies, the merchants called upon their radical adversaries—shopkeepers, artisans, laborers, and small farmers—for support. The most dramatic result was the Boston Tea Party of 1773, led by Samuel Adams.

This event was of decisive importance in American history. The merchants had hoped to force the British government to rescind the Tea Act, but they did not support any demands beyond this one. They certainly did not seek independence from Britain. Samuel Adams and the other radicals, however, hoped to provoke

---

[1] The social makeup of colonial America and some of the social conflicts that divided colonial society are discussed in Jackson Turner Main, *The Social Structure of Revolutionary America* (Princeton, N.J.: Princeton University Press, 1965).

the British government to take actions that would alienate its colonial supporters and pave the way for a rebellion. This was precisely the purpose of the Boston Tea Party, and it succeeded. By dumping the East India Company's tea into Boston Harbor, Adams and his followers goaded the British into enacting a number of harsh reprisals. The House of Commons closed the port of Boston to commerce, changed the provincial government of Massachusetts, provided for the removal of accused persons to Britain for trial, and, most important, restricted movement to the West—further alienating the southern planters who depended on access to new western lands. These acts of retaliation confirmed the worst criticisms of England and helped radicalize the American colonists.

Thus, the Boston Tea Party set into motion a cycle of provocation and retaliation that in 1774 resulted in the convening of the First Continental Congress—an assembly consisting of delegates from all parts of the country—that called for a total boycott of British goods and, under the prodding of the radicals, began to consider the possibility of independence from British rule. The result was the Declaration of Independence.

The Declaration of Independence

In 1776, the Second Continental Congress appointed a committee consisting of Thomas Jefferson of Virginia, Benjamin Franklin of Pennsylvania, Roger Sherman of Connecticut, John Adams of Massachusetts, and Robert Livingston of New York to draft a statement of American independence from British rule. The Declaration of Independence, written by Jefferson and adopted by the Second Continental Congress, was an extraordinary document in both philosophical and political terms. Philosophically, the Declaration was remarkable for its assertion that certain rights, which it called "unalienable rights"—including life, liberty, and the pursuit of happiness—could not be abridged by governments. In the world of 1776, a world in which some kings still claimed to rule by divine right, this was a dramatic statement. The Declaration was remarkable as a political document because it identified and focused on problems, grievances, aspirations, and principles that might unify the various colonial groups. The Declaration was an attempt to identify and articulate a history and set of principles that might help to forge national unity.[2]

The Articles of Confederation

Having declared independence, the colonies needed to establish a government. In November 1777, the Continental Congress adopted the Articles of Confederation and Perpetual Union—the first written constitution of the United States. Although it was not ratified by all the states until 1781, it served as the country's constitution for almost twelve years, until March 1789.

The **Articles of Confederation** was concerned primarily with limiting the powers of the central government. It created no executive branch. Congress constituted the central government, but it had little power. Execution of its laws was to be left

Articles of Confederation America's first written constitution. Adopted by the Continental Congress in 1777, the Articles of Confederation and Perpetual Union was the formal basis for America's national government until 1789, when it was superseded by the Constitution.

[2] See Carl Becker, *The Declaration of Independence* (New York: Vintage, 1942).

to the individual states. Its members were not much more than messengers from the state legislatures. They were chosen by the state legislature, their salaries were paid out of the state treasuries, and they were subject to immediate recall by state authorities. In addition, each state, regardless of its size, had only a single vote.

Congress was given the power to declare war and make peace, to make treaties and alliances, to coin or borrow money, and to regulate trade with Native Americans. It could also appoint the senior officers of the United States Army. But it could not levy taxes or regulate commerce among the states. Moreover, the army officers it appointed had no army to serve in because the nation's armed forces were composed of the state militias. Probably the most unfortunate part of the Articles of Confederation was that the central government could not prevent one state from discriminating against other states in the quest for foreign commerce.

In brief, the relationship between Congress and the states under the Articles of Confederation was much like the contemporary relationship between the United Nations and its member states, a relationship in which the states retain virtually all governmental powers. It was called a confederation because, as provided under Article II, "each state retains its sovereignty, freedom and independence, and every Power, Jurisdiction and right, which is not by this confederation expressly delegated to the United States, in Congress assembled." Not only was there no executive, there was also no judicial authority and no other means of enforcing Congress's will. If there was to be any enforcement at all, the states would have to do it.[3]

THE SECOND FOUNDING: FROM COMPROMISE TO CONSTITUTION

The Declaration of Independence and the Articles of Confederation were not sufficient to hold the nation together as an independent and effective nation-state. From almost the moment of armistice with the British in 1783, moves were afoot to reform and strengthen the Articles.

International Standing and Domestic Turmoil

Many Americans were concerned about the country's international position. Competition among the states for foreign commerce allowed the European powers to play the states against one another, which created confusion on both sides of the Atlantic. At one point during the winter of 1786–87, John Adams, a leader in the independence struggle, was sent to negotiate a new treaty with the British, one that would cover disputes left over from the war. The British government responded that, since the United States under the Articles of Confederation was unable to enforce existing treaties, it would negotiate with each of the thirteen states separately.

At the same time, well-to-do Americans—in particular the New England merchants and southern planters—were troubled by the influence that "radical" forces

---

[3] See Merrill Jensen, *The Articles of Confederation* (Madison: University of Wisconsin Press, 1963).

exercised in the Continental Congress and in the governments of several of the states. The colonists' victory in the Revolutionary War had not only meant the end of British rule, but it had also significantly changed the balance of political power within the new states. As a result of the Revolution, one key segment of the colonial elite—the royal land, office, and patent holders—was stripped of its economic and political privileges. In fact, many of these individuals, along with tens of thousands of other colonists who considered themselves loyal British subjects, left for Canada after the British surrender. And although the elite was weakened, the radicals were now better organized than ever before. They controlled such states as Pennsylvania and Rhode Island, where they pursued economic and political policies that struck terror into the hearts of the prerevolutionary political establishment. The central government under the Articles of Confederation was powerless to intervene.

The new nation's weak international position and domestic turmoil led many Americans to consider whether a new version of the Articles might be necessary. In the fall of 1786, delegates from five states met in Annapolis, Maryland, and called on Congress to send commissioners to Philadelphia at a later time to devise adjustments to the constitution. Their resolution took on force as a result of an event that occurred the following winter in Massachusetts: Shays's Rebellion. Daniel Shays led a mob of farmers, who were protesting foreclosures on their land, in a rebellion against the state government. The state militia dispersed the mob within a few days, but the threat posed by the rebels scared Congress into action. The states were asked to send delegates to Philadelphia to discuss constitutional revision, and eventually delegates were sent from every state but Rhode Island.

The Constitutional Convention

Twenty-nine of a total of seventy-three delegates selected by the state governments convened in Philadelphia in May 1787, with political strife, international embarrassment, national weakness, and local rebellion fixed in their minds. Recognizing that these issues were symptoms of fundamental flaws in the Articles of Confederation, the delegates soon abandoned the plan to revise the Articles and committed themselves to a second Founding—a second, and ultimately successful, attempt to create a legitimate and effective national system. This effort occupied the convention for the next five months.

The Great Compromise.   The proponents of a new government fired their opening shot on May 29, 1787, when Edmund Randolph of Virginia offered a resolution that proposed corrections and enlargements in the Articles of Confederation. His proposal was not a simple motion. It provided for virtually every aspect of a new government. Randolph later admitted it was intended to be an alternative draft constitution, and it was in fact the framework for what ultimately became the Constitution.[4]

---

[4] There is no verbatim record of the debates, but James Madison, a Virginia delegate, was present during nearly all of the deliberations and kept full notes on them. Madison's notes are included in Max Farrand, ed., *The Records of the Federal Convention of 1787*, rev. ed., 4 vols. (New Haven, Conn.: Yale University Press, 1966).

The portion of Randolph's motion that became most controversial was known as the **Virginia Plan**. This plan provided for a system of representation in the national legislature based upon the population of each state or the proportion of each state's revenue contribution, or both. (Randolph also proposed a second branch of the legislature, but it was to be elected by the members of the first branch.) Because the states varied enormously in size and wealth, the Virginia Plan was thought to be heavily biased in favor of the large states.

While the convention was debating the Virginia Plan, additional delegates arriving in Philadelphia were beginning to mount opposition to it. In particular, delegates from the less populous states, which included Delaware, New Jersey, Connecticut, and New York, asserted that the more populous states, such as Virginia, Pennsylvania, North Carolina, Massachusetts, and Georgia, would dominate the new government if representation were to be determined by population. The smaller states argued that each state should be equally represented in the new regime regardless of its population. The proposal, called the **New Jersey Plan** (it was introduced by William Paterson of New Jersey), focused on revising the Articles rather than replacing them. Their opposition to the Virginia Plan's system of representation was sufficient to send the proposals back to committee for reworking into a common document.

The outcome was the Connecticut Compromise, also known as the **Great Compromise**. Under the terms of this compromise, in the first branch of Congress—the House of Representatives—the representatives would be apportioned according to the number of inhabitants in each state. This, of course, was what delegates from the large states had sought. But in the second branch—the Senate—each state would have an equal vote regardless of its size; this was to deal with the concerns of the small states. This compromise was not immediately satisfactory to all the delegates. In the end, however, both sets of forces preferred compromise to the breakup of the Union, and the plan was accepted. The "Analyzing the Evidence" unit for this chapter explores the states' conflicting interests and how these shaped the eventual compromise in more detail.

The Question of Slavery: The Three-fifths Compromise.

Many of the conflicts that emerged during the Constitutional Convention were reflections of the fundamental differences between the slave and the nonslave states—differences that pitted the southern planters and the New England merchants against one another. This was the first premonition of a conflict that would almost destroy the Republic in later years. In the midst of debate over large versus small states, Madison observed, "The great danger to our general government is the great southern and northern interests of the continent, being opposed to each other. Look to the votes in Congress, and most of them stand divided by the geography of the country, not according to the size of the states."[5]

Over 90 percent of all slaves resided in five states—Georgia, Maryland, North Carolina, South Carolina, and Virginia—where they accounted for 30 percent of the total population. In some places, slaves outnumbered nonslaves by as much

---

[5] Farrand, *Records of the Federal Convention*, vol. 1, p. 476.

as ten to one. Were they to be counted in determining how many congressional seats a state should have? Northerners and southerners eventually reached agreement through the **Three-fifths Compromise**. The seats in the House of Representatives would be apportioned according to a "population" in which five slaves would count as three persons. The slaves would not be allowed to vote, of course, but the number of representatives would be apportioned accordingly. This arrangement was supported by the slave states, which included some of the biggest and some of the smallest states at that time. It was also accepted by delegates from nonslave states who strongly supported the principle of property representation, whether that property was expressed in slaves or in land, money, or stocks.

The issue of slavery was the most difficult one faced by the framers, and it nearly destroyed the Union. Although some delegates believed slavery to be morally wrong, morality was not the issue that caused the framers to support or oppose the Three-fifths Compromise. Whatever they thought of the institution of slavery, most delegates from the northern states opposed counting slaves in the distribution of congressional seats. But southern delegates made it clear that if the northerners refused to give in, they would never agree to the new government. William Davie of North Carolina heatedly asserted that the people of North Carolina would never enter the Union if slaves were not counted as part of the basis for representation. Without such an agreement, he asserted ominously, "the business was at an end." This conflict between the southern and the northern delegates was so divisive that many came to question the possibility of creating and maintaining a union of the two, and a compromise that acknowledged the legitimacy of slavery was probably necessary to keep the South from rejecting the Constitution.

Three-fifths Compromise Agreement reached at the Constitutional Convention of 1787 that stipulated that for purposes of the appointment of congressional seats, every slave would be counted as three-fifths of a person.

THE CONSTITUTION

The political significance of the Great Compromise and the Three-fifths Compromise was to reinforce the unity of those who sought the creation of a new government. The Great Compromise reassured those who feared that the importance of their own local or regional influence would be reduced by the new governmental framework. The Three-fifths Compromise temporarily defused the rivalry between the merchants and the planters. Their unity secured, members of the alliance supporting the establishment of a new government moved to fashion a constitutional framework for this government that would be congruent with their economic and political interests.

In particular, the framers sought a new government that, first, would be strong enough to promote commerce and protect property from radical state legislatures such as Rhode Island's. This goal became the basis for the establishment of national control over commerce and finance, as well as the establishment of national judicial supremacy and a strong presidency. Second, the framers sought to prevent what they saw as the threat posed by the "excessive democracy" of the state and national governments under the Articles of Confederation. This led to such constitutional principles as **bicameralism** (division of the Congress into two chambers), checks

bicameralism Division of a legislative body into two houses, chambers, or branches.

Voting at the Constitutional Convention

Under the Articles of Confederation, there was a unicameral Congress in which each state delegation received a single vote, regardless of state population. So Virginia, with roughly 700,000 people, had the same share of votes as Rhode Island, with a population closer to 70,000.[**] Among the issues considered by the framers at the Constitutional Convention, one of the most contentious involved how representation in the Congress would work under the new Constitution.

On May 29, 1787, Edmund Randolph proposed the Virginia Plan, which later came to be associated with James Madison. This plan initially called for the creation of three semi-independent branches of government with a bicameral legislature and introduced the idea of checks and balances. On June 11, a series of votes were taken on the Virginia Plan, which consistently received the support of the larger, more populous states—because under this plan at least one of the chambers of Congress would be elected with representation proportional to population, giving the more populous states more of a voice in the national government.

Given that the smaller, less populous states were poised to lose representation if votes in Congress were based on population, delegates from those states decided to propose their own plan for the national government. On June 15, William Paterson proposed the New Jersey Plan, which called for the creation of a unicameral legislature with one vote per state. When a vote was scheduled on June 19 that pitted the Virginia Plan against the New Jersey Plan, the states voted exactly the same way as they did on the vote for proportional representation in the Virginia Plan (see below). Moreover, many of the delegates from the smaller states threatened to leave the convention if the Virginia Plan was ratified. In an attempt to prevent the smaller states from departing, Roger Sherman proposed the Connecticut Compromise, which was voted on on June 23. This plan called for a bicameral legislature, with representation based on population in the lower house and equal representation of states in the upper house. The Connecticut Compromise ultimately passed by a 5–4 vote.

State[*]	Total population[**]	Slave population[**]	Vote on Virginia Plan	Vote on Connecticut Compromise
Virginia	747,550	292,627	Y	N
Pennsylvania	433,611	3,707	Y	N
Massachusetts	378,556	0	Y	—
New York	340,241	21,193	N	—
Maryland	319,728	103,036	—	Y
North Carolina	395,005	100,783	Y	Y
South Carolina	249,073	107,094	Y	N
Connecticut	237,655	2,648	Y	Y
New Jersey	184,139	11,423	N	Y
Georgia	82,548	29,264	Y	N
New Hampshire	141,899	157	—	—
Delaware	59,096	8,887	N	Y
Rhode Island	69,112	958	—	—

*Maryland's delegates were split equally and thus did not vote. Delegates from New Hampshire never attended at the same time as those from New York, hence their lack of participation. Rhode Island did not send any delegates to the convention.

**Population data are based on the 1790 census and therefore are only approximate with respect to populations in 1787.

If we consider the number of representatives in Congress that each state would receive under the various plans (see below), it becomes clear why individual states voted the way they did. Under the Articles and the proposed New Jersey Plan, even the smallest states had 1 out of 13 votes in the Congress. We can express their share of the total votes as .077.

State*	Under Articles: Each state has one out of 13 total votes	Population-based system like Virginia Plan: Each state has one vote per 30,000 constituents, out of 65 total votes*
Virginia	.077	10/65 = .154
Pennsylvania	.077	8/65 = .123
Massachusetts	.077	8/65 = .123
New York	.077	6/65 = .092
Maryland	.077	6/65 = .092
North Carolina	.077	5/65 = .077
South Carolina	.077	5/65 = .077
Connecticut	.077	5/65 = .077
New Jersey	.077	4/65 = .062
Georgia	.077	3/65 = .046
New Hampshire	.077	3/65 = .046
Delaware	.077	1/65 = .015
Rhode Island	.077	1/65 = .015

*Note that the framers calculated the number of representatives per state using population estimates. The first census was not taken until 1790.

Under a population-based system such as the Virginia Plan, the smaller states would lose voting power in Congress. For example, in a population-based system with one representative per 30,000 people, Delaware would only have 1 out of 65 votes, or a .015 share of total votes. This is significantly less voting power than the 1 out of 13 (.077) share that these states enjoyed under the Articles and other arrangements that would give each state equal representation in Congress.

By providing for equal representation of the states in one house of Congress and population-weighted representation in the other, the Connecticut Compromise mitigated the loss of voting power that the small states would suffer. As the right-hand column in the table on the previous page indicates, a majority of the states accepted this compromise, which eventually became part of the Constitution. As this case demonstrates, the conflicting interests of the framers are reflected in the rules and procedures of the institutions they established.

Sources: Keith L. Dougherty and Jac C. Heckelman, "A Pivotal Voter from a Pivotal State: Roger Sherman at the Constitutional Convention," *American Political Science Review* 100 (May 2006): 297–302; Clinton L. Rossiter, *1787: The Grand Convention* (New York: Macmillan, 1996.)

and balances, staggered terms in office, and indirect election (selection of the president by an electoral college rather than by voters directly).

Third, hoping to secure support from the states or the public at large for the new form of government they proposed, the framers provided for direct popular election of representatives and, subsequently, for the addition of the Bill of Rights. Finally, to prevent the new government from abusing its power, the framers incorporated principles such as the separation of powers and federalism into the Constitution. Let us now assess the major provisions of the Constitution to see how each relates to these objectives.

The Legislative Branch

The first seven sections of Article I of the Constitution provided for a Congress consisting of two chambers—a House of Representatives and a Senate. Members of the House of Representatives were given two-year terms in office and were to be subject to direct popular election—though generally only white males had the right to vote. State legislatures were to appoint members of the Senate (this was changed in 1913 by the Seventeenth Amendment, providing for direct election of senators) for six-year terms. These terms, moreover, were staggered so that the appointments of one-third of the senators would expire every two years. The Constitution assigned somewhat different tasks to the House and Senate. Though the approval of each body was required for the enactment of a law, the Senate alone was given the power to ratify treaties and approve presidential appointments. The House, on the other hand, was given the sole power to originate revenue bills.

The character of the legislative branch was directly related to the framers' major goals. The House of Representatives was designed to be directly responsible to the people in order to encourage popular consent for the new Constitution and, as we saw in Chapter 1, to help enhance the power of the new government. At the same time, to guard against "excessive democracy," the power of the House of Representatives was checked by the Senate, whose members were to be appointed for long (six-year) terms rather than elected directly by the people for short terms.

Staggered terms of service in the Senate were intended to make that body even more resistant to popular pressure. Because only one-third of the senators would be selected at any given time, the composition of the institution would be protected from changes in popular preferences transmitted by the state legislatures. Thus, the structure of the legislative branch was designed to contribute to governmental power, promote popular consent for the new government, and at the same time place limits on the popular political currents that many of the framers saw as a radical threat to the economic and social order.

The Powers of Congress and the States. The issues of power and consent were important throughout the Constitution. Section 8 of Article I specifically listed the powers of Congress, which include the authority to collect taxes, to borrow money, to regulate commerce, to declare war, and to maintain an army and navy. By granting it these powers, the framers indicated very clearly that they intended the new government to be far more influential than its predecessor. At the

IN BRIEF

The Seven Articles of the Constitution

1. **The Legislative Branch**

   House: two-year terms, elected directly by the people.

   Senate: six-year terms (staggered so that only one-third of the Senate changes in any given election), appointed by state legislature (changed in 1913 to direct election).

   Expressed powers of the national government: collecting taxes, borrowing money, regulating commerce, declaring war, and maintaining an army and a navy; all other power belongs to the states, unless deemed otherwise by the elastic (necessary and proper) clause.

   Exclusive powers of the national government: states are expressly forbidden to issue their own paper money, tax imports and exports, regulate trade outside their own borders, and impair the obligation of contracts; these powers are the exclusive domain of the national government.

2. **The Executive Branch**

   Presidency: four-year terms (limited in 1951 to a maximum of two terms), elected indirectly by the electoral college.

   Powers: can recognize other countries, negotiate treaties, grant reprieves and pardons, convene Congress in special sessions, and veto congressional enactments.

3. **The Judicial Branch**

   Supreme Court: lifetime terms, appointed by the president with the approval of the Senate.

   Powers: include resolving conflicts between federal and state laws, determining whether power belongs to national government or the states, and settling controversies between citizens of different states.

4. **National Unity and Power**

   Reciprocity among states: establishes that each state must give "full faith and credit" to official acts of other states, and guarantees citizens of any state the "privileges and immunities" of every other state.

5. **Amending the Constitution**

   Procedures: requires two-thirds approval in Congress and three-fourths adoption by the states.

6. **National Supremacy**

   The Constitution and national law are the supreme law of the land and cannot be overruled by state law.

7. **Ratification**

   The Constitution became effective when approved by nine states.

---

same time, by giving these important powers to Congress, the framers sought to reassure citizens that their views would be fully represented whenever the government exercised its new powers.

As a further guarantee to the people that the new government would pose no threat to them, the Constitution implied that any powers *not* listed were not granted at all. This is the doctrine of **expressed power**. The Constitution grants only those powers specifically *expressed* in its text. But the framers intended to create an active and powerful government, and so they included the **necessary and proper clause**, sometimes known as the elastic clause, which signified that the enumerated powers were meant to be a source of strength to the national government, not a limitation on it. Each power could be used with the utmost vigor, but no new powers could be seized upon by the national government without a constitutional amendment. Any power not enumerated was conceived to be "reserved" to the states (or the people).

The Executive Branch

The Constitution provided for the establishment of the presidency in Article II. As Alexander Hamilton put it, the presidential article sought "energy in the Executive." It did so in an effort to overcome the natural stalemate that was built into the bicameral legislature as well as into the separation of powers among the legislative, executive, and judicial branches. The Constitution afforded the president a measure of independence from the people and from the other branches of government—particularly Congress.

In line with the framers' goal of increased power to the national government, the president was granted the unconditional power to accept ambassadors from other countries; this amounted to the power to "recognize" other countries. He was also given the power to negotiate treaties, although their acceptance required the approval of the Senate. The president was given the unconditional right to grant reprieves and pardons, except in cases of impeachment. And he was provided with the power to appoint major departmental personnel, to convene Congress in special session, and to veto congressional enactments. (The veto power is formidable, but it is not absolute, since Congress can override it by a two-thirds vote.)

At the same time, the framers sought to help the president withstand (excessively) democratic pressures by making him subject to indirect rather than direct election (through his selection by a separate electoral college). The extent to which the framers' hopes were actually realized will be the topic of Chapter 6.

The Judicial Branch

Article III established the judicial branch. This provision reflects the framers' concern with giving more power to the national government and checking radical democratic impulses, while guarding against abuse of liberty and property by the new national government itself.

The framers created a court that was to be literally a supreme court of the United States, and not merely the highest court of the national government. The Supreme Court was given the power to resolve any conflicts that might emerge between federal and state laws and to determine to which level of government a power belonged. In addition, the Supreme Court was assigned jurisdiction over controversies between citizens of different states. The long-term significance of this was that as the country developed a national economy, it came to rely increasingly on the federal judiciary, rather than on the state courts, for resolution of disputes.

Judges were given lifetime appointments in order to protect them from popular politics and from interference by the other branches. But they would not be totally immune to politics or to the other branches, for the president was to appoint the judges and the Senate was to approve the appointments. Congress would also have the power to create inferior (lower) courts, to change the jurisdiction of the federal courts, to add or subtract federal judges, and even to change the size of the Supreme Court.

No specific mention is made in the Constitution of **judicial review**—the power of the courts to render the final decision when there is a conflict of interpretation of the Constitution or of laws. This conflict could be between the courts and Congress, the courts and the executive branch, or the courts and the states. Scholars generally feel that judicial review is implicit in the very existence of a written Constitution and in the power given explicitly to the federal courts over "all Cases . . . arising under this Constitution, the Laws of the United States, and Treaties made, or which shall be made, under their Authority" (Article III, Section 2). The Supreme Court eventually assumed the power of judicial review. Its assumption of this power, as we shall see in Chapter 8, was based not on the Constitution itself but on the politics of later decades and the membership of the Court.

National Unity and Power

Various provisions in the Constitution addressed the framers' concern with national unity and power. Article IV provided for comity (reciprocity) among states, which we will discuss in more detail in Chapter 3. Each state was also prohibited from discriminating against the citizens of other states in favor of its own citizens, with the Supreme Court being the arbiter in each case.

The framers' concern with national supremacy was also expressed in Article VI, in the **supremacy clause**, which provided that national laws and treaties "shall be the supreme law of the land." This meant that all laws made under the "authority of the United States" would be superior to all laws adopted by any state or any other subdivision, and that the states would be expected to respect all treaties made under that authority. This was a clear effort to keep the states from dealing separately with foreign nations or businesses. The supremacy clause also bound the officials of all state and local as well as federal governments to take an oath of office to support the national Constitution. This meant that every action taken by the U.S. Congress would have to be applied within each state as though the action were in fact state law.

Amending the Constitution

The Constitution established procedures for its own revision in Article V. Its provisions are so difficult that Americans have succeeded in the amending process only seventeen times since 1791, when the first ten amendments were adopted. Many other amendments have been proposed in Congress, but fewer than forty of them have even come close to fulfilling the Constitution's requirement of a two-thirds vote in Congress, and only a fraction have gotten anywhere near adoption by three-fourths of the states. (A breakdown of these figures and further discussion of amending the Constitution appear in Chapter 3.) The Constitution could also be amended by a constitutional convention. Occasionally, proponents of particular measures, such as a balanced-budget amendment, have called for a constitutional convention to consider their proposals. Whatever the purpose for which it was called, however, such a convention would presumably have the authority to revise America's entire system of government.

Ratifying the Constitution

The rules for the ratification of the Constitution of 1787 made up Article VII of the Constitution. This provision actually violated the lawful procedure for constitutional change incorporated in the Articles of Confederation. For one thing, it adopted a nine-state rule in place of the unanimity among the states required by the Articles of Confederation. For another, it provided that ratification would occur in special state conventions called for that purpose rather than in the state legislatures. All the states except Rhode Island eventually did set up state conventions to ratify the Constitution, and none seemed to protest very loudly the extralegal character of the procedure.

Constitutional Limits on the National Government's Power

As we have indicated, though the framers sought to create a powerful national government, they also wanted to guard against possible misuse of that power. To that end, the framers incorporated two key principles into the Constitution—the **separation of powers** and **federalism** (see also Chapter 3). A third set of limitations, in the form of the **Bill of Rights**, was added to the Constitution to help secure its ratification when opponents of the document charged that it paid insufficient attention to citizens' rights.

The Separation of Powers. No principle of politics was more widely shared at the time of the 1787 Founding than the principle that power must be used to balance power. The French political theorist Montesquieu (1689–1755) believed that this balance was an indispensable defense against tyranny, and his writings, especially his major work, *The Spirit of the Laws,* "were taken as political gospel" at the Philadelphia Convention.[6] This principle is not stated explicitly in the Constitution, but it is clearly built into Articles I, II, and III, which provide for

1. Three separate branches of government (see Figure 2.1).
2. Different methods of selecting the top personnel, so that each branch is responsible to a different constituency. This is intended to produce a "mixed regime," in which the personnel of each department will develop very different interests and outlooks on how to govern, and different groups in society will be assured of some access to governmental decision making.

separation of powers The division of governmental power among several institutions that must cooperate in decision making.

federalism System of government in which power is divided by a constitution between a central government and regional governments.

Bill of Rights The first ten amendments to the U.S. Constitution, ratified in 1791. They ensure certain rights and liberties to the people.

---

[6] Max Farrand, *The Framing of the Constitution of the United States* (New Haven, Conn.: Yale University Press, 1962), p. 49.

FIGURE 2.1 THE SEPARATION OF POWERS

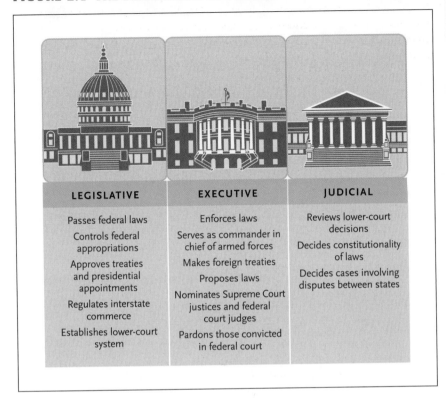

LEGISLATIVE	EXECUTIVE	JUDICIAL
Passes federal laws	Enforces laws	Reviews lower-court decisions
Controls federal appropriations	Serves as commander in chief of armed forces	Decides constitutionality of laws
Approves treaties and presidential appointments	Makes foreign treaties	Decides cases involving disputes between states
Regulates interstate commerce	Proposes laws	
Establishes lower-court system	Nominates Supreme Court justices and federal court judges	
	Pardons those convicted in federal court	

3. **Checks and balances**, a system under which each of the branches is given some power over the others. Familiar examples are the presidential veto power over legislation and the power of the Senate to approve high-level presidential appointments.

One clever formulation conceives of this system not as separated powers but as "separated institutions sharing power,"[7] thus diminishing the chance that power will be misused.

Federalism.   Federalism was a step toward greater centralization of power. The delegates agreed that they needed to place more power at the national governmental level, without completely undermining the power of the state governments. Thus, they devised a system of two sovereigns—the states and the nation—with the hope that competition between the two would be an effective limitation on the power of both.

checks and balances Mechanisms through which each branch of government is able to participate in and influence the activities of the other branches. Major examples include the presidential veto power over congressional legislation, the power of the Senate to approve presidential appointments, and judicial review of congressional enactments.

[7] Richard E. Neustadt, *Presidential Power* (New York: Wiley, 1960), p. 33.

Comparing the Articles of Confederation and the Constitution

	Articles of Confederation	Constitution
Legislative Branch	*Power to:* Declare war and make peace. Make treaties and alliances. Coin or borrow money. Regulate trade with Native Americans. Appoint senior officers of the United States Army. *Limits on power:* Could not levy taxes, regulate commerce among the states, or create national armed forces.	*Power to:* Collect taxes. Borrow money. Regulate commerce. Declare war. Maintain an army and navy. *Limits on power:* All other powers belong to the states.
Executive Branch	*No executive branch was created.*	*Power to:* Recognize other countries. Negotiate treaties. Grant reprieves and pardons. Appoint major departmental personnel. Convene special sessions of Congress. Veto congressional actions. *Limits on power:* Senate must approve treaties. Congress can override a veto by a two-thirds vote.
Judicial Branch	*No judicial branch was created.*	*Power to:* Resolve conflicts between state and federal laws. Determine to which level of government a power belongs. Decide conflicts between citizens of different states. *Limits on power:* Judicial appointments are made by the president and approved by the Senate. Congress creates lower courts and can change the jurisdiction of the federal courts. Congress can add or subtract federal judges and can change the size of the Supreme Court.

The Bill of Rights.   Late in the Philadelphia Convention, a motion was made to include a bill of rights in the Constitution. After a brief debate in which hardly a word was said in its favor and only one speech was made against it, the motion to include it was almost unanimously turned down. Most delegates sincerely believed that since the federal government was already limited to its expressed powers, further protection of citizens was not needed. The delegates argued that the states should adopt bills of rights because their powers needed more limitations than those of the federal government. But almost immediately after the Constitution was ratified, there was a movement to adopt a national bill of rights. This is why the Bill of Rights, adopted in 1791, comprises the first ten amendments to the Constitution rather than being part of the body of it. We will have a good deal more to say about the Bill of Rights in Chapter 4.

THE FIGHT FOR RATIFICATION

The first hurdle faced by the new Constitution was ratification by state conventions of delegates elected by white, propertied males of each state. This struggle for ratification was carried out in thirteen separate campaigns. Each involved different individuals, moved at a different pace, and was influenced by local as well as national considerations. Two sides faced off throughout all the states, however, taking the names of Federalists and Antifederalists.[8] The **Federalists** supported the Constitution and preferred a strong national government. The **Antifederalists** opposed the Constitution and preferred a more decentralized federal system of government; they took on their name by default, in reaction to their better-organized opponents. The Federalists were united in their support of the Constitution. The Antifederalists, although opposing this plan, were divided as to what they believed the alternative should be.

Under the name of "Publius," Alexander Hamilton, James Madison, and John Jay wrote eighty-five articles in the New York newspapers supporting ratification of the Constitution. These *Federalist Papers,* as they are collectively known today, defended the principles of the Constitution and sought to dispel the fears of a national authority.[9] The Antifederalists, however, such as Richard Henry Lee and Patrick Henry of Virginia and George Clinton of New York, argued that the new Constitution betrayed the Revolution and was a step toward monarchy. They accused the

Federalists Those who favored a strong national government and supported the constitution proposed at the American Constitutional Convention of 1787.

Antifederalists Those who favored strong state governments and a weak national government and who were opponents of the constitution proposed at the American Constitutional Convention of 1787.

---

[8] An excellent analysis of the ratification campaigns—based on a quantitative assessment of the campaigners' own words as found in campaign documents, pamphlets, tracts, public letters, and the eighteenth-century equivalent of op-ed pieces (such as the individual essays that make up the *Federalist Papers*)—is William H. Riker, *The Strategy of Rhetoric: Campaigning for the American Constitution* (New Haven, Conn.: Yale University Press, 1996).

[9] Alexander Hamilton, James Madison, and John Jay, *The Federalist Papers,* Isaac Kramnick, ed. (New York: Viking Press, 1987), esp. nos. 10 and 51.

Philadelphia Convention of being a "Dark Conclave" that had worked under a "thick veil of secrecy" to overthrow the law and spirit of the Articles of Confederation.[10]

By the end of 1787 and the beginning of 1788, five states had ratified the Constitution. Delaware, New Jersey, and Georgia ratified it unanimously; Connecticut and Pennsylvania ratified by wide margins. Opposition was overcome in Massachusetts by the inclusion of nine recommended amendments to the Constitution to protect human rights. Ratification by Maryland and South Carolina followed. In June 1788, New Hampshire became the ninth state to ratify. That put the Constitution into effect, but for the new national government to have real power, the approval of both Virginia and New York would be needed. After impassioned debate and a great number of recommendations for future amendment of the Constitution, especially for a bill of rights, the Federalists mustered enough votes for approval of the Constitution in June (Virginia) and July (New York) of 1788. North Carolina joined the new government in 1789, after a bill of rights actually was submitted to the states by Congress, and Rhode Island held out until 1790 before finally voting to become part of the new union.

CHANGING THE FRAMEWORK: CONSTITUTIONAL AMENDMENT

The Constitution has endured for over two centuries as the framework of government. But it has not endured without change. Without change, the Constitution might have become merely a sacred text, stored under glass.

Amendments: Many Are Called, Few Are Chosen

The framers of the Constitution recognized the need for change. The provisions for amendment incorporated into Article V were thought to be "an easy, regular and Constitutional way" to make changes, which would occasionally be necessary because members of Congress "may abuse their power and refuse their consent on that very account . . . to admit to amendments to correct the source of the abuse."[11] James Madison, again writing in *The Federalist Papers*, made a more balanced defense of the amendment procedures: "It guards equally against that extreme facility, which would render the Constitution too mutable; and that extreme difficulty, which might perpetuate its discovered faults."[12]

---

[10] Herbert Storing, ed., *The Anti-Federalist* (Chicago: University of Chicago Press, 1985), "Brutus" letters pp. 108–21 and 133–38. Also, Herbert Storing, *What the Anti-Federalists Were For* (Chicago: University of Chicago Press, 1981).

[11] Observation by Colonel George Mason, delegate from Virginia, early during the convention period. Quoted in Max Farrand, *The Records of the Federal Convention of 1787*, rev. ed. (New Haven, Conn.: Yale University Press, 1966), vol. 1, pp. 202–3.

[12] Clinton Rossiter, ed., *The Federalist Papers* (New York: New American Library, 1961), no. 43, p. 278.

Federalists versus Antifederalists

	Federalists	Antifederalists
Who were they?	Property owners, creditors, merchants	Small farmers, frontiersmen, debtors, shopkeepers
What did they believe?	Believed that elites were best fit to govern; feared "excessive democracy"	Believed that government should be closer to the people; feared concentration of power in the hands of the elites
What system of government did they favor?	Favored strong national government; believed in "filtration" so that only elites would obtain governmental power	Favored retention of power by state governments and protection of individual rights
Who were their leaders?	Alexander Hamilton James Madison George Washington	Patrick Henry George Mason Elbridge Gerry George Clinton

Experience since 1789 raises questions even about Madison's more modest claim. The Constitution has proven to be extremely difficult to amend. In the history of efforts to amend the Constitution, the most appropriate characterization is "many are called, few are chosen." Between 1789 and the present, more than eleven thousand amendments have been formally offered in Congress. Of these, Congress officially proposed only twenty-nine, and only twenty-seven of these were eventually ratified by the states. But the record is even more severe than that. Since 1791, when the first ten amendments, the Bill of Rights, were added, only seventeen amendments have been adopted. And two of them—prohibition of alcohol (Eighteenth) and its repealer (Twenty-first)—cancel each other out, so that for all practical purposes, only fifteen amendments have been added to the Constitution since 1791. Despite vast changes in American society and its economy, only twelve amendments have been adopted since the Civil War amendments (Thirteenth, Fourteenth, and Fifteenth) in 1868.

As Figure 2.2 illustrates, Article V provides four methods of amendment:

1. Passage in House and Senate by two-thirds vote; then ratification by majority vote of the legislatures of three-fourths (thirty-eight) of the states.

2. Passage in House and Senate by two-thirds vote; then ratification by conventions called for the purpose in three-fourths of the states.

FIGURE 2.2 ROUTES OF AMENDMENT

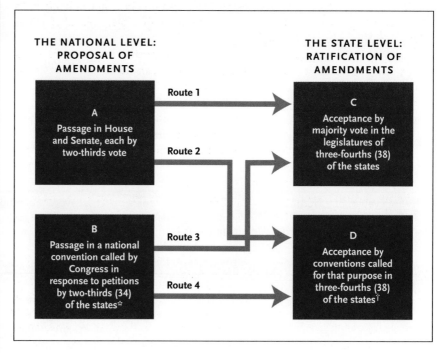

*This method of proposal has never been employed. Thus, amendment routes 3 and 4 have never been attempted.

†For each amendment proposal, Congress has the power to choose the method of ratification, the time limit for consideration by the states, and other conditions of ratification.

3. Passage in a national convention called by Congress in response to petitions by two-thirds of the states; ratification by majority vote of the legislatures of three-fourths of the states.

4. Passage in a national convention, as in method 3; then ratification by conventions called for the purpose in three-fourths of the states.

Because no amendment has ever been proposed by national convention, however, routes 3 and 4 have never been employed. And route 2 has been employed only once (for the Twenty-first Amendment, which repealed the Eighteenth, or Prohibition, Amendment). Thus, route 1 has been used for all the others.

Now we should be better able to explain why it has been so difficult to amend the Constitution. The main reason is the requirement of a two-thirds vote in the House and the Senate, which means that any proposal for an amendment in Congress can be killed by only 34 senators *or* 136 members of the House. The amendment can also be killed by the refusal or inability of only thirteen state legislatures to ratify it. Since each state has an equal vote regardless of its population, the thirteen holdout states may represent a small fraction of the total American population. In the 1970s, the Equal Rights Amendment (ERA), granting protection from denial of rights on account of sex, got the necessary two-thirds vote in Congress but failed by three states to get the necessary three-fourths votes of the states, even after a three-year extension for its ratification.[13]

If the ERA was a defeat for liberal forces, conservatives have done no better. The school prayer amendment proposed in 2002 sought to restore power to the states to require selected religious observances, thereby reversing a whole series of earlier Supreme Court decisions.[14] The pro-life amendment proposed in 1981 sought to reverse *Roe v. Wade* in order to restore to the states the power to outlaw abortions. And Republicans have made frequent efforts to get Congress to adopt an amendment outlawing the burning or other desecration of the American flag. On four occasions—most recently in 2006—a resolution for a flag-burning amendment passed in the House of Representatives but never found enough support in the Senate. Republicans have also proposed an amendment to define marriage as a union of one man and one woman, but even some opponents of gay marriage are reluctant to change the Constitution to outlaw it.[15]

The Twenty-seven Amendments

All but two of the Constitution's twenty-seven amendments are concerned with the structure or composition of the government. This is consistent with the concept of a constitution as "higher law," because the whole point and purpose of a higher law is to establish a framework within which government and the process of making ordinary law can take place. Even those who would have preferred more changes in the Constitution would have to agree that there is great wisdom in this principle. A constitution ought to enable legislation and public policies to take place, but it should not attempt to determine what that legislation or those policies ought to be.

The purpose of the ten amendments in the Bill of Rights was basically to give each of the three branches clearer and more restricted boundaries (see Table 2.1). The First Amendment clarified Congress's turf. Although the powers of Congress under Article I, Section 8, would not have justified laws regulating religion, speech, and the like, the First Amendment made this limitation explicit: "Congress shall make no law. . . ." The Second, Third, and Fourth Amendments similarly spelled out limits on the executive branch, a necessity given the abuses of executive power Americans had endured under British rule.

The Fifth, Sixth, Seventh, and Eighth Amendments contain some of the most important safeguards for individual citizens against the arbitrary exercise of

---

[13] Marcia Lee, "The Equal Rights Amendment—Public Policy by Means of a Constitutional Amendment," in *The Politics of Policy Making in America*, David Caputo, ed. (San Francisco: Freeman, 1977); Gilbert Steiner, *Constitutional Inequality: The Political Fortunes of ERA* (Washington, D.C.: Brookings Institution, 1985); and Jane Mansbridge, *Why We Lost the ERA* (Chicago: University of Chicago Press, 1986).

[14] For judicial action, see *Engel v. Vitale*, 370 U.S. 421 (1962). For the efforts of states to get around the Supreme Court requirement that public schools be secular, see John A. Murley, "School Prayer: Free Exercise of Religion or Establishment of Religion?" in *Social Regulatory Policy*, Raymond Tatalovich and Byron Daynes, eds. (Boulder, Colo.: Westview Press, 1988), pp. 5–40.

[15] Evan Gerstmann, *Same Sex Marriage and the Constitution* (New York: Cambridge University Press, 2003).

TABLE 2.1 THE BILL OF RIGHTS: ANALYSIS OF ITS PROVISIONS

Amendment	Purpose
I	*Limits on Congress:* Congress is not to make any law establishing a religion or abridging the freedom of speech, press, assembly, or the right to petition freedoms.
II, III, IV	*Limits on Executive:* The executive branch is not to infringe on the right of people to keep arms (II), is not arbitrarily to take houses for a militia (III), and is not to engage in the search for or seizure of evidence without a court warrant swearing to a belief in the probable existence of a crime (IV).
V, VI, VII, VIII	*Limits on Courts:* The courts are not to hold trials for serious offenses without provision for a grand jury (V), a petit (trial) jury (VII), a speedy trial (VI), presentation of charges, and confrontation of hostile witnesses (VI). Immunity from testimony against oneself (V) and immunity from trial more than once for the same offense (V). Neither bail nor punishment can be excessive (VIII), and no property can be taken without just compensation (V).
IX, X	*Limits on National Government:* All rights not enumerated are reserved to the states or the people.

government power. And these amendments sought to accomplish their goal by defining the judicial branch more concretely and clearly than had been done in Article III of the Constitution.

Five amendments adopted since 1791 are directly concerned with expansion of the electorate (see Table 2.2).[16] The Founders were unable to establish a national electorate with uniform voting qualifications. They decided to evade the issue by providing in the final draft of Article I, Section 2, that eligibility to vote in a national election would be the same as "the Qualification requisite for Elector of the most numerous branch of the state Legislature." Article I, Section 4, added that Congress could alter state regulations as to the "Times, Places and Manner of holding Elections for Senators and Representatives," but this meant that any important expansion of the American electorate would almost certainly require a constitutional amendment.

---

[16] The Fourteenth Amendment is included in this table as well as in Tables 2.3 and 2.4 because it seeks not only to define citizenship but seems to intend also that this definition of citizenship included, along with the right to vote, all the rights of the Bill of Rights, regardless of the state in which the citizen resided. A great deal more will be said about this in Chapter 4.

TABLE 2.2 AMENDING THE CONSTITUTION TO EXPAND THE ELECTORATE

Amendment	Purpose	Year Proposed	Year Adopted
XIV	Section 1 provided national definition of citizenship*	1866	1868
XV	Extended voting rights to all races	1869	1870
XIX	Extended voting rights to women	1919	1920
XXIII	Extended voting rights to residents of the District of Columbia	1960	1961
XXIV	Extended voting rights to all classes by abolition of poll taxes	1962	1964
XXVI	Extended voting rights to citizens aged 18 and over	1971	1971

*In defining *citizenship*, the Fourteenth Amendment actually provided the constitutional basis for expanding the electorate to include all races, women, and residents of the District of Columbia. Only the "eighteen-year-olds' amendment" should have been necessary, since it changed the definition of citizenship. The fact that additional amendments were required after the Fourteenth suggests that voting is not considered an inherent right of U.S. citizenship. Instead, it is viewed as a privilege.

Six more amendments are also electoral in nature, although not concerned directly with voting rights and the expansion of the electorate. These six amendments are concerned with the elective offices themselves or with the relationship between elective offices and the electorate (see Table 2.3).

Another five amendments have sought to expand or to limit the powers of the national and state governments (see Table 2.4). The Eleventh Amendment protected the states from suits by private individuals and took away from the federal courts any power to take suits by private individuals of one state (or a foreign country) against another state. The other three amendments in Table 2.4 are obviously designed to reduce state power (Thirteenth), to reduce state power and expand national power (Fourteenth), and to expand national power (Sixteenth). The Twenty-seventh put a moderate limit on Congress's ability to raise its own salary.

The Eighteenth, or Prohibition, Amendment underscores the meaning of the rest: This is the only amendment that the country used to try to *legislate*. In other words, it is the only amendment that was designed to deal directly with some substantive social problem. And it was the only amendment ever to have been repealed. Two other amendments—the Thirteenth, which abolished slavery, and the Sixteenth, which established the power to levy an income tax—can be said to have had the effect of legislation. But the purpose of the Thirteenth was to restrict the power of the states by forever forbidding them to treat any human being as property. As for

TABLE 2.3 AMENDING THE CONSTITUTION TO CHANGE THE RELATIONSHIP BETWEEN THE ELECTED OFFICES AND THE ELECTORATE

Amendment	Purpose	Year Proposed	Year Adopted
XII	Created separate ballot for vice president in the electoral college	1803	1804
XIV	Section 2 eliminated counting of slaves as "three-fifths" citizens for apportionment of House seats	1866	1868
XVII	Provided direct election of senators	1912	1913
XX	Eliminated "lame duck" session of Congress	1932	1933
XXII	Limited presidential term	1947	1951
XXV	Provided presidential succession in case of disability	1965	1967

the Sixteenth, it is certainly true that income tax legislation followed immediately; nevertheless, the amendment concerns itself strictly with establishing the power of Congress to enact such legislation. The legislation came later; and if down the line a majority in Congress had wanted to abolish the income tax, they could also have done this by legislation rather than through the arduous path of a constitutional amendment repealing the income tax.

DOES THE CONSTITUTION WORK?

The final product of the Constitutional Convention would have to be considered an extraordinary victory for those who wanted a new system of government to replace the Articles of Confederation. The new Constitution laid the groundwork for a government that would be sufficiently powerful to promote trade, to protect property, and to check the activities of radical state legislatures. Moreover, this new government was so constructed through internal checks and balances, indirect selection of officeholders, lifetime judicial appointments, and other similar provisions to preclude the "excessive democracy" feared by many of the Founders. Some of the framers favored going even further in limiting popular influence, but the general consensus at the convention was that a thoroughly undemocratic document would never receive the popular approval needed to be ratified by the states.[17]

---

[17] See Farrand, *The Records of the Federal Convention*, vol. 1, p. 132.

TABLE 2.4 AMENDING THE CONSTITUTION TO EXPAND OR LIMIT THE POWER OF GOVERNMENT

Amendment	Purpose	Year Proposed	Year Adopted
XI	Limited jurisdiction of federal courts over suits involving the states	1794	1798
XIII	Eliminated slavery and eliminated the right of states to allow property in persons	1865*	1865
XIV	(Part 2) Applied due process of Bill of Rights to the states	1866	1868
XVI	Established national power to tax incomes	1909	1913
XXVII	Limited Congress's power to raise its own salary	1789	1992

*The Thirteenth Amendment was proposed on January 31, 1865, and adopted less than a year later, on December 18, 1865.

Though the Constitution was the product of a particular set of political forces, the principles of government it established have a significance that goes far beyond the interests of its authors. Two of these principles, federalism and civil liberties, will be discussed in Chapters 3 and 4. A third important constitutional principle that has affected America's government for the past two hundred years is the principle of checks and balances. As we saw earlier, the framers gave each of the three branches of government a means of intervening in and blocking the actions of the others. Often, checks and balances have seemed to prevent the government from getting much done. During the 1960s, for example, liberals were often infuriated as they watched Congress stall presidential initiatives in the area of civil rights. More recently, conservatives were outraged when President Clinton thwarted congressional efforts to enact legislation promised in the Republican "Contract with America." At various times, all sides have vilified the judiciary for invalidating legislation enacted by Congress and signed by the president.

Over time, checks and balances have acted as brakes on the governmental process. Groups hoping to bring about changes in policy or governmental institutions seldom have been able to bring about decisive and dramatic transformations in a short period of time. Instead, checks and balances have slowed the pace of change and increased the need for compromise and accommodation.

Groups able to take control of the White House, for example, must negotiate with their rivals who remain entrenched on Capitol Hill. New forces in Congress must reckon with the influence of other forces in the executive branch and in the courts. Checks and balances inevitably frustrate those who desire change, but they also function as a safeguard against rash action. During the 1950s, for example, Congress was caught up in a nearly hysterical effort to unmask subversive activities in the United States, which might have led to a serious erosion of American liberties if not for the checks and balances provided by the executive branch and the courts. Thus, a governmental principle that serves as a frustrating limitation one day may become a vitally important safeguard the next.

Yet, although the Constitution sought to lay the groundwork for a powerful government, the framers struggled to reconcile government power with freedom. The framers surrounded the powerful institutions of the new regime with a variety of safeguards—a continual array of checks and balances—designed to make certain that the power of the national government could not be used to undermine the states' power and their citizens' freedoms. Thus, the framers were the first Americans to confront head on the dilemma of coercion and power that we discussed briefly in Chapter 1. Whether their solutions to this dilemma were successful is the topic of the remainder of our chapters.

To Whose Benefit?

Of course, the groups whose interests were served by the Constitution in 1789, mainly the merchants and planters, are not the same groups that benefit from the Constitution's provisions today. Once incorporated into the law, political principles often take on lives of their own and have consequences that were never anticipated by their original champions. Indeed, many of the groups that benefit from constitutional provisions today did not even exist in 1789. Who would have thought that the principle of free speech would influence the transmission of data on the Internet? Who would have predicted that commercial interests that once sought a powerful government might come, two centuries later, to denounce governmental activism as "socialistic"? Perhaps one secret of the Constitution's longevity is that it did not confer permanent advantage on any one set of economic or social forces.

Although they were defeated in 1789, the Antifederalists present us with an important picture of a road not taken and of an America that might have been. Would the country have been worse off if it had been governed by a confederacy of small republics linked by a national administration with severely limited powers? Were the Antifederalists correct in predicting that a government given great power in the hope that it might do good would, through "insensible progress," inevitably turn to evil purposes? Two hundred years of government under the federal Constitution are not necessarily enough to definitively answer these questions. Time must tell.

To What Ends?

The Constitution's framers placed individual liberty ahead of all other political values. Their concern for liberty led many of the framers to distrust both democracy and equality. They feared that democracy could degenerate into a majority tyranny in which the populace, perhaps led by a rabble-rousing demagogue, would trample on liberty. As for equality, the framers were products of their time and place; our contemporary ideas of racial and gender equality would have been foreign to them. The framers were concerned primarily with another manifestation of equality: They feared that those without property or position might be driven by what some called a "leveling spirit" to infringe on liberty in the name of greater economic or social equality. Indeed, the framers believed that this leveling spirit was most likely to produce demagoguery and majority tyranny. As a result, the basic structure of the Constitution—separated powers, internal checks and balances, and federalism—was designed to safeguard liberty, and the Bill of Rights created further safeguards for liberty. At the same time, however, many of the Constitution's other key provisions, such as indirect election of senators and the president, as well as the appointment of judges for life, were designed to limit democracy and, hence, the threat of majority tyranny.

By championing liberty, however, the framers virtually guaranteed that democracy and even a measure of equality would sooner or later evolve in the United States. For liberty inevitably leads to the growth of political activity and the expansion of political participation. In James Madison's famous phrase, "Liberty is to faction as air is to fire."[18] Where they have liberty, more and more people, groups, and interests will almost inevitably engage in politics and gradually overcome whatever restrictions might have been placed on their participation. This is precisely what happened in the early years of the American Republic. During the Jeffersonian period, political parties formed. During the Jacksonian period, many state suffrage restrictions were removed, and popular participation greatly expanded. Over time, liberty is conducive to democracy.

Liberty does not guarantee that everyone will be equal. It does, however, reduce the threat of inequality in one very important way. Historically, the greatest inequalities of wealth, power, and privilege have arisen where governments have used their power to allocate status and opportunity among individuals or groups. The most extreme cases of inequality are associated with the most tyrannical regimes. In the United States, however, by promoting a democratic politics, over time liberty unleashed forces that militated against inequality. As a result, over the past two hundred years, groups that have learned to use the political process have achieved important economic and social gains.

One limitation of liberty as a political principle, however, is that the idea of limits on government action can also inhibit effective government. Take one of the basic tasks of government, the protection of citizens' lives and property. A government limited by concerns over the rights of those accused of crimes may be limited in its ability to maintain public order. Currently, the U.S. government is asserting that protecting the nation against terrorists requires law enforcement measures that seem at odds with legal and constitutional formalities. The conflict between liberty and governmental effectiveness is another tension at the heart of the American constitutional system.

---

[18] E. M. Earle, ed., *The Federalist* (New York: Modern Library, 1937), no. 10.

CHAPTER REVIEW

Political conflicts between the colonies and England, and among competing groups within the colonies, led to the first Founding as expressed by the Declaration of Independence. The first constitution, the Articles of Confederation, was adopted one year later (1777). Under this document, the states retained their sovereignty. The central government, composed solely of the Continental Congress, had few powers and no means of enforcing its will. The national government's weakness soon led to the second Founding as expressed by the Constitution of 1787.

In this second Founding, the framers sought, first, to fashion a new government sufficiently powerful to promote commerce and protect property from radical state legislatures. Second, they sought to bring an end to the "excessive democracy" of the state and national governments under the Articles of Confederation. Third, they sought to introduce mechanisms that would secure popular consent for the new government. Finally, the framers sought to make certain that their new government would not itself pose a threat to liberty and property.

The Constitution consists of seven articles. In part, Article I provides for a Congress of two chambers (Sections 1–7), defines the powers of the national government (Section 8), and interprets the national government's powers as a source of strength rather than a limitation (necessary and proper clause). Article II describes the presidency and establishes it as a separate branch of government. Article III is the judiciary article. Although there is no direct mention of judicial review in this article, the Supreme Court eventually assumed that power. Article IV addresses reciprocity among states and their citizens. Article V describes the procedures for amending the Constitution. Thousands of amendments have been offered, but only twenty-seven have been adopted. With the exception of the two Prohibition amendments, all amendments were oriented toward some change in the framework or structure of government. Article VI establishes that national laws and treaties are "the supreme law of the land." And finally, Article VII specifies the procedure for ratifying the Constitution of 1787.

FOR FURTHER READING

Amar, Akhil Reed. *America's Constitution: A Biography.* New York: Random House, 2005.

Bailyn, Bernard. *The Ideological Origins of the American Revolution.* Cambridge, Mass.: Harvard University Press, 1967.

Beard, Charles A. *An Economic Interpretation of the Constitution of the United States.* New York: Macmillan, 1913.

Breyer, Stephen. *Active Liberty: Interpreting our Democratic Constitution.* New York: Knopf, 2005.

Chernow, Ron. *Alexander Hamilton.* New York: Penguin, 2004.

Ellis, Joseph. *Founding Brothers: The Revolutionary Generation.* New York: Knopf, 2000.

————. *His Excellency, George Washington*. New York: Knopf, 2004.

Farrand, Max, ed. *The Records of the Federal Convention of 1787*. Rev. ed. 4 vols. New Haven, Conn.: Yale University Press, 1966.

Hamilton, Alexander, James Madison, and John Jay. *The Federalist Papers*. Isaac Kramnick, ed. New York: Viking Press, 1987.

Riker, William H. *The Strategy of Rhetoric: Campaigning for the American Constitution*. New Haven, Conn.: Yale University Press, 1996.

Storing, Herbert J., ed. *The Complete Anti-Federalist*. 7 vols. Chicago: University of Chicago Press, 1981.

reader selection

reader selection

Additional study and review materials are available online at wwnorton.com/studyspace/

3

Federalism and the Separation of Powers

HOW DO FEDERALISM AND THE SEPARATION OF POWERS WORK AS POLITICAL INSTITUTIONS?

The great achievement of American politics was the fashioning of an effective constitutional structure of political institutions. Although it is an imperfect and continuously evolving work in progress, this structure of law and political practice has served its people well for more than two centuries. Two of America's most important institutional features are federalism and the separation of powers. Federalism seeks to limit government by dividing it into two levels, national and state, each with sufficient independence to compete with the other, thereby restraining the power of both.[1] The separation of powers seeks to limit the power of the national government by dividing government against itself—by giving the legislative, executive, and judicial branches separate functions, thus forcing them to share power.

Both federalism and the separation of powers complicate policy making in the United States. If governmental power were arranged neatly and simply in a single hierarchy, decisions could certainly be made more easily and more efficiently. But would they be better decisions? The framers thought that complexity, multiple checks, and institutionalized second-guessing, though messy, would allow more

---

[1] The notion that federalism requires separate spheres of jurisdictions in which lower and higher levels of government are uniquely decisive is developed fully in William H. Riker, *Federalism: Origin, Operation, Significance* (Boston: Little, Brown, 1964). This American version of federalism is applied to the emerging federal arrangements in the People's Republic of China during the 1990s in a paper by Barry R. Weingast, "The Economic Role of Political Institutions: Market-Preserving Federalism and Economic Development," *Journal of Law, Economics, and Organization* 11 (1995): 1–32.

interests to have a voice and would eventually produce better results. And along the way, messy decision processes might preserve liberty and prevent tyranny. Yet, although the constitutional dispersion of power among federal institutions and between the federal government and the states may well protect our liberties, it often seems to make it impossible to get anything done collectively. This lack of decisiveness sometimes appears to negate the most important reason for building institutions in the first place.

Since the adoption of the Constitution, ambitious politicians and decision makers have developed a variety of strategies for overcoming the many impediments to policy change that inevitably arise in our federal system of separated powers. Most commonly, those seeking to promote a new program may try to find ways of dispersing the program's benefits so that other politicians controlling institutional veto powers will be persuaded that it is in their interest to go along. Thus, federalism and the separation of powers have given rise to the federal pork barrel, to the defense subcontracting system, and to grants-in-aid and other forms of policy that reflect the dispersion of power. For example, if the executive branch hopes to win congressional support for a new weapons system, it generally sees to it that portions of the new system are subcontracted to firms in as many congressional districts as possible. In this way, dispersion of benefits helps to overcome the separation of powers between the executive and legislative branches. Similarly, as we will see below, federal officials often secure state cooperation with national programs by offering the states funding, called grants-in-aid, in exchange for their compliance. These programs help to overcome the limitations of federalism.

However, these American political institutions are not carved in stone. Although the Constitution initially set a broad framework for the division of authority between the national government and the states, and the division of labor among the branches of the national government, much adaptation and innovation took place as these institutions themselves were bent to the purposes of various political players. Politicians are goal oriented and are constantly exploring the possibilities provided them by their institutional positions and political situations. As we will see in this chapter, the Supreme Court has also been a central player in settling the ongoing debate over how power should be divided between the national government and the states and between Congress and the president.

FEDERALISM

federalism
System of government in which power is divided by a constitution between a central government and regional governments (in the United States, between the national government and state governments).

Federalism can be defined as the division of powers and functions between the national government and the state governments. As we saw in Chapter 2, the states were individual colonies before independence, and for nearly thirteen years they were virtually autonomous units under the Articles of Confederation. In effect, the states had retained too much power relative to the national government, a problem that led directly to the Annapolis Convention in 1786 and the Constitutional Convention in 1787. Under the Articles, disorder within states was beyond the reach of the national government, and conflicts of interest between states were not manageable. For example, states were making their own trade agreements with foreign countries and companies, which might then play one state against another for special advantages. Some states adopted special trade tariffs and further barriers to foreign commerce that were contrary to the interests of another state.[2] Tax and other barriers were also being erected between the states.[3] But even after the ratification of the Constitution, the states continued to be more important than the national government. For nearly a century and a half, virtually all of the fundamental policies governing the lives of American citizens were made by the state legislatures, not by Congress.

Federalism in the Constitution

The United States was the first nation to adopt federalism as its governing framework. With federalism, the framers sought to limit the national government by creating a second layer of state governments. American federalism recognized two sovereigns in the original Constitution and reinforced the principle in the Bill of Rights by granting a few **expressed powers** to the national government and reserving all the rest to the states.

expressed powers
(Congress) Specific powers granted to the federal government under Article I, Section 8, of the Constitution.

---

[2] For a good treatment of these conflicts of interests between states, see Forrest McDonald, *E Pluribus Unum—The Formation of the American Republic, 1776–1790* (Boston: Houghton Mifflin, 1965), chap. 7, especially pp. 319–38.

[3] See David O'Brien, *Constitutional Law and Politics* (New York: Norton, 1997), vol. 1. pp. 602–3.

The Powers of the National Government.   As we saw in Chapter 2, the expressed powers granted to the national government are found in Article I, Section 8, of the Constitution. These seventeen powers include the power to collect taxes, to coin money, to declare war, and to regulate commerce (which, as we will see, became a very important power for the national government). Article I, Section 8, also contains another important source of power for the national government: the **implied powers** that enable Congress "to make all Laws which shall be necessary and proper for carrying into Execution the foregoing Powers." Not until several decades after the Founding did the Supreme Court allow Congress to exercise the power granted in this **necessary and proper clause**, but, as we shall see later in this chapter, this doctrine allowed the national government to expand considerably the scope of its authority, although the process was a slow one. In addition to these expressed and implied powers, the Constitution affirmed the power of the national government in the supremacy clause (Article VI), which made all national laws and treaties "the supreme Law of the Land."

The Powers of State Government.   One way in which the framers sought to preserve a strong role for the states was through the Tenth Amendment to the Constitution. The Tenth Amendment states that the powers that the Constitution does not delegate to the national government or prohibit to the states are "reserved to the States respectively, or to the people." The Antifederalists, who feared that a strong central government would encroach on individual liberty, repeatedly pressed for such an amendment as a way of limiting national power. Federalists agreed to the amendment because they did not think it would do much harm, given the powers of the Constitution already granted to the national government. The Tenth Amendment is also called the **reserved powers** amendment because it aims to reserve powers to the states.

The most fundamental power that is retained by the states is that of coercion—the power to develop and enforce criminal codes, to administer health and safety rules, to regulate the family via marriage and divorce laws. The states have the power to regulate individuals' livelihoods; if you're a doctor or a lawyer or a plumber or a barber, you must be licensed by the state. Even more fundamental, the states have the power to define private property—private property exists because state laws against trespassing define who is and is not entitled to use a piece of property. If you own a car, your ownership isn't worth much unless the state is willing to enforce your right to possession by making it a crime for anyone else to take your car. These are fundamental matters, and the powers of the states regarding these domestic issues are much greater than the powers of the national government, even today.

A state's authority to regulate these fundamental matters is commonly referred to as the **police power** of the state and encompasses the state's power to regulate the health, safety, welfare, and morals of its citizens. Policing is what states do—they coerce you in the name of the community in order to maintain public order. And this was exactly the type of power that the Founders intended the states to exercise.

In some areas, the states share **concurrent powers** with the national government, whereby they retain and share some power to regulate commerce and to affect the currency—for example, by being able to charter banks, grant or deny corporate

implied powers
Powers derived from the necessary and proper clause of Article I, Section 8, of the Constitution. Such powers are not specifically expressed but are implied through the expansive interpretation of delegated powers.

necessary and proper clause
From Article I, Section 8, of the Constitution, it provides Congress with the authority to make all laws "necessary and proper" to carry out its expressed powers.

reserved powers
Powers, derived from the Tenth Amendment of the Constitution, that are not specifically delegated to the national government or denied to the states.

police power
Power reserved to the state to regulate the health, safety, and morals of its citizens.

concurrent powers
Authority possessed by *both* state and national governments, such as the power to levy taxes.

charters, grant or deny licenses to engage in a business or practice a trade, and regulate the quality of products or the conditions of labor. This issue of concurrent versus exclusive power has come up from time to time in our history, but wherever there is a direct conflict of laws between the federal and the state levels, the issue will most likely be resolved in favor of national supremacy.

State Obligations to Each Other. The Constitution also creates obligations among the states. These obligations, spelled out in Article IV, were intended to promote national unity. By requiring the states to recognize actions and decisions taken in other states as legal and proper, the framers aimed to make the states less like independent countries and more like parts of a single nation.

Article IV, Section 1, calls for "Full Faith and Credit" among states, meaning that each state is normally expected to honor the "public Acts, Records, and judicial Proceedings" that take place in any other state. So, for example, if a couple is married in Texas—marriage being regulated by state law—Missouri must also recognize that marriage, even though they were not married under Missouri state law.

This **full faith and credit clause** has recently become entangled in the controversy over gay marriage. In several states individuals of the same gender may marry. A number of other states, though, have passed "defense of marriage acts" that define marriage only as a union between a man and a woman. Eager to show its disapproval of gay marriage, Congress passed the federal Defense of Marriage Act in 1996, declaring that states will *not* have to recognize a same-sex marriage legally contracted in another state. The Supreme Court may eventually be asked to clarify this issue.

Article IV, Section 2, known as the "comity clause," also seeks to promote national unity. It provides that citizens enjoying the **privileges and immunities** of one state should be entitled to similar treatment in other states. What this has come to mean is that a state cannot discriminate against someone from another state or give special privileges to its own residents. For example, in the 1970s, when Alaska passed a law that gave residents preference over nonresidents in obtaining work on the state's oil and gas pipelines, the Supreme Court ruled the law illegal because it discriminated against citizens of other states.[4] This clause also regulates criminal justice among the states by requiring states to return fugitives to the states from which they have fled. Thus, in 1952, when an inmate escaped from an Alabama prison and sought to avoid being returned to Alabama on the grounds that he was being subjected to "cruel and unusual punishment" there, the Supreme Court ruled that he must be returned according to Article IV, Section 2.[5] This example highlights the difference between the obligations among states and those among different countries. In 1997, France refused to return an American fugitive because he might be subject to the death penalty, which does not exist in France.[6] The Constitution clearly forbids states to do something similar.

full faith and credit clause Article IV, Section 1, of the Constitution provides that each state must accord the same respect to the laws and judicial decisions of other states that it accords to its own.

privileges and immunities clause Provision from Article IV, Section 2, of the Constitution that a state cannot discriminate against someone from another state or give its own residents special privileges.

---

[4] *Hicklin v. Orbeck,* 437 U.S. 518 (1978).

[5] *Sweeny v. Woodall,* 344 U.S. 86 (1953).

[6] Marlise Simons, "France Won't Extradite American Convicted of Murder," *New York Times,* December 5, 1997, p. A9.

States' relationships to one another are also governed by the interstate compact clause (Article I, Section 10), which states that "No State shall, without the Consent of Congress . . . enter into any Agreement or Compact with another State." The Court has interpreted the clause to mean that states may enter into agreements with one another, subject to congressional approval. Compacts are a way for two or more states to reach a legally binding agreement about how to solve a problem that crosses state lines. In the early years of the Republic, states turned to compacts primarily to settle border disputes. Today they are used for a wide range of issues but are especially important in regulating the distribution of river water, addressing environmental concerns, and operating transportation systems that cross state lines.[7]

Local Government and the Constitution.   Local government, including counties, cities, and towns, occupies a peculiar but very important place in the American system. In fact, the status of American local government is probably unique in world experience. First, it must be pointed out that local government has no status in the American Constitution. *State* legislatures created local governments, and *state* constitutions and laws permit local governments to take on some of the responsibilities of the state governments. Most states amended their own constitutions to give their larger cities **home rule**—a guarantee of noninterference in various areas of local affairs. But local governments enjoy no such recognition in the Constitution. Local governments have always been mere conveniences of the states.[8]

> **home rule** Power delegated by the state to a local unit of government to manage its own affairs.

Local governments became administratively important in the early years of the Republic because the states possessed little administrative capability. They relied on local governments—cities and counties—to implement the laws of the state. Local government was an alternative to a statewide bureaucracy.

The Slow Growth of the National Government's Power

Before the 1930s, America's federal system was one of **dual federalism**, a two-layered system—national and state—in which the states and their local principalities did most of the governing. This arrangement is demonstrated in Table 3.1, which shows the types of public policies that fell under national, state, and local jurisdiction during the first century and a half under the Constitution (disregarding the local-level functions discussed in the previous section). We refer to it here as the traditional system precisely because almost nothing about our pattern of government changed during two-thirds of our history. That is, of course, with the exception of the four years of the Civil War, after which we returned to the traditional system.

> **dual federalism** The system of government that prevailed in the United States from 1789 to 1937 in which most fundamental governmental powers were shared between the federal and state governments, with the states exercising the most important powers.

---

[7] Patricia S. Florestano, "Past and Present Utilization of Interstate Compacts in the United States," *Publius* 24 (Fall 1994): 13–26.

[8] A good discussion of the constitutional position of local governments is in York Y. Willbern, *The Withering Away of the City* (Bloomington: Indiana University Press, 1971). For more on the structure and theory of federalism, see Thomas R. Dye, *American Federalism: Competition among Governments* (Lexington, Mass.: Lexington Books, 1990), chap. 1; and Martha Derthick, "Up-to-Date in Kansas City: Reflections on American Federalism," *PS: Political Science & Politics* 25 (December 1992): 671–75.

TABLE 3.1 THE FEDERAL SYSTEM: SPECIALIZATION OF GOVERNMENTAL FUNCTIONS IN THE TRADITIONAL SYSTEM, 1789–1937

National Government Jurisdiction (Domestic)	State Government Jurisdiction	Local Government Jurisdiction
Internal improvements	Property laws (including slavery)	Adaptation of state laws to local conditions (variances)
Subsidies	Estate and inheritance laws	Public works
Tariffs	Commerce laws	Contracts for public works
Public lands disposal	Banking and credit laws	Licensing of public accommodations
Patents	Corporate laws	Assessable improvements
Currency	Insurance laws	Basic public services
	Family laws	
	Morality laws	
	Public health laws	
	Education laws	
	General penal laws	
	Eminent domain laws	
	Construction codes	
	Land-use laws	
	Water and mineral laws	
	Criminal procedure laws	
	Electoral and political party laws	
	Local government laws	
	Civil service laws	
	Occupations and professions laws	

But there was more to dual federalism than merely the existence of two tiers. The two tiers were functionally quite different from one another. There have been debates every generation over how to divide responsibilities between the two tiers. As we have seen in this chapter, the Constitution delegated a list of specific powers to the national government and reserved all the rest to the states. That left a lot of room for interpretation, however, because of the final "elastic" clause of Article I, Section 8. The three formal words *necessary and proper* amounted to an invitation to struggle over the distribution of powers between national and state governments. We shall confront this struggle throughout the book. However, the most remarkable thing about the history of American federalism is that federalism remained dual for nearly two-thirds of that history, with the national government remaining steadfastly within a "strict construction" of Article I, Section 8. The results are clear in Table 3.1.

The best example of the potential elasticity in Article I, Section 8, is in the **commerce clause,** which delegates to Congress the power "to regulate Commerce with foreign Nations, and *among the several States* and with the Indian tribes" [emphasis added]. It is obvious that this clause can be interpreted broadly or narrowly, and in fact the Supreme Court embraced the broad interpretation throughout most of the nineteenth century. Yet Congress chose not to take the Court's invitation to be expansive. The first and most important case favoring national power was *McCulloch v. Maryland.*[9] The issue was whether Congress had the power to charter a bank, in particular the Bank of the United States (created by Congress in 1791 over Thomas Jefferson's constitutional opposition), because no power to create banks was found anywhere in Article I, Section 8. Chief Justice John Marshall, speaking for the Supreme Court, answered that such a power could be "implied" from the other specific powers in Article I, Section 8, plus the final clause enabling Congress "to make all Laws which shall be necessary and proper for carrying into Execution the foregoing Powers." Thus the Court created the potential for significant increases in national governmental power.

A second question of national power arose in *McCulloch v. Maryland:* the question of whether Maryland's attempt to tax the bank was constitutional. Once again Marshall and the Supreme Court took the side of the national government, arguing that a legislature representing all the people (Congress) could not be taxed out of business by a state legislature (Maryland) representing only a small portion of the American people. This opinion was accompanied by Marshall's immortal dictum that "the power to tax is the power to destroy." It was also in this case that the Supreme Court recognized and reinforced the supremacy clause: Whenever a state law conflicts with a federal law, the state law should be deemed invalid because "the Laws of the United States . . . shall be the supreme Law of the Land." (This concept was introduced in Chapter 2 and will come up again in Chapter 8.)

This nationalistic interpretation of the Constitution was reinforced by another major case, that of *Gibbons v. Ogden* in 1824. The important but relatively narrow issue was whether the state of New York could grant a monopoly to Robert Fulton's steamboat company to operate an exclusive service between New York and New

commerce clause Article 1, Section 8, of the Constitution delegates to Congress the power "to regulate commerce with Foreign nations, and among the several States and with the Indian tribes. . . ." The Supreme Court interpreted this clause in favor of national power over the economy.

---

[9] *McCulloch v. Maryland,* 4 Wheaton 316 (1819).

Jersey. Aaron Ogden had secured his license from Fulton's company. Thomas Gibbons, a former partner of Ogden's, secured a competing license from the U.S. government. Chief Justice Marshall argued that Gibbons could not be kept from competing because the state of New York did not have the power to grant this particular monopoly. To reach his decision, Marshall had to define what Article I, Section 8, meant by "Commerce . . . among the several States." Marshall insisted that the definition was "comprehensive" but added that the comprehensiveness was limited "to that commerce which concerns more states than one." This opinion gave rise to what later came to be called interstate commerce.[10]

Although *Gibbons* was an important case, the precise meaning of interstate commerce would remain uncertain for several decades of constitutional discourse. However, one thing was certain: "Interstate commerce" was a source of power for the national government as long as Congress sought to improve commerce through subsidies, services, and land grants (Table 3.1, col. 1). Later in the nineteenth century, when the national government sought to use its power to *regulate* the economy rather than merely promote economic development, the concept of interstate commerce began to operate as a restraint rather than as a source of national power. Any effort by the federal government to regulate commerce in such areas as fraud, the production of impure goods, the use of child labor, or the existence of dangerous working conditions or long hours was declared unconstitutional by the Supreme Court as a violation of the concept of interstate commerce. Regulation in these areas would mean the federal government was entering the factory and the workplace, areas inherently local because the goods produced there had not yet passed into commerce and crossed state lines. Any effort to enter these local workplaces was an exercise of police power, a power reserved to the states. No one questioned the power of the national government to regulate certain kinds of businesses, such as railroads, gas pipelines, and waterway transportation, because they intrinsically involved interstate commerce.[11] But well into the twentieth century, most other efforts by Congress to regulate commerce were blocked by the Supreme Court's interpretation of federalism, with the concept of interstate commerce as the primary barrier.

After 1937, the Supreme Court threw out the old distinction between interstate and intrastate commerce, converting the commerce clause from a barrier to a source of power. The Court began to refuse even to review appeals challenging acts of Congress that protected the rights of employees to organize and engage in collective bargaining, regulated the amount of farmland in cultivation, extended low-interest credit to small businesses and farmers, and restricted the activities of corporations dealing in the stock market, as well as many other laws that contributed to the construction of the "regulatory state" and the "welfare state."

---

[10] *Gibbons v. Ogden*, 9 Wheaton 1 (1824).

[11] In *Wabash, St. Louis, and Pacific Railway Company v. Illinois,* 118 U.S. 557 (1886), the Supreme Court struck down a state law prohibiting rate discrimination by a railroad. In response, Congress passed the Interstate Commerce Act of 1887, creating the Interstate Commerce Commission (ICC), the first federal regulatory agency.

Cooperative Federalism and Grants-in-Aid

If the traditional system of two sovereigns performing highly different functions could be called dual federalism, the system since the 1930s could be called **cooperative federalism,** which generally refers to supportive relations, sometimes partnerships, between national government and the state and local governments. It comes in the form of federal subsidization of special state and local activities; these subsidies are called **grants-in-aid.** But make no mistake about it: Although many of these state and local programs would not exist without the federal grant-in-aid, the grant-in-aid is also an important form of federal influence. (Another form of federal influence, the mandate, will be covered in the next section.)

A grant-in-aid is really a kind of bribe or "carrot"—Congress gives money to state and local governments, but with the condition that the money will be spent for a particular purpose as designed by Congress. Congress uses grants-in-aid because it does not usually have the direct political or constitutional power to command the cities to do its bidding.

This same approach was applied to cities beginning in the late 1930s. Congress set national goals such as public housing and assistance to the unemployed and provided grants-in-aid to meet these goals. The value of these **categorical grants-in-aid** increased from $2.3 billion in 1950 to over $450 billion in 2008 (see Figure 3.1). Sometimes Congress requires the state or local government to match the national contribution dollar for dollar; but for some programs, such as the interstate highway system, the congressional grant-in-aid provides 90 percent of the cost of the program.

For the most part, the categorical grants created before the 1960s simply helped the states perform their traditional functions.[12] In the 1960s, however, the national role expanded and the number of categorical grants increased dramatically. For example, during the Eighty-ninth Congress (1965–66) alone, the number of categorical grant-in-aid programs grew from 221 to 379.[13] The grants authorized during the 1960s announced national purposes much more strongly than did earlier grants. Central to that national purpose was the need to provide opportunities to the poor.

Many of the categorical grants enacted during the 1960s were **project grants,** which require state and local governments to submit proposals to federal agencies. In contrast to the older **formula grants,** which used a formula (composed of such elements as need and state and local capacities) to distribute funds, the new project grants made funding available on a competitive basis. Federal agencies would give grants to the proposals they judged to be the best. In this way, the national government acquired substantial control over which state and local governments got money, how much they got, and how they spent it.

The most important scholar of the history of federalism, Morton Grodzins, characterized this as a move from "layer cake federalism" to "marble cake federalism," in which intergovernmental cooperation and sharing have blurred the line

cooperative federalism A type of federalism existing since the New Deal era in which grants-in-aid have been used strategically to encourage states and localities (without commanding them) to pursue nationally defined goals. Also known as intergovernmental cooperation.

grant-in-aid A general term for funds given by Congress to state and local governments.

categorical grant-in-aid A grant by Congress to states and localities, given with the condition that expenditures be limited to a problem or group specified by the national government.

project grants A grant program in which state and local governments submit proposals to federal agencies and for which funding is provided on a competitive basis.

formula grant A grant-in-aid in which a formula is used to determine the amount of federal funds a state or local government will receive.

---

[12] Kenneth T. Palmer, "The Evolution of Grant Policies," in *The Changing Politics of Federal Grants,* by Lawrence D. Brown, James W. Fossett, and Kenneth T. Palmer (Washington, D.C.: Brookings Institution, 1984), p. 15.

[13] Palmer, "The Evolution of Grant Policies," p. 6.

FIGURE 3.1 THE HISTORICAL TREND OF FEDERAL GRANTS-IN-AID, 1950–2010*

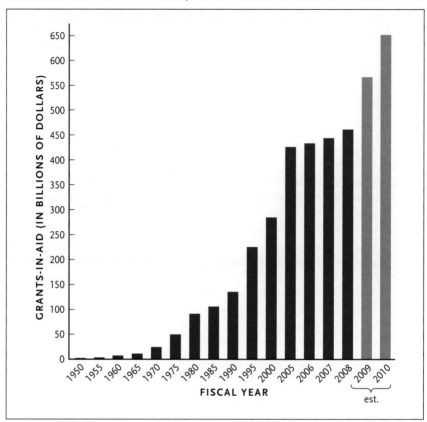

*Excludes outlays for national defense, international affairs, and net interest. 2009 and 2010 are estimates.

SOURCE: Office of Management and Budget, *Budget of the U.S. Government, Fiscal Year 2010,* www.whitehouse.gov/omb/budget/fy2010/pdf/hist.pdf.

between where the national government ends and the state and local governments begin (see Figure 3.2).[14] Figure 3.3 demonstrates the basis of the marble-cake idea. At the high point of grant-in-aid policies in the late 1970s, federal aid contributed about 25–30 percent of the operating budgets of all the state and local governments in the country.

Regulated Federalism and National Standards. Developments from the 1960s to the present have moved well beyond marble cake federalism to what might

---

[14] Morton Grodzins, "The Federal System," in *Goals for Americans: The President's Commission on National Goals* (Englewood Cliffs, N.J.: Prentice Hall, 1960), p. 265. In a marble cake, the white cake is distinguishable from the chocolate cake, but the two are streaked rather than in distinct layers.

FIGURE 3.2 EVOLVING FEDERALISM

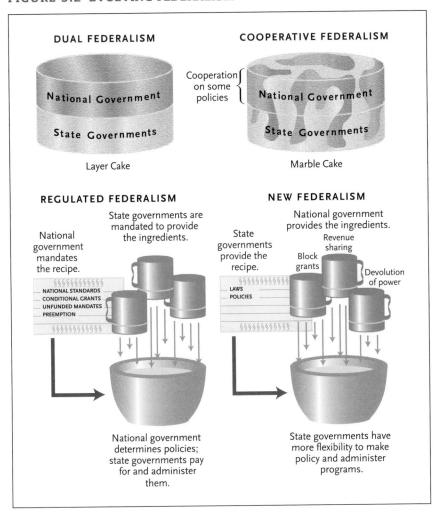

DUAL FEDERALISM

National Government

State Governments

Layer Cake

Cooperation on some policies

COOPERATIVE FEDERALISM

National Government

State Governments

Marble Cake

REGULATED FEDERALISM

National government mandates the recipe.

State governments are mandated to provide the ingredients.

NATIONAL STANDARDS
CONDITIONAL GRANTS
UNFUNDED MANDATES
PREEMPTION

National government determines policies; state governments pay for and administer them.

NEW FEDERALISM

National government provides the ingredients.

State governments provide the recipe.

Revenue sharing

Block grants

Devolution of power

LAWS
POLICIES

State governments have more flexibility to make policy and administer programs.

be called **regulated federalism**.[15] In some areas the national government actually regulates the states by threatening to withhold grant money unless state and local governments conform to national standards. The most notable instances of this regulation are in the areas of civil rights, poverty programs, and environmental protection. In these instances, the national government provides grant-in-aid financing but sets conditions the states must meet in order to keep the grants. The national government refers to these policies as "setting national standards." Important cases of such efforts are in interstate highway use, social services, and education. The net

regulated federalism A form of federalism in which Congress imposes legislation on the states and localities requiring them to meet national standards.

---

[15] The concept and the best discussion of this modern phenomenon will be found in Donald F. Kettl, *The Regulation of American Federalism* (Baltimore: Johns Hopkins University Press, 1983 and 1987), especially pp. 33–41.

FIGURE 3.3 THE RISE, DECLINE, AND RECOVERY OF FEDERAL AID

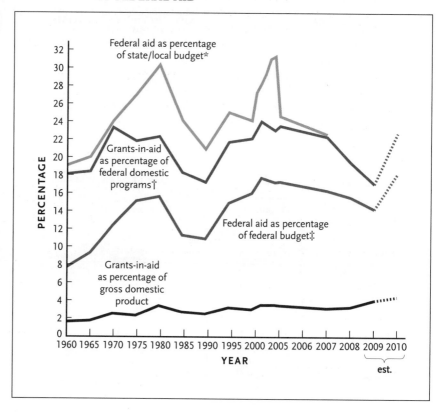

*Federal aid as a percentage of state and local expenditures after transfers.

†Federal aid as a percentage of federal expenditures from the federal government's own funds.

‡Excludes outlays for national defense, international affairs, and net interest.

SOURCE: Office of Management and Budget, *Budget of the U.S. Government, Fiscal Year 2010*, www.whitehouse.gov/omb/budget/fy2010/pdf/hist.pdf.

effect of these national standards is that state and local policies are more uniform from coast to coast. However, in a number of other programs the national government engages in regulated federalism by imposing obligations on the states *without providing any funding at all*. These have come to be called **unfunded mandates**.[16]

These burdens became a major part of the rallying cry that produced the famous Republican Congress elected in 1994, with its Contract with America. One

unfunded mandates Regulations or conditions for receiving grants that impose costs on state and local governments for which they are not reimbursed by the federal government.

---

[16] John DiIulio and Don Kettl report that in 1980 there were thirty-six laws that could be categorized as unfunded mandates. And despite the concerted opposition of the Reagan and Bush administrations, another twenty-seven laws qualifying as unfunded mandates were adopted between 1982 and 1991. See John DiIulio, Jr., and Donald F. Kettl, *Fine Print: The Contract with America, Devolution, and the Administrative Realities of American Federalism* (Washington, D.C.: Brookings Institution, 1995), p. 41.

of the first measures adopted by the 104th Republican Congress was an act to limit unfunded mandates—the Unfunded Mandates Reform Act (UMRA). This was considered a triumph of lobbying efforts by state and local governments, and it was "hailed as both symbol and substance of a renewed congressional commitment to federalism."[17] Under this law, a point of order raised on the House or Senate floor can stop any mandate with an uncompensated state and local cost estimated at greater than $50 million a year as determined by the Congressional Budget Office (CBO). This was called a "stop, look, and listen" requirement, forcing Congress to take positive action to own up to the mandate and its potential costs. During 1996, its first full year of operation, only eleven bills included mandates that exceeded the $50 million threshold—from a total of sixty-nine estimates of actions in which mandates were included. Examples included minimum wage increase, parity for mental health and health insurance, mandated use of Social Security numbers on drivers' licenses, and extension of Federal Occupation Safety and Health to state and local employees. Most of them were modified in the House to reduce their costs. However, as one expert put it, "The primary impact of UMRA came not from the affirmative blockage of [mandate] legislation, but rather from its effect as a deterrent to mandates in the drafting and early consideration of legislation."[18]

As indicated by the first year of its operation, the effect of UMRA is not revolutionary. UMRA does not prevent congressional members from passing unfunded mandates; it only makes them think twice before they do. Moreover, UMRA exempts several areas from coverage. And states must still enforce antidiscrimination laws and meet other requirements to receive federal assistance. But on the other hand, UMRA is a serious effort to shift power in the national–state relationship a bit further toward the state side.

New Federalism and the National–State Tug of War. Presidents Nixon and Reagan called their efforts to reverse the trend toward national standards the new federalism. They helped craft policies to return more discretion to the states. Examples of these policies include Nixon's revenue sharing and Reagan's **block grants**, which consolidated a number of categorical grants into one larger category, leaving the state (or local) government more discretion to decide how to use the money. Presidents Nixon and Reagan, as well as former President George H. W. Bush, were sincere in wanting to return somewhat to a traditional notion of freedom of action for the states. They called it new federalism, but their concept and their goal were really much closer to the older, traditional federalism that predated the 1930s.

President Clinton adopted the new federalism of Nixon and Reagan even though he gave the appearance of expanding federal government activity. He signed the Unfunded Mandates Reform Act of 1995 as well as the Personal Responsibility and Work Opportunity Reconciliation Act of 1996 (PRA), which went further than any other act of Congress in the previous sixty years to relieve the states from both funded and unfunded national mandates. The PRA replaced the sixty-one-year-old

block grant
A federal grant-in-aid that allows states considerable discretion in how the funds should be spent.

---

[17] Paul Posner, "Unfunded Mandate Reform: How Is It Working?" *Rockefeller Institute Bulletin* (Albany, N.Y.: Nelson A. Rockefeller Institute of Government, 1998): 35.

[18] Posner, "Unfunded Mandate Reform," p. 36.

Aid to Families with Dependent Children (AFDC) program with block grants to states for the Temporary Assistance to Needy Families program (TANF). Although some national standards remain, the place of the states in the national welfare system has been virtually revolutionized through **devolution**, the strategy of delegating to the states more and more authority over a range of policies that had been under national government authority, plus providing the states with a substantial portion of the cost of these programs. Since the mid-1990s, devolution has been quite consequential for the national-state tug of war.

By changing welfare from a combined federal-state program into a block grant to the states, Congress gave the states more responsibility for programs that serve the poor. One argument in favor of devolution is that states can act as "laboratories of democracy" by experimenting with many different approaches to find one that best meets the needs of their citizens.[19] As states have altered their welfare programs in the wake of the new law, they have indeed designed diverse approaches. For example, Minnesota has adopted an incentive-based approach that offers extra assistance to families that take low-wage jobs. Other states, such as California, have more sticks than carrots in their new welfare programs.

Former president George W. Bush, though sometimes compared with Reagan, was not an unwavering supporter of new federalism and states' rights. On certain matters dear to his heart, Bush was closer to the spirit of regulated federalism. Some of the expansions of national government under George W. Bush were clearly attributable to September 11 and the gigantic reaction to world terrorism. They include the creation of the Department of Homeland Security, the war in Iraq, and the cost of Hurricane Katrina, all complicated by failed implementation. But President Bush had other plans for the national government that he brought with him from his experience as a governor. His No Child Left Behind Act increased by 51 percent the budget of the Department of Education, a department that conservatives had vowed since the Reagan administration to abolish. The prescription drug benefit that he added to Medicare was another enormous national government commitment; its estimated cost is $534 billion, the largest expansion of the welfare state since Lyndon Johnson.[20]

The Supreme Court as Referee.   For much of the nineteenth century, federal power remained limited. The Tenth Amendment was used to bolster arguments about **states' rights**, which in their extreme version claimed that the states did not have to submit to national laws when they believed the national government had exceeded its authority. These arguments in favor of states' rights were voiced less often after the Civil War. But the Supreme Court continued to use the Tenth Amendment to strike down laws that it thought exceeded national power, including the Civil Rights Act passed in 1875.

devolution
A policy to remove a program from one level of government by delegating it or passing it down to a lower level of government, such as from the national government to the states.

states' rights
The principle that states should oppose increasing authority of the national government. This view was most popular before the Civil War.

---

[19] The phrase "laboratories of democracy" was coined by Supreme Court Justice Louis Brandeis in his dissenting opinion in *New State Ice Co. v. Liebman*, 285 U.S. 262 (1932).

[20] The figures and judgments in this paragraph are provided by George F. Will, one of America's most distinguished conservative columnists and philosophers, in "The Last Word," *Newsweek*, October 27, 2005, p. 78.

In the early twentieth century, however, the Tenth Amendment appeared to lose its force. Reformers began to press for national regulations to limit the power of large corporations and to preserve the health and welfare of citizens. The Supreme Court approved of some of these laws, but it struck others down, including a law combating child labor. The Court stated that the law violated the Tenth Amendment because only states should have the power to regulate conditions of employment. By the late 1930s, however, the Supreme Court had approved such an expansion of federal power that the Tenth Amendment appeared irrelevant. In fact, in 1941, Justice Harlan Fiske Stone declared that the Tenth Amendment was simply a "truism," that it had no real meaning.[21]

Recent years have seen a revival of interest in the Tenth Amendment and important Supreme Court decisions limiting federal power. Much of the interest in the Tenth Amendment stems from conservatives who believe that a strong federal government encroaches on individual liberties. They believe such freedoms are better protected by returning more power to the states through the process of devolution. In 1996, the Republican presidential candidate Bob Dole carried a copy of the Tenth Amendment in his pocket as he campaigned, pulling it out to read at rallies.[22] Around the same time, the Court revived the Eleventh Amendment concept of **state sovereign immunity**. This legal doctrine holds that states are immune from lawsuits by private persons or groups claiming that the state violated a statute enacted by Congress.

> **state sovereign immunity** A legal doctrine that holds that states cannot be sued for violating an act of Congress.

The Supreme Court's ruling in *United States v. Lopez* in 1995 fueled further interest in the Tenth Amendment. In that case, the Court, stating that Congress had exceeded its authority under the commerce clause, struck down a federal law that barred handguns near schools. This was the first time since the New Deal that the Court had limited congressional powers in this way. (The New Deal is discussed in Chapter 6.) The Court further limited the power of the federal government over the states in a 1996 ruling based on the Eleventh Amendment that prevented Native Americans from the Seminole tribe from suing the state of Florida in federal court. A 1988 law had given Indian tribes the right to sue a state in federal court if the state did not negotiate in good faith over issues related to gambling casinos on tribal land. The Supreme Court's ruling appeared to signal a much broader limitation on national power by raising new questions about whether individuals can sue a state if it fails to uphold federal law.[23]

Another significant decision involving the relationship between the federal government and state governments was the 1997 case *Printz v. United States* (joined with *Mack v. United States*),[24] in which the Court struck down a key provision of the Brady Bill, enacted by Congress in 1993 to regulate gun sales. Under the terms of the act, state and local law enforcement officers were required to conduct background checks on prospective gun purchasers. The Court held that the federal government cannot require states to administer or enforce federal regulatory

---

[21] *United States v. Darby Lumber Co.*, 312 U.S. 100 (1941).

[22] W. John Moore, "Pleading the 10th," *National Journal*, July 29, 1995, p. 1940.

[23] *Seminole Indian Tribe v. Florida*, 116 S. Ct. 1114 (1996).

[24] *Printz* and *Mack*, 521 U.S. 898, 117 S. Ct. 2365 (1997).

Federalism

Consequences of Federalism as Established in the Constitution

Existence of two sovereigns—the national government and the state governments, with state governments wielding more power for the first 150 years after the writing of the Constitution.

Particular restraint on the power of the national government to affect economic policy.

Great variations from state to state in terms of citizens' rights, role of government, and judicial activity.

Evolution of the Federal System

1789–1834	*Nationalization:* The Marshall Court interprets the Constitution broadly so as to expand and consolidate national power.
1835–1930s	*Dual federalism:* The functions of the national government are very specifically enumerated. States do much of the fundamental governing that affects citizens' day-to-day life. There is tension between the two levels of government, and the power of the national government begins to increase.
1930s–70s	*Cooperative federalism:* The national government uses grants-in-aid to encourage states and localities to pursue nationally defined goals.
1970s–	*Regulated federalism:* The national government sets conditions that states and localities must meet in order to keep certain grants. The national government also sets national standards in areas without providing funding to meet them.
	New federalism: The national government attempts to return more power to the states through block grants to the states.

programs. Since the states bear administrative responsibility for a variety of other federal programs, this decision could have far-reaching consequences. Finally, in another major ruling from the 1996–97 term, in *City of Boerne v. Flores,*[25] the Court ruled that Congress had gone too far in restricting the power of the states to enact regulations they deemed necessary for the protection of public health, safety, or welfare. These rulings signal a move toward a much more restricted federal government.

In 1999, the Court's ruling on another Eleventh Amendment case further strengthened the doctrine of state sovereign immunity, finding that "The federal system established by our Constitution preserves the sovereign status of the States. . . . The generation that designed and adopted our federal system considered immunity from private suits central to sovereign dignity."[26] In 2000 in *United States v. Morrison,* the Supreme Court invalidated an important provision of the 1994 Violence against Women Act, which permitted women to bring private damage suits

---

[25] *City of Boerne v. Flores,* 521 U.S. 507, 117 S. Ct. 2157 (1997).

[26] *Alden v. Maine.*

if their victimization was "gender-motivated." Although the 1994 act did not add any new national laws imposing liability or obligations on the states, the Supreme Court still held the act to be "an unconstitutional exercise" of Congress's power. And, although *Morrison* is a quite narrow federalism decision, when it is coupled with *United States v. Lopez* (1995)—the first modern holding against national authority to use commerce power to reach into the states—we see a definite trend toward strict scrutiny of the federal intervention aspects of all national civil rights, social, labor, and gender laws.[27] This trend had continued with the 2006 *Gonzales v. Oregon* case, in which the Court ruled that the federal government could not use federal drug laws to interfere with Oregon's assisted-suicide law.[28]

This tug-of-war between the states and national government will certainly continue, especially because the Roberts Court under Chief Justice John Roberts seems likely to pull us back further toward states' rights.

THE SEPARATION OF POWERS

James Madison quoted the French political thinker the baron de Montesquieu on the **separation of powers**:

> There can be no liberty where the legislative and executive powers are united in the same person . . . [or] if the power of judging be not separated from the legislative and executive powers.[29]

Using this same reasoning, many of Madison's contemporaries argued that there was not *enough* separation among the three branches, and Madison had to backtrack to insist that complete separation was not required:

> . . . unless these departments [branches] be so far connected and blended as to give each a constitutional control over the others, the degree of separation which the maxim requires, as essential to a free government, can never in practice be duly maintained.[30]

This is the secret of how we have made the separation of powers effective: We made the principle self-enforcing by giving each branch of government the means to participate in and partially or temporarily obstruct the workings of the other branches.

Checks and Balances

The means by which each branch of government interacts with each other branch is known informally as **checks and balances**. The best-known examples are shown in

separation of powers The division of governmental power among several institutions that must cooperate in decision making.

checks and balances Mechanisms through which each branch of government is able to participate in and influence the activities of the other branches. Major examples include the presidential veto power over congressional legislation, the power of the Senate to approve presidential appointments, and judicial review of congressional enactments.

---

[27] *United States v. Morrison,* 529 U.S. 598 (2000).

[28] *Gonzales v. Oregon,* 546 U.S. 243 (2006).

[29] Clinton Rossiter, ed., *The Federalist Papers* (New York: New American Library, 1961), no. 47, p. 302.

[30] Rossiter's *Federalist Papers,* no. 48, p. 308.

Figure 3.4. The framers sought to guarantee that the three branches would in fact use these checks and balances as weapons against one another by giving each branch a different political constituency and therefore a different perspective on what the government ought to do: direct, popular election for the members of the House; indirect election of senators (until the Seventeenth Amendment, adopted in 1913); indirect election of the president through the electoral college; and appointment of federal judges for life. All things considered, the best characterization of the separation of powers principle in action is "separated institutions sharing power."[31]

Legislative Supremacy

legislative supremacy The preeminence of Congress among the three branches of government, as established by the Constitution.

Although each branch was to be given adequate means to compete with the other branches, it is also clear that within the system of separated powers the framers provided for **legislative supremacy** by making Congress the preeminent branch. Legislative supremacy made the provision of checks and balances in the other two branches all the more important.

The most important indication of the intentions of the framers were the provisions in Article I, to treat the powers of the national government as powers of Congress. The Founders also provided for legislative supremacy in their decision to give Congress the sole power over appropriations.

divided government The condition in American government wherein one party controls the presidency while the opposing party controls one or both houses of Congress.

Although "presidential government" gradually supplanted legislative supremacy after 1937, the relative power of the executive and legislative branches has varied. The power play between the president and Congress is especially intense during periods of **divided government**, when one party controls the White House and another controls Capitol Hill, as has been the case almost continuously since 1969. The "Analyzing the Evidence" unit on page 68 takes a closer look at efforts by Congress to check the president.

The Role of the Supreme Court

The role of the judicial branch in the separation of powers has depended on the power of judicial review, a power not provided for in the Constitution but asserted by Chief Justice Marshall in 1803:

> If a law be in opposition to the Constitution; if both the law and the Constitution apply to a particular case, so that the Court must either decide that case conformable to the law, disregarding the Constitution, or conformable to the Constitution, disregarding the law; the Court must determine which of these conflicting rules governs the case: This is of the very essence of judicial duty.[32]

Review of the constitutionality of acts of the president or Congress is relatively rare. For example, there were no Supreme Court reviews of congressional acts in the fifty plus years between *Marbury v. Madison* (1803) and *Dred Scott v. Sandford* (1857). In the century or so between the Civil War and 1970, eighty-four acts of Congress were held unconstitutional (in whole or in part), but there were long periods of

---

[31] Richard E. Neustadt, *Presidential Power* (New York: Wiley, 1960), p. 33.

[32] *Marbury v. Madison,* 1 Cranch 137 (1803).

FIGURE 3.4 CHECKS AND BALANCES

Executive over Legislative
- President can veto acts of Congress.
- President can call a special session of Congress.
- President carries out, and thereby interprets, laws passed by Congress.
- Vice president casts tie-breaking vote in the Senate.

LEGISLATIVE

Legislative over Judicial
- Congress can change size of federal court system and number of Supreme Court justices.
- Congress can propose constitutional amendments.
- Congress can reject Supreme Court nominees.
- Congress can impeach and remove federal judges.
- Congress can amend court jurisdictions.
- Congress controls appropriations.

Legislative over Executive
- Congress can override presidential veto.
- Congress can impeach and remove president.
- Senate can reject president's appointments and refuse to ratify treaties.
- Congress can conduct investigations into president's actions.
- Congress can refuse to pass laws or provide funding that president requests.

Judicial over Legislative
- Court can declare laws unconstitutional.
- Chief Justice presides over Senate during hearing to impeach the president.

Executive over Judicial
- President nominates Supreme Court justices.
- President nominates federal judges.
- President can pardon those convicted in federal court.
- President can refuse to enforce the court's decisions.

JUDICIAL

EXECUTIVE

Judicial over Executive
- Court can declare executive actions unconstitutional.
- Court has the power to issue warrants.
- Chief Justice presides over impeachment of president.

complete Supreme Court deference to the Congress, punctuated by flurries of judicial review during periods of social upheaval. The most significant of these was 1935–36, when twelve acts of Congress were invalidated, blocking virtually the entire New Deal program.[33] Then, after 1937, when the Court made its great reversals, no significant acts were voided until 1983, when the Court declared the legislative

---

[33] C. Herman Pritchett, *The American Constitution* (New York: McGraw-Hill, 1959), pp. 180–86.

Bypassing Checks and Balances?

Although the system of checks and balances envisioned by the Founders seems to apportion checks equally among the branches, this has not stopped political actors from attempting to consolidate power. A recent example of one branch claiming greater power at the expense of the others is the increased use of presidential *signing statements*. Presidents use signing statements to offer their opinions on legislation and how it should be interpreted and implemented. However, recent presidents have made more frequent and calculated use of signing statements to nullify legislation they disagree with. An April 2006 article in the *Boston Globe* reported that President Bush used the practice to claim the authority to bypass over 750 statutes passed by Congress.[1]

Criticism of this use of signing statements to reinterpret and nullify legislation has been sharp. A *New York Times* editorial blasted the Bush administration for "disrupt[ing] the founders' careful allocation of power among the president, Congress and the courts."[2] Senator Patrick Leahy (D-Vt.) accused the administration of utilizing "an extra-constitutional, extra-judicial step to enhance the power of the president."[3] Senator Arlen Specter (R-Pa.) introduced legislation to curb the practice, and Senator Robert Byrd (D-Va.) and Congressman John Conyers (D-Mich.) commissioned a study to gauge the impact of the practice. As the figure below demonstrates, the threats and rhetoric from critics seem to have effectively reduced the total number of signing statements issued in the last two years of the Bush presidency. Further, soon after taking office in 2009, President Obama announced plans to use the practice much more modestly than the previous administration.[4]

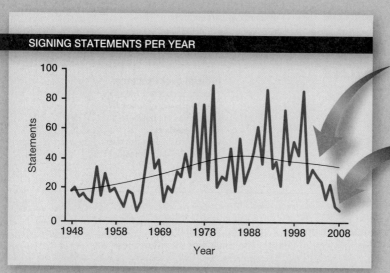

Use of signing statements to bypass Congress was high in the first few years of the Bush presidency.

In 2007 and 2008, Bush's use of signing statements dropped off considerably, suggesting that efforts by members of Congress and others to check the presidency had been effective.

Source: Data from the American Presidency Project, www.presidency.ucsb.edu/index.php (accessed 5/28/09).

[1]Charles Savage, "Bush Challenges Hundreds of Laws," *Boston Globe*, April 30, 2006.
[2]"On Signing Statements," *New York Times*, March 16, 2009.
[3]Carl Hulse, "Lawmakers to Investigate Bush on Laws and Intent," *New York Times*, June 20, 2007.
[4]"Charles Salvage, "Obama Looks to Limit Impact of Tactic Bush Used to Sidestep New Laws," *New York Times*, March 9, 2009.

Presidents have also attempted to circumvent constitutional checks on their power by using the Constitution's *recess appointment clause*. The recess appointment clause in Article II, Section 2 allows presidents to "fill up all Vacancies that may happen during the Recess of the Senate, by granting Commissions which shall expire at the End of their next Session." The George W. Bush administration seized this language and regularly used recess appointments to bypass the Senate, which normally has the power to confirm (or not confirm) appointees to the executive and judicial branches. As the figure below demonstrates, early in his term, Bush used recess appointments at a higher rate than previous administrations.[5]

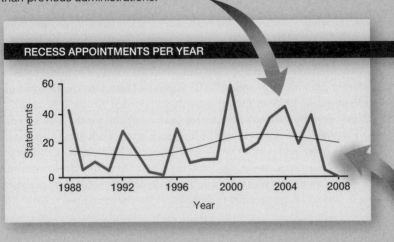

RECESS APPOINTMENTS PER YEAR

Not only did President Bush make a large number of recess appointments, but he made many controversial ones as well. Bush's recess appointments of Charles W. Pickering and William Pryor to federal appellate courts and John Bolton to the United Nations outraged Senate Democrats who had been blocking those nominations. However, it was not until his 2007 recess appointment of Sam Fox to be the United States ambassador to Belgium that the Democrats took action. Fox's nomination was likely to be defeated by the Democratic-controlled Senate Foreign Relations Committee when the president withdrew it and gave him a recess appointment to the position. The move prompted Senate Majority Leader Harry Reid (D-Nev.) to declare his intention of keeping the Senate in permanent session. This maneuver, though highly unorthodox, was aimed at blocking the president from making further recess appointments. As the data demonstrates, it was effective in restoring the Senate's ability to check executive nominations. Following threats by Democrats in Congress, President Bush made a mere four recess appointments in 2007, and none in 2008. In this respect, then, it appears that the system of checks and balances envisioned by the framers had been restored.

[5]Ryan C. Black, Anthony J. Madonna, Ryan J. Owens, and Michael S. Lynch, "Adding Recess Appointments to the President's 'Tool Chest' of Unilateral Powers," *Political Research Quarterly* 60, no. 4 (December 2007): 645–54.

veto unconstitutional.[34] The Supreme Court became much more activist (that is, less deferential to Congress) after the elevation of Justice William H. Rehnquist to chief justice (1986–2005), and "a new program of judicial activism"[35] seemed to be in place. Between 1995 and 2002, at least twenty-six acts or parts of acts of Congress were struck down on constitutional grounds.[36]

The Court has been far more deferential toward the president since the New Deal period, with only five significant confrontations. One was the so-called steel seizure case of 1952, in which the Court refused to permit President Truman to use "emergency powers" to force workers back into the steel mills during the Korean War.[37] A second case was *United States v. Nixon*, in which the Court declared unconstitutional President Nixon's refusal to respond to a subpoena to make available the infamous White House tapes as evidence in a criminal prosecution. The Court argued that although **executive privilege** did protect confidentiality of communications to and from the president, this did not extend to data in presidential files or tapes bearing on criminal prosecutions.[38] During the heat of the scandal over President Clinton's relationship with the intern Monica Lewinsky, the Supreme Court rejected the claim that the pressures and obligations of the office of president were so demanding that all litigation "but the most exceptional cases" should be deferred until his term ended.[39] The Supreme Court also struck down the Line-Item Veto Act of 1996 on the grounds that it violated Article I, Section 7, which prescribed procedures for congressional enactment and presidential acceptance or veto of statutes. Any such change in the procedures of adopting laws would have to be made by amendment to the Constitution, not by legislation.[40] Most recently, and of far greater importance, the Supreme Court repudiated the Bush administration's claims about the president's authority to detain enemy combatants without giving detainees an opportunity to defend themselves in an open court.[41]

executive privilege
The claim that confidential communications between a president and close advisers should not be revealed without the consent of the president.

DO FEDERALISM AND THE SEPARATION OF POWERS WORK?

Federalism and the separation of powers are two of the three most important constitutional principles upon which the United States' system of limited government is based. (The third is the principle of individual rights.) As we have seen, federalism limits the power of the national government in numerous ways. By its

---

[34] *Immigration and Naturalization Service v. Chadha*, 462 U.S. 919 (1983). (See Chapter 7.)

[35] Cass R. Sunstein, "Taking Over the Courts," *New York Times*, November 9, 2002, p. A19.

[36] Sunstein, "Taking Over the Courts."

[37] *Youngstown Sheet & Tube Co. v. Sawyer*, 343 U.S. 579 (1952).

[38] *United States v. Nixon*, 418 U.S. 683 (1974).

[39] *Clinton v. Jones*, 117 S. Ct. 1636 (1997).

[40] *Clinton v. City of New York*, 524 U.S. 417 (1998).

[41] *Hamdi v. Rumsfeld*, 124 S. Ct. 2633 (2004); *Rasul v. Bush*, 542 U.S. 466 (2004).

very existence, federalism recognizes the principle of two sovereigns, the national government and the state governments (hence the term "dual federalism"). In addition, the Constitution specifically restrained the power of the national government to regulate the economy. As a result, the states were free to do most of the fundamental governing for the first century and a half of American government. This began to change during and following the New Deal, as the national government began to exert more influence over the states through grants-in-aid and mandates. But even as the powers of the national government grew, so did the powers of the states. In the last decade, as well, we have noticed a countertrend to the growth of national power as Congress has opted to devolve some of its powers to the states. The most recent notable instance of devolution was the welfare reform plan of 1996.

But the problem that arises with devolution is that programs that were once uniform across the country (because they were the national government's responsibility) can become highly variable, with some states providing benefits not available in other states. To a point, variation can be considered one of the virtues of federalism. But dangers are inherent in large variations and inequalities in the provision of services and benefits in a democracy. For example, the Food and Drug Administration has been under attack in recent years. Could the government address the agency's perceived problems by devolving its regulatory tasks to the states? Would people care if drugs would require "caution" labels in some states but not in others? In 2009, the Obama administration indicated that it would seek more power for the FDA to regulate potentially harmful drugs. Devolution, as attractive as it may be, is not an approach that can be applied across the board without analyzing carefully the nature of the program and of the problems it is designed to solve.

A key puzzle of federalism is deciding when differences across states reflect the proper democratic decisions of the states and when such differences reflect inequalities that should not be tolerated. Sometimes a decision to eliminate differences is made on the grounds of equality and individual rights, as in the Civil Rights Act of 1964, which outlawed segregation. At other times, a stronger federal role is justified on the grounds of national interest, as in the case of the oil shortage and the institution of a fifty-five-mile-per-hour speed limit in the 1970s. Advocates of a more limited federal role often point to the value of democracy. Public actions can more easily be tailored to fit distinctive local or state desires if states and localities have more power to make policy. Viewed this way, variation across states can be an expression of democratic will.

In the 1990s, many Americans seemed to have grown disillusioned with the federal government and have supported efforts to give the states more responsibilities. A 1997 poll, for example, found that nearly two-thirds of those polled believed that shifting some responsibility to states and localities would help achieve excellence in government. After the terrorist attacks of September 11, 2001, however, support for the federal government soared. With issues of security topping the list of citizens' concerns, the federal government, which had seemed less important with the waning of the Cold War, suddenly reemerged as the central actor in American politics. As one observer put it, "Federalism was a luxury of peaceful times."[42] Similarly, as

---

[42] Linda Greenhouse, "Will the Court Reassert National Authority?" *New York Times*, September 30, 2001, Sect. 4, p. 14.

an economic crisis deepened in 2008 and 2009, many Americans looked to the federal government to address the nation's problems. Yet the newfound respect for the federal government is likely to be contingent on how well the government performs. If the federal government does not appear to be effective in the fight against terrorism or the effort to restore prosperity, its stature may once again decline in the minds of many Americans.

The second feature of limited government, separation of powers, is manifested in our system of checks and balances, whereby separate institutions of government share power with each other. Even though the Constitution clearly provided for legislative supremacy, checks and balances have functioned well. Some would say this system has worked too well. The last fifty years have witnessed long periods of divided government, when one party controls the White House while the other party controls Congress. During these periods, the level of conflict between the executive and legislative branches has been particularly divisive, resulting in what some analysts derisively call gridlock.[43]

During President George W. Bush's first six years in office, the separation of powers did not seem to work effectively. Congress gave Bush a free rein in such important matters as the war in Iraq and the war against terrorism. Of course during this period, Congress was controlled by the president's fellow Republicans. In 2006, Democrats won control of both houses and promised to scrutinize the president's actions carefully. However, with the election of the Democrat Barack Obama to the presidency in 2008, Congress and the presidency were once again controlled by the same party, raising new concerns about the separation of powers.

CHAPTER REVIEW

In this chapter we have traced the development of two of the three basic principles of the U.S. Constitution: federalism and the separation of powers. Federalism involves a division between two layers of government, national and state. The separation of powers involves the division of the national government into three branches. These principles are limitations on the powers of government; Americans specified these principles as a condition of giving their consent to be governed. And these principles became the framework within which the government operates. The persistence of local government and of reliance of the national government on grants-in-aid to coerce local governments into following national goals demonstrates the continuing vitality of the federal framework. The intense competition among the president, Congress, and the courts dramatizes the continuing vitality of the separation of powers.

---

[43] Not everybody will agree that divided government is so much less productive than government in which the same party controls both branches. See David Mayhew, *Divided We Govern: Party Control, Law Making and Investigations, 1946–1990* (New Haven, Conn.: Yale University Press, 1991). For another good evaluation of divided government, see Charles O. Jones, *Separate but Equal Branches— Congress and the Presidency* (Chatham, N.J.: Chatham House, 1995).

The purpose of a constitution is to organize the makeup or the composition of the government, the *framework* within which government and politics, including actual legislation, can take place. A country does not require federalism and the separation of powers to have a real constitutional government. And the country does not have to approach individual rights in the same manner as the American Constitution. But to be a true constitutional government, a government must have some kind of framework that consists of a few principles that cannot be manipulated by people in power merely for their own convenience. This is the essence of constitutionalism—principles that are above the reach of everyday legislatures, executives, bureaucrats, and politicians, yet that are not so far above their reach that these principles cannot sometimes be adapted to changing conditions.

FOR FURTHER READING

Bednar, Jenna. *The Robust Federation*. New York: Cambridge University Press, 2008. ○ reader selection

Campbell, Tom. *Separation of Powers in Practice*. Palo Alto, Calif.: Stanford University Press, 2004.

Crenson, Matthew, and Benjamin Ginsberg. *Presidential Power: Unchecked and Unbalanced*. New York: Norton, 2007.

Ferejohn, John A., and Barry R. Weingast, eds. *The New Federalism: Can the States Be Trusted?* Stanford, Calif.: Hoover Institution Press, 1997.

Fisher, Louis. *Congressional Abdication on War and Spending*. College Station: Texas A&M University Press, 2000.

——. *Constitutional Conflicts Between Congress and the President*, 7th ed. Lawrence: University of Kansas Press, 2007.

Karmis, Dimitrios, and Wayne Norman. *Theories of Federalism: A Reader*. New York: Palgrave, Macmillan, 2005.

Kettl, Donald F. *The Regulation of American Federalism*. Baltimore: Johns Hopkins University Press, 1987.

Nagel, Robert. *The Implosion of American Federalism*. New York: Oxford University Press, 2001.

Noonan, John T. *Narrowing the Nation's Power: The Supreme Court Sides with the States*. Berkeley: University of California Press, 2002.

Posner, Richard. *Not a Suicide Pact: The Constitution in a Time of National Emergency*. New York: Oxford University Press, 2006.

Riker, William H. *Federalism: Origin, Operation, Significance*. Boston: Little, Brown, 1964. ○ reader selection

Smith, Rogers M. *Civic Ideals: Conflicting Visions of Citizenship in U.S. History*. New Haven, Conn.: Yale University Press, 1997.

Van Horn, Carol E. *The State of the States*, 4th ed. Washington, D.C.: CQ Press, 2004.

 Additional study and review materials are available online at wwnorton.com/studyspace/

4

Civil Liberties and Civil Rights

The first ten amendments of the United States Constitution, together called the **Bill of Rights**, are the basis for the freedoms we enjoy as American citizens. The Bill of Rights might well have been entitled the "Bill of Liberties," because the provisions that were incorporated in the Bill of Rights were seen as defining a private sphere of personal liberty, free of governmental restrictions. These freedoms include the right to free speech, the right to the free exercise of religion, prohibitions against unreasonable searches and seizures, and guarantees of due process of law.

As Jefferson had put it, a bill of rights "is what people are entitled to against every government on earth. . . ." **Civil liberties** are protections from improper government action. Thus, the Bill of Rights is a series of restraints imposed on government. Some of these restraints are substantive liberties, which put limits on what the government shall and shall not have power to do—such as establishing a religion, quartering troops in private homes without consent, or seizing private property without just compensation. Other restraints are *procedural liberties,* which deal with how the government is supposed to act. These procedural liberties are usually grouped under the general category of *due process of law,* which first appears in the Fifth Amendment provision that "no person shall be . . . deprived of life, liberty, or property, without due process of law." For example, even though the government has the substantive power to declare certain acts to be crimes and to arrest and imprison persons who violate criminal laws, it may not do so without meticulously observing procedures designed to protect the accused person. The best-known procedural rule is that an accused person is presumed innocent until proven guilty. This rule does not question the government's power to punish someone for committing a crime; it questions only the way the government determines who committed the crime. Substantive and procedural restraints together identify the realm of civil liberties.

Whereas civil liberties are phrased as negatives, **civil rights** are obligations imposed on government to guarantee equal citizenship and to protect citizens from discrimination by other private citizens and other government agencies. Civil rights did not become part of the Constitution until 1868, with the adoption of the Fourteenth Amendment, which addressed the issue of who was a citizen and provided for each citizen "equal protection of the laws." In legal terms, civil liberties issues arise under the "due process of law" clause, and civil rights issues arise under the "equal protection of the laws" clause of the Constitution.[1]

We turn first to civil liberties and the long history of the effort to make personal liberty a reality for every citizen in America. The struggle for freedom against arbitrary and discriminatory actions by governments continues to this day. And inevitably it is tied to the continuing struggle for civil rights, to persuade those same governments to take positive action. We deal with that in the second section of this chapter.

Bill of Rights The first ten amendments to the U.S. Constitution.

civil liberties Areas of personal freedom with which governments are constrained from interfering.

civil rights Legal or moral claims that citizens are entitled to make on the government to protect them from the illegal actions of other citizens and government agencies.

---

[1] For recent scholarship on the Bill of Rights and its development, see Geoffrey Stone, Richard Epstein, and Cass Sunstein, eds., *The Bill of Rights and the Modern State* (Chicago: University of Chicago Press, 1992); and Michael J. Meyer and William A. Parent, eds., *The Constitution of Rights* (Ithaca, N.Y.: Cornell University Press, 1992).

CIVIL LIBERTIES: NATIONALIZING THE BILL OF RIGHTS

The First Amendment provides that "Congress shall make no law respecting an establishment of religion . . . or abridging freedom of speech, or of the press; or the right of [assembly and petition]." But this is the only amendment in the Bill of Rights that addresses itself exclusively to the national government. For example, the Second Amendment provides that "the right of the people to keep and bear Arms shall not be infringed." The Fifth Amendment says, among other things, that "no person shall . . . be twice put in jeopardy of life or limb" for the same crime; that no person "shall be compelled in any Criminal Case to be a witness against himself"; that no person shall "be deprived of life, liberty, or property, without due process of law"; and that private property cannot be taken "without just compensation."[2]

Dual Citizenship

Because the First Amendment is the only part of the Bill of Rights that is explicit in its intention to put limits on the national government, a fundamental question inevitably arises: Do the remaining amendments of the Bill of Rights put limits on state governments or only on the national government? This question was settled in 1833 in a way that seems odd to Americans today. The case was *Barron v. Baltimore*, and the facts were simple. In paving its streets, the city of Baltimore had disposed of so much sand and gravel in the water near Barron's wharf that the value of the wharf for commercial purposes was virtually destroyed. Barron brought the city into court on the grounds that it had, under the Fifth Amendment, unconstitutionally deprived him of his property without just compensation. Barron took his case all the way to the Supreme Court. There Chief Justice Marshall, in one of the most significant Supreme Court decisions ever handed down, disagreed with Barron:

> The Constitution was ordained and established by the people of the United States for themselves, for their own government, and not for the government of the individual States. Each State established a constitution for itself, and in that constitution provided such limitations and restrictions on the powers of its particular government as its judgment dictated. . . . If these propositions be correct, the fifth amendment must be understood as restraining the power of the general government, not as applicable to the States.[3]

In other words, if an agency of the national government had deprived Barron of his property, there would have been little doubt about Barron's winning his case. But

---

[2] It would be useful at this point to review all the provisions of the Bill of Rights (in the Appendix) to confirm this distinction between the wording of the First Amendment and the rest of the Bill of Rights. For a spirited and enlightening essay on the extent to which the entire Bill of Rights was about equality, see Martha Minow, "Equality and the Bill of Rights," in Meyer and Parent, eds., *The Constitution of Rights*, pp. 118–28.

[3] *Barron v. Mayor and City of Baltimore*, 7 Peters 243 (1833).

The Bill of Rights

Amendment I: Limits on Congress

Congress cannot make any law establishing a religion or abridging freedoms of religious exercise, speech, assembly, or petition.

Amendments II, III, IV: Limits on the Executive

The executive branch cannot infringe on the right of people to keep arms (II), cannot arbitrarily take houses for militia (III), and cannot search for or seize evidence without a court warrant swearing to the probable existence of a crime (IV).

Amendments V, VI, VII, VIII: Limits on the Judiciary

The courts cannot hold trials for serious offenses without provision for a grand jury (V), a trial jury (VII), a speedy trial (VI), presentation of charges and confrontation by the accused of hostile witnesses (VI), immunity from testimony against oneself, and immunity from trial more than once for the same offense (V). Furthermore, neither bail nor punishment can be excessive (VIII), and no property can be taken without "just compensation" (V).

Amendments IX, X: Limits on the National Government

Any rights not enumerated are reserved to the states or the people (X), and the enumeration of certain rights in the Constitution should not be interpreted to mean that those are the only rights the people have (IX).

if the constitution of the state of Maryland contained no such provision protecting citizens of Maryland from such action, then Barron had no legal leg to stand on against Baltimore, an agency of the state of Maryland.

Barron v. Baltimore confirmed dual citizenship—that is, that each American was a citizen of the national government and separately a citizen of one of the states. This meant that the Bill of Rights did not apply to decisions or procedures of state (or local) governments. Even slavery could continue, because the Bill of Rights could not protect anyone from state laws treating people as property. In fact, the Bill of Rights did not become a vital instrument for the extension of civil liberties for anyone until after a bloody Civil War and a revolutionary Fourteenth Amendment intervened. And even so, as we shall see, nearly a second century would pass before the Bill of Rights would truly come into its own.

The Fourteenth Amendment

From a constitutional standpoint, the defeat of the South in the Civil War settled one question and raised another. It probably settled forever the question of whether secession was an option for any state. After 1865, there was more "united" than "states" to the United States. But this left unanswered just how much the states were obliged to obey the Constitution, in particular, the Bill of Rights. Just reading the words of the Fourteenth Amendment, anyone might think it was almost perfectly designed to impose the Bill of Rights on the states and thereby to reverse *Barron v. Baltimore*. The very first words of the Fourteenth Amendment point in that direction:

> All persons born or naturalized in the United States, and subject to the jurisdiction thereof, are citizens of the United States and of the State wherein they reside.

This provides for a single national citizenship, and at a minimum that means that civil liberties should not vary drastically from state to state. That would seem to be the spirit of the Fourteenth Amendment: to nationalize the Bill of Rights by nationalizing the definition of citizenship.

This interpretation of the Fourteenth Amendment is reinforced by the next clause of the Amendment:

> No state shall make or enforce any law which shall abridge the privileges or immunities of citizens of the United States; nor shall any state deprive any person of life, liberty, or property, without due process of law.

All of this sounds like an effort to extend the Bill of Rights in its entirety to citizens wherever they might reside.[4] But this was not to be the Supreme Court's interpretation for nearly a hundred years. Within five years of ratification of the Fourteenth Amendment, the Court was making decisions as though it had never been adopted.[5] The shadow of Barron grew longer and longer. Table 4.1 outlines the major developments in the history of the Fourteenth Amendment against the backdrop of Barron, citing the particular provisions of the Bill of Rights as they were incorporated by Supreme Court decisions into the Fourteenth Amendment as limitations on all the states. This is a measure of the degree of "nationalization" of civil liberties.

The only change in civil liberties during the first sixty years after the adoption of the Fourteenth Amendment came in 1897, when the Supreme Court held that the due process clause of the Fourteenth Amendment did in fact prohibit states from taking property for a public use without just compensation.[6] This effectively overruled the specific holding in *Barron;* henceforth a citizen of Maryland or any state was protected from a "public taking" of property even if the state constitution did not provide such protection. The power of public agencies to seize private property is called eminent domain. According to the Fifth Amendment, private owners must be paid "just compensation" by the government if it decides that it needs their property. But in a broader sense, *Barron* still cast a shadow, because

---

[4]The Fourteenth Amendment also seems designed to introduce civil rights. The final clause of the all-important Section 1 provides that no state can "deny to any person within its jurisdiction the equal protection of the laws." It is not unreasonable to conclude that the purpose of this provision was to obligate the state governments as well as the national government to take *positive* actions to protect citizens from arbitrary and discriminatory actions, at least those based on race. This will be explored in the second half of the chapter.

[5]The Slaughter-House Cases, 16 Wallace 36 (1873); The Civil Rights Cases, 109 U.S. 3 (1883).

[6]*Chicago, Burlington and Quincy Railroad Company v. Chicago,* 166 U.S. 266 (1897).

TABLE 4.1 INCORPORATION OF THE BILL OF RIGHTS INTO THE FOURTEENTH AMENDMENT

Selected Provisions and Amendments	Date "incorporated"	Key Cases
Eminent domain (V)	1897	Chicago, Burlington and Quincy Railroad v. Chicago
Freedom of speech (I)	1925	Gitlow v. New York
Freedom of the press (I)	1931	Near v. Minnesota ex rel. Olson
Free exercise of religion (I)	1934	Hamilton v. Regents of the University of California
Freedom of assembly (I)	1939	Hague v. Committee for Industrial Organization
Freedom from unnecessary search and seizure (IV)	1949	Wolf v. Colorado
Freedom from warrantless search and seizure ("exclusionary rule") (IV)	1961	Mapp v. Ohio
Freedom from cruel and unusual punishment (VIII)	1962	Robinson v. California
Right to counsel in any criminal trial (VI)	1963	Gideon v. Wainwright
Right against self-incrimination and forced confessions (V)	1964	Mallory v. Hogan Escobedo v. Illinois
Right to privacy (III, IV, and V)	1965	Griswold v. Connecticut
Right to remain silent (V)	1966	Miranda v. Arizona
Right against double jeopardy (V)	1969	Benton v. Maryland

the Supreme Court had "incorporated" into the Fourteenth Amendment *only* the property protection provision of the Fifth Amendment, despite the fact that the due process clause applied to the taking of life and liberty as well as property.

No further expansion of civil liberties through incorporation occurred until 1925, when the Supreme Court held that freedom of speech is "among the fundamental personal rights and 'liberties' protected by the due process clause of the

FIGURE 4.1 THE PROTECTION OF FREE SPEECH BY THE FIRST AMENDMENT

	PROTECTED SPEECH	UNPROTECTED SPEECH
If content is true:	All speech is protected by the First Amendment when it is the truth.	"True" speech can be regulated *only* if: • it fails the clear and present danger test, or • it falls below community standards of obscenity or pornography.
If content is false:	Defamatory speech is protected when: • it is spoken or written by a public official in the course of official business, or • it is spoken or written by a citizen or the press against someone in the public eye.	"False" speech can be regulated or punished *only* when it can be demonstrated that there was a reckless disregard for the truth (as in libel or slander).

Fourteenth Amendment from impairment by the states."[7] In 1931, the Supreme Court added freedom of the press to that short list of civil rights protected by the Bill of Rights from state action; in 1939, it added freedom of assembly.[8]

For the following two decades, this was as far as the Supreme Court was willing to go in the effort to nationalize more of the rights in the Bill of Rights. And it should be made clear at this point that none of the rights in the Bill of Rights is absolute, including the most sacred right of all, freedom of speech. Figure 4.1 shows when free speech is protected and when it is not protected. A similar box could be constructed for each of the rights listed in Table 4.1. The only promise the Supreme Court is willing to make is that it will give "strict scrutiny" to any action taken by a state to limit or abridge a right. Again, no right is absolute; no right is protected at all times, regardless of the circumstances.

The shadow of *Barron* extended into its second century, despite adoption of the Fourteenth Amendment. At the time of World War II, the Constitution, as interpreted by the Supreme Court, left standing the framework in which the states had the power to determine their own law on a number of fundamental issues. It left states with the power to pass laws segregating the races. It also left states with the power to engage in searches and seizures without a warrant, to indict accused persons without benefit of a grand jury, to deprive persons of trial by jury, to force persons to testify against themselves, to deprive accused persons of their right to confront adverse witnesses, and to prosecute accused persons more than once for

---

[7] *Gitlow v. New York*, 268 U.S. 652 (1925).

[8] *Near v. Minnesota*, 283 U.S. 697 (1931); *Hague v. C.I.O.*, 307 U.S. 496 (1939).

the same crime.[9] Few states exercised these powers, but the power was there for any state whose legislative majority chose to use it.

The Constitutional Revolution in Civil Liberties

Signs of change in the constitutional framework came after 1954, in *Brown v. Board of Education*, when the Court found state segregation laws for schools unconstitutional. Even though *Brown* was not a civil liberties case, it indicated rather clearly that the Supreme Court was going to be expansive about civil liberties, because with *Brown* the Court had effectively promised that it would actively subject the states and all actions affecting civil rights and civil liberties to **strict scrutiny.** In retrospect, we could say that this constitutional revolution was given a "jump start" in 1954 by *Brown v. Board of Education*, even though the results were not apparent until after 1961, when the number of incorporated civil liberties increased (see Table 4.1).

Nationalizing the Bill of Rights.   As we saw in Chapter 3, the constitutional revolution in federalism began when the Supreme Court in 1937 interpreted "interstate commerce" in favor of federal government regulation.[10] Both revolutions, then, were movements toward nationalization, but they required opposite motions on the part of the Supreme Court. In the area of commerce (the first revolution), the Court had to decide to assume a *passive* role by not interfering as Congress expanded the meaning of the commerce clause of Article I, Section 8. This expansion has been so extensive that the national government can now constitutionally reach a single farmer growing twenty acres of wheat or a small restaurant selling barbecue to local "whites only" without being anywhere near interstate commerce routes. In the second revolution—involving the Bill of Rights and the Fourteenth Amendment—the Court had to assume an active role. It required close review of the laws of state legislatures and decisions of state courts in order to apply a single national Fourteenth Amendment standard to the rights and liberties of all citizens.

Table 4.1 shows that until 1961, only the First Amendment and one clause of the Fifth Amendment had been clearly incorporated into the Fourteenth Amendment.[11] After 1961, several other important provisions of the Bill of Rights were incorporated. Of the cases that expanded the Fourteenth Amendment's reach, the most famous was *Gideon v. Wainwright*, which established the right to counsel in a criminal trial, because it became the subject of a best-selling book and a popular movie.[12] In *Mapp v. Ohio*, the Court held that evidence obtained in violation of the

strict scrutiny
Higher standard of judicial protection for speech cases and other civil liberties and civil rights cases, in which the burden of proof shifts from the complainant to the government.

---

[9] All of these were implicitly identified in *Palko v. Connecticut*, 302 U.S. 319 (1937), as "not incorporated" into the Fourteenth Amendment as limitations on the powers of the states.

[10] *NLRB v. Jones & Laughlin Steel Corp.*, 301 U.S. 1 (1937).

[11] The one exception was the right to public trial (Sixth Amendment), but a 1948 case (*In re Oliver*, 33 U.S. 257) did not actually mention the right to public trial as such; this right was cited in a 1968 case (*Duncan v. Louisiana*, 391 U.S. 145) as a precedent establishing the right to public trial as part of the Fourteenth Amendment.

[12] *Gideon v. Wainwright*, 372 U.S. 335 (1963); Anthony Lewis, *Gideon's Trumpet* (New York: Random House, 1964).

Fourth Amendment ban on unreasonable searches and seizures would be excluded from trial.[13] This **exclusionary rule** was particularly irksome to the police and prosecutors because it meant that patently guilty defendants sometimes go free because the evidence that clearly incriminated them could not be used. In *Miranda*, the Court's ruling required that arrested persons be informed of the right to remain silent and to have counsel present during interrogation.[14] This is the basis of the **Miranda rule** of reading persons their rights. By 1969, in *Benton v. Maryland,* the Supreme Court had come full circle regarding the rights of the criminally accused, explicitly reversing a 1937 ruling and thereby incorporating double jeopardy.

During the 1960s and early 1970s, the Court also expanded another important area of civil liberties: rights to privacy. When the Court began to take a more activist role in the mid-1950s and 1960s, the idea of a "right to privacy" was revived. In 1958, the Supreme Court recognized "privacy in one's association" in its decision to prevent the state of Alabama from using the membership list of the National Association for the Advancement of Colored People in the state's investigations.[15] As we shall see later in this chapter, legal questions about the right to privacy have come to the fore in more recent cases concerning birth control, abortion, homosexuality, and assisted suicide.

THE BILL OF RIGHTS TODAY

Because liberty requires restraining the power of government, the general status of civil liberties can never be considered fixed and permanent.[16] Every provision in the Bill of Rights is subject to interpretation, and in any dispute involving a clause of the Bill of Rights, interpretations will always be shaped by the interpreter's interest in the outcome. As we have seen, the Court continuously reminds everyone that if it has the power to expand the Bill of Rights, it also has the power to contract it.[17]

The First Amendment and Freedom of Religion

The Bill of Rights begins by guaranteeing freedom, and the First Amendment provides for that freedom in two distinct clauses: "Congress shall make no law [1] respecting an establishment of religion, or [2] prohibiting the free exercise thereof." The first clause is called the establishment clause, and the second is called the free exercise clause.

---

[13] *Mapp v. Ohio*, 367 U.S. 643 (1961).

[14] *Miranda v. Arizona*, 384 U.S. 436 (1966).

[15] *NAACP v. Alabama ex rel. Patterson*, 357 U.S. 449 (1958).

[16] This section is taken from Benjamin Ginsberg, Theodore J. Lowi, and Margaret Weir, *We the People: An Introduction to American Politics*, 8th ed. (New York: Norton, 2009).

[17] For a lively and readable treatment of the possibilities of restricting provisions of the Bill of Rights without actually reversing prior decisions, see David G. Savage, *Turning Right: The Making of the Rehnquist Supreme Court* (New York: Wiley, 1992).

Separation between Church and State. The **establishment clause** and the idea of "no law" regarding the establishment of religion could be interpreted in several possible ways. One interpretation, which probably reflects the views of many of the First Amendment's authors, is that the government is prohibited from establishing an official church. Official state churches, such as the Church of England, were common in the eighteenth century and were viewed by many Americans as inconsistent with a republican form of government. Indeed, many Americans colonists had fled Europe to escape persecution for having rejected state-sponsored churches. A second possible interpretation is the "nonpreferentialist" or "accommodationist" view, which holds that the government may not take sides among competing religions but is not prohibited from providing assistance to religious institutions or ideas so long as it shows no favoritism. The United States accommodates religious beliefs in a variety of ways, from the reference to God on U.S. currency to the prayer that begins every session of Congress. These forms of establishment have never been struck down by the courts.

The third view regarding religious establishment, which for many years dominated Supreme Court decision making in this realm, is the idea of a "wall of separation" between church and state that cannot be breached by the government. Despite the absolute sound of the phrase *wall of separation,* there is ample room to disagree on how high the wall is or of what materials it is composed. For example, the Court has been consistently strict in cases of school prayer, striking down such practices as Bible reading,[18] nondenominational prayer,[19] a moment of silence for meditation, and pregame prayer at public sporting events.[20] On the other hand, the Court has been quite permissive (and some would say inconsistent) about the public display of religious symbols, such as city-sponsored Nativity scenes in commercial or municipal areas.[21] In 1971, after thirty years of cases involving religious schools, the Court attempted to specify some criteria to guide its decisions and those of lower courts, indicating, for example, in a decision invalidating state payments for the teaching of secular subjects in parochial schools, circumstances under which the Court might allow certain financial assistance. The case was *Lemon v. Kurtzman;* in its decision, the Supreme Court established three criteria to guide future cases, in what came to be called the **Lemon test.** The Court held that government aid to religious schools would be accepted as constitutional if (1) it had a secular purpose, (2) its effect was neither to advance nor to inhibit religion, and (3) it did not entangle government and religious institutions in each other's affairs.[22]

More recently, the establishment clause has been put under pressure by the school-voucher and charter-school movements. Vouchers financed by public revenues are supporting tuition to religious schools, where common prayer and religious instruction are known parts of the curriculum. In 2004, the question of whether the phrase "under God" in the Pledge of Allegiance violates the

---

[18] *Abington School District v. Schempp,* 374 U.S. 203 (1963).

[19] *Engel v. Vitale,* 370 U.S. 421 (1962).

[20] *Wallace v. Jaffree,* 472 U.S. 38 (1985).

[21] *Lynch v. Donnelly,* 465 U.S. 668 (1984).

[22] *Lemon v. Kurtzman,* 403 U.S. 602 (1971).

establishment clause The First Amendment clause that says, "Congress shall make no law respecting an establishment of religion." This clause means that a wall of separation exists between church and state.

Lemon test Rule articulated in *Lemon v. Kurtzman* according to which governmental action in respect to religion is permissible if it is secular in purpose, does not lead to "excessive entanglement" with religion, and neither promotes nor inhibits the practice of religion.

establishment clause was brought before the Court, but the Court ruled that the plaintiff lacked a sufficient personal stake in the case to bring the complaint.[23] This inconclusive decision by the Court left "under God" in the Pledge while keeping the issue alive for possible resolution in a future case.

Free Exercise of Religion. The *free exercise clause* protects the right to believe and practice whatever religion one chooses; it also protects the right to be a nonbeliever. Although the Supreme Court has been fairly consistent and strict in protecting the free exercise of religious belief, it has taken pains to distinguish between religious beliefs and *actions* based on those beliefs. In one case, for example, two Native Americans had been fired from their jobs for smoking peyote, an illegal drug. They claimed they had been fired from their jobs illegally because smoking peyote was a religious sacrament protected by the free exercise clause. The Court disagreed with their claim in an important 1990 decision,[24] but Congress literally reversed the Court's decision with the enactment of the Religious Freedom Restoration Act (RFRA) of 1993, which forbids any federal agency or state government to restrict a person's free exercise of religion unless the federal agency or state government demonstrates that its action "furthers a compelling government interest" and "is the least restrictive means of furthering that compelling governmental interest." However, in the *City of Boerne* case, the Supreme Court declared the RFRA unconstitutional, but on grounds rarely utilized, if not unique to this case: Congress had violated the separation-of-powers principle, infringing on the powers of the judiciary by going so far beyond its lawmaking powers.[25] The *City of Boerne* case did settle some matters of constitutional controversy over the religious exercise and the establishment clauses of the First Amendment, but it left a lot more unsettled.

The First Amendment and Freedom of Speech and the Press

Because democracy depends on an open political process, freedom of speech and freedom of the press are considered critical. In 1938, freedom of speech (which in all important respects includes freedom of the press) was given extraordinary constitutional status when the Supreme Court established that any legislation that attempts to restrict these fundamental freedoms "is to be subjected to a more exacting judicial scrutiny . . . than are most other types of legislation."[26]

The Court was saying that the democratic political process must be protected at almost any cost. This higher standard of judicial review came to be called strict scrutiny. Strict scrutiny implies that speech—at least some kinds of speech—occupy a

---

[23] *Elk Grove Unified School District v. Newdow,* 542 U.S. 1 (2004).

[24] *Employment Division v. Smith,* 494 U.S. 872 (1990).

[25] *City of Boerne v. Flores,* 521 U.S. 507 (1997).

[26] *United States v. Carolene Products Company,* 304 U.S. 144 (1938), 384. This footnote is one of the Court's most important doctrines. See Alfred H. Kelly, Winfred A. Harbison, and Herman Belz, *The American Constitution: Its Origins and Development,* 7th ed. (New York: Norton, 1991), 2, pp. 519–23.

"preferred" position and will be protected almost absolutely. But as it turns out, only some types of speech are fully protected against restrictions. As we shall see, many forms of speech are less than absolutely protected—even though they are entitled to strict scrutiny.

Political Speech. Since the 1920s, political speech has been consistently protected by the courts even when it has been deemed "insulting" or "outrageous." Here is the way the Supreme Court put it in one of its most important statements on the subject:

> The constitutional guarantees of free speech and free press do not permit a State to forbid or proscribe advocacy of the use of force or of law violation *except where such advocacy is directed to inciting or producing imminent lawless action and is likely to incite or produce such action.*[27] [emphasis added]

This statement was made in the case of a Ku Klux Klan leader, Charles Brandenburg, who had been arrested and convicted of advocating "revengent" action against the president, Congress, and the Supreme Court, among others, if they continued "to suppress the white, Caucasian race." Although Brandenburg was not carrying a weapon, some members of his audience were. Nevertheless, the Supreme Court reversed the state courts and freed Brandenburg while declaring Ohio's Criminal Syndicalism Act unconstitutional because it punished persons who "advocate, or teach the duty, necessity, or propriety [of violence] as a means of accomplishing industrial or political reform" or who publish materials or "voluntarily assemble . . . to teach or advocate the doctrines of criminal syndicalism." The Supreme Court argued that the statute did not distinguish "mere advocacy" from "incitement to imminent lawless action." It would be difficult to go much further in protecting freedom of speech. Typically, the federal courts will strike down restrictions on speech if they are deemed to be "overbroad," "vague," or lacking "neutrality" in terms of the content of the speech, as for example, if a statute prohibited the views of the political left but not the political right, or vice versa.

Another area of recent expansion of political speech—the participation of wealthy persons and corporations in political campaigns—was opened up in 1976 with the Supreme Court's decision in *Buckley v. Valeo.*[28] Campaign finance reform laws of the early 1970s, arising out of the Watergate scandal, sought to put severe limits on campaign spending, and a number of important provisions were declared unconstitutional on the basis of a new principle that spending money by or on behalf of candidates is a form of speech protected by the First Amendment. The issue came up again in 2003, after passage of a new and more severe campaign finance law, the Bipartisan Campaign Reform Act of 2002 (BCRA). In *McConnell v. Federal Election Commission,* the majority seriously reduced the area of speech protected by the *Buckley v. Valeo* decision by holding that Congress was well within its power to put limits on the amounts individuals could spend, plus severe limits on the amounts of "soft money" that could be spent by corporations and their PACs

---

[27] *Brandenburg v. Ohio,* 395 U.S. 444 (1969).

[28] *Buckley v. Valeo,* 424 U.S. 1 (1976).

and limits on issue advertising prior to Election Day. In 2007, however, in the case of *Federal Election Commission v. Wisconsin Right to Life*, the Supreme Court struck down a key portion of BCRA, finding that the act's limitations on political advertising violated the First Amendment's guarantee of free speech.[29] In 2008, in the case of *Davis v. Federal Election Commission*, the Supreme Court struck down another element of BCRA, the so-called millionaire's amendment, which had increased contribution limits for opponents of self-funded, wealthy candidates.[30] And, in *Citizens United v. Federal Exchange Commission*, the Court ruled that corporate funding of independent electioneering ads could not be limited under the First Amendment. [31]

Symbolic Speech, Speech Plus, and the Rights of Assembly and Petition. The First Amendment treats the freedoms of assembly and petition as equal to the freedoms of religion and political speech. Freedom of assembly and freedom of petition are closely associated with speech but go beyond it to speech associated with action. Since at least 1931, the Supreme Court has sought to protect actions that are designed to send a political message. Thus although the Court upheld a federal statute making it a crime to burn draft cards to protest the Vietnam War on the grounds that the government had a compelling interest in preserving draft cards as part of the conduct of the war itself, it considered the wearing of black armbands to school a protected form of assembly. In these sorts of cases, a court will often use the standard it articulated in the draft card case, *United States v. O'Brien,* and now known as the "*O'Brien* test."[32] Under the terms of the *O'Brien* test, a statute restricting expressive or symbolic speech must be justified by a compelling government interest and be narrowly tailored toward achieving that interest.

Another example is the burning of the American flag as a symbol of protest. In 1984, at a political rally held during the Republican National Convention in Dallas, a political protester burned an American flag in violation of a Texas statute that prohibited desecration of a venerated object. In a 5–4 decision, the Supreme Court declared the Texas law unconstitutional on the grounds that flag burning is expressive conduct protected by the First Amendment.[33] Since 1995, the House of Representatives has four times passed a resolution for a constitutional amendment to ban flag burning, but each time the Senate has failed to go along.[34] Further effort in Congress was probably killed by the Supreme Court's 2003 decision striking down a Virginia cross-burning statute.[35] In that case, the Court ruled that states could make cross burning a crime as long as the statute required prosecutors to prove that the act of setting fire to the cross was intended to intimidate.

Closer to the original intent of the assembly and petition clause is the category of **speech plus**—following speech with physical activity such as picketing, distributing

---

speech plus
Speech accompanied by activities such as sit-ins, picketing, and demonstrations. Protection of this form of speech under the First Amendment is conditional, and restrictions imposed by state or local authorities are acceptable if properly balanced by considerations of public order.

---

[29] *Federal Election Commission v. Wisconsin Right to Life,* 09-969 (2007).

[30] *Davis v. Federal Election Commission,* 07-320 (2008).

[31] *Citizens United v. FEC,* 08-205 (2010).

[32] *United States v. O'Brien,* 391 U.S. 367 (1968).

[33] *Texas v. Johnson,* 491 U.S. 397 (1989).

[34] Carl Hulse, "Flag Amendment Narrowly Fails in Senate Vote," *New York Times,* June 28, 2006.

[35] *Virginia v. Black,* 538 U.S. 343 (2003).

leaflets, and other forms of peaceful demonstration or assembly. Such assemblies are consistently protected by courts under the First Amendment; state and local laws regulating such activities are closely scrutinized and frequently overturned.

Freedom of the Press. For all practical purposes, freedom of speech implies and includes freedom of the press. With the exception of the broadcast media, which are subject to federal regulation, the press is protected under the doctrine prohibiting **prior restraint.** Beginning with the landmark 1931 case of *Near v. Minnesota,*[36] the Supreme Court has held that except under the most extraordinary circumstances, the First Amendment prohibits government agencies from seeking to prevent newspapers or magazines from publishing whatever they wish.

Libel, Slander, Obscenity, and Pornography. Some speech is not protected at all. If a written statement is made in "reckless disregard of the truth" and is considered damaging to the victim because it is "malicious, scandalous, and defamatory," it can be punished as **libel.** If an oral statement of such nature is made, it can be punished as **slander.**

Today most libel suits involve freedom of the press, and the realm of free press is enormous. Historically, newspapers were subject to the law of libel, whereby newspapers that printed false and malicious stories could be compelled to pay damages to those they defamed. In recent years, however, American courts have greatly narrowed the meaning of libel and made it extremely difficult, particularly for politicians or other public figures, to win a libel case against a newspaper.

If libel and slander cases can be difficult because of the problem of determining the truth of statements and whether those statements are malicious and damaging, cases involving pornography and obscenity can be even stickier. It is easy to say that pornography and obscenity fall outside the realm of protected speech, but it is impossible to draw a clear line defining where protection ends and unprotected speech begins. All attempts by the courts to define pornography and obscenity have proved impractical because each instance required courts to screen thousands of pages of print material or feet of film alleged to be pornographic. In recent years, the battle against obscene speech has taken place in the realm of pornography on the Internet. Opponents of this form of expression argue that it should be banned because of the easy access children have to the Internet. The first major effort to regulate the content of the Internet occurred on February 1, 1996, when the 104th Congress passed major telecommunications legislation. Attached to the Telecommunications Act was an amendment, called the Communications Decency Act (CDA), that was designed to regulate the online transmission of obscene material. In the 1997 Supreme Court case of *Reno v. ACLU,* the Court struck down the CDA, ruling that it suppressed speech that "adults have a constitutional right to receive" and that governments may not limit the adult population to messages that are fit for children.[37] Congress again tried limiting children's access to Internet pornography with the 2001 Children's Internet Protection Act, which required public libraries

prior restraint An effort by a government agency to block the publication of material it deems libelous or harmful in some other way; censorship. In the United States, the courts forbid prior restraint except under the most extraordinary circumstances.

libel A written statement made in "reckless disregard of the truth" and considered damaging to a victim because it is "malicious, scandalous, and defamatory."

slander An oral statement made in "reckless disregard of the truth" and considered damaging to a victim because it is "malicious, scandalous, and defamatory."

---

[36] *Near v. Minnesota ex rel. Olson,* 283 U.S. 697 (1931).

[37] *Reno v. ACLU,* 521 U.S. 844 (1997).

to install antipornography filters on all library computers with Internet access. Though the act made cooperation a condition for receiving federal subsidies, it did permit librarians to unblock a site at the request of an adult patron. The law was challenged, and in 2003 the Court upheld it, asserting that its provisions did not violate library patrons' First Amendment rights.[38] In 2003, Congress enacted the Prosecutorial Remedies and Other Tools to end the Exploitation of Children Today (PROTECT) Act, which outlawed efforts to sell child pornography via the Internet. The Supreme Court upheld this act in the 2008 case of *United States v. Williams,* in which the majority said that criminalizing efforts to pander child pornography did not violate free-speech guarantees.[39]

Fighting Words and Hate Speech.   Speech can also lose its protected position when it moves toward the sphere of action. "Expressive speech," for example, is protected until it moves from the symbolic realm to the realm of actual conduct— to direct incitement of damaging conduct with the use of so-called **fighting words.** In 1942, the Supreme Court upheld the arrest and conviction of a man who had violated a state law forbidding the use of offensive language in public. He had called the arresting officer a "goddamned racketeer" and "a damn Fascist." When his case reached the Supreme Court, the arrest was upheld on the grounds that the First Amendment provides no protection for such offensive language because such words "are no essential part of any exposition of ideas."[40] Since that time, however, the Supreme Court has reversed almost every conviction based on arguments that the speaker had used "fighting words." But again, that does not mean this is an absolutely settled area.

Many jurisdictions have drafted ordinances banning forms of expression de-signed to assert hatred toward one or another group, be they African Americans, Jews, Muslims, or others. Such hate speech ordinances seldom pass constitutional muster. The leading Supreme Court case in this realm is the 1992 decision in *R.A.V. v. City of St. Paul.*[41] Here, a white teenager was arrested for burning a cross on the lawn of a black family in violation of a municipal ordinance that banned cross burning. The Court ruled that the ordinance was not content neutral (see above), because it prohibited only cross burning—typically an expression of ha-tred of African Americans. Since a statute banning all forms of hateful expression would be deemed overly broad, the *R.A.V.* standard suggests that virtually all hate speech is constitutionally protected.

Commercial Speech.   Commercial speech, such as newspaper or television advertising, does not have full First Amendment protection because it cannot be considered political speech. Some commercial speech is still unprotected and therefore regulated. For example, the regulation of false and misleading advertis-ing by the Federal Trade Commission is an old and well-established power of the

fighting words
Speech that explic-itly incites damag-ing conduct.

---

[38] *United States v. American Library Association,* 539 U.S. 194 (2003).

[39] *United States v. Williams,* 06-694 (2008).

[40] *Chaplinsky v. State of New Hampshire,* 315 U.S. 568 (1942).

[41] *R.A.V. v. City of St. Paul,* 506 U.S. 377 (1992).

federal government. The Supreme Court long ago upheld the constitutionality of laws prohibiting the electronic media from carrying cigarette advertising.[42] However, the gains far outweigh the losses in the effort to expand the protection commercial speech enjoys under the First Amendment. As the scholar Louis Fisher explains, "In part, this reflects the growing appreciation that commercial speech is part of the free flow of information necessary for informed choice and democratic participation."[43] For example, in a 2001 case, the Court ruled that a Massachusetts ban on all cigarette advertising violated the First Amendment right of the tobacco industry to advertise its products to adult consumers.[44]

The Second Amendment and the Right to Bear Arms

The point and purpose of the Second Amendment is the provision for militias; they were to be the backup of the government for the maintenance of local public order. *Militia* was understood at the time of the Founding to be a military or police resource for state governments, and militias were specifically distinguished from armies and troops, which came within the sole constitutional jurisdiction of Congress. Some groups, though, have always argued that the Second Amendment also establishes an individual right to bear arms. In its 2008 decision in the case of *District of Columbia v. Heller*, the Supreme Court ruled that the federal government could not prohibit individuals from owning guns for self-defense in their homes.[45] The case involved a District of Columbia ordinance that made it virtually impossible for residents to possess firearms legally. The District of Columbia is an entity of the federal government, and the Court did not indicate that its ruling applied to state firearms laws. However, in the 2010 case of *McDonald v. Chicago*, the Court struck down a Chicago firearms ordinance and applied the Second Amendment to the states as well.[46]

Rights of the Criminally Accused

Except for the First Amendment, most of the battle to apply the Bill of Rights to the states was fought over the various protections granted to individuals who are accused of a crime, who are suspects in the commission of a crime, or who are brought before the court as a witness to a crime. The Bill of Rights entitles every American to **due process** of law. The Fourth, Fifth, Sixth, and Eighth Amendments, taken together, are the essence of the due process of law, even though this fundamental concept does not appear until the very last words of the Fifth Amendment.

due process To proceed according to law and with adequate protection for individual rights.

The Fourth Amendment and Searches and Seizures. The purpose of the Fourth Amendment is to guarantee the security of citizens against unreasonable

---

[42] *Capital Broadcasting Company v. Acting Attorney General*, 405 U.S. 1000 (1972).

[43] Fisher, *American Constitutional Law*, 7th ed. (Durham, N.C.: Academic Press, 2007), 2, p. 546.

[44] *Lorillard Tobacco v. Reilly*, 533 U.S. 525 (2001).

[45] *District of Columbia v. Heller*, 07-290 (2008).

[46] *McDonald v. Chicago*, 08-1251 (2010).

(that is, improper) searches and seizures. In 1990, the Supreme Court summarized its understanding of the Fourth Amendment brilliantly and succinctly: "A search compromises the individual interest in privacy; a seizure deprives the individual of dominion over his or her person or property."[47]

The exclusionary rule, which prohibits evidence obtained during an illegal search from being introduced in a trial, is the most severe restraint ever imposed by the Constitution and the courts on the behavior of the police. The exclusionary rule is a dramatic restriction because it rules out precisely the evidence that produces a conviction; it frees those people who are *known* to have committed the crime of which they have been accused. Because it works so dramatically in favor of persons known to have committed a crime, the Court has since softened the application of the rule. In recent years, the federal courts have relied on a discretionary use of the exclusionary rule, whereby they make a judgment as to the "nature and quality of the intrusion." It is thus difficult to know ahead of time whether a defendant will or will not be protected from an illegal search under the Fourth Amendment.[48]

The Fifth Amendment. The first clause of the Fifth Amendment, the right to have a **grand jury** determine whether a trial is warranted, is considered "the oldest institution known to the Constitution."[49] Grand juries play an important role in federal criminal cases. However, the provision for a grand jury is the one important civil liberties provision of the Bill of Rights that was not incorporated by the Fourteenth Amendment to apply to state criminal prosecutions. Thus some states operate without grand juries. In such states, the prosecuting attorney simply files a "bill of information" affirming that sufficient evidence is available to justify a trial.

The Fifth Amendment also provides the constitutional protection from double jeopardy, or being tried more than once for the same crime, and the guarantee that no citizen "shall be compelled in any criminal case to be a witness against himself." This protection against self-incrimination led to the *Miranda* case and the *Miranda* rules that police must follow when questioning an arrested criminal suspect.

Another fundamental clause of the Fifth Amendment is the "takings clause," which extends to each citizen a protection against the taking of private property "without just compensation." Although this part of the amendment is not specifically concerned with protecting persons accused of crimes, it is nevertheless a fundamentally important instance where the government and the citizen are adversaries. As discussed earlier in this chapter, the power of any government to take private property for a public use is called **eminent domain**.

The Sixth Amendment and the Right to Counsel. Like the exclusionary rule of the Fourth Amendment and the self-incrimination clause of the Fifth Amendment, the "right to counsel" provision of the Sixth Amendment is notable for freeing defendants who seem to the public to be patently guilty as charged. Other

grand jury A jury that determines whether sufficient evidence is available to justify a trial. Grand juries do not rule on the accused's guilt or innocence.

eminent domain The right of the government to take private property for public use, with reasonable compensation awarded for the property.

---

[47] *Horton v. California*, 496 U.S. 128 (1990).

[48] For a good discussion of the issue, see Fisher, *American Constitutional Law*, pp. 884–89.

[49] E. S. Corwin and Jack Peltason, *Understanding the Constitution*, 13th ed. (Fort Worth, Tex.: Harcourt Brace, 1994), p. 286.

provisions of the Sixth Amendment, such as the right to a speedy trial and the right to confront witnesses before an impartial jury, are less controversial in nature.

Gideon v. Wainwright is the perfect case study because it involved a disreputable person who seemed patently guilty of the crime for which he was convicted. In and out of jails for most of his fifty-one years, Clarence Earl Gideon received a five-year sentence for breaking into and entering a poolroom in Panama City, Florida. While serving time in jail, Gideon became a fairly well qualified "jailhouse lawyer," made his own appeal on a handwritten petition, and eventually won the landmark ruling on the right to counsel in all felony cases.[50] In 1964, the year after the *Gideon* decision, the Supreme Court ruled in *Escobedo v. Illinois* that suspects had a right to counsel during police interrogations, not just when their cases reached trial.[51] The right to counsel has been expanded further during the past few decades. For example, in 2003 the Supreme Court overturned the death sentence of a Maryland death-row inmate, holding that the defense lawyer had failed to fully inform the jury of the defendant's history of "horrendous childhood abuse."[52]

The Eighth Amendment and Cruel and Unusual Punishment. The Eighth Amendment prohibits "excessive bail," "excessive fines," and "cruel and unusual punishment." Virtually all the debate over Eighth Amendment issues focuses on the last clause of the amendment: the protection from "cruel and unusual punishment." One of the greatest challenges in interpreting this provision consistently is that what is considered "cruel and unusual" varies from culture to culture and from generation to generation. And unfortunately, it also varies by class and race.

By far the biggest issue in the inconsistency of class and race as constituting cruel and unusual punishment arises over the death penalty. In 1972, the Supreme Court overturned several state death-penalty laws not because they were cruel and unusual but because they were being applied in a capricious manner.[53] Since 1976, the Court has consistently upheld state laws providing for capital punishment, although it also continues to review numerous death-penalty appeals each year.

Constitutional objections to the death penalty often invoke the Eighth Amendment's protection against punishments that are "cruel and unusual." Yet supporters of the death penalty say it can hardly be considered a violation of this protection, since it was commonly used in the eighteenth century and was supported by most early American leaders.

The Right to Privacy

When the Court began to take a more activist role in the mid-1950s and 1960s, the idea of a **right to privacy** gained traction. The Constitution does not specifically mention a right to privacy, but the Ninth Amendment declares that the rights

right to privacy
The right to be let alone, which has been interpreted by the Supreme Court to entail free access to birth control and abortions.

---

[50] For a full account of the story of the trial and release of Clarence Earl Gideon, see Lewis, *Gideon's Trumpet*. See also David M. O'Brien, *Storm Center*, 7th ed. (New York: Norton, 2005).

[51] *Escobedo v. Illinois*, 378 U.S. 478 (1964).

[52] *Wiggins v. Smith*, 539 U.S. 510 (2003).

[53] *Furman v. Georgia*, 408 U.S. 238 (1972).

enumerated in the Constitution are not an exhaustive list. In 1958, the Supreme Court recognized "privacy in one's association" in its decision to prevent the state of Alabama from using the membership list of the NAACP in the state's investigations. The sphere of privacy was drawn in earnest in 1965, when the Court ruled that a Connecticut statute forbidding the use of contraceptives violated the right of marital privacy. Justice William O. Douglas, author of the majority decision in the *Griswold* case, argued that this right of privacy is also grounded in the Constitution because it fits into a "zone of privacy" created by a combination of the Third, Fourth, and Fifth Amendments. The right to privacy was confirmed and extended in 1973 in the most important of all privacy decisions and one of the most important Supreme Court decisions in American history: *Roe v. Wade*. This decision established a woman's right to seek an abortion and prohibited states from making abortion a criminal act.[54]

In the last three decades, the right to be left alone began to include the privacy rights of homosexuals. One morning in Atlanta in the mid-1980s, Michael Hardwick was arrested by a police officer who discovered him in bed with another man. Hardwick was charged under Georgia's laws against heterosexual and homosexual sodomy. Hardwick filed a lawsuit against the state, challenging the constitutionality of the Georgia law, and won his case in the federal court of appeals. The state of Georgia, in an unusual move, appealed the court's decision to the Supreme Court. The majority of the Court reversed the lower-court decision, holding against Hardwick on the grounds that "the federal Constitution confers [no] fundamental right upon homosexuals to engage in sodomy" and that there was therefore no basis to invalidate "the laws of the many states that still make such conduct illegal and have done so for a very long time."[55] With *Lawrence v. Texas* in 2003, the Court overturned its 1986 decision in *Bowers v. Hardwick*, and state legislatures no longer had the authority to make private sexual behavior a crime.[56] Drawing from the tradition of negative liberty, the Court maintained, "In our tradition the State is not omnipresent in the home. And there are other spheres of our lives and existence outside the home, where the State should not be a dominant presence." Explicitly encompassing lesbians and gay men within the umbrella of privacy, the Court concluded that the "petitioners are entitled to respect for their private lives. The State cannot demean their existence or control their destiny by making their private sexual conduct a crime." This decision added substance to the Ninth Amendment "right of privacy."

Another area ripe for litigation and public discourse is the so-called right to die. A number of highly publicized physician-assisted suicides have focused attention on whether people have a right to choose their own death and receive assistance in carrying it out. Can this become part of the privacy right, or is it a new substantive right? A tentative answer came in 1997, when the Court ruled that a

---

[54] *Roe v. Wade*, 410 U.S. 113 (1973).

[55] *Bowers v. Hardwick*, 478 U.S. 186 (1986). The dissenters were quoting an earlier case, *Olmstead v. United States*, 277 U.S. 438 (1928), to emphasize the nature of their disagreement with the majority in the *Bowers* case.

[56] *Lawrence and Garner v. Texas*, 539 U.S. 558 (2003).

Washington State law establishing a ban on "causing" or "aiding" a suicide did not violate the Fourteenth Amendment or any clauses of the Bill of Rights incorporated into the Fourteenth Amendment. Thus if a state can constitutionally adopt such a prohibition, there is no constitutional right to suicide or assisted suicide. However, the Court left open the narrower question of "whether a mentally competent person who is experiencing great suffering has a constitutionally cognizable interest in controlling the circumstances of his or her imminent death."

The War on Terrorism. In response to the September 11, 2001, terrorist attacks on the United States, Congress enacted new legislation—the USA PATRIOT Act—designed to make it easier for federal law enforcement agencies to investigate and prosecute suspected terrorists. In addition, the president issued a series of orders allowing the National Security Agency to eavesdrop on domestic communications and the military to detain and try terrorism suspects. Civil libertarians have argued that the government's new surveillance and eavesdropping authority poses a threat to free speech and privacy. Critics have also declared that the open-ended military detention of terrorism suspects, along with the special military tribunals and procedures established by the president to try such suspects, violates many of the fundamental constitutional protections provided to those accused of criminal actions.

Some of these questions have been raised in the federal courts. In June 2004, the Supreme Court ruled in three cases involving the president's antiterrorism initiatives and claims of executive power and in two of those cases appeared to place some limit on presidential authority.[57] In these rulings, the Supreme Court asserted that presidential actions were subject to judicial scrutiny and placed some constraints on the president's unfettered power. At the same time, the Court affirmed the president's single most important claim: the unilateral power to declare individuals, including U.S. citizens, "enemy combatants" who can be detained by federal authorities under adverse legal circumstances. Future presidents are likely to cite the Court's decisions as precedents for, rather than limits on, the exercise of executive power. The same is likely to be true of the Court's June 2006 decision in the case of *Hamdan v. Rumsfeld.*[58] Salim Ahmed Hamdan, a Taliban fighter captured in Afghanistan in 2001 and held at Guantánamo starting in 2002, was slated for trial by a special military tribunal. Such tribunals, operating outside both the civilian and the military court systems, were created by the Bush administration to deal with suspected terrorists in the wake of the September 11 attacks and the U.S. invasion of Afghanistan. The Court found that President Bush's tribunals were not authorized by statute and were operating under procedures that provided defendants with fewer rights and safeguards than they would receive under the Uniform Code of Military Justice. But while invalidating these particular tribunals, the Supreme Court accepted the principle that the president could order persons he deemed unlawful combatants to be tried by military tribunals so long as the tribunals were lawfully constituted.

---

[57] *Hamdi v. Rumsfeld,* 542 U.S. 507 (2004); *Rasul v. Bush,* 542 U.S. 466 (2004); *Rumsfeld v. Padilla,* 542 U.S. 426 (2004).

[58] *Hamdan v. Rumsfeld,* 548 U.S. (2006).

CIVIL RIGHTS

With the adoption of the Fourteenth Amendment in 1868, civil rights became part of the Constitution, guaranteed to each citizen through "equal protection of the laws." These words launched a century of political movements and legal efforts to press for racial equality. African Americans' quest for civil rights in turn inspired many other groups—including members of other racial and ethnic groups, women, people with disabilities, and gay men and lesbians—to seek new laws and constitutional guarantees of their civil rights.

Congress passed the Fourteenth Amendment and the states ratified it in the aftermath of the Civil War. Together with the Thirteenth Amendment, which abolished slavery, and the Fifteenth Amendment, which guaranteed voting rights to black men, it seemed to provide a guarantee of civil rights for the newly freed enslaved blacks. But the general language of the Fourteenth Amendment meant that its support for civil rights could be far reaching. The very simplicity of the **equal protection clause** of the Fourteenth Amendment left it open to interpretation:

> No State shall make or enforce any law which shall . . . deny to any person within its jurisdiction the equal protection of the laws.

equal protection clause A clause in the Fourteenth Amendment that requires that states provide citizens "equal protection of the laws."

Plessy v. Ferguson: "Separate but Equal"

Following its initial decision making "equal protection" a right, the Supreme Court was no more ready to enforce the civil rights aspects of the Fourteenth Amendment than it was to enforce the civil liberties provisions. The Court declared the Civil Rights Act of 1875 unconstitutional on the ground that the act sought to protect blacks against discrimination by private businesses, whereas the Fourteenth Amendment, according to the Court's interpretation, was intended to protect individuals only against discrimination by *public* officials of state and local governments.

In 1896, the Court went still further, in the infamous case of *Plessy v. Ferguson,* by upholding a Louisiana statute that required segregation of the races on trolleys and other public carriers (and by implication in all public facilities, including schools). The Supreme Court held that the Fourteenth Amendment's "equal protection of the laws" was not violated by racial distinction as long as the law applied to both races equally.[59] People generally pretended they were treated as equal as long as some accommodation existed. What the Court was saying, in effect, was that it was not unreasonable to use race as a basis of exclusion in public matters. This was the origin of the **"separate but equal" rule** that was not reversed until 1954.

"separate but equal" rule Doctrine that public accommodations could be segregated by race but still be equal.

Racial Discrimination after World War II

The Supreme Court had begun to change its position regarding racial discrimination just before World War II by being stricter about what the states would have to do to provide equal facilities under the "separate but equal" rule. In 1938, the Court

---

[59] *Plessy v. Ferguson,* 163 U.S. 537 (1896).

rejected Missouri's policy of paying the tuition of qualified blacks to out-of-state law schools rather than admitting them to the University of Missouri Law School.[60] After the war, modest progress resumed. In 1950, the Court rejected Texas's claim that its new "law school for Negroes" afforded education equal to that of the all-white University of Texas Law School; without confronting the "separate but equal" principle itself, the Court's decision anticipated *Brown v. Board* by opening the question of whether *any* segregated facility could be truly equal.[61]

As the Supreme Court was ordering the admission of blacks to all-white state laws schools, it was also striking down the southern practice of "white primaries," which legally excluded blacks from participation in the nominating process.[62] The most important pre-1954 decision was probably *Shelley v. Kraemer*,[63] in which the Court ruled against the practice of "restrictive convenants," whereby the seller of a home added a clause to the sales contract requiring the buyer to agree not to resell the home to a non-Caucasian, non-Christian, and so on.

Although none of those cases confronted "separate but equal" and the principle of racial discrimination as such, they were extremely significant to black leaders and gave them encouragement enough to believe that at last they had an opportunity and enough legal precedent to change the constitutional framework itself. By the fall of 1952, the Court had on its docket cases from Kansas, South Carolina, Virginia, Delaware, and the District of Columbia challenging the constitutionality of school segregation. Of these, the Kansas case became the chosen one. It seemed to be ahead of the pack in its district court, and it had the special advantage of being located in a state outside the Deep South.[64]

Oliver Brown, the father of three girls, lived "across the tracks" in a low-income, racially mixed Topeka neighborhood. Every school-day morning, one of his daughters, Linda Brown, took the school bus to the Monroe School for black children about a mile away. In September 1950, Oliver Brown took Linda to the all-white Sumner School, which was actually closer to home, to enter her into the third grade in defiance of state law and local segregation rules. When they were refused, Brown took his case to the NAACP, and soon thereafter *Brown v. Board of Education* was born.

In deciding the case, the Court, to the surprise of many, rejected as inconclusive all the learned arguments about the intent of the Fourteenth Amendment and committed itself to considering only the consequences of segregation:

> Does segregation of children in public schools solely on the basis of race, even though the physical facilities and other "tangible" factors may be equal, deprive

---

[60] *Missouri ex rel. Gaines v. Canada*, 305 U.S. 337 (1938).

[61] *Sweatt v. Painter*, 339 U.S. 629 (1950).

[62] *Smith v. Allwright*, 321 U.S. 649 (1944).

[63] *Shelley v. Kraemer*, 334 U.S. 1 (1948).

[64] The District of Columbia case came up too, but since the District of Columbia is not a state, it did not directly involve the Fourteenth Amendment and its equal protection clause. It confronted the Court on the same grounds, however—that segregation is inherently unequal. Its victory in effect was "incorporation in reverse," with equal protection moving from the Fourteenth Amendment to become part of the Bill of Rights. See *Bolling v. Sharpe*, 347 U.S. 497 (1954).

the children of the minority group of equal educational opportunities? We believe that it does. . . . We conclude that in the field of public education the doctrine of "separate but equal" has no place. Separate educational facilities are inherently unequal.[65]

The *Brown* decision altered the constitutional framework in two fundamental respects. First, after *Brown,* the states would no longer have the power to use race as a basis of discrimination in law. Second, the national government would from then on have the power (and eventually the obligation) to intervene with strict regulatory policies against the discriminatory actions of state or local governments, school boards, employers, and others in the private sector.

Civil Rights after *Brown v. Board of Education*

Although *Brown v. Board of Education* withdrew all constitutional authority to use race as a criterion of exclusion, this historic decision was merely a small opening move. First, most states refused to cooperate until sued, and many ingenious schemes were employed to delay obedience (such as paying the tuition for white students to attend newly created "private" academies). Second, even as southern school boards began to cooperate by eliminating their legally enforced (**de jure**) school segregation, extensive actual (**de facto**) school segregation persisted in the North as well as the South. *Brown* could not affect de facto segregation, which was not legislated but happened as a result of racially segregated housing. Third, *Brown* did not directly touch discrimination in employment, public accommodations, juries, voting, and other areas of social and economic activity.

A decade of frustration following *Brown* made it fairly obvious to all that the goal of "equal protection" required positive, or affirmative, action by Congress and by administrative agencies. And given massive southern resistance and a generally negative national public opinion toward racial integration, progress would not be made through courts, Congress, or agencies without intense, well-organized support.

School Desegregation.   Although the District of Columbia and some of the school districts in the border states began to respond almost immediately to court-ordered desegregation, the states of the Deep South responded with a well-planned delaying tactic. Southern legislatures passed laws ordering school districts to maintain segregated schools and state superintendents to withhold state funding from racially mixed classrooms. Some southern states centralized public school authority to give them power to close the schools that might tend to obey the Court and to provide alternative private schooling.

Most of these plans of "massive resistance" were tested in the federal courts and were struck down as unconstitutional.[66] But southern resistance was not

de jure segregation Racial segregation that is a direct result of law or official policy.

de facto segregation Racial segregation that is not a direct result of law or government policy but is, instead, a reflection of residential patterns, income distributions, or other social factors.

---

[65] *Brown v. Board of Education of Topeka, Kansas,* 347 U.S. 483 (1954).

[66] The two most important cases were *Cooper v. Aaron,* 358 U.S. 1 (1958), which required Little Rock, Arkansas, to desegregate; and *Griffin v. Prince Edward County School Board,* 337 U.S. 218 (1964), which forced all the schools of that Virginia county to reopen after five years of being closed to avoid desegregation.

confined to legislation. For example, in Arkansas in 1957, Governor Orval Faubus ordered the National Guard to prevent enforcement of a federal court order to integrate Central High School of Little Rock. President Eisenhower was forced to deploy U.S. troops and place the city under martial law. The Supreme Court handed down a unanimous decision requiring desegregation in Little Rock.[67] The end of massive resistance, however, became simply the beginning of still another southern strategy. "Pupil placement" laws authorized school districts to place each pupil in a school according to a whole variety of academic, personal, and psychological considerations, never mentioning race at all. This put the burden of transferring to an all-white school on the nonwhite children and their parents.[68] It was thus almost impossible for a single court order to cover a whole district, let alone a whole state. This delayed desegregation a while longer. As Figure 4.2 shows, southern schools remained largely segregated for a decade after *Brown*.

As the southern states invented new devices to avoid desegregation, it was becoming unmistakably clear that the federal courts could not do the job alone.[69] The first modern effort to legislate in the field of civil rights was made in 1957, but the law contained only a federal guarantee of voting rights without any powers of enforcement, although it did create the Civil Rights Commission to study abuses. Much more important legislation for civil rights followed during the 1960s, especially the Civil Rights Act of 1964 (see Timeline, pages 106–7).

Further progress in the desegregation of schools came in the form of busing[70] and redistricting, but it was slow. It is likely to continue to be slow unless the Supreme Court decides to permit federal action against de facto segregation and against the varieties of private schools and academies that have sprung up for the purpose of avoiding integration.[71] A Supreme Court decision handed down in 1995, in which the Court signaled to the lower courts to "disengage from desegregation efforts," dimmed the prospects for further school integration. Moreover, school desegregation has been made more problematic by the Supreme Court's

---

[67] In *Cooper v. Aaron*, the Supreme Court ordered immediate compliance with the lower court's desegregation order and went beyond that with a stern warning that it is "emphatically the province and duty of the judicial department to say what the law is." The justices also took the unprecedented action of personally signing the decisions.

[68] *Shuttlesworth v. Birmingham Board of Education*, 358 U.S. 101 (1958). This decision upheld a "pupil placement" plan purporting to assign pupils on various bases, with no mention of race. This case interpreted *Brown v. Board of Education* to mean that school districts must stop explicit racial discrimination but were under no obligation to take positive steps to desegregate. For a while, black parents were doomed to case-to-case approaches.

[69] For good treatments of that long stretch of the struggle of the federal courts to integrate the schools, see Paul Brest, Sanford Levinson, et al., *Processes of Constitutional Decisionmaking*, 5th ed. (New York: Aspen Publishers, 2006), pp. 471–80; and Kelly, Harbison, and Boltz, *The American Constitution*, pp. 610–16.

[70] *Swann v. Charlotte-Mecklenburg Board of Education*, 402 U.S. 1 (1971). See also Bernard Schwartz, *Swann's Way: The School Busing Case and the Supreme Court* (New York: Oxford University Press, 1986).

[71] For a good evaluation, see Gary Orfield, *Must We Bus? Segregated Schools and National Policy* (Washington, D.C.: Brookings Institution, 1978), pp. 144–46. See also Bob Woodward and Scott Armstrong, *The Brethren: Inside the Supreme Court* (New York: Simon and Schuster, 1979), pp. 426–27; and J. Anthony Lukas, *Common Ground* (New York: Random House, 1986).

Racial Equality

As we discuss in this chapter, civil rights is a major political issue in the United States. Especially since the 1960s, most forms of racial discrimination have been prohibited by law, and a large number of government programs have been designed to promote greater political, social, and economic equality between black and white Americans. Despite these efforts, progress in the direction of racial equality has been uneven. As we can see in the following figures and tables, some data suggest that the United States has made great strides toward the color-blind society envisioned by the early leaders of the civil rights movement. Other data, though, indicate that we have a long way to go. The fact that America's president is black does not mean that complete racial equality has been achieved in the U.S.

In assessing racial equality in the United States, we could also consider numerous other statistics and other racial and ethnic groups. Depending upon which evidence is selected, one might argue that racial equality in the United States has increased substantially in recent years or that it has not.

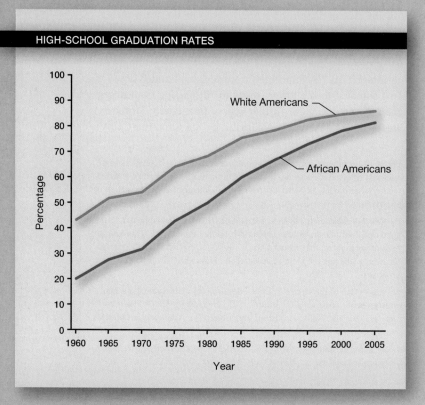

HIGH-SCHOOL GRADUATION RATES

Percentage / Year

White Americans

African Americans

One encouraging statistic is the change in black versus white levels of educational attainment over the past 45 years. In 1960, black Americans were less than half as likely to finish high school or graduate from college as whites. Today, the percentage of blacks graduating from high school is nearly identical to the percentage of whites who earn diplomas.

Source: U.S. Census Bureau, www.census.gov (accessed 6/22/09).

AFRICAN AMERICANS ELECTED TO OFFICE

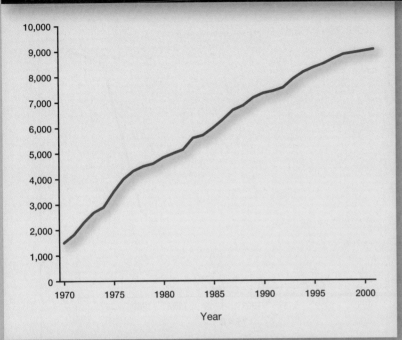

Year

Progress has also been made in the political arena. As recently as 1970, only 1,469 African Americans held elected office in the United States—out of approximately half a million federal, state, and local offices. By 2001, the last year for which the government collected data, there were more than 9,000 black elected officials, an increase of more than 600 percent.

Source: Joint Center for Political and Economical Studies, "Black Elected Officials," http://jointcenter.org/BD/detail/BEO.htm (accessed 6/22/09).

In the economic realm the gap between blacks and whites has decreased more slowly. In 2007, the *mean* income of black men was only 66 percent of the mean income for white men. This represented only slight progress for black men since 1980. Although black women's mean income was close to that of white women in 2007, it was even closer in 1980—so black women have lost ground relative to white women during this period. The table below shows *median* incomes, which also reflect the gap between blacks and whites, especially among men.

MEDIAN INCOME (2005 Dollars)

	Men				Women			
	1980	1990	2000	2007	1980	1990	2000	2007
White	31,931	32,557	35,877	35,141	11,852	15,866	19,360	21,069
Black	19,188	19,789	25,698	25,822	10,973	12,807	19,121	19,752

Source: U.S. Census Bureau, www.census.gov (accessed 6/22/09).

FIGURE 4.2 THE PERCENTAGE OF SOUTHERN BLACK SCHOOLCHILDREN ATTENDING SCHOOL WITH WHITES, 1955–73

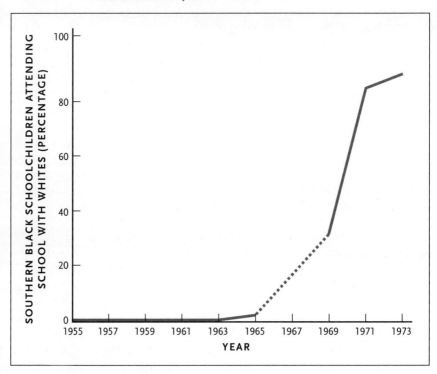

NOTE: Dashed line indicates missing data.

SOURCE: Gerald N. Rosenberg, *Hollow Hope: Can Courts Bring About Social Change?* (Chicago: University of Chicago Press, 1991), pp. 50–51.

2007 decision in the consolidated cases of *County Schools v. Seattle School District No. 1* and *Meredith v. Jefferson County Board of Education*. In both instances, school districts had categorized students by race and assigned them to schools partly on the basis of plans designed to achieve racial diversity. The Supreme Court, however, said that racial classifications were potentially "too pernicious" to be used except under the most compelling circumstances. Rights activists pointed out that it is difficult to see how school systems might achieve greater racial diversity if they are prohibited from taking account of students' race when making school assignments. The "Analyzing the Evidence" unit for this chapter looks at progress toward racial equality in recent decades.

The Rise of the Politics of Rights

Outlawing Discrimination in Employment. Despite the agonizingly slow progress of school desegregation, there was some progress in other areas of civil rights during the 1960s and 1970s. Voting rights were established and fairly quickly began to revolutionize southern politics. Service on juries was no longer denied to minorities. But progress in the right to participate in politics and government dramatized the relative lack of economic progress, and it was in this area that battles over civil rights were increasingly fought.

The federal courts and the Justice Department entered this area through Title VII of the Civil Rights Act of 1964. Title VII outlawed job discrimination by all private and public employers, including governmental agencies (such as fire and police departments), that employed more than fifteen workers. We have already seen that the Supreme Court gave "interstate commerce" such a broad definition that Congress had the constitutional authority to outlaw discrimination by virtually any local employer.[72] Title VII made it unlawful to discriminate in employment on the basis of color, religion, sex, or national origin, as well as race.

One problem with Title VII was that the complaining party had to show that deliberate discrimination was the cause of the failure to get a job or a training opportunity. Rarely does an employer explicitly admit discrimination on the basis of race, sex, or any other illegal reason. For a time, courts allowed the complaining parties to make their case if they could show that an employer's hiring practices, whether intentional or not, had the *effect* of exclusion. Employers, in effect, had to justify their actions.[73] In recent years, though, the Supreme Court has placed a number of limits on employment discrimination suits. In 2007, for example, in the case of *Ledbetter v. Goodyear Tire and Rubber Co.* the court said that a complaint of gender discrimination must be brought within 180 days of the time the discrimination was alleged to have occurred.[74] This blocks suits based on events that might have taken place in the past. In 2009, Congress effectively overturned the Court's decision by enacting legislation greatly extending the amount of time available to workers filing such suits.

Gender Discrimination.   Title VII provided a valuable tool for the growing women's movement in the 1960s and 1970s.[75] In fact, in many ways the law fostered the growth of the women's movement. The first major campaign of the National Organization for Women (NOW) involved picketing the Equal Employment Opportunity Commission (EEOC) for its refusal to ban sex-segregated employment advertisements. NOW also sued the *New York Times* for continuing to publish

---

[72] See especially *Katzenbach v. McClung,* 379 U.S. 294 (1964). Almost immediately after passage of the Civil Rights Act of 1964, a case was brought challenging the validity of Title II, which covered discrimination in public accommodations. Ollie's Barbecue was a neighborhood restaurant in Birmingham, Alabama. It was located eleven blocks away from an interstate highway and even farther from railroad and bus stations. Its table service was for whites only; there was only a take-out service for blacks. The Supreme Court agreed that Ollie's was strictly an intrastate restaurant, but since a substantial proportion of its food and other supplies were bought from companies outside the state of Alabama, there was sufficient connection to interstate commerce; therefore, racial discrimination at such restaurants would "impose commercial burdens of national magnitude upon interstate commerce." Although this case involved Title II, it had direct bearing on the constitutionality of Title VII.

[73] *Griggs v. Duke Power Company,* 401 U.S. 24 (1971).

[74] *Ledbetter v. Goodyear Tire and Rubber Co.,* 05-1074 (2007).

[75] This and the next five sections are from Ginsberg et al., *We the People,* 8th ed.

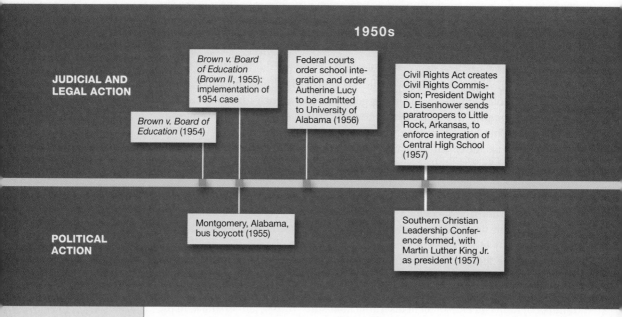

1950s

JUDICIAL AND LEGAL ACTION

Brown v. Board of Education (1954)

Brown v. Board of Education (*Brown II*, 1955): implementation of 1954 case

Federal courts order school integration and order Autherine Lucy to be admitted to University of Alabama (1956)

Civil Rights Act creates Civil Rights Commission; President Dwight D. Eisenhower sends paratroopers to Little Rock, Arkansas, to enforce integration of Central High School (1957)

POLITICAL ACTION

Montgomery, Alabama, bus boycott (1955)

Southern Christian Leadership Conference formed, with Martin Luther King Jr. as president (1957)

such ads after the passage of Title VII. Another organization, the Women's Equity Action League (WEAL), pursued legal action on a wide range of sex discrimination issues, filing lawsuits against law schools and medical schools for their discriminatory admission policies, for example.

Building on these victories and the growth of the women's movement, feminist activists sought an equal rights amendment (ERA) to the Constitution. The proposed amendment was short: Its substantive passage stated that "equality of rights under the law shall not be denied or abridged by the United States or by any State on account of sex." The amendment's supporters believed that such a sweeping guarantee of equal rights was a necessary tool for ending all discrimination against women and for making gender roles more equal. Opponents charged that it would be socially disruptive and would introduce changes—such as coed restrooms—that most Americans did not want. The amendment easily passed Congress in 1972 and won quick approval in many state legislatures but fell three states short of the thirty-eight needed to ratify the amendment by the 1982 deadline for its ratification.[76]

Despite the failure of the ERA, gender discrimination expanded dramatically as an area of civil rights law. In the 1970s, the conservative Burger Court helped to establish gender discrimination as a major and highly visible civil rights issue. Although the Burger Court refused to treat gender discrimination as the equivalent

---

[76] See Jane J. Mansbridge, *Why We Lost the ERA* (Chicago: University of Chicago Press, 1986); and Gilbert Steiner, *Constitutional Inequality* (Washington, D.C.: Brookings Institution, 1985).

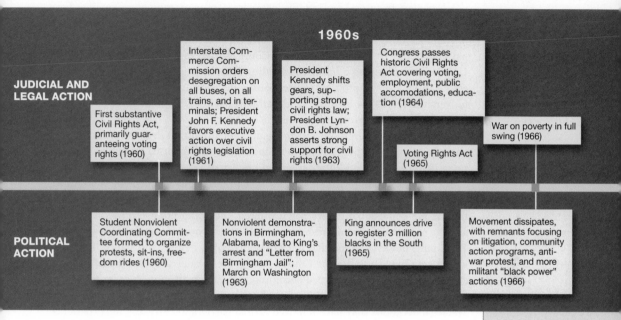

1960s

JUDICIAL AND LEGAL ACTION

First substantive Civil Rights Act, primarily guaranteeing voting rights (1960)

Interstate Commerce Commission orders desegregation on all buses, on all trains, and in terminals; President John F. Kennedy favors executive action over civil rights legislation (1961)

President Kennedy shifts gears, supporting strong civil rights law; President Lyndon B. Johnson asserts strong support for civil rights (1963)

Congress passes historic Civil Rights Act covering voting, employment, public accomodations, education (1964)

Voting Rights Act (1965)

War on poverty in full swing (1966)

POLITICAL ACTION

Student Nonviolent Coordinating Committee formed to organize protests, sit-ins, freedom rides (1960)

Nonviolent demonstrations in Birmingham, Alabama, lead to King's arrest and "Letter from Birmingham Jail"; March on Washington (1963)

King announces drive to register 3 million blacks in the South (1965)

Movement dissipates, with remnants focusing on litigation, community action programs, antiwar protest, and more militant "black power" actions (1966)

---

of racial discrimination,[77] it did make it easier for plaintiffs to file and win suits on the basis of gender discrimination by applying an "intermediate" level of review to these cases.[78] This **intermediate scrutiny** is midway between traditional rules of evidence, which put the burden of proof on the plaintiff, and the doctrine of strict scrutiny, which requires the defendant to show not only that a particular classification is reasonable but also that there is a need or compelling interest for it. Intermediate scrutiny shifts the burden of proof partially onto the defendant, rather than leaving it entirely on the plaintiff.

One major step was taken in 1992, when the Court decided in *Franklin v. Gwinnett County Public Schools* that violations of Title IX of the 1972 Education Act could be remedied with monetary damages.[79] Title IX forbids gender discrimination in education, but it initially sparked little litigation because of its weak enforcement provisions. The Court's 1992 ruling opened the door for more legal action in the area of education. The greatest impact has been in the areas of sexual harassment—the subject of the *Franklin* case—and in equal treatment of women's athletic programs. The potential for monetary damages has made universities and public schools take the problem of sexual harassment more seriously. Colleges and universities have also started to pay more attention to women's athletic programs. In the two years after the *Franklin* case, complaints to the Education Department's

intermediate scrutiny The test used by the Supreme Court in gender discrimination cases. Intermediate scrutiny places the burden of proof partially on the government and partially on the challengers to show that the law in question is constitutional.

---

[77] See *Frontiero v. Richardson*, 411 U.S. 677 (1973).

[78] See *Craig v. Boren*, 423 U.S. 1047 (1976).

[79] *Franklin v. Gwinnett County Public Schools*, 503 U.S. 60 (1992).

Office for Civil Rights about unequal treatment of women's athletic programs nearly tripled. In several high-profile legal cases, some prominent universities have been ordered to create more women's sports programs; many other colleges and universities have begun to add more women's programs in order to avoid potential litigation.[80] In 1997, the Supreme Court refused to hear a petition by Brown University challenging a lower-court ruling that the university establish strict sex equity in its athletic programs. The Court's decision meant that in colleges and universities across the country, varsity athletic positions for men and women must reflect their overall enrollment numbers.[81]

In 1996, the Supreme Court made another important decision about gender and education by putting an end to all-male schools supported by public funds. It ruled that the Virginia Military Institute's policy of not admitting women was unconstitutional.[82] Along with the Citadel, an all-male military college in South Carolina, Virginia Military Institute (VMI) had never admitted women. It argued that the unique educational experience it offered, including intense physical training and the harsh treatment of freshmen, would be destroyed if women were admitted. The Court, however, ruled that the male-only policy denied "substantial equality" to women. Two days after the Court's ruling, the Citadel announced that it would accept women. VMI considered becoming a private institution in order to remain all-male, but in September 1996 the school board finally voted to admit women. The legal decisions may have removed formal barriers to entry, but the experience of the female cadets at these schools has not been easy. The first female cadet at the Citadel, Shannon Faulkner, won admission in 1995 under a federal court order but quit after four days. Although four women were admitted to the Citadel after the Supreme Court decision, two of them quit several months later. They charged harassment by male students, including attempts to set the female cadets on fire.[83]

Courts began to find sexual harassment a form of sex discrimination during the late 1970s. Although sexual harassment law applies to education, most of the law of sexual harassment has been developed by courts through interpretation of Title VII of the Civil Rights Act of 1964. In 1986, the Supreme Court recognized two forms of sexual harassment—the quid pro quo type, which involves sexual extortion, and the hostile-environment type, which involves sexual intimidation.[84] Employers and many employees have worried that hostile-environment sexual harassment is too ambiguous. When can an employee bring charges? When is the employer liable? In 1986, the Court said that sexual harassment may be legally actionable even if the employee did not suffer tangible economic or job-related losses in relation to it. And in 1993, the Court said that sexual harassment may be legally

[80] Jennifer Halperin, "Women Step Up to Bat," *Illinois Issues* 21 (September 1995): 11–14.

[81] Joan Biskupic and David Nakamura, "Court Won't Review Sports Equity Ruling," *Washington Post*, April 22, 1997, p. A1.

[82] *United States v. Virginia*, 518 U.S. 515 (1996).

[83] Judith Havemann, "Two Women Quit Citadel over Alleged Harassment," *Washington Post*, January 13, 1997, p. A1.

[84] *Meritor Savings Bank v. Vinson* (1986).

actionable even if the employee did not suffer tangible psychological costs as a result of it.[85] In two 1998 cases, the Court further strengthened the law when it said that whether or not sexual harassment results in economic harm to the employee, an employer is liable for the harassment if it was committed by someone with authority over the employee—by a supervisor, for example. But the Court also said that an employer may defend itself by showing that it had a sexual harassment prevention and grievance policy in effect.[86]

The development of gender discrimination as an important part of the civil rights struggle has coincided with the rise of women's politics as a discrete movement in American politics. As with the struggle for racial equality, the relationship between changes in government policies and political action suggests that changes in government policies to a great degree produce political action. Today the existence of a powerful women's movement derives in large measure from the enactment of Title VII of the Civil Rights Act of 1964 and from the Burger Court's vital steps in applying that law to the protection of women. The recognition of women's civil rights has become an issue that in many ways transcends the usual distinctions of American political debate. In the heavily partisan debate over the federal crime bill enacted in 1994, for instance, the section of the bill that enjoyed the widest support was the Violence against Women Act, whose most important feature was that it defined gender-biased violent crimes as a matter of civil rights and created a civil rights remedy for women who have been the victims of such crimes. But since the act was ruled unconstitutional by the Supreme Court in 2000, the struggle for women's rights will likely remain part of the political debate.

Latinos and Asian Americans.

The labels "Latino" or "Hispanic" and "Asian American" encompass a wide range of groups with diverse national origins, distinctive cultural identities, and particular experiences. For example, the early political experiences of Mexican Americans were shaped by race and region. In 1898, Mexican Americans were given formal political rights, including the right to vote. In many places, however, and especially in Texas, Mexican Americans were segregated and prevented from voting by such means as the white primary and the poll tax.[87] Region made a difference too. In contrast to the northeastern and midwestern cities in which most European immigrants settled, the Southwest did not have a tradition of ethnic mobilization associated with machine politics. Particularly after the political reforms enacted in the first decade of the twentieth century, city politics in the Southwest was dominated by a small group of white elites. In the countryside, when Mexican Americans participated in politics, it was often as part of a political organization dominated by a large white landowner, or *patron*.

---

[85] *Harris v. Forklift Systems*, 510 U.S. 17 (1993).

[86] *Burlington Industries v. Ellerth*, 524 U.S. 742 (1998); *Faragher v. City of Boca Raton*, 524 U.S. 775 (1998).

[87] New Mexico had a different history because not many Anglos settled there initially. (*Anglo* is the term for a non-Hispanic white of European background.) Mexican Americans had considerable power in territorial legislatures between 1865 and 1912. See Lawrence H. Fuchs, *The American Kaleidoscope* (Hanover, N.H.: University Press of New England, 1990), pp. 239–40.

The earliest independent Mexican American political organizations, the League of United Latin American Citizens (LULAC) and the American GI Forum, worked to stem discrimination against Mexican Americans in the years after World War II. By the late 1950s, the first Mexican American had been elected to Congress, and four others followed in the 1960s. In the late 1960s, a new kind of Mexican American political movement was born. Inspired by the black civil rights movement, Mexican American students launched boycotts of high-school classes in Los Angeles, Denver, and San Antonio. Students in colleges and universities across California joined in as well. Among their demands were bilingual education, an end to discrimination, and greater cultural recognition. In Crystal City, Texas, which had been dominated by Anglo politicians despite a population that was overwhelmingly Mexican American, the newly formed La Raza Unida Party took over the city government.[88]

Since that time, Mexican American political strategy has developed along two tracks. One is a traditional ethnic-group path of voter registration and voting along ethnic lines. The second is a legal strategy using the various civil rights laws designed to ensure fair access to the political system. The Mexican American Legal Defense and Education Fund (MALDEF) has played a key role in designing and pursuing the latter strategy.

The early Asian experience in the United States was shaped by a series of naturalization laws dating back to 1790, the first of which declared that only white aliens were eligible for citizenship. Chinese immigrants had begun arriving in California in the 1850s, drawn by the boom of the gold rush. They were immediately met with hostility. The virulent antagonism toward Chinese immigrants in California led Congress in 1870 to declare Chinese immigrants ineligible for citizenship. In 1882, the first Chinese Exclusion Act suspended the entry of Chinese laborers.

At the time of the Exclusion Act, the Chinese community was composed predominantly of single male laborers, with few women and children. The few Chinese children in San Francisco were initially denied entry to the public schools; only after parents of American-born Chinese children pressed legal action were the children allowed to attend public school. Even then, however, they were made to attend a separate Chinese school. American-born Chinese children could not be denied citizenship, however; this right was confirmed by the Supreme Court in 1898, when it ruled in *United States v. Wong Kim Ark* that anyone born in the United States was entitled to full citizenship.[89] Still, new Chinese immigrants were barred from the United States until 1943; China by then had become a key wartime ally, and Congress repealed the Chinese Exclusion Act and permitted Chinese residents to become citizens.

Immigration climbed rapidly after the 1965 Immigration and Nationality Services Act, which lifted discriminatory quotas. In spite of this and other developments, limited English proficiency barred many Asian Americans and Latinos

---

[88] On the La Raza Unida Party, see Carlos Muñoz, Jr. and Mario Barrera, "La Raza Unida Party and the Chicano Student Movement in California," in *Latinos and the Political System*, F. Chris Garcia, ed. (Notre Dame, Ind.: University of Notre Dame Press, 1988), pp. 213–35.

[89] *United States v. Wong Kim Ark*, 169 U.S. 649 (1898).

from full participation in American life. Two developments in the 1970s, however, established rights for language minorities. In 1974, the Supreme Court ruled in *Lau v. Nichols,* a suit filed on behalf of Chinese students in San Francisco, that school districts have to provide education for students whose English is limited.[90] It did not mandate bilingual education, but it established a duty to provide instruction that students could understand. The 1970 amendments to the Voting Rights Act of 1965 permanently outlawed literacy tests in all fifty states and mandated bilingual ballots or oral assistance for those who speak Spanish, Chinese, Japanese, Korean, Native American languages, or Inuit languages.

Asian Americans and Latinos have also been concerned about the impact of immigration laws on their civil rights. Many Asian American and Latino organizations opposed the Immigration Reform and Control Act of 1986 because it imposes sanctions on employers who hire undocumented workers. Such sanctions, they feared, would lead employers to discriminate against Latinos and Asian Americans. These suspicions were confirmed in a 1990 report by the General Accounting Office that found employer sanctions had created a "widespread pattern of discrimination" against Latinos and others who appear foreign.[91] Organizations such as MALDEF and the Asian Law Caucus monitor and challenge such discrimination. These groups have turned their attention to the rights of legal and illegal immigrants as anti-immigrant sentiment has grown in recent years.

The Supreme Court has ruled that illegal immigrants are eligible for education and medical care but can be denied other social benefits; legal immigrants are to be treated much the same as citizens. But growing immigration—including an estimated 300,000 illegal immigrants per year—and mounting economic insecurity have undermined these practices. Groups of voters across the country now strongly support drawing a sharper line between immigrants and citizens. Not surprisingly, the movement to deny benefits to noncitizens began in California, which experienced sharp economic distress in the early 1990s and has the highest levels of immigration of any state. In 1994, Californians voted in favor of Proposition 187, which denied illegal immigrants all services except emergency medical care. Supporters of the measure hoped to discourage illegal immigration and pressure illegal immigrants already in the country to leave. Opponents contended that denying basic services to illegal immigrants risked creating a subclass of residents in the United States whose lack of education and poor health would threaten all Americans. In 1994 and 1997, a federal court declared most of Proposition 187 unconstitutional, affirming previous rulings that illegal immigrants should be granted public education. A booming economy helped to reduce public concern about illegal immigration, but supporters of Proposition 187 promised to reintroduce similar measures in the future.

In January 2004, President Bush released a plan to revamp American immigration laws to enable all undocumented immigrants "to obtain legal status as temporary workers." For illegal immigrants, the president proposed a new temporary-worker program, whereby every illegal immigrant could apply for a three-year work

---

[90] *Lau v. Nichols,* 414 U.S. 563 (1974).

[91] Dick Kirschten, "Not Black and White," *National Journal,* March 2, 1991, p. 497.

permit, which would be renewable for another three years provided the temporary, or "guest," worker already had a job. Those who failed to stay employed or who broke the law would be deported. Under the plan, employers would control the work permits so that the continued status of the guest worker wou ld depend entirely on the discretion of the employer. In 2007, President Bush and a number of Democrats, including Senator Ted Kennedy of Massachusetts, supported a new immigration reform bill that would have offered legal status and the possibility of future citizenship to approximately 12 million illegal immigrants currently in the United States, while making it more difficult for new illegals to enter the country. However, the bill was defeated in June 2007, leaving the question of immigration reform unresolved.

The question of the rights of legal immigrants points to an even tougher problem. Congress has the power to deny public benefits to this group, but doing so would go against long-standing traditions in American political culture. Legal immigrants have traditionally enjoyed most of the rights and obligations of citizens (such as paying taxes). As the constitutional scholar Alexander Bickel points out, the Constitution begins with "We the People of the United States"; likewise the Bill of Rights refers to the rights of *people,* not the rights of citizens. But even as Congress continues to debate immigration policy, several states, led by Arizona, have enacted their own laws aimed at identifying and deporting illegal immigrants. Immigration continues to be a divisive issue in American politics.

Native Americans.   The political status of Native Americans was left unclear in the Constitution. But by the early 1800s, the courts had defined each of the Indian tribes as a nation. As members of an Indian nation, Native Americans were declared noncitizens of the United States. The political status of Native Americans changed in 1924, when congressional legislation granted citizenship to those who were born in the United States. A variety of changes in federal policy toward Native Americans during the 1930s paved the way for a later resurgence of their political power. Most important was the federal decision to encourage Native Americans on reservations to establish local self-government.[92]

The Native American political movement gathered force in the 1960s as Indians began to use protest, litigation, and assertion of tribal rights to improve their situation. In 1968, Dennis Banks cofounded the American Indian Movement (AIM), the most prominent Native American protest organization. AIM won national attention in 1969 when 200 of its members, representing twenty tribes, took over the famous prison island of Alcatraz in San Francisco Bay, claiming it for Native Americans. In 1973, AIM members took over the town of Wounded Knee, South Dakota, the site of the massacre of over 200 Sioux men, women, and children by the U.S. Army in December 1890. The federal government responded to the rise in Indian activism with the Indian Self-determination and Education Assistance Act (1975), which began to give Indians more control over their own land.[93]

---

[92] Not all Indian tribes agreed with this, including the Navajos. See Ronald Takaki, *A Different Mirror: A History of Multicultural America* (Boston: Little, Brown, 1993), pp. 238–48.

[93] On the resurgence of Indian political activity, see Stephen Cornell, *The Return of the Native: American Indian Political Resurgence* (New York: Oxford University Press, 1990); and Dee Brown, *Bury My Heart at Wounded Knee (*New York: Holt, 1971).

As a language minority, Native Americans were also affected by the 1975 amendments to the Voting Rights Act and the *Lau* decision, which established the right of Native Americans to be taught in their own languages. This ruling marked quite a change from the boarding schools once run by the Bureau of Indian Affairs, at which members of Indian tribes were forbidden to speak their own languages. Native Americans have also sought to expand their rights on the basis of their sovereign status. Since the 1920s and 1930s, Native American tribes have sued the federal government for illegally seizing land, seeking monetary reparations and land as damages. Both types of damages have been awarded in such suits, but only in small amounts. Native American tribes have been more successful in winning federal recognition of their sovereignty. Sovereign status has, in turn, allowed them to exercise greater self-determination. Most significant economically was a 1987 Supreme Court decision that freed Native American tribes from most state regulations prohibiting gambling.[94] The establishment of casino gambling on Native American lands has brought a substantial flow of new income into desperately poor reservations.

Americans with Disabilities.   The concept of rights for people with disabilities began to emerge in the 1970s as the civil rights model spread to other groups. The seed was planted in a little-noticed provision of the 1973 Rehabilitation Act that outlawed discrimination against individuals on the basis of disabilities. As in many other cases, the law itself helped give rise to the movement demanding rights.[95] Modeling itself on the NAACP's Legal Defense Fund, the disability movement founded a Disability Rights Education and Defense Fund to press its legal claims. The movement achieved its greatest success with the passage of the Americans with Disabilities Act (ADA) of 1990, which guarantees the disabled equal employment rights and access to public businesses. Claims of discrimination in violation of this act are considered by the EEOC. The impact of the law has been far-reaching as businesses and public facilities have installed ramps, elevators, and other devices to meet its requirements.[96]

In 1998, the Supreme Court interpreted the ADA to apply to people with HIV. Until then, ADA was interpreted as applying to people with AIDS but not people with HIV. The case arose when a dentist was asked to fill a cavity for a woman with HIV; he would do it only in a hospital setting. The woman sued, and her complaint was that HIV had already disabled her because it was discouraging her from having children. (The act prohibits discrimination in employment, housing, and health care.) Although there have been widespread concerns that the ADA was being expanded too broadly and the costs were becoming too burdensome, corporate America did not seem to be disturbed by the Court's ruling. Stephen Bokat,

---

[94] *California v. Cabazon Band of Mission Indians*, 480 U.S. 202 (1987).

[95] See the discussion in Robert A. Katzmann, *Institutional Disability: The Saga of Transportation Policy for the Disabled* (Washington, D.C.: Brookings Institution, 1986).

[96] For example, after pressure from the Justice Department, one of the nation's largest rental-car companies agreed to make special hand controls available to any customer requesting them. See "Avis Agrees to Equip Cars for Disabled," *Los Angeles Times*, September 2, 1994, p. D1.

general counsel of the U.S. Chamber of Commerce, said businesses in general had already been accommodating people with HIV as well as those with AIDS and the case presented no serious problem.[97]

The Aged. The 1967 federal Age Discrimination in Employment Act (ADEA) makes age discrimination illegal when practiced by employers with at least twenty employees. Many states have added to the federal provisions with their own age discrimination laws, and some of the state laws are stronger than the federal provisions. The major lobbyist for seniors, AARP (formerly the American Association of Retired Persons), with its claim to more than 30 million members, has been active in keeping these laws on the books and making sure they are vigorously implemented.

Gay Men and Lesbians. In less than thirty years, the gay movement has become one of the largest civil rights movements in contemporary America. Beginning with street protests in the 1960s, it has grown into a well-financed and sophisticated lobby. The Human Rights Campaign is the primary national PAC (political action committee) focused on gay rights; it provides campaign financing and volunteers to work for candidates endorsed by the group. The movement has also formed legal rights organizations, including the Lambda Legal Defense and Education Fund.

Gay rights drew national attention in 1993, when President Bill Clinton confronted the question of whether gays should be allowed to serve in the military. As a candidate, Clinton had said he favored lifting the ban on homosexuals in the military. The issue set off a huge controversy in the first months of his presidency. After nearly a year of deliberation, the administration enunciated a compromise: its "don't ask, don't tell" policy, which allows gay men and lesbians to serve in the military as long as they do not openly proclaim their sexual orientation or engage in homosexual activity. The administration maintained that the ruling would protect gay men and lesbians from witch-hunting investigations, but many gay advocates expressed disappointment, charging the president with reneging on his campaign promise.

But until 1996, no Supreme Court ruling or national legislation explicitly protected gay men and lesbians from discrimination. The first gay rights case that the Court decided, *Bowers v. Hardwick* (1986), ruled against a right to privacy that would protect consensual homosexual activity. After the *Bowers* decision, the gay rights movement sought suitable legal cases to test the constitutionality of discrimination against gay men and lesbians, much as the civil rights movement had done in the late 1940s and 1950s. As one advocate put it, "lesbians and gay men are looking for their *Brown v. Board of Education*."[98] Among the cases tested were those stemming from local ordinances restricting gay rights (including the right to marry),

[97] The case and the interview with Stephen Bokat were reported in Margaret Warner, "Expanding Coverage: Defining Disability," *Online NewsHour*, June 30, 1998, www.pbs.org/newshour/bb/law/jan-june98/hiv_6-30.html.

[98] Quoted in Joan Biskupic, "Gay Rights Activists Seek a Supreme Court Test Case," *Washington Post*, December 19, 1993, p. A1.

job discrimination, and family-law issues such as adoption and parental rights. In 1996, in *Romer v. Evans,* the Supreme Court explicitly extended fundamental civil rights protections to gay men and lesbians by declaring unconstitutional a 1992 amendment to the Colorado state constitution that prohibited local governments from passing ordinances to protect gay rights.[99] The decision's forceful language highlighted the connection between gay rights and civil rights as it declared discrimination against gay people unconstitutional.

In *Lawrence v. Texas* (2003), the Court overturned *Bowers* and struck down a Texas statute criminalizing certain intimate sexual conduct between consenting partners of the same sex. A victory for lesbians and gay men every bit as significant as *Roe v. Wade* was for women, *Lawrence v. Texas* extends at least one aspect of civil liberties to sexual minorities: the right to privacy. However, this decision by itself does not undo the various exclusions that deprive lesbians and gay men of full civil rights, including the right to marry, which became a hot-button issue in 2004.

Early in that year, the Supreme Judicial Court of Massachusetts ruled that under that state's constitution gay men and lesbians were entitled to marry. The state senate then requested the court to rule on whether a civil-union statute (avoiding the word *marriage*) would, as it did in Vermont, satisfy the court's ruling, in response to which the court ruled negatively, asserting that civil unions are too much like the "separate but equal" doctrine that maintained legalized racial segregation from 1896 to 1954. In San Francisco, meanwhile, hundreds of gay men and lesbians responded to the opportunity provided by the mayor, who had directed the city clerk to issue marriage licenses to same-sex couples in defiance of California law. At the same time, signs indicated that Massachusetts might move toward a state constitutional amendment that would ban gay unions by whatever name. Voters in Missouri and Louisiana approved a ban on same-sex marriages, joining Alaska, Hawaii, Nebraska, and Nevada in implementing such a ban. Voters in eleven other states approved similar bans in the November 2004 elections. In 2009, however, the Iowa Supreme Court approved same-sex marriages, and several other states appeared ready to follow suit.

Affirmative Action

The politics of rights not only spread to increasing numbers of groups in society but also expanded its goal. The relatively narrow goal of equalizing opportunity by eliminating discriminatory barriers had been developing toward the far broader goal of **affirmative action**—compensatory action to overcome the consequences of past discrimination and encourage greater diversity. An affirmative action policy tends to involve two novel approaches: (1) positive or benign discrimination in which race or some other status is taken into account, but for compensatory action rather than mistreatment, and (2) compensatory action to favor members of the disadvantaged group who themselves may never have been the victims of discrimination. Quotas may be—but are not necessarily—involved in affirmative action policies.

affirmative action A policy or program designed to redress historic injustices against specified groups by actively promoting equal access to educational and employment opportunities.

---

[99] *Romer v. Evans,* 517 U.S. 620 (1996).

In 1965, President Lyndon Johnson attempted to inaugurate affirmative action by executive orders directing agency heads and personnel officers to pursue vigorously a policy of minority employment in the federal civil service and in companies doing business with the national government. But affirmative action did not become a prominent goal until the 1970s.

The Supreme Court and the Burden of Proof.   As affirmative action spread, it began to divide civil rights activists and their supporters. The whole issue of qualification versus minority preference was addressed in the case of Allan Bakke. Bakke, a white man with no minority affiliation, brought suit against the University of California Medical School at Davis on the grounds that in denying him admission the school had discriminated against him on the basis of his race (that year the school had reserved 16 of 100 available slots for minority applicants). He argued that his grades and test scores had ranked him well above many students who had been accepted at the school and that the only possible explanation for his rejection was that the others were black or Hispanic and he was white. In 1978, Bakke won his case before the Supreme Court and was admitted to the medical school, but he did not succeed in getting affirmative action declared unconstitutional. The Court rejected the procedures at the University of California because its medical school had used both a quota *and* a separate admissions system for minorities. The Court agreed with Bakke's argument that racial categorizations are suspect categories that place a severe burden of proof on those using them to show a "compelling public purpose." The Court went on to say that achieving "a diverse student body" was such a public purpose, but the method of a rigid quota of student slots assigned on the basis of race was incompatible with the equal protection clause. Thus the Court permitted universities (and other schools, training programs, and hiring authorities) to continue to take minority status into consideration but limited severely the use of quotas to situations in which previous discrimination had been shown and the quotas were used more as a guideline for social diversity than as a mathematically defined ratio.[100]

For nearly a decade after *Bakke,* the Supreme Court was tentative and permissive about efforts by corporations and governments to experiment with affirmative action programs in employment.[101] But in 1989, the Court returned to the *Bakke* position, ruling that any "rigid numerical quota" is suspect. In *Wards Cove v. Atonio,* the Court further weakened affirmative action by easing the way for employers to prefer white men, holding that the burden of proof of unlawful discrimination should be shifted from the defendant (the employer) to the plaintiff (the person claiming to be the victim of discrimination).[102] This decision virtually overruled the Court's prior holding.[103] That same year, the Court ruled that any affirmative action program already approved by federal courts could be challenged by white men who alleged that the program discriminated against them.[104]

---

[100] *Regents of the University of California v. Bakke,* 438 U.S. 265 (1978).

[101] *United Steelworkers of America v. Weber,* 443 U.S. 193 (1979), and *Fullilove v. Klutznick,* 448 U.S. 448 (1980).

[102] *Wards Cove Packing Company v. Atonio,* 490 U.S. 642 (1989).

[103] *Griggs v. Duke Power Company* (1971).

[104] *Martin v. Wilks,* 490 U.S. 755 (1989).

In 1995, the Supreme Court's ruling in *Adarand Constructors v. Pena* further weakened affirmative action. This decision stated that race-based policies, such as preferences given by the government to minority contractors, must survive strict scrutiny, placing the burden on the government to show that such affirmative action programs serve a compelling government interest and are narrowly tailored to address identifiable past discrimination.[105] President Clinton responded to the *Adarand* decision by ordering a review of all government affirmative action policies and practices. Although many observers suspected that the president would use the review as an opportunity to back away from affirmative action, the conclusions of the task force largely defended existing policies. Reflecting the influence of the Supreme Court's decision in *Adarand,* President Clinton acknowledged that some government policies would need to change. But on the whole, the review found that most affirmative action policies were fair and did not "unduly burden nonbeneficiaries."[106]

Although Clinton sought to "mend, not end" affirmative action, developments in the courts and the states continued to restrict it in important ways. One of the most significant was the *Hopwood* case, in which white students challenged admissions practices at the University of Texas Law School, charging that the school's affirmative action program discriminated against whites. In 1996, a federal court ruling on the case (the U.S. Court of Appeals for the Fifth Circuit) stated that race could never be considered in granting admissions and scholarships at state colleges and universities.[107] This decision effectively rolled back the use of affirmative action permitted by the 1978 *Bakke* case. In *Bakke,* as noted earlier, the Supreme Court had outlawed quotas but said that race could be used as one factor among many in admissions decisions. Many universities and colleges have since justified affirmative action as a way of promoting racial diversity among their student bodies. What was new in the *Hopwood* decision was the ruling that race could *never* be used as a factor in admissions decisions, even to promote diversity.

In 1996, the Supreme Court refused to hear a challenge to the *Hopwood* case. This meant that its ruling remains in effect in the states covered by the Fifth Circuit—Texas, Louisiana, and Mississippi—but does not apply to the rest of the country. The impact of the *Hopwood* ruling is greatest in Texas because Louisiana and Mississippi are under conflicting court orders to desegregate their universities. In Texas in the year after the *Hopwood* case, minority applications to state universities declined. Concerned about the ability of Texas public universities to serve the state's minority students, the Texas legislature quickly passed a new law granting students who graduate in the top 10 percent of their class automatic admission to the state's public universities. State officials hoped that this measure would ensure a racially diverse student body.[108]

---

[105] *Adarand Constructors v. Pena,* 515 U.S. 200 (1995).

[106] Ann Devroy, "Clinton Study Backs Affirmative Action," *Washington Post,* July 19, 1995, p. A1.

[107] *Hopwood v. State of Texas,* 78 F. 3d 932 (Fifth Cir., 1996).

[108] See Lydia Lum, "Applications by Minorities Down Sharply," *Houston Chronicle,* April 8, 1997, p. A1; R. G. Ratcliffe, "Senate Approves Bill Designed to Boost Minority Enrollments," *Houston Chronicle,* May 8, 1997, p. A1.

The weakening of affirmative action in the courts was underscored in a case the Supreme Court agreed to hear in 1998. A white schoolteacher in New Jersey who had lost her job had sued her school district, charging that her layoff was racially motivated: A black colleague hired on the same day was not laid off. Under former president George H. W. Bush, the Justice Department had filed a brief on her behalf in 1989, but in 1994 the Clinton administration formally reversed course in a new brief supporting the school district's right to make distinctions based on race as long as they did not involve the use of quotas. Three years later, the administration, worried that the case was weak and could result in a broad decision against affirmative action, reversed course again and filed a brief with the Court urging a narrow ruling in favor of the dismissed worker. Because the school board had justified its actions on the grounds of preserving diversity, the administration feared that a broad ruling by the Supreme Court could totally prohibit the use of race in employment decisions, even as one factor among many designed to achieve diversity. But before the Court could issue a ruling, a coalition of civil rights groups brokered and arranged to pay for a settlement. This unusual move reflected the widespread fear of a sweeping negative decision. Cases involving dismissals, as the New Jersey case did, are generally viewed as much more difficult to defend than cases that concern hiring. In addition, the particular facts of the New Jersey case—two equally qualified teachers hired on the same day—were seen as unusual and unfavorable to affirmative action.[109]

This betwixt and between status of affirmative action was where things stood in 2003, when the Supreme Court took two cases against the University of Michigan that were virtually certain to clarify, if not put closure on, affirmative action. The first suit, *Gratz v. Bollinger,* alleged that by using a point-based ranking system that automatically awarded 20 points (out of 150) to African American, Latino, and Native American applicants, the university's undergraduate admissions policy discriminated unconstitutionally against white students with otherwise equal or superior academic qualifications. The Supreme Court agreed, 6–3, arguing that something tantamount to a quota was involved because undergraduate admissions lacked the necessary "individualized consideration," employing instead a "mechanical one," based too much on the favorable minority points.[110] The Court's ruling in *Gratz v. Bollinger* was not surprising, given *Bakke*'s holding against quotas and recent decisions calling for strict scrutiny of all racial classifications, even those that are intended to remedy past discrimination or promote future equality.

The second case, *Grutter v. Bollinger,* broke new ground. Barbara Grutter sued the University of Michigan Law School on the grounds that it had discriminated in a race-conscious way against white applicants with grades and law boards equal or superior to those of minority applicants. A precarious vote of 5–4 aligned the majority of the Supreme Court with Justice Lewis Powell's opinion in *Bakke* for the first time. In *Bakke,* Powell had argued that diversity in education is a compelling

---

[109] Linda Greenhouse, "Settlement Ends High Court Case on Preferences," *New York Times,* November 22, 1997, p. A1; Barry Bearak, "Rights Groups Ducked a Fight, Opponents Say," *New York Times,* November 22, 1997, p. A1.

[110] *Gratz v. Bollinger,* 539 U.S. 244 (2003).

state interest and that constitutionally race could be considered a positive factor in admissions decisions. In *Grutter*, the Court reiterated Powell's holding and, applying strict scrutiny to the law school's policy, found that its admissions process was narrowly tailored to the school's compelling state interest in diversity because it gave a "highly individualized, holistic review of each applicant's file," in which race counted but was not used in a "mechanical way."[111]

Throughout the 1990s, federal courts, including the Supreme Court, had subjected public affirmative action programs to strict scrutiny to invalidate them. *Adarand Constructors v. Pena* (1995) definitively established the Supreme Court's view that constitutionally permissible use of race must serve a compelling state interest. Between *Korematsu v. United States* (1944)[112] and *Grutter,* no consideration of race had survived strict scrutiny. Such affirmative action plans that had survived constitutional review did so before 1995, under a lower standard of review, one reserved for policies intended to remedy racial injustice. For affirmative action to survive under the post-1995 judicial paradigm, the Court needed to find that sometimes racial categories can be deployed to serve a compelling state interest. That the Court found exactly this in *Grutter* puts affirmative action on stronger ground— at least if its specific procedures pass the Supreme Court's muster and until the Court's majority changes.

Referendums on Affirmative Action.   The courts have not been the only center of action: Challenges to affirmative action have also emerged in state and local politics, in the form of ballot initiatives or referendums that ask voters to decide the issue. One of the most significant state actions was the passage of the California Civil Rights Initiative, also known as Proposition 209, in 1996. Proposition 209 outlawed affirmative action programs in the state and local governments of California, thus prohibiting state and local governments from using race or gender preferences in their decisions about hiring, contracting, and university admissions. The political battle over Proposition 209 was heated, and supporters and defenders took to the streets and airwaves to make their case. When the referendum was held, the measure passed with 54 percent of the vote, including 27 percent of the black vote, 30 percent of the Latino vote, and 45 percent of the Asian American vote.[113] In 1997, the Supreme Court refused to hear a challenge to the new law.

Many observers predicted that the success of California's ban on affirmative action would provoke similar movements in states and localities across the country. But the political factors that contributed to the success of Proposition 209 in California may not exist in many other states. Winning a controversial state referendum takes leadership and lots of money. The popular California Republican governor Pete Wilson led with a strong anti–affirmative action stand (favoring Proposition 209), and his campaign had a lot of money for advertising. But similar conditions did not exist elsewhere. Few prominent Republican leaders in other

---

[111] *Grutter v. Bollinger,* 539 U.S. 306 (2003).

[112] *Korematsu v. United States,* 323 U.S. 214 (1944).

[113] Michael A. Fletcher, "Opponents of Affirmative Action Heartened by Court Decision," *Washington Post,* April 13, 1997, p. A21.

states were willing to come forward to lead the anti–affirmative action campaign. Moreover, the outcome of any referendum, especially a complicated and controversial one, depends greatly on how the issue is drafted and placed on the ballot. California's Proposition 209 was framed as a civil rights initiative: "The state shall not discriminate against, or grant preferential treatment to, any individual or group on the basis of race, sex, color, ethnicity, or national origin." Different wording can produce quite different outcomes, as a 1997 vote on affirmative action in Houston revealed. There the ballot initiative asked voters whether they wanted to ban affirmative action in city contracting and hiring, not whether they wanted to end preferential treatment. In that city, 55 percent of voters decided in favor of affirmative action.[114]

CHAPTER REVIEW

Civil liberties and *civil rights* are two quite different phenomena and have to be treated legally and constitutionally in two quite different ways. We have defined civil liberties as that sphere of individual freedom of choice created by restraints on governmental power. The Bill of Rights explicitly placed an entire series of restraints on government. Some of these restraints were *substantive*, regarding *what* government could do; other restraints were *procedural*, regarding *how* the government was permitted to act. We call the rights listed in the Bill of Rights civil liberties because they are the rights of citizens to be free from arbitrary government interference.

But *which* government? This was settled in the *Barron v. Baltimore* case in 1833 when the Supreme Court held that the restraints in the Bill of Rights were applicable only to the national government and not to the states. The Court was recognizing "dual citizenship." At the time of its adoption in 1868, the Fourteenth Amendment was considered by many observers as a deliberate effort to reverse *Barron*, to put an end to the standard of dual citizenship, and to nationalize the Bill of Rights, applying its restrictions to state governments as well as to the national government. But the post–Civil War Supreme Court interpreted the Fourteenth Amendment otherwise. Dual citizenship remained almost as it had been before the Civil War, and the shadow of *Barron* extended across the rest of the nineteenth century and well into the twentieth century.

The slow process of nationalizing the Bill of Rights began in the 1920s, when the Court recognized that at least the restraints of the First Amendment had been "incorporated" into the Fourteenth Amendment as restraints on the state governments. But it was not until the 1960s that most of the civil liberties in the Bill of Rights were also incorporated into the Fourteenth Amendment.

The second aspect of protection of the individual, *civil rights*, stresses the expansion of governmental power rather than restraints on it. If the constitutional base of

---

[114] See Sam Howe Verhovek, "Houston Vote Underlined Complexity of Rights Issue," *New York Times*, November 6, 1997, p. A1.

civil liberties is the due process clause of the Fourteenth Amendment, the constitutional base of civil rights is the equal protection clause. This clause imposes a positive obligation on government to advance civil rights, and its original motivation seems to have been to eliminate the gross injustices suffered by "the newly emancipated Negroes . . . as a class." But as with civil liberties, there was little advancement in the interpretation or application of the equal protection clause until after World War II. The major breakthrough came in 1954 with the case of *Brown v. Board of Education*, and advancements came in fits and starts during the succeeding ten years.

After 1964, Congress finally supported the federal courts with effective civil rights legislation. From that point, civil rights developed in two ways. First, the definition of civil rights was expanded to include victims of discrimination other than blacks. Second, the definition of civil rights became increasingly positive through affirmative action policies. Judicial decisions, congressional statutes, and administrative agency actions all have moved beyond the original goal of eliminating discrimination toward creating opportunities for minorities and, in some areas, compensating present individuals for the consequences of discriminatory actions against members of their group in the past. This kind of compensation has sometimes relied on quotas. The use of quotas, in turn, has given rise to intense debate over the constitutionality as well as the desirability of affirmative action.

The story has not ended and is not likely to end. The politics of rights will remain an important part of American political discourse.

FOR FURTHER READING

Ackerman, Bruce. *Before the Next Attack: Preserving Civil Liberties in an Age of Terrorism*. New Haven, Conn.: Yale University Press, 2006.

Baer, Judith, and Leslie Goldstein. *The Constitutional and Legal Rights of Women*. Los Angeles: Roxbury, 2006.

Dawson, Michael. *Behind the Mule: Race and Class in African-American Politics*. Princeton, N.J.: Princeton University Press, 1995.

Dworkin, Ronald. *Justice in Robes*. Cambridge, Mass.: Belknap Press, 2006.

Garrow, David J. *Bearing the Cross: Martin Luther King, Jr., and the Southern Christian Leadership Conference: A Personal Portrait*. New York: Morrow, 1986.

Gerstmann, Evan. *Same-Sex Marriage and the Constitution*. New York: Cambridge University Press, 2004.

Glendon, Mary Ann. *Rights Talk: The Impoverishment of Political Discourse*. New York: Free Press, 1991.

Greenberg, Jack. *Crusaders in the Courts: How a Dedicated Band of Lawyers Fought for the Civil Rights Revolution*. New York: Basic Books, 1994.

Jackson, Thomas. *From Civil Rights to Human Rights*. Philadelphia: University of Pennsylvania Press, 2006.

Klarman, Michael. *From Jim Crow to Civil Rights: The Supreme Court and the Struggle for Racial Equality*. New York: Oxford University Press, 2004.

reader selection

Levy, Leonard W. *Freedom of Speech and Press in Early America: Legacy of Suppression.* New York: Harper & Row, 1963.

Lewis, Anthony. *Gideon's Trumpet.* New York: Random House, 1964.

Meltsner, Michael. *The Making of a Civil Rights Lawyer.* Charlottesville: University of Virginia Press, 2006.

Posner, Richard. *Not a Suicide Pact: The Constitution in a Time of National Emergency.* New York: Oxford University Press, 2006.

Rosenberg, Gerald N. *The Hollow Hope: Can Courts Bring About Social Change?* Chicago: University of Chicago Press, 1991.

Thernstrom, Abigail M. *Whose Votes Count? Affirmative Action and Minority Voting Rights.* Cambridge, Mass.: Harvard University Press, 1987.

Tushnet, Mark, and Michael Olivas. *Colored Men and Hombres Aqui: Hernandez v. Texas and the Emergence of Mexican American Lawyering.* Houston, Tex.: Arte Publico Press, 2006.

Yoshino, Kenji. *Covering: The Hidden Assault on Our Civil Rights.* New York: Random House, 2007.

Additional study and review materials are available online at wwnorton.com/studyspace/

Congress: The First Branch

5

HOW DOES CONGRESS WORK?

The U.S. Congress is the "first branch" of government under Article I of our Constitution and is also among the world's most important representative bodies. Many of the world's representative bodies only represent—that is, their governmental functions consist mainly of affirming and legitimating the national leadership's decisions. The only national representative body that actually possesses powers of governance is the U.S. Congress. For example, although the U.S. Congress never accedes to the president's budget proposals without making major changes, both the British House of Commons and the Japanese Diet always accept the budget exactly as proposed by the government.

In this chapter, we will try to understand how the U.S. Congress is able to serve simultaneously as a representative assembly and a powerful agency of government. Congress has vast authority over the two most important powers given to any government: the power of force (control over the nation's military forces) and the power over money. Specifically, according to Article I, Section 8, Congress can "lay and collect Taxes," deal with indebtedness and bankruptcy, impose duties, borrow and coin money, and generally control the nation's purse strings. It also may "provide for the common Defence and general Welfare," regulate interstate commerce, undertake public works, acquire and control federal lands, promote science and "useful Arts" (pertaining mostly to patents and copyrights), and regulate the militia.

In the realm of foreign policy, Congress has the power to declare war, deal with piracy, regulate foreign commerce, and raise and regulate the armed forces and military installations. These powers over war and the military are supreme—even

- Congress is the most important representative institution in American government.
- Constituents hold their representatives to account through elections.
- Congress also makes the law. Before a bill can become law, it must pass through the legislative process, a complex set of procedures in Congress.
- The legislative process is driven by numerous political forces: political parties, committees, staffs, caucuses, rules of lawmaking, and the president.

the president, as commander in chief of the military, must obey the laws and orders of Congress *if* Congress chooses to assert its constitutional authority. (In the past century, Congress has usually surrendered this authority to the president.) Further, the Senate has the power to ratify treaties (by a two-thirds vote) and to approve the appointment of ambassadors. Capping these powers, Congress is charged to make laws "which shall be necessary and proper for carrying into Execution the foregoing Powers, and all other Powers vested by this Constitution in the Government of the United States, or in any Department or Officer thereof."

It is extraordinarily difficult for a large, representative assembly to formulate, enact, and implement the laws. The internal complexities of conducting business within Congress—the legislative process—are daunting. In addition, many individuals and institutions have the capacity to influence the legislative process. To exercise its power to make the law, Congress must first bring about something close to an organizational miracle. In this chapter, after a brief consideration of representation, we will examine the organization of Congress and the legislative process. Throughout, we point out the connections between these two aspects—the ways in which representation affects congressional operations (especially through the "electoral connection") and the ways in which congressional institutions enhance or diminish representation (especially Congress's division- and specialization-of-labor committee system).

REPRESENTATION

constituency
Members of the district from which an official is elected.

Congress is the most important representative institution in American government. Each member's primary responsibility is to the district, to his or her **constituency**, not to the congressional leadership, a party, or even Congress itself. Yet the task of representation is not a simple one. Views about what constitutes fair and effective representation differ, and constituents can make very different kinds of demands on their representatives. Members of Congress must consider these diverse views and demands as they represent their districts (Figure 5.1).

FIGURE 5.1 HOW MEMBERS OF CONGRESS REPRESENT THEIR DISTRICTS

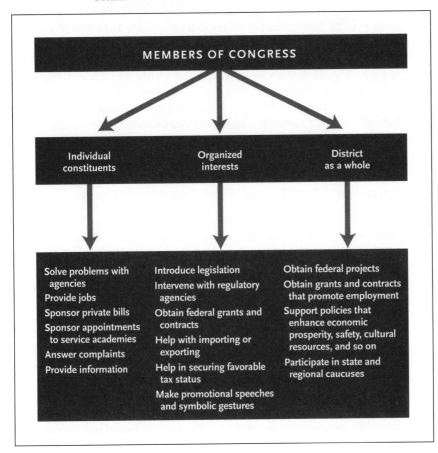

MEMBERS OF CONGRESS

Individual constituents	Organized interests	District as a whole
Solve problems with agencies	Introduce legislation	Obtain federal projects
Provide jobs	Intervene with regulatory agencies	Obtain grants and contracts that promote employment
Sponsor private bills	Obtain federal grants and contracts	Support policies that enhance economic prosperity, safety, cultural resources, and so on
Sponsor appointments to service academies	Help with importing or exporting	Participate in state and regional caucuses
Answer complaints	Help in securing favorable tax status	
Provide information	Make promotional speeches and symbolic gestures	

Some legislators see themselves as perfect agents of others: They have been elected to do the bidding of those who sent them to the legislature, and they act as **delegates**. Others see themselves as having been selected by their fellow citizens to do what they think is "right," and they act as **trustees**. Most legislators are a mix of these two types. And all, one way or another, need to survive the next election in order to pursue whatever role they formulate for themselves.

As we discussed in Chapter 1, **agency representation** takes place when constituents have the power to hire and fire their representatives. Frequent competitive elections constitute an important means by which constituents hold their representatives to account and keep them responsive to constituency views and preferences. The idea of a representative as agent is similar to the relationship of lawyer and client. True, the relationship between the member of Congress and as many as 630,000 "clients" in the district or that between the senator and millions of clients in the state is very different from that of lawyer and client. But the criteria of performance are comparable.

delegate A representative who votes according to the preferences of his or her constituency.

trustee A representative who votes based on what he or she thinks is best for his or her constituency.

agency representation The type of representation by which representatives are held accountable to their constituents if they fail to represent them properly.

One expects at the very least that each representative will constantly be seeking to discover the interests of the constituency and will be speaking for those interests in Congress and other centers of government.[1] We expect this because we believe that members of Congress, like politicians everywhere, are ambitious. For many, this ambition is satisfied simply by maintaining a hold on their present office and advancing up the rungs of power in that legislative body. Some may be looking ahead to the next level—to higher legislative office, as when a representative seeks a Senate seat, or to an executive office, as when a legislator returns home to run for the state's governorship, or at the highest level, when a legislator seeks the presidency.[2] In each of these cases the legislator is eager to serve the interests of constituents, either to enhance his or her prospects of contract renewal at the next election or to improve the chances of moving to another level.[3]

House and Senate: Differences in Representation

bicameralism
Division of a legislative body into two houses, chambers, or branches.

The framers of the Constitution provided for **bicameralism**—that is, a legislative body consisting of two chambers. As we saw in Chapter 2, the framers intended each of these chambers, the House and Senate, to serve a different constituency. Members of the Senate, appointed by state legislatures for six-year terms, were to represent the elite members of society and to be more attuned to the interests of property than to those of population. Today, members of the House and Senate are elected directly by the people. The 435 members of the House are elected from districts apportioned according to population: the 100 members of the Senate are elected by state, with two senators from each. Senators continue to have much longer terms in office and usually represent much larger and more diverse constituencies than do their counterparts in the House (see the "In Brief" box on the following page).

The House and Senate play different roles in the legislative process. In essence, the Senate is the more deliberative of the two bodies—the forum in which any and all ideas can receive a thorough public airing. The House is the more centralized and organized of the two bodies—better equipped to play a role in the routine governmental process. In part, this difference stems from the different rules governing the two bodies. These rules give House leaders more control over the legislative process and provide for House members to specialize in certain legislative areas.

---

[1] The classic description of interactions between politicians and "the folks back home" is given by Richard F. Fenno, Jr., in *Home Style: House Members in Their Districts* (Boston: Little, Brown, 1978). Essays elaborating on Fenno's classic are found in Morris P. Fiorina and David W. Rhode, eds., *Home Style and Washington Work* (Ann Arbor: University of Michigan Press, 1989).

[2] For more on political careers generally, see John R. Hibbing, "Lesiglative Careers: Why and How We Should Study Them," *Legislative Studies Quarterly* 24 (1999): 149–71. See also Cherie D. Maestas, Sarah Fulton, L. Sandy Maisel, and Walter J. Stone, "When to Risk It? Institutions, Ambitions, and the Decision to Run for the U.S. House," *American Political Science Review* 100, no. 2 (May 2006): 195–208.

[3] Constituents are not a legislative agent's only principals. He or she may also be beholden to party leaders and special interests, as well as to members and committees in the chamber. See Forrest Maltzman, *Competing Principals* (Ann Arbor: University of Michigan Press, 1997).

Major Differences between the House and the Senate

	House	Senate
Minimum age of member	25 years	30 years
U.S. citizenship	At least 7 years	At least 9 years
Length of term	2 years	6 years
Number per state	Depends on population: 1 per 30,000 in 1789; now 1 per 630,000	2 per state
Constituency	Tends to be local	Both local and national

The rules of the much-smaller, more free-wheeling Senate give its leadership relatively little power and discourage specialization.

Both formal and informal factors contribute to differences between the two chambers of Congress. Differences in the length of terms and requirements for holding office specified by the Constitution in turn generate differences in how members of each body develop their constituencies and exercise their powers of office. The result is that members of the House most effectively and frequently are the agents of well-organized local interests with specific legislative agendas—used-car dealers seeking relief from regulation, labor unions seeking more favorable legislation, or farmers looking for higher subsidies. The small size and relative homogeneity of their constituencies and the frequency with which they must seek reelection make House members more attuned to the legislative needs of local interest groups. This, too, was the intent of the Constitution's drafters—namely, that the House of Representatives would be the "people's house" and that its members would reflect and represent public opinion in a timely manner.

Senators, on the other hand, serve larger and more heterogeneous constituencies. As a result, they are somewhat better able than members of the House to be the agents for groups and interests organized on a statewide or national basis. Moreover, with longer terms in office, senators have the luxury of considering new ideas or seeking to bring together new coalitions of interests, rather than simply serving existing ones. This is what the framers intended when they drafted the Constitution.

In recent years, the House has exhibited considerably more intense partisanship and ideological division than the Senate. Because of their diverse constituencies, senators are more inclined to seek compromises that will offend as few voters and interest groups as possible. Members of the House, in contrast, typically represent more homogeneous districts in which their own party is dominant. This situation has tended to make House members less inclined to seek compromises and more willing than their Senate counterparts to stick to partisan and ideological guns during the policy debates of the past several decades. For example, in 2006 and 2007 the House was considerably more partisan than the Senate in a number of votes on President Bush's policies in Iraq.

The Electoral System

In light of their role as agents for various constituencies in their states and districts, and the importance of elections as a mechanism by which principals (constituents) reward and punish their agents, representatives are very much influenced by electoral considerations. Three factors related to the U.S. electoral system affect who gets elected and what he or she does once in office. The first set of issues concerns who decides to run for office and which candidates have an edge over others. The second issue is that of the incumbency advantage. Finally, the way congressional district lines are drawn can greatly affect the outcome of an election. Let us examine more closely the impact these considerations have on who serves in Congress.

Running for Office.   Voters' choices are restricted from the start by who decides to run for office. In the past, decisions about who would run for a particular elected office were made by local party officials. A person who had a record of service to the party, or who was owed a favor, or whose "turn" had come up might be nominated by party leaders for an office.[4] Today few party organizations have the power to slate candidates in that way. Instead, the decision to run for Congress is a more personal choice. One of the most important factors determining who runs for office is a candidate's individual ambition.[5] A potential candidate may also assess whether he or she can attract enough money to mount a credible campaign. The ability to raise money depends on connections to other politicians, interest groups, and the national party organization.

Features distinctive to each congressional district also affect the field of candidates. For any candidate, decisions about running must be made early because once money has been committed to already declared candidates, it is harder for new candidates to break into a race. Thus the outcome of a November election is partially determined many months earlier, when decisions to run are finalized.[6]

---

[4] In the nineteenth century, it was often an *obligation*, not an honor, to serve in Congress. The real political action was back home in the state capital or a big city, not in Washington. So the practice of "rotation" was devised, whereby a promising local politician would do a tour of duty in Washington before being slated for an important local office. This is not to say that electoral incentives—the so-called electoral connection in which a legislator's behavior was motivated by the desire to retain the seat for himself or his party—was absent in nineteenth-century America. See, for example, Jamie L. Carson and Erik J. Engstrom, "Assessing the Electoral Connection Evidence from the Early United States," *American Journal of Political Science* 49 (2005): 746–57. See also William T. Bianco, David B. Spence, and John D. Wilkerson, "The Electoral Connection in the Early Congress: The Case of the Compensation Act of 1816," *American Journal of Political Science* 40 (1996): 145–71.

[5] See Linda L. Fowler and Robert D. McClure, *Political Ambition: Who Decides to Run for Congress* (New Haven, Conn.: Yale University Press, 1989); and Alan Ehrenhalt, *The United States of Ambition: Politicians, Power, and the Pursuit of Office* (New York: Times Books, 1991).

[6] On the thesis of "strategic candidacy," see Gary C. Jacobson, *The Politics of Congressional Elections*, 6th ed. (New York: Pearson Longman, 2004).

Incumbency. **Incumbency** plays a very important role in the American electoral system and in the kind of representation citizens get in Washington. Once in office, members of Congress are typically eager to remain in office and make politics a career. The career ambitions of members of Congress are helped by an array of tools that they can use to stack the deck in favor of their reelection. Through effective use of these tools, an incumbent establishes a reputation for competence, imagination, and responsiveness—the attributes most principals look for in an agent. One tool of incumbency is the franking privilege. Under a law enacted by the first U.S. Congress in 1789, members of Congress may send mail to their constituents free of charge to keep them informed of government business and public affairs. The franking privilege provides incumbents with a valuable resource for publicizing their activities and making themselves visible to voters.

A particularly important tool is the incumbent's reputation for constituency service: taking care of the problems and requests of individual voters. Through such services and their advertisement by word of mouth, the incumbent seeks to establish an attractive political reputation and a "personal" relationship with his or her constituents. Well over a quarter of the representatives' time and nearly two-thirds of the time of their staff members is devoted to constituency service (termed **casework**). This service includes talking to constituents, providing them with minor services, presenting special bills for them, and attempting to influence decisions by regulatory commissions on their behalf.

One very direct way in which incumbent members of Congress serve as the agents of their constituencies is through the venerable institution of **patronage**. Patronage refers to a variety of forms of direct services and benefits that members provide for their districts. One of the most important forms of patronage is **pork-barrel legislation**. Through pork-barrel legislation, representatives seek to capture federal projects and federal funds for their own districts (or states in the case of senators) and thus "bring home the bacon" for their constituents. A common form of pork barreling is the "earmark," the practice by which members of Congress insert into otherwise pork-free bills language that provides special benefits for their own constituents.[7]

The incumbency advantage is evident in the high rates of reelection for congressional incumbents: over 95 percent for House members and nearly 90 percent for members of the Senate in recent years.[8] The advantage is also evident in what is called sophomore surge—the tendency for candidates to win a higher percentage

incumbency Holding a political office for which one is running.

casework An effort by members of Congress to gain the trust and support of constituents by providing them with personal service. One important type of casework consists of helping constituents obtain favorable treatment from the federal bureaucracy.

patronage The resources available to higher officials, usually opportunities to make partisan appointments to offices and to confer grants, licenses, or special favors to supporters.

pork-barrel legislation Appropriations made by legislative bodies for local projects that are often not needed but that are created so that local representatives can win reelection in their home district.

---

[7] For an excellent study of academic earmarking, see James D. Savage, *Funding Science in America: Congress, Universities, and the Politics of the Academic Pork Barrel* (New York: Cambridge University Press, 1999). For a general study of pork-barrel activity, see Diana Evans, *Greasing the Wheels: Using Pork-Barrel Projects to Build Majority Coalitions in Congress* (New York: Cambridge University Press, 2004).

[8] Norman J. Ornstein, Thomas E. Mann, and Michael J. Malbin, *Vital Statistics on Congress, 1995–1996* (Washington, D.C.: Congressional Quarterly Press, 1996), pp. 60–61 (see also subsequent editions); Robert S. Erickson and Gerald C. Wright, "Voters, Candidates, and Issues in Congressional Elections," in *Congress Reconsidered*, 5th ed., Lawrence C. Dodd and Bruce I. Oppenheimer, eds. (Washington, D.C.: Congressional Quarterly Press, 1993), p. 99; John R. Alford and David W. Brady, "Personal and Partisan Advantage in U.S. Congressional Elections, 1846–1990," in *Congress Reconsidered*, pp. 141–57.

FIGURE 5.2 THE POWER OF INCUMBENCY

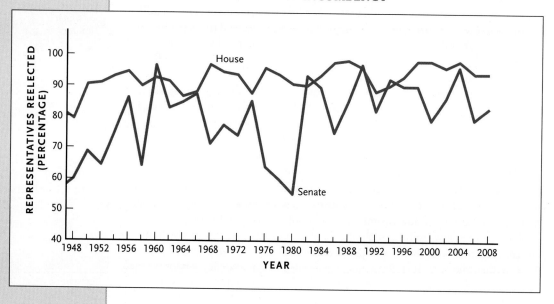

SOURCE: Center for Resposive Politics, www.opensecrets.org/big picture/reelect, and authors' update.

of the vote when seeking their second term in office than in their initial election victory. Once in office, members of Congress find it much easier to raise campaign funds and are thus able to outspend their challengers (Figure 5.2).[9] Over the past quarter century, and despite many campaign-finance regulations to level the playing field, the gap between incumbent and challenger spending has grown (House) or held steady (Senate). Members of the majority party in the House and Senate are particularly attractive to donors who want access to those in power.[10] Incumbency can help a candidate by scaring off potential challengers. In many races, potential candidates may decide not to run because they fear that the incumbent simply has brought too many benefits to the district, has too much money, or is too well liked or too well known.[11]

The role of incumbency also has implications for the social composition of Congress. For example, the incumbency advantage makes it harder for women to increase their numbers in Congress because most incumbents are men. Women who run for open seats (for which there are no incumbents) are just as likely to win

[9] Stephen Ansolabehere and James Snyder, "Campaign War Chests and Congressional Elections," *Business and Politics* 2 (2000): 9–34.

[10] Gary W. Cox and Eric Magar, "How Much Is Majority Status in the U.S. Congress Worth?" *American Political Science Review* 93, no. 2 (June 1999): 299–309.

[11] Kenneth Bickers and Robert Stein, "The Electoral Dynamics of the Federal Pork Barrel," *American Journal of Political Science* 40 (1996): 1300–26.

FIGURE 5.3 APPORTIONMENT OF HOUSE SEATS BY REGION, 1910 AND 2000

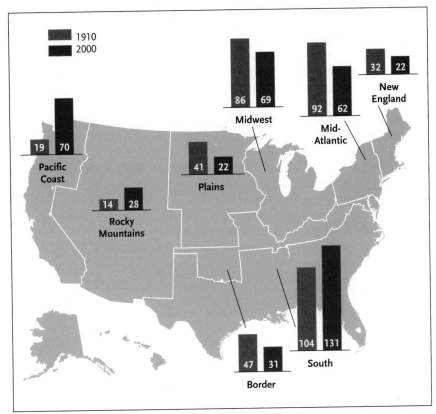

SOURCE: Norman J. Ornstein, Thomas E. Mann, and Michael J. Malbin, eds., *Vital Statistics on Congress, 2001–2002* (Washington, D.C.: American Enterprise Institute, 2002), p. 59.

as male candidates.[12] Supporters of term limits argue that such limits are the best way to get new faces into Congress. They believe that the incumbency advantage and the tendency of many legislators to view politics as a career mean that very little turnover will occur in Congress unless limits are imposed on the number of terms a legislator can serve.

Congressional Districts. The final factor that affects who wins a seat in Congress is the way congressional districts are drawn. Every ten years, state legislatures must redraw congressional districts to reflect population changes. In 1929, Congress enacted a law fixing the total number of congressional seats at 435. As a result, when states with growing populations gain districts, they do so at the expense

---

[12] See Barbara C. Burrell, *A Woman's Place Is in the House: Campaigning for Congress in the Feminist Era* (Ann Arbor: University of Michigan Press, 1994), chap. 6; and David Broder, "Key to Women's Political Parity: Running," *Washington Post*, September 8, 1994, p. A17.

of states with slower population growth. In recent decades, this has meant that the nation's growth areas in the South and West have gained congressional seats at the expense of the Northeast and the Midwest (Figure 5.3). After the 2000 Census, for example, Arizona, Texas, Florida, and Georgia each gained two seats, whereas New York and Pennsylvania each lost two seats. Redrawing congressional districts is a highly political process: Districts are shaped to create an advantage for the majority party in the state legislature, which controls the redistricting process. As we will see in Chapter 10, **gerrymandering** can have a major effect on the outcome of congressional elections.

Since the passage of the 1982 amendments to the 1965 Voting Rights Act, race has become a major—and controversial—consideration in drawing voting districts. These amendments, which encouraged the creation of districts in which members of racial minorities have decisive majorities, have greatly increased the number of minority representatives in Congress. After the 1991–92 redistricting, the number of predominantly minority districts doubled, rising from twenty-six to fifty-two. Among the most fervent supporters of the new minority districts were white Republicans, who used the opportunity to create more districts dominated by white Republican voters.[13] These developments raise thorny questions about representation. Some analysts argue that the system may grant minorities greater sociological representation, but it has made it more difficult for them to win substantive policy goals.[14]

gerrymandering
Apportionment of voters in districts in such a way as to give an unfair advantage to one political party.

THE ORGANIZATION OF CONGRESS

We will now examine the organization of Congress and the legislative process, particularly the basic building blocks of congressional organization: political parties, the committee system, congressional staff, the caucuses, and the parliamentary rules of the House and Senate. Each of these factors plays a key role in the organization of Congress and in the process through which Congress formulates and enacts laws. We will also look at powers Congress has in addition to lawmaking and explore the future role of Congress in relation to the powers of the executive.

Party Leadership and Organization in the House and the Senate

One significant aspect of legislative life is not even part of the *official* organization: political parties. The legislative parties—primarily Democratic and Republican in

---

[13] David Lublin, *The Paradox of Representation: Racial Gerrymandering and Minority Interests in Congress* (Princeton, N.J.: Princeton University Press, 1997).

[14] Lani Guinier, *The Tyranny of the Majority: Fundamental Fairness in Representative Democracy* (New York: Free Press, 1995). See also David Epstein and Sharyn O'Halloran, "Measuring the Electoral and Policy Impact of Majority-Minority Voting Districts," *American Journal of Political Science* 42 (1999): 36–95.

modern times, but also numerous others over the course of American history—foster cooperation, coalitions, and compromise. They are the vehicles of collective action, both for legislators sharing common policy objectives inside the legislature and for those very same legislators as candidates in periodic election contests back home.[15] In short, political parties in Congress are the fundamental building blocks from which policy coalitions are fashioned to pass legislation and monitor its implementation, thereby providing a track record on which members build electoral support.

Every two years, at the beginning of a new Congress, the members of each party gather to elect their House leaders. This gathering is traditionally called the **party caucus**, or, in the case of Republicans, the **party conference**.

The elected leader of the majority party is later proposed to the whole House and is automatically elected to the position of **Speaker of the House**, with voting along straight party lines. The House majority caucus (or conference) then also elects a **majority leader**. The minority party goes through the same process and selects the **minority leader**. Both parties also elect whips to line up party members on important votes and relay voting information to the leaders.

At one time, party leaders strictly controlled committee assignments, using them to enforce party discipline. Today, representatives expect to receive the assignments they want and resent leadership efforts to control assignments. The leadership's best opportunities to use committee assignments as rewards and punishments come when more than one member seeks a seat on a committee.

Generally, representatives seek assignments that will allow them to influence decisions of special importance to their districts. Representatives from farm districts, for example, may request seats on the Agriculture Committee.[16] Seats on powerful committees such as Ways and Means, which is responsible for tax legislation, and Appropriations are especially popular.

Within the Senate, the president pro tempore exercises mainly ceremonial leadership. Usually, the majority party designates a member with the greatest seniority to serve in this capacity. Real power is in the hands of the majority leader and minority leader, each elected by party caucus or conference. The majority and minority leaders, together, control the Senate's calendar or agenda for legislation. In addition, the senators from each party elect a whip. (The whip system is discussed in the Party Discipline section of this chapter.)

In recent years, party leaders have sought to augment their formal powers by reaching outside Congress for resources that might enhance their influence within Congress. One aspect of this external strategy is the increased use of national communications media, including televised speeches and talk show appearances by

party caucus, or party conference A normally closed meeting of a political or legislative group to select candidates, plan strategy, or make decisions regarding legislative matters.

Speaker of the House The chief presiding officer of the House of Representatives. The speaker is elected at the beginning of every Congress on a straight party vote. The Speaker is the most important party and House leader, and can influence the legislative agenda, the fate of individual pieces of legislation, and members' positions within the House.

majority leader The elected leader of the party holding a majority of the seats in the House of Representatives or in the Senate. In the House, the majority leader is subordinate in the party hierarchy to the Speaker.

minority leader The elected leader of the party holding less than a majority of the seats in the House or Senate.

---

[15] For a historically grounded analysis of the development of political parties as well as a treatment of their general contemporary significance, see John H. Aldrich, *Why Parties? The Origin and Transformation of Political Parties in America* (Chicago: University of Chicago Press, 1995). For an analysis of the parties in the legislative process, see Gary W. Cox and Mathew D. McCubbins, *Legislative Leviathan: Party Government in the House* (Berkeley: University of California Press, 1993). A provocative essay questioning the role of parties is Keith Krehbiel, "Where's the Party?" *British Journal of Political Science* 23 (1993): 235–66.

[16] Richard Fenno, Jr., *Home Style: House Members in Their Districts* (Boston: Little, Brown, 1978).

party leaders. The former Republican House Speaker Newt Gingrich, for example, used television extensively to generate support for his programs among Republican loyalists.[17] As long as it lasted, Gingrich's support among the Republican rank and file gave him an added measure of influence over Republican members of Congress.

A second external strategy involves fundraising. In recent years, congressional leaders have frequently established their own political action committees. Interest groups are usually eager to contribute to these "leadership PACs" to curry favor with powerful members of Congress. The leaders, in turn, use these funds to support the various campaigns of their party's candidates in order to create a sense of obligation.

In addition to the tasks of organizing Congress, congressional party leaders may also seek to set the legislative agenda. Since the New Deal, presidents have taken the lead in creating legislative agendas. (This trend will be discussed in the next chapter.) But in recent years, congressional leaders, especially when facing a White House controlled by the opposing party, have attempted to devise their own agendas. The "Analyzing the Evidence" unit for this chapter takes a closer look at parties and agenda setting in Congress.

The Committee System

The committee system provides Congress with its second organizational structure, but it is more a division and specialization of labor than the hierarchy of power that determines leadership arrangements.

Six fundamental characteristics define the congressional committee system:

1. *The official rules give each* **standing committee** *a permanent status*, with a fixed membership, officers, rules, staff, offices, and, above all, a jurisdiction that is recognized by all other committees and usually the leadership as well (see Table 5.1).

2. *The jurisdiction of each standing committee is defined according to the subject matter of basic legislation.* Except for the House Rules Committee, all the important committees are organized to receive proposals for legislation and to process them into official bills. The House Rules Committee decides the order in which bills come up for a vote and determines the specific rules that govern the length of debate and the opportunity for amendments. Rules can be used to help or hinder particular proposals.

3. *Standing committees' jurisdictions usually parallel those of the major departments or agencies in the executive branch.* There are important exceptions—Appropriations (House and Senate) and Rules (House), for example—but by and large, the division of labor is self-consciously designed to parallel executive-branch organization.

standing committee A permanent committee with the power to propose and write legislation that covers a particular subject, such as finance or appropriations.

---

[17] Douglas Harris, *The Public Speaker* (Ph.D. diss., Johns Hopkins University, 1998).

TABLE 5.1 STANDING COMMITTEES OF CONGRESS, 2009

House Committees

Agriculture	Natural Resources
Appropriations	Oversight and Government Reform
Armed Services	Rules
Budget	Science and Technology
Education and Labor	Small Business
Energy and Commerce	Standards of Official Conduct (Ethics)
Financial Services	Transportation and Infrastructure
Foreign Affairs Homeland Security	Veterans' Affairs
House Administration	Ways and Means
Judiciary	

Senate Committees

Agriculture, Nutrition, and Forestry	Foreign Relations
Appropriations	Health, Education, Labor, and Pensions
Armed Services	
Banking, Housing, and Urban Affairs	Homeland Security and Governmental Affairs
Budget	Judiciary
Commerce, Science, and Transportation	Rules and Administration
Energy and Natural Resources	Small Business and Entrepreneurship
Environment and Public Works	Veterans' Affairs
Finance	

4. *Bills are assigned to standing committees on the basis of subject matter,* but the Speaker of the House and the Senate's presiding officer have some discretion in the allocation of bills to committees. Most bills "die in committee"—that is, they are not reported out favorably. Ordinarily this ends a bill's life. There is only one way for a legislative proposal to escape committee processing: A bill passed in one chamber may be permitted to move directly to the calendar of the other chamber. Even here, however, the bill has received the full committee treatment before passage in the first chamber.

5. *Each standing committee is unique.* No effort is made to compose the membership of any committee to be representative of the total House or Senate membership.

Parties and Agenda Control in Congress

In assessing the influence of political parties on legislative politics, political scientists often ask how parties affect outcomes in Congress. One approach might be to look for evidence of arm twisting or promised favors by party leaders, both of which can be used to influence members' roll-call vote choices. Yet, increasingly, scholars have responded to this question by looking for evidence of agenda manipulation by the majority party. If the majority party can control *what* gets voted on—through its control of committees, including the Rules Committee, and the party leaders' scheduling power—then it can affect outcomes even when the party leaders cannot effectively twist arms or promise favors. Thus, a question that has taken center stage in congressional research is, Who controls the agenda in Congress?

REPUBLICAN AGENDA (Pre-Obama)	DEMOCRATIC AGENDA (Post-Obama)
Tax Cuts	Economic Recovery
War in Iraq and Afghanistan	Energy Independence
Education (No Child Left Behind)	Iraq Troop Withdrawal
National Security	Health Care Reform
Budget Management	College Access
Terrorism (Homeland Security)	Mortgage Reform
Social Security Reform	Banking Industry Reform
Faith Based and Community Initiatives	Equal Pay

Source: Republican National Committee, www.rnc.org; Office of the Speaker, U.S. House of Representatives, "A New Direction for America," www.speaker.gov/pdf/thebook.pdf (accessed 7/9/09).

Why is majority party status so important in Congress? Whichever party controls a greater number of seats in either the House or the Senate decides which issues will come to the floor for consideration. To illustrate this point, consider the recent instances when the Republicans controlled both chambers of Congress and the presidency (from 2003–2006) and when the Democrats achieved unified party control of these two branches of government (beginning in 2009). In addition to all the other perks that come with majority control, each party was able to push its specific agenda. As we see from the table above, there are clear differences between Republicans and Democrats in terms of the legislative policies they chose to pursue.

HOUSE ROLLS ON FINAL-PASSAGE VOTES, 99TH—110TH CONGRESSES

Congress	Majority Party	Total Final Passage Votes	Majority Party Rolls	Majority Party Roll Rate (%)	Minority Party Rolls	Minority Party Roll Rate (%)
99th	Democrats	89	1	1.1	35	39.3
100th	Democrats	116	2	1.7	40	34.5
101th	Democrats	108	1	0.93	39	36.1
102th	Democrats	142	0	0	39	27.5
103th	Democrats	160	1	0.63	56	35
104th	Republicans	136	1	0.74	63	46.3
105th	Republicans	133	3	2.3	51	38.4
106th	Republicans	136	4	2.9	51	37.5
107th	Republicans	93	1	1.1	31	33.3
108th	Republicans	119	1	0.84	46	38.7
109th	Republicans	146	2	1.37	64	43.8
110th	Democrats	161	4	2.48	102	63.4

Source: Gary W. Cox and Mathew D. McCubbins *Setting the Agenda: Responsible Party Government in the U.S. House of Representatives* New York: Cambridge University Press, 2005; calculated by author.

One specific way to think about agenda control in Congress is in terms of the winners and losers on particular pieces of legislation, because this may tell us how much influence the majority party actually has. The most prominent example of this approach has been to look at partisan roll rates. A party (or group of members) is "rolled" when a majority of its members winds up on the losing side of a vote that passes. In focusing specifically on final passage votes in the U.S. House, the political scientists Gary Cox and Mathew McCubbins have found that, at the aggregate level, the majority party is almost never rolled. In contrast, and as we see from the table above, the minority party is significantly more likely to be on the losing side of final-passage votes. This suggests that the majority party controls the agenda and prevents legislation that it opposes (and is likely to lose on) from coming to a vote.

Members with a special interest in the subject matter of a committee are expected to seek membership on it. In both the House and the Senate, each party has established a Committee on Committees, which determines the committee assignments of new members and of established members who wish to change committees. Ordinarily, members can keep their committee assignments as long as they like.

seniority Priority or status ranking given to an individual on the basis of length of continuous service in a committee in Congress.

6. *Each standing committee's hierarchy is based on seniority.* **Seniority** is determined by years of continuous service on a particular committee, not by years of service in the House or Senate. In general, each committee is chaired by the most senior member of the majority party. Although the power of committee chairs is limited, they play an important role in scheduling hearings, selecting subcommittee members, and appointing committee staff. Because Congress has a large number of subcommittees and has given each representative a larger staff, the power of the committee chairs has been diluted.

The Staff System: Staffers and Agencies

A congressional institution second in importance only to the committee system is the staff system. Every member of Congress employs a large number of staff members, whose tasks include handling constituency requests and, to a large and growing extent, dealing with legislative details and overseeing the activities of administrative agencies. Increasingly, staffers bear the primary responsibility for formulating and drafting proposals, organizing hearings, dealing with administrative agencies, and negotiating with lobbyists. Indeed, legislators typically deal with each other through staff rather than through direct, personal contact. Representatives and senators together employ nearly 11,000 staffers in their Washington and home offices.

In addition to the personal staffs of individual senators and representatives, Congress also employs roughly two thousand committee staffers. These individuals are the permanent staff, who stay regardless of turnover in Congress, attached to every House and Senate committee, and who are responsible for organizing and administering the committee's work, including research, scheduling, organizing hearings, and drafting legislation.

Not only does Congress employ personal and committee staffs, but it has also established three *staff agencies* designed to provide the legislative branch with resources and expertise independent of the executive branch. These agencies enhance Congress's capacity to oversee administrative agencies and to evaluate presidential programs and proposals. They are the Congressional Research Service, which performs research for legislators who wish to know the facts and competing arguments relevant to policy proposals or other legislative business; the General Accounting Office, through which Congress can investigate the financial and administrative affairs of any government agency or program; and the Congressional Budget Office, which assesses the economic implications and likely costs of proposed federal programs, such as health care reform proposals and the rescue packages for the failing financial system in 2008 and 2009.

Informal Organization: The Caucuses

In addition to the official organization of Congress, an unofficial organizational structure also exists—the caucuses, formally known as *legislative service organizations* (*LSOs*). Caucuses are groups of senators or representatives who share certain opinions, interests, or social characteristics. They include ideological caucuses such as the liberal Democratic Study Group and the conservative Democratic Forum. There are also a large number of caucuses composed of legislators representing particular economic or policy interests, such as the Travel and Tourism Caucus, the Steel Caucus, the Mushroom Caucus, and the Concerned Senators for the Arts. Legislators who share common backgrounds or social characteristics have organized caucuses such as the Congressional Black Caucus, the Congressional Caucus for Women's Issues, and the Hispanic Caucus. All these caucuses seek to advance the interests of the groups they represent by promoting legislation, encouraging Congress to hold hearings, and pressing administrative agencies for favorable treatment.

RULES OF LAWMAKING: HOW A BILL BECOMES A LAW

The institutional structure of Congress is one key factor that helps to shape the legislative process. A second and equally important factor is the rules of congressional procedures. These rules govern everything from the introduction of a bill through its submission to the president for signing. Not only do these regulations influence the fate of each and every bill, they also help to determine the distribution of power in Congress (see Figure 5.4).

Committee Deliberation

Even if a member of Congress, the White House, or a federal agency has spent months developing and drafting a piece of legislation, it does not become a bill until it is submitted officially by a senator or representative to the clerk of the House or Senate and referred to the appropriate committee for deliberation. No floor action on any bill can take place until the committee with jurisdiction over it has taken all the time it needs to deliberate. During the course of its deliberations, the committee typically refers the bill to one of its subcommittees, which may hold hearings, listen to expert testimony, and amend the proposed legislation before referring it to the full committee for its consideration. The full committee may accept the recommendation of the subcommittee or hold its own hearings and prepare its own amendments. Or, even more frequently, the committee and subcommittee may do little or nothing with a bill that has been submitted to them. Many bills are simply allowed to die in committee with little or no serious consideration ever given to them. In a typical congressional session, 85 to 90 percent of the roughly 8,000 bills introduced die in committee—an indication of the power of the congressional committee system.

FIGURE 5.4 HOW A BILL BECOMES A LAW

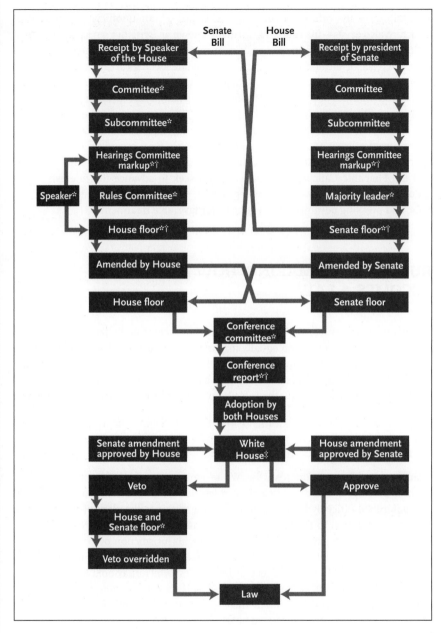

*Points at which the bill can be amended.

†Points at which the bill can die.

‡If the president neither signs nor vetoes the bill within ten days, it automatically becomes law.

Once a bill's assigned committee or committees in the House have reported it, the bill must pass one additional hurdle: the Rules Committee. This powerful committee determines the rules that will govern action on the bill on the House floor. In particular, the Rules Committee allots the time for debate and decides to what extent amendments to the bill can be proposed from the floor. A bill's supporters generally prefer what is called a **closed rule**, which severely limits floor debate and amendments. Opponents of a bill usually prefer an **open rule**, which permits potentially damaging floor debate and makes it easier to add amendments that may cripple the bill or weaken its chances for passage.

Debate

Party control of the agenda is reinforced by the rule giving the Speaker of the House and the majority leader of the Senate the power of recognition during debate on a bill. Usually the chair knows the purpose for which a member intends to speak well in advance of the occasion. Spontaneous efforts to gain recognition are often foiled. For example, the Speaker may ask, "For what purpose does the member rise?" before deciding whether to grant recognition.

In the House, virtually all of the time allotted by the Rules Committee for debate on a given bill is controlled by the bill's sponsor and by its leading opponent. In almost every case, these two people are the committee chair and the ranking minority member of the committee that processed the bill—or those they designate. These two participants are, by rule and tradition, granted the power to allocate most of the debate time in small amounts to members who are seeking to speak for or against the measure.

In the Senate, other than the power of recognition, the leadership has much less control over the floor debate. Indeed, the Senate is unique among the world's legislative bodies for its commitment to unlimited debate. Once given the floor, a senator may speak as long as he or she wishes. On a number of memorable occasions, senators have used this right to prevent action on legislation that they opposed. Through this tactic, called the **filibuster**, small minorities or even one individual in the Senate can force the majority to give in to their demands. During the 1950s and 1960s, for example, opponents of civil rights legislation often sought to block its passage by adopting the tactic of filibuster. Sixty votes are needed to end a filibuster. This procedure is called **cloture**.

In general, the party leadership in the House has total control over debate. In the Senate, each member has substantial power to block debate. This is one reason that the Senate tends to be a less partisan body than the House. A House majority can override opposition, whereas it takes a three-fifths vote in the Senate; thus the Senate tends to be more accommodating of various views.

Conference Committee: Reconciling House and Senate Versions of a Bill

Getting a bill out of committee and through one of the houses of Congress is no guarantee that a bill will be enacted into law. Frequently, bills that began with

closed rule Provision by the House Rules Committee limiting or prohibiting the introduction of amendments during debate.

open rule Provision by the House Rules Committee that permits floor debate and the addition of amendments to a bill.

filibuster A tactic used by members of the Senate to prevent action on legislation they oppose by continuously holding the floor and speaking until the majority backs down. Once given the floor, senators have unlimited time to speak, and it requires sixty votes to end the filibuster.

cloture Rule allowing a supermajority of the members in a legislative body to set a time limit on debate over a given bill.

conference committee A joint committee created to work out a compromise on House and Senate versions of a piece of legislation.

similar provisions in both chambers emerge with little resemblance to one another. Alternatively, a bill may be passed by one chamber but undergo substantial revision in the other chamber. In such cases, a **conference committee** composed of the senior members of the committees or subcommittees that initiated the bills may be required to iron out differences between the two pieces of legislation. Sometimes members or leaders will let objectionable provisions pass on the floor with the idea that they will get the change they want in conference. Usually, conference committees meet behind closed doors. Agreement requires majority support from the two delegations. Legislation that emerges from a conference committee is more often a compromise than a clear victory of one set of political forces over another.

When a bill comes out of conference, it faces one more hurdle. Before a bill can be sent to the president for signing, the House-Senate conference report must be approved on the floor of each chamber. Usually, such approval is given quickly. Occasionally, however, a bill's opponents use approval as one last opportunity to defeat a piece of legislation.

Presidential Action

veto The president's constitutional power to turn down acts of Congress. A presidential veto may be overridden by a two-thirds vote of each house of Congress.

pocket veto A presidential veto of legislation wherein the president takes no formal action on a bill. If Congress adjourns within ten days of passing a bill, and the president does not sign it, the bill is considered to be vetoed.

Once adopted by the House and Senate, a bill goes to the president, who may choose to sign the bill into law or veto it. The **veto** is the president's constitutional power to reject a piece of legislation. To veto a bill, the president returns it within ten days to the house of Congress in which it originated, along with his objections to the bill. If Congress adjourns during the ten-day period, and the president has taken no action, the bill is also considered to be vetoed. This latter method is known as the **pocket veto**. The possibility of a presidential veto affects how willing members of Congress are to push for different pieces of legislation at different times. If they think the president is likely to veto a proposal, they might shelve it for a later time. Alternatively, the sponsors of a popular bill opposed by the president might push for passage in order to force the president to pay the political costs of vetoing it.[18]

A presidential veto may be overridden by a two-thirds vote in both the House and the Senate. A veto override says much about the support that a president can expect from Congress, and it can deliver a stinging blow to the executive branch. Presidents will often back down from a veto threat if they believe that Congress will override the veto.

HOW CONGRESS DECIDES

What determines the kinds of legislation that Congress ultimately produces? The process of creating a legislative agenda, drawing up a list of possible measures, and deciding among them is very complex, and a variety of influences from inside

---

[18] John Gilmour, *Strategic Disagreement* (Pittsburgh: University of Pittsburgh Press, 1995).

and outside government play important roles. External influences include a legislator's constituency and various interest groups. Influences from inside government include party leadership, congressional colleagues, and the president. Let us examine each of these influences individually and then consider how they interact to produce congressional policy decisions.

Constituency

Because members of Congress want to be reelected, we would expect the views of their constituents to have a key influence on the decisions that legislators make. Yet constituency influence is not so straightforward. In fact, most constituents do not even know what policies their representatives support. The number of citizens who *do* pay attention to such matters—the attentive public—is usually very small. Nonetheless, members of Congress spend a lot of time worrying about what their constituents think, because these representatives realize that the choices they make may be scrutinized in a future election and used as ammunition by an opposing candidate. Because of this possibility, members of Congress try to anticipate their constituents' policy views.[19] Legislators are more likely to act in accordance with their constituents' views if they think that voters will take them into account during elections. In this way, constituents may affect congressional policy choices even when there is little direct evidence of their influence.[20]

Interest Groups

Interest groups are another important external influence on the policies that Congress produces. When members of Congress are making voting decisions, those interest groups that have some connection to constituents in particular members' districts are most likely to be influential. For this reason, interest groups with the ability to mobilize followers in many congressional districts may be especially influential in Congress. The small-business lobby, for example, played an important role in defeating President Clinton's proposal for comprehensive health care reform in 1993–94. Because of the mobilization of networks of small businesses across the country, virtually every member of Congress had to take their views into account.

In the 2010 electoral cycle, interest groups and political action committees (PACs) donated many millions of dollars in campaign contributions to incumbent legislators and challengers. What does this money buy? A popular conception is that campaign contributions buy votes. In this view, legislators vote for whichever

---

[19] See John W. Kingdon, *Congressmen's Voting Decisions* (New York: Harper & Row, 1973), chap. 3, and R. Douglas Arnold, *The Logic of Congressional Action* (New Haven, Conn.: Yale University Press, 1990). See also Joshua Clinton, "Representation in Congress: Constituents and Roll Calls in the 106th House," *Journal of Politics* 68 (2006): 397–409.

[20] Interest groups from the state or district (which we discuss below) can be useful to legislators in this respect, when they provide information concerning the significance of particular issues for various constituency groups. See Kenneth W. Kollman, *Outside Lobbying: Public Opinion and Interest Group Strategies* (Princeton, N.J.: Princeton University Press, 1998).

proposal favors the bulk of their contributors. Although the vote-buying hypothesis makes for good campaign rhetoric, it has little factual support. Empirical studies by political scientists show little evidence that contributions from large PACs influence legislative voting patterns.[21]

If contributions don't buy votes, what do they buy? Our claim is that campaign contributions influence legislative behavior in ways that are difficult for the public to observe and for political scientists to measure. The institutional structure of Congress provides opportunities for interest groups to influence legislation outside the public eye.

Committee proposal power enables legislators, if they are on the relevant committee, to introduce legislation that favors contributing groups. Gatekeeping power enables committee members to block legislation that harms contributing groups. The fact that certain provisions are *excluded* from a bill is as much an indicator of PAC influence as the fact that certain provisions are *included*. The difference is that it is hard to measure what you don't see. Committee oversight powers enable members to intervene in bureaucratic decision making on behalf of contributing groups.

The point here is that voting on the floor, the alleged object of campaign contributions according to the vote-buying hypothesis, is a highly visible, highly public act, one that could get a legislator in trouble with his or her broader electoral constituency. The committee system, on the other hand, provides loads of opportunities for legislators to deliver to PAC contributors and other donors "services" that are more subtle and disguised from broader public view. Thus, we suggest that the most appropriate places to look for traces of campaign contribution influence on the legislative process are in the manner in which committees deliberate, mark up proposals, and block legislation from the floor; outside public view, these are the primary arenas for interest-group influence.

Party Discipline

In both the House and the Senate, party leaders have a good deal of influence over the behavior of their party members. This influence, sometimes called "party discipline," was once so powerful that it dominated the lawmaking process. At the turn of the century, because of their control of patronage and the nominating process, party leaders could often command the allegiance of more than 90 percent of their members. A vote on which 50 percent or more of the members of one party take a particular position while at least 50 percent of the members of the other party take the opposing position is called a **party vote**. At the beginning of the twentieth century, most **roll-call votes** in the House of Representatives were party votes. Today, primary elections have deprived party leaders of the power to decide who receives

party vote A roll-call vote in the House or Senate in which at least 50 percent of the members of one party take a particular position and are opposed by at least 50 percent of the members of the other party. Party votes are rare today, although they were fairly common in the nineteenth century.

roll-call vote A vote in which each legislator's yes or no vote is recorded as the clerk calls the names of the members alphabetically.

[21] See Janet M. Grenke, "PACs and the Congressional Supermarket: The Currency Is Complex," *American Journal of Political Science* 33, no. 1 (February 1989): 1–24. More generally, see Jacobson, *The Politics of Congressional Elections.* For a view that too little, not too much, money is spent by interest groups, see Stephen Ansolabehere, John de Figueiredo, and James Snyder, "Why Is There So Little Money in U.S. Politics?" *Journal of Economic Perspectives* 17 (2003): 105–30.

FIGURE 5.5 PARTY UNITY SCORES BY CHAMBER, 1955–2009

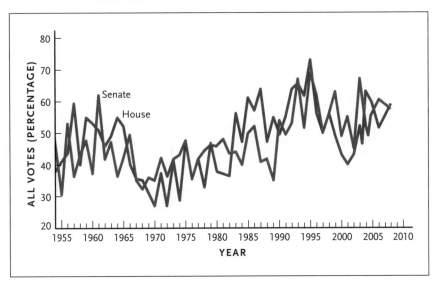

NOTE: The scores represent the percentage of recorded votes on which the majority of one party voted against the majority of the other party.

SOURCE: Party Polarization: 1879–2009, updated January 2, 2009, http://voteview.com/polarized_America.htm#politicalpolarization (accessed 6/18/09).

the party's official nomination. The patronage resources available to the leadership, moreover, have become quite limited. As a result, party-line voting happens less often. It is, however, fairly common to find at least a majority of Democrats opposing a majority of Republicans on any given issue.

Typically, party unity is greater in the House than in the Senate. House rules grant greater procedural control of business to the majority party leaders, which gives them more influence over their members. In the Senate, however, the leadership has few sanctions over its members. The former Senate minority leader Tom Daschle once observed that a Senate leader seeking to influence other senators has as incentives "a bushel full of carrots and a few twigs."[22] Party unity has increased in recent sessions of Congress as a consequence of the intense partisan struggles during the 1980s and 1990s (see Figure 5.5). On the whole, there was more party unity in the House during 1995 than in any year since 1954. By 1996, the level of party unity was back to average. In 1997, party unity diminished as House Republicans divided over budget and tax cut negotiations with President Clinton. Following the election of George W. Bush in 2000, accompanied by Republican control of Congress, party voting again ticked upward. And in the first two years of the Obama administration, party voting in both chambers was strong. Republican votes supporting Obama initiatives have been quite rare.

---

[22] Holly Idelson, "Signs Point to Greater Loyalty on Both Sides of the Aisle," *Congressional Quarterly Weekly Report*, December 19, 1992, p. 3849.

FIGURE 5.6 THE WIDENING IDEOLOGICAL GAP BETWEEN THE PARTIES

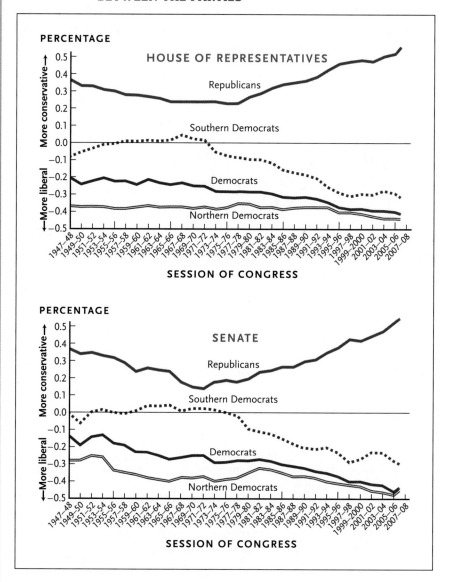

SOURCE: Party Polarization: 1879–2009, updated January 2, 2009, http://voteview.com/polarized_America .htm#politicalpolarization (accessed 6/18/09).

To some extent, party divisions are based on ideology and background. Republican members of Congress are more likely than Democrats to be drawn from rural or suburban areas. Democrats are likely to be more liberal on economic and social questions than their Republican colleagues. This ideological gap has been especially pronounced since 1980 (see Figure 5.6). These differences certainly help to explain roll-call divisions between the two parties. Ideology and background, however, are only part of the explanation of party unity. The other part has to do with organization and leadership.

Although party organization has weakened since the turn of the century, today's party leaders still have some resources at their disposal: (1) committee assignments, (2) access to the floor, (3) the whip system, (4) logrolling, and (5) the presidency. These resources are regularly used and are often very effective in securing the support of party members.

Committee Assignments. Leaders can create debts among members by helping them get favorable committee assignments. These assignments are made early in the congressional careers of most members and cannot be taken from them if they later balk at party discipline. Nevertheless, if the leadership goes out of its way to get the right assignment for a member, this effort is likely to create a bond of obligation that can be called on without any other payments or favors.

Access to the Floor. The most important everyday resource available to the parties is control over access to the floor. With thousands of bills awaiting passage and most members clamoring for access in order to influence a bill or to publicize themselves, floor time is precious. In the House, the Speaker, as head of the majority party (in consultation with the minority leader), allocates large blocks of floor time. More important, the Speaker of the House and the majority leader in the Senate possess the power of recognition. Although this power may not appear to be substantial, it is a formidable authority and can be used to block a piece of legislation completely or to frustrate a member's attempts to speak on a particular issue. Because the power is significant, members of Congress usually attempt to stay on good terms with the Speaker and the majority leader to ensure that they will continue to be recognized.[23]

The Whip System. Some influence accrues to party leaders through the **whip system**, which is primarily a communications network. Between twelve and twenty assistant and regional whips are selected by zones to operate at the direction of the majority or minority leader and the whip. They take polls of all the members in order to learn their intentions on specific bills. This tells the leaders whether they have enough support to allow a vote, as well as whether the vote is so close that they need to put pressure on a few swing votes. Leaders also use the whip system to convey their wishes and plans to the members, but only in very close votes do they actually exert pressure on a member. In those instances, the speaker or a lieutenant will go to a few party members who have indicated they will switch if their vote is essential. The whip system helps the leaders limit pressuring members to a few times per session.

The whip system helps maintain party unity in both houses of Congress, but it is particularly critical in the House of Representatives because of the large number

whip system Primarily a communications network in each house of Congress, whips take polls of the membership in order to learn their intentions on specific legislative issues and to assist the majority and minority leaders in various tasks.

---

[23] A recent analysis of how floor time is allocated is found in Gary C. Cox and Matthew D. McCubbins, *Setting the Agenda: Responsible Party Government in the U.S. House of Representatives* (New York: Cambridge University Press, 2005).

Party Discipline

The influence party leaders have over the behavior of their party members is maintained through a number of sources:

Committee assignments—By giving favorable committee assignments to members, party leaders create a sense of debt.

Access to the floor—Ranking committee members in the Senate and the Speaker of the House control the allocation of floor time, so House and Senate members want to stay on good terms with these party leaders so that their bills get time on the floor.

Whip system—The system allows party leaders to keep track of how many votes they have for a given piece of legislation; if the vote is close, they can try to influence members to switch sides.

Logrolling—Members who have nothing in common agree to support one another's legislation because each needs the vote.

Presidency—The president's legislative proposals are often the most important part of Congress's agenda. Party leaders use the president's support to rally members.

of legislators whose positions and votes must be accounted for. The majority and minority whips and their assistants must be adept at inducing compromise among legislators who hold widely differing viewpoints. The whips' personal styles and their perception of their function significantly affect the development of legislative coalitions and influence the compromises that emerge.

logrolling A legislative practice whereby reciprocal agreements are made between legislators, usually in voting for or against a bill. In contrast to bargaining, parties to logrolling have nothing in common but their desire to exchange support.

Logrolling.   An agreement between two or more members of Congress who have nothing in common except the need for support is called **logrolling**. The agreement states, in effect, "You support me on bill X and I'll support you on another bill of your choice." Since party leaders are the center of the communications networks in the two chambers, they can help members create large logrolling coalitions. Hundreds of logrolling deals are made each year. Although there are no official record-keeping books, it would be a poor party leader whose whips did not know who owed what to whom.

The Presidency.   Of all the influences that maintain the clarity of party lines in Congress, the influence of the presidency is probably the most important. Indeed, it is a touchstone of party discipline in Congress. Since the late 1940s, under President Truman, presidents each year have identified a number of bills to be considered part of the administration's program. By the mid-1950s, both parties in Congress began to look to the president for these proposals, which became the most significant part of Congress's agenda. The president's support is a criterion for party loyalty, and party leaders in Congress are able to use it to rally some members.

Weighing Diverse Influences

Clearly, many factors affect congressional decisions. But at various points in the decision-making process, some factors are likely to be more influential than others. For example, interest groups may be more effective at the committee stage, when their expertise is especially valued and their visibility is less obvious. Because committees play a key role in deciding what legislation actually reaches the floor of the House or Senate, interest groups can often put a halt to bills they dislike, or they can ensure that the options that do reach the floor are those that the group's members support.

Once legislation reaches the floor and members of Congress are deciding among alternatives, constituent opinion will become more important. Legislators are also influenced very much by other legislators: Many of their assessments about the substance and politics of legislation come from fellow members of Congress.

The influence of the external and internal forces described in the preceding section also varies according to the kind of issue being considered. On policies of great importance to powerful interest groups—farm subsidies, for example—those groups are likely to have considerable influence. On other issues, members of Congress may be less attentive to narrow interest groups and more willing to consider what they see as the general interest.

Finally, the mix of influences varies according to the historical moment. The 1994 electoral victory of Republicans allowed their party to control both houses of Congress for the first time in forty years. That fact, combined with an unusually assertive Republican leadership, meant that party leaders became especially important in decision making. The willingness of moderate Republicans to support measures they had once opposed indicated the unusual importance of party leadership in this period.[24]

BEYOND LEGISLATION: ADDITIONAL CONGRESSIONAL POWERS

In addition to the power to make the law, Congress has at its disposal an array of other instruments through which to influence the process of government. The Constitution gives the Senate the power to approve treaties and appointments. And Congress has drawn to itself a number of other powers through which it can share with the other branches the capacity to administer the laws. The powers of Congress can be called "weapons of control" to emphasize Congress's power to govern and to call attention to what governmental power means.

---

[24] David Broder, "At 6 Months, House GOP Juggernaut Still Cohesive," *Washington Post*, July 17, 1995, p. A1.

Oversight

Oversight, as applied to Congress, refers not to something neglected but to the effort to oversee or to supervise how the executive branch carries out legislation. Individual senators and members of the House can engage in a form of oversight simply by calling or visiting administrators, sending out questionnaires, or talking to constituents about programs. But in a more formal sense, oversight is carried out by committees or subcommittees of the Senate or House, which conduct hearings and investigations in order to analyze and evaluate bureaucratic agencies and the effectiveness of their programs. The purpose may be to locate inefficiencies or abuses of power, to explore the relationship between what an agency does and what a law intended, or to change or abolish a program. Most programs and agencies are subject to some oversight every year during the course of hearings on **appropriations**, that is, the funding of agencies and government programs.

Committees or subcommittees have the power to subpoena witnesses, administer oaths, cross-examine, compel testimony, and bring criminal charges for contempt (refusing to cooperate) and perjury (lying).

Hearings and investigations resemble each other in many ways, but they differ on one fundamental point. A hearing is usually held on a specific bill, and the questions asked there are usually intended to build a record with regard to that bill. In an investigation, the committee or subcommittee does not begin with a particular bill, but examines a broad area or problem and then concludes its investigation with one or more proposed bills. One example of an investigation is the Senate hearings on the abuse of prisoners in Iraq's Abu Ghraib prison. Many Democrats and some Republicans complained that congressional oversight of the entire Iraq war had been too lax. Reflecting on the prison abuse scandal, Representative Christopher Shays (R-Conn.) stated, "I believe our failure to do proper oversight has hurt our country and the administration. Maybe they wouldn't have gotten into some of this trouble if our oversight had been better."[25]

Advice and Consent: Special Senate Powers

The Constitution has given the Senate a special power, one that is not based on lawmaking. The president has the power to make treaties and to appoint top executive officers, ambassadors, and federal judges—but only "with the Advice and Consent of the Senate" (Article II, Section 2). For treaties, two-thirds of those present must concur; for appointments, a majority is required.

The power to approve or reject presidential requests also involves the power to set conditions. The Senate only occasionally exercises its power to reject treaties and appointments. The Senate has rejected only nine judicial nominees during the past century, whereas many times that number have been approved. In 2009, Republicans criticized President Obama's nominee to the Supreme Court,

---

[25] Carl Hulse, "Even Some in G.O.P. Call for More Oversight of Bush," *New York Times*, May 31, 2004, p. A13.

Sonia Sotomayor, but her nomination was easily approved, thanks in part to a large Democratic majority in the chamber.

More common than Senate rejection of presidential appointees is a senatorial "hold" on an appointment. By Senate tradition, any member may place an indefinite hold on the confirmation of a mid- or lower-level presidential appointment. The hold is typically used by senators trying to wring concessions from the White House on matters having nothing to do with the appointment in question. After George W. Bush took office in January 2001, the Democratic minority in the Senate scrutinized judicial nominations and prevented final confirmation votes on a dozen especially conservative nominees, a matter about which the president frequently complained during the 2004 reelection campaign.

Most presidents make every effort to take potential Senate opposition into account in treaty negotiations and will frequently resort to **executive agreements** with foreign powers instead of treaties. The Supreme Court has held that such agreements are equivalent to treaties, but they do not need Senate approval.[26] In the past, presidents sometimes concluded secret agreements without informing Congress of the agreements' contents, or even their existence. American involvement in the Vietnam War grew in part out of a series of secret arrangements made between American presidents and the South Vietnamese during the 1950s and 1960s. Congress did not even learn of these agreements until 1969.

> **executive agreement** Agreement between the president and another country, which has the force of a treaty but does not require the Senate's "advice and consent."

In 1972, Congress passed the Case Act, which requires that the president inform Congress of any executive agreement within sixty days of its having been reached. This provides Congress with the opportunity to cancel agreements that it opposes. In addition, Congress can limit the president's ability to conduct foreign policy through executive agreement by refusing to appropriate the funds needed to implement an agreement. In this way, for example, Congress can modify or even cancel executive agreements to provide economic or military assistance to foreign governments.

Impeachment

The Constitution also grants Congress the power of **impeachment** over the president, vice president, and other executive officials. To impeach means to charge a government official (president or other) with "Treason, Bribery, or other high Crimes and Misdemeanors," and bring him or her before Congress to determine guilt. The procedure is similar to a criminal indictment in that the House of Representatives acts like a grand jury, voting (by simple majority) on whether the accused ought to be impeached. If a majority of the House votes to impeach, the impeachment trial moves to the Senate, which acts like a trial jury by voting whether to convict and forcibly remove the person from office. (This vote requires a two-thirds majority.)

> **impeachment** The charging of a governmental official (president or other) with "Treason, Bribery, or other high Crimes and Misdemeanors" and bring him or her before Congress to determine guilt.

---

[26] *U.S. v. Pink*, 315 U.S. 203 (1942). For a good discussion of the problem, see James W. Davis, *The American Presidency* (New York: Harper & Row, 1987), chap. 8.

Controversy over Congress's impeachment power has arisen over the meaning of "high Crimes and Misdemeanors." A strict reading of the Constitution suggests that the only impeachable offense is an actual crime. But a more commonly agreed-on definition is that an impeachable offense is whatever the majority of the House of Representatives considers it to be at a given time. In other words, impeachment, especially the impeachment of a president, is a political decision.

During the course of American history, only two presidents have been impeached. In 1867, President Andrew Johnson, a Southern Democrat who had battled a congressional Republican majority over Reconstruction, was impeached by the House but saved from conviction by one vote in the Senate. In 1998, President Bill Clinton was impeached by the House for perjury and obstruction of justice arising from his sexual relationship with a former White House intern, Monica Lewinsky. At the conclusion of a Senate trial in 1999, Democrats, joined by a handful of Republicans, acquitted the president of both charges.

The impeachment power is an important one. The framers of the Constitution gave Congress the power to impeach in order to guard against executive tyranny.

DOES CONGRESS WORK?

Congress is both a representative assembly and a powerful institution of government. In assessing the effectiveness of Congress, we will focus on both its representative character and the efficiency with which Congress is able to get things done.

Congress is the most important representative institution in American government. Each member's primary responsibility is to the district, to his or her constituency, not to the congressional leadership, a party, or even Congress itself. Yet the task of representation is not a simple one. Views about what defines fair and effective representation differ, and constituents can make very different kinds of demands on their representatives. Members of Congress must consider these diverse views and demands as they represent their districts (see Figure 5.1). A representative claims to act or speak for some other person or group. But how can one person be trusted to speak for another? How do we know that those who call themselves our representatives are actually speaking on our behalf, rather than simply pursuing their own interests?

As we saw earlier in this chapter, legislators vary in the weight they give to personal priorities and the things desired by campaign contributors and past supporters. Some see themselves as delegates, elected to do the bidding of those who sent them to the legislature. Other legislators see themselves as trustees, selected by their fellow citizens to do what the legislator thinks is "right." Most legislators are mixes of these two types. Frequent competitive elections are an important means by which constituents hold their representatives in account and keep them responsive to constituency views and preferences.

Indeed, taking care of constituents explains a lot of the legislation that Congress produces. It is not too much of an exaggeration to suggest the following list of individuals whose support is necessary in order to get a measure through Congress and signed into law:

- A majority of the authorizing subcommittees in the House and Senate (probably including the subcommittee chairs)
- A majority of the full authorizing committees in the House and Senate (probably including committee chairs)
- A majority of the appropriations subcommittees in the House and Senate (probably including the subcommittee chairs)
- A majority of the full appropriations committees in the House and Senate (probably including committee chairs)
- A majority of the House Rules Committee (including its chair)
- A majority of the full House
- A majority—possibly as many as sixty votes, if needed to shut off a filibuster—of the Senate
- The Speaker and majority leader in the House
- The majority leader in the Senate
- The president

This list includes an extraordinarily large number of public officials.

With so many hurdles to clear for a legislative initiative to become a public law, the benefits must be spread broadly. It is as though a bill must travel on a toll road past a number of tollbooths, each one containing a collector with his or her hand out for payment. Frequently, features of the bill are drafted initially or revised so as to be more inclusive, spreading the benefits widely among members' districts. This is the **distributive tendency**.

The distributive tendency is part of the American system of representative democracy. It is as American as apple pie! Legislators, in advocating the interests of their constituents, are eager to advertise their ability to deliver for their state or district. They maneuver to put themselves in a position to claim credit for good things that happen there and to duck blame for bad things. This is the way they earn trust back home, deter strong challengers in upcoming elections, and defeat those who run against them. This means that legislators must take advantage of every opportunity that presents itself. In some instances, as in our earlier discussion of the pork barrel, the results may seem bizarre. Nevertheless, the distributive tendency is a consequence of how Congress was designed to work.

Another consequence of Congress's design is almost the opposite of the distributive tendency: the tendency toward the status quo. The U.S. Congress has more veto points than any other legislative body in the world. If any of the individuals listed above says no, a bill dies. Some celebrate this design. As a result, the government is unlikely to change in response to superficial fluctuations in public sentiment. Congress's design does mean greater representation of minority interests in the legislative process (at least to say no to the majority). But it also creates the impression of gridlock, leading some to question Congress's effectiveness.

Critics of Congress want it to be both more representative and more effective. On the one hand, Congress is frequently criticized for falling victim to "gridlock"

distributive tendency The tendency of Congress to spread the benefits of a bill over a wide range of members' districts.

and failing to reach decisions on important issues such as Social Security reform. This was one reason why, in 1995, the Republican House leadership reduced the number of committees and subcommittees in the lower chamber. Having fewer committees and subcommittees generally means greater centralization of power and more expeditious decision making. On the other hand, critics demand that Congress become more representative of the changing makeup and values of the American populace. In recent years, for example, some reformers have demanded limits on the number of terms that any member of Congress can serve. Term limits are seen as a device for producing a more rapid turnover of members and, hence, a better chance for new political and social forces to be represented in Congress. The problem, however, is that although reforms such as term limits and greater internal diffusion of power may make Congress more representative, they may also make it less efficient and effective. By the same token, reforms that may make Congress better able to act—such as strong central leadership, reduction of the number of committees and subcommittees, and retention of members with seniority and experience—may make Congress less representative. This is the dilemma of congressional reform. Efficiency and representation are often competing principles in our system of government; we must be wary of gaining one at the expense of the other.

CHAPTER REVIEW

The legislative process must provide the order necessary for legislation to take place amid competing interests. It is dependent on a hierarchical organizational structure within Congress. Six basic dimensions of Congress affect the legislative process: (1) the parties, (2) the committees, (3) the staff, (4) the caucuses (or conferences), (5) the rules, and (6) the presidency.

Since the Constitution provides only for a presiding officer in each house, some method had to be devised for conducting business. Parties quickly assumed the responsibility for this. In the House, the majority party elects a leader every two years. This individual becomes Speaker. In addition, a majority leader and a minority leader (from the minority party) and party whips are elected. Each party has a committee whose job it is to make committee assignments. Party structure in the Senate is similar, except that the vice president of the United States is the president of the Senate.

The committee system surpasses the party system in its importance in Congress. In the early nineteenth century, standing committees became a fundamental aspect of Congress. They have, for the most part, evolved to correspond to executive branch departments or programs and thus reflect and maintain the separation of powers.

The Senate has a tradition of unlimited debate, on which the various cloture rules it has passed have had little effect. Filibusters still occur. The rules of the House restrict talk and support committees; deliberation is recognized as committee business. The House Rules Committee has the power to control debate and floor amendments. The rules prescribe the formal procedure through which bills become law. Generally, the parties control scheduling and agenda, but the committees determine action on the floor. Committees, seniority, and rules all limit the ability of members to represent their constituents. Yet these factors enable Congress to maintain its role as a major participant in government.

Although party voting regularity remains strong, party discipline has declined. Still, parties do have several means of maintaining discipline: (1) favorable committee assignments create obligations; (2) floor time in the debate on one bill can be allocated in exchange for a specific vote on another; (3) the whip system allows party leaders to assess support for a bill and convey their wishes to members; (4) party leaders can help members create large logrolling coalitions; and (5) presidents, by identifying pieces of legislation as their own, can muster support along party lines. In most cases, party leaders accept constituency obligations as a valid reason for voting against the party position.

FOR FURTHER READING

Adler, E. Scott. *Why Congressional Reforms Fail: Reelection and the House Committee System.* Chicago: University of Chicago Press, 2002.

Arnold, R. Douglas. *The Logic of Congressional Action.* New Haven, Conn.: Yale University Press, 1990. ○ reader selection

Binder, Sarah. *Stalemate: Causes and Consequences of Legislative Gridlock.* Washington, D.C.: Brookings Institution, 2003.

———— and Paul Quirk, eds. *Institutions of Democracy: The Legislative Branch.* New York: Oxford University Press, 2004.

Brady, David, and Mathew D. McCubbins, eds. *Party, Process, and Political Change in Congress: New Perspectives on the History of Congress.* Palo Alto, Calif.: Stanford University Press, 2002.

Cox, Gary C., and Jonathon Katz, *Elbridge Gerry's Salamander: The Electoral Consequences of the Reapportionment Revolution.* Cambridge: Cambridge University Press, 2002.

————, and Mathew D. McCubbins. *Legislative Leviathan: Party Government in the House.* 2nd ed. Berkeley: University of California Press, 2006.

————. *Setting the Agenda: Responsible Party Government in the U.S. House of Representatives.* New York: Cambridge University Press, 2005. ○ reader selection

Dodd, Lawrence C., and Bruce I. Oppenheimer, eds. *Congress Reconsidered.* 8th ed. Washington, D.C.: Congressional Quarterly Press, 2005.

Fenno, Richard F., Jr. *Home Style: House Members in Their Districts.* Boston: Little, Brown, 1978.

————. *The United States Senate: A Bicameral Perspective.* Washington, D.C.: American Enterprise Institute, 1982.

Fiorina, Morris P. *Congress: Keystone of the Washington Establishment.* 2nd ed. New Haven, Conn.: Yale University Press, 1989.

Frisch, Scott A., and Sean Q. Kelly. *Committee Assignment Politics in the U.S. House of Representatives*. Norman: University of Oklahoma Press, 2006.

Krehbiel, Keith. *Pivotal Politics: A Theory of U.S. Lawmaking*. Chicago: University of Chicago Press, 1998.

reader selection Mayhew, David. *Congress: The Electoral Connection*. New Haven, Conn.: Yale University Press, 1974.

Polsby, Nelson W. *How Congress Evolves*. New York: Oxford University Press, 2004.

Schickler, Eric. *Disjointed Pluralism*. Princeton, N.J.: Princeton University Press, 2001.

Sinclair, Barbara. *Unorthodox Lawmaking: New Legislative Processes in the U.S. Congress*. 3rd ed. Washington, D.C.: CQ Press, 2007.

Smith, Steven, Jason M. Roberts, and Ryan J. Vander Wielen. *The American Congress*. New York: Cambridge University Press, 2009.

Stewart, Charles H. *Analyzing Congress*. New York: Norton, 2001.

Sundquist, James L. *The Decline and Resurgence of Congress*. Washington, D.C.: Brookings Institution, 1981.

Ⓢ Additional study and review materials are available online at wwnorton.com/studyspace/

6

The Presidency

HOW DOES PRESIDENTIAL POWER WORK?

Presidential power generally seems to increase during times of war. For example, President Abraham Lincoln's 1862 declaration of martial law and Congress's 1863 legislation giving the president the power to make arrests and imprisonments through military tribunals amounted to a "constitutional dictatorship" that lasted through the war and Lincoln's reelection in 1864. But these measures were viewed as emergency powers that could be revoked once the crisis of union was resolved. In less than a year after Lincoln's death, Congress had reasserted its power, leaving the presidency in many respects the same as, if not weaker than, it had been before the war.

During World War II, Franklin D. Roosevelt, like Lincoln, did not bother to wait for Congress but took executive action first and expected Congress to follow. Roosevelt brought the United States into an undeclared naval war against Germany a year before Pearl Harbor, and he ordered the unauthorized use of wiretaps and other surveillance as well as the investigation of suspicious persons for reasons not clearly specified. The most egregious (and revealing) of these was his segregation and eventual confinement of 120,000 individuals of Japanese descent, many of whom were American citizens. Even worse, the Supreme Court validated Roosevelt's treatment of the Japanese, on the flimsy grounds of military necessity. One dissenter on the Court called the president's assumption of emergency powers "a loaded weapon ready for the hand of any authority that can bring forward a plausible claim of an urgent need."[1]

---

[1] Quoted from the dissenting opinion of Justice Robert Jackson in *Korematsu v. United States*, 323 U.S. 214 (1944).

- Since the 1930s, the presidency has been the dominant branch of American government.

- Most of the real power of the modern presidency comes from the powers granted by the Constitution and the laws made by Congress. Mass public opinion, however, is also a source of presidential power.

- Contemporary presidents have also increased the power of the executive branch through "administrative strategies" that often allow them to achieve policy goals without congressional approval.

The "loaded weapon" was seized again on September 14, 2001, when Congress defined the World Trade Center and Pentagon attacks as an act of war and proceeded to adopt a joint resolution authorizing the president to use "all necessary and appropriate force against those nations, organizations or persons he determines planned, authorized, committed or aided the terrorist attacks that occurred on September 11, 2001, or harbored such organizations or persons. . . ."[2] On the basis of this authorization, President Bush ordered the invasion of Afghanistan and began the reorganization of the nation's "homeland security."

In this chapter, we will examine the foundations of the American presidency and assess the origins and character of presidential power in the twenty-first century. National emergencies are one source of presidential power, but presidents are also empowered by democratic political processes and, increasingly, by their ability to control and expand the institutional resources of the office. The Supreme Court, to be sure, can sometimes check presidential power. For example, in the 2006 *Hamdan v. Rumsfeld* decision, the Court invalidated the military tribunals established by President Bush to try terror suspects. And, of course, through legislative investigations and its budgetary powers, Congress can oppose the president. With Democratic majorities in both houses of Congress after the 2006 elections, congressional opposition to President Bush's policies in Iraq and the war on terrorism increased. And even though President Obama enjoyed solid Democratic majorities in Congress, he encountered congressional opposition to several proposed spending cuts in 2009.

This chapter explains why the American system of government could be described as presidential government and how it got to be that way. We also explore how and why the president, however powerful, is nevertheless vulnerable to the popular will. But first, we begin with powers provided for in the Constitution.

THE CONSTITUTIONAL BASIS OF THE PRESIDENCY

The presidency was established by Article II of the Constitution. Article II begins by asserting, "The executive power shall be vested in a President of the United States of America." It goes on to describe the manner in which the president is to

---

[2] *Authorization for Use of Military Force*, Public Law 107-40, *U.S. Statutes at Large* 115 (2001): 224.

be chosen and defines the basic powers of the presidency. By vesting the executive power in a single president, the framers were emphatically rejecting proposals for various forms of collective leadership. Some delegates to the Constitutional Convention had argued in favor of a multiheaded executive or an "executive council" in order to avoid undue concentration of power in the hands of one individual. Most of the framers, however, were anxious to provide for "energy" in the executive. They hoped to have a president capable of taking quick and aggressive action. They believed that a powerful executive would help to protect the nation's interests vis-à-vis other nations and promote the federal government's interests relative to the states.

Immediately following the first sentence, Section 1, Article II, defines the manner in which the president is to be chosen. This is an odd sequence, but it does say something about the struggle the delegates were having over how to give power to the executive and at the same time how to balance that power with limitations. The struggle was between those delegates who wanted the president to be selected by Congress, and thus responsible to it, and those delegates who preferred that the president be elected directly by the people. Direct popular elections would create a more independent and more powerful presidency. The framers finally agreed on a scheme of indirect election through an electoral college, the electors to be selected by the state legislatures (and close elections would be resolved in the House of Representatives). In this way, the framers hoped to achieve a "republican" solution: a strong president who would be responsible to state and national legislators rather than directly to the electorate.

THE CONSTITUTIONAL POWERS OF THE PRESIDENCY

While Section 1 of Article II explains how the president is to be chosen. Sections 2 and 3 outline the powers and duties of the president. These two sections identify two sources of presidential power. Some presidential powers are specifically established by the language of the Constitution. For example, the president is authorized to make treaties, grant pardons, and nominate judges and other public officials. These specifically defined powers are called the **expressed powers** of the office and cannot be revoked by the Congress or any other agency without an amendment to the Constitution. Other expressed powers include the power to receive ambassadors and command of the military forces of the United States.

In addition to establishing the president's expressed powers, Article II declares that the president "shall take Care that the Laws be faithfully executed." Since the laws are enacted by Congress, this language implies that Congress is to delegate to the president the power to implement or execute its will. Powers given to the president by Congress are called **delegated powers.** In principle, Congress delegates to the president only the power to identify or develop the means to carry out Congressional decisions. So, for example, if Congress determines that air quality should be improved, it might delegate to the executive branch the power to determine the

expressed powers of the president Specific powers granted to the president under Article II, Sections 2 and 3, of the Constitution.

delegated powers Constitutional powers that are assigned to one governmental agency but that are exercised by another agency with the express permission of the first.

best means of improvement as well as the power to implement the cleanup process. In practice, of course, decisions about how to clean the air are likely to have an enormous impact on businesses, organizations, and individuals throughout the nation. As it delegates power to the executive, Congress substantially enhances the importance of the presidency and the executive branch. In most cases, Congress delegates power to executive agencies rather than to the president. As we shall see, however, contemporary presidents have found ways to capture a good deal of this delegated power for themselves.

Presidents have claimed a third source of institutional power beyond expressed and delegated powers. These are powers not specified in the Constitution or the law but said to stem from "the rights, duties and obligations of the presidency."[3] They are referred to as the **inherent powers** of the presidency and are most often asserted by presidents in times of war or national emergency. For example, after the fall of Fort Sumter and the outbreak of the Civil War, President Abraham Lincoln issued a series of executive orders for which he had no clear legal basis. Without even calling Congress into session, Lincoln combined the state militias into a ninety-day national volunteer force, called for forty thousand new volunteers, enlarged the regular army and navy, diverted $2 million in unspent appropriations to military needs, instituted censorship of the U.S. mails, ordered a blockade of Southern ports, suspended the writ of *habeas corpus* in the border states, and ordered the arrest by military police of individuals whom he deemed to be guilty of engaging in or even contemplating treasonous actions.[4] Lincoln asserted that these extraordinary measures were justified by the president's inherent power to protect the nation.[5] Subsequent presidents, including Franklin D. Roosevelt and George W. Bush, have had similar views.

inherent powers
Powers claimed by a president that are not expressed in the Constitution, but are inferred from it.

Expressed Powers

The president's expressed powers, as defined by Sections 2 and 3 of Article II, fall into several categories:

1. *Military.* Article II, Section 2, provides for the power as "Commander in Chief of the Army and Navy of the United States, and of the Militia of the several States, when called in to the actual Service of the United States."

2. *Judicial.* Article II, Section 2, also provides the power to "grant Reprieves and Pardons for Offenses against the United States, except in Cases of Impeachment."

3. *Diplomatic.* Article II, Section 3, provides the power to "receive Ambassadors and other public Ministers."

4. *Executive.* Article II, Section 3, authorizes the president to see to it that all the laws are faithfully executed; Section 2 gives the chief executive the power to appoint, remove, and supervise all executive officers and to appoint all federal judges.

---

[3] *In re Neagle*, 135 U.S. 1 (1890).

[4] James G. Randall, *Constitutional Problems under Lincoln* (New York: Appleton, 1926), chap. 1.

[5] Edward S. Corwin, *The President: Office and Powers*, 4th rev. ed. (New York: New York University Press, 1957), p. 229.

5. *Legislative.* Article I, Section 7, and Article II, Section 3, give the president the power to participate authoritatively in the legislative process.

Military. The president's military powers are among the most important that the chief executive exercises. The position of **commander in chief** makes the president the highest military officer in the United States, with control of the entire military establishment. The president is also the head of the nation's intelligence hierarchy, which includes not only the Central Intelligence Agency (CIA) but also the National Security Council (NSC), the National Security Agency (NSA), the Federal Bureau of Investigation (FBI), and a host of lesser-known but very powerful international and domestic security agencies.

War and Inherent Presidential Power. The Constitution gives Congress the power to declare war. Presidents, however, have gone a long way toward capturing this power for themselves. Congress has not declared war since December 1941, yet since then American military forces have engaged in numerous campaigns throughout the world under the orders of the president. When North Korean forces invaded South Korea in June 1950, Congress was prepared to declare war, but President Harry S. Truman decided not to ask for congressional action. Instead, Truman asserted the principle that the president and not Congress could decide when and where to deploy America's military might. He dispatched American forces to Korea without a congressional declaration, and in the face of the emergency, Congress felt it had to acquiesce. It passed a resolution approving the president's actions, and this became the pattern for future congressional-executive relations in the military realm. The wars in Vietnam, Bosnia, Afghanistan, and Iraq, as well as a host of smaller scale conflicts, were all fought without declarations of war.

In 1973, Congress responded to presidential unilateralism by passing the **War Powers Resolution** over President Nixon's veto. This resolution reasserted the principle of congressional war power, required the president to inform Congress of any planned military campaign, and stipulated that forces must be withdrawn within sixty days in the absence of a specific congressional authorization for their continued deployment. Presidents, however, have generally ignored the War Powers Resolution, claiming inherent executive power to defend the nation. Thus, for example, in 1989, President George H. W. Bush ordered an invasion of Panama without consulting Congress. In 1990 the same President Bush received congressional authorization to attack Iraq but had already made it clear that he was prepared to go to war with or without congressional assent. President Clinton ordered a massive bombing campaign against Serbian forces in the former nation of Yugoslavia without congressional authorization. And, of course, President George W. Bush responded to the 2001 attacks by Islamic terrorists by organizing a major military campaign to overthrow the Taliban regime in Afghanistan, which had sheltered the terrorists. In 2002, Bush ordered a major American campaign against Iraq, which he accused of posing a threat to the United States. U.S. forces overthrew the government of Iraqi dictator Saddam Hussein and occupied the country. In both instances, Congress passed resolutions approving the president's actions, but the president was careful to assert that he did not need congressional authorization. The War Powers Resolution was barely mentioned on Capital Hill and was ignored by the White House.

commander in chief The position of the president as commander of the national military and the state National Guard units (when they are called into service).

War Powers Resolution A resolution of Congress that the president can send troops into action only by authorization of Congress, or if American troops are already under attack or serious threat.

Military Sources of Domestic Power. The president's military powers extend into the domestic sphere although Article IV, Section 4, provides that the "United States shall [protect] . . . every State . . . against Invasion . . . and . . . domestic Violence," Congress has made this an explicit presidential power through statutes directing the president as commander in chief to discharge these obligations.[6] The Constitution restrains the president's use of domestic force by providing that a state legislature (or governor when the legislature is not in session) must request federal troops before the president can send them into the state to provide public order. Yet this proviso is not absolute. First, presidents are not obligated to deploy national troops merely because the state legislature or governor makes such a request. And more important, presidents may deploy troops in a state or city without a specific request if they consider it necessary to maintain an essential national service, to enforce a federal judicial order, or to protect federally guaranteed civil rights.

A famous example of the unilateral use of presidential power to protect the states against domestic disorder occurred in 1957 under President Eisenhower. He decided to send troops into Little Rock, Arkansas, against the wishes of the state of Arkansas, to enforce court orders to integrate Little Rock's Central High School. Governor Orval Faubus had posted the Arkansas National Guard at the entrance of the school to prevent the court-ordered admission of nine black students. After an effort to negotiate with Governor Faubus failed, President Eisenhower reluctantly sent to Little Rock a thousand paratroopers, who stood watch while the black students took their places in the all-white classrooms. This case makes quite clear that the president does not have to wait for a request by a state legislature or governor before acting as domestic commander in chief.[7] However, in most instances of domestic disorder—whether from human or from natural causes—presidents tend to exercise unilateral power justified by declaring a "state of emergency," thereby making available federal grants, insurance, and direct assistance as well as troops. After hurricanes Katrina and Rita struck the Gulf Coast in fall 2005, President Bush declared a state of emergency, using both state militias and federal troops for rescue operations, the prevention of looting and violence, and the delivery of medical, health, and food services.

Military emergencies have typically also led to expansion of the domestic powers of the executive branch. This was true during World Wars I and II and has been true during the "war on terrorism" as well. Within a month of the 9/11 attacks, the White House drafted and Congress enacted the USA PATRIOT Act, expanding the power of government agencies to engage in domestic surveillance activities, including electronic surveillance, and restricting judicial review of such efforts. The act also gave the attorney general greater authority to detain and deport aliens suspected of having terrorist affiliations. The following year, Congress created the Department of Homeland Security, combining offices from twenty-two federal agencies into one huge new cabinet department responsible for protecting the nation from attack. The new agency, with a tentative budget of $40 billion, includes

---

[6] These statutes are contained mainly in Title 10 of the United States Code, Sections 331, 332, and 333.

[7] An excellent study covering all aspects of the domestic use of the military is that of Adam Yarmolinsky, *The Military Establishment* (New York: Harper & Row, 1971).

the Coast Guard, Transportation Safety Administration, Federal Emergency Management Administration, Immigration and Naturalization Service, and offices from the departments of Agriculture, Energy, Transportation, Justice, Health and Human Services, Commerce, and the General Services Administration. The White House drafted the reorganization plan, but Congress weighed in to make certain that the new agency's workers had civil service and union protections.

Judicial Power. The presidential power to grant reprieves, pardons, and amnesties as well as to "commute" or reduce the severity of sentences, literally gives the president the power of life and death over individuals. Presidents may use this power on behalf of a particular individual, as did Gerald Ford when he pardoned Richard Nixon in 1974 "for all offenses against the United States which he . . . has committed or may have committed." Similarly, in 2007, President Bush commuted the sentence handed down to Lewis "Scooter" Libby, one of Vice President Cheney's top aides. Libby had been found guilty of perjury and obstruction of justice and was sentenced to several years in prison as well as ordered to pay a steep fine. President Bush declared that Libby would not go to prison, though he would still have to pay the fine.

Diplomatic Power. The president is America's "head of state"—its chief representative in dealings with other nations. As head of state, the president has the power to make treaties for the United States (with the advice and consent of the Senate). When President George Washington received Edmond Genêt ("Citizen Genêt") as the formal emissary of the revolutionary government of France in 1793, he transformed the power to "receive Ambassadors and other public Ministers" into the power to "recognize" other countries. That power gives the president the almost unconditional authority to review the claims of any new ruling groups to determine whether they indeed control the territory and population of their country, so that they can commit it to treaties and other agreements.

In recent years, presidents have expanded the practice of using executive agreements to conduct foreign policy.[8] An **executive agreement** is like a treaty because it is a contract between two countries, but an executive agreement does not require a two-thirds vote of approval by the Senate (a treaty does require this approval). Ordinarily, executive agreements are used to carry out commitments already made in treaties, or to arrange for matters well below the level of policy. But when presidents have found it expedient to use an executive agreement in place of a treaty, Congress has typically acquiesced.

executive agreement An agreement between the president and another country, which has the force of a treaty but does not require the Senate's "advice and consent."

Executive Power. The most important basis of the president's power as chief executive is to be found in the sections of Article II that stipulate that the president must see that all the laws are faithfully executed and that provide that the president will appoint all executive officers and all federal judges. In this manner, the Constitution focuses executive power and legal responsibility upon the president. The

---

[8] In *United States v. Pink*, 315 U.S. 203 (1942), the Supreme Court confirmed that an executive agreement is the legal equivalent of a treaty, despite the absence of Senate approval.

famous sign on President Truman's desk, "The buck stops here," was not merely an assertion of Truman's personal sense of responsibility. It acknowledged his acceptance of the constitutional imposition of that responsibility upon the president. The president is subject to some limitations, because the appointment of all the top officers, including ambassadors and ministers and federal judges, is subject to a majority approval by the Senate. But these appointments are at the discretion of the president.

executive privilege The claim that confidential communications between a president and close advisers should not be revealed without the consent of the president.

Another component of the president's power as chief executive is **executive privilege**, which is the claim that confidential communications between a president and close advisers should not be revealed without the consent of the president. Presidents have made this claim ever since George Washington refused a request from the House of Representatives to deliver documents concerning negotiations of an important treaty. Washington refused (successfully) on the grounds that, first, the House was not constitutionally part of the treaty-making process, and, second, that diplomatic negotiations required secrecy.

Executive privilege became a popular part of the "checks and balances" between president and Congress, and presidents have usually had the upper hand when invoking it. Although many presidents have claimed executive privilege, the concept was not tested in the courts until the 1971 Watergate affair, during which President Nixon refused congressional demands that he turn over secret White House tapes that congressional investigators thought would establish Nixon's complicity in illegal activities. In *United States v. Nixon*, the Supreme Court ordered Nixon to turn over the tapes.[9] The president complied with the order and was forced to resign from office. *United States v. Nixon* is often seen as a blow to presidential power, but in actuality the Court's ruling recognized for the first time the validity of a claim of executive privilege, although holding that it did not apply in this instance. Subsequent presidents have cited *United States v. Nixon* in support of their claims of executive privilege. For example, the administration of George W. Bush invoked executive privilege when it refused to give Congress documents relating to the president's decision to make use of warrantless wiretaps and the so-called CIA leak case, in which the identity of a CIA operative was revealed after her husband criticized the administration. The Bush administration also invoked executive privilege when it refused to obey congressional subpoenas demanding materials pertaining to the firing of a number of assistant U.S. attorneys. The exercise of presidential power through the executive-privilege doctrine has been all the more frequent in the past twenty years, when we have been living nearly 90 percent of the time under conditions of "divided government"; that is, the party that is not in control of the White House is in control of one or both chambers of Congress.[10]

The President's Legislative Power.   The president plays a role not only in the administration of government but also in the legislative process. Two constitutional

---

[9] *United States v. Nixon*, 418 U.S. 683 (1974).

[10] A recent extension of executive power by President George W. Bush is the "signing statement," which is discussed later in this chapter.

provisions are the primary sources of the president's power in the legislative arena. Article II, Section 3, provides that the president "shall from time to time give to the Congress Information of the State of the Union, and recommend to their Consideration such Measures as he shall judge necessary and expedient." This first legislative power has been important especially since Franklin Delano Roosevelt began to use the provision to initiate proposals for legislative action in Congress. Roosevelt established the presidency as the primary initiator of legislation.

The second of the president's legislative powers is the "**veto** power" assigned by Article I, Section 7. The veto power is the president's constitutional power to turn down acts of Congress. This power alone makes the president the most important single legislative leader. No bill vetoed by the president can become law unless both the House and the Senate override the veto by a two-thirds vote. In the case of a **pocket veto**, Congress does not even have the option of overriding the veto, but must reintroduce the bill in the next session. The president may exercise a pocket veto when presented with a bill during the last ten days of a legislative session. Usually, if a president does not sign a bill within ten days, it automatically becomes law. But this is true only while Congress is in session. If a president chooses not to sign a bill within the last ten days that Congress is in session, then the ten-day limit does not expire until Congress is out of session, and instead of becoming law, the bill is vetoed. Figure 6.1 illustrates the president's veto option. In 1996, a new power was added—the **line-item veto**—giving the president power to strike specific spending items from appropriations bills passed by Congress, unless reenacted by a two-thirds vote of both the House and Senate. In 1997, President Clinton used this power eleven times to strike eighty-two items from the federal budget. But, as we saw in Chapter 5, in 1998 the Supreme Court ruled that the Constitution does not authorize the line-item veto power.[11] Only a constitutional amendment would restore this power to the president.

The Games Presidents Play: The Veto.

Use of the veto varies according to the political situation that each president confronts. George W. Bush vetoed no bill during his first term, a period in which his party controlled both houses of Congress. After the Democrats won control of Congress in 2006, Bush's use of the veto increased markedly. In general, presidents have used the veto to equalize or perhaps upset the balance of power with Congress. Although the simple power to reject or accept legislation in its entirety might seem like a crude tool for making sure that legislation adheres to a president's preferences, the politics surrounding the veto is complicated, and it is rare that vetoes are used simply as bullets to kill legislation. Instead, vetoes are usually part of an intricate bargaining process between the president and Congress, involving threats of vetoes, repassing legislation, re-vetoes.[12]

veto The president's constitutional power to turn down acts of Congress. A presidential veto may be overridden by a two-thirds vote of each house of Congress.

pocket veto A presidential veto of legislation wherein the president takes no formal action on a bill. If Congress adjourns within ten days of passing a bill, and the president does not sign it, the bill is considered to be vetoed.

line-item veto Power that allows a governor (or the president) to strike out specific provisions (lines) of bills that the legislature passes. Without a line-item veto, the governor (or president) must accept or reject an entire bill. The line-item veto is no longer in effect for the president.

---

[11] *Clinton v. City of New York*, 524 U.S. 417 (1998).

[12] Charles M. Cameron, *Veto Bargaining: Presidents and the Politics of Negative Power* (New York: Cambridge University Press, 2000). See also David W. Rohde and Dennis Simon, "Presidential Vetoes and Congressional Response: A Study of Institutional Conflict," *American Journal of Political Science* 29 (1985): 397–427.

FIGURE 6.1 THE VETO PROCESS

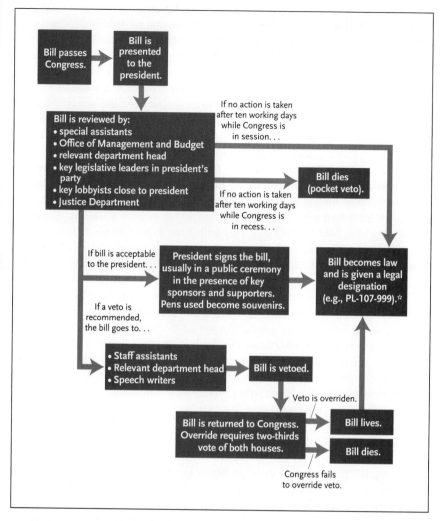

*PL stands for "public law"; 107 is the Congress (e.g., the 107th Congress was in session in 2001–2); 999 is the number of the law.

Although presidents rarely veto legislation, this does not mean vetoes and veto bargaining have an insignificant influence over the policy process. The fact that presidents vetoed only 434 of the 17,000 public bills that Congress sent to them between 1945 and 1992 belies the centrality of the veto to presidential power. Many of these bills were insignificant and not worth the veto effort. Thus it is important to separate "significant" legislation, against which vetoes frequently occur, from insignificant legislation.[13] Vetoes can also be effective—even though they are rarely

---

[13] David R. Mayhew, *Divided We Govern: Party Control, Lawmaking, and Investigations, 1946–1990* (New Haven, Conn.: Yale University Press, 1991).

employed because the threat of a veto may be sufficient. This means that members of Congress will alter the content of a bill to make it more to a president's liking to preempt a veto. Thus the veto power can be influential even when the veto pen rests in its inkwell, particularly when it comes to the content of legislation. The "Analyzing the Evidence" unit on the following pages takes a closer look at veto politics.

What about the relationship between mass public support for the president and the use of the veto? At least for the modern presidency, a crucial resource for the president in negotiating with Congress has been his public approval as measured by opinion polls.[14] In some situations, members of Congress pass a bill not because they want to change policy but because they want to force the president to veto a popular bill that he disagrees with in order to hurt his approval ratings.[15] The key is that the public, uncertain of the president's policy preferences, uses information conveyed by vetoes to reassess what it knows about his preferences. As a result, vetoes may come at a price to the president.

Legislative Initiative. Although this power is not explicitly stated, the Constitution provides the president with the power of **legislative initiative.** To initiate means to originate, and in government that can mean power. The framers of the Constitution clearly saw legislative initiative as one of the keys to executive power. Initiative obviously implies the ability to formulate proposals for important policies, and the president, as an individual with a great deal of staff assistance, is able to initiate decisive action more frequently than Congress, with its large assemblies that have to deliberate and debate before taking action. With some important exceptions, Congress banks on the president to set the agenda of public policy. And quite clearly, there is power in initiative; there is power in being able to set the terms of discourse in the making of public policy.

For example, during the weeks immediately following September 11, 2001, George W. Bush took many presidential initiatives to Congress, and each was given almost unanimous support—from commitments to pursue Al Qaeda to the removal of the Taliban, the reconstitution of the Afghanistan regime, all the way to almost unlimited approval for mobilization of both military power and power over the regulation of American civil liberties. Bush's second term, however, was difficult. Growing problems (and casualties) in Iraq, administrative scandals, and a financial crisis plagued Bush. As presidential popularity ebbed in the polls, so too did Bush's agenda power. In 2009, President Obama presented Congress with major health care and energy programs, hoping to seize the initiative before his opponents had an opportunity to mobilize their own forces.

The president's initiative does not end with policy making involving Congress and the making of laws in the ordinary sense of the phrase. The president has still another legislative role (in all but name) within the executive branch. This is

legislative initiative The president's inherent power to bring a legislative agenda before Congress.

---

[14] Theodore J. Lowi, *The Personal President: Power Invested, Promise Unfulfilled* (Ithaca, N.Y.: Cornell University Press, 1985).

[15] Timothy Groseclose and Nolan McCarty, "The Politics of Blame: Bargaining before an Audience," *American Journal of Political Science* 45 (2001): 100–19.

Veto Politics

Although vetoes are relatively rare in the legislative process, scholars are drawn to study them because vetoes carry clear policy implications. Indeed, a president's use of the veto is an ideal example of negative agenda control—it creates an opportunity to block legislative action, but does not give the executive the power to alter proposed legislation after the fact. Nonetheless, chief executives regularly use the threat of a veto in their attempts to shape legislative outcomes.[1] In many cases, a credible veto threat may be sufficient to force compliance on the part of reluctant legislators who would like to avoid a prolonged legislative battle over a controversial bill or resolution, especially near the end of a legislative session. Instead of "losing" to the president, one or both chambers of the legislature may be willing to make concessions if the price of passage necessitates it.

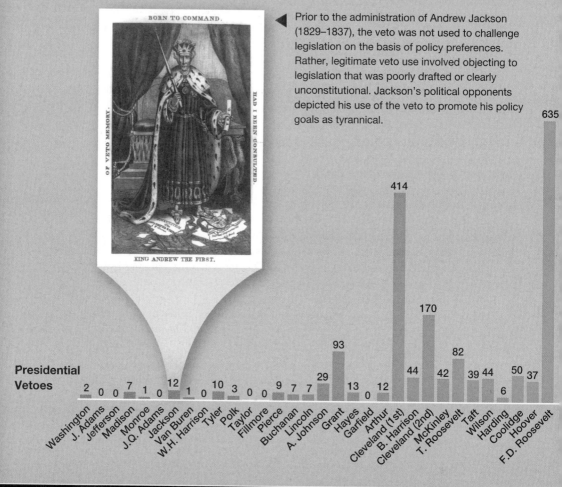

Prior to the administration of Andrew Jackson (1829–1837), the veto was not used to challenge legislation on the basis of policy preferences. Rather, legitimate veto use involved objecting to legislation that was poorly drafted or clearly unconstitutional. Jackson's political opponents depicted his use of the veto to promote his policy goals as tyrannical.

Presidential Vetoes

President	Vetoes
Washington	2
J. Adams	0
Jefferson	0
Madison	7
Monroe	1
J.Q. Adams	0
Jackson	12
Van Buren	1
W.H. Harrison	0
Tyler	10
Polk	3
Taylor	0
Fillmore	0
Pierce	9
Buchanan	7
Lincoln	7
A. Johnson	29
Grant	93
Hayes	13
Garfield	0
Arthur	12
Cleveland (1st)	414
B. Harrison	44
Cleveland (2nd)	170
McKinley	42
T. Roosevelt	82
Taft	39
Wilson	44
Harding	6
Coolidge	50
Hoover	37
F.D. Roosevelt	635

Veto power is by no means absolute. Consistent with the Madisonian notion of checks and balances, the legislature has the opportunity to override a veto if legislators can muster the necessary votes. In the U.S. Congress, two-thirds of both chambers must successfully vote to override a presidential veto. Although many override attempts fail as a result of this supermajority requirement, the risk of a successful override attempt provides an important check on executive power.[2]

PRESIDENTIAL VETOES AND CONGRESSIONAL OVERRIDES, 1945–2009

	Years in Office	Vetoes	Divided Government	Override Attempts		Successes	
Truman	1945–1953	250	1947–1949	22	8.8%	12	54.5%
Eisenhower	1953–1961	181	1955–1961	11	6.1%	2	18.2%
Kennedy	1961–1963	21		0	0.0%	0	0.0%
Johnson	1963–1969	30		0	0.0%	0	0.0%
Nixon	1969–1974	43	1969–1974	21	48.8%	7	33.3%
Ford	1974–1977	66	1974–1977	28	42.4%	12	42.9%
Carter	1977–1981	31		4	12.9%	2	50.0%
Reagan	1981–1989	78	1981–1989	15	19.2%	9	60.0%
G. H. W. Bush	1989–1993	44	1989–1993	21	47.7%	1	4.8%
Clinton	1993–2001	37	1995–2001	11	29.7%	2	5.4%
G. W. Bush	2001–2009	12	2007–2009	6	50.0%	4	33.3%

Sources: "Congressional Bills Vetoed: 1789–2001." Contributed by John P. McIver. *Historical Statistics of the United States,* Millennial Edition On Line, edited by Susan B. Carter, Scott S. Gartner, Michael R. Haines, Alan L. Olmstead, Richard Sutch, and Gavin Wright. © Cambridge University Press, 2006; calculated by author.

Veto override attempts and successes are more likely to occur under divided government than unified government, which is most likely a function of divergent preferences across the institutions. Note that few or no overrides were attempted during presidencies that enjoyed unified government, with the president's party controlling at least one chamber of Congress.

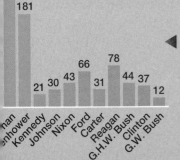

Since Jackson left office in 1837, presidents have routinely vetoed legislation for political reasons. During the twentieth century, for instance, the incidence of presidential vetoes was almost always greater under divided government, in which the executive is controlled by one political party and at least one chamber of Congress by the other.

[1]Charles M. Cameron, *Veto Bargaining: Presidents and the Politics of Negative Power* (New York: Cambridge University Press, 2000).
[2]David W. Rohde and Dennis M. Simon, "Presidential Vetoes and Congressional Response: A Study of Institutional Conflict," *American Journal of Political Science* 29 (1985): 397–427.

executive order
A rule or regulation
issued by the presi-
dent that has the
effect and formal
status of legislation.

designated as the power to issue **executive orders**. The executive order is first and foremost simply a management tool, a power possessed by virtually any CEO to make "company policy"—rules setting procedures, etiquette, chains of command, functional responsibilities, and so on. But evolving out of this normal management practice is a recognized presidential power to promulgate rules that have the effect and the formal status of legislation. Most of the executive orders of the president provide for the reorganization of structures and procedures or otherwise direct the affairs of the executive branch—either to be applied across the board to all agencies or applied in some important respect to a single agency or department. The power to issue executive orders illustrates that although reputation and persuasion are typically required in presidential policy making, the practice of issuing executive orders, within limits, allows a president to govern without the necessity to persuade.[16]

THE RISE OF PRESIDENTIAL GOVERNMENT

Most of the real influence of the modern presidency derives from the powers granted by the Constitution and the laws made by Congress. Presidential power is institutional. Thus, any person properly elected and sworn in as president will possess all of the power held by the strongest presidents in American history. But what variables account for a president's success in exercising these powers? Why are some presidents considered to be great successes and others colossal failures? The answer relates broadly to the very concept of presidential power. Is that power a reflection of the attributes of the person or is it more characteristic of the political situations that a president encounters?

The personal view of presidential power dominated political scientists' view for several decades,[17] but recent scholars have argued that presidential power should be analyzed in terms of the strategic interactions that a president has with other political actors. The veto, which we reviewed in the last section, is one example of this sort of strategic interaction, but there are many other "games" that presidents play: the Supreme-Court-nomination and treaty-ratification games with the Senate, the executive-order game, the agency-supervision-and-management game with the executive branch. As the political scientist Charles M. Cameron has argued, "Understanding the presidency means understanding these games."[18] Success in these "games" translates into presidential power. With the occasional exception, however,

---

[16] This point is developed in both Kenneth R. Mayer, *With the Stroke of a Pen: Executive Orders and Presidential Power* (Princeton, N.J.: Princeton University Press, 2001), and William G. Howell, *Power without Persuasion: The Politics of Direct Presidential Action* (Princeton, N.J.: Princeton University Press, 2003).

[17] Richard Neustadt, *Presidential Power: The Politics of Leadership* (New York: Wiley, 1960).

[18] Charles M. Cameron, "Bargaining and Presidential Power," in *Presidential Power: Forging the Presidency for the Twenty-first Century*, Robert Y. Shapiro, Martha Joynt Kumar, and Lawrence R. Jacobs, eds. (New York: Columbia University Press, 2000), p. 47.

it took more than a century, perhaps as much as a century and a half, before presidents came to be seen as consequential players in these strategic encounters. A bit of historical review will be helpful in understanding how the presidency has risen to its current level of influence.

The Legislative Epoch, 1800–1933

In 1885, a then-obscure political science professor named Woodrow Wilson entitled his general textbook *Congressional Government* because American government was just that, "congressional government." The clear intent of the framers of the Constitution was for legislative supremacy. The strongest evidence of this original intent is the fact that the powers of the national government were listed in Article I, the legislative article. Madison had laid it out explicitly in *The Federalist*, No. 51: "In republican government, the legislative authority necessarily predominates."[19]

By the second term of President Jefferson (1805–9), the executive branch was beginning to play the secondary role anticipated by the Constitution. The quality of presidential performance and then of presidential personality and character declined accordingly. The president was seen by some observers as little more than America's "chief clerk." It was said of President James Madison, who had been the principal author of the Constitution, that he knew everything about government except how to govern. Indeed, after Jefferson and until the beginning of the twentieth century, most historians agree that presidents Jackson and Lincoln were the only exceptions to what was the rule of weak presidents.

One reason that so few great men became presidents in the nineteenth century is that there was only occasional room for greatness in such a weak office.[20] As Chapter 3 indicated, the national government of that period was not particularly powerful. Another reason is that during this period, the presidency was not closely linked to major national political and social forces. Federalism had taken very good care of ensuring this by fragmenting political interests and diverting the energies of interest groups toward state and local governments, where most key decisions were being made.

---

[19] The Library of Congress believes that *Federalist* No. 51 could have been written by Hamilton or by Madison, and it is true that the authorship of certain of the *Federalist Papers* is still in dispute. But we insist on Madison's authorship of *Federalist* No. 51 for two important reasons: First, the style of the essay and the political theory underlying the essay are, to us, clearly Madisonian. Second, Madison's authorship of *Federalist* No. 51 seems to be the consensus among academic political scientists and historians, and we find our strongest support in three of the most esteemed and admirable students of the Founding: the historian Forrest McDonald, *Novus Ordo Seclorum—The Intellectual Origins of the Constitution* (Lawrence: University Press of Kansas, 1985), p. 258; the political theorist Isaac Kramnick in his edition of *The Federalist Papers* (New York: Viking Penguin, 1987), Editor's Introduction, especially p. 53; and the late Clinton Rossiter, *The Federalist Papers* (New York: New American Library, 1961), pp. xiii–xiv.

[20] For related appraisals, see Jeffrey Tulis, *The Rhetorical Presidency* (Princeton, N.J.: Princeton University Press, 1988); Stephen Skowronek, *The Politics Presidents Make: Presidential Leadership from John Adams to George Bush* (Cambridge, Mass.: Harvard University Press, 1993); and Robert Spitzer, *President and Congress: Executive Hegemony at the Crossroads of American Government* (New York: McGraw-Hill, 1993).

The presidency was strengthened somewhat in the 1830s with the introduction of the national convention system of nominating presidential candidates. Until then, presidential candidates had been nominated by their party's congressional delegates. This was the caucus system of nominating candidates, and it was derisively called "King Caucus" because any candidate for president had to defer to the party's leaders in Congress in order to get the party's nomination and the support of the party's congressional delegation in the election. The national nominating convention arose outside Congress in order to provide some representation for a party's voters who lived in districts where they weren't numerous enough to elect a member of Congress. The political party in each state made its own provisions for selecting delegates to attend the presidential nominating convention, and in virtually all states, the selection was dominated by the party leaders (called "bosses" by the opposition party). Only in recent decades have state laws intervened to regularize the selection process and provide (in all but a few instances) for open election of delegates.

In the nineteenth century, the national nominating convention was seen as a victory for democracy against the congressional elite. And the national convention gave the presidency a base of power independent of Congress. Eventually, though more slowly, the presidential selection process began to be democratized further, with the adoption of primary elections through which millions of ordinary citizens were given an opportunity to take part in the presidential nominating process by popular selection of convention delegates.

This independence did not immediately transform the presidency into the office we recognize today, because Congress was able to keep tight reins on the president's power. The real turning point came during the administration of Franklin Delano Roosevelt. The New Deal was a response to political forces that had been gathering national strength and focus for fifty years. What is remarkable is not that they gathered but that they were so long in gaining influence in Washington.

The New Deal and the Presidency

The "first hundred days" of the Roosevelt administration in 1933 have no parallel in U.S. history. But this period was only the beginning. The policies proposed by President Roosevelt and adopted by Congress during the first thousand days of his administration so changed the size and character of the national government that they constitute a moment in American history equivalent to the Founding or to the Civil War. The president's constitutional obligation to see "that the laws be faithfully executed" became, during Roosevelt's presidency, virtually a responsibility to shape the laws before executing them.

New Programs Expand the Role of National Government.   Many of the New Deal programs were extensions of the traditional national government approach, which was described in Chapter 3 (see especially Table 3.1, page 54). But the New Deal also adopted policies never before tried on a large scale by the national government. It began intervening into economic life in ways that had hitherto been reserved to the states. In other words, the national government discovered that it, too, had "police power" and that it could directly regulate individuals as well as provide roads and other services.

The new programs were such dramatic departures from the traditional policies of the national government that their constitutionality was in doubt. The turning point came in 1937 with *National Labor Relations Board v. Jones & Laughlin Steel Corporation.* At issue was the National Labor Relations Act, or Wagner Act, which prohibited corporations from interfering with the efforts of employees to engage in union activities. The newly formed National Labor Relations Board (NLRB) had ordered Jones & Laughlin to reinstate workers fired because of their union activities. The appeal reached the Supreme Court because Jones & Laughlin had made a constitutional issue over the fact that its manufacturing activities were local and therefore beyond the national government's reach. The Supreme Court rejected this argument with the response that a big company with subsidiaries and suppliers in many states was innately involved in interstate commerce.[21] Since the end of the New Deal, the Supreme Court has never again seriously questioned the constitutionality of an important act of Congress broadly authorizing the executive branch to intervene into the economy or society.[22]

Delegation of Power.   The most important constitutional effect of Congress's actions and the Supreme Court's approval of those actions during the New Deal was the enhancement of presidential power. Most major acts of Congress in this period involved significant exercises of control over the economy. But few programs specified the actual controls to be used. Instead, Congress authorized the president or, in some cases, a new agency to determine what the controls would be. Some of the new agencies were independent commissions responsible to Congress. But most of the new agencies and programs of the New Deal were placed in the executive branch directly under presidential authority.

This form of congressional act is called the "delegation of power." In theory, the delegation of power works as follows: (1) Congress recognizes a problem; (2) Congress acknowledges that it has neither the time nor the expertise to deal with the problem; and (3) Congress therefore sets the basic policies and then delegates to an agency the power to "fill in the details." But in practice, Congress was

---

[21] *NLRB v. Jones & Laughlin Steel Corporation,* 301 U.S. 1 (1937). Congress had attempted to regulate the economy before 1933, with the Interstate Commerce Act and Sherman Antitrust Act of the late nineteenth century and with the Federal Trade Act and the Federal Reserve in the Wilson period. But these were rare attempts, and each was restricted very carefully to a narrow and acceptable definition of "interstate commerce." The big break did not come until after 1933.

[22] Some will argue that there are some exceptions to this statement. One was the 1976 case declaring unconstitutional Congress's effort to supply national minimum wage standards to state and local government employees (*National League of Cities v. Usery,* 426 U.S. 833 [1976]). But the Court reversed itself on this nine years later, in 1985 (*Garcia v. San Antonio Metropolitan Transit Authority,* 469 U.S. 528 [1985]). Another was the 1986 case declaring unconstitutional the part of the Gramm-Rudman law authorizing the comptroller general to make "across the board" budget cuts when total appropriations exceeded legally established ceilings (*Bowsher v. Synar,* 478 U.S. 714 [1986]). In 1999, executive authority was compromised somewhat by the Court's decision to question the Federal Communication Commission's authority to supervise telephone deregulation under the Telecommunications Act of 1996. But cases such as these are rare, and they touch on only part of a law, not the constitutionality of an entire program.

delegating not merely the power to "fill in the details," but actual and real policy-making powers—that is, real legislative powers—to the executive branch.

No modern government can avoid the delegation of significant legislative powers to the executive branch. But the fact remains that these delegations of power cumulatively produced a fundamental shift in the American constitutional framework. During the 1930s, the growth of the national government through acts delegating legislative power tilted the American national structure away from a Congress-centered government toward a president-centered government. Congress continues to be the constitutional source of policy, and Congress can rescind these delegations of power or restrict them with later amendments, committee oversight, or budget costs. But since Congress has continued to enact large new programs involving very broad delegations of legislative power to the executive branch, and since the Court has gone along with such actions,[23] we can say that presidential government has become an established fact of American life.

PRESIDENTIAL GOVERNMENT

There was no great mystery in the shift from Congress-centered government to president-centered government. Congress simply delegated its own powers to the executive branch. Congressional delegations of power, however, are not the only resources available to the president. Presidents have at their disposal a variety of other formal and informal resources that enable them to govern. Indeed, without these other resources, presidents would lack the tools needed to make much use of the power and responsibility given to them by Congress. Let us first consider the president's formal or official resources (see Figure 6.2). Then, in the section following, we will turn to the more informal resources that affect a president's capacity to govern, in particular the president's popular support.

Formal Resources of Presidential Power

The Cabinet. In the American system of government, the **Cabinet** is the traditional but informal designation for the heads of all the major federal government departments. The Cabinet has no constitutional status. Unlike that of England and many other parliamentary countries, where the cabinet *is* the government, the American Cabinet is not a collective body. It meets but makes no decisions as a group. Each appointment must be approved by the Senate, but the person

---

[23] The Supreme Court did in fact *dis*approve broad delegations of legislative power by declaring the National Industrial Recovery Act of 1933 unconstitutional on the grounds that Congress did not accompany the broad delegations with sufficient standards or guidelines for presidential discretion (*Panama Refining Co. v. Ryan*, 293 U.S. 388 [1935], and *Schechter Poultry Corp. v. U.S.*, 295 U.S. 495 [1935]). The Supreme Court has never reversed those two decisions, but it has also never really followed them. Thus, broad delegations of legislative power from Congress to the executive branch can be presumed to be constitutional.

FIGURE 6.2 THE INSTITUTIONAL PRESIDENCY, 2009

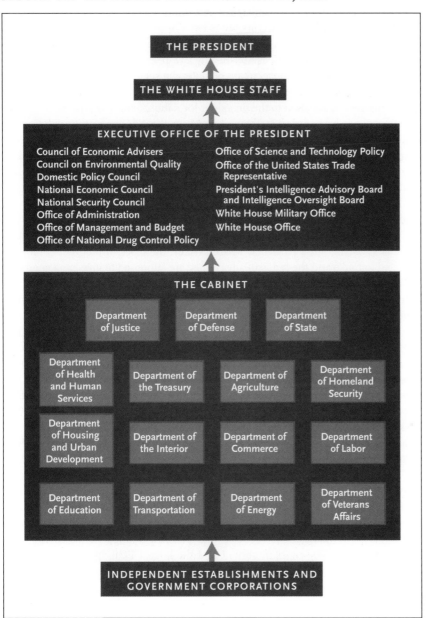

NOTE: Arrows are used to indicate lines of legal responsibility.

appointed is not responsible to the Senate or to Congress at large. Cabinet appointments help build party and popular support, but the Cabinet is not a party organ. The cabinet is made up of directors but is not a board of directors.

National Security Council (NSC) A presidential foreign policy advisory council composed of the president; the vice president; the secretary of state; the secretary of defense; and other officials invited by the president. The NSC has a staff of foreign policy specialists.

Some presidents have relied heavily on an "inner cabinet," the **National Security Council (NSC).** The NSC, established by law in 1947, is composed of the president; the vice president; the secretary of state; the secretary of defense; and other officials invited by the president. It has its own staff of foreign-policy specialists run by the special assistant to the president for national security affairs.

Presidents have varied in their reliance on the NSC and other sub-Cabinet bodies, because executive management is inherently a personal matter. However, despite all the personal variations, one generalization can be made: Presidents have increasingly preferred the White House staff to the Cabinet as their means of managing the gigantic executive branch.

The White House Staff.   The White House staff is composed mainly of analysts and advisers. Although many of the top White House staffers are given the title "special assistant" for a particular task or sector, the types of judgments they are expected to make and the kinds of advice they are supposed to give are a good deal broader and more generally political than those that come from the Cabinet departments or the Executive Office of the President. The White House staff has grown substantially under recent presidents (see Table 6.1).[24]

The White House staff is a crucial information source and management tool for the president. But it may also insulate the president from other sources of information. Managing this trade-off between in-house expertise and access to independent outside opinion is a major challenge for the president. Sometimes it is botched, as when President George W. Bush depended too heavily on his staff for information about WMDs in Iraq, leading him to erroneous conclusions. In 2009, President Obama merged the White House Homeland Security staff with the National Security Council staff to create a new National Security staff to deal with all security problems.[25]

The Executive Office of the President.   The development of the White House staff can be appreciated only in relation to the still larger Executive Office of the President (EOP). Created in 1939, the EOP is what is often called the "institutional presidency"—the permanent agencies that perform defined management tasks for the president. The most important and the largest EOP agency is the Office of Management and Budget (OMB). Its roles in preparing the national budget,

---

[24] All the figures since 1967, and probably 1957, are understated; additional White House staff members who were on "detailed" service from the military and other departments are not counted here because they were not on the White House payroll.

[25] See George Krause, "The Secular Decline in Presidential Domestic Policymaking: An Organizational Perspective," *Presidential Studies Quarterly* 34 (2004): 779–92. On the general issue, see James P. Pfiffner, ed., *The Managerial Presidency*, 2nd ed. (College Station: Texas A&M University Press, 1999).

TABLE 6.1 THE EXPANDING WHITE HOUSE STAFF

Year	President	Full-time Employees	Year	President	Full-time Employees*
1937	Franklin D. Roosevelt	45	1980	Jimmy Carter	488
1947	Harry S. Truman	190	1984	Ronald Reagan	575
1957	Dwight D. Eisenhower	364	1992	George H. W. Bush	605
1967	Lyndon B. Johnson	251	1996	Bill Clinton	511
1972	Richard M. Nixon	550	2001	George W. Bush	507
1975	Gerald R. Ford	533	2009	Barack Obama	487

*The vice president employs over twenty staffers, and there are at least one hundred on the staff of the National Security Council. These people work in and around the White House and Executive Office but are not included in the preceding totals.

SOURCES: U.S. Office of Personnel Management, *Federal Civilian Workforce Statistics, Employment and Trends as of January 1990* (Washington, D.C.: Government Printing Office, 1990), p. 29. For 1992, 1996, 2001, and 2009: OMB and the White House.

designing the president's program, reporting on agency activities, and overseeing regulatory proposals make OMB personnel part of virtually every conceivable presidential responsibility. The status and power of the OMB within the EOP has grown in importance from president to president.

The process of budgeting was at one time a bottom-up procedure, with expenditure and program requests passing from the lowest bureaus through the departments to "clearance" in OMB and hence to Congress, where each agency could be called in to reveal what its original request had been before OMB got hold of it. Now the process is top-down, with OMB setting the budget guidelines for agencies as well as for Congress.

The Vice Presidency. The Constitution created the vice presidency along with the presidency, and the office exists for two purposes only: to succeed the president in the case of a vacancy[26] and to preside over the Senate, casting the tie-breaking

---

[26]This provision was clarified by the Twenty-fifth Amendment (1967), which provides that the president (with majority confirmation of House and Senate) must appoint someone to fill the office of vice president if the vice president should die or should fill a vacancy in the presidency. This procedure has been invoked twice—once in 1973 when President Nixon nominated Gerald Ford, and the second time in 1974 when President Ford, having automatically succeeded the resigned President Nixon, filled the vice presidential vacancy with Nelson Rockefeller.

vote when necessary.[27] The main value of the vice presidency as a political resource for the president is electoral. Traditionally, a presidential candidate's most important rule for the choice of a running mate is that he or she bring the support of at least one state (preferably a large one) not otherwise likely to support the ticket. Another rule holds that the vice-presidential nominee should come from a region and, where possible, from an ideological or ethnic subsection of the party differing from the presidential nominee's. It is very doubtful that John Kennedy would have won in 1960 without his vice-presidential candidate, Lyndon Johnson, and the contribution Johnson made to carrying Texas. The emphasis has recently shifted away from geographical to ideological balance. George W. Bush's choice of Dick Cheney in 2000 was completely devoid of direct electoral value since Cheney came from one of our least populous states (Wyoming, which casts only three electoral votes). But given Cheney's stalwart right-wing record both in Congress and as President George H. W. Bush's secretary of defense, his inclusion on the Republican ticket was clearly an effort to consolidate the support of the restive right wing of his party. In 2008, the Republican candidate, John McCain, chose Alaska's governor, Sarah Palin, as his running mate. Palin had no national visibility or experience but was well liked on the Republican right for her conservative views. Many conservative Republicans thought McCain was too liberal and had been threatening to sit out the election. Palin ignited their enthusiasm. At the same time, the Democratic candidate, Barack Obama, chose Senator Joseph Biden of Delaware as his vice-presidential running mate. Obama had often been criticized for lacking background in the realm of foreign policy. Biden, the chair of the Senate Foreign Relations Committee, brought considerable foreign-policy experience to the ticket.

As the institutional presidency has grown in size and complexity, most presidents of the past twenty-five years have sought to use their vice presidents as a management resource after the election. George H. W. Bush, as vice president, was "kept within the loop" of decision making because President Reagan delegated so much power. A copy of virtually every document made for Reagan was made for Bush, especially during the first term, when Bush's close friend James Baker was chief of staff. Former President Bush did not take such pains to keep Dan Quayle "in the loop," but President Clinton relied greatly on his vice president, Al Gore, who emerged as one of the most trusted and effective figures in the Clinton White House. Gore's most important task was to oversee the National Performance Review (NPR), an ambitious program to "reinvent" the way the federal government conducts its affairs. The presidency of George W. Bush resulted in unprecedented power and responsibility for his vice president, Dick Cheney.

The Contemporary Bases of Presidential Power

Generally, presidents can expand their power in three ways: party, popular mobilization, and administration. In the first instance, presidents may construct or strengthen national partisan institutions with which to exert influence in the

---

[27] Article I, Section 3, provides that the vice president "shall be President of the Senate, but shall have no Vote, unless they be equally divided."

legislative process and through which to implement their programs. Alternatively, or in addition to the first tactic, presidents may use popular appeals to create a mass base of support that will allow them to subordinate their political foes. This tactic has sometimes been called the strategy of "going public" or the "rhetorical" presidency.[28] Third, presidents may seek to bolster their control of established executive agencies or to create new administrative institutions and procedures that will reduce their dependence on Congress and give them a more independent governing and policy-making capability. Presidents' use of executive orders to achieve their policy goals in lieu of seeking to persuade Congress to enact legislation is, perhaps, the most obvious example.

Party as a Source of Power.   All presidents have relied on the members and leaders of their own party to implement their legislative agendas. President George W. Bush, for example, worked closely with congressional GOP leaders on such matters as energy policy and Medicare reform and President Obama depended on Democratic leaders to secure enactment of his budget and his health care and energy proposals. But the president does not control his own party; party members have considerable autonomy. Moreover, in America's system of separated powers, the president's party may be in the minority in Congress and unable to do much for the chief executive's programs (Figure 6.3). Consequently, although their party is valuable to chief executives, it has not been a fully reliable presidential tool. The more unified the president's party is behind his legislative requests, the more unified the opposition party is also likely to be. Unless the president's party majority is very large, he must also appeal to the opposition to make up for the inevitable defectors within the ranks of his own party. Thus the president often poses as being above partisanship to win "bipartisan" support in Congress. But to the extent that he pursues a bipartisan strategy, he cannot throw himself fully into building the party loyalty and the party discipline that would maximize the value of his own party's support in Congress. This is a dilemma for every president, particularly one faced with an opposition-controlled Congress.

Going Public.   Popular mobilization as a technique of presidential power has its historical roots in the presidencies of Theodore Roosevelt and Woodrow Wilson and has, subsequently, became a weapon in the political arsenals of most presidents since the mid-twentieth century. During the nineteenth century, it was considered inappropriate for presidents to engage in personal campaigning on their own behalf or in support of programs and policies. When Andrew Johnson broke this unwritten rule and made a series of speeches vehemently seeking public support for his Reconstruction program, even some of Johnson's most ardent supporters were shocked at what they saw as his lack of decorum.

The president who used public appeals most effectively was Franklin D. Roosevelt. The political scientist Sidney Milkis observes that FDR was "firmly

---

[28] Samuel Kernell, *Going Public: New Strategies of Presidential Leadership*, 3rd ed. (Washington, D.C.: Congressional Quarterly Press, 1997); also Jeffrey Tulis, *The Rhetorical Presidency* (Princeton, N.J.: Princeton University Press, 1987).

FIGURE 6.3 THE PRESIDENTIAL BATTING AVERAGE: PRESIDENTIAL SUCCESS ON CONGRESSIONAL VOTES, 1953–2008

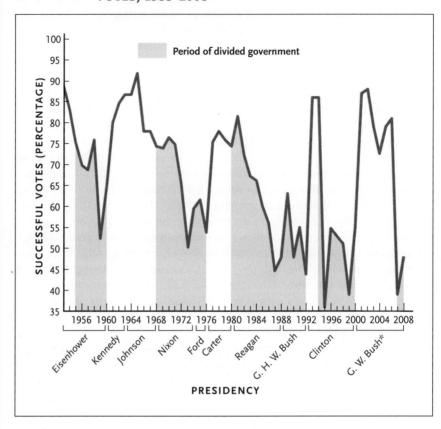

*In 2001, the government was divided for only part of the year.

NOTE: Percentages are based on votes on which presidents took a position.

SOURCE: *Congressional Quarterly Weekly Report,* January 3, 2004, p. 18; and authors' update.

persuaded of the need to form a direct link between the executive office and the public."[29] FDR developed a number of tactics aimed at forging such a link. Like his predecessors, he often embarked on speaking trips around the nation to promote his programs. In addition, FDR made limited but important use of the new electronic medium, the radio, to reach millions of Americans. In his famous "fireside chats," the president, or at least his voice, came into every living room in the country to discuss programs and policies and generally to assure Americans that Franklin Delano Roosevelt was aware of their difficulties and working diligently toward solutions.

---

[29] Sidney M. Milkis, *The President and the Parties* (New York: Oxford, 1993), p. 97.

Roosevelt also made himself available for biweekly press conferences, during which he offered candid answers to reporters' questions and made certain to make important policy announcements that would provide the reporters with significant stories to file with their papers.[30] Roosevelt was the first president to designate a press secretary (Stephen Early), who was charged with organizing the press conferences and making certain that reporters observed the informal rules distinguishing presidential comments that were off the record from those that could be attributed directly to the president.

Every president since FDR has sought to craft a public-relations strategy that would emphasize the incumbent's strengths and maximize his popular appeal. One Clinton innovation was to make the White House Communications Office an important institution within the EOP. In a practice continued by George W. Bush, the Communications Office became responsible not only for responding to reporters' queries but for developing and implementing a coordinated communications strategy—promoting the president's policy goals, developing responses to unflattering news stories, and making certain that a favorable image of the president would, insofar as possible, dominate the news. To be effective, the president's communications staff must have good access to the chief executive. President Obama's communications director, Ellen Moran, left after only three months in office, in part because she did not enjoy a close relationship with the president and his senior advisors.

In addition to using the media, recent presidents have reached out directly to the American public to gain its approval. This is an expression of the presidency as a **permanent campaign** for reelection. A study by the political scientist Charles O. Jones shows that President Bill Clinton engaged in campaignlike activity throughout his presidency and was the most-traveled American president in history. In his first twenty months in office, he made 203 appearances outside of Washington, compared with 178 for George H. W. Bush and 58 for Ronald Reagan. Time will tell whether President Obama will challenge Clinton's record.

However, popular support has not been a firm foundation for presidential power. To begin with, popular support is notoriously fickle. President George W. Bush maintained an approval rating of over 70 percent for more than a year after the September 11 terrorist attacks. By 2003, however, his approval rating had fallen nearly twenty points as American casualties in Iraq mounted; by the end of 2005 it had fallen almost another twenty points, to the high-30s range. Such declines in popular approval during a president's term in office are nearly inevitable and follow a predictable pattern (see Figure 6.4).[31] Presidents generate popular support by promising to undertake important programs that will contribute directly to the well-being of large numbers of Americans. Almost inevitably, presidential performance falls short of those promises and popular expectations, leading to a sharp decline in public support and an ensuing collapse of presidential influence.[32]

permanent campaign Description of presidential politics in which all presidential actions are taken with re-election in mind.

---

[30] Kernell, *Going Public*, p. 79.

[31] Theodore J. Lowi, *The Personal President: Power Invested, Promise Unfulfilled* (Ithaca, N.Y.: Cornell University Press, 1985).

[32] Lowi, *The Personal President*, p. 11.

FIGURE 6.4 PUBLIC APPEARANCES BY PRESIDENTS

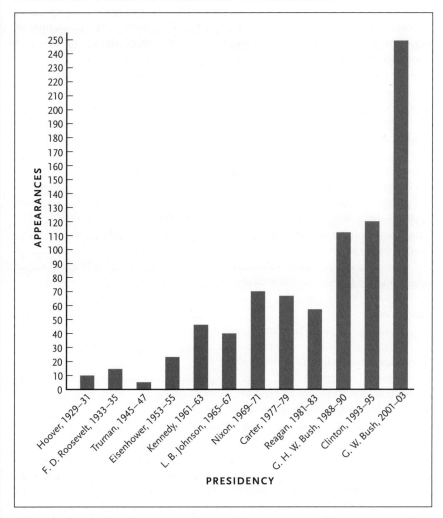

NOTE: Only the first two years of each term are included, because the last two years include many purely political appearances for the president's reelection campaign.

SOURCE: Samuel Kernell, *Going Public: New Strategies of Presidential Leadership*, 3rd ed. (Washington, D.C.: Congressional Quarterly Press, 1998), p. 118; updated by authors.

Presidents have certainly not abandoned "going public," but they no longer do so as frequently as they once did—there has been, for example, a decline in presidential appearances on prime-time television.[33] Instead, presidents have employed institutionalized public and media relations efforts more to create a generally favorable public image than to promote specific policies. Thus, in 2002, President George W. Bush made several speeches to boost the proposed creation of the

---

[33] Kernell, *Going Public*, p. 114.

homeland security department. At the same time, however, the White House Communications Office was engaged in a nonstop, seven-day-a-week effort to promote news and feature stories aimed at bolstering the president's more general public image. Stories emphasized the president's empathy for retirees hurt by the downturn of stock prices, the president's anger over corporate abuses, the president's concern for the environment, the president's determination to prevent terrorism, the president's support for Israel, and so forth. These are all examples of image-polishing rather than going public on behalf of specific programs. Confronted with the limitations of a strategy of popular mobilization, presidents have shifted from an offensive strategy to a more defensive mode in this domain. The limitations of going public as a route to presidential power have also led contemporary presidents to make use of a third technique: expansion of their administrative capabilities.

The Administrative State

Contemporary presidents have increased the administrative capabilities of their office in three ways. First, they have enhanced the reach and power of the EOP. Second, they have sought to increase White House control over the federal bureaucracy. Third, they have expanded the role of executive orders and other instruments of direct presidential governance. Taken together, these components of what might be called the White House "administrative strategy" have given presidents the potential to achieve their programmatic and policy goals even when they are unable to secure congressional approval. Indeed, some recent presidents have been able to accomplish quite a bit without much congressional, partisan, or even public support.

The Executive Office of the President. The Executive Office of the President has grown from six administrative assistants in 1939 to today's 400 employees working directly for the president in the White House office along with some 1,400 individuals staffing the several (currently eight) divisions of the Executive Office.[34] The growth of the White House staff gives the president an enormously enhanced capacity to gather information, plan programs and strategies, communicate with constituencies, and exercise supervision of the executive branch. In particular, the OMB serves as a potential instrument of presidential control over federal spending and hence as a mechanism through which the White House has greatly expanded its power. The OMB has the capacity to analyze and approve all legislative proposals, not only budgetary requests, emanating from all federal agencies before being submitted to Congress. Thus in one White House agency, the president has the means to exert major influence over the flow of money as well as the shape and content of national legislation.

Regulatory Review. A second tactic that presidents have used to increase their power and reach is the process of regulatory review, through which presidents have sought to seize control of rule making by the agencies of the executive branch. Whenever Congress enacts a statute, its actual implementation requires

---

[34] Harold W. Stanley and Richard G. Niemi, *Vital Statistics on American Politics, 2001–2002* (Washington, D.C.: Congressional Quarterly Press, 2001), pp. 250–51.

the promulgation of hundreds of rules by the agency charged with administering the law and giving effect to the will of Congress. Some congressional statutes are quite detailed and leave agencies with relatively little discretion. Typically, however, Congress enacts a relatively broad statement of legislative intent and delegates to the appropriate administrative agency the power to fill in many important details.[35] In other words, Congress typically says to an administrative agency, "Here is the problem: deal with it."[36]

The discretion Congress delegates to administrative agencies has provided recent presidents with an important avenue for expanding their power. For example, Clinton ordered the Food and Drug Administration (FDA) to develop rules designed to restrict the marketing of tobacco products to children. White House and FDA staffers then spent several months preparing nearly 1,000 pages of new regulations affecting tobacco manufacturers and vendors.[37] Republicans denounced Clinton's actions as a usurpation of power.[38] However, after he took office, President George W. Bush made no move to surrender the powers Clinton had claimed.

In September 2001, John D. Graham, President Bush's newly appointed administrator of the Office of Information and Regulatory Affairs (OIRA), issued a memorandum asserting that the president's chief of staff expected the agencies to "implement vigorously" the principles and procedures outlined in former president Clinton's Executive Order 12866. During the first seven months of Bush's presidency, OIRA returned twenty major rules to agencies for further analysis. At the same time, Bush continued the Clinton-era practice of issuing presidential directives to agencies to spur them to issue new rules and regulations. These directives are contained in "prompt letters" from the OIRA to agency administrators. Five such letters were sent during Bush's first year, alone.[39] One "prompt" encouraged the Occupational Safety and Health Administration (OSHA) to require companies to use automated external defibrillators to prevent heart-attack deaths. Another told HHS to require food labels to disclose transfatty acid content.[40] Since both agencies were eager to adopt the presidentially mandated regulations, it appeared that Bush was following the Clinton example of ordering agencies to undertake actions they favor in order to establish helpful precedents for the use of presidential mandates. During the Bush years, OIRA became an increasingly powerful force in the rule-making process. The extent of OIRA's influence became evident in 2003 when the GAO examined eighty-five important rules adopted by federal agencies during the prior year. In twenty-five of these eighty-five cases, it turned out that OIRA had a significant impact on the substance and character of the rules adopted by federal agencies.

---

[35] The classic critique of this process is Theodore J. Lowi, *The End of Liberalism* (New York: Norton, 1979).

[36] Kenneth Culp Davis, *Administrative Law Treatise* (St. Paul, Minn.: West Publishing, 1958), p. 9.

[37] Elena Kagan, "Presidential Administration," *Harvard Law Review* 2245 (2001): 2265.

[38] For example, Douglas W. Kmiec, "Expanding Power," in *The Rule of Law in the Wake of Clinton*, Roger Pilon, ed. (Washington, D.C.: Cato Institute Press, 2000), pp. 47–68.

[39] Ellen Nakashima, "Chief Plans Overhaul of Regulatory Process," *Washington Post*, March 20, 2002, p. A31.

[40] Robert V. Percival, "Presidential Management of the Administrative State: The Not-So-Unitary Executive," *Duke Law Journal* 51, no. 3 (December 2001), 963–1013.

Soon after he took office, President Obama announced that he was nominating the Harvard law professor Cass Sunstein to head OIRA. Sunstein is an expert on the regulatory process and is one of the president's former University of Chicago colleagues. His appointment seemed to signal that Obama plans to increase OIRA's role.

Executive Orders. A third mechanism through which contemporary presidents have sought to enhance their power to govern unilaterally is through the use of executive orders and other forms of presidential decrees, including executive agreements, national security findings and directives, proclamations, reorganization plans, signing statements, and a host of others.[41] Presidents may not use executive orders to issue whatever commands they please. The use of such decrees is bound by law. If a president issues an executive order, proclamation, directive, or the like, in principle he does so pursuant to the powers granted to him by the Constitution or delegated to him by Congress, usually through a statute. When presidents issue such orders, they generally state the constitutional or statutory basis for their actions. For example, when President Truman ordered the desegregation of the armed services, he did so pursuant to his constitutional powers as commander in chief. In a similar vein, when President Johnson issued Executive Order No. 11246, he asserted that the order was designed to implement the 1964 Civil Rights Act, which prohibited employment discrimination. Where an executive order has no statutory or constitutional basis, the courts have held it to be void. The most important case illustrating this point is *Youngstown Sheet & Tube Co. v. Sawyer*, the so-called steel seizure case of 1952.[42] Here the Supreme Court ruled that President Truman's seizure of the nation's steel mills during the Korean War had no statutory or constitutional basis and was thus invalid.

A number of court decisions, though, have established broad boundaries that leave considerable room for presidential action. By illustration, the courts have held that Congress might approve a presidential action after the fact or, in effect, ratify a presidential action through "acquiescence"—for example, by not objecting for long periods of time or by continuing to provide funding for programs established by executive orders. In addition, the courts have indicated that some areas, most notably the realm of military policy, are presidential in character and have allowed presidents wide latitude to make policy by executive decree. Thus, within the very broad limits established by the courts, presidential orders can be and have been important policy tools (see Figure 6.5).

President George W. Bush did not hesitate to use executive orders, issuing more than forty during his first year in office alone and continuing to employ this device (along with signing statements) regularly during his presidency. During his first months in office, Bush issued orders prohibiting the use of federal funds to support international family-planning groups that provided abortion-counseling services and placing limits on the use of embryonic stem cells in federally funded research projects. Bush also made very aggressive use of executive orders in

---

[41] A complete inventory is provided in Harold C. Relyea, "Presidential Directives: Background and Review," The Library of Congress, *Congressional Research Service Report 98–611*, 9 November 2001.

[42] *Youngstown Sheet & Tube Co. v. Sawyer*, 346 U.S. 579 (1952).

FIGURE 6.5 SIGNIFICANT EXECUTIVE ORDERS, 1900–1995

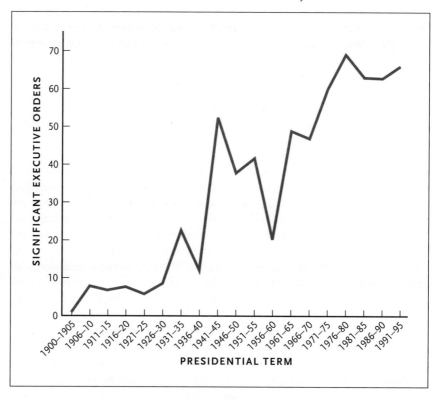

SOURCE: William G. Howell, "The President's Powers of Unilateral Action: The Strategic Advantages of Acting Alone" (Ph.D. diss., Stanford University, 1999).

response to the threat of terrorism, which the president declared to be his administration's most important policy agenda. In November 2001, for example, Bush issued a directive authorizing the creation of military tribunals to try noncitizens accused of involvements in acts of terrorism against the United States.

Soon after taking office in 2009, President Obama issued executive orders reversing a number of Bush-era orders. Obama ordered the closing of the Guantánamo prison holding terror suspects, ordered that federal funding be made available for stem-cell research, and ordered an end to some Bush-mandated limits on abortion funding.

Signing Statements.　The signing statement has become another instrument of presidential power. To negate congressional actions to which they objected, recent presidents have made frequent and calculated use of presidential signing statements when signing bills into law.[43] A **signing statement** is an announcement made by the president at the time of signing a congressional enactment into law,

signing statement An announcement made by the president when signing bills into law, often presenting the president's interpretation of the law.

---

[43] Mark Killenback, "A Matter of Mere Approval: The Role of the President in the Creation of Legislative History," 48 *University of Arkansas Law Review* 239 (1995).

sometimes presenting the president's interpretation of the law as well as usually innocuous remarks predicting the many benefits the new law will bring to the nation. Occasionally, presidents have used signing statements to point to sections of the law they deemed improper or even unconstitutional, and to instruct executive branch agencies how they were to execute the law.[44] President Harry Truman, for example, accompanied his approval of the 1946 Hobbs Anti-Racketeering Act with a message offering his interpretation of ambiguous sections of the statute and indicating how the federal government would implement the new law.[45]

Presidents have made signing statements throughout American history, though many were not recorded and so did not become part of the official legislative record. Ronald Reagan's attorney general, Edwin Meese, is generally credited with transforming the signing statement into a routine tool of presidential direct action.[46] With the way paved, Reagan proceeded to use detailed and artfully designed signing statements—prepared by the Department of Justice—to attempt to reinterpret congressional enactments. When he signed the Competition in Contracting Act in 1984, President Reagan declared that portions of the law were unconstitutional and directed executive branch officials not to comply with them. Subsequently, U.S. District Court Judge Harold Ackerman upheld the act and decried the notion that the president had the power to declare acts of Congress unconstitutional.[47] The same conclusion was later reached by the Ninth Circuit Court of Appeals, which declared that the president did not have the authority to "excise or sever provisions of a bill with which he disagrees."[48]

Despite these adverse rulings, however, the same tactic of reinterpreting and nullifying congressional enactments was continued by Reagan's successor, George H. W. Bush. For the most part, Presidents Reagan and Bush used signing statements to limit the scope of affirmative action programs, to block expansion of business regulation, to reduce the impact of environmental programs and to thwart new labor laws. Bill Clinton followed the examples set by Reagan and Bush and made extensive use of signing statements both to reinterpret and nullify congressional enactments. But, of course, Clinton's agenda was far different from that of his two immediate predecessors. Faced with Republican-controlled congresses for six of his eight years in office, Clinton used his signing statements to attempt to block constriction of affirmative action programs, to limit efforts to weaken environmental standards, and to protect the rights of individuals with disabilities.

Presidential use of signing statements to challenge legislative provisions increased sharply during the George W. Bush years. President Reagan used signing statements to attack 71 legislative provisions, and President Clinton made 105 significant signing statements. Bush challenged more than 800 legislative provisions with his signing statements, including a number of important domestic and security matters, such as a congressional effort, led by Senator John McCain,

---

[44] Cooper, p. 201.

[45] Edward S. Corwin, *The President: Office and Powers*, 4th ed. (New York: New York University Press, 1957), p. 283.

[46] Cooper, p. 201.

[47] *AMERON, Inc. v. U.S. Army Corps of Engineers*, 610 F.Supp. 750 (D.N.J. 1985).

[48] *Lear, Siegler v. Lehman*, 842 F.2nd 1102 (1988).

to ban the use of torture by American interrogators. Though he had denounced Bush's use of signing statements during the campaign, soon after taking office President Obama begin to make use of she same tactic. In March 2009, for example, when Obama signed a $400 billion spending bill, he declared that five of the bill's provisions were unconstitutional and nonbinding. These included a provision aimed at preventing the punishment of whistle-blowers.

IS THE PRESIDENCY TOO STRONG?

The framers of the Constitution, as we saw, created a unitary executive branch because they thought this would make the presidency a more energetic institution. At the same time, they checked the powers of the executive branch by creating a system of separated powers. Did the framers' work make the presidency a strong or weak institution?

At one time, historians and journalists liked to debate the question of strong versus weak presidents. Some presidents, such as Lincoln and FDR, were called "strong" for their leadership and ability to guide the nation's political agenda. Others, such as James Buchanan and Calvin Coolidge, were seen as "weak" for failing to develop significant legislative programs and seeming to observe rather than shape political events. Today, the strong versus weak categorization has become moot. *Every president is strong.* This strength is not so much a function of personal charisma as it is a reflection of the increasing powers of the institution of the presidency. Of course, as we noted earlier, political savvy in strategic interactions with other politicians and mobilizing public opinion can account for a president's success in exercising these powers. But contemporary presidents all possess a vast array of resources and powers.

Indeed, presidents seek to dominate the policy-making process and claim the inherent power to lead the nation in time of war. The expansion of presidential power over the past century has not come about by accident but as the result of an ongoing effort by successive presidents to expand the power of the office. Some presidential efforts have succeeded and others have failed. One recent president, Richard Nixon, was forced to resign, and others have left office under clouds. Most presidents, nevertheless, have sought to increase the office's power. As the framers of the Constitution predicted, presidential ambition has been a powerful and unrelenting force in American politics. Why has presidential ambition gone virtually unchecked? What are the consequences of such a development?

As is often noted by the media and in the academic literature, popular participation in American political life has declined precipitously since its nineteenth-century apogee. Voter turnout in national presidential elections barely exceeds the 50 percent mark; hardly a third of those eligible participate in off-year congressional races. Turnout in state and local contests is typically even lower. These facts are well known, and their implications for the representative character of American government frequently deplored.

The decay of popular political participation, however, also has institutional implications that are not often fully appreciated. To put the matter succinctly, the decline of voting and other forms of popular involvement in American political life reduce congressional influence while enhancing the power of the presidency. This is a development with which we should be deeply concerned. For all its faults and foibles, the Congress is the nation's most representative political institution and remains the only entity capable of placing limits on unwise or illegitimate presidential conduct. Certainly, the courts have seldom been capable of thwarting a determined president, especially in the foreign policy realm. Unfortunately, however, in recent decades our nation's undemocratic politics has undermined the Congress while paving the way for aggrandizement of power by the executive and the presidential unilateralism that inevitably follows.

The framers of the Constitution created a system of government in which the Congress and the executive branch were to share power. In recent years, however, the powers of Congress have waned while those of the presidency have expanded dramatically. To take a recent instance of congressional retreat in the face of presidential assertiveness, in October 2002, pressed by President George W. Bush, both houses of Congress voted overwhelmingly to authorize the White House to use military force against Iraq. The resolution adopted by Congress allowed the president complete discretion to determine whether, when, and how to attack Iraq. The president had rejected language that might have implied even the slightest limitations on his prerogatives. Indeed, Bush's legal advisers had pointedly declared that the president did not actually need specific congressional authorization to attack Iraq if he deemed such action to be in America's interest. "We don't want to be in the legal position of asking Congress to authorize the use of force when the president already has that full authority," said one senior administration official. Few members of Congress even bothered to object to this apparent rewriting of the U.S. Constitution.

There is no doubt that Congress continues to be able to harass presidents and even, on occasion, to hand the White House a sharp rebuff. In the larger view, however, presidents' occasional defeats—however dramatic—have to be seen as temporary setbacks in a gradual and decisive shift toward increased presidential power in the twenty-first century.

CHAPTER REVIEW

The foundations for presidential government were set down in the Constitution, which provided for a unitary executive and made the president head of state as well as head of government. The first section of this chapter reviewed the powers of each: the head of state with its military, judicial, and diplomatic powers; and the head of government with its executive, military, and legislative powers. But the presidency was subordinated to congressional government during the nineteenth century and part of the twentieth, as the national government took part in few domestic functions and was inactive or sporadic in foreign affairs.

The second section of the chapter showed the rise of modern presidential government following the long period of congressional government. There is no mystery in the shift to government centered on the presidency. Congress built the modern presidency essentially in the 1930s by delegating to it not only the power to implement the vast new programs of the New Deal but also by delegating its own legislative power to make policy.

The next sections focused on the president's informal resources. The Cabinet, the other top presidential appointments, the White House staff, and the Executive Office of the President are some of the impressive formal resources of presidential power. Informal resources include the president's political party, the supportive group coalitions, access to the media, and, through that, access to the millions of Americans who make up the general public. Contemporary presidents have also made use of administrative strategies, such as regulatory review, executive orders, and signing statements, to achieve their goals even when they are unable to secure congressional approval.

FOR FURTHER READING

Cameron, Charles M. *Veto Bargaining: Presidents and the Politics of Negative Power.* New York: Cambridge University Press, 2000.

reader selection Canes-Wrone, Brandice. *Who Leads Whom? Presidents, Policy, and the Public.* Chicago: University of Chicago Press, 2006.

Crenson, Matthew, and Benjamin Ginsberg. *Presidential Power: Unchecked and Unbalanced.* New York: Norton, 2007.

Deering, Christopher, and Forrest Maltzman. "The Politics of Executive Orders: Legislative Constraints on Presidential Power." *Political Research Quarterly* 52 (1999): 767–83.

Krutz, Glen, and Jeffrey Peake. *Presidential-Congressional Governance and the Rise of Executive Agreements.* Ann Arbor: University of Michigan Press, 2009.

Lowi, Theodore J. *The Personal President: Power Invested, Promise Unfulfilled.* Ithaca, N.Y.: Cornell University Press, 1985.

Milkis, Sidney M. *The President and the Parties: The Transformation of the American Party System since the New Deal.* New York: Oxford University Press, 1993.

Nelson, Michael, ed. *The Presidency and the Political System.* 8th ed. Washington, D.C.: Congressional Quarterly Press, 2005.

reader selection Neustadt, Richard E. *Presidential Power and the Modern Presidents: The Politics of Leadership from Roosevelt to Reagan.* 1960. Rev. ed., New York: Free Press, 1990.

Pfiffner, James P. *The Modern Presidency.* 4th ed. Belmont, Calif.: Wadsworth, 2005.

Skowronek, Stephen. *The Politics Presidents Make: Leadership from John Adams to Bill Clinton.* Cambridge, Mass.: Harvard University Press, 1997.

Yoo, John. *The Powers of War and Peace.* Chicago: University of Chicago Press, 2005.

 Additional study and review materials are available online at wwnorton.com/studyspace/

Analyzing the Obama Presidency:
The First Two Years

In a historic election in November 2008, Barack Obama was chosen as the forty-fourth president of the United States. Inaugurated on January 20, 2009, he has served during a particularly rocky period of American history—two active wars, increased global economic competition, the most significant economic downturn since the Great Depression, and constituencies clamoring for action on the education, immigration, and environmental fronts: in short, a very full plate for any president. Though many problems were inherited from the Bush administration, President Obama was quickly forced to take ownership of these issues. Obama may have won the election partly because of his predecessor's poor performance, but now the performance under the microscope is his.

Although our focus in this secction is on the Obama administration, we will see that the story of Obama's presidency is inseparable from the stories of the other branches of government. We will also see how the concepts we have covered in this book so far can help us analyze and understand the politics of Obama's first two years. We can think of the Bush years as important background, but a new set of interests and objectives have been formulated under Obama. The attempt to pursue a very full agenda has constituted the stuff of politics these last two years and provides an illustration of how politicians act strategically in pursuit of their goals. The story of that effort is an institutional one, as the Obama administration decided on a strategy that put the U.S. Congress square in the middle and had the opportunity to appoint two new justices to the Supreme Court.

THE TEAM

The first task of any president-elect is, together with his transition team, to select a governing team—his cabinet and senior advisors. With his choice of Representative Rahm Emanuel (D-IL) to be White House chief of staff, President-elect Obama signaled to the political class that his administration was going to focus on securing an expansive legislative agenda. The rest of the administration was pieced together with this objective in mind, as well as other goals, including countering perceived weaknesses in the president's resumé, demonstrating seriousness of purpose, and repaying politicians who supported the president's election.

Throughout the primary and general election campaigns, Obama had to fend off criticisms of inexperience in foreign policy. The selection of Joe Biden of Delaware, a senator with extensive foreign policy experience, as Obama's running mate was one way his advisors attempted to address this. To shore up Obama's foreign policy credentials, the transition team surrounded the president with noted national security experts. Retaining Robert Gates, President Bush's secretary of defense, provided some continuity between administrations during a time in which the country was involved in two wars. The addition of General Jim Jones as the national security advisor lent even more weight to the national security team. Appointing his former rival Senator Hillary Clinton (D-NY) as the secretary of state harnessed the good will and energy of Senator Clinton and her husband, former president Bill Clinton. It also moved a potential critic into the administration.

Obama's nominee for treasury secretary, Timothy Geith- ▶
ner, was initially seen by some as too cozy with Wall
Street to push through needed financial reforms. How-
ever, Geithner was eventually confirmed and has been
instrumental in crafting and implementing Obama's
economic and financial initiatives.

On the domestic front, the transition team faced the daunting task of finding candidates for cabinet positions who could play to the president's political supporters and at the same time get confirmed by the Senate. In addition, several of them had to be credible with the financial industry. The principal financial appointee was Timothy Geithner to head the Treasury Department. Unfortunately, there were a few revelations of unpaid taxes, which were humbling for a man who would be chief of the department that oversees the Internal Revenue Service. However, the greater problem for Geithner's confirmation was the role he had played as head of the Federal Reserve Bank of New York in the period leading up to the financial crisis of late 2008. He had credibility on Wall Street, but this wasn't the best character reference in the stormy weeks following the passage of the Troubled Assets Relief Program (TARP), as many Americans held Wall Street responsible for the problems in the economy. Nonetheless, Geithner was confirmed. Another important member of the economic team was Lawrence Summers, the former vice president of the World Bank, Clinton treasury secretary and, more recently, president of Harvard University. Summers became the principal economic advisor to the president.

President Obama's focus on health care reform led to great speculation about whom he would choose to head the Department of Health and Human Services. His first choice, former South Dakota senator Tom Daschle, provided another strong signal that the president intended to get health care reform through Congress. Daschle had served as majority leader in the Senate and knew the inner workings of Congress. However, a significant tax delinquency derailed this nomination. Instead, the president settled on Kathleen Sebelius, the governor of Kansas.

In an attempt to repay an early declaration of support, President Obama named New Mexico governor Bill Richardson to be secretary of commerce. This bid failed when it was revealed that the governor was under investigation for improper conduct in his home state. The Commerce hot potato then landed in the lap of Senator Judd Gregg (R-NH), but Gregg later publicly repudiated the nomination in a spat with the president. The vacancy was finally filled by the former two-term governor of Washington, Gary Locke.

As all this suggests, former office holders were a major presence in the cabinet. Ray LaHood at the Department of Transportation had been a member of the House. The secretary of agriculture position went to a farm-state politician, Tom Vilsack, the former governor of Iowa. Janet Napolitano, the governor of Arizona, became the secretary of homeland security. Ron Kirk, the former mayor of Dallas, became the

U.S. trade representative. President Obama nominated Congresswoman Hilda Solis (D-CA) to head the Department of Labor. He named Senator Ken Salazar (D-CO) to become the secretary of the interior. The Obama cabinet also included academics like Secretary of Energy Steven Chu, Ambassador to the UN Susan Rice, and Chair of the Council on Economic Advisors Christina Romer. Eric Holder's appointment as attorney general added another former Clinton appointee to a top Obama administration post. David Axelrod, Obama's campaign manager, moved into a position as an advisor to the president, while Robert Gibbs took on the role of press secretary.

The diversity of backgrounds, genders, and races was an important sign of Obama's commitment to the different political constituencies within the Democratic Party. In addition to their political qualifications, that Salazar and Solis were Hispanic was important to the new administration. Eric Holder's appointment as attorney general was historic in that he was the first African American to hold that office. Kirk and Rice are also African American. Clinton, Napolitano, Romer, Rice, Sebelius, and Solis are women. Chu and Locke are Asian American. It is important to remember that every action a president takes is interpreted as a signal of support for different electoral constituencies. With his team in place, the president went to work on some of his legislative goals.

EARLY LEGISLATIVE ACHIEVEMENTS

Together with the Democratic 111th Congress, President Obama achieved a number of legislative results in his first two years. This section discusses some of Obama's significant legislative victories: the Lilly Ledbetter Fair Pay Act, the Children's Health Insurance Program Reauthorization Act of 2009, the American Recovery and Reinvestment Act of 2009, and financial reform legislation. The next section looks at the case of health care reform legislation in some detail and analyzes the politics surrounding its passage. Table 1 shows how Congress voted on each of these bills. In working to get these bills passed, Obama's team was strategic in how they pursued their goals and mindful of the institutional rules and practices that would affect the outcomes.

The Lilly Ledbetter Fair Pay Act

Obama championed the cause of Lilly Ledbetter, a former employee of the Goodyear Tire & Rubber Company, and other women who shared her plight. When Ledbetter retired from Goodyear in 1998, she was earning significantly less than her male peers. She sued the company, claiming that she was a victim of discrimination based on gender, and arguing that supervisors had prevented her from receiving the same pay raises as her male peers. The central claim of her case was that her current state of reduced retirement income was the result of previous acts of discrimination. Ledbetter won her case at the district court level, where she was awarded both back pay and damages. Goodyear then appealed the case based on the fact that her complaint was filed in 1998, which meant that the alleged discrimination took place well outside the 180-day time limit imposed by the Civil Rights Act of 1964. The appellate court agreed with Goodyear and overturned the lower court's decision. Ledbetter pursued an appeal to the Supreme Court, where she argued that pay discrimination was not a discrete event like being fired or other more overt job actions and that therefore the Court should use a different rule for establishing when the 180-day clock starts. The Court rejected her claim. Justice Samuel Alito, writing the majority opinion, cited several precedents where petitioners' claims had been rejected as a result of untimely filings. The Lilly Ledbetter Fair Pay Act, which Obama actively supported and signed into law in 2009, legislatively overturned the Supreme Court's decision. It amended U.S. law so that the 180-day time period starts each time the employee receives a paycheck that is affected by a discriminatory decision instead of when the discriminatory pay decision was made.

The Children's Health Insurance Program Reauthorization Act of 2009

Although the bill enjoyed considerable bipartisan support, President George W. Bush vetoed the Children's Health Insurance Plan Reauthorization Act of 2007 (CHIP). His principal objection to the bill was his belief that it was a step toward socialized medicine and that it provided incentives to middle- and upper-income parents to move their children off private insurance plans and onto the public plan. There was tremendous political fallout over this decision. Calling it a "heartless veto," Senate Majority Leader Harry Reid (D-NV) accused President Bush of denying health care to millions of children. Reauthorizing and expanding CHIP became a Democratic campaign promise that President Obama fulfilled early in his administration.

The American Recovery and Reinvestment Act of 2009

The economic downturn of 2008 gave a major boost to the campaign of Barack Obama. In fact, throughout most of the end stages of the presidential campaign, Senator Obama drew distinctions between his plan to get the economy growing, what his opponent, Senator John McCain (R-AZ), would do, and what the Republican Party, under President George W. Bush,

Although most Americans agreed that the gov- ▶
ernment needed to address the economic crisis,
Obama's specific plans for the economy were
controversial. Some Democrats complained that
the government was "bailing out" Wall Street
rather than ordinary Americans, while some Re-
publicans objected to the deep deficit that would
result from increased government spending.

had done. Obama proposed enacting a large stimulus package of federal spending mixed with some targeted tax cuts. The purpose of this spending was to spur economic demand. This constituted a 180-degree departure from the more conservative Republican emphasis on supply-side economics, which calls for stimulating the economy by giving incentives to producers, through tax breaks and subsidies, to employ their capital. Supply-side prescriptions for helping the economy favor reducing taxes and eliminating governmental regulation. The demand-side proponents argued that producers were not going to produce more when consumers were not inclined to buy what was being produced. The stimulus would put money into the hands of consumers, which would then enable producers to get back to employing their capital and ultimately would lead the economy out of the recession. As a result of this sharp ideological divide, support for the American Recovery and Reinvestment Act of 2009, Public Law 111-5, ran almost completely along partisan lines (see Table 1). No Republican members of the House and only three Republican senators supported passage.

Financial Reform Legislation

If the economic downturn gave the Obama campaign a general boost, the near complete meltdown of the global financial system created a major challenge for the new president. Political pressure for a response was intense. The Obama administration, along with its allies in Congress, delivered by enacting laws to protect consumers, restructure the financial system, and prevent a recurrence of the factors that led to the collapse in the first place. The Democrats enacted the Fraud Enforcement and Recovery Act of 2009, the Helping Families Save Their Homes Act of 2009, the Credit Card Accountability Responsibility and Disclosure Act of 2009, and the Dodd-Frank Wall Street Reform and Consumer Protection Act. As Table 1 shows, the Republicans were more supportive of these acts than of Obama's other major initiatives.

HEALTH CARE REFORM

No discussion of President Obama's legislative track record would be complete without treating the passage of the Patient Protection and Affordable Care Act and the Health Care and Education Reconciliation Act of 2010. Together, the two laws comprised Obama's landmark health care reform legislation. The last attempt at comprehensive health care reform in the United States, a failure, had severely weakened President Clinton. In fact, some argued that President Obama's plan to enact health care reform was based on a study of how opponents of health care reform had defeated the Clinton attempt.

Where President Clinton had used an executive branch approach to fashioning a plan, President Obama chose a plan driven by the legislative branch. He outlined the basic goals but left the details to the legislative leaders who would be responsible for getting the plan through Congress. Where Clinton's plan faced intense industry opposition, Obama sought buy-in from the industries to be regulated by his plan. Another crucial difference between the approaches of Clinton and Obama

The issue of health care reform was highly divi- ▶
sive. Even Democrats who supported reform in
general disagreed over the details. Obama and
his allies in Congress struggled to devise a plan
that would win the necessary votes.

arose from the facts that Obama enjoyed
a bigger partisan seat advantage in each
chamber of Congress and that the Democrats were more ideologically unified than
they had been in 1993–94.

Even with this more inclusive strategy,
however, securing passage of Obama's
health care reform legislation was far from
simple. While the Democrats in the 111th
Congress were more ideologically unified
than their predecessors in Clinton's 103rd,
there was still a considerable diversity of
preferences. Some on the liberal end of
the spectrum wanted a single-payer system that was flatly opposed by all Republicans
and most centrist Democrats. At the same time, the minor modifications to the current system that more conservative members favored were insufficient for liberals.
Social issues that had not previously divided Democrats in the health care debate
started to gain traction when Democrats representing socially conservative districts
demanded provisions limiting funding for abortions and stem cell research.

Not to be completely left out of the debate, opponents of health care reform
used the opportunity of Democratic intra-party squabbling to project their own
views on the issue. Former Alaska governor Sarah Palin, the 2008 Republican vice-
presidential candidate, a vocal critic of the president, and a potential presidential
challenger in 2012, weighed in with her concerns about bureaucratic determination of end-of-life care, which she termed "death panels." The politics of the matter were further confused when opponents of health care reform argued that the
president's plan would endanger current Medicare benefits, leaving some Medicare recipients to object to "socialized medicine" even though they were already on
government-provided health insurance.

By late fall 2009, it had become clear that health care reform remained highly
divisive. In the January 2010 special election in Massachusetts to fill the U.S. Senate seat of Ted Kennedy, the eventual winner, Republican Scott Brown, campaigned
as being *the* vote to stop Obamacare. Ironically, Senator Brown's election may well
have made passage of health care reform possible, because it put to rest some of
the squabbles within the Democratic party over policy alternatives. The loss of the
Kennedy seat to the Republicans meant that some of the features preferred by
more liberal Democrats in the House were no longer viable. To understand why
requires an appreciation of the institutional context in which the parties and politicians contest policy.

When President Obama announced that he intended to make health care reform part of his legislative agenda for the 111th Congress, he had to rebut critics

TABLE 1 FINAL PASSAGE VOTE TALLIES: HOUSE OF REPRESENTATIVES

HOUSE OF REPRESENTATIVES						
	Total		Democrats		Republicans	
Legislation	Yeas	Nays	Yeas	Nays	Yeas	Nays
The Lilly Ledbetter Fair Pay Act	250	177	247	5	3	172
The Children's Health Insurance Program Reauthorization Act of 2009	290	135	250	2	40	133
The American Recovery and Reinvestment Act of 2009	246	183	246	7	0	163
The Fraud Enforcement and Recovery Act of 2009	338	52	224	0	114	52
The Helping Families Save Their Homes Act of 2009	367	54	244	3	123	51
The Credit Card Accountability Responsibility and Disclosure Act of 2009	279	147	105	145	174	2
The Dodd-Frank Wall Street Reform and Consumer Protection Act	237	192	234	19	3	173
The Patient Protection and Affordable Care Act	219	212	219	34	0	178
The Health Care and Education Reconciliation Act of 2010	220	207	220	32	0	175

SOURCE: The Library of Congress, http://thomas.loc.gov/ (accessed 10/21/10).

who argued that his young administration already had too many issues to address. Obama faced the immediate tasks of waging the wars in Iraq and Afghanistan simultaneously and rescuing an economy on the brink of collapse. Both his supporters and his opponents suggested that attempting to pass health care reform was an unnecessary burden. However, reviewing the political situation from Obama's viewpoint allows one to see why a newly elected president would go for big-ticket legislative items early in his first term.

It may help to use an example from the military. When developing combat orders, military planners first assess the terrain, then try to determine the ways in which the enemy can use the terrain, and finally take stock of their assets and allies in order to try to use them to counter what the enemy might do to prevent the unit from achieving its objectives. This is summed up by three short commands: "see the terrain, see the enemy, see yourself." Upon becoming president of the United States of America, Barack Obama, along with his advisors, must have conducted a similar strategic review of the situation.

TABLE 1 (CONT.) FINAL PASSAGE VOTE TALLIES: SENATE

| | SENATE | | | | | |
| | Total | | Democrats | | Republicans | |
Legislation	Yeas	Nays	Yeas	Nays	Yeas	Nays
The Lilly Ledbetter Fair Pay Act	61	36	56	0	5	36
The Children's Health Insurance Program Reauthorization Act of 2009	66	32	57	0	9	32
The American Recovery and Reinvestment Act of 2009	60	38	57	0	3	38
The Fraud Enforcement and Recovery Act of 2009	92	4	56	0	36	4
The Helping Families Save Their Homes Act of 2009	91	5	56	0	35	5
The Credit Card Accountability Responsibility and Disclosure Act of 2009	90	5	55	1	35	4
The Dodd-Frank Wall Street Reform and Consumer Protection Act	60	39	57	1	3	38
The Patient Protection and Affordable Care Act	60	39	60	0	0	39
The Health Care and Education Reconciliation Act of 2010	56	43	56	3	0	40

"See the Terrain"

Instead of a physical terrain, political strategists see their battlefield as the institutions in which political actions take place. Instead of in mountains, forests, valleys, and rivers, political fights take place on the floor of the House and Senate, in the committee chambers, at the party caucuses/conferences, in political action committees, at regulatory commission hearings, in administrative law courts, in the judicial courts, and indeed in the "court" of public opinion. For achieving the president's agenda, the terrain is the Congress.

Barack Obama took office with huge majorities in both houses of Congress. Only Lyndon Johnson in 1965 enjoyed larger majorities. Possession of these majorities, however, is tempered by the fact that, with few exceptions, the party of the president loses seats in the president's first midterm election; accomplishments must come early.

The president also had to adapt to the unexpected. During Obama's inaugural luncheon on Capitol Hill, Senator Ted Kennedy (D-MA), one of Obama's key supporters, had to be taken away by ambulance. In a situation where every single vote counts, the age and relative health of the members of Congress start to factor into legislative strategies. The lesson here is that new presidents should go for the big-ticket items early in their terms because they may not get a second chance.

Strategists must also consider the rules of both bodies and their implications for the president's agenda. A central concern for the administration and in the media was the possibility of obstruction in the Senate. As we discussed in Chapter 5, 60 votes are needed to overcome a filibuster. So, the administration would need to assemble a coalition of 60 senators whose votes could close down debate. The necessity of "getting to 60" in the Senate means that an essential senator can hold hostage the policy preferences of majorities in both legislative chambers. President Obama's team was very close to "getting to 60" and knew the identity of the one or two senators who could take them over the top. These senators, in turn, knew their value to the president and were in a position to extract maximum reward for their votes.

Political terrain is different from geographic terrain. While mountains and valleys are relatively stable, political terrain is dynamic. The essential senators alluded to in the previous paragraph changed as the composition and/or political affiliation of the U.S. Senate changed for various reasons, one member at a time. The initial seating of 99 senators—the outcome of the Minnesota Senate race had not been determined—left the filibuster pivot among a trio of moderate Republicans: Arlen Specter (PA), Susan Collins (ME), and Olympia Snowe (ME). However, Specter's switching of his party affiliation from Republican to Democrat as a result of an intra-party challenge in Pennsylvania coupled with the declaration that Al Franken (D) had won the hotly contested Minnesota Senate seat changed the identity of the pivotal senator to Ben Nelson (D-NE).

"See the Enemy"

Military planners say that the enemy gets a vote. In the case of the president, the enemy is any political actor who wants to prevent the president from securing parts of his legislative agenda. There are different categories of those who oppose the president's goals. The Republicans in Congress executed a simple policy of confronting the president; they opted for no compromise, voting against almost everything he wanted to accomplish. As Table 1 shows, not a single Republican voted for either of the two health care bills passed in 2010. It is easy to suggest that this is just a case of sour grapes and of being ornery for the sake of being ornery. However, a more sophisticated reading of this tactic is that by forcing the administration to rely on strict party votes to pass legislation, it actually pulls the Democratic administration policy toward its most conservative members, instead of making it appealing to moderate Republicans. A secondary benefit of such opposition is that it frees the Republican Party from blame if something goes wrong. One of the few benefits of being in the minority is that the minority's political task is to point out how the majority party has screwed things up. The minority party is free of the responsibilities of governing.

In addition to members of the minority party in Congress, Republicans with national election ambitions made themselves known by going public in opposition. Sarah Palin was a constant critic of the Obama administration. Other high-profile critics—former speaker of the House Newt Gingrich, former governor of Massachusetts Mitt Romney, and former governor of Arkansas Mike Huckabee—were all rumored to be considering presidential bids in 2012.

"See Yourself"

Having a good understanding of the political situation in which he finds himself, the president is better able to evaluate methods for implementing his legislative agenda. What tools does the president have to get things done? Within the bounds of legislative and legal restrictions, he has nominal control over the immense federal bureaucracy and the resources it controls. The president has sticks and carrots to encourage legislators to work with him instead of against him. For example, suppose a vote in favor of health care reform will be secured if a senator is able to obtain more federal assistance for her state. Several years after Hurricane Katrina, mobile teams of federal health clinics descended upon Louisiana. One of Louisiana's senators, Mary Landrieu (D), initially uncertain, came to support Obamacare. In short, the president can, and President Obama did, use discretionary authority over federal activity and, as leader of his party, exert legislative guidance over the exact language and structure of legislation to assemble a winning coalition.

What Obama won did not please all his supporters; indeed, it undoubtedly fell short of his own aspirations. But a win is a win, and in this case a bare win was about as good as he could do. The point of this section has been to drive home the idea that the president must know the rules of the institutional game, the capabilities of his opponents, and the tools he controls in order to implement his legislative agenda. We devoted special attention to health care since passing health care reform was one of Obama's major domestic achievements.

LEGISLATIVE DISAPPOINTMENTS AND CHALLENGES

Obama took on enormous political risks when he staked his presidency on legislative accomplishments. The first risk was that he would fail to accomplish what he had set out to do. For example, President Jimmy Carter's inability to realize his big plans contributed greatly to his defeat in the 1980 election and to the impression that his presidency was "a failure," and Obama risks suffering the same consequences.

The second risk is that the messy and often ugly process of legislation will frustrate the president's efforts to meet these goals. There is a reason that the German statesman Otto von Bismarck said, "Laws are like sausages. It's better not to see them being made." Compromise is at the heart of politics in a democracy. When the president gives special favors to those whose vote might help his legislation pass or when the majority leader tries to pass amendments that favor a particular senator or representative, the seamy side of politics is rearing its head. During the attempt to pass health care reform, critics of bartering political favors for crucial votes had a field day. For example, Nebraska was given a Medicare exemption that no other state received solely to secure the vote for Obamacare of the pivotal Nebraska senator, something the media publicized and Obama opponents took great pains to point out. For a president who campaigned on "changing politics as we know it," it looked an awful lot like old-school politics. The Republicans were free to point out the inconsistencies between Democratic pledges for open, honest government and the closed-door negotiations, proposals, and counterproposals that were taking place. Even worse, elements of the coalitions that supported President Obama in the campaign had to watch as their objectives were sacrificed or ignored in the quest to get *something* done. Compromise is all well and good unless your pet policy is the one that's about to be compromised away, and public legislative bargaining alienated some supporters. In short, the messiness of the political process negatively affected the Democrats and left the Republicans largely unscathed.

Even when the president takes great pains to understand his political situation, he sometimes fails to meet his objectives. Most notably, Obama has not passed significant environmental legislation nor has he secured comprehensive immigration reform.

Environmental Legislation

Although the Democratic platform called for "implement[ing] a market-based cap and trade system to reduce carbon emissions by the amount scientists say is necessary to avoid catastrophic change and [setting] interim targets along the way to ensure that we meet our goal," Democrats were unable to muster the votes to pass the legislation in the Senate. Furthermore, the filibuster did not come into play as Democrats in the House were unable to obtain even a simple majority to pass the proposed legislation.

Immigration Reform

When Arizona governor Jan Brewer signed Arizona Senate Bill 1070, a controversial law that permitted Arizona police to stop and require identification from individuals who might be illegal aliens, comprehensive immigration reform jumped back to the forefront of U.S. political conversation. It is a topic that previous presidents have faced and not handled well. President George W. Bush attempted (and failed) to pass comprehensive immigration reform during his second term. A great deal of the opposition came from members of the president's own party.

Most federal immigration laws have aimed at limiting or reducing the immigration of national and racial minorities. In the wake of the terrorist attacks of September 11, 2001, the immigration debate became enmeshed in the dramatic confusion of national security policy, economic policy, and human rights. The Democrats recognized the intricacies of dealing with immigration reform, stating in their 2008 platform that "our current immigration system has been broken for far too long. We need comprehensive immigration reform, not just piecemeal efforts. We are committed to pursuing tough, practical, and humane immigration reform in the first year of the next administration."

With so many different dimensions, immigration reform is a topic with many losing positions and few winning ones. Even Senator John McCain (R-AZ), Obama's opponent in the 2008 presidential election and a strong supporter of President Bush's plans for comprehensive immigration reform, faced a tough primary challenge from the *right* in his 2010 bid for reelection to the Senate and altered his position on immigration to shore up his conservative credentials. It is no wonder that politicians avoid the topic of immigration reform even when they declare it to be a top priority.

This all leads us to ask how these apparently hopeless items end up on the president's legislative agenda. Some of these policy positions are personal preferences that stem from life experiences. Others result from trying to persuade large groups of voters to support one's candidacy for office. Obama, for example, sought the support of young voters and of highly educated ones, both of which groups would support increases in federal assistance for higher education. He also sought the support of Hispanic Americans; hence his emphasis on immigration reform.

OBAMA'S USE OF EXECUTIVE ORDERS

In many cases, the president opts to use nonlegislative tools to achieve his policy objectives. Clearly, the fastest, most direct, and easiest way to implement change is to issue an executive order. As we saw in Chapter 6, executive orders are instructions the president gives to the government, implementing his policy objectives using authority granted to the president by Congress through previous laws. Sometimes a president issues an executive order when attempts to arrive at a legislative solution fail.

The earliest actions of the Obama presidency were executive orders rescinding some of the more controversial policies of his predecessor. With the stroke of a pen, President Obama changed government policy on detention operations at the naval base at Guantanamo Bay; clarified his administration's stance on the use of torture and/or controversial interrogation techniques; reversed the previous administration's ban on certain types of stem cell research; and reversed the so-called "Mexico City gag rule," which restricted federal funding for groups who performed or advocated abortion in other countries as a component of family-planning services.

The executive order reversing the gag rule is a good example of why executive orders are in some ways less desirable than new laws. As easy as it was for President Obama to rescind the old order, it will be equally as easy for a future president to reinstate it. In fact, the gag rule was first imposed by President Reagan in 1984. Shortly after his inauguration, President Clinton issued an executive order rescinding Reagan's policy. Shortly after his inauguration, President George W. Bush issued an executive order rescinding President Clinton's executive order.

Finally, the president as a unitary actor and as the commander-in-chief of the military is free to issue commands that are either inherently beyond the scope of legislation or create a very high cost for Congress to do anything to reverse. While many Republicans supported President Obama's expansion of the war in Afghanistan, many Democrats in Congress were upset. Ultimately, both Republicans and Democrats have little control over the president's options in this realm. While

TABLE 2 NOMINATIONS TO FEDERAL COURTS

President	Congress	Nominations	Confirmed	Withdrawn	Rejected	Expired	Pending
George W. Bush	110th	104	68	6	0	30	N/A
Barack H. Obama	111th	97	41	1	7	N/A	48

SOURCE: The Library of Congress, http://thomas.loc.gov/ (accessed 10/21/10)

Congress does hold the purse strings, the political reality is that Congress will back down in the face of the president in his role as commander-in-chief. Congress will not allow itself to be accused of failing to support the members of the American military while they are engaged in foreign conflict.

CHANGES ON THE SUPREME COURT

Presidents have many opportunities to fill posts in the federal judiciary, the most common of which are naming district and appeals court judges. Table 2 compares President Obama's federal court nominations in his first two years in office to President Bush's from his last half-term. More than half of Obama's nominees have yet to be decided on. Rarer for presidents are opportunities to name justices to the Supreme Court. President Obama has been fortunate in his first two years; he has been able to fill *two* Supreme Court vacancies. Obama's selections partly reflected his commitment to diversity. He named, and the Senate confirmed, two women: Sonia Sotomayor, a Catholic Hispanic, and Elena Kagan, a Jew. The court now consists of six Catholics and three Jews (the first time in living memory that no Protestant serves), a Hispanic for the first time, and three women (a historical high). Given the age and health of the sitting justices, Obama may have additional opportunities before his present term concludes.

Sonia Sotomayor, Obama's first nominee, had served for eight years as a federal district judge (nominated by President George H. W. Bush) and for an additional ten years as a court of appeals judge (nominated by President Bill Clinton). Shortly after Justice David Souter announced his retirement in spring 2009, Obama nominated Sotomayor to the Supreme Court, and she was confirmed by the Senate in August 2009 by a 68–31 vote. Perhaps her most famous ruling as a federal judge was one in which she prevented major league baseball owners from hiring replacements for striking baseball players, thus bringing the 1994 baseball strike to an end. Her "paper trail" as a federal judge was quite extensive, with a mainly liberal cast (though she was not always predictable, especially on business-related issues). This provided her opponents with many opportunities to try to derail the nomination. But, after following the tried-and-true practice of nominees to provide little indication of their inclinations on current hot-button legal issues during confirmation hearings, Sotomayor was confirmed relatively easily.

Prior to her nomination to the Supreme Court, Elena Kagan had a varied legal career. From 1995 to 1999 she served as President Clinton's White House counsel. He nominated her to a federal judgeship in 1999, but the Republican-controlled Senate did not schedule a hearing and her nomination lapsed when Clinton left office at the end of the year. After returning to academia—she had been a professor of law at the University of Chicago—she was named professor, and then dean, at the Harvard Law School. In early 2009 President Obama appointed her solicitor general. A year later, Justice John Paul Stevens, the oldest member of the Supreme Court, announced he would retire that summer. Kagan was nominated by the president in May 2010 and confirmed later that summer, after another uneventful confirmation hearing, by a 63–37 vote.

EVALUATING THE OBAMA PRESIDENCY

As we have already noted, it is too early to evaluate Obama's record and the impact of his first two years as president. However, we can make a few observations about how Obama's early record might eventually be assessed.

President Obama will be evaluated not only for his legislative hits and misses but also for the implementation of policy during his administration. There his record of accomplishments is less clear. One way to assess the president is to look

FIGURE 1 PRESIDENT OBAMA'S APPROVAL RATING AND MONTHLY EMPLOYMENT, JANUARY 2008–SEPTEMBER 2010 (SEASONALLY ADJUSTED)

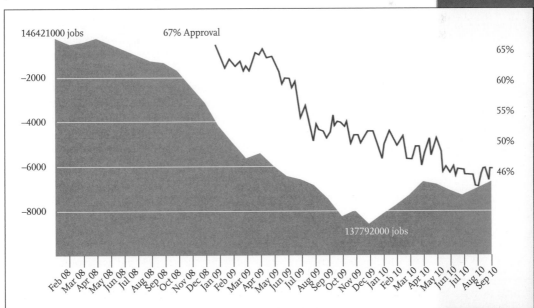

at the stated goals of his presidency before he took office and evaluate his success so far. As part of the party's platform, "Renewing America's Promise," the president vowed to renew the American dream, renew American leadership, renew the American community, and renew American democracy.

If the economic stimulus package and health care reform bring about the objectives of the laws, the president will have succeeded in renewing economic and social well-being. Renewing American leadership in the world is much more questionable. The situation in Afghanistan is deeply problematic; Pakistan remains a questionable ally; and the dismissal of the director of National Intelligence bodes poorly for intelligence reform. Iran seems on the brink of developing nuclear weapons, and North Korea will likely retain its nuclear capacity. American combat brigades have withdrawn from Iraq on schedule, but a resurgence of coordinated terrorist attacks is making permanent peace in the country questionable. Recent cyber-attacks on Google in China and U.S. government networks indicate that much work remains to be done on strengthening cyber-security. The successes in this broader category of American leadership largely stem from policies that focus on "revitalizing and supporting our military, keeping faith with veterans." The country is still a long way off from establishing energy security; and its efforts to provide international leadership to combat climate change are currently dead in Congress.

Renewing the American community is also a mixed bag for the president. The failure to enact significant immigration reform is a gaping hole. The catastrophic oil spill in the Gulf of Mexico underscores the federal government's Katrina-like inability to handle large-scale environmental crises. Of course, the president has also not scored many points for the government's continuing efforts to rebuild New Orleans and other areas affected by Hurricane Katrina.

Ultimately, President Obama's term in office will be judged by whether he is reelected in 2012. Research has shown that the economy is the single most important indicator of how well presidents will do in their bids for reelection. According to the Bureau of Economic Analysis, the economy had begun to expand by the end of Obama's first two years, but the rate of growth is slow. The rule of thumb is that voters punish incumbents when the economy underperforms. Figure 1 illustrates the relationship between presidential approval rating and economic performance with regards to employment. If the economy rebounds, all will be forgiven and President Obama will likely cruise to reelection. If the economy stagnates or deteriorates further, then the president's chances of remaining in office decline.

The Executive Branch

7

WHY BUREAUCRACY?

The bureaucracy is the administrative heart and soul of government. It is literally where the rubber meets the road—where policies formulated, incubated, perfected, and ultimately passed into law by elected officials (legislators, executives) are interpreted, implemented, and ultimately delivered to a nation's citizens. Government touches the life of the ordinary citizen most directly in his or her interactions with bureaucratic agents—at the Department of Motor Vehicles when obtaining a driver's license; in filing one's income-tax return with the Internal Revenue Service; at the recruiting center when enlisting in one of the armed services; at the Board of Elections when registering to vote.

Public bureaucracies are powerful because legislatures and chief executives— and, indeed, the people—delegate to them vast power to make sure a particular job is done, enabling the rest of us to be freer to pursue our private ends. The public sentiments that emerged after September 11 revealed this underlying appreciation of public bureaucracies. When faced with the challenge of making air travel safe again, the public strongly supported giving the federal government responsibility for airport security even though this meant increasing the size of the federal bureaucracy in order to make the security screeners federal workers. In 2008 and 2009, Americans again looked to the federal bureaucracy to help solve the financial crisis. However, Americans have often been more suspicious of bureaucracy.

We can shed some systematic light on public attitudes toward government bureaucracy by examining one of the standard questions posed in election years by the American National Election Studies (ANES). As part of its survey of the American public, the ANES asks a range of questions, among which is "Do you think that people in the government waste a lot of money we pay in taxes, waste some of it, or don't waste very much of it?" Although not perfect for eliciting from the public a nuanced assessment of bureaucratic performance, the question allows respondents to register a blunt evaluation. Results from the past several decades are given in Figure 7.1.

We examine the federal bureaucracy in this chapter both as an organizational setting within which policies are interpreted and implemented and as a venue in which politicians (called bureaucrats or bureaucratic agents) pursue their own (and sometimes public) interests. We will first seek to define and describe bureaucracy as a social and political phenomenon. Second, we will look in detail at American bureaucracy in action by examining the government's major administrative agencies, their role in the governmental process, and their political behavior.

HOW DOES BUREAUCRACY WORK?

Despite the tendency to criticize bureaucracy, most Americans recognize that maintaining order in a large society is impossible without some sort of large governmental apparatus staffed by professionals with some expertise in public administration. When we approve of what a government agency is doing, we give the phenomenon a positive name, *administration;* when we disapprove, we call the phenomenon *bureaucracy.*

bureaucracy The complex structure of offices, tasks, rules, and principles of organization that are employed by all large-scale institutions to coordinate the work of their personnel.

Although the terms "administration" and "bureaucracy" are often used interchangeably, it is useful to distinguish between the two. Administration is the more general of the two terms; it refers to all the ways human beings might rationally coordinate their efforts to achieve a common goal. This applies to private as well as public organizations. **Bureaucracy** refers to the actual offices, tasks, and principles of organization that are employed in the most formal and sustained administration. The "In Brief" box on page 190 defines bureaucracy by identifying its basic characteristics.

FIGURE 7.1 THE PUBLIC THINKS THERE IS A LOT OF WASTE IN GOVERNMENT

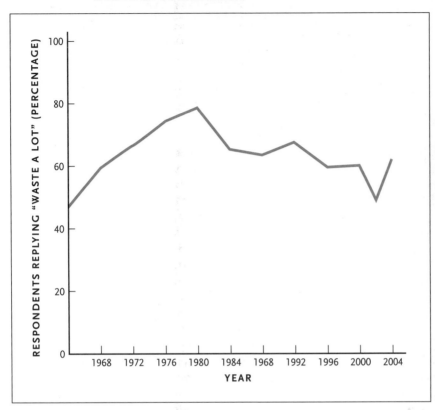

SOURCE: American National Election Studies, Cumulative Data File, 1948–2004, www.electionstudies.org/index.htm.

Bureaucratic Organization Enhances Efficiency

The core of bureaucracy is the *division of labor*. The key to bureaucratic effectiveness is the coordination of experts performing complex tasks. If each job is specialized in order to gain efficiencies, then each worker must depend on the output of other workers, and that requires careful *allocation* of jobs and resources. Inevitably, bureaucracies become hierarchical, often approximating a pyramid in form. At the base of the organization are workers with the fewest skills and specializations; one supervisor can deal with a relatively large number of these workers. At the next level of the organization, where workers are more highly specialized, the supervision and coordination of work involves fewer workers per supervisor. Toward the top of the organization, a very small number of high-level executives engages in the "management" of the organization, meaning the coordination and oversight of all the tasks and functions, plus the allocation of the appropriate supplies, and the distribution of the outputs of the organization to the market (if it is a "private sector" organization) or to the public.

Six Primary Characteristics of Bureaucracy

Division of Labor

To increase productivity, workers are specialized.

Each develops a skill in a particular job and then performs that job routinely.

Allocation of Functions

Each worker depends on the output of other workers.

No worker makes an entire product alone.

Allocation of Responsibility

A task becomes a personal and contractual responsibility.

Supervision

An unbroken chain of command ties superiors to subordinates from top to bottom to ensure orderly communication between workers and levels of the organization.

Each superior is assigned a limited number of subordinates to supervise—this is the span of control.

Purchase of Full-time Employment

The organization controls all the time the worker is on the job, so each worker can be assigned and held to a task.

Identification of Career within the Organization

Paths of seniority along with pension rights and promotions are all designed to encourage workers to identify with the organization.

Bureaucracies Allow Governments to Operate

Bureaucracy, when used pejoratively, conjures up images of endless paperwork, red tape, and lazy, uncaring employees. In fact, the term refers to a rather spectacular human achievement. By dividing up tasks, matching tasks to a labor force that develops appropriately specialized skills, routinizing procedures, and providing the incentive structure and oversight arrangements to get large numbers of people to operate in a coordinated, purposeful fashion, bureaucracies accomplish tasks and missions in a manner that would otherwise be unimaginable. The provision of "government goods" as broad as the defense of people, property, and national borders or as narrow as a subsidy to a wheat farmer, beef rancher, or manufacturer of specialty steel requires organization, routines, standards, and, at the end of the day, the authority for someone to cut a check and put it in the mail. Bureaucracies are created to do these things. No large organization would be larger than the sum of its parts, and many would be smaller, without bureaucratizing its activities.

Bureaucracy also consolidates a range of complementary programs and insulates them from the predatory ambitions of out-of-sympathy political forces. Nothing in this world is permanent, but bureaucracies come close. By creating clienteles—in the legislature, the world of interest groups, and public opinion—a bureaucracy establishes a coalition of supporters, some of whom will fight to the end to keep it in place. It is a well-known rule of thumb that everyone in the political world cares deeply and intensely about a subset of policies and the agencies that produce them, and opposes other policies and agencies but not with nearly the same passion. Opponents, to succeed, must clear many hurdles, whereas proponents, to maintain the status quo, must only marshall their forces at a few veto points. In the final analysis, opponents typically meet obstacle after obstacle and eventually give up their uphill battles and concentrate on protecting and expanding that about which they care most deeply. In a complex political system such as that of the United States, it is much easier to do the latter. Politicians acknowledge this fact of life. Consequently, both opponents and proponents of a particular set of government activities wage the fiercest battles at the time programs are enacted and a bureaucracy is created. Once created, these organizations assume a position of relative permanence.

So, in response to the question of how bureaucracy makes government possible, there is an *efficiency* part to the answer and a *credibility* part. The creation of a bureau is a way to deliver government goods efficiently *and* a device by which to "tie one's hands," thereby providing a credible commitment to the long-term existence of a policy.

Bureaucrats Fulfill Important Roles

"Government by offices and desks" conveys to most people a picture of hundreds of office workers shuffling millions of pieces of paper. There is a lot of truth in that image, but we have to look more closely at what papers are being shuffled and why. More than fifty years ago, an astute observer defined bureaucracy as "continuous routine business."[1] Almost any organization succeeds by reducing its work to routines, with each routine being given to a different specialist. But specialization separates people from each other; one worker's output becomes another worker's input. The timing of such relationships is essential, and this requires these workers to stay in communication with each other. Communication is the key. In fact, bureaucracy was the first information network. Routine came first; voluminous routine came as bureaucracies grew and specialized.

Bureaucrats Implement Laws. Bureaucrats, whether in public or in private organizations, communicate with each other in order to coordinate all the specializations within their organization. This coordination is necessary to carry out the primary task of bureaucracy, which is **implementation**, that is, implementing

implementation
The efforts of departments and agencies to translate laws into specific bureaucratic routines.

[1] Arnold Brecht and Comstock Glaser, *The Art and Techniques of Administration in German Ministries* (Cambridge, Mass.: Harvard University Press, 1940), p. 6.

the objectives of the organization as laid down by its board of directors (if a private company) or by law (if a public agency). In government, the "bosses" are ultimately the legislature and the elected chief executive.

Bureaucrats Make and Enforce Rules. When the bosses—Congress, in particular, when it is making the law—are clear in their instructions to bureaucrats, implementation is a fairly straightforward process. Bureaucrats translate the law into specific routines for each of the employees of an agency. But what happens to routine administrative implementation when several bosses disagree as to what the instructions ought to be? This requires a fourth job for bureaucrats: interpretation. Interpretation is a form of implementation, in that the bureaucrats still have to carry out what they believe to be the intentions of their superiors. But when bureaucrats have to interpret a law before implementing it, they are in effect engaging in lawmaking.[2] Congress often deliberately delegates to an administrative agency the responsibility of lawmaking. Members of Congress often conclude that some area of industry needs regulating or some area of the environment needs protection, but they are unwilling or unable to specify just how that should be done. In such situations, Congress delegates to the appropriate agency a broad authority within which the bureaucrats have to make law, through the procedures of rule making and administrative adjudication.

Rule making is exactly the same as legislation; in fact it is often referred to as quasilegislation. The rules issued by government agencies provide more detailed and specific indications of what the policy actually will mean. For example, the Forest Service is charged with making policies that govern the use of national forests. Just before President Clinton left office, the agency issued rules that banned new road building and development in the forests. This was a goal long sought by environmentalists and conservationists. In 2005, the Forest Service relaxed the rules, allowing states to make proposals for building new roads within the national forests. Just as the timber industry opposed the Clinton rule banning road building, environmentalists challenged the new ruling and sued the Forest Service in federal court for violating clean-water and endangered-species legislation.

New rules proposed by an agency take effect only after a period of public comment. Reaction from the people or businesses that are subject to the rules may cause an agency to modify the rules they first issue. The rule-making process is thus highly political. Once rules are approved, they are published in the *Federal Register* and have the force of law.

Bureaucrats Settle Disputes. Administrative adjudication is very similar to what the judiciary ordinarily does: applying rules and precedents to specific cases in order to settle disputes. In administrative adjudication, the agency charges the person or business suspected of violating the law. The ruling in an adjudication

---

[2] When bureaucrats engage in interpretation, the result is what political scientists call bureaucratic drift. Bureaucratic drift occurs because, as we've suggested, the "bosses" (in Congress) and the "agents" (within the bureaucracy) don't always share the same purposes. Bureaucrats also have their own agendas to fulfill.

dispute applies only to the specific case being considered. Many regulatory agencies use administrative adjudication to make decisions about specific products or practices. For example, product recalls are often the result of adjudication.

In sum, government bureaucrats do essentially the same things that bureaucrats in large private organizations do. But because of the authoritative, coercive nature of government, far more constraints are imposed on public bureaucrats than on private bureaucrats, even when their jobs are the same. Public bureaucrats are required to maintain a far more thorough paper trail. Public bureaucrats are also subject to a great deal more access from the public. Newspaper reporters, for example, have access to public bureaucrats. Public access has been vastly facilitated in the past half-century; the adoption of the Freedom of Information Act (FOIA) in 1966 gave ordinary citizens the right of access to agency files and agency data to determine whether derogatory information exists in the file about citizens themselves and to learn about what the agency is doing in general.

Moreover, citizens are given far more opportunities to participate in the decision-making processes of public agencies. There are limits of time, money, and expertise to this kind of access, but it does exist, and it occupies a great deal of the time of mid-level and senior public bureaucrats. This public exposure and access serves a purpose, but it also cuts down significantly on the efficiency of public bureaucrats. Thus, much of the lower efficiency of public agencies can be attributed to the political, judicial, legal, and publicity restraints put on public bureaucrats.

Legislatures Find It Valuable to Delegate

In principle, the legislature could make all bureaucratic decisions itself, writing very detailed legislation each year, dotting every *i* and crossing every *t*. In some jurisdictions—tax policy, for example—this is in fact done. Tax policy is promulgated in significant detail by the House Ways and Means Committee, the Senate Finance Committee, and the Joint Committee on Taxation. The Internal Revenue Service, the administrative agency charged with implementation, engages in relatively less discretionary activity than many other regulatory and administrative agencies. But this is the exception.

The norm is for statutory authority to be delegated to the bureaucracy, sometimes with specificity but often in relatively vague terms. The bureaucracy is expected to fill in the gaps. This, however, is not a blank check to exercise unconstrained discretion. The bureaucracy is expected to be guided by legislative intent, and it will be held to account by the legislature's oversight of bureaucratic performance. The latter is monitored by the staffs of relevant legislative committees, which also serve as repositories for complaints from affected parties.[3] Poor performance or the exercise of discretion inconsistent with the preferences of the important legislators invites sanctions ranging from the browbeating of senior bureaucrats to the trimming of budgets and the clipping of authority.

---

[3] See Mathew D. McCubbins and Thomas Schwartz, "Congressional Oversight Overlooked: Police Patrols versus Fire Alarms," *American Journal of Political Science* 28 (1984): 165–79.

The delegation relationship will be revisited later in this chapter. For now, simply note that over and above the more conventional reasons for bureaucracy, politicians find it convenient to delegate many of the nuts-and-bolts decisions to bureaucratic agents. We will take up the reasons shortly.

HOW IS THE EXECUTIVE BRANCH ORGANIZED?

Cabinet departments, agencies, and bureaus are the operating parts of the bureaucratic whole. These parts can be separated into four general types: (1) cabinet departments, (2) independent agencies, (3) government corporations, and (4) independent regulatory commissions.

Although Figure 7.2 is an "organizational chart" of the Department of Agriculture, any other department could have been used as an illustration. At the top is the head of the department, who in the United States is called the "secretary" of the department. Below the department head are several top administrators, such as the general counsel and the chief financial officer, whose responsibilities cut across the various departmental functions and enable the secretary to manage the entire organization. Of equal status are the assistant and undersecretaries, each of whom has management responsibilities for a group of operating agencies, which are arranged vertically below each of the undersecretaries.

The next tier, generally called the bureau level, is the highest level of responsibility for specialized programs. The names of these bureau-level agencies are often very well known to the public: The Forest Service and the Food Safety and Inspection Service are two examples. Sometimes they are officially called bureaus, as in the Federal Bureau of Investigation (FBI), which is a bureau in the Department of Justice. Nevertheless, "bureau" is also the generic term for this level of administrative agency. Within the bureaus, there are divisions, offices, services, and units—sometimes designating agencies of the same status, sometimes designating agencies of lesser status.

Not all government agencies are part of cabinet departments. Some independent agencies are set up by Congress outside the departmental structure altogether, even though the president appoints and directs the heads of these agencies. Independent agencies usually have broad powers to provide public services that are either too expensive or too important to be left to private initiatives. Some examples of independent agencies are the National Aeronautics and Space Administration (NASA), the Central Intelligence Agency (CIA), and the Environmental Protection Agency (EPA). Government corporations are a third type of government agency, but are more like private businesses performing and charging for a market service, such as delivering the mail (the United States Postal Service) or transporting railroad passengers (Amtrak).

A fourth type of agency is the independent regulatory commission, given broad discretion to make rules. The first regulatory agencies established by Congress, beginning with the Interstate Commerce Commission in 1887, were set up

FIGURE 7.2 ORGANIZATIONAL CHART OF THE DEPARTMENT OF AGRICULTURE

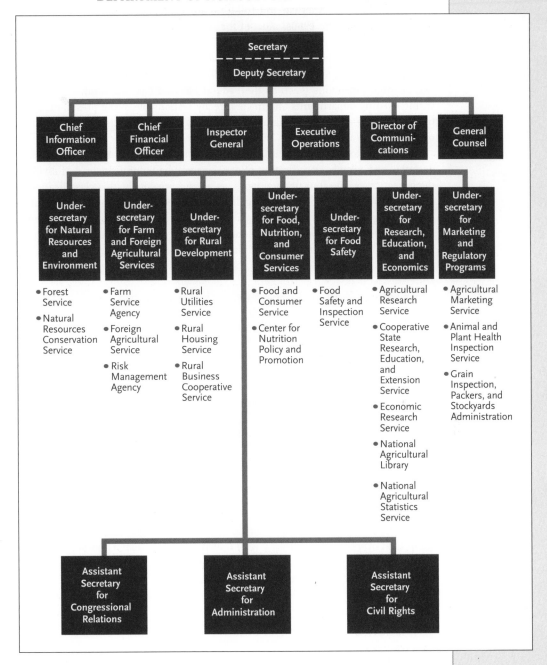

SOURCE: U.S. Department of Agriculture, www.usda.gov/img/content/org_chart_enlarged.jpg (accessed 5/21/09).

as independent regulatory commissions because Congress recognized that regulatory agencies are "minilegislatures," whose rules are the same as legislation but require the kind of expertise and full-time attention that is beyond the capacity of Congress. Until the 1960s, most of the regulatory agencies that were set up by Congress, such as the Federal Trade Commission (1914) and the Federal Communications Commission (1934), were independent regulatory commissions. But beginning in the late 1960s and the early 1970s, all new regulatory programs, with two or three exceptions (such as the Federal Election Commission), were placed within existing departments and made directly responsible to the president. Since the 1970s, no major new regulatory programs have been established, independent or otherwise.

There are too many agencies in the executive branch to identify, much less to describe, so a simple classification of agencies will be helpful. Instead of dividing the bureaucracy into four general types, as we did previously, this classification is organized by the mission of each agency, as defined by its jurisdiction: clientele agencies, agencies for maintenance of the Union, regulatory agencies, and redistributive agencies. We will examine each of these types of agencies, focusing on both their formal structure and their place in the political process.

Clientele Agencies Serve Particular Interests

clientele agency
Department or bureau of government whose mission is to promote, serve, or represent a particular interest.

The entire Department of Agriculture is an example of a **clientele agency**. So are the departments of the Interior, Labor, and Commerce. Although all administrative agencies have clienteles, certain agencies are singled out and called by that name because they are directed by law to foster and promote the interests of their clientele. For example, the Department of Commerce and Labor was founded in 1903 as a single department "to foster, promote, and develop the foreign and domestic commerce, the mining, the manufacturing, the shipping, and fishing industries, and the transportation facilities of the United States."[4] It remained a single department until 1913, when the law created the two separate departments of Commerce and Labor, with each statute providing for the same obligation: to support and foster their respective clienteles.[5] The Department of Agriculture serves the many farming interests that, taken together, are one of the United States' largest economic sectors.

Most clientele agencies locate a relatively large proportion of their total personnel in field offices dealing directly with the clientele. The Extension Service of the Department of Agriculture is among the most familiar, with its numerous local "extension agents" who consult with farmers on farm productivity. These same agencies also seek to foster the interests of their clientele by providing "functional representation"; that is, they try to learn what their clients' interests and needs are and then operate almost as a lobby in Washington on their behalf. In addition to

---

[4] 32 Stat. 825; 15 USC 1501.

[5] For a detailed account of the creation of the Department of Commerce and Labor and its split into two separate departments, see Theodore J. Lowi, *The End of Liberalism* (New York: Norton, 1979), pp. 78–84.

the Department of Agriculture, other clientele agencies include the Department of Interior and five of the newest cabinet departments: Housing and Urban Development (HUD), created in 1966; Transportation (DOT), created in 1966; Energy (DOE), created in 1977; and Education (ED) and Health and Human Services (HHS), both created in 1979.[6]

Agencies for Maintenance of the Union Keep the Government Going

These agencies could be called public-order agencies were it not for the fact that the Constitution entrusts so many of the vital functions of public order, such as the police, to the state governments. But some agencies vital to maintaining *national* bonds do exist in the national government, and they can be grouped for convenience into three categories: (1) agencies for control of the sources of government revenue, (2) agencies for control of conduct defined as a threat to internal national security, and (3) agencies for defending American security from external threats. The departments of greatest power in these three areas are Treasury, Justice, Defense, State, and Homeland Security.

Revenue Agencies.   The Internal Revenue Service (IRS) is the most important revenue agency. The IRS is also one of the federal government's largest bureaucracies. Over 100,000 employees are spread through four regions, sixty-three districts, ten service centers, and hundreds of local offices.

Agencies for Internal Security.   As long as the country is not in a state of insurrection, most of the task of maintaining the Union takes the form of legal work, and the main responsibility for that lies with the Department of Justice. It is indeed a luxury, and rare in the world, when national unity can be maintained by routines of civil law rather than imposed by an army with guns. The largest and most important agency in the Justice Department is the Criminal Division, which is responsible for enforcing all the federal criminal laws except a few specifically assigned to other divisions. Criminal litigation is actually done by the U.S. attorneys. A presidentially appointed U.S. attorney is assigned to each federal judicial district, and he or she supervises the work of assistant U.S. attorneys. The work or jurisdiction of the Antitrust and Civil Rights Divisions is described by their official names. Although it looms so very large in American folklore, the FBI is simply another bureau of the Department of Justice. The FBI handles no litigation but instead is the information-gathering agency for all the other divisions.

In 2002, Congress created the Department of Homeland Security to coordinate the nation's defense against the threat of terrorism. The new department is responsible for a number of tasks, including protecting commercial airlines from would-be hijackers.

---

[6] The departments of Education and of Health and Human Services until 1979 were joined in a single department, the Department of Health, Education, and Welfare (HEW), which had been established by Congress in 1953.

Agencies for External National Security. Two departments occupy center stage here, State and Defense. A few key agencies outside State and Defense also have external national-security functions. They are treated in this chapter only as bureaucratic phenomena and as examples of the political problems relevant to administration.

Although diplomacy is generally considered the primary task of the State Department, diplomatic missions make up only one of its organizational dimensions. The State Department is also composed of geographic, or regional, bureaus concerned with all problems within the defined regions of the world; "functional" bureaus, which handle such things as economic and business affairs, intelligence, and research; and international organizations and bureaus of internal affairs, which handle such areas as security, finance and management, and legal issues.

Despite the importance of the State Department in foreign affairs, fewer than 20 percent of all U.S. government employees working abroad are directly under its authority. By far the largest number of career government professionals working abroad are under the authority of the Defense Department.

The creation of the Department of Defense by legislation enacted between 1947 and 1949 was an effort to unify the two historic military departments, the War Department and the Navy Department, and integrate into them a new department, the Air Force Department. Real unification did not occur, however. Instead, the Defense Department added more pluralism to national security.

America's primary political problem with its military has not been the historic one of how to keep the military out of the politics of governing, a problem that has plagued so many countries in Europe and Latin America. The American military problem is instead the politics of the pork barrel. President Clinton's long list of proposed military-base closings, a major part of his budget-cutting drive for 1993, caused a firestorm of opposition even in his own party, with some of the opposition coming from members of Congress who otherwise prominently favored significant reductions in the Pentagon budget. Emphasis on jobs rather than strategy and policy means pork-barrel use of the military for political purposes. This is a classic way for a bureaucracy to defend itself politically in a democracy. It is an example of the distributive tendency, in which the bureaucracy ensures political support among elected officials by making sure to distribute things—military bases, contracts, facilities, and jobs—to the states and districts that elected the legislators. As is commonly known, it is hard to bite the hand that feeds you! Thus the best way to understand the military in American politics is to study it within the bureaucratic framework that is used to explain the domestic agencies.

Regulatory Agencies Guide Individual Conduct

regulatory agency A department, bureau, or independent agency whose primary mission is to impose limits, restrictions, or other obligations on the conduct of individuals or companies in the private sector.

The United States has no Department of Regulation but has many **regulatory agencies**. Some of these are bureaus within departments, such as the Food and Drug Administration (FDA) in the Department of Health and Human Services, the Occupational Safety and Health Administration (OSHA) in the Department of Labor, and the Animal and Plant Health and Inspection Service (APHIS) in the Department of Agriculture. Other regulatory agencies are independent regulatory commissions. An example is the Federal Trade Commission (FTC). But whether departmental or independent, an agency or commission is regulatory if Congress delegates to it relatively broad powers over a sector of the economy or a type of commercial activity and authorizes it to make rules governing the conduct of people and businesses within that jurisdiction. Rules made by regulatory agencies have the force and effect of legislation; indeed, the rules they make are referred to as **administrative legislation**. And when these agencies make decisions or orders settling disputes between parties or between the government and a party, they are really acting like courts.

Agencies for Redistribution Implement Fiscal/Monetary and Welfare Policies

Welfare agencies and fiscal/monetary agencies are responsible for the transfer of hundreds of billions of dollars annually between the public and the private spheres, and through such transfers these agencies influence how people and corporations spend and invest trillions of dollars annually. We call them agencies of redistribution because they influence the amount of money in the economy and because they directly influence who has money, who has credit, and whether people will want to invest or save their money rather than spend it.

Fiscal and Monetary Agencies. Government activity affecting or relating to money may be partitioned into *fiscal* and *monetary* policy. Fiscal policy includes taxing and spending activities. Monetary policies have to do with banks, credit, and currency.

Administration of fiscal policy is primarily performed in the Treasury Department. It is no contradiction to include the Treasury here as well as with the agencies for maintenance of the Union. This indicates that (1) the Treasury is a complex department performing more than one function of government, and (2) traditional controls have had to be adapted to modern economic conditions and new technologies.

Today, in addition to administering and policing income tax and other tax collections, the Treasury is responsible for managing the enormous federal debt. The Treasury Department is responsible for printing the currency that we use, but currency represents only a tiny proportion of the entire money economy. Most of the trillions of dollars used in the transactions that compose the private and public sectors of the U.S. economy exist on printed accounts and computers, not in currency.

Another important fiscal agency (although for technical reasons it is called an agency of monetary policy) is the **Federal Reserve System**, headed by the Federal Reserve Board. The Federal Reserve System (the Fed) has authority over the credit rates and lending activities of the nation's most important banks. Established by Congress in 1913, the Fed is responsible for adjusting the supply of money to the needs of banks in the different regions and of the commerce and industry in each. The Fed helps shift money from where there is too much to where it is needed. It also ensures that the banks do not overextend themselves by having lending policies that are too liberal, out of fear that if there is a sudden economic scare, a run

administrative legislation Rules made by regulatory agencies and commissions.

Federal Reserve System (the Fed) Consisting of twelve Federal Reserve Banks, an agency that facilitates exchanges of cash, checks, and credit; it regulates member banks, and it uses monetary policies to fight inflation and deflation.

on a few banks might be contagious and cause another terrible stock market crash like the one in 1929. The Federal Reserve Board sits at the top of the pyramid of twelve district Federal Reserve Banks, which are "bankers' banks," serving the monetary needs of the hundreds of member banks in the national bank system (see also Chapter 13).

Welfare Agencies.   No single government agency is responsible for all the programs that make up the "welfare state." The largest agency in this field is the Social Security Administration (SSA), which manages the social insurance aspects of Social Security and SSI. Other agencies in the Department of Health and Human Services administer Temporary Assistance to Needy Families (TANF) and Medicaid, and the Department of Agriculture is responsible for the food stamp program. With the exception of Social Security, these are means-tested programs, requiring applicants to demonstrate that their total annual cash earnings fall below an officially defined poverty line. These public assistance programs compose a large administrative burden. In 1996, Congress enacted the Personal Responsibility and Work Opportunity Reconciliation Act (PRA), which abolished virtually all *national means-tested* public assistance programs, devolving that power to state governments.

THE PROBLEM OF BUREAUCRATIC CONTROL

Two centuries, millions of employees, and trillions of dollars after the Founding, we must return to James Madison's observation that "you must first enable the government to control the governed; and in the next place oblige it to control itself."[7] Today the problem is the same, but the form has changed. Our problem now is bureaucracy and our inability to keep it accountable to elected political authorities.

Bureaucrats Have Their Own Motivational Considerations

The economist William Niskanen proposed that we consider a bureau or department of government as analogous to a division of a private firm and conceive of the bureaucrat just as we would the manager who runs that division.[8] In particular, Niskanen stipulated that a bureau chief or department head can be thought of as trying to maximize his or her budget (just as the private-sector counterpart tries to maximize his or her division's profits).

There are quite a number of motivational bases on which bureaucratic budget maximizing might be justified. A cynical (though some would say realistic) basis for budget maximizing is that the bureaucrat's own compensation is often tied to the size of his or her budget. A second, related motivation for large budgets is nonmaterial personal gratification. An individual understandably enjoys the prestige

---

[7] Alexander Hamilton, James Madison, and John Jay, *The Federalist Papers*, Clinton L. Rossiter, ed. (New York: New American Library, 1961), no. 51.

[8] William A. Niskanen Jr., *Bureaucracy and Representative Government* (Chicago: Aldine, 1971).

and respect that comes from running a major enterprise. You can't take these things to the bank or put them on your family's dinner table, but your self-esteem and your status are surely buoyed by the conspicuous fact that your bureau or division has a large budget.

But salary and power tripping are not the only forces driving a bureaucrat toward gaining as large a budget as possible. Some bureaucrats, perhaps most, actually *care* about their mission.[9] They initially choose to go into public safety, or the military, or health care, or social work, or education because they believe in the importance of helping people in their community. As they rise through the ranks of a public bureaucracy and assume management responsibilities, they take this mission orientation with them. Thus they try to secure as large a budget as they can to succeed in achieving the mission to which they have devoted their professional lives.

This does not mean that the legislature, which controls the bureau's budget, has to fork over whatever the bureau requests. Critics of the budget-maximizing theory call into question its assumption about the passivity of the legislature. The legislature, the only customer of the bureau's product, in essence tells the bureau how much it is willing to pay for various production levels. The critics suggest that this is akin to a customer walking onto a used-car lot and telling the salesman precisely how much he or she is willing to spend for each vehicle.[10]

In a representative democracy, it may be difficult for the legislature to keep silent about its own willingness to pay. The bureau, at any rate, can do some research to judge the preferences of various legislators based on who their constituents are. But legislators can do research, too. Indeed, we suggested in Chapter 5 that the collection, evaluation, and dissemination of information are precisely the things in which specialized legislative committees engage. After the fact, the committees engage in oversight, making sure that what the legislature was told at the time when authorization and appropriations were voted on actually holds in practice. In short, the legislature can be much more proactive than the Niskanen budget-maximizing theory gives it credit for.

Before leaving motivational considerations, we should remark that budget maximizing is not the only objective that bureaucrats pursue. It needs to be emphasized and reemphasized that career civil servants and high-level political appointees are *politicians*. They spend their professional lives pursuing political goals, bargaining, forming alliances and coalitions, solving cooperation and collective-action problems, making policy decisions, operating within and interfacing with political institutions—in short, doing what other politicians do. As politicians subject to the oversight and authority of others, bureaucrats must be strategic and forward thinking. Whichever party wins control of the House or the Senate, whichever candidate wins the presidency, whoever becomes chair of the legislative committee with authorization or appropriation responsibility over their agency, life will go on, and bureau chiefs will have to adjust to the prevailing political winds. To

---

[9] John Brehm and Scott Gates, *Working, Shirking, and Sabotage: Bureaucratic Response to a Democratic Public* (Ann Arbor: University of Michigan Press, 1997).

[10] This and other related points are drawn from Gary J. Miller and Terry M. Moe, "Bureaucrats, Legislators, and the Size of Government," *American Political Science Review* 77, no. 2 (June 1983): 297–323.

protect and expand authority and resources, bureaucratic politicians seek, in the form of autonomy and discretion, insurance against political change. They don't always succeed in acquiring this freedom, but they do try to insulate themselves from changes in the broader political world.[11] So bureaucratic motivations include budget-maximizing behavior, to be sure, but bureaucrats also seek the autonomy to weather changes in the political atmosphere and the discretion and flexibility to achieve their goals.

Control of the Bureaucracy Is a Principal-Agent Problem

How does the principal-agent problem apply to the president's and Congress's control of the bureaucracy? Suppose the legislation that created the EPA required that after ten years new legislation be passed renewing its existence and mandate. The issue facing the House, the Senate, and the president in their consideration of renewal involves how much authority to give this agency and how much money to permit it to spend. Eventually relevant majorities in the House and the Senate and the president agree on a policy reflecting a compromise among their various points of view.

The bureaucrats are not particularly pleased with this compromise because it gives them considerably less authority and funding than they had hoped for. If they flout the wishes of their principals and implement a policy exactly to their liking, they risk the unified wrath of the House, the Senate, and the president. Undoubtedly the politicians would react with new legislation (and they would also presumably find other political appointees and career bureaucrats at the EPA to replace the current bureaucratic leadership). If, however, the EPA implements some policy located between its own preferences and the preferences of its principals, it might be able to get away with it.

Thus we have a principal-agent relationship in which a political principal—a collective principal consisting of the president and coalitions in the House and Senate—formulates policy and creates an implementation agent to execute its details. The agent, however, has policy preferences of its own and, unless subjected to further controls, will inevitably implement a policy that drifts toward its ideal.

A variety of controls might conceivably restrict this **bureaucratic drift**. Indeed, legislative scholars often point to congressional hearings in which bureaucrats may be publicly humiliated, annual appropriations decisions that may be used to punish out-of-control bureaus, and watchdog agents, such as the Government Accountability Office, that may be used to monitor and scrutinize the bureau's performance. But these all come after the fact and may be only partially credible threats to the agency. The most powerful before-the-fact political weapon is the appointment process. The adroit control of the political stance of a given bureau by the president and Congress, through their joint powers of nomination and confirmation (especially if they can arrange for appointees who closely share the political consensus on policy)

bureaucratic drift The oft-observed phenomenon of bureaucratic implementation that produces policy more to the liking of the bureaucracy than to the original intention of the legislation that created it, but without triggering a political reaction from elected officials.

---

[11] For an expanded view of bureaucratic autonomy and insulation with historical application to the U.S. Department of Agriculture and the Post Office Department, see Daniel P. Carpenter, *The Forging of Bureaucratic Autonomy: Reputations, Networks, and Policy Innovation in Executive Agencies, 1862–1928* (Princeton, N.J.: Princeton University Press, 2001).

is a self-enforcing mechanism for ensuring reliable agent performance. A second powerful before-the-fact weapon is procedural controls. The general rules and regulations that direct the manner in which federal agencies conduct their affairs are contained in the Administrative Procedure Act. This act is almost always the boilerplate of legislation creating and renewing federal agencies. It is not uncommon, however, for an agency's procedures to be tailored to suit particular circumstances.

The President, as Chief Executive, Can Direct Agencies

In 1937, President Franklin Roosevelt's Committee on Administrative Management gave official sanction to an idea that had been growing increasingly urgent: "The president needs help." The national government had grown rapidly during the preceding twenty-five years, but the structures and procedures necessary to manage the burgeoning executive branch had not yet been established. The response to the call for help for the president initially took the form of three management policies: (1) All communications and decisions that related to executive policy decisions must pass through the White House; (2) to cope with such a flow, the White House must have an adequate staff of specialists in research, analysis, legislative and legal writing, and public affairs; and (3) the White House must have additional staff to follow through on presidential decisions—to ensure that those decisions are made, communicated to Congress, and carried out by the appropriate agency.

Establishing a management capacity for the presidency began in earnest with FDR, but it did not stop there. The story of the modern presidency can be told largely as a series of responses to the plea for managerial help. Indeed, each expansion of the national government into new policies and programs in the twentieth century was accompanied by a parallel expansion of the president's management authority. This pattern began even before FDR's presidency, with the policy innovations of President Woodrow Wilson between 1913 and 1920. Congress responded to Wilson's policies with the 1921 Budget and Accounting Act, which conferred on the White House agenda-setting power over budgeting. The president, in his annual budget message, transmits comprehensive budgetary recommendations to Congress. Because Congress retains ultimate legislative authority, a president's proposals are sometimes said to be dead on arrival on Capitol Hill. Nevertheless, the power to frame deliberations is potent and constitutes an important management tool. Each successive president has continued this pattern of setting the congressional agenda, creating what we now know as the managerial presidency.

For example, President Clinton inaugurated one of the most systematic efforts to change the way government does business in his National Performance Review. Heavily influenced by the theories of management consultants who prize decentralization, customer responsiveness, and employee initiative, Clinton sought to infuse these new practices into government.[12] George W. Bush was the first president with a graduate degree in business. His management strategy followed a standard business-school dictum: Select skilled subordinates and delegate responsibility to them. Bush followed this model closely in his appointment of highly experienced

---

[12] See John Micklethwait, "Managing to Look Attractive," *New Statesman*, November 8, 1996, p. 24.

officials to cabinet positions. This was no guarantee of policy success, as doubts emerged about the conduct of the Iraq war, and especially about the leadership of the highly experienced secretary of defense Donald Rumsfeld.

Congress Can Promote Responsible Bureaucracy through Oversight and Incentives

Congress is constitutionally essential to responsible bureaucracy because, in a "government of laws," legislation is the key to government responsibility. When a law is passed and its intent is clear, the president knows what to "faithfully execute," and the agency understands its guidelines. But when Congress enacts vague legislation, everybody, from president to agency to courts to interest groups, gets involved in the interpretation of legislation. In that event, to whom is the agency responsible?

The answer lies in **oversight**. The more legislative power Congress delegates to the executive branch, the more power it seeks to regain through committee and subcommittee oversight of executive branch agencies. The standing committee system of Congress is well suited for oversight, inasmuch as most congressional committees and subcommittees have jurisdictions roughly parallel to one or more executive departments or agencies. Appropriations committees and authorization committees have oversight powers—and delegate their respective oversight powers to their subcommittees. In addition, there is a committee on government operations both in the House and the Senate, and these committees have oversight powers not limited by departmental jurisdiction.

Committees and subcommittees oversee agencies through public hearings. Representatives from each agency, the White House, major interest groups, and other concerned citizens are called as witnesses to present testimony at these hearings. These are printed in large volumes and are widely circulated. Detailed records of the recent activities and expenditures of each and every agency can be found in these volumes. The number of hearings and equivalent public meetings (sometimes called investigations) rose steadily from 1950 to 1980, as Congress tried through oversight to keep pace with the expansion of the executive branch.[13] However, around 1980 the number began to decline. New questions about the ability of Congress to exercise oversight arose when the Republicans took over Congress in 1995. Reductions in committee staffing and an emphasis on using investigative oversight to uncover scandal meant much less time spent on programmatic oversight. On issues of major national importance, multiple committees may initiate oversight hearings simultaneously. No less than a dozen congressional committees (along with the Justice Department and the Securities and Exchange Commission) launched investigations into the collapse of the giant energy company Enron.

oversight The effort by Congress, through hearings, investigations, and other techniques, to exercise control over the activities of executive agencies.

---

[13] For figures on the frequency and character of oversight, see Lawrence Dodd and Richard Schott, *Congress and the Administrative State* (New York: Wiley, 1979), p. 169. See also Norman Ornstein et al., *Vital Statistics on Congress, 1987–88* (Washington, D.C.: Congressional Quarterly Press, 1987), pp. 161–62. For a valuable and skeptical assessment of legislative oversight of administration, see James W. Fesler and Donald F. Kettl, *The Politics of the Administrative Process* (Chatham, N.J.: Chatham House, 1991), chap. 11.

Although congressional oversight is potent because of Congress's power to make—and, therefore, to change—the law, often the most effective and influential lever over bureaucratic accountability is "the power of the purse"—the ability of the House and Senate committees and subcommittees on appropriations to look at agency performance through the microscope of the annual appropriations process. This annual process makes bureaucrats attentive to Congress because they know that Congress has a chance each year to reduce their funding.[14] This may be another explanation for why there may be some downsizing but almost no terminations of federal agencies.

Congressional Oversight: Abdication or Strategic Delegation? Congress often grants the executive-branch bureaucracies discretion in determining certain features of a policy during the implementation phase. Although the complexities of governing a modern industrialized democracy make the granting of discretion necessary, some argue that Congress not only gives unelected bureaucrats too much discretion but also delegates too much policy-making authority to them. By enacting vague statutes that give bureaucrats broad discretion, so the argument goes, members of Congress effectively abdicate their constitutionally designated roles and effectively remove themselves from the policy-making process.

Others claim that even though Congress may possess the tools to engage in effective oversight, it fails to use them simply because we do not see Congress actively engaging in much oversight activity.[15] However, Mathew McCubbins and Thomas Schwartz argue that these critics have focused on the wrong type of oversight and have missed a type of oversight that benefits members of Congress in their bids for reelection.[16] McCubbins and Schwartz distinguish between two types of oversight: police patrol and fire alarm. Under the police-patrol variety, Congress systematically initiates investigation into the activity of agencies. Under the fire-alarm variety, members of Congress do not initiate investigations but wait for adversely affected citizens or interest groups to bring bureaucratic perversions of legislative intent to the attention of the relevant congressional committee. To make sure that individuals and groups bring these violations to members' attention—set off the fire alarm, so to speak—Congress passes laws that help individuals and groups make claims against the bureaucracy, granting them legal standing before administrative agencies and federal courts.

McCubbins and Schwartz argue that given the incentives of elected officials, it makes sense that we would see Congress engaging more in fire-alarm oversight than police-patrol oversight. Why should members spend their scarce resources (mainly time) to initiate investigations without having any evidence that they will reap electoral rewards? Police-patrol oversight can waste taxpayers' dollars too,

---

[14] See Aaron Wildavsky, *The New Politics of the Budgetary Process*, 2nd ed. (New York: HarperCollins, 1992), pp. 15–16.

[15] Morris S. Ogul, *Congress Oversees the Bureaucracy: Studies in Legislative Supervision* (Pittsburgh: University of Pittsburgh Press, 1976); and Peter Woll, *American Bureaucracy*, 2nd ed. (New York: Norton, 1977).

[16] See Mathew D. McCubbins and Thomas Schwartz, "Congressional Oversight Overlooked: Police Patrols versus Fire Alarms," *American Journal of Political Science* 28 (1984): 165–79.

because many investigations will not turn up any evidence of violations of legislative intent. It is much more cost effective for members to conserve their resources and then claim credit for fixing the problem (and saving the day) after the fire alarms have been sounded. The "Analyzing the Evidence" unit on page 208 takes a closer look at the problem of congressional oversight.

On the other hand, bureaucratic drift might be contained if Congress spent more of its time clarifying its legislative intent and less of its time on oversight activity. If its original intent in the law were clearer, Congress could then afford to defer to presidential management to maintain bureaucratic responsibility. Bureaucrats are more responsive to clear legislative guidance than to anything else. But when Congress and the president are at odds (or coalitions within Congress are at odds), bureaucrats have an opportunity to evade responsibility by playing one side off against the other.

HOW CAN BUREAUCRACY BE REDUCED?

Americans like to complain about bureaucracy. Americans don't like big government because big government means big bureaucracy, and bureaucracy means the federal service—about 2.7 million civilian and 1.4 million military employees.[17] Promises to cut the bureaucracy are popular campaign appeals; "cutting out the fat" with big reductions in the number of federal employees is held up as a sure-fire way of cutting the deficit.

Despite fears of bureaucratic growth getting out of hand, however, the federal service has hardly grown at all during the past thirty years; it reached its peak postwar level in 1968 with 2.9 million civilian employees plus an additional 3.6 million military personnel (a figure swollen by Vietnam). The number of civilian federal executive-branch employees has since remained close to that figure. The growth of the federal service is even less imposing when placed in the context of the total workforce and when compared with the size of state and local public employment, which was 19.4 million full- and part-time employees in 2009.[18] Figure 7.3 indicates that, since 1950, the ratio of federal service employment to the total workforce has been steady and in fact has declined slightly in the past twenty-five years. Another useful comparison is to be found in Figure 7.4. Although the dollar increase in federal spending shown by the bars looks very impressive, the horizontal line indicates that even here the national government has simply kept pace with the growth of the economy.

To sum up, the national government is indeed "very large," but the federal service has not been growing any faster than the economy or society. The same is

---

[17] This is just under 99 percent of all national government employees. About 2 percent work for the legislative branch and for the federal judiciary. U.S. Bureau of the Census, *Statistical Abstract of the U.S. 2009.*

[18] Ibid.

FIGURE 7.3 EMPLOYEES IN THE FEDERAL SERVICE

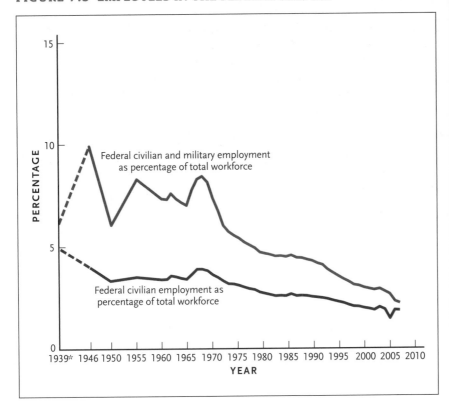

*Lines between 1939 and 1946 are broken because they connect the last prewar year with the first postwar year, disregarding the temporary ballooning of federal employees, especially in the military, during the war years.

NOTE: Workforce includes unemployed persons.

SOURCE: Tax Foundation, *Facts and Figures on Government Finance* (Baltimore: Johns Hopkins University Press, 1990), pp. 22, 44; Office of Management and Budget, *Budget of the U.S. Government, Fiscal Year 2009*, Table 17.5; and U.S. Bureau of Labor Statistics, "Employment Status of the Civilian Population by Sex and Age," *Labor Force Statistics from the Current Population Survey*, Table A1, www.bls.gov/news.release/empsit.t01.htm (accessed 5/22/09).

roughly true of the growth pattern of state and local public personnel. Bureaucracy keeps pace with our society, despite our seeming dislike for it, because we can't operate the control towers, the prisons, the Social Security system, and other essential elements without bureaucracy. And we certainly could not conduct wars in Iraq and Afghanistan without a gigantic military bureaucracy.

Nevertheless some Americans continue to argue that bureaucracy is too big and should be reduced. In the 1990s, Americans seemed particularly enthusiastic about reducing (or to use the popular contemporary word, "downsizing") the federal bureaucracy.

Keeping a Growing Bureaucracy in Check

The federal government is the United States's largest employer, with over 1.8 million civilian employees. This graph shows how the overall size of the federal bureaucracy has changed from 1940 to the present. During World War II, the number of civilian employees vastly increased, although the growth was largely concentrated in the Department of Defense. Since the war ended, the number of other civilian employees has steadily increased.

We can also use this graph to evaluate the views of the two political parties on the size of government. Generally speaking, Democrats are in favor of more government intervention and programs, while Republicans support a more limited role for the federal government. If this translates into policy, we should observe an increased number of federal employees during Democratic administrations. However, based on the figure, there does not seem to be a distinct pattern for either party. The total number of non-military federal employees ("other civilian employees") has risen steadily since the 1940s, regardless of which party was in power.

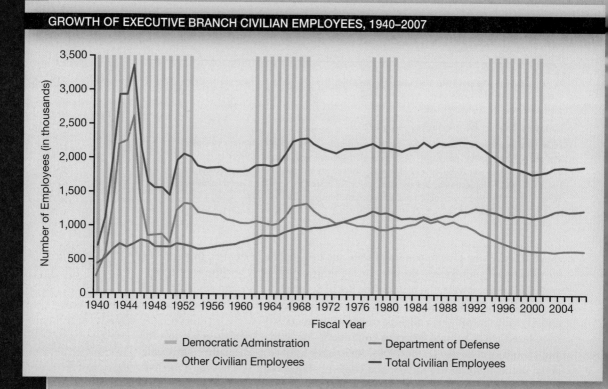

GROWTH OF EXECUTIVE BRANCH CIVILIAN EMPLOYEES, 1940–2007

Number of Employees (in thousands)

Fiscal Year

— Democratic Adminstration

— Other Civilian Employees

— Department of Defense

— Total Civilian Employees

As the size of the government increases, it may become more difficult to make sure the bureaucrats are doing their jobs. Although we often think of the Congress as a lawmaking body, it also carries out another important task—checking the executive branch through the oversight process. If Congress thinks the bureaucracy is no longer serving the public's interest as defined by the legislative branch, it can use its oversight powers to pull the agency back where it belongs. The political scientists Mathew McCubbins and Thomas Schwartz (1984) define two types of oversight: Police-Patrols and Fire-Alarms.

Under the police-patrol method, Congress systematically initiates investigations into the activity of agencies. The goal is to catch and punish enough violators so that the rest of the bureaucracy will be discouraged from straying too far from legislative intent. However, Congress cannot monitor all agencies at once. Police-patrol oversight is especially difficult because of the vast number of employees spread out over many government departments and agencies. The table below lists the number of employees in each of the fifteen executive Cabinet departments and the six largest independent agencies.

EXECUTIVE BRANCH EMPLOYEES

Executive Departments		Independent Agencies	
Defense	623,000	Social Security Administration	62,000
Veterans Affairs	239,000	National Aeronautics and Space Administration	18,000
Homeland Security	149,000		
Justice	105,000	Environmental Protection Agency	18,000
Agriculture	92,000	Tennessee Valley Authority	12,000
Treasury	109,000	General Services Administration	12,000
Interior	66,000	Federal Deposit Insurance Corporation	5,000
Health and Human Services	60,000		
Transportation	53,000		
Commerce	39,000		
Labor	16,000		
Energy	15,000		
State	14,000	Source: Bureau of Labor Statistics, U.S. Department of Labor, *Career Guide to Industries*, Federal Government, Excluding the Postal Service, www.bls.gov/oco/cg/cgs041.htm (accessed 4/28/09).	
Housing and Urban Development	10,000		
Education	4,000		

The fire-alarm method relies on the public. Members of Congress do not initiate investigations but wait for adversely affected citizens or interest groups to bring bureaucratic perversions of legislative intent to the attention of the relevant congressional committee. McCubbins and Schwartz argue that this method is more effective because, "Instead of sniffing for fires, Congress places fire-alarm boxes on street corners, builds neighborhood fire houses and sometimes dispatches its own hook-and-ladder in response to an alarm."[1] Since concerned citizens are out looking for bureaucratic fires, members of Congress will have more time to engage in other activities, such as securing reelection.

[1]Mathew McCubbins and Thomas Schwartz, "Congressional Oversight Overlooked: Police Patrols and Fire Alarms," *American Journal of Political Science* 28, no.1 (1984): 165–179.

FIGURE 7.4 ANNUAL FEDERAL OUTLAYS

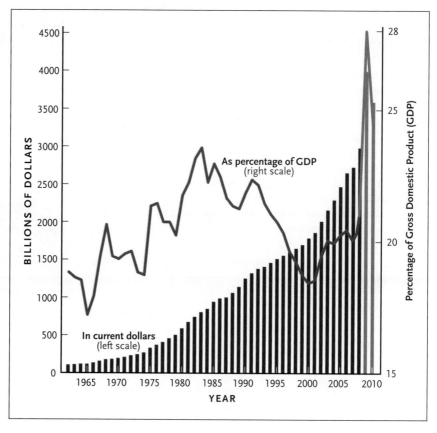

*Data for 2009–2010 are estimated.

SOURCE: Office of Management and Budget, *Budget of the U.S. Government, Fiscal Year 2010,* Tables 1.1 and 1.2.

Termination

The only *certain* way to reduce the size of the bureaucracy is to eliminate programs. But most agencies have a supportive constituency that will fight to reinstate any cuts that are made. Termination is the only way to ensure an agency's reduction, and it is a rare occurrence.

The Republican-led 104th Congress (1995–96) was committed to the termination of programs. Newt Gingrich, Speaker of the House, took Congress by storm with his promises of a virtual revolution in government. But when the dust had settled at the end of the first session of the first Gingrich-led Congress, no significant progress had been made toward downsizing through termination of agencies or programs.[19] The only two agencies eliminated were the Office of Technology

---

[19] A thorough review of the first session of the 104th Congress will be found in "Republican's Hopes for 1996 Lie in Unfinished Business," *Congressional Quarterly Weekly Report,* January 6, 1996, pp. 6–18.

Assessment, which provided research for Congress, and the Advisory Council on Intergovernmental Relations, which studied the relationship between the federal government and the states. Significantly, neither of these agencies had a strong constituency to defend it.

The overall lack of success in terminating bureaucracy is a reflection of Americans' love/hate relationship with the national government. As antagonistic as Americans may be toward bureaucracy in general, they grow attached to the services being rendered and protections being offered by particular bureaucratic agencies—that is, they fiercely defend their favorite agencies while perceiving no inconsistency between that defense and their antagonistic attitude toward the bureaucracy in general. A good case in point was the agonizing problem of closing military bases in the wake of the end of the Cold War with the former Soviet Union, when the United States no longer needed so many bases. Since every base is in some congressional member's district, it proved impossible for Congress to decide to close any of them. Consequently, between 1988 and 1990, Congress established a Defense Base Closure and Realignment Commission to decide on base closings, taking the matter out of Congress's hands altogether.[20] And even so, the process has been slow and agonizing.

Elected leaders have come to rely on a more incremental approach to downsizing the bureaucracy. Much has been done by budgetary means, reducing the budgets of all agencies across the board by small percentages and cutting some less-supported agencies by larger amounts. Yet these changes are still incremental, leaving the existence of agencies unaddressed.

An additional approach has been taken to thwart the highly unpopular regulatory agencies, which are so small (relatively) that cutting their budgets contributes virtually nothing to reducing the deficit. This approach is called **deregulation**, simply defined as a reduction in the number of rules promulgated by regulatory agencies. But deregulation by rule reduction is still incremental and has certainly not satisfied the hunger of the American public in general and Washington representatives in particular for a genuine reduction of bureaucracy.

deregulation A policy of reducing or eliminating regulatory restraints in the conduct of individuals or private institutions.

Devolution

An alternative to genuine reduction of the size of the bureaucracy is **devolution**—downsizing the federal bureaucracy by delegating the implementation of programs to state and local governments. Indirect evidence for this is seen in Figure 7.5, which shows the increase in state and local government employment against a backdrop of flat or declining federal employment. This evidence suggests a growing share of governmental actions taking place on the state and local levels. Devolution often alters the pattern of who benefits most from government programs. In the early 1990s, a major devolution of transportation policy sought to open up decisions about transportation to a new set of interests. Since the 1920s, transportation policy had been dominated by road-building interests in the federal and state governments. Many advocates for cities and many environmentalists believed

devolution A policy to remove a program from one level of government by delegating it or passing it down to a lower level of government, such as from the national government to the states.

---

[20] Public Law 101-510, Title XXIX, Sections 2,901 and 2,902 of Part A (Defense Base Closure and Realignment Commission).

FIGURE 7.5 GOVERNMENT EMPLOYMENT

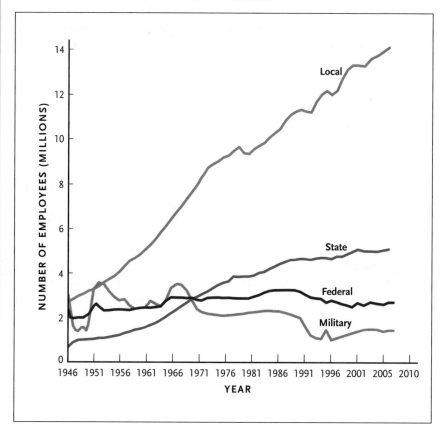

NOTE: Federal government employment figures include civilians only. Military employment figures include only active-duty personnel.

SOURCE: U.S. Bureau of the Census, *Statistical Abstract of the United States 2009* (Washington, D.C.: Government Printing Office, 2009), Tables 443 and 478.

that the emphasis on road building hurt cities and harmed the environment. The 1992 reform, initiated by environmentalists, put more power in the hands of metropolitan planning organizations and lifted many federal restrictions on how the money should be spent. Reformers hoped that these changes would open up the decision-making process so those advocating alternatives to road building, such as mass transit, bike paths, and walking, would have more influence over how federal transportation dollars were spent. Although the pace of change has been slow, devolution has indeed brought new voices into decisions about transportation spending, and alternatives to highways have received increasing attention.

Often the central aim of devolution is to provide more efficient and flexible government services. Yet, by its very nature, devolution entails variation across the states. In some states, government services may improve as a consequence of devolution. In other states, services may deteriorate as the states use devolution as an opportunity to cut spending and reduce services. This has been the pattern in the implementation of the welfare reform passed in 1996, the most significant devolution of federal government social programs in many decades. Some states, such as Wisconsin, have used the flexibility of the reform to design innovative programs that respond to clients' needs; other states, such as Idaho, have virtually dismantled their welfare programs. Because the legislation placed a five-year lifetime limit on receiving welfare, the states will take on an even greater role in the future as existing clients lose their eligibility for federal benefits. Welfare reform has been praised by many for reducing welfare rolls and responding to the public desire that welfare be a temporary program. At the same time, it has placed more low-income women and their children at risk for being left with no form of assistance at all, depending on the state in which they live.

This variation is the dilemma that devolution poses. Up to a point, variation can be considered one of the virtues of federalism. But there are dangers inherent in large variations in the provisions of services and benefits in a democracy.

Privatization

Privatization, another downsizing option, seems like a synonym for termination, but that is true only at the extreme. Most of what is called "privatization" is not termination at all but the provision of government goods and services by private contractors under direct government supervision. Except for top-secret strategic materials, virtually all of the production of military hardware, from boats to bullets, is done on a privatized basis by private contractors. Billions of dollars of research services are bought under contract by governments; these private contractors are universities as well as ordinary industrial corporations and private "think tanks." **Privatization** simply means that a formerly public activity is picked up under contract by a private company or companies. But such programs are still very much government programs; they are paid for and supervised by government. Privatization downsizes the government only in that the workers providing the service are no longer counted as part of the government bureaucracy.

privatization Removing all or part of a program from the public sector to the private sector.

The central aim of privatization is to reduce the cost of government. When private contractors can perform a task as well as government but for less money, taxpayers win. Often the losers in such situations are the workers. Government workers are generally unionized and, therefore, receive good pay and benefits. Private sector workers are less likely to be unionized, and private firms often provide lower pay and fewer benefits. For this reason, public sector unions have been one of the strongest voices arguing against privatization. Other critics of privatization observe that private firms may not be more efficient or less costly than government. This is especially likely when there is little competition among private firms and when public bureaucracies are not granted a fair chance to bid in the contracting competition. When private firms have a monopoly on service provision, they may be less efficient than government and more expensive. This problem raises important questions about how private contractors can be held accountable. As one analyst of Pentagon spending put it, "The Pentagon is supposed to be representing the taxpayer and the public interest—its national security. So it's really important to have transparency, to be able to see these competitions and hold people accountable."[21] As security has become the nation's paramount concern, new worries about privatization have surfaced. Some Pentagon officials fear that too many tasks vital to national security may have already been contracted out and that national security might best be served by limiting privatization.

The new demands of domestic security have altered the thrust of bureaucratic reform. The emphasis on reducing the size of government that was so prominent during the previous two decades is gone. Instead, there is an acceptance that the federal government will grow as needed to ensure the safety of American citizens. The administration's effort to focus the entire federal bureaucracy on a single central mission will require unprecedented levels of coordination among federal agencies. Despite the strong agreement on the goal of fighting terrorism, the effort to streamline the bureaucracy around a single purpose is likely to face considerable obstacles along the way. Reform of public bureaucracies is always complex because strong constituencies may attempt to block changes that they believe will harm them. Initiatives that aim to improve coordination among agencies can easily provoke political disputes if the proposed changes threaten to alter the access of groups to the bureaucracy. And groups that oppose bureaucratic changes can appeal to Congress to intervene on their behalf.

DOES BUREAUCRACY WORK?

Bureaucracy is one of humanity's most significant inventions. It is an institutional arrangement that employs both division and specialization of labor, harnesses expertise, and coordinates collective action for social, political, and economic purposes. It enables governments to exist and perform. In this chapter, we have focused on what public bureaucracies do, how they are organized at the national level in the United States, and how they are controlled (or not) by elected politicians.

At a theoretical level, public bureaucracy is the concrete expression of rational, purposeful, political action. Elected politicians have goals—as broad as defending the realm, maintaining public health and safety, or promoting economic growth; as narrow as securing a post office for Possum Hollow, Pennsylvania, or an exit off the interstate highway for Springfield, Massachusetts. Bureaucracy is the instrument by which political objectives, established by elected legislators and executives, are transformed from ideas, concepts, and intentions into the actual "bricks and mortar" of implemented policies.

At a practical level, this transformation depends upon the motivations of bureaucratic agents and the institutional machinery created when a bureaucratic entity is formed or reformed. Elected politicians engage in institutional design in creating agencies. They have their greatest impact at this point. Once an agency is up and running, elected officials only imperfectly control their bureaucratic agents.

---

[21] Ellen Nakashima, "Defense Balks at Contract Goals; Essential Services Should Not Be Privatized, Pentagon Tells OMB," *Washington Post*, January 30, 2002, p. A21.

Institutional arrangements, and simple human nature, provide a certain amount of insulation to agencies, enabling bureaucrats to march to their own drummers, at least some of the time. Of course, bureaucrats are not entirely free agents. But control is a constant and recurring problem for elected officials.

We cannot live without bureaucracy—it is the most efficient way to organize people to get a large collective job done. But we can't live comfortably with bureaucracy either. Bureaucracy requires hierarchy, appointed authority, and professional expertise. Those requirements make bureaucracy the natural enemy of representation, which requires discussion and reciprocity among equals. Yet the task is not to retreat from bureaucracy but to take advantage of its strengths while trying to make it more accountable to the demands that democratic policies and representative government make upon it.

Indeed, as the president and Congress seek to translate the ideal of democratic accountability into practice, they struggle to find the proper balance between administrative discretion and the public's right to know. An administration whose every move is subject to intense public scrutiny may be hamstrung in its efforts to carry out the public interest. On the other hand, a bureaucracy that is shielded from the public eye may wind up pursuing its own interests rather than those of the public. The last century has seen a double movement toward strengthening the managerial capacity of the presidency and making bureaucratic decision making more transparent. The purpose of these reforms has been to create an effective, responsive bureaucracy. But reforms alone cannot guarantee democratic accountability. Presidential and congressional vigilance in the defense of the public interest is essential.

Another approach to bureaucratic accountability is for Congress to spend more of its time clarifying its legislative intent and less of its time on committee or individual oversight. If the intent of the law were clear, Congress could then count on the president to maintain a higher level of bureaucratic responsibility, because bureaucrats are more responsive to clear legislative guidance than to anything else. Nevertheless, this is not a neat and sure solution, because Congress and the president can still be at odds, and when they are at odds, bureaucrats have an opportunity to evade responsibility by playing one branch off against the other.

As to the vast apparatus, bureaucracy is here to stay. The administration of myriad government functions and responsibilities in a large, complex society will always require "rule by desks and offices" (the literal meaning of *bureaucracy*). No "reinvention" of government, however well conceived or executed, can alter that basic fact, nor can it resolve the problem of reconciling bureaucracy in a Democracy. President Clinton's National Performance Review accomplished some impressive things: The national bureaucracy has become somewhat smaller, and in the next few years, it will become smaller still; government procedures are being streamlined and are under tremendous pressure to become even more efficient. But these efforts are no guarantee that the bureaucracy itself will become more malleable. Congress will not suddenly change its practice of loose and vague legislative draftsmanship. Presidents will not suddenly discover new reserves of power or vision to draw more tightly the reins of responsible management. No deep solution can be found in quick fixes. As with all complex social and political problems, the solution lies mainly in a sober awareness of the nature of the problem.

How the Three Branches Regulate Bureaucracy

The president may	appoint and remove agency heads.
	reorganize the bureaucracy (with congressional approval).
	make changes in agencies' budget proposals.
	initiate or adjust policies that would alter the bureaucracy's activities.
Congress may	pass legislation that alters the bureaucracy's activities.
	abolish existing programs.
	investigate bureaucratic activities and force bureaucrats to testify about them.
	influence presidential appointments of agency heads and other officials.
The judiciary may	rule on whether bureaucrats have acted within the law and require policy changes to comply with the law.
	force the bureaucracy to respect the rights of individuals through hearings and other proceedings.
	rule on the constitutionality of all rules and regulations.

This awareness enables people to avoid fantasies and myths about the abilities of a democratized presidency—or the potential of a reform effort, or the powers of technology, or the populist rhetoric of a new Congress—to change the nature of governance by bureaucracy.

CHAPTER REVIEW

Most American citizens possess less information and more misinformation about bureaucracy than about any other feature of government. We therefore began the chapter with an elementary definition of bureaucracy, identifying its key characteristics and demonstrating the extent to which bureaucracy is not only a phenomenon but an American phenomenon. In the second section of the chapter, we showed how all essential government services and controls are carried out by bureaucracies—or to be more objective, administrative agencies. Following a very general description of the different general types of bureaucratic agencies in the executive branch, we divided the agencies of the executive branch into four categories according to mission: the clientele agencies, the agencies for maintaining the

Union, the regulatory agencies, and the agencies for redistribution. These illustrate the varieties of administrative experience in American government. Although the bureaucratic phenomenon is universal, not all the bureaucracies are the same in the way they are organized, in the degree of their responsiveness, or in the way they participate in the political process.

The chapter concluded with a review of all three of the chapters on "representative government" in order to assess how well the two political branches (the legislative and the executive) do the toughest job any government has to do: making the bureaucracy accountable to the people it serves and controls. "Bureaucracy in a Democracy" is the theme of the chapter not because we have succeeded in democratizing bureaucracies but because it is the never-ending task of politics in a democracy.

FOR FURTHER READING

Aberbach, Joel, and Bert A. Rockman. *In the Web of Politics: Three Decades of the U.S. Federal Executive.* Washington, D.C.: Brookings Institution, 2000.

Arnold, Peri E. *Making the Managerial Presidency: Comprehensive Reorganization Planning, 1905–1980.* Princeton, N.J.: Princeton University Press, 1986.

Downs, Anthony. *Inside Bureaucracy.* Boston: Little, Brown, 1966.

Esman, Milton J. *Government Works: Why Americans Need the Feds.* Ithaca, N.Y.: Cornell University Press, 2000.

Goodsell, Charles. *The Case for Bureaucracy.* 4th ed. Washington, D.C.: Congressional Quarterly Press, 2003.

Heclo, Hugh. *On Thinking Institutionally.* Boulder, Colo.: Paradigm, 2007.

Kerwin, Cornelius M. *Rulemaking.* 3rd ed. Washington, D.C.: Congressional Quarterly Press, 2003.

Kettl, Donald F., and James Fesler. *The Politics of the Administrative Process.* 3rd ed. Washington, D.C.: Brookings Institution, 2005.

Light, Paul C. *The True Size of Government.* Washington, D.C.: Brookings Institution, 1999.

Meier, Kenneth J., and John Bohte. *Politics and the Bureaucracy.* 5th ed. Belmont, Calif.: Wadsworth, 2006.

Seidman, Harold. *Politics, Position, and Power: The Dynamics of Federal Organization.* 5th ed. New York: Oxford University Press, 1998.

Wilson, James Q. *Bureaucracy: What Government Agencies Do and Why They Do It.* New reader selection
York: Basic Books, 1989.

 Additional study and review materials are available online at wwnorton.com/studyspace/

8

The Federal Courts

Courts serve an essential and ancient function. When disputes arise, those involved need an impartial arbiter to help settle the matter. When laws must be enforced, justice requires an impartial judge to determine guilt and innocence and, if the accused is found guilty, the appropriate punishment. And when questions arise about the meaning of the laws, we rely on the wisdom of judges to divine what Congress meant and how that applies in a given circumstance. It is not possible, or even wise, to pass a law to cover every contingency. Nearly every nation today has established a system of courts—the judiciary—to satisfy the need for an arbiter and interpreter.

The significant and, at the time of the nation's Founding, novel feature of the American judiciary is that it is independent, with powers to check the Congress and president. As it was written and as it has evolved over time, the Constitution of the United States sets up the system of courts as a separate entity from the legislature, the executive, and the states, and insulated from electoral politics. Four important features of the institutions of the American Judiciary ensure a powerful, independent judiciary: First, the Constitution establishes the federal courts as a separate branch of government from Congress and the president. Second, authority among the courts is hierarchical, with federal courts able to overturn state courts and the United States Supreme Court the ultimate authority. Third, the U.S. Supreme Court and other federal courts of appeals can strike down actions of Congress, the president, or states if the judges deem those acts to be violations of the constitution. This is the power of judicial review. Fourth, federal judges are appointed for life. Federal judges are not subject to the pressures of running for reelection and need not be highly responsive to changes in public opinion.[1]

---

[1] Justices in many state and local courts are elected.

CORE OF THE ANALYSIS

- The power of judicial review makes the Supreme Court more than a judicial agency; it also makes the Court a major lawmaking body.

- Judicial decisions are highly constrained by the past, in the form of common law and precedents, but every decision also contributes to the evolution of the law.

- The courts maintain their independence from the legislature and executive because federal judges are appointed for life and not elected. Independence allows the courts to act as a check on the democratically chosen branches of government, to protect individual rights.

An independent judiciary has been one of the most distinctive and successful aspects of the American government. It has settled constitutional crises when Congress and the president are at odds. It has guaranteed that no person is above the law (the rule of law), not even members of Congress or the president.[2] It has guaranteed that all people, even noncitizens, enjoy the equal protection of the laws. It has meant that small businesses, large corporations, and workers can engage in economic activities and agreements with the assurance that their rights will be protected. It has even ensured that the democratic branches of government operate in a democratic manner and that all votes count the same in the selection of the legislature. The cumulative effect of an independent judiciary has been a stable, successful economy and democracy.[3]

In this chapter, we will first examine the judicial process, including the types of cases that the federal courts consider. Second, we will assess the organization and structure of the federal court system as well as the flow of cases through the courts. Third, we will consider judicial review and how it makes the Supreme Court a "lawmaking body." Fourth, we will examine various influences on the Supreme Court. Finally, we will analyze the role and power of the federal courts in the American political process, looking in particular at the growth of judicial power in

---

[2] The case of *U.S. v. Nixon* (418 U.S. 683 [1974]) dealt head on with the question of whether President Nixon was beyond prosecution for alleged obstruction of justice in the case of the break-in at the Democratic Party headquarters in the Watergate Hotel.

[3] Douglass C. North, *Institutions, Institutional Change, and Economic Performance* (New York: Cambridge University Press, 1990).

the United States. The framers of the American Constitution called the Court the "least dangerous branch" of American government. Today, it is not unusual to hear friends and foes of the Court alike refer to it as the "imperial judiciary."[4] Before we can understand this transformation and its consequences, however, we must look in some detail at America's judicial process.

HOW COURTS WORK

Court cases in the United States proceed under three broad categories of law: criminal law, civil law, and public law.

Cases of **criminal law** are those in which the government charges an individual with violating a statute that has been enacted to protect the public health, safety, morals, or welfare. In criminal cases, the government is always the **plaintiff** (the party that brings charges) and alleges that a criminal violation has been committed by a named **defendant**. Most criminal cases arise in state and municipal courts and involve matters ranging from traffic offenses to robbery and murder. Although the great bulk of criminal law is still a state matter, a growing body of federal criminal law deals with such matters as tax evasion, mail fraud, and the sale of narcotics. Defendants found guilty of criminal violations may be fined or sent to prison.

Cases of **civil law** involve disputes among individuals or between individuals and the government where no criminal violation is charged. But unlike in criminal cases, the losers in civil cases cannot be fined or sent to prison, although they may be required to pay monetary damages for their actions. In a civil case, the one who brings a complaint is the plaintiff and the one against whom the complaint is brought is the defendant. The two most common types of civil cases involve contracts and torts. In a typical contract case, an individual or corporation charges that it has suffered because of another's violation of a specific agreement between the two. For example, the Smith Manufacturing Corporation may charge that Jones Distributors failed to honor an agreement to deliver raw materials at a specified time, causing Smith to lose business. Smith asks the court to order Jones to compensate it for the damage allegedly suffered. In a typical tort case, one individual charges that he or she has been injured by another's negligence or malfeasance. Medical malpractice suits are one example of tort cases.

In deciding cases, courts apply statutes (laws) and legal **precedents** (prior decisions). State and federal statutes, for example, often govern the conditions under which contracts are and are not legally binding. Jones Distributors might argue that it was not obliged to fulfill its contract with the Smith Corporation because actions by Smith, such as the failure to make promised payments, constituted fraud under state law. Attorneys for a physician being sued for malpractice, on the other hand, may search for prior instances in which courts ruled that actions similar to those

criminal law The branch of law that deals with disputes or actions involving criminal penalties (as opposed to civil law). It regulates the conduct of individuals, defines crimes, and provides punishment for criminal acts.

plaintiff The individual or organization that brings a complaint in court.

defendant The individual or organization against which a complaint is brought in criminal or civil cases.

civil law A system of jurisprudence, including private law and governmental actions, to settle disputes that do not involve criminal penalties.

precedent A prior case whose principles are used by judges as the bases for their decisions present case.

---

[4] See Richard Neely, *How Courts Govern America* (New Haven, Conn.: Yale University Press, 1981).

IN BRIEF

Types of Laws and Disputes

Type of law	Type of case or dispute	Form of case
Criminal law	Cases arising out of actions that violate laws protecting the health, safety, and morals of the community. The government is always the plaintiff.	*U.S. (or state) v. Jones* *Jones v. U.S. (or state)*, if Jones lost and is appealing
Civil law	"Private law," involving disputes between citizens or between government and citizen where no crime is alleged. Two general types are contract and tort. *Contract cases* are disputes that arise over voluntary actions. *Tort cases* are disputes that arise out of obligations inherent in social life. Negligence and slander are examples of torts.	*Smith v. Jones* *New York v. Jones* *U.S. v. Jones* *Jones v. New York*
Public law	All cases where the powers of government or the rights of citizens are involved. The government is the defendant. *Constitutional law* involves judicial review of the basis of a government's action in relation to specific clauses of the Constitution as interpreted in Supreme Court cases. *Administrative law* involves disputes of the statutory authority, jurisdiction, or procedures of administrative agencies.	*Jones v. U.S. (or state)* *In re Jones* *Smith v. Jones*, if a license or statute is at issue in their private dispute

of their client did not constitute negligence. Such precedents are applied under the doctrine of ***stare decisis***, a Latin phrase meaning "let the decision stand."

A case becomes a matter of the third category, **public law**, when plaintiffs or defendants in a civil or criminal case seeks to show that their case involves the powers of government or rights of citizens as defined under the Constitution or by statute. One major form of public law is constitutional law, under which a court will examine the government's actions to see if they conform to the Constitution as it has been interpreted by the judiciary. Thus, what began as an ordinary criminal case may enter the realm of public law if a defendant claims that the police violated his or her constitutional rights. Another important arena of public law is administrative law, which involves disputes over the jurisdiction, procedures, or authority of administrative agencies. Under this type of law, civil litigation between an individual and the government may become a matter of public law if the individual

stare decisis Literally "let the decision stand." A previous decision by a court applies as a precedent in similar cases until that decision is overruled.

public law Cases in private law, civil law, or criminal law in which one party to the dispute argues that a license is unfair, a law is inequitable or unconstitutional, or an agency has acted unfairly, violated a procedure, or gone beyond its jurisdiction.

asserts that the government is violating a statute or abusing its power under the Constitution. For example, landowners have asserted that federal and state restrictions on land use constitute violations of the Fifth Amendment's restrictions on the government's ability to confiscate private property. Recently, the Supreme Court has been very sympathetic to such claims, which effectively transform an ordinary civil dispute into a major issue of public law.

Most of the important Supreme Court cases we will examine in this chapter involve judgments concerning the constitutional or statutory basis of the actions of government agencies. As we shall see, it is in this arena of public law that the Supreme Court's decisions can have significant consequences for American politics and society.

Types of Courts

In the United States, systems of courts have been established both by the federal government and by the governments of the individual states. Both systems have several levels, as shown in Figure 8.1. More than 99 percent of all court cases in the United States are heard in state courts. The overwhelming majority of criminal cases, for example, involves violations of state laws prohibiting such actions as murder, robbery, fraud, theft, and assault. If such a case is brought to trial, it will be heard in a state **trial court**, in front of a judge and sometimes a jury, who will determine whether the defendant violated state law. If the defendant is convicted, he or she may appeal the conviction to a higher court, such as a state **court of appeals**,

trial court The first court to hear a criminal or civil case.

court of appeals A court that hears the appeals of trial court decisions.

FIGURE 8.1 THE U.S. COURT SYSTEM

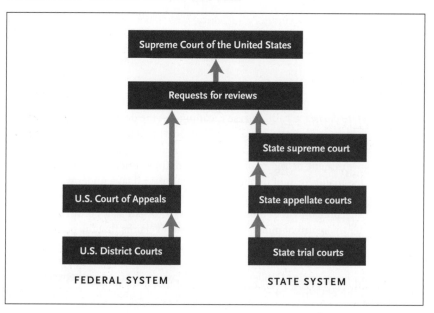

and from there to a state's **supreme court**. Similarly, in civil cases, most litigation is brought in the courts established by the state in which the activity in question took place. For example, a patient bringing suit against a physician for malpractice would file the suit in the appropriate court in the state where the alleged malpractice occurred. The judge hearing the case would apply state law and state precedent to the matter at hand. (It should be noted that in both criminal and civil matters, most cases are settled before trial through negotiated agreements between the parties. In criminal cases, these agreements are called plea bargains.)

FEDERAL JURISDICTION

Cases are heard in the federal courts if they involve federal laws, treaties with other nations, or the U.S. Constitution; these areas are the official **jurisdiction** of the federal courts. In addition, any case in which the U.S. government is a party is heard in the federal courts. If, for example, an individual is charged with violating a federal criminal statute, such as evading the payment of income taxes, charges would be brought before a federal judge by a federal prosecutor. Civil cases involving the citizens of more than one state and in which more than $70,000 is at stake may be heard in either the federal or the state courts, usually depending on the preference of the plaintiff.

But even if a matter belongs in federal court, how do we know which federal court should exercise jurisdiction over the case? The answer to this seemingly simple question is somewhat complex. The jurisdiction of each federal court is derived from the U.S. Constitution and federal statutes. Article III of the Constitution gives the Supreme Court appellate jurisdiction in all federal cases and original jurisdiction in cases involving foreign ambassadors and issues in which a state is a party. Article III assigns original jurisdiction in all other federal cases to the lower courts that Congress was authorized to establish. Over the years, as Congress enacted statutes creating the federal judicial system, it specified the jurisdiction of each type of court it established. For the most part, Congress has assigned jurisdictions on the basis of geography. The nation is currently, by statute, divided into ninety-four judicial districts, including one court for each of three U.S. territories: Guam, the U.S. Virgin Islands, and the Northern Marianas. Each of the ninety-four U.S. district courts exercises jurisdiction over federal cases arising within its territorial domain. The judicial districts are, in turn, organized into eleven regional circuits and the District of Columbia circuit. Each circuit court exercises appellate jurisdiction over cases heard by the district courts within its region.

Geography is not the only basis for federal court jurisdiction. Congress has also established several specialized courts that have nationwide original jurisdiction in certain types of cases. These include the U.S. Court of International Trade, created to deal with trade and customs issues, and the U.S. Court of Federal Claims, which handles damage suits against the United States. Congress has, in addition, established a court with nationwide appellate jurisdiction. This is the U.S. Court of

Appeals for the Federal Circuit, which hears appeals involving patent law and those arising from the decisions of the trade and claims courts.

The appellate jurisdiction of the federal courts also extends to cases originating in the state courts. In both civil and criminal cases, a decision of the highest state court can be appealed to the U.S. Supreme Court by raising a federal issue. Appellants might assert, for example, that they were denied the right to counsel or otherwise deprived of the **due process** guaranteed by the federal Constitution, or they might assert that important issues of federal law were at stake in the case. The U.S. Supreme Court is not obligated to accept such appeals and will accept them only if it believes that the matter has considerable national significance. (We shall return to this topic later in this chapter.) In addition, in criminal cases defendants who have been convicted in a state court may request a writ of ***habeas corpus*** from a federal district court. *Habeas corpus* is a court order to the authorities to release a prisoner deemed to be held in violation of his or her legal rights. Generally speaking, state defendants seeking a federal writ of *habeas corpus* must show that they have exhausted all available state remedies and raise issues not previously raised in their state appeals. Federal courts of appeals and, ultimately, the U.S. Supreme Court have appellate jurisdiction over federal district court *habeas* decisions.

Although the federal courts hear only a small fraction of all the civil and criminal cases decided each year in the United States, their decisions are extremely important. It is in the federal courts that the Constitution and federal laws that govern all Americans are interpreted and their meaning and significance established. Moreover, it is in the federal courts that the powers and limitations of the increasingly powerful national government are tested. Finally, through their power to review the decisions of the state courts, it is ultimately the federal courts that dominate the American judicial system.

The Federal Trial Courts

The federal district courts handle most of the cases of original federal jurisdiction. These trial courts have general jurisdiction, and their cases are, in form, indistinguishable from cases in the state trial courts.

There are eighty-nine district courts in the fifty states, plus one in the District of Columbia and one in Puerto Rico, and three territorial courts. These courts are staffed by 678 federal district judges. District judges are assigned to district courts according to the workload; the busiest of these courts may have as many as twenty-eight judges. The routines and procedures of the federal district courts are essentially the same as those of the lower state courts, except that federal procedural requirements tend to be stricter. States, for example, do not have to provide a grand jury, a twelve-member trial jury, or a unanimous jury verdict. Federal courts must provide all of these.

Federal Appellate Courts

Roughly 20 percent of all lower court cases along with appeals from some federal agency decisions are subsequently reviewed by a federal appeals court. The country

due process To proceed according to law and with adequate protection for individual rights.

habeas corpus A court order demanding that an individual in custody be brought into court and shown the cause for detention. *Habeas corpus* is guaranteed by the Constitution and can be suspended only in cases of rebellion or invasion.

is divided into twelve judicial circuits, each of which has a U.S. Court of Appeals. A thirteenth appellate court, the U.S. Court of Appeals for the Federal Circuit, is defined by subject matter rather than geographical jurisdiction. This court accepts appeals regarding patents, copyrights, and international trade.

Except for cases selected for review by the Supreme Court, decisions made by the appeals courts are final. Because of this finality, certain safeguards have been built into the system. The most important is the provision of more than one judge for every appeals case. Each court of appeals has three to twenty-eight permanent judgeships, depending on the workload of the circuit. Although normally three judges hear appealed cases, in some instances a larger number of judges sit together *en banc*.

Another safeguard is provided by the assignment of a Supreme Court justice as the circuit justice for each of the eleven circuits. The circuit justice deals with requests for special action by the Supreme Court. The most frequent and best-known action of circuit justices is that of reviewing requests for stays of execution when the full Court is unable to do so—mainly during the summer, when the Court is in recess.

The Supreme Court

The Supreme Court is America's highest court. Article III of the Constitution vests "the judicial power of the United States" in the Supreme Court, and this court is supreme in fact as well as form. The Supreme Court is made up of a chief justice and eight associate justices. The **chief justice** presides over the Court's public sessions and conferences. In the Court's actual deliberations and decisions, however, the chief justice has no more authority than his or her colleagues. Each justice casts one vote. The chief justice, though, is always the first to speak and the last to vote when the justices deliberate. In addition, if the chief justice has voted with the majority, he decides which of the justices will write the formal opinion for the court. The character of the opinion can be an important means of influencing the evolution of the law beyond the mere affirmation or denial of the appeal at hand. To some extent, the influence of the chief justice is a function of his or her own leadership ability. Some chief justices, such as the late Earl Warren, have been able to lead the court in a new direction. In other instances, a forceful associate justice, such as the late Felix Frankfurter, is the dominant figure on the Court.

The Constitution does not specify the number of justices who should sit on the Supreme Court; Congress has the authority to change the Court's size. In the early nineteenth century, there were six Supreme Court justices; later there were seven. Congress set the number of justices at nine in 1869, and the Court has remained that size ever since. In 1937, President Franklin D. Roosevelt, infuriated by several Supreme Court decisions that struck down New Deal programs, asked Congress to enlarge the court so that he could add a few sympathetic justices to the bench. Although Congress balked at Roosevelt's "court packing" plan, the Court gave in to FDR's pressure and began to take a more favorable view of his policy initiatives. The president, in turn, dropped his efforts to enlarge the Court. The Court's surrender to FDR came to be known as "the switch in time that saved nine."

chief justice Justice on the Supreme Court who presides over the Court's public sessions.

How Judges Are Appointed

Federal judges are appointed by the president and are generally selected from among the more prominent or politically active members of the legal profession. Many federal judges previously served as state court judges or state or local prosecutors. Before the president makes a formal nomination, however, the senators from the candidate's own state must indicate that they support the nominee. This is an informal but seldom violated practice called **senatorial courtesy**. If one or both senators from a prospective nominee's home state belong to the president's political party, the president will almost invariably consult them and secure their blessing for the nomination. Because the president's party in the Senate will rarely support a nominee opposed by a home-state senator from their ranks, this arrangement gives these senators virtual veto power over appointments to the federal bench in their own states. Senators often see such a nomination as a way to reward important allies and contributors in their states. If the state has no senator from the president's party, the governor or members of the state's House delegation may make suggestions. In general, presidents endeavor to appoint judges who possess legal experience and good character and whose partisan and ideological views are similar to the president's own. During the presidencies of Ronald Reagan and George H. W. Bush, most federal judicial appointees were conservative Republicans. Bush established an advisory committee to screen judicial nominees to make certain that their legal and political philosophies were sufficiently conservative. Bill Clinton's appointees to the federal bench, on the other hand, tended to be liberal Democrats. Clinton also made a major effort to appoint women and African Americans to the federal courts. He drew nearly half of his nominees from these groups.

Once the president has formally nominated an individual, the nominee must be considered by the Senate Judiciary Committee and confirmed by a majority vote in the full Senate. In recent years, the Senate Judiciary Committee has sought to signal the president when it has had qualms about a judicial nomination. After the Republicans won control of the Senate in 1994, for example, Judiciary Committee Chair Orrin Hatch of Utah let President Clinton know that he considered two of Clinton's nominees to be too liberal. The president withdrew the nominations.

Federal appeals court nominations follow much the same pattern. Since appeals court judges preside over jurisdictions that include several states, however, senators do not have as strong a role in proposing potential candidates. Instead, the Justice Department or important members of the administration usually suggest potential appeals court candidates to the president. The senators from the nominee's own state are still consulted before the president will formally act.

During President George W. Bush's first two years in office, Democrats controlled the Senate and used their majority on the Judiciary Committee to block eight of the president's first eleven federal court nominations. After the GOP won a narrow Senate majority in the 2002 national elections, Democrats used a filibuster to block action on several other Bush federal appeals court nominees. Both Democrats and Republicans saw struggles over lower court slots as practice and preparation for all-out partisan warfare over the next Supreme Court vacancy. In June 2009, President Obama nominated Judge Sonia Sotomayor to fill the Supreme Court seat vacated by the retirement of Justice David Souter. Republicans promised to oppose

senatorial courtesy The practice whereby the president, before formally nominating a person for a federal judgeship, will seek approval of the nomination from the senators who represent the candidate's own state.

TABLE 8.1 SUPREME COURT JUSTICES, 2009

Name	Year of Birth	Prior Experience	Appointment by	Year of Appointment
John G. Roberts, Jr. *Chief Justice*	1955	Federal judge	G. W. Bush	2005
Antonin Scalia	1936	Law professor, federal judge	Reagan	1986
Anthony Kennedy	1936	Federal judge	Reagan	1988
Clarence Thomas	1948	Federal judge	G. H. W. Bush	1991
Ruth Bader Ginsburg	1933	Federal judge	Clinton	1993
Stephen Breyer	1938	Federal judge	Clinton	1994
Samuel Alito	1950	Federal judge	G. W. Bush	2006
Sonia Sotomayor	1954	Federal judge	Barack Obama	2009
Elena Kagan	1960	Solicitor General	Barack Obama	2010

Sotomayor but, given their depleted ranks after the 2008 elections, had little chance of blocking the appointment.

If political factors play an important role in the selection of district and appellate court judges, they are decisive when it comes to Supreme Court appointments. For example, presidents Ronald Reagan and George H. W. Bush appointed five justices whom they believed to have conservative perspectives: Justices Sandra Day O'Connor, Antonin Scalia, Anthony Kennedy, David Souter, and Clarence Thomas. Reagan also elevated William Rehnquist to the position of chief justice. Reagan and Bush sought appointees who believed in reducing government intervention in the economy and who supported the moral positions taken by the Republican Party in recent years, particularly opposition to abortion. However, not all the Reagan and Bush appointees fulfilled their sponsors' expectations. Bush appointee David Souter, for example, was attacked by conservatives as a turncoat for his decisions on school prayer and abortion rights. Nevertheless, through their appointments, Reagan and Bush were able to create a far more conservative Supreme Court. For his part, President Bill Clinton named Ruth Bader Ginsburg and Stephen Breyer to the Court, hoping to counteract the influence of the Reagan and Bush appointees. But George W. Bush's appointees, John Roberts and Samuel Alito helped bolster the conservative bloc.

Similarly, President Obama hoped that Sonia Sotomayor and Elena Kagan would add strong voices to the Court's liberal wing. Sotomayor became the first Supreme Court justice of Hispanic origin and thus made judicial history even before participating in the Court's deliberations. (Table 8.1 shows more information about the current Supreme Court justices.)

Typically, in recent decades, after the president has named a nominee, interest groups opposed to the nomination have mobilized opposition in the media, the public, and the Senate. When former President George H. W. Bush proposed the conservative judge Clarence Thomas for the Court in 1991, for example, liberal groups launched a campaign to discredit Thomas. After extensive research into his background, opponents of the nomination were able to produce evidence suggesting that Thomas had sexually harassed a former subordinate, Anita Hill. Thomas denied the charge. After contentious Senate Judiciary Committee hearings, highlighted by testimony from both Thomas and Hill, Thomas narrowly won confirmation.

Likewise, conservative interest groups carefully scrutinized Bill Clinton's somewhat more liberal nominees, hoping to find information about them that would sabotage their appointments. During his two opportunities to name Supreme Court justices, Clinton was compelled to drop several potential appointees because of information unearthed by political opponents.

These struggles over judicial appointments indicate the growing intensity of partisan struggle in the United States today. They also indicate how much importance competing political forces attach to Supreme Court appointments. Because these contending forces see the outcome as critical, they are willing to engage in a fierce struggle when Supreme Court appointments are at stake.

JUDICIAL REVIEW

judicial review
Power of the courts to declare actions of the legislative and executive branches invalid or unconstitutional. The Supreme Court asserted this power in *Marbury v. Madison* (1803).

The phrase **judicial review** refers to the power of the judiciary to examine and, if necessary, invalidate actions undertaken by the legislative and executive branches (see Figure 8.2). Sometimes the phrase is also used to describe the scrutiny that appeals courts give to the actions of trial courts, but, strictly speaking, this is an improper usage. A higher court's examination of a lower court's decision might be called "appellate review" but it is not "judicial review."

Judicial Review of Acts of Congress

Because the Constitution does not give the Supreme Court the power of judicial review of congressional enactments, the Court's exercise of it may be seen as something of a usurpation. Among the proposals debated at the Constitutional Convention was one to create a council composed of the president and the judiciary that would share the veto power over legislation. Another proposal was to route all legislation through both the Court and the president; overruling a veto by either one would have required a two-thirds vote of the House and the Senate. Those and other proposals were rejected by the delegates, and no further effort was made to give the Supreme Court review power over the other branches. This does not prove that the framers of the Constitution opposed judicial review, but it does indicate

FIGURE 8.2 JUDICIAL REVIEW

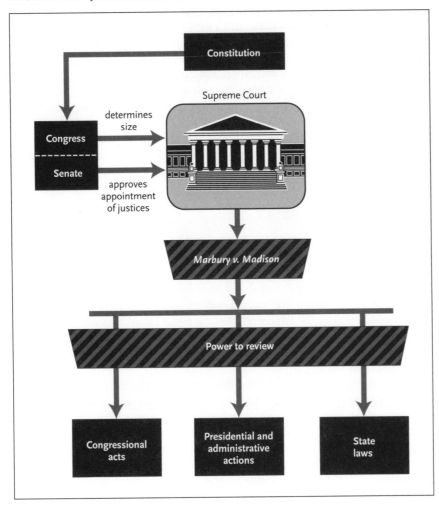

that "if they intended to provide for it in the Constitution, they did so in a most obscure fashion."[5]

Disputes over the intentions of the framers were settled in 1803 in the case of *Marbury v. Madison*.[6] In that case, William Marbury sued Secretary of State James Madison for Madison's failure to complete Marbury's appointment to a lower judgeship that had been initiated by the outgoing administration of President John Adams. Quite apart from the details of the case, Chief Justice John Marshall, speaking on behalf of the court, used the case to declare a portion of a law

---

[5] C. Herman Pritchett, *The American Constitution* (New York: McGraw-Hill, 1959), p. 138.

[6] *Marbury v. Madison*, 1 Cranch 137 (1803).

unconstitutional. In effect, he stated that although the substance of Marbury's request was not unreasonable, the Court's jurisdiction in the matter was based on a section of the Judiciary Act of 1789, which the Court declared unconstitutional.

Although Congress and the president have often been at odds with the Court, its legal power to review acts of Congress has not been seriously questioned since 1803. One reason is that judicial power has been accepted as natural, if not intended. Another reason is that during the early years of the Republic, the Supreme Court was careful to use its power sparingly, striking down only two pieces of legislation during the first seventy-five years of its history. In recent years, with the power of judicial review securely accepted, the Court has been more willing to use it. Just since 1995, the Supreme Court has struck down more than forty acts of Congress, in part or in their entirety.

Judicial Review of State Actions

The power of the Supreme Court to review state legislation or other state action and to determine its constitutionality is neither granted by the Constitution nor inherent in the federal system. But the logic of the **supremacy clause** of Article VI of the Constitution, which declares that it and laws made under its authority to be the supreme law of the land, is very strong. Furthermore, in the Judiciary Act of 1789, Congress conferred on the Supreme Court the power to reverse state constitutions and laws whenever they are clearly in conflict with the U.S. Constitution, federal laws, or treaties.[7] This power gives the Supreme Court jurisdiction over all of the millions of cases handled by American courts each year.

The supremacy clause of the Constitution not only established the federal Constitution, statutes, and treaties as the "supreme law of the land," but also provided that "the Judges in every State shall be bound thereby, any Thing in the Constitution or Laws of the State to the Contrary notwithstanding." Under this authority, the Supreme Court has frequently overturned state constitutional provisions or statutes and state court decisions that it feels are counter to rights or privileges guaranteed under the Constitution or federal statutes.

Judicial Review of Federal Agency Actions

Although Congress makes the law, as we saw in Chapters 5 and 7, it can hardly administer the thousands of programs it has enacted and must delegate power to the president and to a huge bureaucracy to achieve its purposes. For example, if Congress wishes to improve air quality, it cannot possibly anticipate all the conditions and circumstances that may arise with respect to that general goal. Inevitably, Congress must delegate to the executive substantial discretionary power to make judgments about the best ways to improve air quality in the face of changing circumstances. Thus, over the years, almost any congressional program will result in

supremacy clause Article VI of the Constitution, which states that laws passed by the national government and all treaties are the supreme laws of the land and superior to all laws adopted by any state or any subdivision.

---

[7]This review power was affirmed by the Supreme Court in *Martin v. Hunter's Lessees,* 1 Wheaton 304 (1816).

thousands of pages of administrative regulations developed by executive agencies nominally seeking to implement the will of the Congress.

The issue of delegation of power has led to a number of court decisions over the past two centuries generally revolving around the question of the scope of the delegation. Courts have also been called on to decide whether the rules and regulations adopted by federal agencies are consistent with Congress's express or implied intent.

As presidential power expanded during the New Deal era, one measure of increased congressional subordination to the executive was the enactment of laws that contained few, if any, principles limiting executive discretion. Congress enacted legislation, often at the president's behest, that gave the executive virtually unfettered authority to address a particular concern. For example, the Emergency Price Control Act of 1942 authorized the executive to set "fair and equitable" prices without offering any indication of what those terms might mean.[8] Although the Court initially challenged these delegations of power to the president during the New Deal, a confrontation with President Franklin D. Roosevelt caused the Court to retreat from its position. Perhaps as a result, no congressional delegation of power to the president has been struck down as impermissibly broad in more than six decades. In the last two decades in particular, the Supreme Court has found that as long as federal agencies developed rules and regulations "based upon a permissible construction" or "reasonable interpretation" of Congress's statute, the judiciary would accept the views of the executive branch.[9] Generally, the courts give considerable deference to administrative agencies as long as those agencies have engaged in a formal rule-making process and can show that they have carried out the conditions prescribed by the various statutes governing agency rule making. These include the 1946 Administrative Procedure Act, which requires agencies to notify parties affected by proposed rules as well as allow them ample time to comment on such rules before they go into effect.

Judicial Review and Presidential Power

The federal courts are also called on to review the actions of the president. As we saw in Chapter 6, presidents increasingly make use of unilateral executive powers rather than relying on congressional legislation to achieve their objectives. On many occasions, presidential orders and actions have been challenged in the federal courts by members of Congress and by individuals and groups opposing the president's policies. In recent years, assertions of presidential power in such realms as foreign policy, war and emergency powers, legislative power, and administrative authority have, more often than not, been upheld by the federal bench. Indeed, the federal judiciary has sometimes taken extraordinary presidential claims made for limited and temporary purposes and rationalized them, that is, converted them into routine and permanent instruments of presidential government. Take,

---

[8] 56 Stat. 23 (30 January 1942).

[9] *Chevron v. Natural Resources Defense Council,* 467 U.S. 837 (1984).

for example, Richard Nixon's sweeping claims of executive privilege. In *U.S. v. Nixon*, the Court, to be sure, rejected the president's refusal to turn over tapes to congressional investigators. For the first time, though, the justices also recognized the validity of the principle of executive privilege and discussed the situations in which such claims might be appropriate.[10] This judicial recognition of the principle encouraged Presidents Bill Clinton and George W. Bush to make broad claims of executive privilege during their terms in office.[11] Executive privilege has been invoked to protect even the deliberations of the vice president from congressional scrutiny in the case of Dick Cheney's consultations with representatives of the energy industry.

This pattern of judicial deference to presidential authority is also manifest in the Supreme Court's decisions regarding President Bush's war on terrorism. In June 2004, the Supreme Court ruled in three cases involving the president's anti-terrorism initiatives and claims of executive power and in two of the three cases appeared to place some limits on presidential authority. Indeed, the justices had clearly been influenced by revelations that U.S. troops had abused prisoners in Iraq and sought in these cases to make a statement against the absolute denial of procedural rights to individuals in the custody of American military authorities. But although the Court's decisions were widely hailed as reining in the executive branch, they actually fell far short of stopping presidential power in its tracks.

The most important case decided by the Court was *Hamdi v. Rumsfeld*.[12] Yaser Esam Hamdi, apparently a Taliban soldier, was captured by American forces in Afghanistan and brought to the United States, where he was incarcerated at the Norfolk Naval Station. Hamdi was classified as an enemy combatant and denied civil rights, including the right to counsel, despite the fact that he had been born in Louisiana and held American citizenship. A federal district court scheduled a hearing on Hamdi's *habeas corpus* petition and ordered that he be given unmonitored access to counsel. This ruling, however, was reversed by the Fourth Circuit Court of Appeals. In its opinion the court held that in the national security realm, the president wields "plenary and exclusive power." This power was even greater, said the court, when the president acted with statutory authority from Congress. The court did not indicate which statute, in particular, might have authorized the president's actions, but went on to affirm the president's constitutional power, as supported in many prior rulings, to conduct military operations, decide who is and is not an enemy combatant, and determine the rules governing the treatment of such individuals. In essence, said the court, the president had virtually unfettered discretion to deal with emergencies, and it was inappropriate for the judiciary to saddle presidential decisions with what the court called the "panoply of encumbrances associated with civil litigation."

---

[10] *U.S. v. Nixon*, 418 U.S. 683 (1974).

[11] On Clinton, see Jonathan Turley, "Paradise Lost: The Clinton Administration and the Erosion of Executive Privilege," 60 *Maryland Law Review* 205 (2001). On Bush, see Jeffrey P. Carlin, *"Walker v. Cheney:* Politics, Posturing and Executive Privilege," 76 *Southern California Law Review* 235 (November 2002).

[12] *Hamdi v. Rumsfeld*, 542 U.S. 507 (2004).

In June 2004, the Supreme Court ruled that Hamdi was entitled to a lawyer and "a fair opportunity to rebut the government's factual assertions." However, the Supreme Court affirmed that the president possessed the authority to declare a U.S. citizen to be an enemy combatant and to order such an individual held in federal detention. Several of the justices intimated that once designated an enemy combatant, a U.S. citizen might be tried before a military tribunal and the normal presumption of innocence suspended. In 2006, in *Hamdan v. Rumsfeld,* the Court ruled that the military commissions established to try enemy combatants and other detainees violated both the Uniform Code of Military Justice and the Geneva Conventions.[13]

Two years later the Supreme Court intervened again on the rights of those detained at Guantánamo Bay. Lakhdar Boumediene, a naturalized citizen of Bosnia and Herzegovina, sued to challenge the legality of his detention under the Military Combatants Act of 2006. Boumediene's attorneys argued that the U.S. Constitution guarantees the right of *habeas corpus,* the right of any person detained by the government to challenge his or her detention in federal court. The only exceptions allowed under the constitution are situations of rebellion or invasion. In a 5–4 vote, the Supreme Court sided with Boumediene.[14]

Thus, the Supreme Court did assert that presidential actions were subject to judicial scrutiny and placed some constraints on the president's power. But at the same time the Court affirmed the president's single most important claim—the unilateral power to declare individuals, including U.S. citizens, "enemy combatants" who could be detained by federal authorities under adverse legal circumstances.

Judicial Review and Lawmaking

Much of the work of the courts involves the application of statutes to the particular case at hand. Over the centuries, however, judges have developed a body of rules and principles of interpretation that are not grounded in specific statutes. This body of judge-made law is called common law.

The appellate courts are a different realm. When a court of appeals hands down its decision, it accomplishes two things. First, of course, it decides who wins—the person who won in the lower court or the person who lost in the lower court. But at the same time, it expresses its decision in a manner that provides guidance to the lower courts for handling future cases in the same area. Appellate judges try to give their reasons and rulings in writing so the "administration of justice" can take place most of the time at the lowest judicial level. They try to make their ruling or reasoning clear, so as to avoid confusion, which can produce a surge of litigation at the lower levels. These rulings can be considered laws, but they are laws governing the behavior only of the judiciary. Decisions by appellate courts affect citizens by giving them a cause of action or by taking it away from them. That is, they open or close access to the courts.

---

[13] *Hamdan v. Rumsfeld,* 548 U.S. (2006).

[14] *Boumediene v. Bush,* 06-1195 (2008).

THE SUPREME COURT IN ACTION

How Cases Reach the Supreme Court

Given the millions of disputes that arise every year, the job of the Supreme Court would be impossible if it were not able to control the flow of cases and its own caseload. The Supreme Court has original jurisdiction in a limited variety of cases defined by the Constitution. The original jurisdiction includes (1) cases between the United States and one of the fifty states, (2) cases involving two or more states, (3) cases involving foreign ambassadors or other ministers, and (4) cases brought by one state against citizens of another state or against a foreign country. The most important of these cases are disputes between states over land, water, or old debts. Generally, the Supreme Court deals with these cases by appointing a "special master," usually a retired judge, who actually hears the case and presents a report. The Supreme Court then allows the parties involved in the dispute to present arguments for or against the master's opinion.[15]

Rules of Access. Over the years, the courts have developed specific rules that govern which cases within their jurisdiction they will and will not hear. To have access to the courts, cases must meet certain criteria that are initially applied by the trial court but may be reconsidered by appellate courts. These rules of access can be broken down into three major categories: case or controversy, standing, and mootness.

Article III of the Constitution and Supreme Court decisions define judicial power as extending only to "cases and controversies." This means that the case before a court must be an actual controversy, not a hypothetical one, with two truly adversarial parties. The courts have interpreted this language to mean that they do not have power to render advisory opinions to legislatures or agencies about the constitutionality of proposed laws or regulations. Furthermore, even after a law is enacted, the courts will generally refuse to consider its constitutionality until it is actually applied.

standing The right of an individual or organization to initiate a court case.

Parties to a case must also have **standing**, that is, they must show that they have a substantial stake in the outcome of the case. The traditional requirement for standing has been to show injury to oneself; that injury can be personal, economic, or even aesthetic, for example. For a group or class of people to have standing (as in class action suits), each member must show specific injury. This means that a general interest in the environment, for instance, does not provide a group with sufficient basis for standing.

mootness A criterion used by courts to screen cases that no longer require resolution.

The Supreme Court also uses a third criterion in determining whether it will hear a case: that of **mootness**. In theory, this requirement disqualifies cases that are brought too late—after the relevant facts have changed or the problem has been resolved by other means. The criterion of mootness, however, is subject to the discretion of the courts, which have begun to relax the rules of mootness, particularly in cases where a situation that has been resolved is likely to come up again. In

---

[15] Walter F. Murphy, "The Supreme Court of the United States," in *Encyclopedia of the American Judicial System*, Robert J. Janosik, ed. (New York: Scribner's, 1987).

the abortion case *Roe v. Wade*, for example, the Supreme Court rejected the lower court's argument that because the pregnancy had already come to term, the case was moot. The Court agreed to hear the case because no pregnancy was likely to outlast the lengthy appeals process.

Putting aside the formal criteria, the Supreme Court is most likely to accept cases that involve conflicting decisions by the federal circuit courts, cases that present important questions of civil rights or civil liberties, and cases in which the federal government is the appellant.[16] Ultimately, however, the question of which cases to accept can come down to the preferences and priorities of the justices. If a group of justices believes that the Court should intervene in a particular area of policy or politics, they are likely to look for a case or cases that can be vehicles for judicial intervention. For many years, for example, the Court was not interested in considering challenges to affirmative action or other programs designed to provide particular benefits to minorities. In recent years, however, several of the Court's more conservative justices have been eager to push back the limits of affirmative action and racial preference, and have therefore accepted a number of cases that would allow them to do so. In 1995, the Court's decision in *Adarand Constructors v. Peña, Missouri v. Jenkins*, and *Miller v. Johnson* placed new restrictions on federal affirmative action programs, school desegregation efforts, and attempts to increase minority representation in Congress through the creation of "minority districts" (see Chapter 10).[17] Similarly, because some justices have felt that the Court had gone too far in the past in restricting public support for religious ideas, the Court accepted the case of *Rosenberger v. University of Virginia*. This case was brought by a Christian student group against the University of Virginia, which had refused to provide student activities fund support for the group's magazine, *Wide Awake*. Other student publications received subsidies from the activities fund, but university policy prohibited grants to religious groups. Lower courts supported the university, finding that support for the magazine would violate the Constitution's prohibition against government support for religion. The Supreme Court, however, ruled in favor of the students' assertion that the university's policies amounted to support for some ideas but not others. The Court said this violated the First Amendment right of freedom of expression.[18]

Writs. Most cases reach the Supreme Court through a **writ of *certiorari***. Certiorari is an order to a lower court to deliver the records of a particular case to be reviewed for legal errors (see Figure 8.3). The term *certiorari* is sometimes shortened to *cert*; cases deemed to merit certiorari are referred to as "certworthy." An individual who loses in a lower federal court or state court and wants the Supreme Court to review the decision has 90 days to file a petition for a writ of *certiorari* with

writ of *certiorari* A decision of at least four of the nine Supreme Court justices to review a decision of a lower court; from the Latin "to make more certain."

---

[16] Gregory A. Caldeira and John R. Wright, "Organized Interests and Agenda Setting in the U.S. Supreme Court," *American Political Science Review* 82 (1988): 1109–27.

[17] *Adarand Constructors, Inc. v. Pena*, 115 S. Ct. 2097 (1995); *Missouri v. Jenkins*, 115 S. Ct. 2038 (1995); *Miller v. Johnson*, 115 S. Ct. 2475 (1995).

[18] *Rosenberger v. University of Virginia*, 115 S. Ct. 2510 (1995).

FIGURE 8.3 REACHING THE SUPREME COURT THROUGH *CERTIORARI*

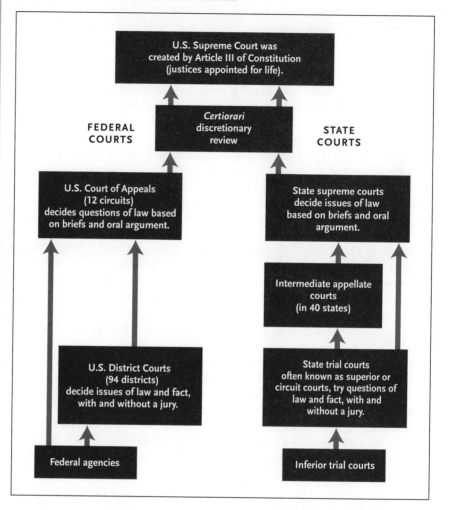

the clerk of the U.S. Supreme Court. There are two types of petitions, paid petitions and petitions *in forma pauperis* (in the form of a pauper). The former requires payment of filing fees, submission of a certain number of copies and compliance with a variety of other rules. For *in forma pauperis* petitions, usually filed by prison inmates, the Court waives the fees and most other requirements.

Since 1972, most of the justices have participated in a *"certiorari* pool" in which they pool their law clerks to evaluate the petitions. Each petition is reviewed by one clerk who writes a memo for all the justices participating in the pool. The memo summarizes the facts and issues and makes a recommendation. Clerks for the other justices add their comments to the memo. After they review the memos, any justice may place any case on the "discuss list." This is a list circulated by the Chief Justice of all the petitions to be talked about and voted on at the Court's conference. If a case is not placed on the discuss list it is automatically denied *certiorari*. Cases placed on the discuss list are considered and voted on during the justices' closed-door conference.

For *certiorari* to be granted four justices must be convinced that the case satisfies Rule 10 of the Rules of the U.S. Supreme Court. Rule 10 states that *certiorari* is not a matter of right but is to be granted only where there are special and compelling reasons. These include conflicting decisions by two or more circuit courts;

FIGURE 8.4 CASES FILED IN THE U.S. SUPREME COURT, 1938–2008

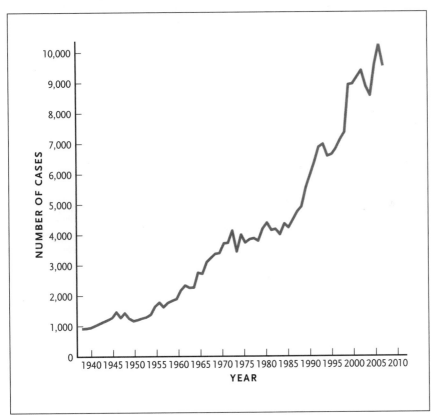

NOTE: Graph indicates the number of cases filed in the term beginning in the year indicated.

SOURCE: Years 1938–69 and 2000–2008: successive volumes of U.S. Bureau of the Census, *Statistical Abstract of the United States* (Washington, D.C.: Government Printing Office); 1970–83: Office of the Clerk of the Supreme Court; 1984–99: reprinted with permission from *The United States Law Week* (Washington, D.C.: Bureau of National Affairs), vol. 56, 3102; vol. 59, 3064; vol. 61, 3098; vol. 63, 3134; vol. 65, 3100; vol. 67, 3167; vol. 69, 3134.

conflicts between circuit courts and state courts of last resort; conflicting decisions by two or more state courts of last resort; decisions by circuit courts on matters of federal law that should be settled by the Supreme Court; or a circuit court decision on an important question that conflicts with Supreme Court decisions. It should be clear from this list that the Court will usually take action only under the most compelling circumstances—where there are conflicts among the lower courts about what the law should be; where an important legal question has been raised in the lower courts but not definitively answered; and where a lower court deviates from the principles and precedents established by the high court. The support of four justices is needed for *certiorari* and few cases are able to satisfy this requirement. In recent sessions, though thousands of petitions have been filed (see Figure 8.4), the Court has granted *certiorari* to hardly more than eighty petitioners each year—about 1 percent of those seeking a Supreme Court review.

A handful of cases reach the Supreme Court through avenues other than certiorari. One of these is the "writ of certification." This writ can be used when a U.S. Court of Appeals asks the Supreme Court for instructions on a point of law that has never been decided. A second avenue is the "writ of appeal," used to appeal the decision of a three-judge district court.

Controlling the Flow of Cases: The Role of the Solicitor General

solicitor general
The top government lawyer in all cases before the appellate courts to which the government is a party.

If any single person has greater influence than the individual justices over the work of the Supreme Court, it is the **solicitor general** of the United States. The solicitor general is third in status in the Justice Department (below the attorney general and the deputy attorney general, who are the government's chief prosecutors) but is the top government defense lawyer in almost all cases before the appellate courts to which the government is a party. Although others can regulate the flow of cases, the solicitor general has the greatest control, with no review of his or her actions by any higher authority in the executive branch. More than half the Supreme Court's total workload consists of cases under the direct charge of the solicitor general.

The solicitor general exercises especially strong influence by screening cases long before they approach the Supreme Court; the justices rely on the solicitor general to "screen out undeserving litigation and furnish them with an agenda to government cases that deserve serious consideration."[19] Agency heads may lobby the president or otherwise try to circumvent the solicitor general, and a few of the independent agencies have a statutory right to make direct appeals, but without the solicitor general's support, these are seldom reviewed by the Court.

amicus curiae Literally, "friend of the court"; individuals or groups who are not parties to a lawsuit but who seek to assist the court in reaching a decision by presenting additional briefs.

The solicitor general can enter a case even when the federal government is not a direct litigant by writing an *amicus curiae* ("friend of the court") brief. A "friend of the court" is not a direct party to a case but has a vital interest in its outcome.

---

[19] Robert Scigliano, *The Supreme Court and the Presidency* (New York: Free Press, 1971), p. 162. For an interesting critique of the solicitor general's role during the Reagan administration, see Lincoln Caplan, "Annals of the Law," *New Yorker*, August 17, 1987, pp. 30–62.

FIGURE 8.5 THE SUPREME COURT'S DECISION-MAKING PROCESS

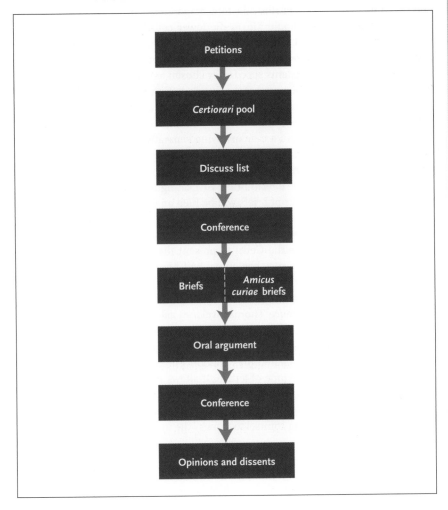

Thus, when the government has such an interest, the solicitor general can file an *amicus curiae*, or the Court can invite such a brief because it wants an opinion in writing. Other interested parties may file briefs as well.

The Supreme Court's Procedures

The Preparation.   The Supreme Court's decision to accept a case is the beginning of what can be a lengthy and complex process (see Figure 8.5). First, the attorneys on both sides must prepare **briefs**—written documents in which the attorneys explain why the Court should rule in favor of their client. The document filed by the individual bringing the case is called the petitioner's brief. This brief summarizes

brief A written document in which attorneys explain why a court should rule in favor of their client.

the facts of the case and presents the legal basis on which the Supreme Court is being asked to overturn the lower court's decision. The document filed by the side that prevailed in the lower court is called the respondent's brief. This brief explains why the Supreme Court should affirm the lower court's verdict. The petitioners will then file a brief answering and attempting to refute the points made in the respondent's brief. This document is called the petitioner's reply brief. Briefs are filled with referrals to precedents specifically chosen to show that other courts have frequently ruled in the same way that the Supreme Court is being asked to rule.

As the attorneys prepare their briefs, they often ask sympathetic interest groups for their help. Groups are asked to file *amicus curiae* briefs that support the claims of one or the other litigant. In a case involving separation of church and state, for example, liberal groups such as the ACLU and Citizens for the American Way are likely to file *amicus* briefs in support of strict separation, whereas conservative religious groups are likely to file *amicus* briefs advocating increased public support for religious ideas. Often, dozens of briefs will be filed on each side of a major case.

Oral Argument.   The next stage of a case is **oral argument**, in which attorneys for both sides appear before the Court to present their positions and answer the justices' questions. Each attorney has only a half hour to present his or her case, and this time includes interruptions for questions. Certain members of the Court, such as Justice Antonin Scalia, are known to interrupt attorneys dozens of times. Others, such as Justice Clarence Thomas, seldom ask questions. For an attorney, the opportunity to argue a case before the Supreme Court is a singular honor and a mark of professional distinction. It can also be a harrowing experience, as justices interrupt a carefully prepared presentation. Nevertheless, oral argument can be very important to the outcome of a case. It allows justices better to understand the heart of the case and to raise questions that might not have been addressed in the opposing side's briefs. It is not uncommon for justices to go beyond the strictly legal issues and ask opposing counsel to discuss the implications of the case for the Court and the nation at large.

The Conference.   Following oral argument, the Court discusses the case in its Wednesday or Friday conference. The chief justice presides over the conference and speaks first; the other justices follow in order of seniority. The Court's conference is secret, and no outsiders are permitted to attend. The justices discuss the case and eventually reach a decision on the basis of a majority vote. While the case is discussed, justices may try to influence or change one another's opinions. At times, this may result in compromise decisions.

Opinion Writing.   After a decision has been reached, one of the members of the majority is assigned to write the **opinion**. This assignment is made by the chief justice, or by the most senior justice in the majority if the chief justice is on the losing side. The assignment of the opinion can make a significant difference to the interpretation of a decision. Every opinion of the Supreme Court sets a major precedent for future cases throughout the judicial system. Lawyers and judges in the lower courts will examine the opinion carefully to ascertain the Supreme Court's

oral argument Oral presentations to a court made by attorneys for both sides in a dispute.

opinion The written explanation of the Supreme Court's decision in a particular case.

meaning. Differences in wording and emphasis can have important implications for future litigation. Thus, in assigning an opinion, the justices must give serious thought to the impression the case will make on lawyers and on the public, as well as to the probability that one justice's opinion will be more widely accepted than another's.

One of the more dramatic instances of this tactical consideration occurred in 1944, when Chief Justice Harlan F. Stone chose Justice Felix Frankfurter to write the opinion in the "white primary" case *Smith v. Allwright*. The chief justice believed that this sensitive case, which overturned the Southern practice of prohibiting black participation in nominating primaries, required the efforts of the most brilliant and scholarly jurist on the Court. But the day after Stone made the assignment, Justice Robert H. Jackson wrote a letter to Stone urging a change of assignment. In his letter, Jackson argued that Frankfurter, a foreign-born Jew from New England, would not win the South with his opinion, regardless of its brilliance. Stone accepted the advice and substituted Justice Stanley Reed, an American-born Protestant from Kentucky and a Southern Democrat in good standing.[20]

Once the majority opinion is drafted, it is circulated to the other justices. Some members of the majority may agree with both the outcome and the rationale but wish to emphasize or highlight a particular point and so will draft a concurring opinion for that purpose. In other instances, one or more justices may agree with the majority but may disagree with the rationale presented in the majority opinion. These justices may draft special concurrences, explaining their disagreements with the majority.

Dissent. Justices who disagree with the majority decision of the Court may choose to publicize the character of their disagreement in the form of a **dissenting opinion**. A dissenting opinion is generally assigned by the senior justice among the dissenters. Dissenting opinions can be used to express irritation with an outcome or to signal to defeated political forces in the nation that their position is supported by at least some members of the Court. Ironically, the most dependable way an individual justice can exercise a direct and clear influence on the Court is to write a dissent. Because there is no need to please a majority, dissenting opinions are often more eloquent and less guarded that majority opinions.

The size of the division on the Court, as well as the reasons for dissent, are often taken as an indication of the strength of the position and principles espoused by the majority. A large majority of, say seven or more, indicates that it will be hard to overturn an opinion in the future, but the one-vote margin of a 5–4 decision might be hard to sustain in future cases involving a given question. In recent years, the Supreme Court often splits 5–4, with dissenters writing long and detailed opinions that they hope will help convince a swing justice to join their side on the next round of cases dealing with a similar topic. In 1950, Justice William O. Douglas wrote the dissent in *South v. Peters*, a case challenging the election of the governor

dissenting opinion Decision written by a justice in the minority in a particular case in which the justice wishes to express his or her reasoning in the case.

---

[20] *Smith v. Allwright*, 321 U.S. 649 (1944).

of Georgia by a vote of counties rather than a vote of the people.[21] Thirteen years later, Justice Douglas echoed that opinion, but this time writing for the majority in the case of *Gray v. Sanders*.[22] In this opinion, Douglas penned one of the most famous phrases of any court decision. In choosing the representatives of the people, equal protection of the laws means "one person, one vote." More recently, Justice David Souter wrote a thirty-four-page dissent in a 2002 case upholding the use of government-funded school vouchers to pay for parochial school tuition. Souter called the decision "a dramatic departure from basic establishment clause principle" and went on to say that he hoped it would be reconsidered by a future court.[23]

Dissent plays a special role in the work and impact of the Court because it amounts to an appeal to lawyers all over the country to keep bringing cases of the sort at issue. Therefore, an effective dissent influences the flow of cases through the Court as well as the arguments that will be used by lawyers in later cases.

Judicial Decision Making

The judiciary is conservative in its procedures, but its impact on society can be radical. That impact depends on a variety of influences, two of which stand out above the rest. The first influence is the individual members of the Supreme Court, their attitudes, and their relationships with each other. The second is the other branches of government, particularly Congress.

The Supreme Court Justices. The Supreme Court explains its decisions in terms of law and precedent. But although law and precedent do have an effect on the Court's deliberations and eventual decisions, it is the Supreme Court that decides what laws actually mean and what importance precedent will actually have. Throughout its history, the Court has shaped and reshaped the law. If any individual judges in the country influence the federal judiciary, they are the Supreme Court justices.

From the 1950s to the 1980s, the Supreme Court took an activist role in such areas as civil rights, civil liberties, abortion, voting rights, and police procedures. For example, the Supreme Court was more responsible than any other governmental institution for breaking down America's system of racial segregation. The Supreme Court virtually prohibited states from interfering with the right of a woman to seek an abortion and sharply curtailed state restrictions on voting rights. And it was the Supreme Court that placed restrictions on the behavior of local police and prosecutors in criminal cases.

But since the early 1980s, resignations, deaths, and new judicial appointments have led to many shifts in the mix of philosophies and ideologies represented on the Court. In a series of decisions between 1989 and 2001, the conservative justices

---

[21] *South v. Peters*, 339 U.S. 276 (1950).

[22] *Gray v. Sanders*, 372 U.S. 368 (1963).

[23] Warren Richey, "Dissenting Opinions as a Window on Future Rulings," *Christian Science Monitor*, July 1, 2002, p. 1.

appointed by Ronald Reagan and George H. W. Bush were able to swing the Court to a more conservative position on civil rights, affirmative action, abortion rights, property rights, criminal procedure, voting rights, desegregation, and the power of the national government.

Precisely because the Court has been so evenly split in recent years, the conservative bloc has not always prevailed. Among the justices serving at the beginning of 2005, Rehnquist, Scalia, and Thomas took conservative positions on most issues and were usually joined by O'Connor and Kennedy. Breyer, Ginsburg, Souter, and Stevens were reliably liberal. This produced many 5-4 splits. On some issues, though, Justice O'Connor or Justice Kennedy tended to side with the liberal camp, producing a 5-4 and sometimes a 6-3 victory for the liberals.

The departure of Justice Sandra Day O'Connor was widely touted in the media as heralding a shift in the Supreme Court in a much more conservative direction. Justice Samuel Alito, who replaced O'Connor, holds more conservative views than Justice O'Connor. O'Connor's departure, however, moved the pivotal vote on the Court only somewhat, from O'Connor to Kennedy. During the 2007 term, Justice Kennedy found himself the swing voter on numerous 5–4 decisions. One-third of all cases in 2007 were decided by just one vote. The appointments of Sonia Sotomayor and Elena Kagan to replace Souter and Stevens, respectively, did not promise to alter this arithmetic. The "Analyzing the Evidence" section on the following page looks at the trend toward more closely decided cases in recent years.

Of course, the meaning of any decision rests not just on which justices vote with the majority but also on the majority's written opinion, which presents the constitutional or statutory rationale for future policy. These options establish the guidelines that govern how federal courts must decide similar cases in the future.

Activism and Restraint.   One element of judicial philosophy is the issue of activism versus restraint. Over the years, some justices have believed that courts should interpret the Constitution according to the stated intentions of its framers and defer to the views of Congress when interpreting federal statutes. The late justice Felix Frankfurter, for example, advocated judicial deference to legislative bodies and avoidance of the "political thicket," in which the Court would entangle itself by deciding questions that were essentially political rather than legal in character. Advocates of **judicial restraint** are sometimes called "strict constructionists," because they look strictly to the words of the Constitution in interpreting its meaning.

The alternative to restraint is **judicial activism**. Activist judges such as the late chief justice Earl Warren believe that the Court should go beyond the words of the Constitution or a statute to consider the broader societal implications of its decisions. Activist judges sometimes strike out in new directions, promulgating new interpretations or inventing new legal and constitutional concepts when they believe these to be socially desirable. For example, Justice Harry Blackmun's opinion in *Roe v. Wade* was based on a constitutional right to privacy that is not found in the words of the Constitution. Blackmun and the other members of the majority in the *Roe* case argued that other constitutional provisions implied the right to privacy. In this instance of judicial activism, the Court knew the result it wanted to achieve and was not afraid to make the law conform to the desired outcome.

judicial restraint
Judicial deference to the views of legislatures and adherence to strict jurisdictional standards.

judicial activism
Proclivity of a court to select cases because of their importance to society rather than adhering to strict legal standards of jurisdiction.

Consensus on the U.S. Supreme Court

For much of the nineteenth century and through the early part of the twentieth century, the Supreme Court publicly operated under what many considered to be a "norm of consensus." Justices believed that unanimity in decision making would serve to strengthen the authority of the Court and its rulings, even if disagreements persisted in private.[1] Over time, however, this behavioral norm appears to have declined among the justices serving on the Court.

▶

The proportion of unanimous decisions handed down by the Court declined sharply between 1930 and 1950, dropping from 90 percent of the cases heard to less than 20 percent. While a number of changes occurred within the judiciary during this period, no definitive explanation exists to account for this trend. Since the 1950s, there has been a modest increase in the proportion of unanimous decisions, but not to anywhere near the level that was common prior to the 1930s.

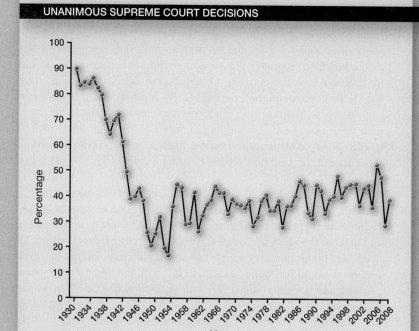

UNANIMOUS SUPREME COURT DECISIONS

Source: Lee Epstein, Jeffrey A. Segal, Harold J. Spaeth, and Thomas G. Walker, *The Supreme Court Compendium: Data, Decisions, and Developments,* 3rd edition (Washington, D.C.: CQ Press, 2003). Updated by author.

[1]On these points, see Lee Epstein, Jeffrey A. Segal, and Harold J. Spaeth, "The Norm of Consensus on the U.S. Supreme Court," *American Journal of Political Science* 45 (April 2001): 362–77.

As Alexander Hamilton observed in *Federalist 78*, the federal judiciary was designed to be the weakest of the three branches of government. Given that the Supreme Court is reliant upon the other branches of government to enforce its decisions, it is much easier to defend a unanimous Court decision than one that reveals a sharp divide among the justices.

Federalist 78

The judiciary…has no influence over either the sword or the purse; no direction either of the strength or of the wealth of the society; and can take no active resolution whatever. It may truly be said to have neither FORCE nor WILL, but merely judgment; and must ultimately depend upon the aid of the executive arm even for the efficacy of its judgments.[2]

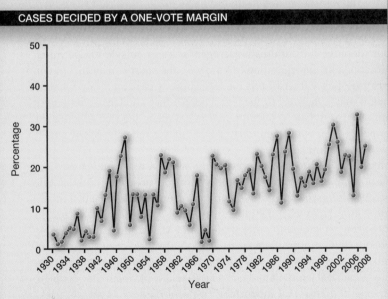

CASES DECIDED BY A ONE-VOTE MARGIN

Source: Lee Epstein, Jeffrey A. Segal, Harold J. Spaeth, and Thomas G. Walker, *The Supreme Court Compendium: Data, Decisions, and Developments,* 3rd edition (Washington, D.C.: CQ Press, 2003). Updated by author.

What are the implications of the precipitous decline in unanimous decisions after 1930? Unanimously decided cases are less likely to be interpreted differently by lower court judges who consider these decisions to be established precedents, whereas decisions supported by a bare majority of justices may not be followed as strictly. Indeed, the proportion of Supreme Court cases decided by a one-vote margin has been steadily increasing since 1930.

[2]Alexander Hamilton, *Federalist* No. 78, in *The Federalist Papers*, Clinton Rossiter, ed. (New York, Penguin: 1961).

Political Ideology. The second component of judicial philosophy is political ideology. The liberal or conservative attitudes of justices play an important role in their decisions.[24] Indeed, the philosophy of activism versus restraint is, to a large extent, a smoke screen for political ideology. In the past, liberal judges have often been activists, willing to use the law to achieve social and political change, whereas conservatives have been associated with judicial restraint. Interestingly, however, in recent years some conservative justices who have long called for restraint have actually become activists in seeking to undo some of the work of liberal jurists over the past three decades.

Other Institutions of Government

Congress. At both the national and state level in the United States, courts and judges are "players" in the policy game because of the separation of powers. Essentially, this means that the legislative branch formulates policy (defined constitutionally and institutionally by a legislative process); that the executive branch implements policy (according to well-defined administrative procedures, and subject to initial approval by the president or the legislative override of his veto); and that the courts, when asked, rule on the faithfulness of the legislated and executed policy either to the substance of the statute or to the Constitution itself. The courts, that is, may strike down an administrative action either because it exceeds the authority granted in the relevant statute (statutory rationale) or because the statute itself exceeds the authority granted the legislature by the Constitution (constitutional rationale).

If the court declares the administrative agent's act as outside the permissible bounds prescribed by the legislation, we suppose the court's majority opinion can declare whatever policy it wishes. If the legislature is unhappy with this judicial action, then it may either recraft the legislation (if the rationale for striking it down was statutory)[25] or initiate a constitutional amendment that would enable the stricken-down policy to pass constitutional muster (if the rationale for originally striking it down was constitutional).

In reaching their decisions, Supreme Court justices must anticipate Congress's response. As a result, judges will not always vote according to their true preferences because doing so may provoke Congress to enact legislation that moves the policy further away from what the judges prefer. By voting for a lesser preference, the justices can get something they prefer to the status quo without provoking congressional action to overturn their decision. The most famous example of this phenomenon is the "switch in time that saved nine," when several justices voted in favor of New Deal legislation, the constitutionality of which they doubted, in order to diminish congressional support for President Roosevelt's plan to "pack"

---

[24] C. Herman Pritchett, *The Roosevelt Court* (New York: Macmillan, 1948).

[25] William N. Eskridge, Jr., "Overriding Supreme Court Statutory Interpretation Decisions," *Yale Law Journal* 101 (1991): 331–55.

the Court by increasing the number of justices. In short, the interactions between the Court and Congress are part of a complex strategic game.[26]

The President.   The president's most direct influence on the Court is the power to nominate justices. Presidents typically nominate judges who they believe are close to their policy preferences and close enough to the preferences of a majority of senators, who must confirm the nomination.

Yet the efforts by presidents to reshape the federal judiciary are not always successful. Often in American history, judges have surprised and disappointed the presidents who named them to the bench. Justice Souter, for example, has been far less conservative than President George H. W. Bush and the Republicans who supported Souter's appointment in 1990 thought he would be. Likewise, Justices O'Connor and Kennedy have disappointed conservatives by opposing limitations on abortion.

THE EXPANDING POWER OF THE JUDICIARY

Over the past fifty years, the place of the judiciary in American politics and society has changed dramatically. Demand for legal solutions has increased, and the reach of the judiciary has expanded. There are now calls to rein in the power of the courts and the discretion of judges in areas ranging from criminal law and sentencing to property rights to liability and torts. How our society deals with these issues will shape the nature of the judiciary—its independence and effectiveness over the generations to come. All indications now are that even the most conservative justices are reluctant to relinquish their newfound power—authority that, once asserted, has become accepted and, thus, established.

To summarize what we have learned so far, judges enjoy great latitude because they are not subject to electoral pressures. Judges and justices, more than any other politicians in America, can pursue their own ideas about what is right and their own ideologies. They are, however, constrained by rules governing access to the courts, by other courts, by Congress and the president, by their lack of enforcement powers, and most important, by the past in the form of precedent and common law. For much of its history, the federal judiciary acted very cautiously. The Supreme Court rarely challenged Congress or the president. Instead the justices tended to legitimate laws passed by Congress and the actions of the president. The scope of the Court's decisions was limited only to those individuals granted access to the courts.

---

[26] A full strategic analysis of the maneuvering among the legislative, executive, and judicial branches in the separation-of-powers arrangement choreographed by the U.S. Constitution may be found in William Eskridge and John Ferejohn, "The Article I, Section 7 Game," *Georgetown Law Review* 80 (1992): 523–65. The entire issue of this journal is devoted to the theme of strategic behavior in American institutional politics.

Two judicial revolutions have expanded the power and reach of the federal judiciary over the decades since World War II. The first of these revolutions brought about the liberalization of a wide range of public policies in the United States. As we saw in Chapter 4, in policy areas—including school desegregation, legislative apportionment, and criminal procedure, as well as obscenity, abortion, and voting rights—the Supreme Court was at the forefront of a series of sweeping changes in the role of the U.S. government and, ultimately, the character of American society. The Court put many of these issues before the public long before Congress or the president were prepared to act.

At the same time that the courts were introducing important policy innovations, they were also bringing about a second, less visible revolution. During the 1960s and 1970s, the Supreme Court and other federal courts instituted a series of institutional changes in judicial procedure that had major consequences by fundamentally expanding the power of the courts in the United States. First, the federal courts liberalized the concept of standing to permit almost any group to bring its case before the federal bench. This change has given the courts a far greater role in the administrative process than ever before. Many federal judges are concerned that federal legislation in areas such as health care reform would create new rights and entitlements that would give rise to a deluge of court cases. "Any time you create a new right, you create a host of disputes and claims," warned Barbara Rothstein, chief judge of the federal district court in Seattle, Washington.[27]

In a second institutional change, the federal courts broadened the scope of relief to permit action on behalf of broad categories or classes of persons in "class action" cases, rather than just on behalf of individuals.[28] A **class action suit** permits large numbers of persons with common interests to join together under a representative party to bring or defend a lawsuit.

In the third major judicial change, the federal courts began to employ so-called structural remedies, in effect retaining jurisdiction of cases until the court's mandate had actually been implemented to its satisfaction.[29] Perhaps the best known of these instances was the federal judge W. Arthur Garrity's effort to operate the Boston school system from his bench in order to ensure its desegregation. Between 1974 and 1985, Judge Garrity issued fourteen decisions relating to different aspects of the Boston school desegregation plan that had been developed under his authority and put into effect under his supervision.[30]

Through these three judicial mechanisms, the federal courts paved the way for an unprecedented expansion of national judicial power. In essence, liberalization of the rules of standing and expansion of the scope of judicial relief drew the federal courts into linkages with important social interests and classes, while the introduction of structural remedies enhanced the courts' abilities to serve these constituencies. Thus, during the 1960s and 1970s, the power of the federal courts expanded in

class action suit
A lawsuit in which large numbers of persons with common interests join together under a representative party to bring or defend a lawsuit, such as hundreds of workers together suing a company.

---

[27] Toni Locy, "Bracing for Health Care's Caseload," *Washington Post*, August 22, 1994, p. A15.

[28] See "Developments in the Law—Class Actions," *Harvard Law Review* 89 (1976): 1318.

[29] See Donald Horowitz, *The Courts and Social Policy* (Washington, D.C.: Brookings Institution, 1977).

[30] *Moran v. McDonough*, 540 F. 2nd 527 (1 Cir., 1976; *cert denied* 429 U.S. 1042 [1977]).

the same way that the power of the executive expanded during the 1930s—through links with constituencies, such as civil rights, consumer, environmental, and feminist groups, that staunchly defended the Supreme Court in its battles with Congress, the executive, or other interest groups.

During the 1980s and 1990s, the Reagan and Bush administrations sought to end the relationship between the Court and liberal political forces. Conservative judges appointed by these Republican presidents modified the Court's position in areas such as abortion, affirmative action, and judicial procedure, though not as completely as some conservative writers and politicians had hoped. Within a one-week window in 2003, for example, the Supreme Court affirmed the validity of affirmative action, reaffirmed abortion rights, strengthened gay rights, offered new protection to individuals facing the death penalty, and issued a ruling in favor of a congressional apportionment plan that dispersed minority voters across several districts—a practice that appeared to favor the Democrats.[31] The Court hadn't changed; rather, it had made these decisions based on the justices' interpretations of precedent and law, not simply personal belief.

The current Court has not been conservative in another sense. It has not been eager to surrender the expanded powers carved out by earlier Courts, especially in areas that assert the power of the national government over the states. Indeed, the early opponents to the U.S. Constitution (the Antifederalists discussed in Chapter 2) feared the assertion of the national interest over the states through the independent judiciary. Over more than two centuries of U.S. history, the reach and authority of the federal judiciary has expanded greatly, and the judiciary has emerged as a powerful arm of our national politics. Whatever their policy beliefs or partisan orientations, judges and justices understand the new importance of the courts among the three branches of American government and act not just to interpret and apply the law but also to maintain the power of the courts.

CHAPTER REVIEW

Millions of cases come to trial every year in the United States. The great majority—nearly 99 percent—are tried in state and local courts. The types of law are civil law, criminal law, and public law. Cases are heard at the state level before three types of courts: trial court, appellate court, and (state) supreme court.

There are three kinds of federal cases: (1) civil cases involving diversity of citizenship, (2) civil cases in which a federal agency is seeking to enforce federal laws that provide for civil penalties, and (3) cases involving federal criminal statutes or in which state criminal cases have been made issues of public law.

Each district court is in one of the twelve appellate districts, called circuits, presided over by a court of appeals. Appellate courts admit no new evidence; their

---

[31] David Van Drehle, "Court That Liberals Savage Proves to Be Less of a Target," *Washington Post*, June 29, 2003, p. A18.

rulings are based solely on the records of the court proceedings or agency hearings that led to the original decision. Appeals court rulings are final unless the Supreme Court chooses to review them.

The Supreme Court has some original jurisdiction, but its major job is to review lower court decisions involving substantial issues of public law. Congress and the state legislatures can reverse Supreme Court decisions, but seldom do. There is no explicit constitutional authority for the Supreme Court to review acts of Congress. Nonetheless, the 1803 case of *Marbury v. Madison* established the Court's right to review congressional acts. The supremacy clause of Article VI and the Judiciary Act of 1789 give the Court the power to review state constitutions and laws.

Cases reach the Court mainly through the writ of *certiorari*. The Supreme Court controls its case load by issuing few writs and by handing down clear leading opinions that enable lower courts to resolve future cases without further review.

Judge-made law is like a statute in that it articulates the law as it relates to future controversies. It differs from a statute in that it is intended to guide judges rather than the citizenry in general.

The judiciary as a whole is subject to two major influences: (1) the individual members of the Supreme Court, who have lifetime tenure; and (2) the Justice Department—particularly the solicitor general, who regulates the flow of cases.

The influence of an individual member of the Supreme Court is limited when the Court is polarized, and close votes in a polarized Court impair the value of the decision rendered. Writing the majority opinion for a case gives a justice an opportunity to influence the judiciary. But the need to frame an opinion in such a way as to develop majority support on the Court may limit such opportunities. Dissenting opinions can have more impact than the majority opinion; they stimulate a continued flow of cases around that issue. The solicitor general is the most important single influence outside the Court itself because he or she controls the flow of cases brought by the Justice Department and also shapes the argument in those cases.

In recent years, the importance of the federal judiciary—the Supreme Court in particular—has increased substantially as the courts have developed new tools of judicial power and forged alliances with important forces in American society.

FOR FURTHER READING

Abraham, Henry J. *The Judicial Process: An Introductory Analysis of the Courts of the United States, England, and France.* 7th ed. New York: Oxford University Press, 1998.

reader selection ○   Baum, Lawrence. *Judges and Their Audiences: A Perspective on Judicial Behavior.* Princeton, N.J.: Princeton University Press, 2006.

reader selection ○   Bickel, Alexander M. *The Least Dangerous Branch: The Supreme Court at the Bar of Politics.* Indianapolis, Ind.: Bobbs-Merrill, 1962.

Epstein, Lee, and Jack Knight. *The Choices Justices Make.* Washington, D.C.: Congressional Quarterly Press, 1998.

Kahn, Ronald. *The Supreme Court and Constitutional Theory, 1953–1993.* Lawrence: University Press of Kansas, 1994.

O'Brien, David M. *Storm Center: The Supreme Court in American Politics*. 8th ed. New York: Norton, 2008.

Perry, H. W., Jr. *Deciding to Decide: Agenda Setting in the United States Supreme Court*. Cambridge, Mass.: Harvard University Press, 1991.

Segal, Jeffrey A., and Harold J. Spaeth. *The Supreme Court and the Attitudinal Model Revisited*. New York: Cambridge University Press, 2002.

Silverstein, Mark. *Judicious Choices: The New Politics of Supreme Court Confirmations*. 2nd ed. New York: Norton, 2007.

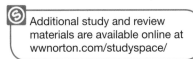

Additional study and review materials are available online at wwnorton.com/studyspace/

9

Public Opinion and the Media

Public support is the coin of the realm in Washington politics. Popular presidents succeed; unpopular presidents struggle. A president who has the backing of a large majority of the public gains leverage in dealing with Congress and the bureaucracy, but a president who lacks public support often meets resistance from members of Congress, even those in his own party. In 1981, Republican president Ronald Reagan had just won a landslide election when he proposed massive cuts in income and capital taxes. Reluctant to oppose such a popular president, the Democratic-controlled Congress readily passed the cuts, allowing Reagan to reduce radically the number of federal regulations. President George W. Bush later described Reagan's popularity as political capital, an asset that must be spent wisely on a few well-chosen issues.[1]

Members of Congress are perhaps even more attuned than presidents to the ups and downs of public opinion. Representatives in the U.S. House must run for reelection every two years, a very short election cycle. They cannot afford to make many unpopular decisions for fear of being punished by their constituents in the next election. A saying among members of Congress goes, "It's okay to be on the losing side of a vote, but you don't want to be on the wrong side." That is, they

---

[1] Chris Suellentrop, "America's New Political Capital," *Slate*, November 30, 2004, www.slate.com/id/2110256/ (accessed 3/18/09). John Fortier of the American Enterprise Institute noted that after 2005 Bush lost his political capital irrevocably: "Spend Your Political Capital Before It's Gone," *Politico*, January 14, 2009, http://mobile.politico.com/story.cfm?id=17395&cat=ideas (accessed 3/18/09). See Richard Neustadt, *Presidential Power and the Modern Presidents*, 4th ed. (New York: Free Press, 1990) and Brandice Canes-Wrone, *Who Leads Whom? Presidents, Policy, and the Public* (Chicago: University of Chicago Press, 2006).

CORE OF THE ANALYSIS

- There are a wide range of interests at stake in any question that the government must decide, as well as differing preferences, beliefs, and opinions about what ought to be done.

- Public opinion is the aggregation of individuals' views. It expresses the range of attitudes and beliefs and on which side of any question a majority of people fall.

- Politicians follow public opinion as part of the representative process. They take signals from polls and other indicators of public sentiment to gauge whether a particular decision might affect their prospects at the next election.

- Among the most important influences shaping public opinion are the media.

worry about going against their constituents' preferences. Members of Congress and party leaders pay close attention to various indicators of public sentiment, including polls; visits back to their districts or home states; and letters, phone calls, and e-mails from constituents.

Even the courts are not immune to the influence of public opinion. Courts lack the power to enforce their decisions; they depend on the compliance of those affected and the cooperation of Congress, the president, and political leaders in the states. That cooperation is not always forthcoming, especially when it is at odds with public opinion. As we saw in Chapter 4, *Brown v. Board of Education*, perhaps the most important Supreme Court decision of the twentieth century, met with immediate opposition in the southern states. In 1963, Governor George Wallace of Alabama stood on the statehouse steps and declared his firm opposition to the Court's edict that the states desegregate "with all deliberate speed." Desegregation occurred slowly, often in the face of violent protests. Only after public opinion turned in support of equal rights for all races did Congress and the president act, accelerating the pace of desegregation.[2]

---

[2] Gerald Rosenberg, *The Hollow Hope* (Chicago: University of Chicago Press, 1991).

Aside from particular government decisions, public opinion is also the standard by which we judge democracy in America. Ideally, representative democracy approximates what the nation as a whole would choose to do were all 300 million Americans to consider a given matter. Congress and the president are supposed to act as the public's agents, enacting laws that a clear majority of the public wants and rejecting laws that fail to achieve widespread support. Also ideally, representative democracy in the United States enacts laws that benefit society and that respond to changes in public sentiment, with the constraint that the laws not violate the freedoms and rights guaranteed in the Bill of Rights. If the norms of society shift strongly in one direction for a period of time, so too should the laws of the land. The nature and origins of public opinion are among the central concerns of modern political science precisely because democratic government is supposed to reflect the wants of the people.

In this chapter, we will examine the role of public opinion in American politics, including questions such as, Do Americans know enough to form meaningful opinions about important policy issues? What factors account for differences in opinion? How do the media influence public opinion? To what extent can the government manipulate popular sentiment? To what extent do—or should—the government's policies respond to public opinion? Then we will take a closer look at one of the most important influences on public opinion, the media.

WHAT IS PUBLIC OPINION?

public opinion
Citizens' attitudes about political issues, personalities, institutions, and events.

Public opinion is the aggregation of many citizens' views and interests. It encompasses assessments of those in office, attitudes toward political organizations and social groups, and preferences about how government ought to address important problems. The term sometimes gives the impression that the public has a single opinion on a given matter; however, that is rarely the case.

Americans do hold common views on questions vital to governance and society. There is consensus on the legitimacy of the Constitution of the United States and trust in the rule of law, the principle that no one is above the law. There is consensus that we are a democratic society and that the outcomes of elections, whether or not a person likes the winners, determine who governs. These commonly held opinions and values are essential to maintaining a well-functioning democracy in the United States. They ensure peaceful transitions of government after each election and respect for laws produced by a legitimately chosen government.

There is also wide agreement on fundamental political values, such as equality of opportunity, liberty, and democracy.[3] Nearly all Americans agree that all people should have equal rights, regardless of race, gender, or social standing. Americans

---

[3] See Louis Hartz, *The Liberal Tradition in America: An Interpretation of American Political Thought since the Revolution* (New York: Harcourt, Brace, 1955).

hold a common commitment to freedom. People who live in the United State are free to live where they want, travel where they want, work where they want, say what they want, and practice whatever religion they wish, including no religion at all. And Americans have an undying belief in democracy, that whenever possible public officials should be chosen by majority vote.[4] It makes sense to think of the American public as having a single opinion on these elemental questions.

On most matters that come before the government, however, the public does not hold a single view. Usually, opinions are divided between those who support the government or a proposed action and those who do not. Politicians are still attuned to public opinion when it is divided, but what matters most are the balance and direction of opinion. What do the majority of constituents want? Which way is opinion trending? Is it possible to find a popular middle ground?

People express their views to those in power in a variety of ways. Constituents contact their members of Congress directly through letters, phone calls, e-mails, and even personal visits to their representatives' offices. Most questions before Congress elicit little reaction from the public, but some questions start a maelstrom of objections. During the fall of 2008, Congress considered a $700 billion bailout of financial institutions. The volume of e-mail on this bill was so great that at one point the House of Representatives had to limit incoming e-mail to keep its computers from crashing.[5]

People also express their opinions more publicly, through blogs, letters to newspapers and op-ed pieces, and conversations with others. They express their support for candidates with lawn signs and bumper stickers; by working on campaigns; giving money to candidates, groups, and party organizations; and, most simply, by voting.

Such expressions of opinions and preferences are not always easy to interpret. If a constituent votes against a member of Congress, did the voter do so because of a controversial decision that the legislator made in Congress, or because the voter decided to vote against all politicians from the legislator's party?

Political scientists and political consultants try to provide more refined and structured descriptions of public opinion using surveys. On any important issue, the government may pursue different policies. Public opinion on a given issue can often be thought of as the distribution of opinion across the different options. Likewise, public opinion may represent the division of support for a leader or party. We try to gauge where majority support lies and how intensely or firmly citizens across the spectrum hold their views. More and more, politicians rely on opinion polls to anticipate the effects of their decisions, to identify opportunities, and to develop ways to blunt the objections to controversial decisions. Answering a survey, then, can also be a form of political action, because it may influence political decisions.

---

[4] For a discussion of political beliefs of Americans, see Everett Carl Ladd, *The American Ideology* (Storrs, Conn: Roper Center, 1994).

[5] Jordy Yeager, "House Limits Constituent e-mail to prevent crash," *The Hill*, September 30, 2008, http://thehill.com/leading-the-news/house-limits-constituent-e-mails-to-prevent-crash-2008-09-30.html (accessed 3/24/09).

ORIGINS OF PUBLIC OPINION

Public opinion is, ultimately, the reflection of millions of individuals' preferences and beliefs. To understand the meaning and origins of the public's opinions, we must have some sense of the basis for individual choice. An individual's opinions are the products of his or her personality, social characteristics, and interests. They mirror who a person is, what she wants, and the manner in which she is embedded in a family and community, and the broader economy and society. But opinions are also shaped by institutional, political, and governmental forces that make it more likely that an individual will hold some beliefs and less likely that he will hold others.

Self-Interest

Individuals' preferences about politics and public policy are rooted partly in self-interest. Laws and other governmental actions directly affect people's interests—their disposable income, the quality of public services and goods, and personal safety, to give just a few examples. It is not surprising, then, that when people express their political opinions, they react to the effects that government actions have had on them personally.

Economic interests are perhaps the most salient preferences when it comes to people's opinions. Virtually every American has an interest in the government's role in the nation's economy and strong preferences about tax rates and expenditure priorities. Public opinion about taxes and spending reflect these preferences. Given the enormous influence of the federal government in the macro economy, assessments of the president and the party in power often correspond to how well the nation's economy performs.

Individuals' attitudes toward government reflect other forms of self-interest as well. Laws affect families, the status of civic and religious organizations, and neighborhoods. Zoning laws and urban redevelopment programs shape the nature of neighborhoods, including the mix of commercial and residential housing and the density of low-income housing in an area. Family law affects how easy it is for families to stay together, what happens when they break down, and what rights and responsibilities parents have. Individuals have a personal stake in decisions bearing on their own communities and families. Proposed changes in such laws bring immediate reaction from those affected.

Political Socialization

The attitudes that individuals hold about political issues and personalities tend to be shaped by their underlying political beliefs and values. For example, someone who has basically negative feelings about government intervention into America's economy and society would probably be predisposed to oppose the development of new health care and social programs. Similarly, someone who distrusts the military would likely be suspicious of any call for the use of American troops. The processes through which these underlying political beliefs and values are formed are collectively called **political socialization.**

The process of political socialization is important. Probably no nation, and certainly no democracy, could survive if its citizens did not share some fundamental beliefs. If Americans had few common values or perspectives, it would be very difficult for them to reach agreement on particular issues. In contemporary America, some elements of the socialization process tend to produce differences in outlook, whereas others promote similarities. Four of the most important **agents of socialization** that foster differences in political perspectives are the family, membership in social groups, education, and prevailing political conditions.

Although these factors cannot fully explain the development of any given individual's political outlook, let us look at some of the most important ways in which they tend to influence most people.

The Family. Most people acquire their initial orientation to politics from their families. As might be expected, differences in family background tend to produce divergent political outlooks. Although relatively few parents spend much time teaching their children about politics, political conversations occur in many households and children tend to absorb the political views of parents and other caregivers, perhaps without realizing it. Studies have suggested, for example, that party preferences are initially acquired at home. Children raised in households in which the primary caregivers are Democrats tend to become Democrats themselves, whereas children raised in homes where their caregivers are Republicans tend to favor the GOP (Grand Old Party, a traditional nickname for the Republican Party).[6] Similarly, children reared in politically liberal households are more likely than not to develop a liberal outlook, whereas children raised in politically conservative settings are likely to see the world through conservative lenses. Obviously, not all children absorb their parents' political views. Moreover, even those children whose views are initially shaped by parental values may change their minds as they mature and experience political life for themselves. Nevertheless, the family is an important initial source of political orientation for everyone.

Social Groups. Another important source of divergent political orientations and values are the social groups to which individuals belong. Social groups include those to which individuals belong involuntarily—gender and racial groups, for example—as well as those to which people belong voluntarily—such as political parties, labor unions, and educational and occupational groups. Some social groups have both voluntary and involuntary attributes. For example, individuals are born with a particular social-class background, but as a result of their own efforts people may move up—or down—the class structure.

Membership in social groups can affect political values in a variety of ways. Membership in a particular group can give individuals important experiences and

political socialization The induction of individuals into the political culture; learning the underlying beliefs and values upon which the political system is based.

agents of socialization Social institutions, including families and schools, that help to shape individuals' basic political beliefs and values.

---

[6] See Angus Campbell, Philip E. Converse, Warren E. Miller, and Donald E. Stokes, *The American Voter* (New York: Wiley, 1960), p. 147.

perspectives that shape their view of political and social life. In American society, for example, the experiences of blacks and whites can differ significantly. Blacks are a minority and have been victims of persecution and discrimination throughout American history. Blacks and whites also have different educational and occupational opportunities and often live in separate communities; many attend separate schools. Such differences tend to produce distinctive political outlooks.

According to recent surveys, blacks and whites in the United States differ on a number of issues. For example, in surveys conducted by the Pew Research Center, clear majorities of whites supported the ideas that government should do more to guarantee food and shelter (62 percent in a 2003 survey) and generally help the needy (55 percent in a 2005 survey). Much larger majorities of blacks expressed support for the guarantee of food and shelter (80 percent) and the provision of help for the needy (72 percent).[7] Other issues show a similar pattern of disagreement, reflecting the differences in experience, background, and interests between blacks and whites in America (Figure 9.1).

Of course, disagreements between blacks and whites are not the only important racial or ethnic differences to be found in contemporary America. Latinos are another major American subgroup with distinctive opinions on some public issues. A 2008 survey by the Pew Hispanic Center found that education is the top concern of Hispanic voters; the economy ranked highest among white non-Hispanic voters.[8] Often immigrants or the children of immigrants, Hispanics view education as the ticket to a better life in America and attach great value to educational opportunity. As a population currently moving to the United States, Latinos also have a distinctive view of immigration. A 2004 Pew Hispanic Center survey found that more than 60 percent of Latinos believe that immigration is good for America. Among non-Latinos, though, more than 60 percent believe that immigration poses a major threat to the country.

Religion has become another important source of variation in opinion. In recent years, contending political forces have placed a number of religious and moral issues on the national political agenda. The Republican Party, in particular, has emphasized its support for traditional "family values" and its opposition to abortion, same-sex marriage, and other practices opposed by conservative religious leaders. It is not surprising that public opinion on these issues differs along religious lines, with evangelical Protestants being most supportive of traditional values and respondents identifying themselves as "secular" manifesting the least support for them. Take the issue of same-sex marriage, for example (Table 9.1).

Men and women have important differences of opinion as well. Reflecting differences in social roles, political experience, and occupational patterns, women tend to be less militaristic than men on issues of war and peace, more likely than men to favor measures to protect the environment, and more supportive than men

---

[7] Pew Research Center for the People and the Press, "The Black and White of Public Opinion," October 31, 2005, http://people-press.org/commentary/?analysisid=121 (accessed 6/8/09).

[8] Mark Lopez and Susan Minushkin, *2008 National Survey of Latinos: Hispanic Voter Attitudes*, Pew Hispanic Center, July 24, 2008, http://pewhispanic.org/files/reports/90.pdf (accessed 3/24/09).

FIGURE 9.1 DISAGREEMENT AMONG BLACKS AND WHITES

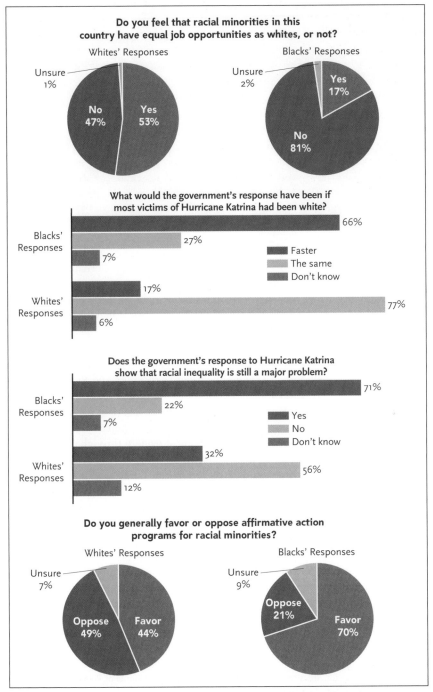

SOURCE: Gallup polls, June 8–25, 2006 and June 12–15, 2003, www.pollingreport.com; Pew Research Center for the People and the Press, "The Black and White of Public Opinion," October 31, 2005, http:people-press.org/commentary/?analysisid=121 (accessed 6/8/09).

TABLE 9.1 SHOULD SAME-SEX MARRIAGE BE LEGALIZED?

Religious Group	In Favor (%)	Opposed (%)
White evangelical Protestant	14	81
White nonevangelical Protestant	43	47
White non-Hispanic Catholic	41	49
Black Protestant	15	79
Secular	60	30

SOURCE: "A Stable Majority: Most Americans Still Oppose Same-Sex Marriage," April 1, 2008, http://pewforum.org/docs/?DocID=290 (accessed 3/24/09).

of government social and health-care programs (Table 9.2). Perhaps because of these differences on issues, women are more likely than men to vote for Democratic candidates, while men have become increasingly supportive of the GOP.[9] This tendency for men's and women's opinions to differ is called the **gender gap.**

As we will see in Chapter 11, political party membership can be another factor affecting political orientation. Partisans tend to rely on party leaders and spokespersons for cues on the appropriate position to take on major political issues. According to recent studies, differences between Democratic and Republican partisans on a variety of political and policy questions are greater today than they were during any other period for which data are available. On issues of national security, for example, Republicans have become very "hawkish," whereas Democrats have become quite "dovish." This polarization was most evident throughout the war in Iraq. Nine months into the war, a large majority of Democrats opposed the war and supported withdrawal. A large majority of Republicans supported the war and the continued efforts to stabilize the situation.[10]

Membership in a social group can affect individuals' political orientations in another way: through the efforts of groups themselves to influence their members. Labor unions, for example, often seek to "educate" their members through meetings, rallies, and literature. These activities are designed to shape union members' understanding of politics and to make them more amenable to supporting the political positions favored by union leaders. Similarly, organization can sharpen the impact of membership in an involuntary group. Women's groups, black groups, religious groups, and the like usually endeavor to structure their members' political views through intensive educational programs. The importance of such group efforts can

gender gap A distinctive pattern of voting behavior reflecting the differences in views between women and men.

---

[9] For data, see Center for American Women and Politics, Eagleton Institute of Politics, Rutgers, State University of New Jersey, "Sex Differences in Voter Turnout," 2005.

[10] Jeffrey M. Jones, "Iraq War Attitudes Politically Polarized," Gallup News, April 8, 2008, www.gallup.com/poll/106309/Iraq-War-Attitudes-Politically-Polarized.aspx (accessed 3/24/09).

TABLE 9.2 DISAGREEMENTS AMONG MEN AND WOMEN ON ISSUES OF WAR AND PEACE

Government Action	Approve of Action (%)	
	Men	Women
Going to war against Iraq (2003)	66	50
Brokering a cease-fire in Yugoslavia instead of using NATO air strikes (1999)	44	51
Ending the ban on homosexuals in the military (1993)	34	51
Engaging in a military operation against a Somali warlord (1993)	72	60
Going to war against Iraq (1991)	72	53

SOURCE: Gallup polls, 1991, 1993, and 1999; *Washington Post*, 2003.

be seen from the impact of group membership on political opinion. Women who belong to women's organizations, for example, are likely to differ more from men in their political views than women without such group affiliation.[11] Other analysts have found that African Americans who belong to black organizations are more likely than blacks who lack such affiliations to differ from whites in their political orientations.[12]

In many cases, no particular efforts are required by groups to affect their members' beliefs and opinions. Often, individuals will consciously or unconsciously adapt their views to those of the groups with which they identify. For example, an African American who is dubious about affirmative action is likely to come under considerable peer pressure and internal pressure to modify his or her views. In this and other cases, dissenters are likely gradually to shift their own views to conform to those of the group. The political psychologist Elisabeth Noelle-Neumann has called this process the "spiral of silence."[13]

Another way that membership in social groups can affect political beliefs is through what might be called objective political interests. On many economic issues, for example, the interests of the rich and poor differ significantly. Inevitably, these differences of interest will produce differences of political outlook. James Madison and other framers of the Constitution thought that the inherent gulf between the rich and the poor would always be the most important source of conflict

---

[11] Pamela Johnston Conover, "The Role of Social Groups in Political Thinking," *British Journal of Political Science* 18 (1988): 51–78.

[12] See Michael C. Dawson, "Structure and Ideology: The Shaping of Black Opinion," paper presented to the 1995 annual meeting of the Midwest Political Science Association, Chicago, Illinois, April 7–9, 1995. See also Michael C. Dawson, *Behind the Mule: Race and Class in African-American Politics* (Princeton, N.J.: Princeton University Press, 1994).

[13] Elisabeth Noelle-Neumann, *The Spiral of Silence: Public Opinion, Our Social Skin* (Chicago: University of Chicago Press, 1984).

in political life. Certainly today, struggles over tax policy, welfare policy, health-care policy, and so forth are fueled by differences of interest between wealthier and poorer Americans. In a similar vein, objective differences of interest between senior citizens and younger Americans can lead to very different views on such diverse issues as health care policy, Social Security, and criminal justice.

It is worth pointing out again that, like the other agencies of socialization, group membership can never fully explain a given individual's political views. One's unique personality and life experiences may produce political views very different from those of the group to which one might nominally belong. Group membership is conducive to particular outlooks, but it is not determinative.

Differences in Education.   A third important source of differences in political perspectives comes from a person's education. In some respects, of course, schooling is a great equalizer. Governments use public education to try to teach all children a common set of civic values. It is mainly in school that Americans acquire their basic belief in liberty, equality, and democracy. In history classes, students are taught that the Founders fought for the principle of liberty. Through participation in class elections and student government, students are taught the virtues of democracy. In the course of studying such topics as the Constitution, the Civil War, and the civil rights movement, students are taught the importance of equality. These lessons are repeated in every grade in a variety of contexts. No wonder they are such an important element in Americans' beliefs.

At the same time, however, differences in educational attainment are strongly associated with differences in political outlook. In particular, those who attend college are often exposed to philosophies and modes of thought that will forever distinguish them from their friends and neighbors who do not pursue college diplomas. Table 9.3 outlines some general differences of opinion found in one survey taken in 2008 comparing college graduates and other Americans. One of the major differences between college graduates and other Americans can be seen in levels of political participation. College graduates vote, write "letters to the editor," join campaigns, take part in protests, and, generally, make their voices heard.

Political Conditions.   A fourth set of factors that shape political orientations and values are the conditions under which individuals and groups are recruited into and involved in political life. Although political beliefs are influenced by family background and group membership, the precise content and character of these views is, to a large extent, determined by political circumstances. For example, many Americans who came of political age during the Great Depression and World War II developed an intense sense of loyalty to President Franklin Delano Roosevelt and became permanently attached to his Democratic Party. In a similar vein, the Vietnam War and social upheavals of the 1960s produced lasting divisions among Americans of the "baby boomer" generation. Indeed, arguments over Vietnam persisted into the 2004 presidential election, some thirty years after American troops left Southeast Asia. Perhaps the 9/11 terrorist attacks and ongoing threats to America's security will have a lasting impact on the political orientations of contemporary Americans.

TABLE 9.3 EDUCATION AND PUBLIC OPINION

Issues	Level of Education			
	Grade School	High School	Some College	College Graduate
Women and men should have equal roles.	73	82	90	90
Abortion should never be permitted.	27	17	12	9
The government should adopt national health insurance.	66	58	50	49
Helping to bring democracy to other nations.	36	27	21	12
Government should see to fair treatment in jobs for African Americans.	80	58	54	60
Government should provide fewer services to reduce government spending.	10	18	21	25

NOTE: The figures show the percentage of respondents in each category agreeing with the statement.

SOURCE: American National Election Studies 2008 data, Center for Political Studies, University of Michigan, www.electionstudies.org.

In a similar vein, the views held by members of a particular group can shift drastically over time, as political circumstances change. For example, American white Southerners were staunch members of the Democratic Party from the Civil War through the 1960s. As members of this political group, they became key supporters of liberal New Deal and post–New Deal social programs that greatly expanded the size and power of the American national government. Since the 1960s, however, Southern whites have shifted in large numbers to the Republican Party. Now they provide a major base of support for efforts to scale back social programs and sharply reduce the size and power of the national government. The South's move from the Democratic to the Republican camp took place because of white Southern opposition to the Democratic Party's racial policies and because of determined Republican efforts to win white Southern support. It was not a change in the character of white Southerners but a change in the political circumstances in which they found themselves that induced this major shift in political allegiances and outlooks in the South.

The moral of this story is that a group's views cannot be inferred simply from the character of the group. College students are not inherently radical or inherently conservative. Jews are not inherently liberal. Southerners are not inherently conservative. Men are not inherently supportive of the military. Any group's political outlooks and orientations are shaped by the political circumstances in which that group finds itself, and those outlooks can change as circumstances change. The "Analyzing the Evidence" unit for this chapter looks at how public opinion on taxes has shifted over time.

Political Ideology

As we have seen, people's beliefs about government can vary widely. But for some individuals, this set of beliefs can fit together into a coherent philosophy about government. This set of underlying orientations, ideas, and beliefs through which we come to understand and interpret politics is called a political ideology.

In America today, people often describe themselves as liberals or conservatives. Liberalism and conservatism are political ideologies that include beliefs about the role of the government, ideas about public policies, and notions about which groups in society should properly exercise power. Historically these terms were defined somewhat differently than they are today. As recently as the nineteenth century, a liberal was an individual who favored freedom from state control, whereas a conservative was someone who supported the use of governmental power and favored continuation of the influence of church and aristocracy in national life.

liberal A liberal today generally supports political and social reform; extensive governmental intervention in the economy; the expansion of federal social services; more vigorous efforts on behalf of the poor, minorities, and women; and greater concern for consumers and the environment.

Today, the term **liberal** has come to imply support for political and social reform; support for extensive governmental intervention in the economy; the expansion of federal social services; more vigorous efforts on behalf of the poor, minorities, and women; and greater concern for consumers and the environment. In social and cultural areas, liberals generally support abortion rights and oppose state involvement with religious institutions and religious expression. In international affairs, liberal positions are usually seen as including support for aid to poor nations, opposition to the use of American troops to influence the domestic affairs of developing nations, and support for international organizations such as the United Nations.

Of course, liberalism is not monolithic. For example, among individuals who view themselves as liberal, many support American military intervention when it is tied to a humanitarian purpose, as in the case of America's military action in Kosovo in 1998–99. Most liberals initially supported President George W. Bush's war on terrorism, even when some of the president's actions seemed to curtail civil liberties.

conservative Today this term refers to one who generally supports the social and economic status quo and is suspicious of efforts to introduce new political formulae and economic arrangements. Conservatives believe that a large and powerful government poses a threat to citizens' freedom.

By contrast, the term **conservative** today is used to describe those who generally support the social and economic status quo and are suspicious of efforts to introduce new political formulae and economic arrangements. Conservatives believe strongly that a large and powerful government poses a threat to citizens' freedom. Thus, in the domestic area, conservatives generally oppose the expansion of governmental activity, asserting that solutions to social and economic problems can be developed in the private sector. Conservatives particularly oppose efforts to impose government regulation on business, pointing out that such regulation is frequently economically inefficient and costly and can ultimately lower the entire nation's standard of living. As for social and cultural positions, many conservatives oppose abortion and support school prayer. In international affairs, conservatism has come to mean support for the maintenance of American military power. Like liberalism, conservatism is far from a monolithic ideology. Some conservatives support many government social programs. George W. Bush called himself a "compassionate conservative" to indicate that he favored programs that assist the poor and needy. Other conservatives oppose efforts to outlaw abortion, arguing that government intrusion in this area is as misguided as government intervention in the economy. The real political world is far too complex to be seen in terms of a simple struggle between liberals and conservatives.

There are many other ideologies besides liberal and conservative. Some people seek to expand liberty above all other principles and wish to minimize government intervention in the economy and society. Such a position is sometimes called liberation. Other ideologies espouse a particular outcome, such as environmental protection, which may lead to emphasis on some issues, such as economic growth, and de-emphasis of other issues, such as abortion. Communism and fascism are ideologies that involve government control of all aspects of the economy and society. These ideologies dominated politics in many European countries from the 1920s through the 1940s. Political discourse in the United States, however, has revolved around the division between liberals and conservatives for most of the last century.

Of course, it is important to note that many people who call themselves liberals or conservatives accept only part of the liberal or conservative ideology. Although it appears that Americans have adopted more conservative outlooks on some issues, their views in other areas have remained largely unchanged or even become more liberal in recent years. Thus, many individuals are liberal on social issues but conservative on economic issues. There is nothing illogical about these mixed positions. They indicate the relatively open and fluid character of American political debate.

HOW ARE POLITICAL OPINIONS FORMED?

An individual's opinions on particular issues, events, and personalities emerge as he or she evaluates these phenomena through the lenses of the beliefs and orientations that, taken together, compose his or her political ideology. Thus, if a conservative is confronted with a plan to expand federal social programs, he or she is likely to express opposition to the endeavor without spending too much time pondering the specific plan. Similarly, if a liberal is asked to comment on former president Ronald Reagan, he or she is not likely to hesitate long before offering a negative view. Underlying beliefs and ideologies tend to automatically color people's perceptions and opinions about politics.

Opinions on particular issues, however, are seldom fully shaped by underlying ideologies. It is true that most people have underlying beliefs that help to shape their opinions on particular issues,[14] but other factors are also important: a person's knowledge of political issues, and outside influences on that person's views.

---

[14] R. Michael Alvarez and John Brehm, *Hard Choices, Easy Answers: Values, Information, and American Public Opinion* (Princeton, N.J.: Princeton University Press, 2002).

Public Opinion and Taxes

Nobody likes to pay taxes. The United States was founded in part due to disputes over taxes. Talk of taxes dominates political campaigns. Americans simply hate taxes, right?

That wasn't always the case. Both the importance of taxes to politics and American dislike of taxes were lower during the 1950s and 1960s than during the period from the 1970s to the present. What changed after the 1960s? Why did taxes become more important to the public? What encouraged politicians to campaign on tax issues?

One measure of the centrality of taxes in political campaigns is the number of times the topic is mentioned in presidential nomination acceptance speeches. These data show that the word *taxes* barely passed the lips of the major-party nominees until after the 1960s. The numbers on the vertical axis represent the number of sentences mentioning taxes in nomination acceptance speeches.

Source: Author content analysis of acceptance speeches as compiled by the Woolley and Peters American Presidency Project.

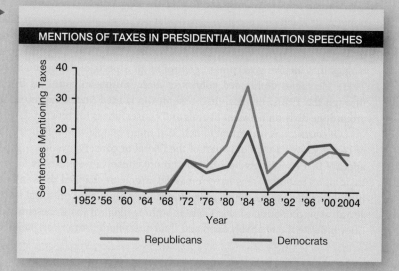

MENTIONS OF TAXES IN PRESIDENTIAL NOMINATION SPEECHES

Republicans   Democrats

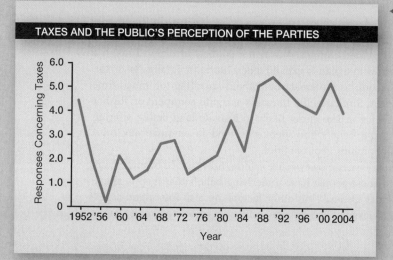

TAXES AND THE PUBLIC'S PERCEPTION OF THE PARTIES

Source: National Election Studies Cumulative File.

In earlier decades, taxes weren't very important to members of the public, either. The National Election Study has asked respondents what they like and dislike about each of the political parties at least every four years since 1952. With the exception of 1952, when the presidential election featured talk of lowering taxes after World War II, the percentages of all "likes" and "dislikes" that concerned taxes were much lower during the 1950s and 1960s than in later decades. Here the vertical axis shows the percentages of all "likes" and "dislikes" (for Republicans and Democrats combined) that concern taxes.

Political scientists don't have a definitive answer, but there are a number of plausible explanations. One factor could be the increasing effective costs of taxes. During the 1950s and 1960s, per capita taxes increased rapidly, but real wages grew even faster. With Americans' disposable income growing, the impact of taxes was muted. But during the 1970s, oil shocks and worldwide economic slowdown reduced wage growth. High inflation both ate into Americans' purchasing power and pushed them into higher and higher tax brackets (a phenomenon called *bracket creep*). As taxes took a bigger bite, their salience to the public grew.

Another explanation, popularized by the journalists Thomas and Mary Edsall in their 1992 book *Chain Reaction*, is that taxes became linked in the public mind with race-related policies. They hypothesized that with the Great Society policies of the 1960s, white Americans in particular came to resent the use of their tax dollars for welfare and other means-tested policies they believed they would never benefit from themselves.

The salience of taxes may also have been fueled by institutional changes within Congress. During the 1950s and 1960s, tax policy was dominated by the House Ways and Means Committee and its powerful chairman for much of this period, Wilbur Mills. The committee and its chair held both tight jurisdiction over taxes and tremendous power within the chamber, which allowed the containment of politics around taxes to a small tax policy community. Reforms in the late 1960s and early 1970s reduced the power of Ways and Means, which had to establish subcommittees for the first time, open its hearings to the public, and give up its control over committee assignments, previously an important source of leverage over House members. These changes opened up the insulated tax policy–making community, paving the way for tax politics as public spectacle.

Finally, tax revolts in some states demonstrated to politicians the expediency of taxes as a political issue. In 1978, California voters, frustrated that the state legislature had done nothing to cut taxes in a period of large budget surpluses and growing state and local tax burdens, took matters into their own hands by passing Proposition 13. The ballot initiative capped property tax rates and also instituted a two-thirds majority requirement in both houses of the state legislature for any subsequent increases in state taxes. Prop 13 convinced politicians, including the presidential candidate Ronald Reagan, that "tax cuts were good politics," according to the sociologist Isaac Martin.[1] Other entrepreneurial politicians, particularly in the Republican Party, strove to keep taxes on the public agenda and to cement the GOP's image as the party of tax cuts.

It is likely that all of these factors contributed to the heightening of taxes as a political issue. And given the current budget deficit, growing national debt, and mismatch between projected revenues and likely spending on Social Security, Medicare, and Medicaid over the long term, taxes will undoubtedly be high on the political agenda for some time to come.

[1]Isaac William Martin, *The Permanent Tax Revolt* (Palo Alto, Calif.: Stanford University Press, 2008), p. 15.

Source: Adapted from *How Americans Think about Taxes* by Andrea Louise Campbell (Princeton, N.J.: Princeton University Press, 2009).

Knowledge and Information

As they read newspapers, listen to the radio, watch television, and chat with their friends and associates, citizens are constantly confronted by new political events, issues, and personalities. Often they will be asked what they think about a particular issue or whether they plan to support a particular candidate. Indeed, in our democracy we expect every citizen to have views about the major problems of the day as well as opinions about who should be entrusted with the nation's leadership.

Some Americans know quite a bit about politics, and many have general views and hold opinions on several issues. Few Americans, though, devote sufficient time, energy, or attention to politics to really understand or evaluate the myriad issues with which they are bombarded on a regular basis. In fact, many studies have shown that the average American knows very little about politics. In one major study, for example, only 25 percent of respondents could name their two senators, only 29 percent could name their U.S. representative, and fewer than half knew that the Constitution's first ten amendments are called the Bill of Rights.[15] Evidence that half of America's citizens—particularly those who have not attended college—are so unaware of the nation's history and politics is troubling.

Yet ignorance is probably a predictable and inevitable fact of political life. Some analysts have argued that political attentiveness is costly; it means spending time at the very least, and often money as well, to collect, organize, and digest political information.[16] Balanced against this cost to an individual is the very low probability that he or she will, on the basis of this costly information, take an action that would not otherwise have been taken *and* that such a departure in behavior would make a beneficial difference to him or her *and* that such a difference, if it existed, would exceed the cost of acquiring the information in the first place. Because individuals anticipate that informed actions they take will rarely make much difference, whereas the costs of informing oneself are often not trivial, it may be rational to remain ignorant. A more moderate conception of "rational ignorance" recognizes that some kinds of information are inexpensive to acquire, such as sound bites from the evening news, or can be pleasant, such as reading the front page of the newspaper while drinking a cup of coffee. In such cases, an individual may become somewhat informed, but usually not in detail.

Precisely because becoming truly knowledgeable about politics requires a substantial investment of time and energy, many Americans seek to acquire political information and to make political decisions on the cheap, using shortcuts that seem to relieve them of having to engage in information gathering and evaluation. One "inexpensive" way to become informed is to take cues from trusted others—the local minister, the television commentator or newspaper editorialist, an interest-group leader, friends, and relatives.[17] Sometimes the cue giver is dis-

---

[15] Michael X. Delli Carpini and Scott Keeter, *What Americans Know about Politics and Why It Matters* (New Haven, Conn.: Yale University Press, 1996), pp. 307–28.

[16] Anthony Downs, *An Economic Theory of Democracy* (New York: Harper & Row, 1957).

[17] For a discussion of the role of information in democratic politics, see Arthur Lupia and Mathew D. McCubbins, *The Democratic Dilemma: Can Citizens Learn What They Need to Know?* (New York: Cambridge University Press, 1998).

trusted, in which case the cue leads the receiver in the opposite direction. For example, if a liberal is told that a Republican president is backing a major overhaul of the Social Security system, he or she will probably not read thousands of pages of economic projections before exhibiting suspicion of the president's efforts. Along the same lines, a common shortcut for political evaluation and decision making is to assess new issues and events through the lenses of one's general beliefs and orientation. Thus if a conservative learns of a plan to expand federal social programs, he or she might express opposition to the endeavor without carefully pondering the specifics of the proposal.

Neither of these shortcuts is entirely reliable, however. Taking cues from others may lead individuals to accept positions that they would not support if they had more information. And general ideological orientations are usually poor guides to decision making in concrete instances. For one thing, especially when applied to discrete issues, most individuals' beliefs turn out to be filled with contradictions. For example, what position should a liberal take on immigration? Should a liberal favor keeping America's borders open to poor people from all over the world, or should he or she be concerned that America's open borders might create a pool of surplus labor that would permit giant corporations to drive down the wages of poor American workers? Many issues are too complex to lend themselves to simple ideological interpretation.

Although understandable and perhaps inevitable, widespread inattentiveness to politics weakens American democracy in two ways. First, those who lack political information or resort to inadequate shortcuts to acquire and assess information cannot effectively defend their political interests and can easily become victims or losers in political struggles. Second, the presence of large numbers of politically inattentive or ignorant individuals means that the political process can be more easily manipulated by the various institutions and forces that seek to shape public opinion.

As for the first of these problems, in our democracy millions of ordinary citizens take part in political life, at least to the extent of voting in national elections. Those with little knowledge of the election's issues or candidates or procedures can find themselves acting against their own preferences and interests. One example is U.S. tax policy. Over the past several decades, the United States has substantially reduced the rate of taxation for its wealthiest citizens.[18] Tax cuts signed into law by President Bush in 2001 and mostly maintained until the Obama administration took office in 2009 provided a tax break mainly for the top 1 percent of the nation's wage earners. Surprisingly, however, polling data showed that millions of middle-class and lower-middle-class Americans who did not stand to benefit from the president's tax cuts seemed to favor them nonetheless. The explanation for this odd state of affairs appears to be a lack of political knowledge. Millions of individuals who were unlikely to derive much advantage from President Bush's tax policy thought they would. The political scientist Larry Bartels has called this

---

[18] One of the most detailed analyses of the distribution of the tax burden in advanced industrial democracies in the past half century is Thomas Piketty and Emmanuel Saez, "How Progressive Is the U.S. Federal Tax System? Historical and International Perspectives," working paper 12404, National Bureau of Economic Research, August 2006, www.nber.org/papers/w12404 (accessed 6/8/04).

phenomenon "misplaced self-interest."[19] Upper-bracket taxpayers, who are usually served by an army of financial advisers, are unlikely to suffer from this problem. Knowledge may not always translate into political power, but lack of knowledge is almost certain to translate into political weakness.

Government and Political Leaders

All governments attempt, to a greater or lesser extent, to influence, manipulate, or manage their citizens' beliefs. But the extent to which public opinion is actually affected by governmental public relations efforts is probably limited. The government—despite its size and power—is only one source of information and evaluation in the United States. Very often, governmental claims are disputed by the media, by interest groups, and at times by opposing forces within the government itself.

Often, too, governmental efforts to manipulate public opinion backfire when the public is made aware of the government's tactics. Thus, in 1971, the United States government's efforts to build popular support for the Vietnam War were hurt when CBS News aired its documentary *The Selling of the Pentagon*, which revealed the extent and character of government efforts to sway popular sentiment. In this documentary, CBS demonstrated the techniques, including planted news stories and faked film footage, that the government had used to misrepresent its activities in Vietnam. These revelations, of course, had the effect of undermining popular trust in all government claims.

A hallmark of the Clinton administration was the steady use of campaign techniques such as those used in election campaigns to bolster popular enthusiasm for White House initiatives. The president established a "political war room" in the Executive Office Building similar to the one that operated in his campaign headquarters. Representatives from all departments met in the war room every day to discuss and coordinate the president's public-relations efforts. Many of the same consultants and pollsters who directed the successful Clinton campaign were employed in the selling of the president's programs.[20]

After he assumed office in 2001, President George W. Bush asserted that political leaders should base their programs on their own conception of the public interest rather than the polls. This, however, did not mean that Bush ignored public opinion. Bush relied on the pollster Jan van Lohuizen to conduct a low-key operation, sufficiently removed from the limelight to allow the president to renounce polling while continuing to make use of survey data.[21] At the same time, the Bush White House developed an extensive public relations program to bolster popular support for the president's policies. These efforts included presidential speeches, media appearances by administration officials, numerous press conferences, and thousands of press releases presenting the administration's views. The White

---

[19] Larry M. Bartels, "Homer Gets a Tax Cut: Inequality and Public Policy in the American Mind," *Perspectives on Politics* 3 (2005): 15–31.

[20] Gerald F. Seib and Michael K. Frisby, "Selling Sacrifice," *Wall Street Journal*, February 5, 1993, p. 1.

[21] Joshua Green, "The Other War Room," *Washington Monthly*, April 2002.

House also made a substantial effort to sway opinion in foreign countries, even sending officials to present the administration's views on television networks serving the Arab world.

Private Groups

We have already seen how the government tries to shape opinion. But the ideas that become prominent in political life are also developed and spread by important economic and political groups searching for issues that will advance their causes. In some instances, private groups espouse values in which they truly believe in the hope of bringing others over to their side. Take, for example, the campaign against so-called partial birth abortion that resulted in the Partial Birth Abortion Ban Act of 2003. Proponents of the act believed that prohibiting particular sorts of abortions would be a first step toward eliminating all abortions—something they viewed as a moral imperative.[22] In other cases, groups will promote principles designed mainly to further hidden agendas of political and economic interests. One famous example is the campaign against cheap, imported handguns—the so-called Saturday night specials—covertly financed by domestic manufacturers of more expensive firearms. The campaign's organizers claimed that cheap handguns posed a grave risk to the public and should be outlawed. The real goal, though, was not safeguarding the public but protecting the economic well-being of the domestic gun industry. A more recent example is the campaign against the alleged "sweatshop" practices of some American companies manufacturing products in Third World countries. This campaign is mainly financed by U.S. labor unions seeking to protect their members' jobs by discouraging American firms from manufacturing products abroad.

Typically, ideas are best marketed by groups with access to financial resources, public or private institutional support, and sufficient skill or education to select, develop, and draft ideas that will attract interest and support. Thus, the development and promotion of conservative themes and ideas in recent years has been greatly facilitated by the millions of dollars that conservative corporations and business organizations, such as the Chamber of Commerce and the Public Affairs Council, spend each year on public information and what is now called in corporate circles "issues management." In addition, conservative businesses have contributed millions of dollars to such conservative institutions as the Heritage Foundation, the Hoover Institution, and the American Enterprise Institute.[23]

Although they often do not have access to financial assets that match those available to their conservative opponents, liberal intellectuals and professionals have ample organizational skills, access to the media, and practice in creating, communicating, and using ideas. During the past three decades, the chief vehicle through which liberal intellectuals and professionals have advanced their ideas has been the "public interest group," an institution that relies heavily upon voluntary

---

[22] Cynthia Gorney, "Gambling with Abortion," *Harper's Magazine*, November 2004, pp. 33–46.

[23] See David Vogel, "The Power of Business in America: A Reappraisal," *British Journal of Political Science* 13 (January 1983): 19–44.

contributions of time, effort, and interest on the part of its members. Through groups such as Common Cause, the National Organization for Women, the Sierra Club, Friends of the Earth, and Physicians for Social Responsibility, intellectuals and professionals have been able to use their organizational skills and educational resources to develop and promote ideas.[24]

The Media

The communications media are among the most powerful forces operating in the marketplace of ideas. Most Americans say that their primary source of information about public affairs is news media—newspapers, broadcast and cable news, radio, and Internet news providers. The alternative sources of political information are direct contact with politics, information provided by groups, and information conveyed by other individuals, such as family members or coworkers. Certainly few people actually go to Washington to find out what's going on in American politics, and the broad access people have to media outlets dwarfs the number of households that receive direct mail from organizations and elected officials. Personal conversation is also an important source for information, but people tend to avoid controversial topics. For example, at work or school, sports and weather are much safer topics for casual conversation than politics.

The mass media, as the term suggests, can be thought of as mediators. They are the conduits through which information flows. Through newspapers, radio, television, magazines, and the Internet we can learn about what's going on in our world and in our government. As we will see in the following section, providing this opportunity to learn about the world and politics is the most important way the media contribute to public opinion.

THE MEDIA AS AN INSTITUTION

People rely on the media, rather than other sources of information, to find out what's going on in politics and public affairs because it is easy to do so. Media outlets are ubiquitous. More households in the United States have television than have indoor plumbing. Radio penetration is nearly as universal. Almost every community has a newspaper, with 1,500 daily newspapers published throughout the United States. The number of news programs and the availability of news has also expanded tremendously in recent decades. In the 1960s there were only three television news outlets—CBS, NBC, and ABC. They aired evening and nightly news programs and allowed a half-hour slot for news from local affiliates. The rise of cable television in the 1980s brought a twenty-four-hour news station, CNN; expanded news programming through the Public Broadcasting System (PBS); and

---

[24] See David Vogel, "The Public Interest Movement and the American Reform Tradition," *Political Science Quarterly* 96 (Winter 1980): 607–27.

created a network devoted exclusively to broadcasting proceedings of Congress and government agencies, C-SPAN. Important competitors to the big three networks emerged, including FOX, UPN, WB, and the Spanish-language networks Univision and Telemundo. There is, today, no shortage of televised news programming available at all hours.[25]

Technological innovations continue to push change in political communication in the United States. Today, more than 75 percent of Americans have Internet access.[26] To put that in historical perspective, Internet penetration in the United States today is comparable to television penetration in the late 1950s. This technology, then, has yet to reach its full power and potential. Nevertheless, the rise of the Internet has already opened the flow of communication further. Conventional media have moved much of their content online, provided for free. Internet users can gain access not only to U.S. media but also to media from around the world. The Internet has also changed the traditional media, leading to the development of interactive graphics and reader forums. We have also witnessed the rise of new forms of communications, most notably Web logs ("blogs" for short), which provide a platform for anyone to have their say. Several Web sites, such as Google News and realclearpolitics.com, are clearinghouses for traditional media, newswire stories, and blogs. The new, highly competitive media environment has put increased financial pressures on the traditional media, and it has radically changed the flow and nature of communication in the United States and the availability of information to the public.

Types of Media

Americans obtain their news from three main sources: broadcast media (radio and television), print media (newspapers and magazines), and, increasingly, the Internet. Each of these sources has distinctive institutional characteristics that help to shape the character of their coverage of political events.

Broadcast Media.   Television news reaches more Americans than any other single news source. Tens of millions of individuals watch national and local news programs every day. Television news, however, covers relatively few topics and provides little depth of coverage. Television news is more like a series of newspaper headlines connected to pictures. It serves the extremely important function of alerting viewers to issues and events but provides little else.

The twenty-four-hour news stations such as Cable News Network (CNN) offer more detail and commentary than the networks' half-hour evening news shows. In 2003, at the start of the war in Iraq, CNN, Fox, and MSNBC provided twenty-four-hour-a-day coverage of the war, including on-the-scene reports from embedded reporters, expert commentary, and interviews with government officials. In

---

[25] See Stephen Ansolabehere, Roy Behr, and Shanto Iyengar, *The Media Game* (New York: Macmillan, 1993).

[26] These figures are tracked regularly by the Nielsen Corporation, www.nielsen-online.com/pr/pr_040318.pdf (accessed 3/25/09).

this instance, these networks' depth of coverage rivaled that of the print media. Normally, however, CNN and the others offer more headlines than analysis, especially during their prime-time broadcasts. In recent years, cable has been growing in importance as a news source (Table 9.4).

Politicians generally view the local broadcast news as a friendlier venue than the national news. National reporters are often inclined to criticize and question, whereas local reporters often accept the pronouncements of national leaders at face value. For this reason, presidents often introduce new proposals in a series of short visits to a number of cities—indeed, sometimes flying from airport stop to airport stop—in addition to or instead of making a national presentation. For example, in February 2002, President Bush introduced his idea for a new national volunteer corps during his State of the Union message and then made a number of local speeches around the country promoting the theme. Although national reporters questioned the president's plans, local news coverage was overwhelmingly positive.

Radio news is also essentially a headline service without pictures. In the short time—usually five minutes per hour—that they devote to news, radio stations announce the day's major events without providing much detail. In major cities, all-news stations provide a bit more coverage of major stories, but for the most part these stations fill the day with repetition rather than detail. All-news stations such as WTOP (Washington, D.C.) and WCBS (New York City) assume that most listeners are in their cars and that, as a result, the people who constitute the audience change markedly throughout the day as they reach their destination. Thus, rather than use their time to flesh out a given set of stories, these stations repeat the same stories each hour to present them to new listeners.

TABLE 9.4 WHERE DO AMERICANS GET THEIR NEWS?

	1993 (%)	1996 (%)	2000 (%)	2002 (%)	2004 (%)	2006 (%)
Local TV news	77	65	56	57	59	54
Cable TV news	—	—	—	33	38	34
Nightly network news	60	42	30	32	34	28
Radio	47*	44	43	41	40	36
Newspaper	58*	50	47	41	42	40
Online news	—	2†	23	25	29	31

*Data from 1994.
†Data from 1995.
SOURCES: Pew Research Center for the People and the Press, "Maturing Internet News Audience—Broader Than Deep: Online Papers Modestly Boost Newspaper Readership," July 30, 2006, http://people-press.org/reports/pdf/282.pdf (accessed 6/8/09).

In recent years, much of the content of the news, especially local news, has shifted away from politics and public affairs toward "soft news"—coverage focusing on celebrities, health tips, advice to consumers, and other topics more likely to provide entertainment than enlightenment. Even a good deal of political coverage is soft. For example, media coverage of the 2008 presidential inauguration devoted nearly as much attention to the dresses worn by President Obama's wife and daughters as it did to the content of the president's address.

Print Media.   Newspapers remain an important source of news even though they are not the primary news source for most Americans. The print media are important for two reasons. First, as we shall see later in this chapter, the broadcast media rely on leading newspapers such as the *New York Times* and the *Washington Post* to set their news agenda. The broadcast media engage in very little actual reporting; they primarily cover stories that have been "broken," or initially reported, by the print media. For example, sensational charges that President Bill Clinton had an affair with a White House intern were reported first by the *Washington Post* and *Newsweek* before being trumpeted around the world by the broadcast media. It is only a slight exaggeration to observe that if an event is not covered in the *New York Times,* it is not likely to appear on the *CBS Evening News.* One important exception, obviously, is the case of "breaking" news, which can be carried by the broadcast media as it unfolds or soon after, while the print media are forced to catch up later in the day. Recall the dramatic real-time videos of the collapsing Twin Towers seen by tens of millions of Americans. Second, the print media provide more detailed and more complete information, offering a better context for analysis. Third, the print media are also important because they are the prime source of news for educated and influential individuals. The nation's economic, social, and political elites rely on the detailed coverage provided by the print media to inform and influence their views about important public matters. The print media may have a smaller audience than their cousins in broadcasting, but they have an audience that matters.

Today, however, the newspaper industry is in serious economic trouble. The rise of Web sites advertising jobs, items for sale, and personal ads has dramatically reduced newspapers' revenues from traditional advertising, such as "help wanted" and personal ads. The *Rocky Mountain News* in Denver closed in 2008, and the *Seattle Post-Intelligencer* announced it would adopt an online format only. Major newspapers serving dozens of large U.S. cities and metropolitan areas have announced that they face serious financial difficulties. It is widely believed that the shakeout at these papers is just the beginning of a wider transformation of the print media in the United States, which may leave the country with few or no print newspapers—the traditional "press"—by 2020. The great unknown is whether other venues can adequately replace newspapers, especially in the provision of news about local area politics and public affairs.[27]

---

[27] "The 10 Most Endangered Newspapers in America," *Time,* March 9, 2009, www.time.com/time/business/article/0,8599,1883785,00.html (accessed 6/8/09).

The Internet. A relatively new source of news is the Internet. Every day several million Americans, especially younger Americans, scan one of many news sites on the Internet for coverage of current events. For the most part, however, the Internet provides electronic versions of coverage offered by print sources. One great advantage of the Internet is that it allows frequent updating. It can potentially combine the depth of coverage of a newspaper with the timeliness of television and radio and probably will become a major news source in the next decade. Already most political candidates and interest groups have sites on the World Wide Web. Some of the more sensational aspects of President Clinton's relationship with Monica Lewinsky were first reported on a Web site maintained by Matt Drudge, who specializes in posting sensational charges about public figures. Though many deny it, most reporters scan Drudge's site regularly, hoping to pick up a bit of salacious gossip. Many Americans relied on Web sites such as CNN.com for up-to-the-minute election news in the days after the 2000 presidential election, the dramatic postelection battle in Florida, the 2001 terrorist attacks on New York City and Washington, D.C., the war in Iraq, and Hurricane Katrina.[28] Acknowledging the growing importance of the Internet as a political communications medium, the U.S. Supreme Court posted its decisions in the Florida election cases as soon as they were issued. Reflecting the importance of the Internet, in January 2007, two days after announcing her bid for the 2008 Democratic presidential nomination, Senator Hillary Rodham Clinton fielded questions from voters in an online chat. Speaking into a Webcam, Clinton discussed health care, energy policy, and even her favorite movies with a group of preselected voters.

In addition, hundreds of thousands of readers turn to more informal sources of Internet news and commentary: Web logs, or blogs. Blogs are intermittently published online by thousands of individuals and generally feature personal opinion and commentary on national and world events. In recent years, some news stories first discussed by bloggers have been picked up by mainstream journalists and have had a major impact on political events. In December 2002, for example, bloggers criticized Senator Trent Lott for praising the one-time segregationist Senator Strom Thurmond at a birthday party for Thurmond. A few days later the mainstream press focused on the story, and Lott was forced to resign his post as Senate majority leader. In 2004, after CBS aired a story claiming that George W. Bush had received preferential treatment while serving in the Air National Guard, conservative bloggers mounted a campaign charging that the documents presented by CBS had been forged. The network ultimately admitted that the documents had not been properly authenticated, and the CBS anchor Dan Rather was forced to resign. In 2006, bloggers and other avid Internet users, sometimes called netroot activists, helped bring about the defeat of the Virginia Republican senator and presidential hopeful George Allen. After it was shown on the YouTube Web site, a video clip of Allen directing what appeared to be a racial slur at a Democratic campaign worker

---

[28] For a discussion of the growing role of the Internet, see Leslie Wayne, "On Web, Voters Reinvent Grass-Roots Activism," *New York Times,* May 21, 2000, p. 22. See also James Fallows, "Internet Illusions," *New York Review of Books,* November 16, 2000, p. 28.

was downloaded to hundreds of thousands of computers and discussed by thousands of bloggers. The story was then featured by the television networks. Allen was defeated in his bid for reelection and saw his presidential hopes destroyed.

Regulation of the Media

In some countries, the government controls media content. In other countries, the government owns the broadcast media but does not tell the media what to say (as is the case with the BBC in Great Britain). In the United States, the government neither owns nor controls the communications networks, but it does regulate the content and ownership of the broadcast media. The print media, on the other hand, are essentially free from government interference.

Broadcast Media. American radio and television are regulated by the Federal Communications Commission (FCC), an independent regulatory agency established in 1934. Radio and TV stations must renew their FCC licenses every five years. Through regulations prohibiting obscenity, indecency, and profanity, the FCC has also sought to prohibit radio and television stations from airing explicit sexual and excretory references between 6 A.M. and 10 P.M., the hours when children are most likely to be in the audience. The FCC has enforced these rules haphazardly. Since 1990, nearly half the $5 million in fines levied by the agency have involved Howard Stern, the "shock jock" whose programs are often built around sexually explicit material.

For more than sixty years, the FCC also sought to regulate and promote competition in the broadcast industry, but in 1996 Congress passed the Telecommunications Act, a broad effort to do away with most regulations in effect since 1934. The act loosened restrictions on media ownership and allowed for telephone companies, cable television providers, and broadcasters to compete with each other for the provision of telecommunication services. Following the passage of the act, several mergers between telephone and cable companies and among different segments of the entertainment media produced an even greater concentration of media ownership.

The federal government has used its licensing power to impose several regulations that can affect the political content of radio and TV broadcasts. The first of these is the **equal time rule**, under which broadcasters must provide candidates for the same political office equal opportunities to communicate their messages to the public. The second regulation affecting the content of broadcasts is the **right of rebuttal**, which requires that individuals be given the opportunity to respond to personal attacks. For many years, a third important federal regulation was the **fairness doctrine**—under which broadcasters who aired programs on controversial issues were required to provide air time for opposing views. In 1985, the FCC stopped enforcing the fairness doctrine on the grounds that there were so many radio and television stations—to say nothing of newspapers and newsmagazines—that in all likelihood many different viewpoints were being presented even without the requirement that each station present all sides of an argument.

equal time rule The requirement that broadcasters provide candidates for the same political office an equal opportunity to communicate their messages to the public.

right of rebuttal An FCC regulation giving individuals the right to have the opportunity to respond to personal attacks made on a radio or TV broadcast.

fairness doctrine An FCC requirement that broadcasters who air programs on controversial issues provide time for opposing views.

prior restraint An effort by a government agency to block the publication of material it deems libelous or harmful in some other way; censorship. In the United States, the courts forbid prior restraint except under the most extraordinary circumstances.

Freedom of the Press.   Unlike the broadcast media, the print media are not subject to federal regulation. Indeed, the great principle underlying the federal government's relationship with the press is the doctrine against **prior restraint**. Beginning with the landmark 1931 case of *Near v. Minnesota*, the U.S. Supreme Court has held that, except under the most extraordinary circumstances, the First Amendment of the Constitution prohibits government agencies from seeking to prevent newspapers or magazines from publishing whatever they wish.[29]

Even though newspapers may not be restrained from publishing whatever they want, they may be subject to sanctions after the fact. Historically, newspapers have been subject to the law of libel, which provides that newspapers that print false and malicious stories can be compelled to pay damages to those they defame. In recent years, however, American courts have greatly narrowed the meaning of libel and made it extremely difficult, particularly for politicians and other public figures, to win a libel case against a newspaper.

Sources of Media Power

The power of the media to affect political knowledge and public opinion stems from several sources. Learning through mass media occurs both actively and passively. Active learning occurs when people search for a particular type of program or a particular type of information. If you turn on the nightly news to find out what has happened in national and international affairs, you are engaged in active learning. If you search the Web for information about your member of Congress, you are engaged in active learning. Passive learning may be just as important. Many entertainment programs discuss current affairs and issues, such as social issues or an election. When that occurs, learning takes a passive form. You watch the program for entertainment but gain information about politics. One study of information gain among voters found that people learned as much from Oprah as from the evening news.[30] Political advertising is perhaps the most common form of passive information. During the last month of national political campaigns, it is not uncommon to see three or four political advertisements during one commercial break in a prime-time (7:00 to 11:00 P.M.) television program.

Mass media are our primary source for information about current affairs. They influence how Americans understand politics not just through the volume of information available but also through what is presented and how. Editors, reporters, and others involved in preparing the content of the news must ultimately decide what topics to cover, what facts to include, and whom to interview. Journalists usually try to present issues fairly, but it is difficult, perhaps impossible, to be perfectly objective. C-SPAN takes an unusual approach. It sets up a camera at an event and simply records what occurs; it adds no commentary and does not edit the material. Just the facts. However, even that approach necessarily involves some slant, depending on what events C-SPAN decides to cover. By choosing to cover some events and not others, it sends a message about what, in its view, is important.

---

[29] *Near v. Minnesota ex rel.*, 283 U.S. 697 (1931).

[30] See Matthew Baum, *Soft News Goes to War* (Princeton, N.J.: Princeton University Press, 2006).

What the media cover and how news is presented and interpreted can affect public opinion. Psychologists have identified two potential pathways through which media coverage shapes what people think. First, the news sets the public's agenda. Through this **agenda-setting** function, the media cue people to think about some issues rather than others; it makes some considerations more salient than others. Suppose, for example that the local news covers crime to the exclusion of all else. When someone who watches the local news regularly thinks about the mayoral election, crime is more likely to be his or her primary consideration, compared with someone who does not watch the local news. Psychologists call this *priming*.

Second, news coverage of an issue frames the way the issue is defined. News coverage of crime, to continue the example, may include a report on every murder that happens in a large city. Such coverage would likely make it seem that murder occurs very often and is much more common than it actually is. This in turn might heighten viewers' sense of insecurity or threat, leading to an exaggerated sense of risk of violent crime and increased support for tough police practices.[31] *Framing* refers to the media's power to influence how events and issues are interpreted.

Priming and framing are often viewed as twin evils. One can distract us from other important problems, and the other can make us think about an issue or a politician in a biased way. The cumulative effects of priming and framing on public opinion depend ultimately on the variety of issues covered and the diversity of perspectives represented. That, after all, is the idea behind the guarantee of a free press in the First Amendment to the Constitution. Free and open communication media allow the greatest likelihood that people will learn about important issues, that they will gain the information they need to distinguish good ideas from bad ones, and that they will learn which political leaders and parties can best represent their interests.

In this regard, the most significant framing effects take the form of the balance in the information available to people. Those in politics—elected officials, candidates, leaders of organized groups—work hard to influence what the news covers. A competitive political environment usually translates into a robust flow of information. However, some political environments are not very competitive. Only one view gets expressed and only one view is reflected in the media. Congressional elections are a case in point. Incumbent politicians today are able to raise much more money than their challengers (an advantage of about 3 to 1). As a result, House elections often have a significant imbalance in the amount of advertising and news coverage between the two campaigns, that of the incumbent member of Congress and that of the challenger. This will likely affect public opinion, because voters hear the incumbent's views and message more often than the challenger's.

A further example of an imbalance in news coverage arises with the president and Congress. Presidential press conferences and events receive much more coverage than the press events of the leaders of the House or Senate. This gives the president the upper hand in setting the public agenda through the media, because members of the public are more likely to hear the president's arguments for

agenda-setting
The power of the media to bring public attention to particular issues and problems.

---

[31] The seminal work on priming and framing in public policy and politics is Shanto Iyengar and Donald Kinder, *News That Matters* (Chicago: University of Chicago Press, 1987).

a particular policy. That opportunity and power, of course, must be used wisely. A president who pursues an ill-advised policy can easily squander the advantage that is gained from disproportionate attention from the media. If a policy fails, the president's media advantage can be short lived. President George W. Bush convinced the nation that Iraq was developing weapons of mass destruction and the United States needed to topple the regime of Saddam Hussein immediately. The invasion occurred and Hussein's regime quickly fell, but large caches of chemical and nuclear weapons were never found, and the United States remained in Iraq for the better part of a decade. The backlash against these policies cost the Republicans support among the public, control of Congress in the 2006 election, and ultimately the presidency in 2008. The power of the president is the power to persuade, but control of information for political aims is a power to be used with caution.

Today, it is easy to learn about public affairs and to hear different opinions—even when we don't want to. The rise of cable television and the Internet has weakened the old media outlets, such as ABC, CBS, and NBC, and the newspaper industry. But, it is widely conjectured, the new media have facilitated learning and muted some of the biases that may emerge through priming and framing. No one voice or perspective dominates our multifaceted media environment and competitive political system. And biases in the media often reflect not the lack of outlets or restrictive editorial control but failures of political competition.

HOW DOES PUBLIC OPINION INFLUENCE GOVERNMENT POLICY?

In democratic nations, leaders should pay attention to public opinion, and most evidence suggests that they do. There are many instances in which public policy and public opinion do not coincide, but in general the government's actions are consistent with citizens' preferences. One study, for example, found that between 1935 and 1979, in about two-thirds of all cases, significant changes in public opinion were followed within one year by changes in government policy consistent with the shift in the popular mood.[32] Other studies have come to similar conclusions about public opinion and government policy at the state level.[33] Do these results suggest that politicians pander to the public? The answer is no. Elected leaders don't always pander to the results of public opinion polls, but instead use polling to sell their policy proposals and shape the public's views.[34]

In addition, there are always areas of disagreement between opinion and policy. For example, the majority of Americans favored stricter governmental control of handguns for years before Congress finally adopted the modest restrictions on firearms purchases embodied in the 1994 Brady Bill and the Crime Control Act. Similarly, most Americans—blacks as well as whites—oppose school busing to achieve racial balance, yet such busing continues to be used extensively throughout the nation. Most Americans are far less concerned with the rights of the accused than the federal courts seem to be. Most Americans oppose U.S. military intervention in other nations' affairs, yet interventions continue to take place and often win public approval after the fact.

Several factors can contribute to a lack of consistency between opinion and governmental policy. First, the national majority on a particular issue may not be as intensely committed to its preference as the adherents of the minority viewpoint. An intensely committed minority may often be more willing to commit its time, energy, efforts, and resources to the affirmation of its opinions than an apathetic, even if large, majority. In the case of firearms, for example, although the proponents of gun control are in the majority by a wide margin, most do not regard the issue as one of critical importance to themselves and are not willing to commit much effort to advancing their cause. The opponents of gun control, by contrast, are intensely committed, well organized, and well financed, and as a result are usually able to carry the day.

A second important reason that public policy and public opinion may not coincide has to do with the character and structure of the American system of government. The framers of the American Constitution, as we saw in Chapter 2, sought to create a system of government that was based on popular consent but that did not invariably and automatically translate shifting popular sentiments into public policies. As a result, the American governmental process includes arrangements such as an appointed judiciary that can produce policy decisions that may run contrary to prevailing popular sentiment—at least for a time.

Perhaps the inconsistencies between opinion and policy could be resolved if broader use were made of the initiative and referendum. This procedure allows propositions to be placed on the ballot and voted into law by the electorate, thereby

---

[32] Benjamin I. Page and Robert Y. Shapiro, "Effects of Public Opinion on Policy," *American Political Science Review* 77 (March 1983): 175–90.

[33] Robert A. Erikson, Gerald Wright, and John McIver, *Statehouse Democracy: Public Opinion and Democracy in the American States* (New York: Cambridge University Press, 1994).

[34] The results of separate studies by the political scientists Lawrence Jacobs, Robert Shapiro, and Alan Monroe were reported by Richard Morin in "Which Comes First, the Politician or the Poll?" *Washington Post National Weekly Edition*, February 10, 1997, p. 35.

eliminating most of the normal machinery of representative government. In recent years, several important propositions sponsored by business and conservative groups have been enacted by voters in the states.[35] For example, in 2008 California voters adopted Proposition 8, amending the state constitution to ban same-sex marriage. In 2009, the California Supreme Court refused to overturn the result. Florida and Arizona voters also banned same-sex marriage in 2008. Proponents and opponents of the California measure spent $73 million in their quests for votes.

Initiatives such as these seem to provide the public with an opportunity to express its will. The major problem, however, is that government by initiative offers little opportunity for reflection and compromise. Voters are presented with a proposition, usually sponsored by a special interest group, and are asked to take it or leave it. Perhaps the true will of the people, not to mention their best interest, might lie somewhere between the positions taken by various interest groups. Perhaps, for example, California voters might have preferred legalization of same-sex unions in some form other than "marriage." In a representative assembly, as opposed to a referendum campaign, a compromise position might have been achieved that was more satisfactory to all the residents of the state. This is one reason the framers of the U.S. Constitution strongly favored representative government rather than direct democracy.

When all is said and done, however, there can be little doubt that in general the actions of the American government do not remain out of line with popular sentiment for very long. A major reason for this is, of course, the electoral process, to which we will turn next.

CHAPTER REVIEW

All governments claim to obey public opinion, and in the democracies politicians and political leaders actually try to do so.

Americans share a number of values and viewpoints but often classify themselves as liberal or conservative in their basic orientations. The meaning of these terms has changed greatly over the past century. Once liberalism meant opposition to big government. Today liberals favor an expanded role for the government. Once conservatism meant support for state power and aristocratic rule. Today conservatives oppose almost all government regulation.

Although the United States relies mainly on market mechanisms, our government does intervene to influence particular opinions and, more important, the general climate of political opinion, often by trying to influence media coverage of events.

Another important force shaping public opinion is the news media, which help to determine the agenda or focus of political debate and to shape popular

---

[35] David S. Broder, *Democracy Detailed: Initiative Campaigns and the Power of Money* (New York: Harcourt, 2000).

understanding of political events. The power of the media stems from their having the freedom to present information and opinion critical of government, political leaders, and policies. Free media are essential ingredients of popular government.

FOR FURTHER READING

Althaus, Scott. *Collective Preferences and Democratic Politics*. New York: Cambridge University Press, 2003.

Ansolabehere, Stephen, Jonathan Rodden, and James M. Snyder Jr., "Purple America." *Journal of Economic Perspectives* 20, no. 2 (Spring 2006): 97–118.

Bartels, Larry. *Unequal Democracy*. Princeton, N.J.: Princeton University Press, 2008.

Cook, Timothy. *Governing with the News: The News Media as a Political Institution*. Chicago: University of Chicago Press, 1997.

Erikson, Robert S., and Kent L. Tedin. *American Public Opinion: Its Origins, Content, and Impact*. 6th ed. New York: Longman, 2001.

Fiorina, Morris, Samuel Abrams, and Jeremy Pope. *Culture War?* 2nd ed. New York: Pearson, Longman, 2005. ○ reader selection

Frank, Thomas. *What's The Matter with Kansas?* New York: Macmillan, 2004.

Ginsberg, Benjamin. *The Captive Public: How Mass Opinion Promotes State Power*. New York: Basic Books, 1986.

Hamilton, James. *All the News That's Fit to Sell*. Princeton, N.J.: Princeton University Press, 2004.

Key, V. O. *Public Opinion and American Democracy*. New York: Knopf, 1961.

Lee, Taeku. *Mobilizing Public Opinion*. Chicago: University of Chicago Press, 2002.

Lupia, Arthur, and Matthew D. McCubbins. *The Democratic Dilemma: Can Citizens Learn What They Need to Know?* New York: Cambridge University Press, 1998. ○ reader selection

Rutherford, Paul. *Weapons of Mass Persuasion*. Toronto: University of Toronto Press, 2004.

Starr, Paul. *The Creation of the Media*. New York: Basic Books, 2004.

Stimson, James A. *Public Opinion in America: Moods, Cycles, and Swings*. 2nd ed. Boulder, Colo.: Westview Press, 1998.

Trippi, Joe. *The Revolution Will Not Be Televised: Democracy, the Internet, and the Overthrow of Everything*. New York: Regan Books, 2004.

Zaller, John R. *The Nature and Origins of Mass Opinion*. New York: Cambridge University Press, 1992.

 Additional study and review materials are available online at wwnorton.com/studyspace/

10 Elections

People convey their opinions to the government through many means, but the simplest and most profound expression of an individual's political preferences is the vote. Through the vote citizens can affirm a commitment to stay the course or to change their government when they think a new direction is needed. The vote, it is often said, is a blunt but effective instrument for controlling the government. In 2004, following a successful invasion of Iraq and with robust economic growth at hand, a majority of American voters reelected George W. Bush president and retained Republican majorities in the House and Senate. In 2006, with discontent over the war in Iraq growing, Americans elected Democratic majorities in the House and Senate. In 2008, facing an economic recession and ongoing involvement in Iraq, a majority of voters elected Barack Obama to the presidency and returned even larger Democratic majorities to the House and Senate. In each of these cases, voters expressed their political preferences through the institution of elections. Following the 2008 election, the administration of Barack Obama and the Democrats in Congress became the focus of the American electorate. As the new administration ascended to power, its members knew that they would be held accountable for their failings and rewarded for their successes. Indeed, only two years later, in the 2010 midterm elections, Republicans took control of the House of Representatives in what was widely seen as an electoral rebuke to the president.

Frequent, regular elections are the hallmark of democracy. Voters in the United States elect the president, governors, and other executive officers every four years, federal and state legislators every two years, and thousands of local mayors, councilors, and commissioners with similar frequency. All told there are over 88,000 governments at the federal, state, and local levels in the United States, nearly all of them run by elected bodies.[1] In a typical election, a voter may choose candidates for

CORE OF THE ANALYSIS

- Frequent, regular elections are the hallmark of democracy. The vote is the simplest and most significant way that people convey their preferences to the government.

- The institutional features of American elections regulate who votes, what form the ballot takes, how voting districts are drawn, and what it takes to win an election. These factors have important consequences for the outcomes of elections.

- The United States uses a system of plurality rule in which the candidate with the most votes wins the electoral district. Plurality rule creates a strong pressure toward two-party politics.

- Voters who identify with a political party vote with that party nearly all of the time. Issues and candidate characteristics also influence voters' decisions.

- Campaigns try to mobilize their candidate's supporters and persuade undecided voters.

a dozen different offices, as well as deciding bond issues and other local questions put before the voters. In parliamentary systems, such as Britain, elections are held when the governing party in the legislature decides to hold elections, typically every four or five years. In parliamentary systems, voters in national elections usually only make one choice—which candidate should serve the district in parliament or which party should rule. In the United States, the regularity of elections makes the prospect of the next race a constant pressure on politicians. The wide use of elections, it is thought, keeps government policy close to the preferences and interests of its constituents. Electoral politics in the United States have functioned in this way for over two centuries. Elections have proved a remarkably successful method of bringing about continual renewal of government through peaceful means.

Why do elections work? How is it that elections generally create a govern-

---

[1] There is one federal government. There are fifty state governments, over 3,000 county governments, 36,000 municipal and town governments, about 13,500 school districts, and over 35,000 special districts (for example, water or utility), http://ftp2.census.gov/govs/cog/2002COGprelim_report.pdf (accessed 3/26/09).

ment and policies that reflect and respond to the preferences of the public? In a representative democracy such as the United States, the electorate selects its leaders and representatives, rather than voting on each law and policy. Voters choose among the people and parties vying for office; they rarely consider the budget and other laws directly, except in the few legislative decisions put before voters in local and state politics, such as issuing school bonds or passing propositions. Elections, then, determine who will govern, not what they should do or what the laws should be. They are, to put the matter in terms we first considered in Chapter 1, occasions when multiple principals—the citizens—choose political agents to act on their behalf.

In this chapter, we will look at how the institutional features of American elections shape the way citizens' goals and preferences are reflected in their government. Then we will consider how voters decide among the candidates and questions put before them on the ballot.

INSTITUTIONS OF ELECTIONS

We have suggested that the relationship between citizens and elected politicians is an instance of a principal-agent relationship. There are two basic approaches to this relationship: the consent approach and the agency approach. The consent approach emphasizes the historical reality that the right of the citizen to participate in his or her own governance, mainly through the act of voting or other forms of consent, arises from an existing governmental order aimed at making it easier for the governors to govern by legitimating their rule. By giving their consent, citizens provide this legitimation. The agency approach treats the typical citizen as someone who would much rather devote scarce time and effort to his or her own private affairs than spend that time and effort on governance. He or she therefore chooses to delegate governance to agents—politicians—who are controlled through elections. In this approach, the control of agents is emphasized.

Whether they are seen as a means to control delegates (the agency approach) or to legitimate governance by politicians (the consent approach), elections allow citizens to participate in political life on a routine and peaceful basis. Indeed, American voters have the opportunity to select and, if they so desire, remove some of their most important leaders. In this way, Americans have a chance to intervene in and influence the government's programs and policies. Yet it is important to recall that elections are not spontaneous affairs. Instead, they are formal governmental institutions. Although elections allow citizens a chance to participate in politics, they also allow the government a chance to exert a good deal of control over when, where, how, and which of its citizens will participate. Electoral processes are governed by a variety of rules and procedures that provide those in power with a significant opportunity to regulate the character—and perhaps also the consequences—of mass political participation.

Four features of U.S. election laws deserve particular emphasis.

- First, *who*. The United States provides for universal adult suffrage—all citizens over the age of eighteen have the right to vote.[2]
- Second, *how*. Americans vote in secret and choose among candidates for office using a form of the ballot called the "Australian ballot."
- Third, *where*. The United States selects almost all elected offices through single-member districts that have equal populations.
- Fourth, *what* it takes to win. For most offices in the United States, the candidate who wins the most votes among all of those competing for a given seat wins the election.

Each of these rules has substantial effects on elections and representation. We will consider each and its consequences in turn. In short, we will see that in the United States these rules create a two-party system that broadly encompasses the entire adult population but that exaggerates the political power of the majority. Other features of American election law and procedure, including rules governing campaign expenditures and fund-raising, party nominations, and ballot access, further shape political competition in the United States. Also notable are rules that the United States does *not* have. Federal and state laws do not limit the amount of television and other forms of advertising, total campaign spending, the activities of groups and parties on behalf of candidates, or how the media cover the campaigns. Most other countries limit the use of television or forbid it altogether, restrict how candidates can campaign and how much they can spend, and tightly regulate the activities of organized interest groups. Compared with other countries, then, the United States has a relatively unregulated electoral system that allows candidates to run on their own separate from the parties and allows candidates to spend relatively freely on media and other aspects of their campaigns.

Before we explore each of these rules in more detail, it is important to note that the rules governing elections are not static. The features of American electoral institutions have evolved over time through legislation, court decisions, administrative rulings of agencies, and public agitation for electoral reform. The nation has gradually converged to our present system of universal suffrage with secret voting and to the use of single-member districts with plurality rule. But this is only one era, and the future will likely bring further innovations in voting and elections. Society is always in flux, with continual changes in the population and its distribution across regions. With waves of immigration, new communication technologies, and other changes reshaping society, the institutions of democracy must change with the times. Perhaps the most dramatic changes under way involve the rise of "convenience voting"— voting by mail or early at a polling center or town hall. In 1972, approximately 5 percent of all votes nationwide were cast in absentia; in 2008, 30 percent of all votes were absentee or early ballots. The state of Oregon votes entirely by mail, as does every county in Washington State but King County. A few states, such as Virginia, accept e-mail absentee ballots, which are particularly convenient for military personnel.

---

[2] In addition there is the restriction that those currently serving sentences for felonies cannot vote; some states prohibit ex-felons from voting.

The rise of this new mode of voting presents new questions about secrecy and about the form of the ballot; it provides new opportunities for reform and modes of voting (such as instant runoff voting). Such changes rarely come about through carefully planned federal legislation. Typically, new voting methods and rules emerge out of the experiences and experiments of local election officials and state laws. Let us now take a closer look at the key institutional features of American elections.

Who Votes: Electoral Composition

Over the course of American history the electorate has expanded greatly. At the beginning of the nineteenth century, America was unusually democratic compared with the rest of the world because the United States provided for universal suffrage for all adult white males, and in some cities even noncitizens. In contrast, during the nineteenth century, property qualifications restricted the electorate in European nations in a manner acceptable to the aristocracy and other ruling classes. In France before 1848, to cite just one example, limiting the suffrage to property owners restricted the electorate to just 240,000 out of 7 million men over age twenty-one.[3] No women were allowed to vote at this time. During the same era, other nations manipulated the electorate's composition by assigning unequal weights to different classes of voters. The 1831 Belgian constitution, for example, assigned individuals anywhere from one to three votes, depending on their property holdings, education, and social position. Even in the American context there were significant restrictions on the size of the electorate, especially on the basis of race and gender. In the southern states, blacks were not allowed to vote before the Civil War. The Fifteenth Amendment to the Constitution in 1870 gave blacks voting rights, but in the late nineteenth century, southern states passed "Jim Crow" laws establishing literacy tests, **poll taxes**, and all-white primaries. Local election officials administered these laws in ways that kept the large majority of blacks from voting. One by one these institutions were struck down by the courts as violations of the Constitution, and finally forbidden by the Voting Rights Act of 1965 and the Twenty-third Amendment. Gender qualifications excluded an even larger segment of the population. In most states, women were not allowed to vote until 1920, following the passage of the Nineteenth Amendment. The most recent expansion of the franchise came in 1971, when Congress decided to lower the voting age from twenty-one to eighteen with the passage of the Twenty-sixth Amendment. If eighteen-year-olds could be drafted to serve their country in the military, it was argued, they deserved the full privileges of citizenship, including the right to vote.

Voting in the United States is treated as a right, not a requirement. Some countries, such as Australia and Germany, have compulsory voting: All eligible voters are required to vote or pay a modest fine. These societies treat electoral participation as a necessity. Americans view voting somewhat differently. Like most other activities in our society, voting is voluntary. If we do not feel strongly about government, we do not have to participate. If we want to send a message of disaffection or dis-

poll tax A state-imposed tax on voters as a prerequisite for registration. Poll taxes were rendered unconstitutional in national elections by the Twenty-fourth Amendment, and in state elections by the Supreme Court in 1966.

---

[3] Stein Rokkan, *Citizens, Elections, Parties* (New York: David McKay, 1970), p. 149. Also see Daron Acemoglu and James A. Robinson, "Why Did the West Extend the Franchise?" *Quarterly Journal of Economics* 115, no. 4 (November 2000): 1167–99.

FIGURE 10.1 VOTER TURNOUT AROUND THE WORLD

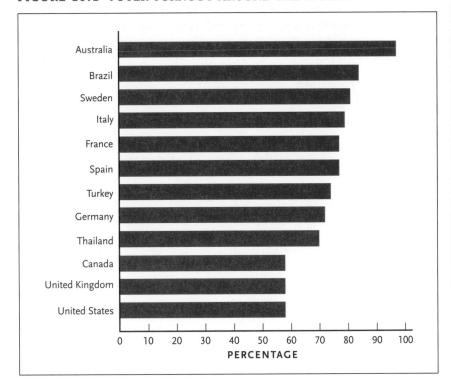

NOTE: Average between 1945 and 2006.

SOURCE: International Institute of Democracy and Electoral Assistance, www.idea.int/vt/ (accessed 4/30/09).

satisfaction, one way to do so is to not vote. Of course, if no one voted, it would be a disaster for American democracy; it would signal the end of Americans' commitment to their form of government. When large numbers of people do participate in the collective decision making of the country at each election, it is evidence of a robust democracy. Governments at all levels in the United States also have so many elections that voters may not feel the need to participate in all elections all the time in order to weigh in on the activities of government. And there are many other ways that we can participate in electoral politics, such as blogging and speaking with others, joining organizations, and giving money. Compared with other nations, the United States is one of the best examples of participatory democracy in the world.[4]

That said, levels of voter participation in the latter half of the twentieth century were quite low in the United States compared with those of the other Western democracies (see Figure 10.1).[5] Indeed, voter participation in U.S. presidential elections barely averaged 50 percent in recent years. Turnout in the 2000 presiden-

---

[4] Sidney Verba, Kay Schlozman, and Henry Brady, *Voice and Equality: Civic Volunteerism in America* (Cambridge, Mass.: Harvard University Press, 1995).

[5] See Walter Dean Burnham, "The Changing Shape of the American Political Universe," *American Political Science Review* 59 (1965): 7–28.

FIGURE 10.2 VOTER TURNOUT IN U.S. PRESIDENTIAL ELECTIONS

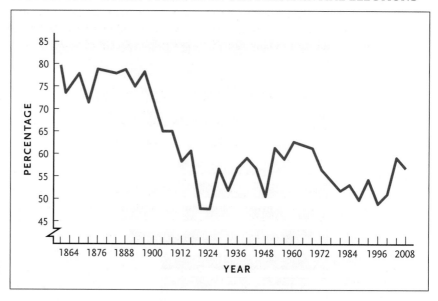

NOTE: Data reflect the population of eligible voters; the percentage of the voting-age population that voted would be smaller.

SOURCES: For 1860–1928, U.S. Bureau of the Census, *Historical Statistics of the United States, Colonial Times to 1970,* pt. 2, p. 1071 (www.census.gov/prod/www/abs/statab.html) (accessed 6/17/08); for 1932–92, U.S. Bureau of the Census, *Statistical Abstract of the United States,* 1993 (Washington, D.C.: Government Printing Office, 1993), p. 284; for 1996–2008, Federal Election Commission data.

tial election was 51 percent; in 2008, it was approximately 57 percent. During the nineteenth century, by contrast, voter turnout in the United States was extremely high, as Figure 10.2 indicates.

Voter turnout declined markedly in the United States between 1890 and 1910 (see Figure 10.2). These years coincide with the adoption of laws across much of the nation requiring eligible citizens to appear personally at a registrar's office to register to vote some time prior to the actual date of an election. Personal registration was one of several "progressive" reforms initiated at the turn of the century. The ostensible purpose of registration was to discourage fraud and corruption. But to many Progressive reformers, "corruption" was a code word referring to the politics practiced in large cities where political parties had organized immigrant and ethnic populations. Reformers not only objected to this corruption but also opposed the growing political power of these urban populations and their leaders.

Personal registration imposed a new burden on potential voters and altered the format of American elections. Under the registration systems adopted after 1890, it became the duty of individual voters to secure their own eligibility. This duty could prove to be a significant burden for potential voters. During a personal appearance before the registrar, individuals seeking to vote were (and are) required to furnish proof of identity, residence, and citizenship. Although the inconvenience of registration varied from state to state, usually voters could register only during business hours on weekdays. Many potential voters could not afford to lose a day's pay in order to register. Second, voters were usually required to register well before the next election, in some states up to several months earlier. Third, since most personal registration laws required a periodic purge of the election rolls to keep them up-to-date, voters often had to reregister to maintain their eligibility. Thus, although personal registration requirements helped to diminish the widespread electoral corruption that accompanied a completely open voting process, they also made it much more difficult for citizens to participate in the electoral process.

Registration requirements particularly depress participation by those with little education and low incomes, for two reasons. First, simply registering on weekdays during business hours is a difficult obstacle for working-class persons to overcome. Second, and more important, registration requires a greater degree of political involvement and interest than does the act of voting itself. To vote, a person need only be concerned with the particular election campaign at hand. Requiring individuals to register before the next election forces them to make a decision to participate on the basis of an abstract interest in the electoral process rather than a simple concern with a specific campaign. Such an abstract interest in electoral politics is typically a product of education. Those with relatively little education may become interested in political events because of a particular campaign, but by that time it may be too late to register. As a result, personal registration requirements not only diminish the size of the electorate but also tend to create an electorate that is, in the aggregate, less representative of the voting-age population. The electorate becomes better educated, higher in income and social status, and composed of fewer African Americans and other minorities than the citizenry as a whole.

Over the years, voter registration restrictions have been modified somewhat to make registration easier. In 1993, for example, Congress approved and President Clinton signed the "motor voter" bill to ease voter registration by allowing individuals to register when they applied for driver's licenses, as well as in public assistance and military recruitment offices.[6] In Europe, there is typically no registration burden on the individual voter; the government handles voter registration automatically. This is one reason that voter turnout rates in Europe are higher than those in the United States.

Another factor explaining low rates of voter turnout in the United States is the relative weakness of the American party system. During the nineteenth century, American political party machines employed hundreds of thousands of workers to organize and mobilize voters and bring them to the polls. The result was an extremely high rate of turnout, typically more than 90 percent of eligible voters.[7] But political party machines began to decline in strength in the early

---

[6] Helen Dewar, " 'Motor Voter' Agreement Is Reached," *Washington Post*, April 28, 1993, p. A6.

twentieth century and by now have largely disappeared. Without party workers to encourage them to go to the polls and even to bring them there if necessary, many eligible voters will not participate. In the absence of strong parties, participation rates drop the most among poorer and less-educated citizens. Because of the absence of such strong political parties, the American electorate is smaller and skewed more toward the middle class than toward the population of all those potentially eligible to vote.

How Americans Vote: The Ballot

The way Americans cast their votes reflects some of our most cherished precepts about voting rights. Most people today view voting as a private matter. They may tell others how they voted, but that is their prerogative. Polling places provide privacy for voters and keep an individual's vote secret. In some respects, the secret ballot seems incongruous with voting, because elections are a very public matter. Indeed, for the first century of the Republic, voting was conducted in the open. Public voting led to vote buying and voter intimidation. American history is full of lore involving urban party workers paying poor voters for their support or intimidating members of the opposing party from voting. The secret ballot

---

[7] Erik Austin and Jerome Chubb, *Political Facts of the United States since 1789* (New York: Columbia University Press, 1986), pp. 378–79.

became widespread at the end of the nineteenth century in response to such corrupt practices.

With the secret ballot came another innovation, the **Australian ballot**. The Australian ballot lists the names of all candidates running for a given office and allows the voter to select any candidate for any office. This way of offering choices to voters was first introduced in Australia in 1851, and in the United States today it is universal. Before the 1880s Americans voted in entirely different ways. Some voted in public meetings; others voted on paper ballots printed by the political parties or by slates of candidates distributed to the voters. Voters chose which ballot they wished to submit—a Republican ballot, a Democratic ballot, a Populist ballot, a Greenback ballot, and so forth. The ballots were often printed on different-colored paper so that voters could distinguish among them—and so that the local party workers could observe who cast which ballots. With party ballots, voters could not choose candidates from different parties for different offices; they had to vote the party line. Under the Australian form, all ballots are identical, making it difficult to observe who votes for which party. More important, voters could choose any candidate for any office, breaking the hold of parties over the vote. The introduction of the Australian ballot gave rise to the phenomenon of split-ticket voting, whereby voters select candidates from different parties for different offices.[8]

The secret and Australian ballot creates the opportunity for voters to choose candidates as well as parties and, as we will discuss in more depth later, created a necessary condition for the rise of the personal vote and the incumbency advantage in American electoral politics. (See Chapter 5's discussion of the incumbency advantage in Congress.) The possibility of split-ticket voting also created greater fragmentation in the control of government in the United States. With the party ballot, an insurgent party could more readily be swept to power at all levels of government in a given election. A strong national tide toward one of the parties in the presidential election, resulting in a landslide victory, would change not just the presidency but also political control of every state and locality that gave a majority of its votes to that presidential candidate's party. The party ballot thus reinforced the effect of elections on party control of government and public policy. In contrast, because the Australian ballot permitted voters to choose for each office separately, it lessened the likelihood that the electorate would sweep an entirely new administration into power. Thus, ticket splitting led to increasingly divided control of government as well as the rise of personal voting.

Where: Electoral Districts

Elected officials in the United States represent places as well as people. Today, the president, representatives, senators, governors, and many other state officers, state legislators, and most local officers are elected by the people through geographic

Australian ballot
An electoral format that presents the names of all the candidates for any given office on the same ballot. Introduced at the turn of the twentieth century, the Australian ballot replaced the partisan ballot and facilitated split-ticket voting.

[8] Jerold G. Rusk, "The Effect of the Australian Ballot Reform on Split Ticket Voting, 1876–1908," *American Political Science Review* 64, no. 4 (December 1970): 1220–38.

areas called electoral districts. Generally speaking, the United States employs **single-member districts** with equal populations. This means that the U.S. House of Representatives, the state legislatures, and almost all local governments have their own districts and elect one representative per district, and all of the districts for a given legislative body must have equal populations.

Elections for the U.S. Senate and the presidency are the odd cases. In the U.S. Senate, the states are the districts. Senate districts, then, have multiple members and unequal populations. In presidential elections, every state is allocated votes in the electoral college equal to the number of U.S. senators (two) plus the number of House members. The states are the districts, and each state chooses all of its electors, who commit to casting their votes for a certain candidate in the electoral college, in a statewide vote.[9] Within the political parties, the nomination process in most states allocates delegates to the parties' national conventions on the basis of House districts and their populations. However, some states choose their delegates on a statewide basis, with all districts selecting multiple delegates to the party conventions.

The United States Senate and the electoral college remain the two great exceptions to the requirements of single-member districts with equal populations. The apportionment of Senate seats to states makes that chamber inherently unequal. California's 35 million people have the same number of senators as Wyoming's 500,000 people. The allocation of electoral college votes creates a population inequity in presidential elections, with larger states selecting fewer electors per capita than smaller states. In the 1960s, the Supreme Court let stand the unequal district populations in the Senate and the electoral college, because the representation of states in the Senate is specified in the Constitution. The reason lies in the politics of the Constitutional Convention (see Chapter 2). That convention, as you may recall, consisted of delegations of states, each of which held equal numbers of votes under the Articles of Confederation. In order to create a House of Representatives to reflect the preferences of the population, the large states had to strike a deal with the smaller states, which stood to lose representation with the initial plan of a single chamber that reflected population. That deal, the Connecticut Compromise, created the U.S. Senate to balance representation of people with representation of places, and led to a clause in Article V of the Constitution that guarantees equal representation of the states in the Senate.

Even though they have unequal populations and select multiple representatives, the Senate and the electoral college share the salient feature of elections for the House and other elections in the use of districts to select representatives. All elections in the United States and all elected officials are tied to geographically based constituencies rather than to the national electorate as a whole. This is certainly true for the House and Senate. It applies also to presidential elections, in which candidates focus on winning key states in the electoral college rather than on

---

[9]The exceptions are Maine and Nebraska, which choose the House electors in individual House districts and the Senate electors in a statewide vote.

winning a majority of the popular vote.

House and state legislative districts are not static. In order to comply with the dictum of equal population representation, they must be remade every decade. Responsibility for drawing new district boundaries rests, in most states, with the state legislatures and the governors, with the supervision of the courts and sometimes with the consultation of commissions (Figure 10.3). Every ten years, the U.S. Census updates the official population figures of the states, as well as population counts, to a fine level of geographical detail (census blocs). The politicians, their staffs, party consultants, and others with a stake in the outcome use the census data to craft a new district map; ultimately, the legislatures must pass and the governors must sign a law defining new U.S. House and state legislative districts. This job is forced on the legislatures by their constitutions and by the courts. As the history of unequal representation suggests, most legislatures would, if left to their own devices, leave the existing boundaries in place. Periodic redistricting, although it corrects one problem, invites another. Those in charge of redistricting may try to manipulate the new map to increase the likelihood of a particular outcome, such as the election of a majority of seats for one party or social interest. This problem arose with some of the earliest congressional district maps. A particularly egregious map of the 1812 Massachusetts House districts drawn with the imprimatur of Governor Elbridge Gerry prompted an editorial writer in the Boston Gazette to dub a very strangely shaped district the "Gerry-Mander." The term stuck, and **gerrymandering** refers broadly to any attempt at creating electoral districts for political advantage.

It is easy to draw an intentionally unfair electoral map, especially with the sophisticated software and data on local voting patterns and demographics that are available today. To facilitate districting, the Census Bureau divides the nation into very small geographic areas, called census blocs, that typically contain a few dozen people. U.S. House districts contain over 700,000 people. Political mapmakers combine various local areas, down to census blocs, to construct legislative districts. Those seeking political advantage try to make as many districts as possible that contain a majority of their own voters, maximizing the number of seats won for a given division of the vote. There are constraints on political cartography: the district populations must be equal, and all parts of the district must touch (be contiguous). Even with those constraints, the number of possible maps that could be drawn for any one state's legislative districts is extremely large.[10] The "Analyzing the Evidence" unit on page 298 shows how this works, using a hypothetical state to explain some basic strategies that parties and politicians might implement to influence elections through the manipulation of district lines, as well as a real-world example of how redistricting of affects election outcomes.

Politicians can use gerrymandering to dilute the strength not only of a party but

gerrymandering Apportionment of voters in districts in such a way as to give unfair advantage to one political party.

---

[10] For definitions of these units, see Bureau of the Census, Geographic Area Reference Manual, www .census.gov/geo/www/garm.html (accessed 6/17/09).

FIGURE 10.3 CONGRESSIONAL REDISTRICTING

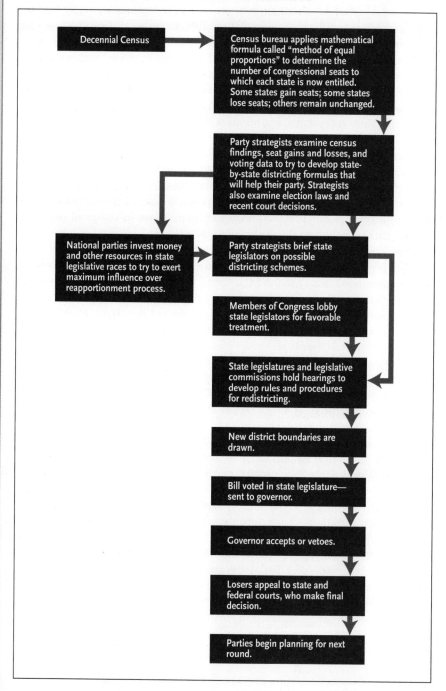

Decennial Census

Census bureau applies mathematical formula called "method of equal proportions" to determine the number of congressional seats to which each state is now entitled. Some states gain seats; some states lose seats; others remain unchanged.

Party strategists examine census findings, seat gains and losses, and voting data to try to develop state-by-state districting formulas that will help their party. Strategists also examine election laws and recent court decisions.

National parties invest money and other resources in state legislative races to try to exert maximum influence over reapportionment process.

Party strategists brief state legislators on possible districting schemes.

Members of Congress lobby state legislators for favorable treatment.

State legislatures and legislative commissions hold hearings to develop rules and procedures for redistricting.

New district boundaries are drawn.

Bill voted in state legislature—sent to governor.

Governor accepts or vetoes.

Losers appeal to state and federal courts, who make final decision.

Parties begin planning for next round.

also of a group. Until recently, many state legislatures employed gerrymandering to dilute the strength of racial minorities. One of the more common strategies involved redrawing congressional district boundaries in such a way as to divide and disperse a black population that would have constituted a majority within the original district. This form of gerrymandering, sometimes called cracking, was used in Mississippi during the 1960s and 1970s to prevent the election of a black candidate to Congress. Historically, the black population of Mississippi was clustered in the western half of the state, along the Mississippi River Delta. From 1882 until 1966, the Delta constituted one congressional district. Although blacks were a clear majority within this district, discrimination against them in voter registration and at the polls guaranteed the continual election of white congressmen. With the passage of the Voting Rights Act in 1965, this district would almost surely be won by a black candidate or one favored by the black majority. To prevent that from happening, the Mississippi state legislature drew new House districts in 1965 in order to minimize the voting power of the black population. Rather than a majority of a single district that encompassed the Delta, the black population was split across three districts and constituted a majority in none. Mississippi's gerrymandering scheme was preserved in the state's redistricting plans in 1972 and 1982 and helped prevent the election of any black representative until 1986, when Mike Espy became the first African American since Reconstruction to represent Mississippi in Congress.

What It Takes to Win: Plurality Rule

The fourth prominent feature of U.S. electoral law is the criterion for winning. Americans often embrace majority rule as a defining characteristic of democracy. However, that is not quite right. The real standard is **plurality rule**. The candidate who receives the most votes in the relevant district or constituency wins the election, even if that candidate doesn't receive a majority of votes. Suppose, for example, three parties nominate candidates for a seat and divide the vote such that one wins 34 percent and the other two each receive 33 percent of the vote. Under plurality rule, the candidate with 34 percent wins the seat. There are different types of plurality systems. The system currently used in the United States combines plurality rule with single-member districts and is called *first past the post*. The electoral college is a plurality system in which the candidate who receives the most votes wins all of the delegates: winner take all.[11] Some states set an even higher standard and require a candidate to receive at least 50 percent of all votes in order to win. This is **majority rule**. Louisiana and Georgia, for instance, require a candidate to receive an outright majority in an election in order to be declared the winner. If no candidate receives a majority in an election, a runoff election is held about one month later between the two candidates who received the most votes in the first round. Other ways of voting also use plurality- and majority-rule criteria. For instance, some city councils

plurality rule Type of electoral system in which, to win a seat in the parliament or other representative body, a candidate need only receive the most votes in the election, not necessarily a majority of votes cast.

majority rule Type of electoral system in which, to win a seat in the parliament or other representative body, a candidate must receive a majority of all the votes cast in the relevant district.

---

[11] Over the centuries, many systems for voting and determining electoral outcomes have been devised. For an excellent analysis of voting systems and a complete classification see Gary Cox, *Making Votes Count* (New York: Cambridge University Press, 1997).

Congressional Redistricting

The method by which electoral districts are drawn following each decennial census may directly impact who gets elected from those districts. Recent decades have witnessed more states utilizing independent commissions or panels to redraw congressional districts in an attempt to limit partisanship in the districting process, but the majority of states still rely on state legislatures to reapportion House seats. At the same time, technological innovations such as Geographic Information Systems (GIS) software allow mapmakers to be extremely precise in terms of how individual voters are allocated among districts. As a result, congressional redistricting remains a focal point for party strategy, with parties looking to increase their advantage after the 2010 census.

Partisan Districting

SCENARIO 1

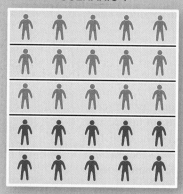

Consider a hypothetical state where Republicans represent 60% of voters and Democrats represent the remaining 40% of voters. As a result of population changes during the preceding decade, this state now has five congressional districts. A state legislature controlled by a Republican majority could draw congressional districts so that Republican voters clearly dominate three of the five districts and Democratic voters dominate the remaining two. In this scenario, the Republicans could expect their candiates to win three of the five House districts.

SCENARIO 2

Another possibility might arise if the Republican state legislature decides to make the districts more competitive, but also attempts to gain control of all five House districts in the upcoming election.

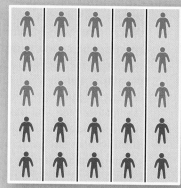

SCENARIO 3

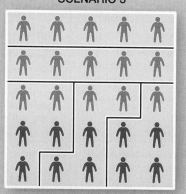

Now, suppose that the Democrats are in control of the state legislature. With the same distribution of voters in the state, they could draw the districts to favor Democratic candidates as much as possible (with Democratic voters dominating three of the districts).

Districting by Commission

IOWA DISTRICTS, 1990s

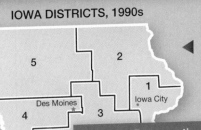

Votes for Democratic candidates: 43%
House seats won by Democrats: 20%

By contrast, a non-partisan, or independent commission may draw more competitive districts, with a more even distribution of Republican and Democratic voters. To take a real-world example, prior to the 2000 census, Iowa's districts were drawn by the state legislature. In the redistricting following the 1990 census, the Republican legislature established district boundaries.

IOWA DISTRICTS, 2000s

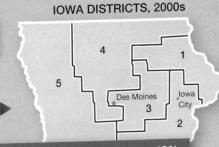

Votes for Democratic candidates: 48%
House seats won by Democrats: 40%

After 2000, Iowa employed a commission to revise district boundaries in an effort to promote greater competitiveness.* Note that under the districting established by the Republican legislature in the 1990s, Democrats won only 20 percent of House races, although they won 43 percent of the vote. After the redistricting by the commission in the 2000s, the Democrats won a share of seats more closely in proportion to their share of total votes.

*Iowa uses both a commission and nonpartisan legislative staff.

The Post–2010 Cycle: Who Draws District Lines?

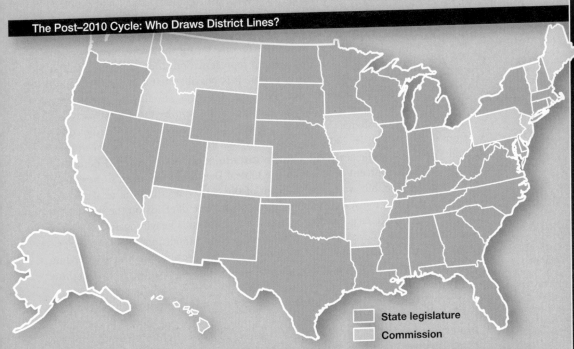

☐ State legislature
☐ Commission

In the redistricting cycle following the 2010 census, the authority to redraw voting districts for congressional and state-level races remains in the hands of the state legislature in most states. In these states, the party with a majority in the legislature has the opportunity to draw districts that favor candidates from that party. However, a growing number of states are using commissions in the post–2010 cycle, which should lead to districts that are more competitive in these states.

Who Wins? Translating Voters' Choices into Electoral Outcomes

Majority System

Winner must receive a simple majority (50 percent plus one).

Example: Formerly used in primary elections in the South.

Plurality System

Winner is the candidate who receives the most votes, regardless of the percentage.

Example: Currently used in almost all general elections throughout the country.

Proportional Representation

Winners are selected to a representative body in proportion to the votes their party received.

Example: Used in New York City in the 1930s, resulting in several communist seats on the City Council.

still have multimember districts. The top vote getters win the seats. If there are, say, seven seats to fill, the seven candidates who win the most votes each win a seat.

Plurality rule is often criticized for yielding electoral results that do not reflect the public's preferences. The votes for the losing candidates seem wasted, because they do not translate directly into representation. Indeed, as the example of the three-candidate race above suggests, it is possible that a majority of voters wanted someone other than the winner. In the aggregate, plurality rule with single-member districts tends to inflate the share of seats won by the largest party and deflate the others' shares. A striking example of the effects of plurality rule comes from Great Britain. In 2005, the British Labour Party won 35 percent of the vote and 55 percent of the seats; the Conservatives finished second, with 31 percent of the vote and 31 percent of the seats; the Liberal Democrats garnered 22 percent of the popular vote, but won just 8 percent of the seats. The shares of all seats won by each party for a given division of the national vote depends on the districts. A particularly egregious gerrymander might bias the results heavily against one party and cause further deviations of election results from proportionality. Nevertheless, plurality rule offers certain advantages. It gives voters the ability to choose individuals to represent them personally, not just political parties, and it picks a definite winner without the need for runoff elections.

Among the democracies of the world, the main alternative to plurality rule is **proportional representation**, also called PR for short. Under proportional representation, competing parties win legislative seats in proportion to their share of the popular vote. For example, if three parties running for seats in the legislature seat divide the vote such that one wins 34 percent and the other two receive 33 percent of the vote, the first party received 34 percent of the seats and the other two receive 33 percent.

PR is used rarely in the United States. The most substantial elections in which

proportional representation A multiple-member district system that awards seats based on the percentage of the vote won by each candidate. By contrast, the "winner-take-all" system of elections awards the seat to the one candidate who wins the most votes.

the status quo, risking an overturn via initiative? The recall complements both of these, keeping institutional agenda setters on their toes to avoid being ousted. As the institution principle implies, these arrangements do not just provide citizens with governance tools. They also affect the strategic calculations of institutional politicians—legislators and governors.

HOW DO VOTERS DECIDE?

An election expresses the preferences of millions of individuals about whom they want as their representatives and leaders. Electoral rules and laws—the institutional side of elections—impose order on that process, but ultimately, elections are a reflection of the people, the aggregation of many millions of individuals' expressions of their preferences about politics.

The voter's decision can be understood as really two linked decisions: whether to vote and for whom. Social scientists have examined both facets of the electoral decision by studying election returns, survey data, and experiments conducted in laboratories as well as field experiments conducted during actual elections. Out of generations of research into these questions, a broad picture emerges of how voters decide. First, the decision to vote or not to vote correlates very strongly with the social characteristics of individuals, especially age and education, but it also depends on the electoral choices and context. An individual who does not know anything about the candidates or dislikes all of the choices is unlikely to vote. Second, which candidates or party voters choose depends primarily on three factors: partisan loyalties, issues, and candidate characteristics. Partisan loyalties have been found to be the strongest single predictor of the vote, though party attachments also reflect issues and experience with candidates. Party, issues, and candidates act together to shape vote choice.

Voters and Nonvoters

As we saw earlier, turnout in modern American presidential elections ranges from 50 to 60 percent of the voting-age population. In other words, roughly half of those who may vote don't. This phenomenon has long puzzled social scientists and motivated reformers. A general explanation is elusive, but what social scientists do know about this phenomenon is that a few demographic characteristics routinely prove to be strong predictors of who votes. The most important of these characteristics are age, education, and residential mobility. Other factors, such as gender, income, and race also matter, but to a much smaller degree. In 2004, the Census Bureau found that 58.3 percent of those of voting age in the survey voted, compared with the actual figure of 55.5 percent. According to the study, 47 percent of those under age thirty voted, fully 11 points below the population average.

Older cohorts exhibit higher turnout rates: 74 percent of those over age 65 voted in 2004. The difference between these groups is 27 percentage points, and the effect of age on voting surely translates into an electoral difference. Education shows similarly large differences. Those without a high school degree voted at half the rate of those with a college education. More than three in four people with a college education vote, and the rate is 84 percent among those with a professional degree. In contrast, slightly fewer than 40 percent of those without a high school diploma voted and 56 percent of those with only a high school degree voted. Finally, consider residency and mobility. Only 53 percent of people who have lived in their current residence less than a year report voting, compared with 76 percent of people who lived in their residence at least five years. Those who own their home or apartment vote at a 69 percent rate, but only 48 percent of those who rent vote.[14] Politicians listen to those who vote, and those who vote are disproportionately older, better educated, and more rooted in their communities.

One important concern is whether differences in voting reflect electoral institutions. Election laws have historically had a large effect on the size and character of the electorate, especially laws preventing racial discrimination at polling places (in 1965) and expanding the suffrage to women (in 1920). Those interested in encouraging greater participation today have focused on voter registration requirements, which are thought to create an unnecessary hurdle and thus to depress turnout. The decision to vote itself consists of two steps—registration and turnout. In 2004, 88.5 percent of those who reported that they registered said they voted. Weakening registration requirements may increase participation. One approach to minimizing such requirements is Election Day registration. As of 2009, seven states allow people to register on Election Day at the polls or at a government office. The three states with the longest experience with same-day registration—Minnesota, Wisconsin, and Maine—do have higher turnout than most other states, and most studies suggest that in a typical state, adopting such a law would increase turnout by about 3 to 5 percent.[15]

Demographics and laws are only part of what accounts for voting and nonvoting. The choices presented to the voters are also quite important. The problem is not that many people have a hard time making up their minds, but that many people do not feel engaged by current elections, or dislike politics altogether. People who are disinterested, "too busy to vote," or do not like the candidates tend not to vote. The Census Bureau survey asks registered nonvoters why they did not vote. The top four reasons are "too busy," "sick or disabled," "not interested," and "did not like the choices."

Partisan Loyalty

The single strongest predictor of how a person will vote is that individual's attachment to a political party. The American National Election Studies (ANES), exit polls, and media polls have found that even in times of great political change in

---

[14] The most reliable source of information about the demographics of voting is the Current Population Survey, conducted by the Bureau of the Census. For these and other statistics see Kelly Holder, "Voting and Registration in the Election of November 2004," March 2006, www.census.gov/prod/2006pubs/p20-556.pdf (accessed 6/18/09).

[15] The classic study in this area is Raymond Wolfinger and Steven Rosenstone, *Who Votes?* (New Haven, Com.: Yale University Press, 1978). See also Steven Rosenstone and John Mark Hansen, *Participation, Mobilization and American Democracy* (New York: Macmillan, 1993).

the United States, the overwhelming majority of Americans identifies with one of the two major political parties and votes almost entirely in accordance with that identity. Survey researchers ascertain **party identification** with simple questions along the following lines: Generally speaking, do you consider yourself to be a Democrat, a Republican, an Independent, or what?[16] Survey researchers further classify people by asking of those who choose a party whether they identify strongly or weakly with that party, and by asking independents whether they lean toward one party or another.

party identification An individual voter's psychological ties to one party or another.

Party identifications capture voters' predisposition toward their party's candidates. Although specific features of the choices and context matter as well, party identifications express how voters would likely vote in a "neutral" election. Party identifications are extremely good predictors of voting behavior in less prominent elections, such as for state legislature or lower-level statewide offices, about which voters may know relatively little. Even in presidential elections, with their extensive advertising and very thorough news coverage, party predispositions predict individual voting behavior. Figure 10.4 displays the percentages of Democratic identifiers, Republican identifiers, and self-described independents who voted for McCain, Obama, or someone else in 2008. Approximately 90 percent of party identifiers voted for their own party's standard bearer. Independents (including independents

FIGURE 10.4 THE EFFECT OF PARTY IDENTIFICATION ON THE VOTE FOR PRESIDENT, 2008

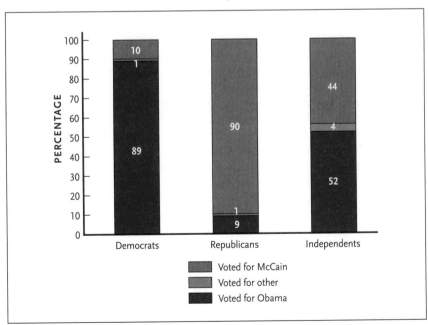

---

[16]This is the wording used by the Gallup Poll. Others ask "In politics today . . ." or offer "or another party" instead of "or what."

who lean toward either party) broke 52 to 44 for Obama. The 2008 election was in this respect quite typical. Partisan loyalty is usually in the range of 90 percent, and the division among independent voters tips the balance.

There are three distinct views about what party identification is. They are not necessarily exclusive of each other, but they point to very different understandings of the nature of party identification and its effect on elections.[17] Debate over the meaning of party identity cuts to the heart of the meaning of elections.

First, party identification is a psychological attachment that individuals hold, often throughout their adulthood, to one of the parties. Individuals learn as children and adolescents from parents, other adults, and even peers about politics, and as part of that socialization they develop attachments to a party, not unlike religion and community. Party identifications continue to form into early adulthood. The first few presidential elections that an individual experiences as an adult are thought to have particularly profound influence on that individual's understanding of the parties and politics. And as different cohorts come into politics, their experiences carry forward throughout their lives. Those who were eighteen to twenty-four years old in 1984, for example, identify overwhelmingly with the Republican Party, because those elections marked the triumph of Ronald Reagan's presidency and political philosophy, the rise of a revitalized Republican Party, and the beginning of the end of the Cold War. Those eighteen to twenty-four years old in 2008, on the other hand, identify disproportionately with the Democratic Party, because the Obama campaign galvanized young voters around a new vision for the future. However it is developed, an individual's psychological affinity for a party makes that person want that party to win and want to support that party, even when he or she disagrees with the party on important policies or disapproves of the party's nominees for office.

Of course, the Democratic and Republican parties are quite different entities today than they were forty years ago or eighty years ago. On matters of race relations, for example, the Democratic Party has moved over the past century from supporting segregation to spearheading civil rights. The Republican Party, once a bastion of economic protectionism, now champions free trade. However strong generational transmission of party identifications may be, the dissonance between identities and issues must surely weaken the pull of party, which suggests a second theory of party. This second idea is that party identifications reflect underlying ideologies of voters and policy positions of parties. Parties in government, as we discussed in Chapter 5, are meaningful organizations for producing public policies. The relatively high degree of party loyalty in Congress and other branches of government means that voters can reasonably anticipate how politicians will act in office. Citizens identify with parties that pursue public policies more to their liking. For example, a union worker will feel a stronger attachment to the Democratic Party because the Democrats have historically protected union interests. A high-income earner may feel a strong pull toward the Republican Party because that party pushes lower taxes overall, and the Democrats promote higher tax rates for higher-income households. In such cases, voters want to choose a party, not just a candidate, to be the agent for their interests.

---

[17] For an excellent treatment of the meanings of party identification and analysis of the implications of different theories, see Donald Green, Bradley Palmquist, and Eric Schickler, *Partisan Hearts and Minds* (New Haven, Conn.: Yale University Press, 2003).

As mentioned in the introduction to this chapter, elections present an informational problem of adverse selection. The party labels act as brand names and help voters choose the candidates that will best match their preferences. Labels carry significant information to voters about the candidates. Voters need not know the details of an individual candidate's voting record or campaign promises in order to understand how that politician will likely behave on important matters. As such, party labels provide an informational short cut for voters. Party identification means, in part, that a voter feels that party represents his or her interests better than other parties; hence, an identifier is highly likely to vote for that party.[18]

A third explanation is that party identification reflects experiences with political leaders and representatives, especially the presidents from each of the parties. As the political scientist Morris Fiorina put it, party identifications are running tallies of experience. Americans hold their presidents, and to a lesser extent Congress, accountable for the economic performance of the country and success in foreign affairs. A bad economy or a disastrous military intervention will lead voters to disapprove of the president and to lower their assessment of the president's party's ability to govern. Parties are, by this account, teams seeking to run the government. They consist of policy experts, managers, and leaders who will conduct foreign policy, economic policy, and domestic policies (such as environmental protection and health care). When things go well, voters infer that the incumbent party has a good approach to running national affairs, but when things go badly, they infer that the party lacks the people needed to run the government competently or the approach needed to produce economic prosperity, international peace, and other outcomes desired by the public. With each successive presidency and their experience of it, individuals update their beliefs about which party is better able to govern.

Psychological attachments, ideological affinities, and past experiences add up to form an individual's current party identifications. But party is not the only factor in voting. Some partisans do defect, especially in elections when voters are dissatisfied with the incumbent party or are especially drawn to a particular candidate.

Issues

Issues and policy preferences constitute a second factor influencing voters' decisions. Voting on issues and policies cuts to the core of our understanding of democratic accountability and electoral control over government. A simple, idealized account of **issue voting** goes as follows. Governments make policies and laws on a variety of issues that affect the public. Voters who disagree with those policies and laws on principle or who think those policies have failed will vote against those who made the decisions. Voters who support the policies or like the outcomes that government has produced will support the incumbent legislatures or party. It is important to note that policies are not taken as constants or fixed attributes of the candidates or parties. Rather, politicians choose what kinds of laws to enact

issue voting
Electoral choice based on issue preferences rather than partisanship, personality, or other factors.

---

[18] For a detailed assessment of the political use of information-economizing devices such as party labels, see Arthur Lupia and Mathew D. McCubbins, *The Democratic Dilemma: Can Citizens Learn What They Need to Know?* (New York: Cambridge University Press, 1998).

and what kinds of administrative actions to take with the express aim of attracting electoral support. Voters, as we discussed in the previous chapter, have preferences about what policies the government pursues or what outcomes result, and they choose the candidates and parties that produce the best results or most preferred laws. Even party identifications, as we have noted, reflect the policy preferences of the voters and the policies pursued by the parties and candidates.

Voters' issue choices usually involve a mix of their judgments about the past behavior of competing parties and candidates and their hopes and fears about candidates' future behavior. Political scientists call choices that focus on future behavior **prospective voting**, while those based on past performance are called **retrospective voting**. To some extent, whether prospective or retrospective evaluation is more important in a particular election depends on the strategies of competing candidates. Candidates always endeavor to define the issues of an election in terms that will serve their interests. Incumbents running during a period of prosperity will seek to take credit for the economy's happy state and define the election as revolving around their record of success. This strategy encourages voters to make retrospective judgments. In contrast, an insurgent running during a period of economic uncertainty will tell voters it is time for a change and ask them to make prospective judgments. Thus, Bill Clinton focused on change in 1992 and prosperity in 1996, and through well-crafted media campaigns was able to define voters' agenda of choices.

In 2004, President Bush emphasized his efforts to protect the nation from terrorists and his strong commitment to religious and moral values. The Democratic candidate, John Kerry, on the other hand, attacked Bush's decision to invade Iraq, questioned the president's leadership in the war on terror, and charged that the president's economic policies had failed to produce prosperity. When asked by exit pollsters which issue mattered most in deciding how they voted for president, 22 percent of all voters cited moral values as their chief concern. More than 80 percent

prospective voting Voting based on the imagined future performance of a candidate.

retrospective voting Voting based on the past performance of a candidate.

IN BRIEF

How Voters Decide

Partisan loyalty—Most Americans identify with either the Democratic or Republican Party and will vote for candidates accordingly. Party loyalty rarely changes and is most influential in less visible electoral contests, such as on the state or local level, where issues and candidates are less well known.

Issues—Voters may choose a candidate whose views they agree with on a particular issue that is very important to them, even if they disagree with the candidate in other areas. It is easier for voters to make choices based on issues if candidates articulate very different positions and policy preferences.

Candidate characteristics—Voters are more likely to identify with and support a candidate who shares their background, views, and perspectives; therefore, race, ethnicity, religion, gender, geography, and social background are characteristics that influence how people vote. Personality characteristics such as honesty and integrity have become more important in recent years.

of these voters supported President Bush. The economy was cited as the most important issue by 20 percent of those who voted and 80 percent of these Americans voted for Senator Kerry. Terrorism ranked third in terms of the percentage of voters who indicated it was the most important issue for them. In 2004, President Bush received more than 80 percent of the votes of those Americans concerned mainly with terrorism. The 2006 midterm elections were portrayed by Democrats as a referendum on President Bush's conduct of the war in Iraq. There was a considerable swing of votes to the Democrats, even in districts that had supported Bush over Kerry in 2004, with the result that the Democrats picked up twenty-five seats in the House and six in the Senate.[19] Similarly, the 2010 midterm elections, which were portrayed by Republicans as a referendum on President Obama's handling of the economy and health care, produced a considerable swing of votes to the GOP.

Economic voting is one way that voters solve the information problems inherent in representative democracy. They cannot monitor every policy that the government initiates. They do, however, have a rudimentary way to hold the government accountable—staying the course when times are good and voting for change when the economy sours. Thus George H. W. Bush lost in 1992 during an economic downturn even though his victory in the Persian Gulf War had briefly given him a 90 percent favorable rating in the polls. And Bill Clinton won in 1996 during an economic boom even though voters had serious concerns about his moral fiber. Over the past quarter century, the Consumer Confidence Index, calculated by the Conference Board, a business research group, has been a fairly accurate predictor of presidential outcomes. The index is based on surveys asking voters how optimistic they are about the future of the economy. It would appear that a generally rosy view, indicated by a score greater than 100, augurs well for the party in power. An index score of less than 100, suggesting that voters are pessimistic about the economy's trend, suggests that incumbents should worry about their job prospects (Figure 10.5).

Candidate Characteristics

Candidates' personal attributes always influence voters' decisions. Some analysts claim that voters prefer tall candidates to short candidates, candidates with shorter names to candidates with longer names, and candidates with lighter hair to candidates with darker hair. Perhaps these rather frivolous criteria do play some role. But the more important candidate characteristics that affect voters' choices are race, ethnicity, religion, gender, geography, and social background. Voters presume that candidates with similar backgrounds to their own are likely to share their views and perspectives. Moreover, they may be proud to see someone of their ethnic, religious, or geographic background in a position of leadership. This is why for many years politicians have sought to "balance the ticket," making certain that their party's ticket included members of as many important groups as possible.

A candidate's personal characteristics may attract some voters, but they may repel others. Many voters are prejudiced against candidates of certain ethnic, racial, or religious groups. And many voters—both men and women—continue to be re-

---

[19] William F. Connelly Jr., "Wall vs. Wave?" *Forum* 4, no. 3, www.bepress.com/forum/vol4/iss3/art3 (accessed 6/18/09).

FIGURE 10.5 CONSUMER CONFIDENCE AND PRESIDENTIAL ELECTIONS

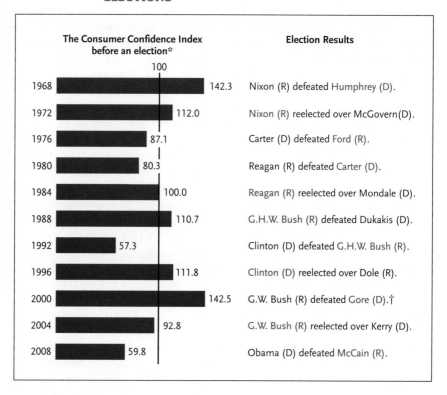

NOTE: The candidate representing the incumbent party appears in red.

*Survey was bimonthly before 1977, so figures for 1968, 1972, and 1976 are for October; from 1980 on, they are for September.

†Gore won the popular vote but Bush was elected by the Electoral College.

SOURCE: *Bloomberg Markets.*

luctant to support the political candidacies of women, although this appears to be changing.

Voters also pay attention to candidates' personality characteristics, such as their "decisiveness," "honesty," and "vigor." In recent years, integrity has become a key election issue. In the 2004 presidential race, President Bush and the Republicans accused Senator Kerry of being inconsistent, a "flip-flopper" who repeatedly changed his positions when it was expedient to do so. Bush, on the other hand, emphasized his own constancy. For their part, Democrats emphasized Senator Kerry's intelligence, empathy for ordinary Americans, and record of wartime heroism, which, they said, stood in sharp contrast to Bush's own somewhat blemished military record. In the end, the GOP's characterization of Kerry as a "flip-flopper" and Bush as an individual with deep moral and religious commitments seemed to resonate with voters.

One of the most distinctive features of American politics is the apparent advantage that incumbents have. Beginning around 1970, political scientists noted a peculiar change overtaking electoral politics, especially in congressional elections. Incumbents were winning reelection at higher rates than in previous generations and by wider margins. Closer examination of the election results revealed that this phenomenon appeared due to incumbency itself. In a simple, natural experiment, Professor Robert Erikson compared the same politician running for election not as an incumbent and as an incumbent. In the first sort of election, the politician ran for a seat left vacant by an incumbent's retirement or against an incumbent and won. In the second sort of election, the politician had just won the previous election and had to defend the seat in the next election as a "sophomore." Erikson called the increase in the politician's vote share from the first election to the second the "sophomore surge." It is the increase in the vote attributable solely to the fact that the politician ran as an incumbent rather than as a nonincumbent. Erikson found an incumbency effect of approximately 5 percentage points around 1970. If the party division of the vote in a congressional district without an incumbent is, say, 50-50, then in a race where one candidate is the incumbent, that same district would vote for the incumbent with 55 percent to 45 percent.

Since Erikson documented it in 1970, the incumbency advantage has grown both in magnitude and in importance in U.S. elections. Incumbency advantages in House elections grew rapidly beginning in the mid-1950s, when they were worth only 1 to 2 percentage points, to 5 to 6 percentage points by the end of the 1960s. They have continued to inch upward, reaching as high as 15 points in the mid-1980s. Today, almost every elective office at the state and federal level exhibits an incumbency advantage. Those advantages have ranged from about 5 percent in state legislative elections to 10 percent for U.S. House, U.S. Senate, and governor. A 10 percent incumbency advantage is a massive electoral edge. It turns a 50-50 seat into a safe seat. It turns a competitive race into a blowout for the incumbent.[20]

Why the incumbency advantage has emerged and grown remains something of a puzzle. Redistricting is almost certainly not the explanation: Incumbency effects are as large in gubernatorial elections, where there are no districts, as in House elections. It is thought that about half of the incumbency advantage reflects the activities of the legislator in office; it is the result of voters rewarding incumbents for their performance. The other half of the incumbency advantage evidently reflects not the incumbents but their opponents.[21] The typical challenger in U.S. elections may not have the personal appeal of the typical incumbent; after all, the typical incumbent has already won office once. Moreover, challengers usually lack the experience and resources that the incumbent has for running a campaign. This is critical. The ability to communicate with the voters can give a politician the edge in close elections.

Although party, issues, and candidate characteristics are perhaps the three

---

[20] See Stephen Ansolabehere and James M. Snyder, Jr., "The Incumbency Advantage in U.S. Elections: An Analysis of State and Federal Offices, 1942–2000," *Election Law Journal* 1, no. 3 (September 2002): 315–38.

[21] The partitioning of the incumbency effect into officeholder advantages and challenger qualities begins with the important work of Gary Jacobson; see for example his excellent text *Congressional Elections*. Estimating exactly what fraction of the incumbency effect is due to office holder benefits is tricky. See Stephen Ansolabehere, James M. Snyder, Jr., and Charles H. Stewart III, "Old Voters, New Voters, and the Personal Vote," *American Journal of Political Science* 44 (2000).

most important factors shaping voting decisions, there is much debate among political scientists as to the relative importance of each. Problems of measurement and the limitations of research methods have made it exceedingly difficult to parse the relative importance of these factors in voters' thinking. Recent scholarship suggests that they have roughly equal weight in explaining the division of the vote in national elections.[22] Part of the difficulty in understanding their importance is that the extent to which these factors matter depends on the information levels of the electorate. In the absence of much information, most voters rely almost exclusively on party cues. A highly informed electorate relies more heavily on issues and candidate characteristics.[23]

CAMPAIGNS: MONEY, MEDIA, AND GRASS ROOTS

American political campaigns are freewheeling events with few restrictions on what candidates may say or do. Candidates in hotly contested House and Senate races spend millions of dollars to advertise on television and radio, as well as direct mail and door-to-door canvassing. Those seeking office are in a race to become as well known and as well liked as possible and to get more of their supporters to vote. Federal laws limit how much an individual or organization may give to a candidate, but with the exception of the presidential campaigns, place no restrictions on how much a candidate or party committee may spend.

Adding to the freewheeling nature of campaigns is their organizational structure. Most political campaigns are temporary organizations. They form for the sole purpose of winning the coming elections and disband shortly afterward. To be sure, political parties in the United States have a set of permanent, professional campaign organizations that raise money, strategize, recruit candidates, and distribute resources. These are, on the Republican side of the aisle, the Republican National Committee, the National Republican Senatorial Committee, and the National Republican Congressional Committee. On the Democratic side of the aisle are the Democratic National Committee, the Democratic Senatorial Campaign Committee, and the Democratic Congressional Campaign Committee. They account for roughly a third of the money in politics and have considerable expertise. But most campaigns are formed by and around individual candidates, who often put up the initial cash to get the campaign rolling and rely heavily on family and friends as volunteers. Thousands of such organizations are at work during an election. The two presidential campaigns operate 50 different state-level operations, with other campaigns competing for 34 Senate seats, 435 House seats, dozens of gubernatorial and other statewide offices, and thousands of state legislative seats. There is relatively little coordination among these myriad campaigns, though they all simul-

---

[22] See Stephen Ansolabehere, Jonathan Rodden, and James M. Snyder, Jr., "Issue Voting," *American Political Science Review* (May 2008).

[23] The classic study showing this is Philip Converse, "The Nature of Belief Systems in Mass Publics," in *Ideology and Discontent*, David Apter, ed. (New York: Free Press, 1964).

taneously work toward the same end—persuading as many people as possible to vote for their candidate on Election Day.

All campaigns, big and small, face similar challenges—how to bring people in, how to raise money, how to coordinate activities, what messages to run, and how to communicate with the public. There is no one best way to run a campaign. There are many tried and true approaches, especially building up a campaign from many local connections, from the grass roots. Candidates have to meet as many people as possible and get their friends and their friends' friends to support them. In-person campaigning becomes increasingly difficult in larger constituencies. Candidates continually experiment with new ways of communicating with the public and new ways of organizing in order to more efficiently reach large segments of the electorate. In the 1920s, radio advertising eclipsed handbills and door-to-door canvassing, as broadcasting captured economies of scale. In the 1960s, television began to eclipse radio. In the 1980s and 1990s, cable television and innovations in marketing (especially phone polling and focus groups) allowed candidates to target very specific demographic groups through the media. The great innovation of the Obama campaign was to meld Internet networking tools with old-style organizing methods to develop a massive communications and fund-raising network that came to be called a "netroots" campaign.

It has become an assumption of American elections and election law that candidates and parties will mount competitive campaigns to win office. They will spend millions, even billions of dollars, to persuade people to vote and how to vote. And because of those efforts voters will understand better what choices they face in the elections. In short, campaigns inform voters, and they do so through competition. In addition to being costly, American political campaigns are long, often spanning years. Campaigns for the presidency officially launch a year and a half to two years in advance of Election Day. Serious campaigns for the U.S. House of Representatives begin at least a year ahead of the general election date and often span the better part of two years. To use the term of the Federal Election Commission, an election is a two-year "cycle," not a single day or even the period between Labor Day and Election Day loosely referred to as "the general election."

The long campaigns in the United States are due in large part to the effort required to mount a campaign. There are roughly 300 million people in the United States, and the voting-age population exceeds 220 million people. Communicating with all of those people is an expensive and time-consuming enterprise. A simple calculation reveals the challenge. Suppose you ran for president of the United States. Sending one piece of mail to each household in the United States would cost approximately $100 million dollars. That is probably the minimum imaginable campaign effort. How long would it take to raise $100 million and mobilize such an effort to communicate with the American people? In the 2008 election cycle, Barack Obama spent $700 million dollars on his presidential bid; John McCain spent $326 million; the Democratic and Republican Party operations spent $1.8 billion. All told, candidates and organizations spent approximately $3 billion on the 2008 presidential election and perhaps another $1 billion on the 2008 congressional elections. The money came primarily from millions of individuals who gave small amounts through the personal networks that the campaigns built up over months, even years, of effort. It takes extensive operations to reach out to so many people and to raise such vast sums. Simply putting such an organization in place takes months. Even a congressional campaign takes considerable time to cultivate. The typical U.S. House campaign raised and spent approximately $700,000 in 2006, with the lion's share of that money coming from hundreds of individual donors. Once a campaign has enough money to initiate operations, it begins to communicate with the voters, often starting small by attending meetings with various groups. A successful campaign builds on early successes, bringing in more supporters and volunteers, and culminating with intensive advertising campaigns in the final months or weeks before election day. Although the Democratic and Republican parties may help campaigns that have a good shot of succeeding, they typically come in late. Every campaign for Congress or president is built by the individual candidates and their close friends and associates from the ground up. The personal style of political campaigning that Americans have come to appreciate reflects an enormous investment of time and resources, an investment that takes the better part of a year to grow.

The campaign season is further extended by the election calendar. American elections proceed in two steps, the party primary elections and the general election. General elections for federal offices are set by the Constitution of the United States to take place on the first Tuesday after the first Monday in November. The first presidential caucuses and primaries come early in January and last through the beginning of June. State and congressional primaries do not follow the same calendar, but most occur in the spring and early summer, with a handful of some states waiting to hold their nominating elections until September of the election year. The immediate result of this year-long calendar of elections is to stretch the campaigns over the entire election year.

The expense, duration, and chaos of American campaigns have prompted many efforts at reform, including attempts to limit campaign spending, shorten the campaign season, and restrict what candidates and organizations may say in advertisements. The most sweeping campaign reforms came in 1971, when Congress passed the Federal Elections Campaign Act (or FECA). It limited the amounts that a single individual could contribute to a candidate or party to $1,000 per election for individuals and $5,000 for organizations (these limits have since been increased, as Table 10.1 indicates). It further regulated how business firms, unions, and other organizations could give money, prohibiting donations directly from the organization's treasury and requiring the establishment of a separate, segregated fund—a **political action committee** (PAC for short). It established public funding for presidential campaigns and tied those funds to expenditure limits. And it set up the Federal Election Commission (FEC) to oversee public disclosure of information and to enforce the laws.[24] Congress has amended the act several times, most importantly in the Bipartisan Campaign Reform Act of 2002 (also called the McCain-Feingold Act, after Senators John McCain and Russell Feingold, its primary sponsors in the Senate). The McCain-Feingold Act prohibited unlimited party spending (called soft money) and banned certain sorts of political attack advertisements from interest groups in the last weeks of a campaign. See Table 10.1 for

political action committee (PAC) A private group that raises and distributes funds for use in election campaigns.

---

[24] The FEC's Web site is an excellent resource for those interested in U.S. campaign finance, www.fec .gov.

TABLE 10.1 FEDERAL CAMPAIGN FINANCE REGULATION

The Rules for Campaign Contributions

Who	may contribute . . .	to . . .	if . . .
Individuals	up to $2,000 ("hard money")	a candidate	they are contributing to a single candidate in a single election.
Individuals	up to $25,000	a national party committee.	
Individuals	up to $5,000	a PAC.	
PACs	up to $5,000	a candidate	they contribute to the campaigns of at least five candidates.
Individuals and PACs	unlimited funds	a 527 committee	the funds are used for issue advocacy and the 527 committee's efforts are not coordinated with any political campaign.
Individuals and PACs	up to $10,000 ("soft money")	a state party committee	the money is used for voter registration and get-out-the-vote efforts.
Individuals and PACs	unlimited funds	an independent expenditure committee (super PAC)	the money is used for political ads advocating for or against candidates and the committee's efforts are not coordinated with the campaign.

The Rules for Campaign Advertising

Who	may not finance . . .	if . . .
Unions, corporations, and nonprofit organizations	broadcast issue ads mentioning federal candidates	they occur within sixty days of a general election or thirty days of a primary.

rules governing campaign finance in federal elections.

The FECA also established public funding for presidential campaigns. If a candidate agrees to abide by spending limits, that candidate's campaign is eligible for matching funds in primary elections and full public funding in the general elec-

The Rules for Presidential Primaries and Elections

Candidates . . .	may receive . . .	if . . .
In primaries	federal matching funds, dollar for dollar, up to $5 million	they raise at least $5,000 in each of twenty states in contributions of $250 or less.
In general elections	full federal funding (but may spend no more than their federal funding)	they belong to a major party (minor-party candidates may receive partial funding).
In any election	money from independent groups (PACs and 527 committees)	the groups' efforts are not tied directly to the official campaign.

Important Definitions for Campaign Finance Regulation

- **Political action committee (PAC):** Private group that raises and distributes funds for use in election campaigns.
- **527 committee:** Tax-exempt organization that engages in political activities, often through unlimited "soft-money" contributions. The committee is not restricted by current law on campaign finance, thus exploiting a loophole in the Internal Revenue Service code.
- **501c committee:** A nonprofit organization that can use some of its funds for political advocacy without disclosing its donors. Some donors prefer this route because their names will not be known.
- **Independent expenditure committee:** Organization that may engage in unlimited political spending to run advertising for and against candidates so long as their efforts are not coordinated with those of the candidates.
- **Federal matching funds:** Federal funds that match, dollar for dollar, all individual contributions of $250 or less received by a candidate. To qualify, the candidate must raise at least $5,000 in individual contributions of $250 or less in each of twenty states.
- **Federal Election Commission:** The commission that oversees campaign finance practices in the United States.

tion. The general election amount was set at $20 million in 1974 and allowed to increase with inflation. Until 2000, nearly all candidates bought into the system. George W. Bush chose to fund his 2000 primary election campaign outside this system and spent $500 million to win the Republican nomination. Barack Obama and Hillary Clinton ignored the public financing system in their 2008 primary contest, and Obama opted out of the public system in the general election as well, allowing him to spend several hundred million more dollars than the Republican nominee, John McCain.

FECA originally went much farther than the law that survives today. Congress originally passed mandatory caps on spending by House and Senate candidates and prohibited organizations from running their own independent campaigns on behalf of or in opposition to a candidate (and not coordinated with any candidate). James Buckley, a candidate for U.S. Senate in New York, challenged the law, arguing that the restrictions on spending and contributions limited his rights to free speech and that FEC had excessive administrative power. In the 1976 landmark case *Buckley v. Valeo*, the U.S. Supreme Court agreed in part.[25] The Court ruled that "money is speech," but the government also has a compelling interest in protecting elections from corrupt practices, such as bribery through large campaign donations. The justices declared the limits on spending unconstitutional because they violated free speech rights of candidates and groups. However, the need to protect the integrity of the electoral process led the justices to leave contribution limits in place. The presidential public-funding system was also validated because it is voluntary. Candidates can opt into the system, but they are not required to; hence, there is no violation of free speech. What survived *Buckley* is a system in which candidates, groups, and parties may spend as much as they like to win office, but donations must come in small amounts. In an expensive election, campaigns must accumulate their resources from large numbers of individuals and groups. This is a more democratic process of campaign finance, but it increases the effort and time needed to construct a campaign.

Today, some observers fear that the incumbency advantage stifles electoral competition. As we noted in the previous section, incumbents enjoy a sizable electoral advantage, a bonus of roughly 10 percentage points. Some of that advantage reflects the voters' reward of the incumbents' performance in office, but some of it may also reflect an imbalance in campaign politics. That imbalance is most obvious in campaign funds. The average House challenger in 2006 raised and spent $430,000; the typical incumbent raised and spent more than three times as much, approximately $1,310,000. To put matters another way, incumbents could spend roughly $2.50 per voting-age person in the district; the typical challenger could spend only $.80 per voting-age person. Incumbents' funding advantages allow them to communicate more extensively with constituents than their opponents.

THE 2008 ELECTION

The 2008 presidential election was in some ways predictable—voters wanted a change from a very unpopular Republican administration and, perhaps predictably, elected a Democrat—but in many ways the 2008 race was a groundbreaking departure from politics as usual. In 2008, for the first time in the nation's history, Americans elected an African American to the White House as the Illinois senator Barack Obama led the Democratic Party to a solid electoral victory, securing 53 percent of the popular vote versus 46 percent for Republican candidate Senator John McCain. Obama won a 365-to-173 majority in the Electoral College (see Figure 10.6), far more than the 270 electoral votes needed to claim the presidency. The 2008 presidential election was also notable because of the prominence of women candidates. Hillary Clinton's strong campaign for the Democratic nomina-

---

[25] *Buckley v. Valeo*, 424 U.S. 1 (1976).

FIGURE 10.6 DISTRIBUTION OF ELECTORAL VOTES IN THE 2008 PRESIDENTIAL ELECTION

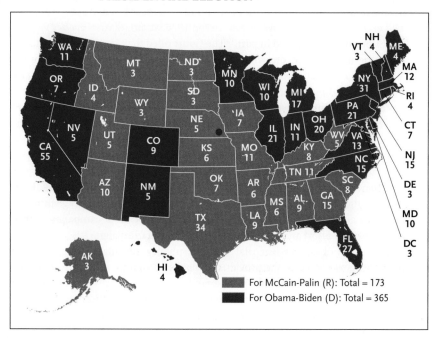

tion shattered the notion that a woman couldn't compete seriously for the nation's highest office, and John McCain's selection of Sarah Palin as his running mate seemed based at least partly on the advantages of having a woman on the ticket. The 2008 campaigns also brought about a significant shift in the electoral map, as states such as Virginia and North Carolina that hadn't supported a Democratic candidate in decades went from "red" to "blue."

The Democrats increased their strength in both houses of Congress. The Democratic Party won eight Senate seats previously held by Republicans and gained one more seat when Senator Arlen Specter of Pennsylvania switched from the GOP to the Democratic camp. This gave the Democrats a majority of 60 to 40,[26] sufficient to close debate if the party voted in unison. The Democrats fared almost as well in the House elections. They captured over two dozen seats previously held by Republicans, mostly open seats and seats defended by Republican freshmen, and the Republicans took five seats from the Democrats. On net, the Democrats added twenty-two seats total to win a 257-to-178 majority in the lower chamber. The defeat of three incumbent Republican senators—Ted Stevens of Alaska, John Sununu of New Hampshire, and Elizabeth Dole of North Carolina—underscored the magni-

---

[26] The Minnesota Senate seat was the subject of a contentious recount. The incumbent, Norm Coleman, beat the challenger, Al Franken, by just two hundred votes in the initial count and retabulation. The fate of the seat hung on a few thousand challenged and absentee ballots, and after the recount gave a narrow victory to Franken, legal challenges prevented Franken from taking his seat in the Senate until nearly eight months after Election Day.

tude of the shift toward the Democrats in 2008. Even the advantages of incumbency could not provide a sufficient levee against the rising tide of the Democratic Party.

The 2008 Primaries

The 2008 Democratic and Republican primaries and caucuses to select the parties' candidates for the presidency began January 3 with the Iowa Democratic caucuses. The actual campaigns, of course, began early in 2007, as ambitious politicians assessed their chances and started the long process of raising the tens of millions of dollars required to launch a presidential candidacy. On the Republican side, the front-runner was John McCain. The Arizona senator had campaigned for the Republican nomination in 2000 only to be defeated by Bush in a primary contest remembered for the victor's smear tactics. McCain, the son and grandson of U.S. Navy admirals, was a Vietnam War hero. McCain had a distinguished career in the Senate and was the chief sponsor of several major pieces of legislation, including the McCain-Feingold campaign reform law. Despite his national prominence, McCain was generally not well liked in Republican circles. Traditional business-oriented Republicans might have preferred Mitt Romney, a successful businessperson and former governor of Massachusetts, but the GOP's evangelical Protestant cadres did not like the idea of Romney, a Mormon, as their party's candidate. Social conservatives supported the former Arkansas governor and evangelical minister Mike Huckabee, an articulate politician whose sense of humor made him a successful guest on *Saturday Night Live*. Establishment Republicans, however, thought Huckabee was too closely associated with the party's religious element and would have no chance in a national campaign. Other Republicans—Ron Paul, Rudy Giuliani, and Fred Thompson—excited little interest. After losing the Iowa caucuses to Huckabee and struggling to raise money, McCain regained his political and financial footing and was able to drive his opponents from the race. McCain had effectively secured the Republican nomination by the beginning of March.

Clinton versus Obama.   On the Democratic side, the early front-runner for the presidential nomination was the New York senator and former first lady Hillary Rodham Clinton. Senator Clinton was famous, her husband was extraordinarily popular among Democrats, and her contacts and position as a New York senator meant that she would be able to count on tens of millions of dollars in campaign contributions. Most pundits predicted an easy Clinton victory, and many leading Democrats quickly endorsed Clinton to make sure that the probable future nominee and likely next president of the United States would remember their early support. Other Democratic contenders included the former North Carolina senator and 2004 vice-presidential candidate John Edwards, the former New Mexico governor Bill Richardson, Congressman Dennis Kucinich, the former Alaska senator Mike Gravel, and senators Joe Biden, Chris Dodd, and Barack Obama. Biden, Dodd, and Richardson, along with Gravel and Kucinich, generated relatively little interest and quickly dropped out. Edwards was popular among his fellow trial lawyers, who contributed enough money to his campaign to keep him in through the end of January, though with little chance of success. The surprise of the Democratic primary contest was, of course, Illinois senator Barack Obama.

Obama was a first-term senator, having arrived in Washington in 2004. He had won a measure of national celebrity by delivering a rousing keynote address at the 2004 Democratic national convention. While Senator Clinton was resolutely marching toward what was widely assumed to be an almost certain victory, Obama was making his own plans. Just before announcing his candidacy in February 2007, Obama had retained the services of a little-known consultancy named Blue State Digital. Blue State had learned how to make use of the new technologies of social networking introduced by such companies as Facebook. For a fee reported to be little more than $1 million, Blue State agreed to undertake an Internet campaign on Obama's behalf. The results were spectacularly successful. Blue State created a social networking site for Obama, called "MyBO," which allowed Obama supporters to communicate directly with one another, organize events, trade ideas, and raise money for the campaign. More than a million Democrats eventually became members of MyBO and gave hundreds of millions of dollars, mostly in small contributions, to the Obama campaign.

However, MyBO and Obama's powerful supporters could not have succeeded if the candidate himself had not been able to inspire and energize the voters who saw him. Obama proved to be an intelligent campaigner and an especially gifted speaker who could hold his own against any competing politician. Many Democrats' first opportunity to see Obama as a serious contender came in the Democratic debates. The Illinois senator was not necessarily more articulate, more knowledgeable, or more passionate about important issues than Clinton, Edwards, and the others, but observers were impressed that at debate after debate the virtually unknown senator stood toe to toe with his more seasoned and famous opponents and remained firm. Obama's impressive performance electrified liberal Democrats, excited young voters, intrigued the media, and ignited the enthusiasm of black Democrats, even if most were initially dubious that Obama could succeed. This enthusiastic response to Obama's debate appearances swelled the ranks of MyBO members, inspired donors to write checks, and gave Obama the means to compete against Clinton.

Throughout the primaries, Clinton and Obama battled furiously in state after state. Obama was particularly popular with younger voters and with liberals who resented what they saw as Clinton's early equivocation on the Iraq war. Black politicians—many of whom had considered Bill Clinton an important ally during his presidency—initially supported Hillary Clinton, assuming she would win. But as their constituents rallied to Obama, and it became clear that Obama's candidacy actually had a chance, the Illinois senator was able to garner overwhelming black support. Some pundits said it was ironic that the first woman to mount a serious presidential bid and the first black person to mount such a bid were pitted against one another. For the news media, however, in this battle of the firsts, Obama's candidacy was the more important first. Clinton was seen as an established figure on the political scene—a powerful senator from New York, former first lady, and wife of perhaps the most influential figure in the Democratic Party. Clinton's status in some ways worked against her. To some commentators it appeared that Clinton had already been co-president for eight years and was no longer a first.

By late spring, it became clear that Obama would be the Democratic presidential nominee. The result was close. Under Democratic rules, 2,118 delegates were needed to win the nomination. In the various primaries and caucuses, Obama had won 1,763 delegates to Clinton's 1,640. This effectively left the decision to the party's 796 "superdelegates," party officials and notables chosen to attend the convention. At the outset, most superdelegates had backed Clinton. As the race wore on, however, sentiment shifted toward Obama. Some saw Obama as the better candidate, while others worried that black Democrats—20 percent of the party's electoral strength—would stay home on Election Day if Obama was denied the nomination. With 438 superdelegates supporting Obama, he could count on 2,201 votes. Clinton briefly weighed taking her candidacy to the floor of the convention to be decided there, but ultimately, on June 3, withdrew and announced that she and her husband would staunchly support Obama in the general election.

The General Election

At the August 2008 Democratic national convention, speaker after speaker extolled Obama's virtues, and even Bill Clinton gave a strong speech supporting Obama, though some still doubted the former president's sincerity. Obama chose the Delaware senator Joseph Biden as his vice-presidential running mate. Biden, chair of the Senate Foreign Relations Committee, was selected at least partly in response to questions about Obama's scant foreign policy experience. In addition, Biden had working-class roots in Pennsylvania. Democrats hoped that Biden would appeal to the so-called Joe Six-pack voters, blue-collar workers whom the Democrats needed in such battleground states as Ohio and Pennsylvania.

The Republican convention, which opened a few days after the Democratic convention ended, began without much fanfare. Although John McCain had won the primary battle and was respected for his military service, he was not an especially beloved figure among rank-and-file Republicans. Nevertheless, McCain excited and energized Republicans when he chose the little-known Alaska governor, Sarah Palin, as his vice-presidential running mate and "introduced" her to the GOP base at the convention. Palin, a religious conservative who opposed abortion, excited many Republicans who had been cool toward McCain. Unfortunately for the GOP, Palin's star faded rapidly as the inexperienced governor proved unequal to the demands of a national campaign. In television interviews, including one with Katie Couric on CBS, Palin seemed to know little about current political issues and problems and could do no more than repeat Republican talking points that she seemed to have committed to memory. Despite her reasonable performance in the nationally televised vice-presidential debate, Palin was declared "clearly out of her league," even by staunchly Republican commentators, who wondered aloud if Palin could seriously be entrusted with the presidency if anything happened to McCain.

Despite the brief surge of enthusiasm generated by the selection of Palin, the McCain ticket struggled throughout the campaign. From the beginning, the deck seemed stacked against the Republicans. Despite his assertions of independence, the fact remained that McCain was a Republican and, hence, was tied to the Bush administration. Obama and the Democrats, moreover, held an enormous fund-raising advantage over McCain and the Republicans. Knowing that he would have difficulty raising money from traditional GOP donors, McCain had decided to accept public funding for the general election. This would give his campaign some $84 million to spend on organizing, advertising, and voter registration. McCain hoped Republican Party fund-raising would add considerably to this figure. Obama, on the other hand, became the first major party candidate since the law was enacted to forgo general election public funding. As a consequence, Obama was able to step up his Internet and conventional fund-raising, which eventually produced in the neighborhood of $700 million, an astonishing total that more than doubled the previous record, which had been set by the Republicans in 2004. His campaign's extraordinary fund-raising prowess gave Obama and the Democrats some $200 million more to spend than was available to McCain and the Republicans.

Lack of money was not McCain's only problem. In September 2008, the nation experienced a serious financial crisis that began with a decline in home sales and a wave of mortgage foreclosures and continued with billions of dollars of losses in mortgage-based securities. Toward the end of September, the stock market lost more than a third of its value, wiping out trillions of dollars in investments. Some of the nation's leading financial institutions, such as the venerable Lehman Brothers, failed, and a host of others seemed poised to close their doors. Since all these events took place while the Republicans controlled the White House, the Democrats were quick to blame the Bush administration's economic policies for the crisis.

The Debates.   Obama helped his cause enormously in the three televised presidential debates held in September and October. He responded with evident knowledge and intelligence to questions of domestic and foreign policy. So, for that matter, did McCain. But McCain, the Washington veteran, was expected to have answers to policy questions. Obama was the newcomer who had been chided for his inexperience. Like Kennedy, Reagan, and Clinton before him, Obama bore the burden of reassuring voters that he measured up to the job of being president. In the debates, Obama spoke clearly and incisively on education, economic policy, health policy, and the wars in Iraq and Afghanistan. Even more important was Obama's manner. By contrast with the often twitchy McCain, Obama was smooth, calm, and reassuring. Many commentators observed that Obama appeared "presidential" and that this helped more and more Americans feel comfortable with his candidacy. Following the debates, Obama's approval ratings rose steadily and the McCain campaign faltered.

Obama's Victory.   Throughout October, Obama consistently led by single-digit margins in the national polls. Given the faltering economy, an unpopular president, and the Democrats' enormous financial advantage, the GOP should have been heading for a train wreck of epic proportions, and yet, until Obama's lead increased in late October, McCain trailed by only three to five points in the polls. Some analysts of opinion data thought the problem was race. A white Democratic candidate, according to some mathematical models of public opinion, would have enjoyed a much stronger lead in the polls, perhaps an additional six or seven points. Some analysts worried whether Obama's lead was even as strong as it looked. These analysts pointed to the so-called Bradley effect, a phantom lead produced when white voters, reluctant to display overt signs of racism, lie to pollsters about their intentions. This is allegedly what happened in 1982, when the Los Angeles mayor Tom Bradley lost the California gubernatorial race after leading his white opponent in the polls. Although asserting that race would not be a factor in the 2008 election, Obama cautioned his supporters not to be overconfident.

In the end, racial antipathy did not determine the outcome of the 2008 presidential election. Some voters undoubtedly opposed Obama because of his race while others supported him on the same grounds. But given America's long history of slavery, segregation, and racial antagonism, the most important fact of the election was that tens of millions of white voters—some reluctantly—voted for a black man for the presidency of the United States. Though many forces were at work in 2008, Obama's victory was made possible by the softening of racial antagonisms in the United States over the past half-century and the delegitimization of overtly racist rhetoric in the public forum. But the election of a black president does not mean the end of racism in America. Obama is an exceptional individual—a graduate of the Harvard Law School with a white mother, an African rather than an African American father, and raised by white grandparents. Some Democratic canvassers emphasized these facts to white voters, describing their candidate as a man from a multiracial background whose father was an African intellectual, not an American from the inner city. Does Obama's victory represent the end of racism and the birth of a new America? Or is Obama an exception? Only time will help us to fully understand the significance of the 2008 election.

The 2008 election was remarkable in another respect. It was the highest-turnout election in the United States since the 1960s. In 2008, 131 million Americans voted out of approximately 231 million voting-age people in the United States. That translates into a turnout rate of about 57 percent, the highest since 1968, and the continuation of a trend. The percentage of the voting-age population that voted was 49 percent in 1996, 51 percent in 2000, and 55 percent in 2004. The last two elections exhibit a tremendous increase in participation and perhaps, if the pattern continues, a resurgence of electoral participation in the United States.

ELECTIONS AND DEMOCRACY

Elections should stir wonder in even the most jaded person. In an election, no one person matters much, and each person acts in apparent isolation, indeed secrecy. The individual voters' decisions reflect diverse experiences, opinions, and preferences about government and public policy. And the millions of votes cumulate into an expression of whom the majority wants to have as its representatives in state government, in Congress, in the presidency.

The institutions of American elections are designed to facilitate majority rule. Single-member districts and plurality rule create strong pressures toward a two-party system and majority rule. Even in elections in which one party wins a plurality but not a majority, that party typically wins an outright majority of legislative seats. The election itself, then, determines the government. Other systems often produce multiparty outcomes, resulting in a period of negotiation and coalition formation among the parties in order to determine who will govern.

The significance of elections derives not so much from the laws as from the preferences of voters. Voting behavior depends in no small part on habit and the tendency to vote for a given party as a matter of ingrained personal identity. If that were all there is to voting behavior, then it is not clear that elections would provide a meaningful way of governing. Elections would be reduced to little more than a sporting event, in which people merely rooted for their own team. Voters' preferences are as strongly rooted in the issues at hand as in the choices themselves, the candidates. Voting decisions reflect individuals' assessments about whether it makes sense to keep public policies on the same track or to change direction, whether those in office have done a good job and deserve to be reelected, or whether they have failed and it is time for new representation. The aggregation of all voters' preferences responds collectively to fluctuations in the economy, to differences in the ideological and policy orientations of the parties, and to the personal abilities of the candidates.

CHAPTER REVIEW

Frequent regular elections are the hallmark of democracy. The vote is the simplest and most significant way that people convey their preferences to the government. Voters in the United States elect the president, governors, and other executive officers every four years, federal and state legislators every two years, and thousands of local officials with similar frequency.

The institutional features of American elections regulate who votes, what form the ballot takes, how voting districts are drawn, and what it takes to win an election.

Voters' choices are based on partisanship, issues, and candidates' personalities. Which of these criteria will be most important varies over time and depends on the factors and issues that opposing candidates choose to emphasize in their campaigns.

FOR FURTHER READING

Ansolabehere, Stephen, and James M. Snyder, Jr. *The End of Inequality: One Person, One Vote and the Transformation of American Politics*. New York: Norton, 2008.

Brady, David W. *Critical Elections and Congressional Policy Making*. Palo Alto, Calif.: Stanford University Press, 1988.

Carmines, Edward G., and James A. Stimson. *Issue Evolution: Race and the Transformation of American Politics*. Princeton, N.J.: Princeton University Press, 1989.

Conway, M. Margaret. *Political Participation in the United States.* 3rd ed. Washington, D.C.: Congressional Quarterly Press, 2000.

Fowler, Linda L. *Candidates, Congress, and the American Democracy.* Ann Arbor: University of Michigan Press, 1994.

Gelman, Andrew, et al. *Red State, Blue State, Rich State, Poor State: Why Americans Vote the Way They Do.* Princeton, N.J.: Princeton University Press, 2008.

Ginsberg, Benjamin, and Martin Shefter. *Politics by Other Means: Politicians, Prosecutors, and the Press from Watergate to Whitewater.* 3rd ed. New York: Norton, 2002.

Green, Donald, and Alan Gerber. *Get Out the Vote!: How to Increase Voter Turnout.* Washington, D.C.: Brookings Institution, 2004.

Ifill, Gwen. *The Breakthrough: Politics and Race in the Age of Obama.* New York: Doubleday, 2009. ○ reader selection

Jacobson, Gary C. *A Divider, Not A Uniter: George W. Bush and the American People.* New York: Longman, 2006. ○ reader selection

———. *The Politics of Congressional Elections.* New York: Longman, 2008.

Morton, Rebecca B. *Analyzing Elections.* New York: Norton, 2006.

Reichley, A. James, ed. *Elections American Style.* Washington, D.C.: Brookings Institution, 1987.

Rosenstone, Steven, and John Mark Hansen. *Participation, Mobilization and Democracy in America.* New York: Macmillan, 1993.

Witt, Linda, Karen M. Paget, and Glenna Matthews. *Running as a Woman: Gender and Power in American Politics.* New York: Free Press, 1994.

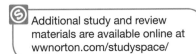

Additional study and review materials are available online at wwnorton.com/studyspace/

11 Political Parties

HOW PARTIES WORK

Political parties are defined as teams of politicians, activists, and voters whose goal is to win control of government. They do so by recruiting and nominating candidates to run for office; by accumulating the resources needed to run political campaigns, especially manpower and money; and by pursuing a policy agenda that can appeal to large numbers of voters and secure electoral majorities. As we saw in Chapter 5, once in office, parties organize the legislature and attempt to put their stamp on the laws passed by Congress and the president. Their potential political power is immense.

The prospect of "party rule" has long made Americans suspicious of these organizations. Indeed, the separation of powers into different branches was meant to blunt any attempts by a "faction" or party to gain control of government, as might more readily occur in a parliament.[1] Divided government, in which one party controls the presidency and the other has a majority in at least one chamber of the legislature, has been the norm in American national and state politics, especially over the past fifty years. In some elections, as in 1980, one party wins a landslide victory for the presidency but still fails to capture control of Congress. And in some midterm elections, as in 1994, 2006, and 2010, the public decides to give control of Congress to the party opposing the president in order to rein in the executive. Our

---

[1] James Madison famously made this argument in *Federalist 51* during the campaign to ratify the Constitution of the United States.

CORE OF THE ANALYSIS

- The United States has a two-party system, in which two major parties, the Democrats and Republicans, compete for most offices.
- Two of the most important functions of American political parties are facilitating nominations and elections.
- Parties also organize the institutions of national government. The legislative and executive branches are organized by the parties, with the party that won a majority of seats controlling most of the key positions and levers of power.
- Although American politics has been characterized by a two-party system, this system has evolved over time and has been influenced at times by third parties.

political system intentionally makes it difficult for any party or organized interest to gain complete control of American government, and when one does, unified government is often short lived. Separation of powers and divided government have not, however, put the parties out of business—quite the contrary.

The Democratic and Republican parties remain essential to the day-to-day operation of the legislature and the conduct of elections. It is difficult to imagine how candidates would emerge and how individuals would vote without political parties to organize the electoral system. Our inability to conceive of democracy without parties is not a failure of our imaginations or an accident of American history. Rather, it reflects a law of democratic politics. Parties form to solve key problems of rationality and collective action in a democracy. They are not unlike businesses providing a service that consumers need. Parties offer clear choices to voters, lowering the costs of collecting information about the candidates and making it easier for voters to hold government accountable. Parties also ease the transition from elections to government. They bear the costs of bringing together representatives of disparate constituencies into coherent coalitions that can act collectively in government. Thus, parties link elections to governing. Throughout this chapter we will highlight some of the general functions of parties in any democracy, but we will be especially attentive to party politics in the United States.

FUNCTIONS OF THE PARTIES

Why Do Political Parties Form?

political party An organized group that attempts to influence the government by electing its members to important government offices.

Political parties, like interest groups, are organizations seeking influence over government. Ordinarily, they can be distinguished from interest groups (which we will consider in more detail in Chapter 12) on the basis of their orientation. A party seeks to control the entire government by electing its members to office, thereby controlling the government's personnel. Interest groups, through campaign contributions and other forms of electoral assistance, are also concerned with electing politicians—in particular, those who are inclined in their policy direction. But interest groups ordinarily do not sponsor candidates directly, and between elections they usually accept government and its personnel as givens and try to influence government policies through them. They are *benefit seekers*, whereas parties are composed largely of *office seekers*.[2]

Parties are mainly involved in nominations and elections—providing the candidates for office, getting out the vote, and facilitating mass electoral choice. They also influence the institutions of government—providing the leadership and organization of the various congressional committees.

Recruiting Candidates

One of the most important but least noticed party activity is the recruitment of candidates for local, state, and national office. Each election year, candidates must be found for thousands of state and local offices as well as congressional seats. Where they do not have an incumbent running for reelection, party leaders attempt to identify strong candidates and to interest them in entering the campaign. One reason for the great success of the Democrats in the 2006 midterm elections was the heightened role played by their campaign committees in the House and Senate and, especially, the active recruitment of new candidates by the chairs of the Democratic Congressional and Senatorial campaign committees.[3] The Democrats were able to recruit well-qualified candidates and to provide them with campaign resources. In 2010, the GOP worked to emulate the Democratic example.

An ideal candidate will have an unblemished record and the capacity to raise enough money to mount a serious campaign. Party leaders are usually not willing to provide financial backing to candidates who are unable to raise substantial funds on their own. For a House seat, this can mean several hundred thousand dollars; for a Senate seat, a serious candidate must be able to raise several million dollars. Often, party leaders have difficulty finding attractive candidates and persuading them to run. Candidate recruitment is problematic in an era when political cam-

---

[2] This distinction is from John H. Aldrich, *Why Parties? The Origin and Transformation of Party Politics in America* (Chicago: University of Chicago Press, 1995).

[3] See Adam Nagourney, "Eyeing '08: Democrats Nurse Freshmen at Risk," *New York Times*, December 22, 2006.

paigns often involve mudslinging, and candidates must assume that their personal lives will be intensely scrutinized in the press.[4]

Nominating Candidates

Nomination is the process of selecting one party candidate to run for each elective office. The nominating process can precede the election by many months, as it does when the many candidates for the presidency are eliminated from consideration through a grueling series of debates and state primaries until there is only one survivor in each party—that party's nominee. Figure 11.1 summarizes the three types of nominating processes described below.

nomination The process through which political parties select their candidate for election to public office.

Nomination by Convention. A nominating convention is a formal caucus bound by a number of rules that govern participation and nominating procedures. Conventions are meetings of delegates elected by party members from the relevant county (county convention) or state (state convention). Delegates to each party's national convention (which nominates the party's presidential candidate) are chosen by party members on a state-by-state basis; there is no single national delegate-selection process.

FIGURE 11.1 TYPES OF NOMINATING PROCESSES

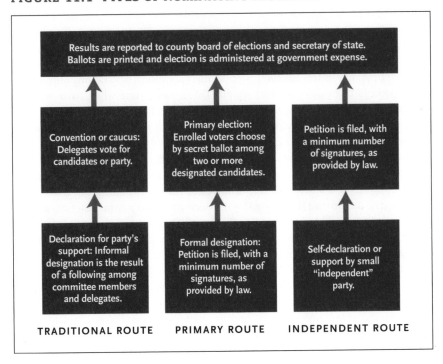

---

[4] For an excellent analysis of the parties' role in recruitment, see Paul Herrnson, *Congressional Elections: Campaigning at Home and in Washington* (Washington, D.C.: Congressional Quarterly Press, 1995).

Nomination by Primary Election.   In primary elections, party members select the party's nominees directly rather than selecting convention delegates who then select the nominees. Primaries are far from perfect replacements for conventions, since it is rare that more than 25 percent of the enrolled voters participate in them. Nevertheless, they have replaced conventions as the dominant method of nomination.[5] Currently, only a few states, such as Connecticut, Delaware, and Utah, provide for state conventions to nominate candidates for statewide offices, and even these states combine them with primaries whenever a substantial minority of delegates vote for one of the defeated aspirants.

Primary elections are of two types: closed and open. In a **closed primary**, participation is limited to individuals who have declared their affiliation by registering with the party. In an **open primary**, individuals declare their party affiliation on the actual day of the primary election—they simply go to the polling place and ask for the ballot of a particular party. The open primary allows each voter an opportunity to consider candidates and issues before deciding whether to participate and in which party's contest to participate. Open primaries, therefore, are less conducive than closed contests to strong political parties. But in either case, primaries are more open than conventions or caucuses to new issues and new types of candidates.

Getting Out the Vote

The election period begins immediately after the nominations. Historically, this has been a time of glory for the political parties, whose popular base of support is fully displayed. All the paraphernalia of party committees and all the committee members are activated into local party workforces.

The first step in the electoral process involves voter registration. This aspect of the process takes place all year round. There was a time when party workers were responsible for virtually all of this kind of electoral activity, but they have been supplemented (and in many states virtually displaced) by civic groups such as the League of Women Voters, unions, and chambers of commerce.

Those who have registered have to decide on Election Day whether to go to the polling place, stand in line, and actually vote for the various candidates and referenda on the ballot. Political parties, candidates, and campaigning can make a big difference in convincing the voters to vote. Because it is costly for voters to participate in elections and because many of the benefits that winning parties bestow are public goods (that is, parties cannot exclude any individual from enjoying them), people will often free ride by enjoying the benefits without incurring the costs of electing the party that provided the benefits. This is the *free-rider problem* (see Chapter 1), and parties are important because they help overcome it by mobilizing the voters to support the candidates.

In recent years, not-for-profit groups such as America Votes and MoveOn have registered and mobilized large numbers of people to vote and raised millions

closed primary A primary election in which voters can participate in the nomination of candidates, but only of the party in which they are enrolled for a period of time prior to primary day.

open primary A primary election in which the voter can wait until the day of the primary to choose which party to enroll in to select candidates for the general election.

---

[5] For a discussion of some of the effects of primary elections, see Peter F. Galderisi and Benjamin Ginsberg, "Primary Elections and the Evanescence of Third Party Activity in the United States," in *Do Elections Matter?* Benjamin Ginsberg and Alan Stone, eds. (Armonk, N.Y.: M. E. Sharpe, 1986), pp. 115–30.

of dollars to devote to election organizing and advertising. These groups have legions of workers, often volunteers, and have proved especially effective at using new technologies to build networks of supporters and communicate through those networks. They are the "netroots" organizations of politics. To comply with federal election and tax law, these groups must maintain their independence from the political parties, although they have the same objectives as the parties and work very hard to elect politicians from just one party. Such organizations act as shadow appendages of the two parties, with some groups mobilizing Democratic supporters and others mobilizing Republicans. They proved vitally important in the political campaigns of 2004, 2006, and 2008. Since 2000 there has been a noticeable uptick in turnout in the United States, possibly attributable to the new partisan netroots organizations.

Facilitating Mass Electoral Choice

Parties make the electoral choice much easier. It is often argued that we should vote for the best person regardless of party affiliation. But on any general election ballot, there are likely to be only two or three candidacies whose characteristics and policy positions are well known to the voters. Without party labels, voters would be constantly confronted by a bewildering array of new faces and new choices, causing them considerable difficulty making informed decisions. Without a doubt, their own party identifications and candidates' party affiliations help voters make reasonable choices.

Parties lower the information costs of participating by providing a recognizable "brand name." Without knowing a great deal about a candidate for office, voters can infer from party labels how the candidate will likely behave once elected. Individuals know about the parties through their past experience with those parties in state and federal office and from the actions of prominent political leaders from both parties. In the United States, the Democratic Party is associated with a commitment to more extensive government regulation of the economy and a larger public sector; the Republican Party favors a limited government role in the economy and reduced government spending paired with tax reductions. The Democrats favor aggressive protection of civil rights and a secular approach to religion in public life. The Republican Party wants to ban abortion and favors government participation in expanding the role of religious organizations in civil society. The parties' positions on the economy were cemented in the 1930s, and their division over civil society emerged during the 1960s and 1970s. The Democratic positions are loosely labeled liberal and those of the Republicans conservative.

The content of the labels is sustained because like-minded people sort themselves into the respective organizations. People who broadly share the principles espoused by a party and who wish to participate on a high level in politics will attend party meetings, run for leadership positions in local and state party organizations, attend state and national conventions, and even run for elected office. Surveys of those who attend national conventions as delegates and of candidates for the U.S. House find that Democratic candidates' personal views on the economy and social issues are quite liberal and that Republican candidates hold very conservative personal views on these matters.[6] Each party, then, draws on a distinct pool for activists and candidates. Each successive election reinforces the existing division between the parties.

Influencing National Government

The ultimate test of the party system is its relationship to and influence on the institutions of national government and the policy-making process. Thus, it is important to examine the party system in relation to Congress and the president.

Parties and Policy.   One of the most familiar observations about American politics is that the two major parties are "big tents." They position themselves to bring in as many groups and ideas as possible. The parties make such broad coalitions as a matter of strategy, much as businesses purchase other companies to expand their market share. Positioning themselves as broad coalitions prevents effective national third parties from emerging and guarantees that the Democrats and Republicans vie for control of Congress.

The coalitions that come together in the Democratic and Republican parties shape the parties' platforms on public policy. The political coalitions that party leaders assemble determine which interests and social groups align with the parties, and also what sorts of issues can emerge. The Democratic Party today embraces a philosophy of active government intervention in the economy, based on the premise that regulation is necessary to ensure orderly economic growth, prevent the emergence of monopolies, and address certain costs of economic activity, such as pollution. In addition, the Democratic Party pushes for aggressive expansion and protection of civil rights, especially for women and racial minorities. The Republican Party espouses a philosophy of laissez-faire economics and a minimal government role in the economy. The coalition that Ronald Reagan built in the late 1970s paired this vision of limited government intervention in the economy with an expanded role for religion in society and strong opposition to immigration, affirmative action, and abortion.

To many European observers, the American parties appear as odd amalgams of contradictory ideas. As it developed as a political philosophy in Europe, liberalism naturally pairs laissez-faire economics with liberal views on civil rights. Conservatism, which maintains a respect for social and political order, advocates a stronger role for social organizations in society, especially religions; a greater respect for existing social hierarchies, most notably social classes and higher educated elites; and government power in the economy. The American parties, partly because of their histories, have scrambled these traditional views and developed their own political philosophies. In the Republican Party today, laissez-faire economics goes hand in hand with conservative views on civil rights and religion in society. In the Democratic Party today, liberal views on civil rights are tied to an

---

[6] The most comprehensive studies of delegates were conducted by Walter J. Stone and Ronald B. Rapoport from 1980 through 1996. See Ronald B. Rapoport and Walter J. Stone, *Three's A Crowd: The Dynamic of Third Parties, Ross Perot, and Republican Resurgence* (Ann Arbor: University of Michigan Press, 1999). Surveys of candidates find similar sorting.

expansive view of government in the economy. The American parties have mixed and matched different ideas as new issues have emerged and as leaders within the parties have seized opportunities. The New Deal coalition that President Franklin Delano Roosevelt assembled consisted of Progressive Republicans, who favored greater economic regulation; the old-line Democrats, especially in the South; and urban political machines in northern and midwestern cities. This peculiar coalition gave rise to the political philosophy and public policies pursued under the New Deal. It also constrained what Roosevelt could do on some issues. Most important, he could not push for expansion of civil rights of blacks without losing the support of southerners. The meaning of Democratic liberalism in the United States, then, was very much a function of the history of the parties.

Even though American liberalism and conservatism do not align neatly with their European counterparts, they still embody distinct views about how government ought to act, and they appeal to distinctly different core constituencies. The Democratic Party at the national level seeks to unite organized labor, the poor, members of racial minorities, and liberal upper-middle-class professionals. The Republicans, by contrast, appeal to business, upper-middle- and upper-class groups in the private sector, and social conservatives. Often, party leaders will seek to develop issues they hope will add new groups to their party's constituent base. During the 1980s, for example, under the leadership of Ronald Reagan, the Republicans devised a series of "social issues," including support for school prayer, opposition to abortion, and opposition to affirmative action, designed to cultivate the support of white southerners. This effort was extremely successful in increasing Republican strength in the once solidly Democratic South. In the 1990s, under the leadership of Bill Clinton, who called himself a "new Democrat," the Democratic Party sought to develop new social programs designed to solidify the party's base among working-class and poor voters, and new, somewhat more conservative economic programs aimed at attracting the votes of middle- and upper-middle-class voters.

As these examples suggest, parties do not always support policies because they are favored by their constituents. Instead, party leaders can play the role of policy entrepreneurs, seeding ideas and programs that will expand their party's base of support while eroding that of the opposition. In recent years, for example, leaders of both major political parties have sought to develop ideas and programs they hoped would appeal to America's most rapidly growing electoral bloc: Latino voters. Thus President George W. Bush recommended a number of proposals designed to help Latinos secure U.S. residence and employment. Democrats, for their part, have proposed education and social service programs designed to appeal to the needs of Latino immigrants. Both parties promoted their ideas extensively within the Latino community in the 2004 presidential campaign, and although the Democrats won more Hispanic votes in 2004, each party claimed to be satisfied with its long-term strategy for building Latino support. The 2006 election campaign, however, produced much more one-sided results. A hard-line view on immigration, especially from Latin America, put Republicans at a competitive disadvantage. Democratic support among Hispanics rose dramatically in the midterm elections, and several prominent Republican incumbents in the southwest lost their seats as a result. The 2008 election saw a continuation of the pattern from 2006. Exit polls revealed that Democrats won 66 percent of Hispanics, a huge swing from 2004, and Hispanics continued their steady rise as a percentage of all voters. In 2000, one out of five voters was Hispanic or black; in 2008, one out of four voters was Hispanic or black.

It is one of the essential characteristics of party politics in America that a party's programs and policies often lead, rather than follow, public opinion. Like their counterparts in the business world, party leaders seek to identify and develop "products" (programs and policies) that will appeal to the public. The public, of course, has the ultimate voice. With its votes it decides whether or not to "buy" new policy offerings.

Through members elected to office, both parties have made efforts to translate their general goals into concrete policies. Republicans, for example, implemented tax cuts, increased defense spending, cut social spending, and enacted restrictions on abortion during the 1980s and 1990s. Democrats were able to defend consumer and environmental programs against GOP attacks and sought to expand domestic social programs in the late 1990s. During his two terms in office, President George W. Bush sought substantial cuts in federal taxes, "privatization" of the social security system, and a larger role for faith-based organizations allied with the Republican Party in the administration of federal social programs. In the context of the nation's campaign against terrorism, Bush also sought to shift America's defense posture from an emphasis on deterrence to a doctrine of preemptive strikes against perceived threats.

The Parties and Congress.   Congress, in particular, depends more on the party system than is generally recognized. First, the speakership of the House is a party office. All the members of the House take part in the election of the speaker. But the actual selection is made by the majority party. When the **majority party** caucus presents a nominee to the entire House, its choice is then invariably ratified in a straight party-line vote.

The committee system of both houses of Congress is also a product of the two-party system. Although the rules organizing committees and the rules defining the jurisdiction of each committee are adopted like ordinary legislation by the whole membership, parties shape all other features of the committees. For example, each party is assigned a quota of members for each committee, depending on the percentage of total seats held by the party. On the rare occasions when an independent or third-party candidate is elected, the leaders of the two parties must agree against whose quota this member's committee assignments will count.

The assignment of individual members to committees is a party decision. Each party has a "committee on committees" to make such decisions. Permission to transfer from one committee to another is also a party decision. Moreover, advancement up the committee ladder toward the chair is a party decision. Since the late nineteenth century, most advancements have been automatic—based upon the length of continual service on the committee. This seniority system has existed only because of the support of the two parties, and either party can depart from it by a simple vote. During the 1970s, both parties reinstituted the practice of reviewing each chair—voting anew every two years on whether each chair would be continued. In 2001, Republicans lived up to their 1995 pledge to limit House committee chairs to three terms. Existing chairpersons were forced to step down, but were replaced generally by the most senior Republican member of each committee.

majority party
The party that holds the majority of legislative seats in either the House or the Senate.

President and Party. As we saw earlier, the party that wins the White House is led, in title anyway, by the president. The president normally depends on fellow party members in Congress to support legislative initiatives. At the same time, members of the party in Congress hope that the president's programs and personal prestige will help them raise campaign funds and secure reelection.

When he assumed office in 2001, President George W. Bush called for a new era of bipartisan cooperation, and the new president did receive the support of some Democratic conservatives. Generally, however, Bush depended on near-unanimous backing from his own party in Congress to implement his plans for cutting taxes as well as other elements of his program. After the terrorist attacks of September 11, both parties united behind Bush's military response. By the end of the president's first term, however, the parties were sharply divided on the administration's policies in Iraq, economic policy, Social Security reform, abortion, other social issues, and the need for enhanced governmental law-enforcement powers to combat terrorism. Ultimately, Bush relied mainly on Republican support to achieve his goals.

In 2009, President Obama took office backed by substantial Democratic majorities in both houses of Congress. For the most part, the president could count on his party's support. However, factional division within the Democratic camp meant that conflicts between Obama and some of his fellow Democrats developed on a number of issues. For example, congressional Democrats were divided on the issue of health care reform, with some backing the president's proposals and others offering their own ideas. On defense policy, the president engaged in a sharp fight with Democrats who supported production of the multibillion-dollar F-22 fighter, which Obama said was not needed.

THE TWO-PARTY SYSTEM IN AMERICA

Although George Washington deplored partisan politics, the two-party system emerged early in the history of the new Republic. Beginning with the Federalists and the Jeffersonian Republicans in the early 1800s, two major parties would dominate national politics, although which particular two parties they were would change with the times and issues. This two-party system has culminated in today's Democrats and Republicans. The evolution of American political parties is shown in Figure 11.2.

The Democrats

When the Jeffersonian party splintered in 1824, Andrew Jackson emerged as the leader of one of its four factions. In 1830, Jackson's group became the Democratic Party. This new party had the strongest national organization of its time and presented itself as the party of the common man. Jacksonians supported reductions in the price of public lands and a policy of cheaper money and credit. Laborers, immigrants, and settlers west of the Alleghenies were quickly attracted to it.

From 1828, when Jackson was elected president, to 1860, the Democratic Party was the dominant force in American politics. For all but eight of those years, the

FIGURE 11.2 HOW THE U.S. PARTY SYSTEM EVOLVED

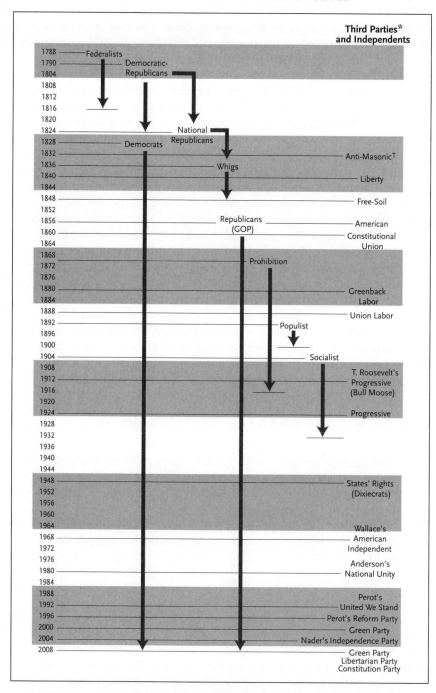

*In some cases, there was even a fourth party. Most of the parties listed here existed for only one term.

†The Anti-Masonics not only had the distinction of being the first third party but also were the first party to hold a national nominating convention and the first to announce a party platform.

Democrats held the White House. In addition, a Democratic majority controlled the Senate for twenty-six years and the House for twenty-four years during the same time period. Nineteenth-century Democrats emphasized the importance of interpreting the Constitution literally, upholding states' rights, and limiting federal spending.

In 1860, the issue of slavery split the Democrats along geographic lines. In the South, many Democrats served in the Confederate government. In the North, one faction of the party (the Copperheads) opposed the war and advocated negotiating a peace with the South. Thus, for years after the war, Republicans denounced the Democrats as the "party of treason."

The Democratic Party was not fully able to regain its political strength until the Great Depression. In 1933, the Democrat Franklin Delano Roosevelt entered the White House, and the Democrats won control of Congress as well. Roosevelt's New Deal coalition, composed of Catholics, Jews, African Americans, farmers, intellectuals, and members of organized labor, dominated American politics until the 1970s and served as the basis for the party's expansion of federal power and efforts to remedy social problems.

The Democrats were never fully united. In Congress, Southern Democrats often aligned with Republicans in the "conservative coalition" rather than with members of their own party. But the Democratic Party remained America's majority party, usually controlling Congress and the White House, for nearly four decades after 1932. By the 1980s, the Democratic coalition faced serious problems. The once-solid South often voted for the Republicans, as did many blue-collar Northern voters. On the other hand, the Democrats increased their strength among African American voters and women. The Democrats maintained a strong base in the bureaucracies of the federal government and the states, in labor unions, and in the not-for-profit sector of the economy. During the 1980s and 1990s, moderate Democrats were able to take control of the party nominating process and sought to broaden middle-class support for the party. This helped the Democrats elect a president in 1992. In 1994, however, the unpopularity of the Democratic president Bill Clinton led to the loss of the Democrats' control of both houses of Congress for the first time since 1946. In 1996, Clinton was able to win reelection to a second term over the weak opposition of the Republican candidate, Robert Dole. Democrats were, however, unable to dislodge their GOP rivals from the leadership of either house of Congress. During the 2000 national presidential elections, Vice President Al Gore won the nomination despite a serious challenge from the former New Jersey senator Bill Bradley. In the general presidential election, Gore outpolled Republican candidate George W. Bush but lost the electoral vote after Bush won a long battle over Florida's votes.

Disagreements between the two wings of the party were evident during the campaign for the Democratic presidential nomination in 2004 and 2008. In 2004, moderate Democrat Joseph Lieberman, for example, supported President Bush's decision to launch a war against Iraq, where as liberal Democrats such as Howard Dean and Al Sharpton strongly criticized the president's military policies. The party's eventual nominee, Senator John Kerry of Massachusetts, had originally supported the war but sought to stake out a position in opposition to Bush's policies that would satisfy liberal Democrats but not appear to be indecisive. In 2009, liberal

Democrats attacked Obama for retaining a number of Bush-era antiterrorism policies and expanding the war in Afghanistan.

The Republicans

The 1854 Kansas-Nebraska Act overturned the Missouri Compromise of 1820 and the Compromise of 1850, which had both barred the expansion of slavery in the American territories. The Kansas-Nebraska Act gave each territory the right to decide whether or not to permit slavery. Opposition to this policy galvanized antislavery groups and led them to create a new party, the Republicans. It drew its membership from existing political groups—former Whigs, Know-Nothings, free soilers, and antislavery Democrats. In 1856, the party's first presidential candidate, John C. Frémont, won one-third of the popular vote and carried eleven states.

The early Republican platforms appealed to commercial as well as antislavery interests. The Republicans favored homesteading, internal improvements, the construction of a transcontinental railroad, and protective tariffs, as well as the containment of slavery. In 1858, the Republican Party won control of the House; in 1860, the Republican presidential candidate, Abraham Lincoln, was victorious.

From the Civil War to the Great Depression, the Republicans were America's dominant political party, especially after 1896. In the seventy-two years between 1860 and 1932, Republicans occupied the White House for fifty-six years, controlled the Senate for sixty years, and controlled the House for fifty. During these years, the Republicans came to be closely associated with big business. The party of Lincoln became the party of Wall Street.

The Great Depression, however, ended Republican supremacy. The voters held the Republican president Herbert Hoover responsible for the economic catastrophe, and by 1936 the party's popularity was so low that Republicans won only eighty-nine seats in the House and seventeen in the Senate. The Republican presidential candidate, Governor Alfred M. Landon of Kansas, carried only two states. The Republicans won only four presidential elections between 1932 and 1980, and they controlled Congress for only four of those years (1947–1949 and 1953–1955).

The Republican Party has widened its appeal over the last five decades. Groups previously associated with the Democratic Party—particularly blue-collar workers and southern Democrats—have been increasingly attracted to Republican presidential candidates (for example, Dwight D. Eisenhower, Richard Nixon, Ronald Reagan, and George W. Bush). But Republicans generally did not do so well at the state and local levels and had little chance of capturing a majority in either the House or Senate. Yet in 1994, the Republican Party finally won a majority in both houses of Congress, in large part because of the party's growing strength in the South.

During the 1990s, conservative religious groups, which had been attracted to the Republican camp by its opposition to abortion and support for school prayer, made a concerted effort to expand their influence within the party. This effort led to conflict between these members of the "religious right" and more traditional "country-club" Republicans, whose major concerns were matters such as taxes and federal regulation of business. This coalition swept the polls in 1994 and maintained its control of both houses of Congress in 1996, despite President Clinton's reelection. In 1998, however, severe strains began to show in the GOP coalition.

In 2000, George W. Bush sought to unite the party's centrist and right wings behind a program of tax cuts, education reform, military strength, and family values. Bush avoided issues that divided the GOP camp, such as abortion. In 2004, he adopted a similar strategy. Bush's candidacy seemed to bode well for the future of the GOP insofar as he was able to find a political formula that could unite the party. By 2008, however, conflicts over the Iraq war undermined Republican unity and the GOP's electoral chances. The "Analyzing the Evidence" unit on page 344 takes a closer look at this recent drop in support for the Republicans.

Electoral Alignments and Realignments

In the United States, party politics has followed a pattern (see Figure 11.3). Typically, during the course of American political history, the national electoral arena has been dominated by one party for a period of roughly thirty years. At the conclusion of this period, a new party has supplanted the dominant party in what political scientists call an **electoral realignment**. The realignment is typically followed by a long period in which the new party is the dominant political force in the United States—not necessarily winning every election but generally maintaining control of the Congress and usually of the White House as well.[7]

Although there are some disputes among scholars about the precise timing of these critical realignments, there is general agreement that at least five have occurred since the Founding of the American Republic. The first took place around 1800 when the Jeffersonian Republicans defeated the Federalists and became the dominant force in American politics. The second realignment occurred in about 1828, when the Jacksonian Democrats took control of the White House and Congress. The third period of realignment centered on 1860. During this period, the newly founded Republican Party led by Abraham Lincoln won power, in the process destroying the Whig Party, which had been one of the nation's two major parties since the 1830s. During the fourth critical period, centered on the election of 1896, the Republicans reasserted their dominance of the national government, which had been weakening since the 1880s. The fifth realignment took place during the period 1932–1936 when the Democrats, led by Franklin Delano Roosevelt, took control of the White House and Congress and, despite sporadic interruptions, maintained control of both through the 1960s. Since that time, American party politics has often been characterized by **divided government**, wherein one party controls the presidency while the other party controls one or both houses of Congress.

Historically, realignments occur when new issues combined with economic or political crises persuade large numbers of voters to reexamine their traditional partisan loyalties and permanently shift their support from one party to another. For example, in the 1850s, diverse regional, income, and business groups supported one of the two major parties, the Democrats or the Whigs, on the basis of their positions on various economic issues, such as internal improvements, the tariff,

electoral realignment The point in history when a new party supplants the ruling party, becoming in turn the dominant political force. In the United States, this has tended to occur roughly every thirty years.

divided government The condition in American government in which one party controls the presidency while the opposing party controls one or both houses of Congress.

---

[7] See Walter Dean Burnham, *Critical Elections and the Mainsprings of American Electoral Politics* (New York: Norton, 1970). See also James L. Sundquist, *Dynamics of the Party System* (Washington, D.C.: Brookings Institution, 1983).

FIGURE 11.3 ELECTORAL REALIGNMENTS

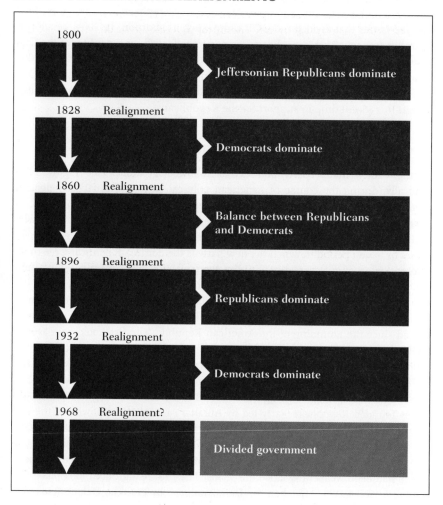

monetary policy, and banking. This economic alignment was shattered during the 1850s. The newly formed Republican Party campaigned on the basis of opposition to slavery and, in particular, opposition to the expansion of slavery into the territories. The issues of slavery and sectionalism produced divisions within both the Democratic and the Whig parties, ultimately leading to the dissolution of the latter, and these issues compelled voters to reexamine their partisan allegiances. Many Northern voters who had supported the Whigs or the Democrats on the basis of their economic stands shifted their support to the Republicans as slavery replaced tariffs and economic concerns as the central item on the nation's political agenda. Many Southern Whigs shifted their support to the Democrats. The new sectional alignment of forces that emerged was solidified by the trauma of the Civil War and persisted almost to the turn of the century.

In 1896, this sectional alignment was at least partially supplanted by an alignment of political forces based on economic and cultural factors. During the economic crises of the 1880s and 1890s, the Democrats forged a coalition consisting of economically hard-pressed midwestern and southern farmers, as well as small-town and rural economic interests. These groups tended to be descendants of British Isles, Dutch, and Hessian fundamentalist Protestants. The Republicans, on the other hand, put together a coalition comprising most of the business community, industrial workers, and city dwellers. In the election of 1896, the Republican candidate, William McKinley, emphasizing business, industry, and urban interests, decisively defeated the Democrat William Jennings Bryan, who spoke for sectional interests, farmers, and fundamentalism. Republican dominance lasted until 1932.

Such periods of critical realignment in American politics have had extremely important institutional and policy results. Realignments occur when new issue concerns coupled with economic or political crises weaken the established political elite and permit new groups of politicians to create coalitions of forces capable of capturing and holding the reins of governmental power. The construction of new governing coalitions during these realigning periods has effected major changes in American governmental institutions and policies. Each period of realignment is a turning point in American politics. The choices made by the national electorate during these periods have helped shape the course of American political history for generations.[8]

American Third Parties

Although the United States is said to possess a two-party system, we have always had more than two parties. Typically, **third parties** in the United States have represented social and economic protests that, for one or another reason, were not given voice by the two major parties.[9] Such parties have had a good deal of influence on ideas and elections in the United States. The Populists, a party centered in the rural areas of the West and the Midwest during the late nineteenth century, and the Progressives, spokesmen for the urban middle classes in the late nineteenth and early twentieth centuries, are among the most important examples. More recently, Ross Perot, who ran in 1992 and 1996 as an independent, impressed some voters with his folksy style in the presidential debates and garnered almost 19 percent of the votes cast in the 1992 presidential election. Earlier, George Wallace received almost 10 percent of the vote in 1968, and John Anderson received about 5 percent in 1980.

Table 11.1 lists parties that fielded candidates in one or more states in the presidential election of 2008, as well as independent candidates who ran. The third-party and independent candidates together polled barely 1 million votes. They gained no electoral votes for president, and most of them disappeared immediately after the presidential election. The significance of Table 11.1 is that it demonstrates the large number of third parties fielding candidates and appealing to voters. Third-party candidacies also arise at the state and local levels. In New York, the Liberal and Conservative parties have been on the ballot for decades. In 1998, Minnesota elected a third-party governor, the former professional wrestler Jesse Ventura.

third party A party that organizes to compete against the two major American political parties.

---

[8] Benjamin Ginsberg, *The Consequences of Consent* (New York: Random House, 1982), chap. 4.

[9] For a discussion of third parties in the United States, see Daniel A. Mazmanian, *Third Parties in Presidential Elections* (Washington, D.C.: Brookings Institution, 1974).

TABLE 11.1 PARTIES AND CANDIDATES, 2008

Candidate	Party	Vote Total	Percent of Vote
Barack Obama	Democrat	69,456,897	52.38%
John McCain	Republican	59,934,814	45.20%
Ralph Nader	Independent	736,804	0.56%
Robert Barr	Libertarian	524,524	0.40%
Charles Baldwin	Constitution	196,461	0.00%
Cynthia McKinney	Green	161,195	0.15%
Richard Duncan	Independent	3,902	0.12%
John Polachek	New Party	1,149	0.00%
Frank McEnulty	New American Independent	828	0.00%
Jeffrey Wamboldt	We the People	764	0.00%
Jeffrey Boss	Vote Here Party	639	0.00%
George Phillies	Libertarian (New Hampshire)	522	0.00%
Ted Weill	Reform	481	0.00%
Bradford Lyttle	U.S. Pacifist	110	0.00%

Total Turnout = 132,588,514

SOURCE: www.census.gov

Although the Republican Party was only the third American political party ever to make itself permanent (by replacing the Whigs), other third parties have enjoyed an influence far beyond their electoral size. This was because large parts of their programs were adopted by one or both of the major parties, which sought to appeal to the voters mobilized by the new party and thereby expand their own electoral strength. The Democratic Party, for example, became a great deal more liberal when it adopted most of the Progressive program early in the twentieth century. Many socialists felt that President Roosevelt's New Deal had adopted most of their party's program, including old-age pensions, unemployment compensation, an agricultural marketing program, and laws guaranteeing workers the right to organize into unions.

This kind of influence explains the short lives of third parties. Their causes are usually eliminated by the ability of the major parties to absorb their programs and to draw their supporters into the mainstream. There are, of course, additional reasons that most third parties are short lived. One is the usual limitation of their electoral support to one or two regions. Populist support, for example, was primarily midwestern. The 1948 Progressive Party, with Henry Wallace as its candidate, drew nearly half its votes from the state of New York. The American Independent Party polled nearly 10 million popular votes and 45 electoral votes for George Wallace in 1968—the most electoral votes ever polled by a third-party candidate. But all of Wallace's electoral votes and the majority of his popular vote came from the states of the Deep South.

Americans usually assume that only the candidates nominated by one of the two major parties have any chance of winning an election. Thus, a vote cast for a third-party or independent candidate is often seen as a wasted vote. Voters who would prefer a third-party candidate may feel compelled to vote for the major party candidate whom they regard as the lesser of two evils to avoid wasting their votes in a futile gesture. Third-party candidates must struggle—usually without success—to overcome the perception that they cannot win. Thus in 2004, many liberals who admired Ralph Nader nevertheless urged him not to mount an independent bid for the presidency for fear he would siphon liberal votes from the Democrats, as he had in 2000. Some former Naderites participated in efforts to keep Nader off the ballot in a number of states. Ultimately Nader did mount a presidential campaign but received 2.5 million fewer votes in 2004 than in 2000. Most of his former adherents, knowing he could not win and might prevent their second-choice candidate from winning, voted for John Kerry.

As many scholars have pointed out, third-party prospects are also hampered by America's **single-member-district** plurality election system. In many other nations, several individuals can be elected to represent each legislative district. This is called a system of **multiple-member districts**. With this type of system, the candidates of weaker parties have a better chance of winning at least some seats. For their part, voters are less concerned about wasting ballots and usually more willing to support minor-party candidates.

Reinforcing the effects of the single-member district, plurality voting rules (as was noted in Chapter 10) generally have the effect of setting what could be called a high threshold for victory. To win a plurality race, candidates usually must secure many more votes than they would need under most European systems of proportional representation. For example, to win an American plurality election in a single-member district where there are only two candidates, a politician must win more than 50 percent of the votes cast. To win a seat from a European multiple-member district under proportional rules, a candidate may need to win only 15 or 20 percent of the votes cast. This high American threshold discourages minor parties and encourages the various political factions that might otherwise form minor parties to minimize their differences and remain within the major-party coalitions.[10]

It would nevertheless be incorrect to assert (as some scholars have maintained) that America's single-member plurality election system is the major cause of our historical two-party pattern. All that can be said is that American election law depresses the number of parties likely to survive over long periods of time in

single-member district An electorate that is allowed to elect only one representative from each district; the normal method of representation in the United States.

multiple-member district An electorate that selects all candidates at large from the whole district; each voter is given the number of votes equivalent to the number of seats to be filled.

---

[10] Maurice Duverger, *Political Parties: Their Organization and Activity in the Modern State*, Barbara North and Robert North, trans. (New York: Wiley, 1954).

How Stable Is Party Identification?

An individual's identification with a party, Democratic or Republican, is thought to be a fundamental psychological attachment and, thus, extremely stable from year to year and election to election. Substantial changes in the percentage of people who identify with one of the two parties do occur. Particularly large changes in party identifications occurred in the mid-1960s and the early 1980s, and between 2005 and 2008. Here lies a puzzle. If individuals' party attachments are stable, why do the aggregate percentages of people who identify with one party or the other vary so much?

Two distinct arguments are often proposed to explain this puzzle and account for broad trends in partisanship. (1) *Generational replacement* may account for the change. By this account, individual party identifications don't change much throughout one's adulthood, but the composition of the electorate changes as new generations emerge and older generations fade. (2) *Conversion* of individuals from one party to the other from one election to the next may contribute to fluctuations in aggregate trends in party attachments. It may be the case that party identification is less stable than political scientists have thought, and that people do change their party allegiances in response to immediate political choices offered by the parties and their assessments of the current president.

Political scientists measure changes in individuals' opinions and attitudes using panel surveys of the same individuals at different points in time. The Cooperative Congressional Election Study conducted an annual survey of the same 2,000 people in 2006, 2007, and 2008, a period that overlaps with the most recent significant shift in party identifications (between 2005 and 2008). The table to the right shows how people changed from 2006 to 2008. Each row of the table shows the identities of respondents in 2006. The percentages in each row show the loyalty and defection rates of those people, that is, the percent of those with a given identity in 2006 who stayed with that identity in 2008 or chose an alternate identification. The partisans are quite loyal, with 89 percent of Democrats and 82 percent of Republicans maintaining their loyalties. There is also very little switching between parties, and it appears to be symmetric—approximately the same percent switch from D to R as from R to D (about 3–4 percent). Most of the defection from each of the two parties is to the category of Independent, with Republicans becoming Independents at a much higher rate than Democrats (14 percent versus 8 percent). And Independents are the source of the uptick in Democratic identifications.

▶

TRANSITIONS FROM 2006 to 2008

		2008 Party Identification		
		D	**I**	**R**
2006 Party Identification	**D**	89%	8%	3%
	I	20%	72%	8%
	R	4%	14%	82%

Can the decline in Republican identification between 2000 and 2008 be traced to the conversion of individuals, or is it attributed to newer, more Democratic generations replacing older, Republican generations? To answer such questions, political scientists conduct a *cohort analysis*. First, we define each generation in terms of when it came of age politically. Over the past several decades the main generations identified by social scientists are the pre–New Deal, New Deal, Baby Boom, Gen X, Gen Y, and Internet generations. Using survey data from each election (in this case, the American National Election Study), we then measure the party identification of the people in each generation, in this case, the percent Democratic minus the percent Republican. In the graph, a higher value on the vertical axis signifies more Democrats. ▼

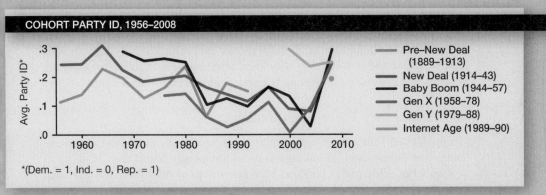

COHORT PARTY ID, 1956–2008

*(Dem. = 1, Ind. = 0, Rep. = 1)

The generational replacement argument would predict that each generation doesn't vary in its net party attachments, because the people don't change much. We would expect each generation to be a horizontal line over time. The conversion hypothesis (in its extreme version) predicts that generations really don't differ in their baseline party attachments and that all generations show the same fluctuations in net party attachments. The graph above reveals that both arguments are in play. The generations clearly differ. The New Deal generation is consistently among the most Democratic, and Gen X is consistently among the most Republican. The net party attachments of the generations also show dramatic ups and downs, and the swings are correlated. All the generations move in the Democratic direction in Democratic years and in the Republican direction in Republican years. The Baby Boomer generation shows the most radical swings in party attachments.

Some simple calculations reveal that the changes in overall party identification in the electorate since 2000 are due to conversion. Overall, Democratic identifications minus Republican identifications rose by 18 percentage points. Consider a hypothetical change that would arise only with replacement. Suppose that the identification of each group remained as it was in 2000, but that only the composition of the electorate changed. That is, suppose that the New Deal generation shrank as a percent of the electorate and that the Gen Y and the Internet generation entered the electorate, but that the party identifications of all the generations remained as they had been in 2000. If only the composition of the electorate had changed from 2000 to 2008, then aggregate party identification would have moved 2 points in the Republican direction!

the United States. There is no requirement that there be even two strong parties. Indeed, the single-member plurality system of election can also discourage second parties. After all, if one party consistently receives a large plurality of the vote, people may eventually come to see their vote *even for the second party* as a wasted effort. This happened to the Republican Party in the Deep South before World War II.

Despite these obstacles, every presidential election brings out a host of minor-party hopefuls (see Table 11.1). Few survive until the next contest.

POLITICAL PARTIES TODAY

As a result of Progressive reform, American party organizations entered the twentieth century with rickety substructures. As the use of civil service, primary elections, and other Progressive innovations spread, the strength of party organizations eroded. By the end of World War II, political scientists were already bemoaning the absence of party discipline and "party responsibility" in the United States.

Contemporary Party Organizations

In the United States, party organizations exist at virtually every level of government (see Figure 11.4). These organizations are usually committees made up of a number of active party members. State law and party rules prescribe how such committees are constituted. Usually, committee members are elected at local party meetings—called **caucuses**—or as part of the regular primary election. The best-known examples of these committees are at the national level—the Democratic National Committee and the Republican National Committee.

The National Convention.   At the national level, the party's most important institution is the quadrennial national convention. The convention is attended by delegates from each of the states; as a group, they nominate the party's presidential and vice-presidential candidates, draft the party's campaign platform for the presidential race, and approve changes in the rules and regulations governing party procedures. Before World War II, presidential nominations occupied most of the time, energy, and effort expended at the national convention. The nomination process required days of negotiation and compromise among state party leaders and often required many ballots before a nominee was selected. In recent years, however, presidential candidates have essentially nominated themselves by winning enough delegate support in primary elections to win the official nomination on the first ballot. The actual convention has played little or no role in selecting the candidates.

The convention's other two tasks, establishing the party's rules and platform, remain important. Party rules can determine the relative influence of competing factions within the party and can also increase or decrease the party's chances for electoral success. In 1972, for example, the Democratic National Convention adopted a new set of rules favored by the party's liberal wing. Under these rules, state delegations to the Democratic convention were required to include women and members of minority groups in rough proportion to those groups'

caucus (political) A normally closed meeting of a political or legislative group to select candidates, plan strategy, or make decisions regarding legislative matters.

FIGURE 11.4 HOW AMERICAN PARTIES ARE ORGANIZED

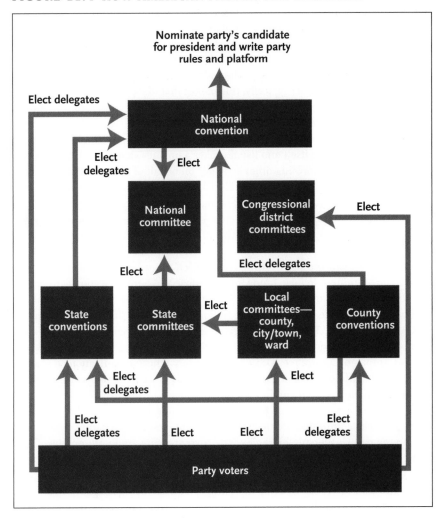

representation among the party's membership in that state. Liberals correctly calculated that women and African Americans would generally support liberal ideas and candidates. The convention also approves the party platform. Platforms are often dismissed as documents filled with platitudes that are seldom read by voters. Furthermore, the parties' presidential candidates make little use of the platforms in their campaigns; usually they prefer to develop and promote their own themes. Nonetheless, the platform should be understood as a "treaty" in which the various factions attending the convention state their terms for supporting the ticket.

The National Committee.   Between conventions, each national political party is technically headed by its national committee. For the Democrats and Republicans, these are called the Democratic National Committee (DNC) and the Republican National Committee (RNC), respectively. These national committees raise campaign funds, head off factional disputes within the party, and endeavor to enhance the party's media image. Since 1972, the size of staff and the amount of money raised have increased substantially for both national committees. The work of each national committee is overseen by its chairperson. Other committee members are generally major party contributors or fund-raisers and serve in a largely ceremonial capacity.

For the party that controls the White House, the national committee chair is appointed by the president. Typically, this means that that party's national committee becomes little more than an adjunct to the White House staff. For a first-term president, the committee devotes the bulk of its energy to the reelection campaign. The national committee chair of the party not in control of the White House is selected by the committee itself and usually takes a broader view of the party's needs, raising money and performing other activities on behalf of the party's members in Congress and in the state legislatures. Barack Obama's presidential campaign was based on a fifty-state strategy. Obama developed extensive grassroots organizations in every state, which registered many new Democratic voters in traditionally Republican areas, a change that will likely benefit the Democrats for years to come.

Congressional Campaign Committees.   Each party forms House and Senate campaign committees to raise funds for the House and Senate election campaigns. The Republicans call their House and Senate committees the National Republican Campaign Committee (NRCC) and the National Republican Senatorial Committee (NRSC), respectively. The Democrats call their House and Senate committees the Democratic Congressional Campaign Committee (DCCC) and the Democratic Senatorial Campaign Committee (DSCC), respectively. These organizations also have professional staff devoted to raising and distributing funds, developing strategies, recruiting candidates, and conducting on-the-ground campaigns. These organizations, however, are accountable to the caucuses inside the House and Senate. The chairs of these committees come from within the respective chambers and rank high in the party leadership hierarchy. The current chairs are Representative Chris Van Hollen (D-Md.) and Senator Charles Schumer (D-N.Y.) on the Democratic side and Representative Tom Cole (R-Okla.) and Senator John Ensign (R-Nev.) on the Republican side. The national committees and the congressional committees are sometimes rivals. Both groups seek donations from the same pool of people but for different candidates: the national committee seeks funds primarily for the presidential race, while the congressional campaign committees focus on House and Senate seats.

State and Local Party Organizations.   Each of the two major parties has a central committee in each state. The parties traditionally also have county committees and, in some instances, state senate district committees, judicial district committees, and, in the case of larger cities, citywide party committees and local assembly district "ward" committees as well. Congressional districts also may have party committees.

State and local party organizations are very active in recruiting candidates and conducting voter-registration drives. Under current federal law, state, and local party organizations can spend unlimited amounts of money on "party-building" activities such as voter registration and get-out-the-vote drives (though in some states such practices are limited by state law). As a result, for many years the national party organizations, which have enormous fund-raising abilities but were restricted by law in how much they could spend on candidates, transferred millions of dollars to the state and local organizations. The state and local parties, in turn, spent these funds, sometimes called soft money, to promote the candidacies of national, as well as state and local, candidates. In this process, as local organizations have become linked financially to the national parties, American political parties became somewhat more integrated and nationalized than ever before. At the same time, the state and local party organizations came to control large financial resources and play important roles in elections despite the collapse of the old patronage machines.[11]

The Contemporary Party as Service Provider to Candidates. Party leaders have adapted parties to the modern age. Parties as organizations are more professional, better financed, and more organized than ever before.[12] Political scientists argue that parties have evolved into "service organizations," which, though they no longer hold a monopoly over campaigns, still provide services to candidates. Without such services, it would be extremely difficult for candidates to win and hold office. Parties have not declined but have simply adapted to serve the interests of political actors.[13]

Many politicians, however, are able to raise funds, attract volunteers, and win office without much help from local party organizations. Once in office, these politicians often refuse to submit to party discipline; instead they steer independent courses. They are often supported by voters who see independence as a virtue and party discipline as "boss rule." Analysts refer to this pattern as a "candidate-centered" politics to distinguish it from a political process in which parties are the dominant forces. The problem with a candidate-centered politics is that it tends to be associated with low turnout, high levels of special-interest influence, and a lack of effective decision making. In short, many of the problems that have plagued American politics in recent years can be traced directly to the independence of American voters and politicians and the candidate-centered nature of American national politics.

PARTIES AND DEMOCRACY

Political parties help make democracy work. We often do not appreciate that democratic government is a contradiction in terms. Government implies policies, programs, and decisive action. Democracy, on the other hand, implies an opportunity

---

[11] For a useful discussion, see John Bibby and Thomas Holbrook, "Parties and Elections," in *Politics in the American States: A Comparative Analysis*, 6th ed., Virginia Gray and Herbert Jacob, eds. (Washington, D.C.: Congressional Quarterly Press, 1996), pp. 78–121.

[12] See John H. Aldrich, *Why Parties? The Origin and Transformation of Party Politics in America* (Chicago: University of Chicago Press, 1995), chap. 8.

[13] See Paul S. Herrnson, *Party Campaigning in the 1980s* (Cambridge, Mass.: Harvard University Press, 1988).

for all citizens to participate fully in the governmental process. Full participation by everyone is inconsistent with getting things done in an efficient and timely manner. How can we balance the ideals of democracy and efficiency in government? How can we make certain that popular participation will result in a government capable of making decisions and developing needed policies? At what point should participation stop and government begin? Strong political parties are a partial antidote to the inherent contradiction between participation and governance. Strong parties can both encourage popular involvement and convert participation into effective government.

As we've seen, parties simplify the electoral process. They set the electoral agenda by laying out party platforms, broad statements of ideas and policies that the party's candidates will pursue in office. They recruit candidates, accumulate and distribute campaign resources, and register and mobilize people to vote. Party control of the nominating process and the pressures toward two-party politics in the United States mean that most voters must decide between just two meaningful or plausible choices in any election. This in turn facilitates voters' decision making. Voters can reasonably expect what sorts of policies a candidate who has a party's endorsement will pursue if elected. Even before a given candidate has received the nomination, most voters have already sorted themselves into one of the two competing camps, Democratic or Republican. They know for whom they will vote before the election begins. This may seem like a gross simplification of politics. It reduces the many complex interests in our society to just two competing teams whose policy platforms must be watered down to accommodate the many subtle differences or ideological nuances among the groups inside the party. It further reduces politics into warring factions that have little hope of finding compromise or common ground. However, the two-party system does give meaning to the vote. It empowers the voter to say, I want to stay the course with the party in power, or, I want to go in a new direction.

CHAPTER REVIEW

Political parties seek to control government by controlling its personnel. Elections are their means to this end. Thus, parties take shape from the electoral process. The formal principle of party organization is this: For every district in which an election is held—from the entire nation to the local county or precinct—there should be some kind of party unit.

The two-party system dominates U.S. politics. Third parties are short lived for several reasons. They have limited electoral support, the tradition of the two-party system is strong, and a major party often adopts their platforms. The American system of single-member districts with two competing parties also discourage third parties.

Nominating and electing are two basic functions of parties. Originally, nominations were made in party caucuses, and individuals who ran as independents had a difficult time getting on the ballot. In the 1830s, dissatisfaction with the cliquish caucuses led to nominating conventions. Although these ended the era in which the party caucuses in Congress controlled the nomination of the presidential candidates and thereby gave the presidency a popular base, they too proved unsatisfactory. Primaries have now replaced the conventions. Primaries can be closed or open. Closed primaries are more supportive of strong political parties than open primaries. Contested primaries sap party strength and financial resources, but they nonetheless resolve important social conflicts and recognize new interest groups.

Congress is organized around the two-party system. The House speakership is a party office. Parties determine the makeup of congressional committees, including their chairs, which are no longer based entirely on seniority.

FOR FURTHER READING

Aldrich, John H. *Why Parties? The Origin and Transformation of Party Politics in America.* Chicago: University of Chicago Press, 1995. ○ reader selection

Beck, Paul Allen, and Marjorie Randon Hershey. *Party Politics in America.* 10th ed. New York: Longman, 2003.

Chambers, William N., and Walter Dean Burnham, eds. *The American Party Systems: Stages of Political Development.* 2nd ed. New York: Oxford University Press, 1975.

Coleman, John J. *Party Decline in America: Policy, Politics, and the Fiscal State.* Princeton, N.J.: Princeton University Press, 1996.

Cox, Gary W., and Mathew D. McCubbins. *Legislative Leviathan: Party Government in the House.* Berkeley: University of California Press, 1993.

———. *Setting the Agenda: Responsible Party Government in the U.S. House of Representatives.* New York: Cambridge University Press, 2005. ○ reader selection

Hofstadter, Richard. *The Idea of a Party System: The Rise of Legitimate Opposition in the United States, 1780–1840.* Berkeley: University of California Press, 1969.

Mayhew, David. *Electoral Realignments: A Critique of an American Genre.* New Haven, Conn.: Yale University Press, 2007.

Miller, Gary, and Norman Schofield. "The Transformation of the Republican and Democratic Party Coalitions in the U.S." *Perspectives on Politics* (September 2008): 433–50. ○ reader selection

Rohde, David W. *Parties and Leaders in the Post-reform House.* Chicago: University of Chicago Press, 1991.

Sundquist, James L. *Dynamics of the Party System: Alignment and Realignment of Political Parties in the United States.* Washington, D.C.: Brookings Institution, 1983.

Wattenberg, Martin P. *The Decline of American Political Parties, 1952–1996.* Cambridge, Mass.: Harvard University Press, 1998.

Ⓢ Additional study and review materials are available online at wwnorton.com/studyspace/

12 Groups and Interests

HOW DO INTEREST GROUPS WORK?

Democratic politics in the United States does not end with elections. Federal, state, and local governments provide many additional avenues through which individuals and organizations can express their preferences. People may, for example, contact elected officials, their staffs, and bureaucrats directly about a particular decision or problem. They may participate in public meetings about legislation or administrative rulings; some private citizens are even selected to serve on special government commissions because of their expertise or particular concerns. They may file lawsuits to request that a government agency take a particular action or to prevent it from doing so. They may give their time and money to elect candidates to their liking. They may express their opinions in newspapers, on television and the Internet, or through other venues, and even hold public protests, without fear of persecution. Individuals, organizations, and even governments make frequent use of these many points of access. Their actions are purposive—they seek something from government that will benefit them. Many of these encounters with government are episodic, as when someone contacts an agency to solve a particular problem. But a substantial amount of political activity in the United States occurs through enduring, organized efforts that bring many individuals into collective action to seek a common goal.

Individuals, firms, and other organizations engage in political activity for very definite purposes. Elections do not fully capture the intensity and range of people's preferences. Those who care a great deal about what government does or are particularly affected by government decisions are usually willing to do more than just vote in order to have their opinions heard. The 1970s, for example, witnessed a massive upsurge in business activity in Washington, D.C., in response to new labor and environmental regulations. The debate over health care reform, which

CORE OF THE ANALYSIS

- Interest groups are organized to influence government decisions.
- Though interest groups sometimes promote public concerns, they more often represent narrow interests.
- Interest groups use various strategies to promote their goals, including lobbying, gaining access to key decision makers, using the courts, going public, and influencing electoral politics.

has stretched out over the better part of two decades, has resulted in a massive new prescription drug benefit and drawn the pharmaceutical industry into Washington politics. The firms and associations in that industry are acutely aware of the economic consequences of particular regulations and benefits (such as the prescription drug benefit); support for and opposition to particular bills reflects the economic gains the firms expect to reap.[1]

Those seeking access to the government may benefit in two distinct ways—shaping policy and gathering information. It is widely understood that organizations try to affect government policy decisions in the legislative, administrative, and legal arenas, but gathering information from agencies and departments may be just as important. For instance, when a commission or department issues a new regulation, firms that are potentially affected must figure out whether the regulation applies to them, how to comply if they are affected, and the exact interpretation of the regulations. That often involves many interactions between the agency and representatives of the firms and sometimes further rulings from agencies clarifying the procedures. Firms frequently hire representation in Washington and state capitals just to stay on top of such matters. One influential study discovered that half of the activities and efforts of businesspeople who contacted the government consisted of gathering information, and half consisted of advocacy for a particular policy or action.[2]

Information gathering seems innocuous. The organizations are just trying to figure out how the regulations work. Influencing policy, on the other hand, is a matter of concern, because it may lead to government policies that protect relatively narrow

---

[1] Thomas B. Edsall, "Two Bills Would Benefit Top Bush Fundraisers," *Washington Post*, November 22, 2003, p. 1; Jeffrey H. Birnbaum, "In the Loop on K Street," *Washington Post*, January 16, 2007, p. A17.

[2] Raymond Bauer, Ithiel de Sola Pool, and Lewis Dexter, *American Business and Public Policy* (Chicago: Atherton Press, 1972).

or special interests at the expense of the majority. Both sorts of benefits, however, may motivate firms, unions, and other organizations to engage in political action.

The government itself encourages participation by such groups. Government agencies and representatives need information about the effects of public policies. Frequent elections provide some guidance from the public, but elected representatives may need more refined information about how a given decision will affect particular constituencies. They also need to know whether those constituencies, even if not a majority, will be sufficiently affected by a decision to base their future electoral behavior—including campaign contributions and votes—on that decision. Bureaucrats typically do not have the time and resources to study all potential problems. Instead they rely on information from individuals, firms, and other organizations to gauge the importance of a given problem and to learn about the consequences of particular decisions. A responsive government needs subtler, more refined information about how a decision will affect people or society or about the best way to implement a law. The solution in American government is to allow, indeed encourage, an open government with many points of access for competing views.

This is pluralism at work. It is messy and often disliked by the public at large, but it is an essential feature of American government. The Constitution embraces this idea fully. The more competition there is among many different interests, the less likely it is that any one will triumph, and the more likely it is that representatives and government officials will learn what they need to know.[3]

In this chapter we examine interest-group politics in the United States. We analyze the group basis of politics, the challenges groups face in getting individuals to act collectively, and some solutions to these problems. We seek to understand the character and balance of the interests promoted through the pluralistic political system in the United States. We further examine the tremendous growth of interest groups in their number, resources, and activity in recent American political history, especially the emergence of public interest groups. Finally, we examine the strategies that groups use to influence politics and whether their influence in the political process has become excessive.

THE CHARACTERISTICS OF INTEREST GROUPS

interest group
A group of people organized around a shared belief or mutual concern who try to influence the government to make policies promoting their belief or concerns.

An **interest group** is an organized group of people that makes policy-related appeals to government. Individuals form groups in order to increase the chance that their views will be heard and their interests treated favorably by the government. Interest groups are organized to influence governmental decisions. They are often referred to as lobbies.

Interest groups are sometimes confused with political action committees (see Chapter 10). The difference is that PACs focus on influencing elections, whereas

---

[3] This sentiment is expressed most eloquently in *Federalist 10*.

interest groups focus on influencing elected officials. Another distinction that we should make is that interest groups are also different from political parties: interest groups tend to concern themselves with the *policies* of government; parties tend to concern themselves with the *personnel* of government.

Enhancing Democracy

There are an enormous number of interest groups in the United States, and millions of Americans are members of one or more groups, at least to the extent of paying dues or attending an occasional meeting. By representing the interests of such large numbers of people and encouraging political participation, organized groups can and do enhance American democracy. Organized groups educate their members about issues that affect them. Groups lobby members of Congress and the executive, engage in litigation, and generally represent their members' interests in the political arena. Groups mobilize their members for elections and grassroots lobbying efforts, thus encouraging participation. Interest groups also monitor government programs to make certain that their members are not adversely affected by these programs. In all these ways, organized interests can be said to promote democratic politics. But because not all interests are represented equally, interest-group politics works to the advantage of some and the disadvantage of others.

"The Evils of Faction"

The framers of the Constitution feared the power that could be wielded by organized interests and that the public good would be "disregarded in the conflict of rival [factions]."[4] Yet they believed that interest groups thrived because of freedom—the freedom that all Americans enjoyed to organize and express their views. To the framers, this problem presented a dilemma—indeed, the dilemma of freedom versus power that is central to our text. If the government were given the power to regulate or in any way to forbid efforts by organized interests to interfere in the political process, the government would in effect have been given the power to suppress freedom. The solution to this dilemma was presented by James Madison:

> ... Take in a greater variety of parties and interest [and] you make it less probable that a majority of the whole will have a common motive to invade the rights of other citizens. . . . [Hence the advantage] enjoyed by a large over a small republic.[5]

According to Madisonian theory, a good constitution encourages multitudes of interests so that no single interest can ever tyrannize the others. The basic assumption is that competition among interests will produce balance and compromise, with all the interests regulating each other.[6] Today, this Madisonian principle of regulation is called **pluralism.**

pluralism The theory that all interests are and should be free to compete for influence in the government. The outcome of this competition is balance and compromise.

---

[4] Clinton Rossiter, ed., *The Federalist Papers* (New York: New American Library, 1961), no. 10, p. 78.

[5] Rositer, ed., *Federalist 10,* p. 83.

[6] Rossiter, ed., *Federalist 10.*

There are tens of thousands of organized groups in the United States, but the huge number of interest groups competing for influence does not mean that all interests are fully and equally represented in the American political process. As we will see, the political deck is heavily stacked in favor of those interests able to organize and to wield substantial economic, social, and institutional resources on behalf of their cause. This means that within the universe of interest-group politics, it is political power—not some abstract conception of the public good—that is likely to prevail. Moreover, this means that interest-group politics, taken as a whole, is a political format that works more to the advantage of some types of interests than others. In general, a politics in which interest groups predominate is a politics with a distinctly upper-class bias.

What Interests Are Represented

When most people think about interest groups, they immediately think of groups with a direct economic interest in governmental actions (see Table 12.1). These groups are generally supported by groups of producers or manufacturers in a particular economic sector. Examples of this type of group include the National Petroleum Refiners Association, the American Farm Bureau Federation, and the National Federation of Independent Business, which represents small business owners. At the same time that broadly representative groups such as these are active in Washington, specific companies—such as Disney, Shell Oil, IBM, and Microsoft—may be active on certain issues that are of particular concern to them.

TABLE 12.1 WHO IS REPRESENTED BY ORGANIZED INTERESTS?

Economic Role of the Individual	U.S. Adults (%)	Orgs. (%)	Type of Org. in Washington	Ratio of Orgs. to Adults
Managerial/administrative	7	71.0	Business association	10.10
Professional/technical	9	17.0	Professional association	1.90
Student/teacher	4	4.0	Educational organization	1.00
Farmworker	2	1.5	Agricultural workers' organization	0.75
Unable to work	2	0.6	Organization for the disabled	0.30
Other nonfarm workers	41	4.0	Union	0.10
Homemaker	19	1.8	Women's organization	0.09
Retired	12	0.8	Senior citizens' organization	0.07
Looking for work	4	0.1	Unemployment organization	0.03

Labor organizations are equally active lobbyists. The AFL-CIO, the United Mine Workers, and the Teamsters's union are all groups that lobby on behalf of organized labor. In recent years, lobbies have arisen to further the interests of public employees, the most significant among these being the American Federation of State, County, and Municipal Employees (AFSCME).

Professional lobbies such as the American Bar Association and the American Medical Association have been particularly successful in furthering their own interests in state and federal legislatures. Financial institutions, represented by organizations such as the American Bankers Association and the National Savings & Loan League, although frequently less visible than other lobbies, also play an important role in shaping legislative policy.

Recent years have witnessed the growth of a powerful "public interest" lobby purporting to represent interests whose concerns are not likely to be addressed by traditional lobbies. These groups have been most visible in the consumer protection and environmental policy areas, although public interest groups cover a broad range of issues. The National Resources Defense Council, the Union of Concerned Scientists, and Common Cause are all examples of public interest groups.

The perceived need for representation on Capitol Hill has generated a public sector lobby, including the National League of Cities and the "research" lobby. The latter group comprises think tanks and universities that have an interest in obtaining government funds for research and support, and it includes such prestigious institutions as Harvard University, the Brookings Institution, and the American Enterprise Institute. Indeed, many universities have expanded their lobbying efforts even as they have reduced faculty positions and course offerings and increased tuition.[7]

The "Free Rider" Problem

Whether organizations need individuals to volunteer or merely to write checks, all must recruit and retain members. Yet many groups find this difficult, even with regard to those who agree strongly with the group's goals. The reason is that, as the economist Mancur Olson explains, the benefits of a group's success are often broadly available and cannot be denied to nonmembers.[8] Such benefits can be called **collective goods.** This term is usually associated with certain government benefits, but it can also be applied to beneficial outcomes of interest-group activity.

To follow Olson's theory, suppose a number of private property owners live near a mosquito-infested swamp. Each owner wants this swamp cleared. But if one or a few of the owners were to clear the swamp alone, their actions would benefit all the other owners as well, without any effort on the part of those other owners. Each of the inactive owners would be a **free rider** on the efforts of the ones who cleared the swamp. Thus, there is a disincentive for any of the owners to undertake the job alone.

Since the number of concerned owners is small in this particular case, they might eventually be able to organize themselves to share the costs as well as enjoy

collective goods Benefits, sought by groups, that are broadly available and cannot be denied to nonmembers.

free rider One who enjoys the benefits of collective goods but did not participate in acquiring them.

---

[7] Betsy Wagner and David Bowermaster, "B.S. Economics," *Washington Monthly*, November 1992, pp. 19–22.

[8] Mancur Olson, *The Logic of Collective Action* (Cambridge, Mass.: Harvard University Press, 1971).

The Character of Interest Groups

What Interests Are Represented

Economic interests—American Farm Bureau Federation

Labor organizations—AFL-CIO, United Mine Workers, International Brotherhood of Teamsters

Professional lobbies—American Bar Association, American Medical Association

Financial institutions—American Bankers Association, National Savings & Loan League

Public interest groups—Common Cause, Union of Concerned Scientists

Public sector lobby—National League of Cities

Organizational Components

Attracting and keeping members

Fund-raising to support the group's infrastructure and lobbying efforts

Leadership and decision-making structure

Agency that carries out the group's tasks

Characteristics of Members

Interest groups tend to attract members from the middle and upper-middle classes because these people are more likely to have the time, the money, and the inclination to take part in such associations. People from less advantaged socioeconomic groups need to be organized on the massive scale of political parties.

the benefits of clearing the swamp. But suppose the numbers of interested people are increased. Suppose the common concern is not the neighborhood swamp but polluted air or groundwater involving thousands of residents in a region, or in fact millions of residents in a whole nation. National defense is the most obvious collective good whose benefits are shared by every resident, regardless of the taxes they pay or the support they provide. As the number of involved persons increases, or as the size of the group increases, the free-rider phenomenon becomes more of a problem. Individuals do not have much incentive to become active members and supporters of a group that is already working more or less on their behalf. The group would no doubt be more influential if all concerned individuals were active members—if there were no free riders. But groups will not reduce their efforts just because free riders get the same benefits as dues-paying activists. In fact, groups may try even harder precisely because there are free riders, with the hope that the free riders will be encouraged to join in.

Organizational Components

Although there are many interest groups, most share certain key organizational components. First and most important, all groups must attract and keep members.

Somehow, groups must overcome the free rider problem and persuade individuals to invest the money, time, energy, or effort required to take part in the group's activities. Members play a larger role in some groups than in others. In membership associations, group members actually serve on committees and engage in projects. In the case of labor unions, members may march on picket lines, and in the case of political or ideological groups, members may participate in demonstrations and protests. In another set of groups, staff organizations, a professional staff conducts most of the group's activities; members are called on only to pay dues and make other contributions. Among the well-known public interest groups, some—such as the National Organization for Women (NOW)—are membership groups; others—such as Defenders of Wildlife and the Children's Defense Fund—are staff organizations.

Usually, groups appeal to members not only by promoting political goals or policies they favor but also by offering them direct **informational**, **material**, or **social benefits**. Thus, for example, AARP, which promotes the interests of senior citizens, offers members information, insurance benefits, and commercial discounts. Many organizations provide information through conferences, training programs, and newsletters and other periodicals sent automatically to those who have paid membership dues. Material benefits can be discount purchasing, shared advertising, and perhaps most valuable of all, health and retirement insurance. Another benefit that can attract members is social interaction, networking, and good fellowship. Thus, the local chapters of many national groups provide their members with a congenial social environment while collecting dues that finance the national office's political efforts.

Another kind of benefit involves the appeal of an interest group's purpose. The best examples of such **purposive benefits** are those of religious interest groups. The Christian right is made up of a number of interest groups that offer virtually no material benefits to their members, depending almost entirely on the religious identifications and affirmations of their members. Many religion-based interest groups have arisen throughout American history, such as those that drove abolition and prohibition.

The second component shared by all groups is that each one must build a financial structure capable of sustaining an organization and funding the group's activities. Most interest groups rely on annual membership dues and voluntary contributions from sympathizers. Many also sell some ancillary services, such as insurance and vacation tours, to members.

Third, every group must have a leadership and decision-making structure. For some groups, this structure is very simple. For others, it can be quite elaborate and involve hundreds of local chapters that are melded into a national apparatus.

Last, most groups include an agency that actually carries out the group's tasks. This may be a research organization, a public relations office, or a lobbying office in Washington or a state capital.

The Characteristics of Members

Membership in interest groups is not randomly distributed in the population. People with higher incomes, higher levels of education, and management or professional occupations are much more likely to become members of groups than

informational benefits Special newsletters, periodicals, training programs, conferences, and other information provided to members of groups to entice others to join.

material benefits Special goods, services, or money provided to members of groups to entice others to join.

social benefits Selective benefits of a group membership that emphasize friendship, networking, and consciousness raising.

purposive benefits Selective benefits of group membership that emphasize the purpose and accomplishments of the group.

those who occupy lower rungs on the socioeconomic ladder.[9] Well-educated, upper-income business and professional people are more likely to have the time and the money, and to have acquired through the educational process the concerns and skills needed to play a role in a group or association. Moreover, for business and professional people, group membership may provide personal contacts and access to information that can help advance their careers. At the same time, of course, corporate entities—businesses and the like—usually have ample resources to form or participate in groups that seek to advance their causes.

The result is that interest-group politics in the United States tends to have a very pronounced upper-class bias. Certainly, many interest groups and political associations have a working-class or lower-class membership—labor organizations or welfare-rights organizations, for example—but the great majority of interest groups and their members are drawn from the middle and upper middle classes. In general, the "interests" served by interest groups are the interests of society's "haves." Even when interest groups take opposing positions on issues and policies, the conflicting positions they espouse usually reflect divisions among upper-income strata rather than conflicts between the upper and lower classes.

In general, to obtain adequate political representation, forces from the bottom rungs of the socioeconomic ladder must be organized on the massive scale associated with political parties. Parties can organize and mobilize the collective energies of large numbers of people who, as individuals, may have very limited resources. Interest groups, on the other hand, generally organize smaller numbers of the better-to-do. Thus, the relative importance of political parties and interest groups in American politics has far-ranging implications for the distribution of political power in the United States.

Response to Changes in the Political Environment

If interest groups and our concerns about them were a new phenomenon, we would not have begun this section with James Madison. As long as there is government, as long as government makes policies that add value or impose costs, and as long as there is liberty to organize, interest groups will abound. And if government expands, so will interest groups. There was, for example, a spurt of growth in the national government during the 1880s and 1890s, arising largely from the first government efforts at economic intervention to fight large monopolies and regulate some aspects of interstate commerce. In the latter decade, a parallel spurt of growth occurred in national interest groups, including the imposing National Association of Manufacturers and numerous other trade associations. Many groups organized around specific agricultural commodities as well. This period also marked the beginning of the expansion of trade unions as interest groups. Later, in the 1930s, interest groups with headquarters and representation in Washington began to grow significantly, concurrent with that decade's expansion of the national government.

---

[9] Kay Lehman Schlozman and John T. Tierney, *Organized Interests and American Democracy* (New York: Harper & Row, 1986), p. 60.

Over recent decades, there has been an enormous increase both in the number of interest groups seeking to play a role in the American political process and in the extent of their opportunity to influence that process. The total number of interest groups in the United States today is not known. There are certainly tens of thousands of groups at the national, state, and local levels. One indication of the proliferation of such groups' activity is the growth over time in the number of PACs attempting to influence U.S. elections. Nearly six times as many PACs operated in 2008 as in the 1970s (Figure 12.1). A *New York Times* report, for example, noted that during the 1970s, expanded federal regulation of the automobile, oil, gas, education, and health-care industries impelled each of these interests to substantially increase its efforts to influence the government's behavior. These efforts, in turn, had the effect of spurring the organization of other groups to augment or counter the activities of the first.[10] Similarly, federal social programs have

FIGURE 12.1 PAC COUNT, 1974–2008

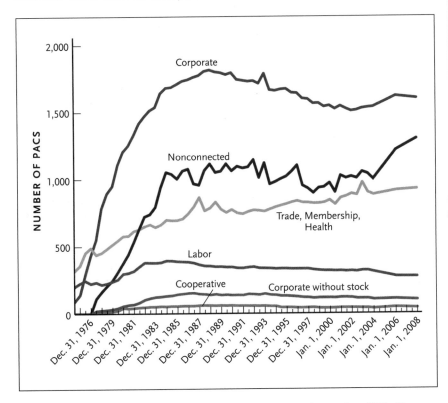

SOURCE: Federal Election Commission, "FEC Records Slight Increase in the Number of PASs," January 17, 2008, www.fec.gov/press/press2008/20080117paccount.shtml (accessed 7/8/09).

---

[10] John Herbers, "Special Interests Gaining Power as Voter Disillusionment Grows," *New York Times*, November 14, 1978.

occasionally sparked political organization and action by clientele groups seeking to influence the distribution of benefits and, in turn, the organization of groups opposed to the programs or their cost. For example, federal programs and court decisions in such areas as abortion and school prayer were the stimuli for political action and organization by fundamentalist religious groups. These groups include the Christian Coalition of America, the Family Research Council, the Traditional Values Coalition, Focus on the Family, and Christian Voice. Struggles over such issues as abortion and gay marriage have helped these groups expand their membership roles and build a network of state and local chapters. As we have noted, religious conservatives played key roles in George W. Bush's presidential victories in both 2000 and 2004. In response, Bush launched his so-called faith-based initiative. Under the terms of this program, federal grants and contracts were given to religious organizations to provide social services to children, seniors, and others. By using so-called faith-based groups as federal contractors, Bush sought to reward religious conservatives for their loyalty to the GOP and ensure that these groups had a continuing stake in Republican success.

Another factor accounting for the explosion of interest-group activity in recent decades was the emergence of new social and political movements. The civil rights and antiwar movements of the 1960s and the reactions against them created a generation of upper-middle-class professionals and intellectuals who have seen themselves as a political force in opposition to the public policies and politicians associated with the nation's postwar regime. Following close on the heels of these movements came the decade-long debate over the equal rights amendment, the Sagebrush Rebellion (concerned with land use in the West), the nuclear disarmament movement, and the antiabortion movement. Such groups sought change in social behavior and public policy, usually through civil disobedience.

Members of these new politics movements constructed or strengthened public interest groups such as Common Cause, the Sierra Club, the Environmental Defense Fund, Physicians for Social Responsibility, the National Organization for Women, and the various organizations formed by the consumer activist Ralph Nader. These groups were able to influence the media, Congress, and even the judiciary and enjoyed a remarkable degree of success during the late 1960s and early 1970s in securing the enactment of policies they favored. New politics activists also played a major role in securing the enactment of environmental, consumer, and occupational health and safety legislation.

Among the factors contributing to the rise and success of new politics forces was technology. In the 1970s and 1980s, computerized direct-mail campaigns allowed public interest groups to reach hundreds of thousands of potential sympathizers and contributors. Today the Internet and e-mail serve the same function. Electronic communication allows relatively small groups to efficiently identify and mobilize their adherents throughout the nation. Individuals with perspectives that might be in the minority everywhere can become conscious of each other and mobilize for national political action through the magic of electronic politics. For example, a relatively small number of Americans scattered across the nation might be intensely concerned with the protection of whales and other aquatic mammals. These individuals form an active and vocal community on the Internet, however.

They communicate with one another, reach out to potential sympathizers, and bombard politicians with e-mail. In this way, the Internet can facilitate group formation and political action, overcoming the limitations of geography and numbers.

STRATEGIES FOR INFLUENCING POLICY

Interest groups work to improve the probability that they and their policy interests will be heard and treated favorably by all branches and levels of the government. The quest for political influence of power takes many forms. We can roughly divide these strategies into "insider strategies" and "outsider strategies."

Insider strategies include gaining access to key decision makers and using the courts. Of course, influencing policy through traditional political institutions requires understanding how those institutions work. A lobbyist who wishes Congress to address a problem with legislation will try to find a sympathetic member of Congress, preferably on a committee with jurisdiction over the problem, and will work directly with the member's staff. If an organization decides to bring suit in the courts, it may want sue in a jurisdiction where it has a good chance of getting a judge favorable to the case or where the immediate appellate courts are likely to support its case. Gaining access is not easy. Legislators and bureaucrats have little time and many requests to juggle; courts have full dockets. Interest groups themselves have limited budgets and staff. They must choose their battles well and map out the strategy most likely to succeed.

Outsider strategies include going public and using electoral tactics. Just as politicians can gain an electoral edge by informing voters, so too can groups. A well-planned public-information campaign or targeted campaign activities and contributions can have as much influence as working the corridors of Congress.

Many groups employ a mix of insider and outsider strategies. For example, environmental groups such as the Sierra Club lobby members of Congress and key congressional staff members, participate in bureaucratic rule making by offering comments and suggestions to agencies on new environmental rules, and bring lawsuits under various environmental acts such as the Endangered Species Act, which authorizes groups and citizens to come to court if they believe the act is being violated. At the same time, the Sierra Club attempts to influence public opinion through media campaigns and to influence electoral politics by supporting candidates whom it believes share its environmental views and opposing candidates whom it views as foes of environmentalism.

Direct Lobbying

Lobbying is an attempt by an individual or a group to influence the passage of legislation by exerting direct pressure on members of the legislature. The First Amendment to the Constitution provides for the right to "petition the Government for a redress of grievances." But as early as the 1870s, "lobbying" became the common term for petitioning.

lobbying An attempt by a group to influence the policy process through persuasion of government officials.

The 1946 Federal Regulation of Lobbying Act defines a lobbyist as "any person who shall engage himself for pay or any consideration for the purpose of attempting to influence the passage or defeat of any legislation to the Congress of the United States." The Lobbying Disclosure Act requires all organizations employing lobbyists to register with Congress and to disclose whom they represent, whom they lobby, what they are lobbying for, and how much they are paid. More than 7,000 organizations, collectively employing many thousands of lobbyists, are currently registered.

Lobbying involves a great deal of activity on the part of someone speaking for an interest. Lobbyists badger and buttonhole legislators, administrators, and committee staff members with facts about pertinent issues and facts or claims about public support of them.[11] Lobbyists can serve a useful purpose in the legislative and administrative process by providing this kind of information. In 1978, during debate on a bill to expand the requirement for lobbying disclosures, the Democratic senators Edward Kennedy of Massachusetts and Dick Clark of Iowa joined with the Republican senator Robert Stafford of Vermont to issue the following statement: "Government without lobbying could not function. The flow of information to Congress and to every federal agency is a vital part of our democratic system."[12]

Lobbying Members of Congress.   Interest groups also have substantial influence in setting the legislative agenda and in helping craft the language of legislation (Figure 12.2). Today sophisticated lobbyists win influence by providing information about policies to busy members of Congress. As one lobbyist noted, "You can't get access without knowledge. . . . I can go in to see John Dingell [chairman of the House Committee on Energy and Commerce], but if I have nothing to offer or nothing to say, he's not going to want to see me."[13] In recent years, interest groups have also begun to build broader coalitions and comprehensive campaigns around particular policy issues.[14] These coalitions do not rise from the grassroots but instead are put together by Washington lobbyists who launch comprehensive campaigns that combine simulated grassroots activity with information and campaign funding for members of Congress.

Some interest groups are able to place their lobbyists directly on congressional staffs. In 2007, several experienced lobbyists and Washington insiders were "borrowed" by the new Democratic leadership to help organize the business of the new Congress. For example, Dennis Fitzgibbons, a lobbyist for DaimlerChrysler, was hired as chief of staff of the House Energy and Commerce Committee. In his capacity as an auto lobbyist, Fitzgibbons attempted to block efforts to force

---

[11] For discussions of lobbying, see John Wright, *Interest Groups and Congress* (New York: Longman, 2009).

[12] "The Swarming Lobbyists," *Time*, August 7, 1978, p. 15.

[13] Daniel Franklin, "Tommy Boggs and the Death of Health Care Reform," *Washington Monthly*, April 1995, p. 36.

[14] Marie Hojnacki, "Interest Groups' Decisions to Join Alliances or Work Alone," *American Journal of Political Science* 41 (1997): 61–87; Kevin W. Hula, *Lobbying Together: Interest Group Coalitions in Legislative Politics* (Washington, D.C.: Georgetown University Press, 1999).

FIGURE 12.2 HOW INTEREST GROUPS INFLUENCE CONGRESS

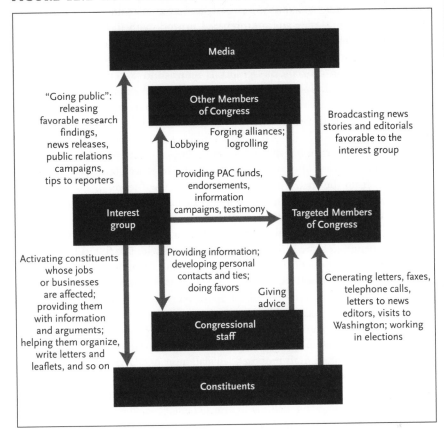

automakers to make vehicles more fuel efficient or to manufacture vehicles that would use alternative fuels. Subsequently, in 2009 Fitzgibbons joined the First Solar energy company as vice president for federal affairs. In his new position Fitzgibbons could take advantage of the contacts he had made in his previous position.[15]

Not every interest group can embed stealth lobbyists in Congress. Many, however, do the next best thing: They hire the spouses and relatives of members of Congress or important staffers to lobby for them. An extensive study of the congressional appropriations process conducted in 2006 found thirty instances in which lobbyists related to members and senior staffers of the House and Senate appropriations committees sought money in the appropriation bills their family members helped to write. In twenty-two cases, relatives were able to get specific language inserted in bills that guaranteed money for their clients.[16]

---

[15] Birnbaum, "In the Loop on K Street."

[16] Matt Kelley and Peter Eisler, "Relatives Have Inside Track in Lobbying for Tax Dollars," *USA Today*, October 17, 2006, p. 1.

Some interest groups have strong ties to the Democrats and others to the Republicans. Most interest groups, however, endeavor to maintain good relations with both political parties and are prepared to work with the party in power to achieve their legislative goals. When Republicans controlled Congress, trade associations and corporate interests hired Republican lobbyists and built close ties to the GOP leadership. In 2007, as Democrats returned to power, the same interest groups hired Democratic lobbyists and worked to build close ties to the new Democratic leadership. And when it came to campaign contributions, corporate interests cheerfully backed both sides, making sure to befriend the winners, whoever they might be.[17]

What happens to interests that do not engage in extensive lobbying? They often find themselves "Microsofted." In 1998, the software giant was facing antitrust action from the Justice Department and had few friends in Congress. One member of the House, Representative Billy Tauzin (R-La.), told Microsoft's chairman, Bill Gates, that without an extensive investment in lobbying, the corporation would continue to be "demonized." Gates responded by quadrupling Microsoft's lobbying expenditures and hiring a group of lobbyists with strong ties to Congress. The result was congressional pressure on the Justice Department, resulting in a settlement of the Microsoft suit on terms favorable to the company.

Providing access is only one of the many services lobbyists perform. Lobbyists often testify on behalf of their clients at congressional committee and agency hearings; lobbyists sometimes help their clients identify potential allies with whom to construct coalitions; lobbyists provide research and information to government officials; lobbyists often draft proposed legislation or regulations to be introduced by friendly lawmakers; lobbyists talk to reporters, place ads in newspapers, and organize letter-writing, e-mail, and telegram campaigns. Lobbyists also play an important role in fund-raising, helping to direct clients' contributions to members of Congress and presidential candidates.

Lobbying the President. So many individuals and groups clamor for the president's time and attention that only the most skilled and well-connected members of the lobbying community can hope to influence presidential decisions. When running for president, Barack Obama laid down a bold promise to "free the executive branch from special interest influence." No political appointee, the Obama team promised, "will be permitted to work on regulations or contracts directly and substantially related to their prior employer for two years." That promise proved exceedingly difficult to adhere to. Many on the Obama transition team, including Obama's nominee for the position of Health and Human Services Secretary, ex-Senate majority leader Thomas Daschle, had close ties to lobbyist or had worked for lobbying firms.[18] Daschle later withdrew his name when it appeared he had not fully paid his income taxes.

---

[17] "Cash Flow: Congress Changes Hands—or Does It?" *Washington Post*, January 7, 2007, p. B2.

[18] David Kirkpatrick, "In Daschle's Tax Woes, A Peek Into Washington," *New York Times*, February 2, 2009, p. A1.

Lobbying the Executive Branch.   Even when an interest group is very success-ful at getting its bill passed by Congress and signed by the president, the prospect of full and faithful implementation of that law is not guaranteed. Often, a group and its allies do not pack up and go home as soon as the president turns their lob-bied-for new law over to the appropriate agency. On average, 40 percent of interest-group representatives regularly contact both legislative and executive branch orga-nizations, whereas 13 percent contact only the legislature and 16 percent only the executive branch.[19]

In some respects, interest-group access to the executive branch is promoted by federal law. The Administrative Procedure Act, first enacted in 1946 and frequently amended in subsequent years, requires most federal agencies to provide notice and an opportunity for comment before implementing proposed new rules and regula-tions. So-called notice and comment rule-making is designed to allow interests an opportunity to make their views known and to participate in the implementation of federal legislation that affects them. In 1990, Congress enacted the Negotiated Rulemaking Act to encourage administrative agencies to engage in direct and open negotiations with affected interests when developing new regulations. These two pieces of legislation—which have been strongly enforced by the federal courts—have played an important role in opening the bureaucratic process to interest-group influence. Today, few federal agencies would consider attempting to implement a new rule without consulting affected interests.[20]

Cultivating Access.   Exerting influence on Congress or government agencies by providing their members with information about issues, support, and even threats of retaliation requires easy and constant access to decision makers. One interesting example of why groups need to cultivate and maintain access is provided by dairy farmers. Until the 1960s, dairy farmers were part of the powerful coalition of ag-ricultural interests that had full access to Congress and the Department of Agri-culture. During the 1960s, a series of disputes over commodities prices broke out between the dairy farmers and the producers of corn, grain, and other agricultural commodities. Dairy farmers, whose cows consume grain, prefer low commodi-ties prices, whereas grain producers obviously prefer high prices. The commodities producers won the battle, and Congress raised commodities prices, in part at the expense of the dairy farmers. In the 1970s, the dairy farmers left the agriculture coalition, set up their own lobby and political action groups, and became heavily involved in public relations campaigns and both congressional and presidential elections. Thus the dairy farmers lost their traditional access and had to pursue an "outsider" strategy. Indeed, the political fortunes of the dairy operations were badly hurt when they were accused of making illegal contributions to President Richard Nixon's reelection campaign in 1972.

---

[19] John P. Heinz et al., *The Hollow Core: Private Interests in National Policy Making* (Cambridge, Mass.: Harvard University Press, 1993).

[20] For an excellent discussion of the political origins of the Administrative Procedure Act, see Martin Shapiro, "APA: Past, Present, Future," 72 *Virginia Law Review* 377 (March 1986): 447–92.

Cultivating access usually requires considerable time and effort, and a successful long-term strategy for gaining access may entail the sacrifice of short-run influence. For example, many of the most important organized interests in agriculture devote far more time and resources to cultivating the staff and trustees of state agriculture schools and county agents back home than to buttonholing members of Congress or bureaucrats in Washington.

Regulations on Lobbying. As a result of the constant access to important decision makers that lobbyists seek out and require, stricter guidelines regulating the actions of lobbyists have been adopted recently. For example, as of 1993, businesses may no longer deduct from their taxes the cost of lobbying. Trade associations must report to members the proportion of their dues that goes to lobbying, and that proportion may not be reported as a business expense. The most important attempt to limit the influence of lobbyists was the 1995 Lobbying Disclosure Act, which significantly broadened the definition of people and organizations that must register as lobbyists. According to the filings under this act, almost 11,500 lobbyists were working the halls of Congress in 2006.

In 1996, Congress passed legislation limiting gifts from a single source to $50 and no more than $100 annually. It also banned the practice of honoraria, which special interests had used to supplement congressional salaries. But Congress did not limit the travel of representatives, senators, their spouses, or congressional staff members. Interest groups can pay for congressional travel as long as a trip is related to legislative business and is disclosed on congressional reports within thirty days. On these trips, meals and entertainment expenses are not limited to $50 per event and $100 annually. The rules of Congress allow its members to travel on corporate jets as long as they pay an amount equal to first-class airfare.

In 2007, congressional Democrats secured the enactment of a package of ethics rules designed to fulfill their 2006 campaign promise to bring an end to lobbying abuses. The new rules prohibited lobbyists from paying for most meals, trips, parties, and gifts for members of Congress. Lobbyists were also required to disclose the amounts and sources of small campaign contributions they collected from clients and "bundled" into large contributions. And interest groups were required to disclose the funds they used to rally voters to support or oppose legislative proposals. As soon as these new rules were enacted, lobbyists and politicians hurried to find ways to cirumvent them, and it remains to be seen whether these reforms will have any major impact.

Using the Courts

Interest groups sometimes turn to the courts to augment other avenues of access. A group can use the courts to affect public policy in at least three ways: (1) by bringing suit directly on behalf of the group itself, (2) by financing suits brought by individuals, or (3) by filing a companion brief as *amicus curiae* (literally "friend of the court") to an existing court case.

Among the most significant modern illustrations of the use of the courts as a strategy for political influence are those that accompanied the "sexual revolution" of the 1960s and the emergence of the movement for women's rights. Beginning in the mid-sixties, a series of cases was brought into the federal courts in an effort to force definition of a right to privacy in sexual matters. The case began with a challenge to state restrictions on obtaining contraceptives for nonmedical purposes, a challenge that was effectively made in *Griswold v. Connecticut*, where the Supreme Court held that states could neither prohibit the dissemination of information about nor prohibit the actual use of contraceptives by married couples. That case was soon followed by *Eisenstadt v. Baird*, in which the Court held that the states could not prohibit the use of contraceptives by single persons any more than they could prohibit their use by married couples. One year later, the Court held, in the 1973 case of *Roe v. Wade*, that states could not impose an absolute ban on voluntary abortions. Each of these cases, as well as others, was part of the Court's enunciation of a constitutional doctrine of privacy.[21]

The 1973 abortion case sparked a controversy that brought conservatives to the fore on a national level. These conservative groups made extensive use of the courts to whittle away the scope of the privacy doctrine. They obtained rulings, for example, that prohibit the use of federal funds to pay for voluntary abortions. And in 1989, right-to-life groups used a strategy of litigation that significantly undermined the *Roe v. Wade* decision in the case of *Webster v. Reproductive Health Services* (see Chapter 4), which restored the right of states to place restrictions on abortion.[22]

Another extremely significant set of contemporary illustrations of the use of the courts as a strategy for political influence is found in the history of the NAACP. The most important of these court cases was, of course, *Brown v. Board of Education of Topeka*, in which the U.S. Supreme Court held that legal segregation of the schools was unconstitutional.[23]

Business groups are also frequent users of the courts because of the number of government programs applied to them. Litigation involving large businesses is most mountainous in such areas as taxation, antitrust cases, interstate transportation, patents, and product quality and standardization. Major corporations and their trade associations pay tremendous fees each year to the most prestigious Washington law firms. Some of this money is expended in gaining access. A great proportion of it, however, is used to keep the best and most experienced lawyers prepared to represent the corporations in court or before administrative agencies when necessary.

The forces of the new politics movement made significant use of the courts during the 1970s and 1980s, and judicial decisions were instrumental in advancing their goals. Facilitated by changes in the rules governing access to the courts (these rules of standing were discussed in Chapter 8), the new politics agenda was clearly visible in court decisions handed down in several key policy areas. In the environmental policy area, new politics groups were able to force federal agencies to pay attention to environmental issues, even when the agency was not directly involved in activities related to environmental quality. By the 2000s, the courts often were the

---

[21] *Griswold v. Connecticut,* 381 U.S. 479 (1965); *Eisenstadt v. Baird,* 405 U.S. 438 (1972); *Roe v. Wade,* 410 U.S. 133 (1973).

[22] *Webster v. Reproductive Health Services,* 109 S. Ct. 3040 (1989).

[23] *Brown v. Board of Education of Topeka,* 347 U.S. 483 (1954).

battleground on which those in the new political movements waged their fights. Perhaps the most dramatic cases were a string of lawsuits spanning twenty years (from 1986 to 2006) in which antiabortion protest organizations, such as Pro-Life Action Network and Operation Rescue, and the National Organization of Women repeatedly took each other to court to establish the rules governing clinic protests. Ultimately, the U.S. Supreme Court sided with the antiabortion organizations, but not before deciding three separate cases on the matter, at extremely high cost to both sides.[24]

Mobilizing Public Opinion

Organizations try to bring pressure to bear on politicians through a variety of methods designed to mobilize public opinion. This strategy is known as **going public**. When groups go public, they use their various resources to try to persuade large numbers of people to pay attention to their concerns. They hope that greater visibility and public support will help underline the importance of such issues to those in power. Advertising campaigns, protests, and grassroots lobbying efforts are all examples of going public. An increased use of this kind of strategy is traced to the rise of modern advertising at the beginning of the twentieth century. As early as the 1930s, political analysts distinguished between the "old lobby" of direct group representatives attempting to influence Congress and the "new lobby" of public-relations professionals addressing the public at large in order to reach Congress indirectly.[25] Going public differs from other strategies that interest groups use to influence public policy. The "new lobby" techniques are designed to change the way people think, rather than just changing the actions of insiders.

One way that groups often go public is conventional advertising. For example, a casual scan of major newspapers, magazines, and Web sites will immediately reveal numerous examples of expensive, well-designed ads by major companies and industry associations, such as those from the oil and gas, automobile, and health and pharmaceutical industries. Such ads are often intended to show what the firms do for the country, not merely the products they develop. Their purpose is to create and maintain a strongly positive association between the organization and the community at large in the hope that the organization can draw on the community's favorable feelings as needed in specific political controversies later.

Sometimes groups advertise expressly to shift public opinion on a question. One of the most famous such advertising campaigns was run by the Health Insurance Association of America in 1993 and 1994 in opposition to President Bill Clinton's proposed national health insurance plan. These ads featured a couple—Harry and Louise (played by the actors Harry Johnson and Louise Caire Clark)—sitting at their kitchen table disparaging the excessive red tape and bureaucratic

---

[24] *Scheidler v. National Organization for Women et al.*, 547 U.S. 9 (2006).

[25] Pendleton Herring, *Group Representation before Congress* (1928; repr.: New York: Russell & Russell, 1967). See also Kenneth W. Kollman, *Outside Lobbying: Public Opinion and Interest Group Strategies* (Princeton, N.J.: Princeton University Press, 1998).

problems that they would face under Clinton's plan. The Harry and Louise ads are widely credited with turning public opinion against Clinton's plan, which never even got off the ground in Congress.

A second strategy that groups use to bring public pressure to bear on a problem is **grassroots lobbying**. Grassroots lobbying entails many of the same organizing methods one sees in political campaigns—developing lists of supporters and having those supporters voice their concern with an issue and recruit others to do so. It is common today to send direct mail that includes a draft letter that recipients can adapt and then send to their representatives in Congress, or to send e-mails urging people to contact their member of Congress regarding a particular bill or controversy. A grassroots campaign can cost anywhere from $40,000 to sway the votes of one or two crucial members of a committee or subcommittee to millions of dollars to mount a national effort aimed at Congress as a whole. Such grassroots campaigns are often organized around controversial, prominent appointments, especially to fill vacancies on the U.S. Supreme Court.

> **grassroots lobbying** A lobbying campaign in which a group mobilizes its membership to contact government officials in support of the group's position.

Grassroots lobbying has become more prevalent in Washington over the last couple of decades because the adoption of congressional rules limiting gifts to members has made traditional lobbying more difficult. This circumstance makes all the more compelling the question of whether grassroots campaigning has reached an intolerable extreme. One case in particular may have tipped it over the edge: in 1992, ten giant companies in the financial services, manufacturing, and high-tech industries began a grassroots campaign and spent millions of dollars over the next three years to influence a decision in Congress to limit the ability of investors to sue for fraud. Retaining an expensive consulting firm, these corporations paid for the use of specialized computer software to persuade Congress that there was "an outpouring of popular support for the proposal." Thousands of letters from individuals flooded Capitol Hill. Many of those letters were written and sent by people who sincerely believed that investor lawsuits are often frivolous and should be curtailed. But much of the mail was phony, generated by the Washington-based campaign consultants; the letters came from people who had no strong feelings or even no opinion at all about the issue. More and more people, including leading members of Congress, are becoming quite skeptical of such methods, charging that these are not genuine grassroots campaigns but instead represent "Astroturf lobbying" (a play on the name of an artificial grass used on many sports fields). Such "Astroturf" campaigns have increased in frequency in recent years as members of Congress grow more skeptical of Washington lobbyists and far more concerned about demonstrations of support for a particular issue by their constituents. But after the firms mentioned above spent millions of dollars and generated thousands of letters to members of Congress, they came to the somber conclusion that "it's more effective to have 100 letters from your district where constituents took the time to write and understand the issue," because "Congress is sophisticated enough to know the difference."[26]

---

[26] Jane Fritsch, "The Grass Roots, Just a Free Phone Call Away," *New York Times*, June 23, 1995, pp. A1, A22.

Finally, groups often organize protests as a means of bringing attention to an issue or pressure on the government. Protests, in fact, are the oldest means of going public. Those who lack other resources, such as money, contacts, and expertise, can always resort to protest as a means of making their concerns public. Indeed, the right to assembly is protected in the First Amendment to the Constitution.

Protests may have many different consequences, depending on how they are managed. One basic consequence of a well-run protest is that it attracts attention. Organized protests also create a sense of community and common interest among those involved and raises the consciousness of people outside the protest. Finally, protests often attempt to impose costs on others by disrupting traffic or commerce, thereby forcing people to strike a bargain with protestors.

Using Electoral Politics

In addition to attempting to influence members of Congress and other government officials, interest groups also seek to use the electoral process to elect the right legislators in the first place and to ensure that those who are elected will owe them a debt of gratitude for their support. To put matters into perspective, groups invest far more resources in lobbying than in electoral politics. Nevertheless, financial support and campaign activism can be important tools for organized interests.

Political Action Committees.   By far the most common electoral strategy that interest groups employ is that of giving financial support to the parties or to particular candidates. But such support can easily cross the threshold into outright bribery. Therefore, Congress has occasionally made an effort to regulate this strategy. One effort was the Federal Election Campaign Act of 1971 (amended in 1974), which we discussed in Chapter 10. This act limits campaign contributions and requires that each candidate or campaign committee itemize the full name and address, occupation, and principal business of each donor who contributes more than $100. These provisions have been effective up to a point, considering the rather large number of embarrassments, indictments, resignations, and criminal convictions in the aftermath of the Watergate scandal.

The Watergate scandal itself was triggered by the illegal entry of Republican workers into the office of the Democratic National Committee in the Watergate apartment building. But an investigation quickly revealed numerous violations of campaign finance laws, involving millions of dollars in unregistered cash from corporate executives to President Nixon's reelection committee. Many of these violations were discovered by the famous Ervin committee, whose official name was the Senate Select Committee to Investigate the 1972 Presidential Campaign Activities.

Reaction to Watergate produced further legislation on campaign finance in 1974 and 1976, but the effect has been to restrict individual rather than interest group campaign activity. Individuals may now contribute no more than $2,300 to any candidate for federal office in any primary or general election. A **political action committee (PAC)**, however, can contribute $5,000, provided it contributes to at least five different federal candidates each year. Beyond this, the laws permit

political action committee (PAC)
A private group that raises and distributes funds for use in election campaigns.

IN BRIEF

Interest Group Strategies

Lobbying

Influencing the passage or defeat of legislation.

Access

Development of close ties to decision makers on Capitol Hill and bureaucratic agencies.

Litigation

Taking action through the courts, usually in one of three ways:

Filing suit against a specific government agency or program.

Financing suits brought against the government by individuals.

Filing companion briefs as *amicus curiae* (friend of the court) to existing court cases.

Going Public

Especially via advertising; also through boycotts, strikes, rallies, marches, and sit-ins, generating positive news coverage.

Electoral Politics

Giving financial support to a particular party or candidate.

Congress passed the Federal Election Campaign Act of 1971 to try to regulate this practice by limiting the amount of funding interest groups can contribute to campaigns.

corporations, unions, and other interest groups to form PACs and to pay the costs of soliciting funds from private citizens for those PACs.

Electoral spending by interest groups has increased steadily despite the campaign finance reforms that followed the Watergate scandal. Total PAC contributions continue to rise, increasing from nearly $260 million in 2000 to just under $413 million in 2008. Interest groups also pursue their electoral strategies by spending money on advertising, get-out-the-vote efforts, and other forms of direct campaigning in support of or against candidates. Such spending—called independent expenditure because it is done independently of the candidates' campaigns—totaled just $21 million in 2000, but rose to $135 million in 2008. Interest groups also give to political parties, especially through nonfederal (mainly state) committees. Such "soft money" donations were restricted after 2004, but still totaled almost $22 million in 2008.

Interest groups focus their direct contributions on Congress, especially the House. Because of the enormous cost of running modern political campaigns (see Chapter 11), most politicians are eager to receive PAC contributions. A typical U.S. House incumbent receives half of his or her campaign funds from interest groups. There is little evidence that interest groups buy roll-call votes or other favors from members of Congress with their donations. Group donations do, however, help to keep those who are sympathetic to groups' interests and views in office.[27] (See "Analyzing the Evidence" on page 376.)

The potential influence of interest group campaign donations and expenditures over the legislature has prompted frequent calls from reformers to abolish PACs or limit their activities. The challenge is how to regulate the participation of groups without violating their members' rights to free speech and free association. In 1976, the U.S. Supreme Court weighed in on this matter in the case *Buckley v. Valeo*, which questioned the constitutionality of the 1974 Federal Elections Campaign Act.[28] In its decision to let the act stand, the majority on the Court ruled that donors' rights of expression were at stake, but that these rights had to be weighed against the government's interest in limiting corruption, or the perception of corruption. The Court has repeatedly up held the key tenets of its decision: (1) that money is a form of speech; but (2) that speech rights must be weighed against concerns about corruption. Most recently the Court upheld the Bipartisan Campaign Reform Act's (BCRA) restrictions on donations to nonfederal (for example, state party) accounts as a necessary reform to limit corruption. Continued growth of PAC contributions since the passage of BCRA in 2002 has raised continued concerns about the campaign finance laws in the United States and their ability to limit interest-group influence. The challenge for future reform efforts is to find the balance between the speech rights of interest groups and the fight to limit corruption. It is especially hard to get the right balance because those who write the regulations, incumbent members of Congress, have a profound stake in the current campaign finance system. For a fuller discussion of the rules governing campaign finance, see Chapter 10.

Campaign Activism. Financial support is not the only way in which organized groups seek influence through the electoral process. Sometimes activism can be even more important than campaign contributions.

Perhaps the most notable instance of such activism occurs on behalf of the Democratic Party and candidates through unions. Labor unions regularly engage in massive get-out-the-vote drives during political campaigns. The largest such activities are those of the Service Employees International Union (SEIU), which represents works ranging from hotel and restaurant workers to clerical staff, and the United Auto Workers (UAW). SEIU, for instance, spent in excess of $30 million to support Barack Obama. Other sorts of groups routinely line up behind the Democratic and Republican campaigns. The National Right to Life Committee, for example, spent $26 million on behalf of John McCain's presidential bid. Moveon.org reported that it spent in excess of $7 million on direct campaigning in the 2008 presidential race.

The cumulative effect of such independent campaign activism is difficult to judge. One important research initiative within political science seeks to measure systematically the marginal effectiveness of campaign contact. Professors Alan Gerber and Donald Green have developed a program of field experiments in which

---

[27] See Stephen Ansolabehere, John M. de Figueiredo, and James M. Snyder, Jr., "Why Is There So Little Money in U.S. Politics?" *Journal of Economic Perspectives* 17, no. 1 (2003): 105–30.

[28] *Buckley v. Valeo*, 424 U.S. 1 (1976).

campaigns agree to assign direct campaign activity randomly to some neighborhoods but not others. They have been able to measure the marginal effect of an additional piece of mail, a direct canvasser, or a phone call. In a typical election context, it costs about $40 to get an additional voter to the polls. Professors Gerber and Green further find that campaign activism can have an initially large impact, but after six or so attempted contacts, the effects diminish dramatically. This important empirical research has given campaigns and reformers some sense of the effectiveness of campaign activism in stimulating turnout and possibly influencing elections. Especially in low-turnout elections, such as those for city councils or state legislatures, interest-group get-out-the-vote activities can have very large effects on who wins. But as other money enters the scene, especially candidates' own campaign expenditures, the effects of interest groups' direct campaign activities becomes muted.[29]

The Initiative.   Another political tactic that interest groups sometimes use is sponsorship of ballot initiatives at the state level. The initiative, a device adopted by a number of states around 1900, allows laws proposed by citizens to be placed on the general election ballot and submitted directly to the state's voters. This procedure bypasses the state legislature and governor. The initiative was originally promoted by late-nineteenth-century Populists as a mechanism that would allow the people to govern directly. Populists saw the initiative as an antidote to interest-group influence in the legislative process.

Ironically, many studies have suggested that most initiative campaigns today are actually sponsored by interest groups seeking to circumvent legislative opposition to their goals. In recent years, for example, initiative campaigns have been sponsored by the insurance industry, trial lawyers' associations, and tobacco companies.[30] The role of interest groups in initiative campaigns should come as no surprise, because such campaigns can cost millions of dollars.

ARE INTEREST GROUPS EFFECTIVE?

Do interest groups have an impact on government and policy? The short answer is yes. One of the best academic studies of the impact of lobbying was conducted in 2001 by John M. de Figueiredo of MIT and Brian Silverman of the University of Toronto.[31] Figueiredo and Silverman focused on a particular form of lobbying: efforts by lobbyists for colleges and universities to obtain "earmarks," special, often disguised, congressional appropriations for their institutions. Millions of dollars in earmarks are written into law every year.

---

[29] Donald Green and Alan Gerber, *Get Out the Vote: How to Increase Voter Turnout*, 2nd ed. (Washington, D.C.: Brookings Institution Press, 2008).

[30] Elisabeth R. Gerber, *The Populist Paradox* (Princeton, N.J.: Princeton University Press, 1999).

[31] John M. P. de Figueiredo and Brian S. Silverman, "Academic Earmarks and the Returns to Lobbying" (May 2002), Harvard Law and Economics Discussion Paper no. 370; MIT Sloan Working Paper no. 4245-02.

Interest Groups and Representation

Americans have long been suspicious of organized interests and the possibly deleterious effects of campaign contributions. Political action committees (PACs) donate large amounts of money to members of Congress for their reelection campaigns. In turn, many observers worry that members may pay closer attention to the desires of the special interest groups than to their constituents.

One can get a sense of the magnitude of PAC contributions from this table. Each row shows the contribution by an industry to members of the committee that has jurisdiction over policies that most concern the industry, as well as contributions to members who are not on the committee. Notice that while the contributions to all members are quite sizable, industries tend to direct most of their money to committee members who are most involved with issues that are important to the industry. Assuming PACs are not making these contributions out of a purely charitable instinct, one can surmise that they expect something in return for their money.

INDUSTRY CONTRIBUTIONS TO HOUSE COMMITTEE MEMBERS, 2008 ELECTION CYCLE

Committee & Industry	Average Amount to Committee Members ($)	Average Amount to Noncommittee Members ($)	Ratio
Agricultural Committee, Agricultural Services and Products	$37,955	$5,877	6.5
Armed Services Committee, Defense Aerospace	$28,289	$11,216	2.5
Education and Labor Committee, Education	$19,523	$11,415	1.7
Energy and Commerce Committee, Health Professionals	$104,616	$56,578	1.8
Financial Services Committee, Commercial Banks	$49,843	$18,387	2.7
Natural Resources Committee, Oil and Gas	$31,098	$18,198	1.7

Source: Center for Responsive Politics, www.opensecrets.org (accessed 5/12/09).

The framers were attuned to the potential problems of factions and special interests. In *Federalist 10* Madison proposed the "extended sphere" of a large and diverse republic as an institutional solution. In a diverse republic, Madison argued, any single faction acting alone would have little influence as competition between the many various groups would prevent any one group from dominating. In addition, in a large republic, representation would "refine and enlarge" public opinion because these opinions pass through a select body.[1] Madison, however, did not foresee our current system of campaign finance. Is there any evidence that this institutional solution works in modern times?

Madison's prescience, perhaps, can be seen in recent research by Kevin Esterling.[2] Esterling shows that PACs tend to direct their contributions to members who have high "analytical capacity," or those members who are attentive to research and analysis in their work in committees. Esterling limited his study to committees with jurisdiction over health policies. We saw in the previous table that health interest groups tend to direct their contributions to these members, and this figure shows they contribute most heavily to members with high analytical capacity (see the red curve in the graph), or the ones who are most likely to "refine and enlarge" public opinion. In addition, these same members tend to attract more contributions from groups that are not health-related (see the blue curve), suggesting that members with high analytical capacity are pressured by groups with diverse interests, exactly as envisioned in Madison's "extended sphere."

While it may be that the groups intend to advance their special interests, the overall pattern of contributions seems to reward legislators who try to inform legislation with research and analysis.

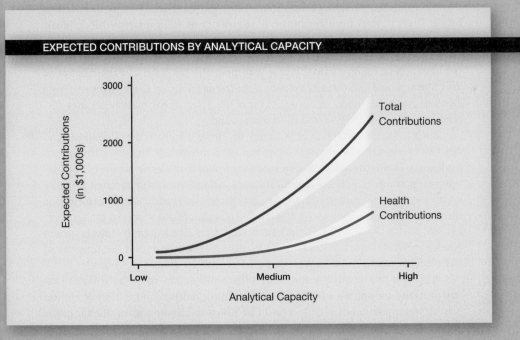

EXPECTED CONTRIBUTIONS BY ANALYTICAL CAPACITY

[1]James Madison, *Federalist* 10, in the *Federalist Papers*, Clinton Rossiter, ed. (New York: Peguin, 1961), pp. 82–83.
[2]Kevin M. Esterling, "Buying Expertise: Campaign Contributions and Attention to Policy Analysis in Congressional Committees," *American Political Science Review* 101 (February 2007): 93–109.

The authors discovered that lobbying had an impact. The more money schools spent on lobbying activities, the larger the total quantity of earmarked funds they received. The extent of lobbying's impact, however, varied with institutional factors. Schools whose state's senator served on the Senate Appropriations Committee received $18 to $29 in earmarks for every dollar spent on lobbying. Schools located in congressional districts whose representative served on the House Appropriations Committee received between $49 and $55 for every dollar spent on lobbying. Schools lacking such representation, however, averaged only about $1.09 for every dollar spent on lobbying—hardly worth the effort.

These results suggest that, as is so often the case, institutions and politics are profoundly related. Schools without access to members of Congress in a position to help them cannot gain much from lobbying. Schools with such access still need to lobby to take advantage of the potential that representation on the Senate and House Appropriations committees can give them. But if they do so, the potential return from lobbying is substantial.

Do Interest Groups Foster or Impede Democracy?

The institutions of American government embrace an open and democratic process in order to ensure that government is responsive to the public's preferences and needs to the society. The Bill of Rights provides for free speech, freedom of the press, and freedom of assembly. The laws of the land have only further cemented this commitment, providing for open meetings, citizen advisory commissions, lobbying, direct contact from constituents, contributions from interested individuals and groups, an open legal system, protests, and many other routes through which individuals and groups may advocate for their interests. Through these many points of access, representatives and government officials learn how their decisions affect groups and individuals. Politics is the arena in which these many interests compete for the attention and imprimatur of the government; sometimes they succeed in coming together to find common ground.

Such a system creates an opportunity for those who have the willingness and capacity to use their resources to represent their interests before the government. Problems of collective action and free riding prevent many latent interests from developing permanent political organizations capable of bringing concerted pressure on the government. Businesses, unions, and professional and industry associations usually have less trouble overcoming the obstacles to organization and group maintenance that many volunteer associations may face. Consequently, interest-group politics in Washington, D.C. and state legislatures tends to reflect the interests of and conflicts among those engaged in economic activity around the country.

Although firms, unions, and other organizations can solve the collective action problem, they do not necessarily succeed in the political arena. They often find politics unfamiliar, even hostile, terrain in which to pursue organizational goals. Unlike economic activity, politics involves power derived from the ability to vote on measures, to introduce legislation or rules, or to block actions from happening. Interest groups are necessarily outsiders and can do none of these things directly. Nonetheless, these organizations find that they can make gains by seeking out the appropriate institutions in which to find support, such as a court with a sympathetic judge or a subcommittee of Congress whose chairperson holds similar views to those of the group. And the way to success is usually quite subtle. Typically, groups succeed not by bringing pressure but by providing expertise to the government and by learning from those in office about the impact of new rules and regulations.

Increasingly over the past thirty to forty years, interest groups have found that the best route to power is through public action and public opinion. It is not enough for a group to hire a lobbyist to advocate on its behalf. Real pressure can be brought on politicians by shaping what other individuals think. Through advertising, protests, and grassroots networks, interest groups have increasingly brought their issues to the attention of the public and through public pressure have been able to influence politics. These new means of shaping public policy and government decision making are increasingly remote from traditional politics. Likewise, it is becoming increasingly difficult for an organization to trace its influence in the political arena. Tens of thousands of organizations compete in the political sphere, alternately pursuing insider and outsider strategies, with each group claiming credit for favorable policies and ducking blame for failures.

Interest group politics at the beginning of the twenty-first century do not neatly fit stereotypical notions. There are certainly as many lobbyists as ever, but the backroom dealings of the "old lobby" are an anachronism. Interest-group politics is diffuse, spread across all branches of government and involving many different interests vying for the attention of politicians in an increasingly crowded and active interest-group ecology. Those who are organized gain advantages from pooling resources, but an interest group's political action today is only one aspect of the debate over any given political issue or decision. Other interests and voices making competing claims may very well cancel out a given organization's efforts. And the activities of all groups amount to just one facet of legislators', judges', and executives' deliberations. Those who must ultimately make political decisions and be held accountable for those decisions weigh other voices as well, especially the opinions and preferences of their constituents. Perhaps a better contemporary characterization is that the organized and disorganized interests participating in politics today are really contributing to a much broader sphere of political discourse and debate. That debate takes place inside the institutions of government—Congress, courts, executives, and elections. It also takes place in another arena, the media. That forum is the final part of our discussion of democracy in America, and to that subject we now turn.

CHAPTER REVIEW

Efforts by organized groups to influence government and policy are an important part of American politics. The expansion of government over the past several decades has fueled an expansion of interest-group activity. In recent years upper-middle-class Americans have organized public interest groups to vie with more specialized interests. All groups use a number of strategies to gain power.

Lobbying is the act of petitioning legislators. Lobbyists—individuals who receive some form of compensation for lobbying—are required to register in the House and the Senate. In addition to pursuing their group's goals, they serve a useful function, providing members of Congress with a vital flow of information.

Access is participation in government. Groups with access have less need for lobbying. Most groups build up access through great effort. They work for years to get their members into positions of influence on congressional committees.

Litigation in the courts sometimes serves interest groups when other strategies fail. Groups may bring suit on their own behalf, finance suits brought by individuals, or file *amicus curiae* briefs.

Going public is an effort to mobilize the widest and most favorable climate of opinion. Advertising is a common technique in this strategy.

Groups engage in electoral politics either by embracing one of the major parties, usually through financial support, or through a nonpartisan strategy. Interest groups' campaign contributions now seem to be flowing into the coffers of candidates at a faster rate than ever before.

FOR FURTHER READING

Ainsworth, Scott. *Analyzing Interest Groups*. New York: Norton, 2002.

Alexander, Robert, ed. *The Classics of Interest Group Behavior*. New York: Wadsworth, 2005.

Ansolabehere, Stephen, John M. de Figuereido, and James M. Snyder, Jr. "Why Is There So Little Money in U.S. Politics?" *Journal of Economic Perspectives* 17, no. 1 (2003): 105–30.

Birnbaum, Jeffrey H. *The Money Men*. New York: Crown, 2000.

Cigler, Allan J., and Burdett A. Loomis, eds. *Interest Group Politics*. 7th ed. Washington, D.C.: Congressional Quarterly Press, 2006.

Esterling, Kevin. *The Political Economy of Expertise*. Ann Arbor: University of Michigan Press, 2004.

reader selection ○ Kollman, Kenneth W. *Outside Lobbying: Public Opinion and Interest Group Strategies*. Princeton, N.J.: Princeton University Press, 1998.

reader selection ○ Moe, Terry M. *The Organization of Interests: Incentives and the Internal Dynamics of Political Interest Groups*. Chicago: University of Chicago Press, 1980.

Nownes, Anthony. *Total Lobbying: What Lobbyists Want and How They Try to Get It*. New York: Cambridge University Press, 2006.

Olson, Mancur, Jr. *The Logic of Collective Action: Public Goods and the Theory of Groups*. 1965. Reprinted with new preface and appendix. Cambridge, Mass.: Harvard University Press, 1965.

Rosenthal, Alan. *The Third House: Lobbyists and Lobbying in the States*. Washington, D.C.: Congressional Quarterly Press, 2001.

Rozell, Mark, Clyde Wilcox, and David Madland. *Interest Groups in American Campaigns*. Washington, D.C.: Congressional Quarterly Press, 2005.

Analyzing the 2010 Midterm Elections

The 2010 elections shifted the balance of power in American government. Approaching the congressional election of November 2010, the Democratic Party enjoyed solid majorities in the U.S. Senate and House of Representatives. In 2010, the Democrats held 59 of 100 Senate seats, including the seats of two independent senators who aligned with the Democratic caucus. In the House, the Democrats, with 257 of 435 seats, held 59 percent as well. But after four years of Democratic control in the House and Senate, the 2010 midterm elections gave Republicans a solid majority in the House and increased their numbers in the Senate. With the House of Representatives now controlled by Republicans, Representative John Boehner (R-OH), the Republican leader, ascended to the position of Speaker of the House, replacing two-term speaker Nancy Pelosi (D-CA). In analyzing what happened in the 2010 elections, why it happened, and what the consequences may be, we observe many of the concepts and principles from Part 3 in action.

WHAT HAPPENED?

Our analysis of the 2010 elections begins with a simple accounting of where Democrats lost races for the House and Senate. Understanding this basic data will take us a long way toward understanding the outcomes of the 2010 elections. We will look first at the races for the Senate and then at the races for the House.

The Senate

In 2010, 37 U.S. Senate races took place. Elections for full six-year terms were held for 34 seats, and 3 other seats had special elections to fill out the remainder of existing six-year terms. New York and Delaware held special elections to complete the terms vacated by Hillary Clinton and Joe Biden, who left the Senate for the positions of secretary of state and vice president, respectively. West Virginia held a special election to fill the remainder of the term of the late senator Robert Byrd, who died in office.

Electoral contests can be divided into open-seat races and non-open-seat races. A Senate seat becomes open when senators retire, leave the Senate for other offices, or lose primary battles. Republican pick-ups in 2010 came both from open-seat elections and from victories over Democratic incumbents.

There were an unusually large number of open Senate seats in 2010. Six Republicans and 6 Democrats retired. In addition, Republican senators Robert Bennett of Utah and Lisa Murkowski of Alaska and Democratic senator Arlen Specter lost their nomination contests. As a result, 12 Democratic incumbents and 10 Republican incumbents stood for reelection. Not a single incumbent Republican senator lost in the general elections. In one of the wildest races of the year, incumbent senator Lisa Murkowski of Alaska lost the Republican primary to a challenger but staged a major comeback in the general election. She mounted a write-in campaign and won more votes than Republican-nominee Joe Miller, the Tea Party favorite who had beaten her in the primary, and Democrat Scott McAdams. Two Democratic incumbents lost. In conservative Arkansas, Senator Blanche Lincoln, first

▲ *Surveys showed Senate majority leader Harry Reid lagging among voters in the days before the November 2010 election, but when the votes were tallied, he held onto his seat. Despite losing several seats in the Senate to Republicans, Democrats held onto a majority.*

elected in 1998, lost to Republican challenger Representative John Boozman, who left his seat in the House to run against Lincoln. In Wisconsin, Democrat Russ Feingold lost to businessman Ron Johnson.

Republicans' biggest gains, though, came in the open Senate seats. The GOP picked up 4 of 7 seats left open by retiring Democrats. These party changes took place in Illinois, Indiana, North Dakota, and Pennsylvania. Of these, the Pennsylvania contest was most unusual, as the seat was previously held by Arlen Specter, who was last elected as a Republican in 2004, then defected to the Democratic Party in 2009, only to lose a primary battle against Representative Joe Sestak. Though Pennsylvania trended Democratic in the last election cycles, voters opted for former congressman Pat Toomey, a Republican, over Sestak. In Illinois, Republican House member Mark Kirk edged by State Treasurer Alexi Giannoulias to take the Senate seat formerly held by President Barack Obama. Democrats won 3 remaining Democratic open seats—in Connecticut, Delaware, and West Virginia. Republican candidates won all 8 of the seats vacated by Republican senators. With two wins against incumbents and four wins in open seats, the Republicans won a total of 6 seats they had not previously held.

The new Senate, with 51 Democrats and 47 Republicans, also has 2 Independents, Bernie Sanders of Vermont and Joe Lieberman of Connecticut, who join the Democratic caucus when the Senate convenes. That brings the Democrats' edge to 53–47. This division is rather typical of the Senate. It is not the filibuster-proof majority that the Democrats won in 2008, nor is it the evenly split Senate that George Bush worked with. The composition of the new Senate is unusual in one important respect. In a body known for its folkways and traditions, nearly half of the 100 senators are in their first term of office. Past senators have often made headlines for their long tenures. For example, Robert Byrd of West Virginia, who died in 2010, served for 51 years. Other recent and current members, such as Strom Thurmond (SC), Daniel Inouye (HI), and Ted Kennedy (MA), served nearly as long. However, a host of retirements and defeats in 2006, 2008, and 2010 have led to a Senate with many more freshmen than is typical. Whether the large number of new members will have any direct political or policy consequences is an open question.

The new Senate remains overwhelmingly white and male. For instance, while just over 50 percent of the country is female, only 17 of the 100 senators in the 112th Congress are female, the same number as in the 111th Congress. Approximately one-quarter of U.S. citizens are nonwhite, but only 4 members of the U.S. Senate are nonwhite: Bob Menendez of New Jersey, Marco Rubio of Florida, and Daniel Inouye and Daniel Akaka, both of Hawaii.

The House

The 2010 elections produced a split Congress. Democrats held their Senate majority, but Republicans gained a majority of seats in the House of Representatives. Coming into the election, Democrats had to defend many more seats than Republicans, and more seats in hostile territory. Democrats held 67 seats in districts that John McCain won in 2008, while Republicans held 8 seats in districts that Barack Obama won. Making matters worse, Democrats did not field as many challengers as Republicans. Republicans failed to field a challenger for only 5 seats, but Democrats did not recruit a challenger in 24 races, and you can't beat somebody with nobody.

One important feature of the 2010 electoral landscape helped buoy the Democrats. Relatively few Democrats retired or were defeated in their primaries. Only 20 of 256 Democratic-held seats were open seats (no incumbent running in the general election), and Republicans had 21 open seats. Incumbents tend to win higher vote margins than nonincumbents. The incumbency advantage has hovered around 8 percentage points since 1990, and 2010 was no exception. Consider, for example, the Florida 12th and 13th congressional districts. In both districts, Republican presidential candidates won, on average, 55 percent of the vote from 2000 through 2008. In 2010, the Florida 12th Congressional District had an open-seat race, and Republican Dennis Ross won 54 percent of the two-party vote to beat Democrat Lori Edwards. In the neighboring 13th, incumbent Republican Vern Buchanan represented the Florida 13th and beat the Democratic challenger 69 percent to 31 percent. Comparing the two suggests a very large incumbency advantage. But even incumbency was not enough to help many House Democrats keep their seats, especially in a year in which economic woes produced high levels of dissatisfaction with the president and in those districts where a Democratic incumbent represented a traditionally Republican constituency.

Many of the Democratic losses in 2010 came from districts that Democrats had won from Republicans in 2006 and 2008. Arizona is a case in point. Prior to the 2006 midterm election, Republicans held 6 of the state's 8 congressional districts. From losses in 2006 and 2008, Republicans held only 3 of those 8 seats. Two of the 3 seats that the Republicans lost were regained in 2010. A similar story can be told about Ohio. In the previous two election cycles, Democrats gained 4 seats in Ohio and lost none. All 4 of these seats were returned to Republicans in 2010. Of the 30 seats that Democrats gained in 2006, only one, held by Joe Courtney of Connecticut, was considered a safe seat in 2010.[1]

The 2010 elections also bore out the continuing regional orientation of the two major political parties in the United States. In House elections, Republicans won the largest majorities in the South, where they took 61 percent of the vote. Democrats, meanwhile, had their strongest showing in the Northeast, where they won 54 percent of the vote. Other regions split more evenly, with the West voting slightly more Democratic and the Midwest voting slightly more Republican.

In addition to Democrats and Republicans representing different regions of the country, the parties represent different kinds of districts within states. In particular, Democrats tend to represent urban districts and Republicans tend to represent rural districts. All congressional districts are required to represent roughly the same number of people. Hence, the smaller the district in physical size, the more densely populated it is. Congressional districts vary greatly in size. The 15th district of New York, in New York City, is only 10 square miles, whereas the at-large district of Alaska is over 570,000 square miles. The median district is about 2,300 square miles in size. Democratic and Republican districts are very different. The 112th Congress continues the trend toward regional separation of Republican and Democratic representatives. Democrats are now even more highly concentrated in urban areas than they were after the 2008 election, and Republicans represent an even larger number of rural districts.

WHY?

We can identify two broad, macro-level reasons for the Democratic losses in 2010. First, we can see the 2010 midterm elections as a "correction" of the 2006 and 2008 elections. Democrats took a net 54 seats from the Republicans in 2006 and 2008, many of them in districts that traditionally leaned Republican. In 2006, the sitting president, George W. Bush, was unpopular; the U.S. war in Iraq was not going well; and several Republicans were involved in scandals. The 2006 election resulted in Democratic control of the House for the first time since 1994 and control of the Senate for the first time since 2002.

As Table 1 shows, from 2006 to 2008, the Democrats expanded the small majorities that they had gained in both chambers of Congress. Riding the coattails of a popular presidential candidate, Barack Obama, and in the midst of an economic crisis, the Democrats made sharp gains in 2008. In the House, the Democrats added 21 seats to their majority. In the Senate, following a contested election and recount for a seat in Minnesota (eventually won by Democrat Al Franken), the Democrats

---

[1] John F. Harris, "Rahm Emanuel's Class of 2006 in Jeopardy," *Politico*, October 14, 2010.

TABLE 1 CONGRESSIONAL ELECTION RESULTS, 1994–2010

HOUSE OF REPRESENTATIVES

Year	Turnout	Party Ratio	Seat Shift	Democrats Reelected	Republicans Reelected
1994	41.1%	204 D, 230 R	+54 R	89.3%	99.4%
1996	51.7	207 D, 227 R	+3 D	98.3	91.4
1998	38.1	211 D, 223 R	+4 D	99.5	97.2
2000	54.2	212 D, 222 R	+1 D	98.0	97.5
2002	39.5	205 D, 229 R	+8 R	97.4	97.5
2004	60.3	201 D, 232 R	+3 R	97.4	99.0
2006	40.2	233 D, 202 R	+30 D	100	89.6
2008	61.0	254 D, 173 R	+21 D	97.9	92.1
2010*	40.3	191 D, 244 R	+71R	78.8	98.7

SOURCE: Michael McDonald, United States Election Project, http://elections.gmu.edu/2010_vote_forecasts.html (accessed 11/4/2010).
*Data for 2010 are preliminary estimates.

went from a 51–49 majority to a "filibuster-proof" majority of 60 seats. This advantage in the Senate, however, was short-lived. The sixtieth vote of Al Franken came not in January 2009, when the other new legislators were sworn into office, but in July 2009, after a lengthy post-election dispute. And after the death of Senator Ted Kennedy less than two months later, the Massachusetts Democrat was replaced in January 2010 by Republican Scott Brown, thus leaving the Democrats with 59 seats for the remainder of the 111th Congress.

That the Democrats controlled an unusually high number of seats going into the 2010 elections is the first reason why they lost so many seats. In the previous two elections, Democratic candidates won seats in districts that normally did not favor Democrats. This means that many incumbent Democrats in 2010 were on the defensive in conservative districts. A useful way to characterize this is by counting the number of congressional districts that were won by Republican presidential candidates but were held by Democratic members of Congress and, vice-versa, the number won by Democratic presidential candidates and held by Republican members of Congress. Districts represented by a politician of one party but won by the presidential candidate of the opposite party may be places where the legislative incumbents are particularly vulnerable. Indeed, going into the 2010 election, 47 Democratic members represented districts that George W. Bush won in 2004 and John McCain won in 2008. Conversely, only 6 Republican members held seats that John Kerry won in 2004 and Barack Obama won in 2008.[2] Thus, Democrats were

---

[2] James E. Campbell, "The Seats in Trouble Forecast of the 2010 Elections to the U.S. House," *PS: Political Science and Politics* (2010), 43: 627-630.

TABLE 1 (CONT.) CONGRESSIONAL ELECTION RESULTS, 1994–2010

		SENATE			
Year	Turnout	Party Ratio	Seat Shift	Democrats Reelected	Republicans Reelected
1994	41.1%	47 D, 53 R	+10 R	87.5%	80.0%
1996	51.7	45 D, 55 R	—	100	85.7
1998	38.1	45 D, 55 R	—	92.3	87.5
2000	54.2	50 D, 50 R	+5 D	93.3	64.3
2002	39.5	48 D, 51 R	+1 R	83.3	93.3
2004	60.3	44 D, 55 R	+4 R	92.9	100
2006	40.2	50 D, 49 R	+6 D	100	57.1
2008	61.0	59 D, 41 R	+8 D	100	66.7
2010*	40.3	53 D, 47 R	+16 R	76.9	100

disproportionately defending seats in areas inclined toward the opposite party. The degree of Democratic vulnerability appears even larger when considering the average presidential vote in the congressional districts from 2000 through 2008. Democrats had to defend seats in nearly 70 Republican-leaning constituencies, while Republicans had fewer than 10 seats in Democrat-leaning constituencies.

A second important, macro-level explanation for losses by the Democratic Party in 2010 is that in midterm elections, the sitting president's party almost always suffers losses in Congress. With just a few notable exceptions, such as Republican gains in 2002, candidates of the president's party tend to do worse in off-year election cycles.[3] This pattern is also visible in Table 1. This regularity in American politics is often explained by the notion that voters collectively penalize the president in power, who inevitably fails to live up to promises made on the campaign trail.

Public disaffection in 2010 can be traced to many things, including a lingering war in Afghanistan, but most important was the state of the economy. Approaching the 2010 elections, the country had not yet recovered from the longest economic recession since the Great Depression. Nearly 10 percent of the workforce was unemployed at the time of the elections, and the unemployment rate had been that high for almost two years. The Democrats' control of the presidency and both chambers of Congress made them a greater target for blame in the recession.

But it wasn't just that the Democrats happened to be in office at the wrong time. In early 2009, President Obama had shepherded through Congress a massive economic stimulus package, which his chief economic advisor, Christina Romer, predicted would help reduce unemployment to 8 percent by 2010, thereby setting up an expectation that was not met. Areas particularly hard-hit by the recession and

---

[3] The 2002 election is widely thought to be unusual in this regard, coming just a year after 9/11.

related collapse of housing and other industries included Arizona, Nevada, Ohio, Indiana, and Florida. In these states Democrats had an especially hard time.

The 2010 Electorate

While at the macro-level the Republicans' 2010 electoral gains can be explained in part by the Democrats' unusual success in Republican areas in 2006 and 2008 and the usual pattern of midterm loss of the president's party, we can also look for explanations at the level of the voters themselves. First, elections are won and lost in part because of who actually shows up on Election Day and, as importantly, who abstains. In the beginning of Chapter 10, we learned that not everyone eligible to vote actually votes. The group that chooses to vote in any particular election is not static—in each election a somewhat different conglomeration of citizens decides to vote, and the differences between the composition of the electorate in each election may influence who wins and who loses.

Turnout in midterm elections is always lower than in presidential election years. Presidential elections capture the public's attention in a way that congressional and gubernatorial elections do not. Voters tend to be more animated by the presidential race than by the congressional and gubernatorial races that top the ballot in off-years. In 2010, approximately 40 percent of adults cast a ballot. This turnout rate is on par with the last midterm election, in 2006, when 40 percent of adults also voted. These midterm turnout rates contrast sharply with the rate in the 2008 presidential election, in which 61 percent of adults voted.

In comparing the electorates across election cycles, let us focus on two important demographic variables: race and age. Racial groups in American politics have different partisan tendencies: African Americans are overwhelmingly Democratic; Latinos are moderately Democratic; whites lean Republican; and Asian voters are split fairly evenly. Because of these differences, even small compositional shifts from one election to the next can affect who wins and loses. Between 2006 and 2008, the fraction of minority voters in the electorate grew by 5 percentage points. And, by 2008, whites made up 74 percent of all voters, according to exit polls. However, in 2010, that trend reversed, with whites composing 78 percent of voters (see Table 2).

We see a similar story with respect to the ages of voters. Currently in American politics, younger people are more likely than older people to vote for Democrats. According to the 2008 national exit polls, over 60 percent of voters under age 30 voted Democratic, whereas only 48 percent of voters over 50 voted for Obama. The composition of the electorate in the 2008 general election contained a higher percentage of young voters more amenable to Democratic candidates than in the 2006 or 2010 elections. In 2006, 12 percent of the voters were under 30 years old. In 2008, the proportion of voters under 30 increased to 18 percent. And in 2010, the participation of young people dropped back down, and just 11 percent of all voters were under 30.

Thus, compared to the 2006 midterm elections and the presidential contest of 2008, the 2010 midterm elections brought fewer young people and fewer minorities to the polls. Because both of these groups tend to vote Democratic, this compositional change in the electorate might have made the difference between winners

TABLE 2 2006 AND 2010 EXIT POLLS, BY DEMOGRAPHICS

	2006			2010		
	% of Group Voting		Group Size	% of Group Voting		Group Size
	D	R	% of Voters	D	R	% of Voters
Gender						
Male	50	47	49	42	56	47
Female	55	43	51	48	49	53
Race						
White	47	51	79	37	60	78
Black	89	10	10	90	9	10
Hispanic	69	30	8	64	34	8
Age						
Under 30	60	38	12	57	40	11
30–59	53	46	58	46	52	59
60+	50	48	29	38	59	29
Religion						
Protestant	44	54	55	39	60	54
Catholic	55	44	26	44	54	25
Other	71	25	6	73	25	8
None	47	22	11	66	32	12
Income						
< $50,000	60	38	40	53	44	37
$50–100,000	51	48	38	44	54	37
>$100,000	47	52	22	40	58	26

and losers in some close races. This element of campaign politics is often referred to as mobilization. With the help of campaign appeals and news media attention, people can be mobilized to vote. As we have seen, the kinds of people that are mobilized to vote can change the composition of the electorate, and thereby change the outcomes of elections.

Another factor in the 2010 elections related to the electorate is the choices made by voters who did go to the polls. Electoral swings are explained not only by who votes, but also by how those people vote. Many voters lend unwavering support to one party, regardless of circumstances. In a typical election 85 to 90 percent of Democratic and Republican identifiers remain loyal. Though some partisans do deflect from their party on occasion, the most closely watched group are Independents. Their votes are less predictable, and candidates often fight hard to win this pivotal voting bloc, just as they campaign hard to get their own supporters to the polls. In 2006 and 2008, Democrats won convincing majorities of the Independent vote in House elections, and they lost this group in 2010 (see Table 3).

TABLE 3 2006 AND 2010 EXIT POLLS, BY POLITICAL ORIENTATION

	2006			2010		
	% of Group Voting		**Group Size**	**% of Group Voting**		**Group Size**
	Dem.	**Rep.**	**% of Voters**	**Dem.**	**Rep.**	**% of Voters**
Party ID						
Democrat	93	7	38	92	7	36
Republican	8	91	36	4	95	36
Independent	57	39	26	38	56	28
Ideology						
Liberal	87	11	20	90	8	20
Moderate	60	38	47	55	42	39
Conservative	20	78	32	14	84	41

Such losses reflect the natural correction that usually occurs in midterm elections and the poor state of the economy in 2010. They also reflect the fact that the Republican Party, or more properly a faction within the Republican Party, had energized and organized many core Republican voters.

The Role of the Tea Party

In the year leading up to the 2010 midterm elections, a movement of conservative citizens, angered by Obama and the Democrats' economic and health care policies, gained force. The Tea Party, organized by both grassroots leaders and professional political elites, held its first nationwide protest on February 27, 2009.[4] By April of the following year, nearly 500,000 people had voted online for what they believed should be the key tenets of the Tea Party platform. The platform's main tenets are demands for a balanced budget, lower taxes, and less government spending. However, the platform also demands a repeal of the healthcare reform bill passed during the 111th Congress and a rejection of cap-and-trade environmental regulation.[5]

Two weeks before the elections, the *New York Times* reported that 138 candidates for the U.S. House and Senate, all running as Republicans, were identified with the Tea Party movement. Of these, more than half were running in solidly Democratic districts where they had little chance of winning the general election.

---

[4]Judson Berger, "Modern-Day Tea Parties Give Taxpayers Chance to Scream for Better Representation," *Foxnews.com,* April 9, 2009.

[5]Bernie Becker, "A Revised Contract for America, Minus 'With' and Newt," *New York Times,* April 14, 2010.

The Tea Party movement emerged in early 2009 in ▶
response to Obama and the Democrats' "bail out" of
Wall Street. Tea Party groups helped mobilize Republican voters in the 2010 elections.

But 33 House candidates and 8 Senate candidates identified with the Tea Party movement
were competitive or even dominating in their
races.[6] What kinds of Americans participated
in the Tea Party movement? What effect did
they have on the 2010 elections?

According to a September 2010 poll by
NBC News and the *Wall Street Journal*, 30 percent of Americans have a favorable view of the
Tea Party, 20 percent have a neutral view, 36
percent have a negative view, and the remainder have no view or are not sure. Among self-
identified Republicans, 71 percent were either
Tea Party supporters, had a favorable view of
the movement, and/or hoped Tea Party candidates would win.[7]

With broad support among Republican
voters, outsider, Tea Party-affiliated Republi-
can candidates were able to defeat more moderate incumbents who had the support of the Republican elites. Sitting Republican senators Lisa Murkowski of Alaska
and Robert Bennett of Utah lost primary fights against Tea Party candidates. While
Bennett retired from politics, Murkowski mounted a general election write-in candidacy against the candidate who had beaten her in the primary, and won the general election as an Independent. In Delaware, early polls showed that the endorsed
Republican candidate, Representative Mike Castle, could easily win the general
election for the seat vacated by Vice President Joe Biden. However, Castle lost the
Republican primary to Tea Party candidate Christine O'Donnell, whose policy priorities were far to the right of Delaware's general election voters. O'Donnell lost
decisively to her Democratic opponent, Chris Coons, who had seemed to stand no
chance had Representative Castle been the Republican nominee instead.

The Tea Party is a geographically disperse movement led not by a single group
but by several organizations that donate money to candidates, offer endorsements,
and organize rallies. However, several key Republican figureheads are at the center
of the movement and act as de facto leaders. Most prominently, Sarah Palin, former vice-presidential candidate and former governor of Alaska, stumped for Tea
Party Republican candidates around the country on a "Tea Party Express" bus tour.

[6]Kate Zernike, "Tea Party Set to Win Enough Races for Wide Influence," *New York Times*, October 14,
2010.

[7]Peter Wallsten and Danny Yadron, "Tea-Party Movement Gains Strength," *Wall Street Journal*, September 29, 2010.

▲ *Christine O'Donnell was one of several Tea Party-backed candidates who won primary elections by appealing to dissatisfied Republican voters, but whose positions on many issues made it difficult to win the general election.*

The other prominent figure in the movement was Fox News host Glenn Beck, who promoted Tea Party activities on his show and attended Tea Party events. Beck also held his own rally in Washington D.C. in August 2010 that drew tens of thousands of activists.

The Tea Party movement played prominently in the news stories of the 2010 elections, but in the days following the elections, it was still unclear whether the movement will have a long-term impact. Will the newly elected Tea Party-backed candidates, such as Senator Marco Rubio of Florida and Senator Mike Lee of Utah, have different policy priorities and vote differently in Congress than Republicans unaffiliated with the Tea Party? Will the Tea Party movement play a prominent role in the next election cycle, or will it fade?

Money in the 2010 General Election

Campaign spending was higher in 2010 than in any other congressional election. In January 2010, in a 5–4 decision, the U.S. Supreme Court ruled on a case called *Citizens United v. Federal Election Commission*. The ruling held that part of the 2002 campaign finance law passed by Congress was unconstitutional. In particular, under the 2002 law, known informally as the McCain-Feingold Act (see Chapter 10), corporations were forbidden to electioneer in the two months before an election. A private entity could not, for example, run a television commercial encouraging viewers to vote for or against a candidate. In 2010, in *Citizens United,* the Court found that this restriction violated the free speech clause of the First Amendment of the Constitution.

The Court ruling drew the attention of critics, including President Obama, who took the unusual step of publicly opposing the case during the 2010 State of the Union address, in the presence of the justices. The case was also mentioned in political campaign ads that criticized the role of anonymous corporate donors in the elections process.

In addition to the money candidates raise in their campaign accounts or from personal wealth, most money spent on campaigns comes from political parties and interest groups. The Democratic and Republican campaign committees for House and Senate candidates collectively spent over $86 million during the 2010 cycle. Other big spenders include business groups, like the U.S. Chamber of Commerce; unions, such as the Service Employees International Union (SEIU); and independent groups, such as American Crossroads, a conservative group advised by leaders from George W. Bush's administration, Karl Rove and Ed Gillespie. With few exceptions, most of the groups taking part in political campaigns support candidates from only one party. All in all, in 2010 political spending was fairly even between Democratic candidates and parties and Republican candidates and parties. However, interest group spending in 2010 strongly favored Republican candidates.

TRENDS IN VOTING METHODS

A trend toward early voting and voting by mail continued in 2010. Until recently, almost all voters in the United States cast a paper ballot in person on Election Day. If a voter wanted to mail in a ballot ahead of the election, he or she needed to provide a valid excuse, such as a religious conflict, illness, or absence from his or her hometown. In the last several elections, alternative voting methods have gained in popularity. Thirty states plus Washington D.C. now permit "no-excuse" absentee voting. In these states, a voter can request a ballot by mail without providing a reason. In three of these states—California, Colorado, and Montana—voters can sign up to be on a permanent absentee ballot list and will then be automatically mailed a ballot for each election. In addition, thirty-two states have in-person early voting. In these states, a voter can visit the election office ahead of Election Day and cast a ballot. In some of these states, early voting takes place not only at government offices but also in churches, community centers, and other satellite locations.

According to state voting records, 10 percent of all voters in the 2008 election voted early in person, and 16 percent voted by mail. The Early Voting Information Center at Reed College estimates that in eleven states, the majority of ballots are cast before Election Day. Early estimates of nontraditional voting in the 2010 elections show that these newer forms of voting are increasing in popularity. Professor

Michael McDonald of George Mason University projects that 29 percent of all ballots cast in 2010 were absentee or early.[8]

Early and absentee voting for the 2010 elections began up to seven weeks before Election Day in some places. For campaigns, these new forms of voting reduce the amount of mobilization work that has to be done on Election Day itself. Campaign volunteers and professionals can go door-to-door, make phone calls, visit community events, and try to convince their supporters to vote before Election Day. Once people cast early votes, campaigns can ask the state and county election authorities for a list that shows which citizens have voted early, and with this list, the campaigns can focus their Election Day Get-Out-The-Vote (GOTV) efforts on those who have not yet cast a ballot. With over 50 percent of voters casting early ballots in some states, campaigns can dramatically increase their overall efficiency in the time leading up to and including Election Day.

Early and absentee voting is more popular in certain regions of the country and among certain demographic groups than others. For instance, in the Northeast fewer than 7 percent of voters cast ballots ahead of Election Day, according to a late October 2010 Gallup poll.[9] In contrast, more than half of voters in the West and nearly a third of voters in the South cast ballots ahead of time. Older voters—those over 65—are the most likely to use these new voting methods. For older citizens who are less mobile, voting by mail makes it easier to cast a ballot than does venturing to the polls in November. In contrast to age and region, there is very little relationship between use of early voting and political affiliation. According to the Gallup poll, Democrats and Republicans tend to use early voting methods at similar rates.

As nontraditional voting opportunities become more available and more popular, there will be a number of questions for scholars, policymakers, and activists. Under what circumstances does early voting increase turnout? Is early voting cost-effective? Does early voting make elections more or less susceptible to fraud? Does early voting reduce the amount of privacy in the voting process? These questions will be of growing importance as more Americans opt for nontraditional voting methods.

ISSUES AND MANDATES

Going into the 2010 elections, the biggest issue for most voters was the economy. With high unemployment and a shaky economy in the two years leading up to the elections, it is not surprising that 57 percent of registered voters told a Gallup poll in spring 2010 that the economy was extremely important to their vote. Republicans, Democrats, and Independents were all likely to focus more on the economy than on any other issue. Health care was the second-most dominant issue, with just under 50 percent of registered voters identifying it as extremely important to their vote.[10]

---

[8]See http://elections.gmu.edu/2010_vote_forecasts.html (accessed 11/4/2010).

[9]Frank Newport. "Early Voting Highest among Older Voters. Those in the West,"*Gallup.com*. October 27, 2010.

[10]Jeffrey M. Jones, "Voters Rate Economy as Top Issue for 2010," *Gallup*, April 8, 2010.

▲ *In August 2010, Missouri voters approved a referendum, Proposition C, that banned the federal government from mandating health insurance. Although the referendum had little legal impact, it was indicative of strong opposition among conservative voters to Obama's health care plan.*

During the 2010 campaign, candidates discussed both the economy and health care. On the economic front, a key issue was whether candidates supported a tax increase on wealthy Americans. At the start of his first term, George W. Bush signed into law a tax break for virtually all Americans. That tax decrease, however, would only last through 2010. When he took office, President Obama proposed that the Bush-era tax rate stay the same for most Americans but revert to its former, higher rate for the wealthiest Americans. When asked how they would vote on this issue in the 112th Congress, the candidates split along partisan lines, with most Democrats seeking increased taxation for the wealthy and most Republicans seeking an extension of the Bush-era tax rate for all.

As for health care, one of the central tenets of the Tea Party movement calls for a repeal of the health care reform bill passed in the 111th Congress, so it is likely that Republican members of the 112th Congress will advocate for scaling back or even repealing the law. However, given the Democratic control of the Senate and the presidency, a major change in the health care law is unlikely.

CONSEQUENCES FOR AMERICAN GOVERNMENT

If the electorate's choice to replace many Democrats with Republicans was fairly predictable, the elections' results seemed unlikely to produce a clear response from the government. The 2010 elections ushered in a period of divided government with the Democrats controlling the Senate and the White House and the Republicans dominating the House of Representatives. Periods of divided government have occurred frequently in American politics, and history (as well as the nature of the institutions) suggests that with control of only one house of Congress, the

▲ *As a new Republican majority took control of the House of Representatives, led by incoming Speaker John Boehner of Ohio, it was unclear how much of their agenda they would be able to implement under divided government.*

GOP will have little chance to implement an agenda of its own. The Republican Party will have to settle for either obstructing the Democrats or reaching out to the president's party in areas amenable to compromise. Given the highly confrontational tone of the 2010 campaign, the former seems to be the more likely approach. Indeed, some Republicans have stated that their major goal will be to block the Obama agenda and have suggested a need to launch legislative investigations into the administration's activities of 2009–2010.

As for the Democrats, with the GOP controlling the House of Representatives, the chance that any substantial portion of the Democratic agenda will be enacted after 2010 seems remote. President Obama has indicated that, like his predecessors, he will make increased use of such presidential tools as executive orders and regulatory review to implement programs whose congressional passage can no longer be secured.

While there remains the chance for the Republican House and the Democratic president and Senate to find common ground on key pieces of legislation like energy reform, the most likely scenario is that both sides will prevent the other from enacting any major changes to existing law as they gear up for another showdown in November 2012.

13

Introduction to Public Policy

HOW DOES PUBLIC POLICY WORK?

public policy A law, rule, statute, or edict that expresses the government's goals and provides for rewards and punishments to promote their attainment.

Public policy is an officially expressed intention backed by a sanction; that sanction can be a reward or a punishment. Thus public policy may be a law, a rule, a statute, an edict, a regulation, or an order. Its purpose is to provide incentives, whether carrotlike rewards or sticklike punishments, to induce people to change what they are currently doing and do something else, or to do more or less of what they are currently doing.

As we said in Chapter 1 and have emphasized elsewhere, governments do what they do in part because of the concerns, ambitions, and purposes of politicians and other government officials and the institutional contexts in which these concerns, ambitions, and purposes play out. Since the policy-making process affords many opportunities to change the purposes of government, politicians and officials constantly take advantage of their capacities as agenda setters. But policy change requires success at every step of the rather lengthy and intricate policy-making process. The institutional arrangements of a government create hurdles that a proposed change in policy must clear. This often means that change is nearly impossible. Because change is difficult, policies—once put in place—possess a degree of durability. This durability, in turn, provides a semblance of order and predictability in an otherwise uncertain world.

Few Americans realize how much their economic freedom owes to government action. Americans often point with pride to their "free-market" economy and view governmental institutions and policies as intrusions on the freedom of the marketplace. Yet the very existence of what we regard as a free market depends heavily on public policies and institutions. Ironically, without ongoing collective action coordinated by the government, individual market freedom would be difficult to exercise and might be limited to small-scale barter and trade. America's huge free-market economy could not exist without the government. Even our increasingly global economy depends on international economic institutions and cooperation among national governments. In the economic realm, as in the realm of national security, maintaining individual freedom ultimately rests on our capacity for collective action.

Consider, for example, the case of home ownership. To many Americans, home ownership and personal freedom are inextricably linked. "A person's home is his or her castle" is a traditional adage that reflects long-held American beliefs. Yet the truth is that "ownership" implies a legal status enforced by the government. There can be no property ownership without collective action. In difficult times, moreover, as in the 2008–2009 financial crisis, millions of Americans demanded that the government help them restructure their mortgages to enable them to keep their homes. The Obama administration responded with several billion dollars in assistance. Once again, individual freedom was closely linked to collective action.

This dependence is brought home during times of economic crisis, but the government's role in maintaining the free market is not simply a matter of occasional crisis intervention. In point of fact, government action actually makes a market economy possible by setting the rules that allow markets to function, as well as maintaining the institutions needed to sustain a market economy. As we will see in this chapter, several prerequisites for a market economy are especially important and illustrate the ways in which collective action is needed to make individual economic freedom possible. We will then turn to some of the ways government uses social policies to address poverty and broaden opportunity.

GOALS OF ECONOMIC POLICY

Governments are neither aloof nor separate from the economy but are inextricably bound up in its activities. Government involvement in the economy is now routine and widespread, touching practically every aspect of economic life. Governments provide a structure and a framework—standards, rules, laws—as well as substantive support in the form of subsidies, regulations, and taxes, all of which allow the economy to operate. Through politics, however, governments and their agents create winners and losers. The winners may think of government's policies as benign; the losers do not.

Three major goals have guided government involvement in the economy since the early years of our nation's history: promoting public order and private property, promoting business development, and maintaining a stable and strong economy. Over time, the federal government has taken on greater responsibility for meeting each of these goals. The Great Depression of the 1930s marked a decisive turning point. As Washington created new agencies and new measures to monitor the nation's economic health, it transformed public expectations of the federal role in the economy. The federal government assumed primary responsibility for achieving established goals, and it faced heightened expectations of its ability to reach those goals.

Promoting Public Order and Private Property

A system of law and order is necessary for a healthy market economy. Participants need to be able to assume that the people with whom they are dealing will be bound by a set of predictable laws. Under the American federalist system, there is no national police force, no national criminal law, no national common law, no national property laws. However, the national government does enforce a few policies directly concerned with public order, most of which are mandated by the Constitution itself. These include laws against counterfeiting, using the mails to defraud, and crossing state lines to avoid arrest for a violation of state laws. A few other offenses against public order have simply been presumed to be interstate crimes against which federal statutes have been enacted, mainly in the twentieth century. Important examples include kidnapping, dealing narcotics, and political subversion. But virtually all of the multitudes of other policies dealing with public order and the foundations of the economy are left to the states and their local governments.

In the wake of the terrorist attacks of September 11, the federal role in public order increased. In one of his first acts in response to the attacks, President George W. Bush announced the creation of a new cabinet-level agency, the Office of Homeland Defense, which became the Department of Homeland Security. Its mission is to coordinate the federal government's role in the preservation of public order.

Another unique feature of the American approach to public order is the emphasis placed on private property. Private property is valued in most of the cultures of the world but not as centrally as in the United States, where it is embodied in the Constitution. Seizing private property for a public use, or **expropriation**, is widely used in the United States, especially in land-use regulation. Almost all public works, from highways to parks to government office buildings, involve the forceful taking of some private property to assemble sufficient land and the correct distribution of land for the necessary construction. The vast interstate highway program required expropriation of thousands of narrow strips of private land. We generally call the power to expropriate **eminent domain,** and the eminent domain power is recognized as inherent in any government. The Fifth Amendment of the U.S. Constitution surrounds this expropriation power with important safeguards against abuse, so that government agencies in the United States are not permitted to use that power except through a strict due process, and they must offer "fair market value" for the land sought.[1]

Many policies positively encourage property ownership on the theory that property owners are better citizens and, therefore, more respectful of public order. One of the most important national policies is the part of the tax code that permits homeowners to deduct from their taxes interest paid on mortgage loans. In addition, three large federal agencies—the Federal Housing Administration (FHA), the Farmers Home Administration, and the Veterans Benefits Administration (VBA)—encourage home ownership by making mortgage loans available at interest rates below the market rate. The Farm Credit Administration operates the extensive Farm Credit System, whose primary function is to make long-term and short-term loans to improve farm and rural real estate.

expropriation
Confiscation of property with or without compensation.

eminent domain
The right of government to take private property for public use, with reasonable compensation awarded for the property.

Promoting Business Development

During the nineteenth century, the national government was almost exclusively a promoter of markets. National roads and canals were built to tie states and regions together. National tariff policies promoted domestic markets by restricting imported goods; a tax on an import raised its price and weakened its ability to compete with similar domestic products. The national government also heavily subsidized the railroad. Until the 1840s, railroads were thought to be of limited commercial value. But between 1850 and 1872, Congress granted over 100 million acres of public

---

[1] For an evaluation of the politics of eminent domain, see Theodore J. Lowi, Benjamin Ginsberg, et al., *Poliscide: Big Government, Big Science, Lilliputian Politics,* 2nd ed. (Lanham, Md.: University Press of America, 1990), p. 235 and passim, esp. chaps. 11 and 12, by Julia Vitullo-Martin and Thomas Vitullo-Martin.

domain land to railroad interests, and state and local governments pitched in an estimated $280 million in cash and credit. Before the end of the century, the United States had 35,000 miles of track—almost half the world's total.

Railroads were not the only clients of federal support aimed at fostering the expansion of private markets. Many sectors of agriculture also received federal subsidies during the nineteenth century. Agriculture remains highly subsidized. In 2001, an environmental group caused a stir by putting the exact amounts of subsidies received by individual farmers on a widely publicized Web site.[2] The top recipient of government aid in Texas, for example, received $1.3 million in 2001. President Bush continued the tradition of generous agricultural subsidies. The Obama administration has not yet tackled the problem.

In the twentieth century, traditional promotional techniques were expanded, and some new ones were invented. For example, a great proportion of the promotional activities of the national government are now done indirectly through **categorical grants-in-aid** (see Chapter 3). The national government offers grants to states on the condition that the state (or local) government undertake a particular activity. Thus to use motor transportation to improve national markets, a national highway system of 900,000 miles was built during the 1930s, based on a formula whereby the national government would pay 50 percent of the cost if the state would provide the other 50 percent. And then for over twenty years, beginning in the late 1950s, the federal government constructed over 45,000 miles of interstate highways. This project came about through a program whereby the national government agreed to pay 90 percent of the construction costs on the condition that each state provide for 10 percent of the costs of any portion of a highway built within its boundaries.[3] More recently, the federal government has been involved in the subsidization of urban mass transit, airport construction and modernization, and port improvements—a combination of promotional and security concerns at work.

The government also fosters business development by regulating competition. Federal economic regulation aims to protect the public from potential abuses by concentrated economic power in two ways. First, the federal government can establish conditions that govern the operation of big businesses to ensure fair competition. For example, it can require business to make available to the public information about its activities and its account books. Second, the federal government can force a large business to break up into smaller companies if it finds that the business has established a monopoly. This is called **antitrust policy**. In addition to economic regulation, the federal government engages in social regulation. Social regulation imposes conditions on businesses to protect workers, the environment, and consumers.

The modern epoch of comprehensive national regulation began in the 1930s. However, the extent to which government should regulate businesses is

---

[2] Farm Subsidy Database: A Project of Environmental Working Group, www.ewg.org/farm.

[3] A congressional act of 1956 officially designated the interstate highways the National System of Interstate and Defense Highways. It was indirectly a major part of President Eisenhower's defense program. But it was just as obviously a pork-barrel policy as any rivers and harbors legislation.

---

categorical grant-in-aid A grant by Congress to states and localities given with the condition that expenditures be limited to a problem or group specified by the national government.

antitrust policy Government regulation of large businesses that have established monopolies.

controversial. In the late 1970s, many economists began to argue that excessive regulation was hurting the economy. Congress and the president responded with a wave of **deregulation.** Economic conservatives are in principle opposed to virtually any sort of government intervention in the economy.[4] As President Ronald Reagan once put it, they see government not as part of the solution, but as part of the problem. They adamantly oppose intervention by techniques of promoting commerce and are even more opposed to intervention through techniques of regulation. They believe that markets would be bigger and healthier if not regulated at all.

President George W. Bush's support of deregulation contributed to the trend away from government intervention. In response to the nation's 2008–2009 economic crisis, however, the Obama administration supported a substantial program of new regulations in the banking and financial services sector designed to prevent some of the lending practices associated with the collapse of several financial institutions. The Obama administration also supported new regulations in the realms of food and drug safety designed to increase the power of the Food and Drug Administration to protect the nation's consumers. The Reagan era of deregulation seemed to be at an end.

Maintaining a Stable and Strong Economy

A stable and strong economy is the basic goal of all economic policy. What makes reaching this goal so difficult is that the key elements of a strong economy— economic growth, full employment, and low inflation—often appear to conflict with each other. Economic policy must manage the trade-offs among these goals. This is a complicated task because there is much disagreement about whether pursuing one of these economic goals really does mean sacrificing the others. Let us now turn to the actual policies designed to accomplish economic stability and growth.

Monetary Policies. **Monetary policies** manipulate the growth of the entire economy by controlling the availability of money to banks.

But banks did not become the core of the American economic system without intense political controversy. The Federalist majority in Congress, led by Alexander Hamilton, did in fact establish a Bank of the United States in 1791, but it was vigorously opposed by the agrarian interests, led by Thomas Jefferson, based on the fear that the interests of urban, industrial capitalism would dominate such a bank. The Bank of the United States was finally terminated during the administration of Andrew Jackson, but the fear of a central, *public* bank still existed eight decades later, when Congress in 1913 established an institution—the **Federal Reserve System**—to integrate private banks into a single system. The Federal Reserve System did not

deregulation
A policy of reducing or eliminating regulatory restraints in the conduct of individuals or private institutions.

monetary policy (technique)
Effort to regulate the economy through manipulation of the supply of money and credit. America's most powerful institution in the area of monetary policy is the Federal Reserve Board.

Federal Reserve System Consisting of twelve Federal Reserve Banks, an agency that facilitates exchanges of cash, checks, and credit; it regulates member banks; and it uses monetary policies to fight inflation and deflation.

---

[4] Actually, this point of view is better understood as nineteenth-century liberalism, or free-market liberalism, following the theories of Adam Smith. However, after the New Deal appropriated "liberal" for its progovernment point of view, the Republican antigovernment wing got tagged with the conservative label. With Reagan, the conservative label took on more popular connotations, while "liberal" became stigmatized as the "L-word."

become a central bank in the European tradition, but rather is composed of twelve Federal Reserve banks, each located in a major commercial city. The Federal Reserve banks are not ordinary banks but banker's banks: they make loans to other banks, clear checks, and supply the economy with currency and coins. They also play a regulatory role in relation to the member banks. Every national bank must be a member of the Federal Reserve System; each must follow national banking rules and must purchase stock in the Federal Reserve System (which helps make the system self-financing). State banks and savings and loan associations may also join if they accept the national rules. At the top of the system is the Federal Reserve Board (the Fed), made up of seven members appointed by the president (with Senate confirmation) for fourteen-year terms. The chairman of the Fed is selected by the president from among the seven members of the board for a four-year term. In all other concerns, however, the Fed is an independent agency inasmuch as its members cannot be removed during their terms except "for cause," and the president's executive power does not extend to them or their policies.

The major advantage of belonging to the federal system is that each member bank can borrow money from the Fed, using as collateral the notes on loans already made. This privilege enables them to expand their loan operations continually, as long as there is demand for new loans. The ability of a member bank to borrow money from the Fed is a profoundly important monetary policy. The Fed charges interest, called a **discount rate**, on its loans to member banks.

If the Fed significantly decreases the discount rate—that is, the interest it charges member banks when they apply for credit—that can be a good shot in the arm for a sagging economy. Manipulating interest rates is the Fed's most powerful tool. During 2001, the Fed cut interest rates eleven times to combat the combined effects of recession and the terrorist attacks. As the economy began to sag in late 2007, all eyes were on the Fed to reduce interest rates. By March 2008, the Fed had cut rates six times from their high in September 2007. If the Fed adopts a policy of higher discount rates, it will put a brake on the economy if the economy is expanding too fast, because the higher rate pushes up the interest rates charged by leading private banks to their customers.

Other monetary policies implemented by the Fed include increasing or decreasing the **reserve requirement**, which sets the proportion of deposited money that a bank must keep "on demand" as it makes all the rest of its deposits available for new loans. A third important technique used by the Fed is **open-market operations**—the buying and selling of Treasury securities to absorb excess dollars or to release more dollars into the economy. Finally, a fourth power is derived from one of the important services rendered by the Federal Reserve System, which is the opportunity for member banks to borrow from each other. This exchange is called the federal funds market, and the interest rate charged by one bank to another, the **federal funds rate**, can be manipulated just like the discount rate, to expand or contract credit.

The federal government also provides insurance to foster credit and encourage private capital investment. The Federal Deposit Insurance Corporation (FDIC) protects bank deposits up to $100,000. Another important promoter of investment

discount rate
The interest rate charged by the Federal Reserve when commercial banks borrow in order to expand their lending operations; an effective tool of monetary policy.

reserve requirement The amount of liquid assets and ready cash that the Federal Reserve requires banks to hold to meet depositors' demands for their money.

open-market operations The buying and selling of government securities to help finance government operations and to loosen or tighten the total amount of credit circulating in the economy.

federal funds rate
The interest rate on loans between banks that the Federal Reserve Board influences by affecting the supply of money available.

is the federal insurance of home mortgages provided by the Department of Housing and Urban Development. This system began to unravel in the first decade of the 2000s with the growth of the subprime market for lending. This market made home loans available to people who could not otherwise afford to buy a home. At the same time, however, it created new instabilities in the market by offering risky loans that would become costlier due to adjustable interest rates. The slowing housing market in 2007 set off a wave of foreclosures when many home owners discovered that they could not pay back their loans. Some analysts predicted that as many as 2 million home owners could lose their homes by the end of 2009. The foreclosure crisis in turn set shock waves through the financial system, as investment banks found themselves holding worthless loans.

Fiscal Policies. **Fiscal policies** include the government's taxing and spending powers. Personal and corporate income taxes, which raise most government revenues, are the most prominent examples (Table 13.1). Although the direct purpose

fiscal policy (technique) The government's use of taxing, monetary, and spending powers to manipulate the economy.

TABLE 13.1 FEDERAL REVENUES BY TYPE OF TAX AS PERCENTAGE OF TOTAL RECEIPTS, 1960–2010

Year	Individual Income Tax	Corporation Income Tax	Social Insurance and Retirement Receipts	Excise Taxes	Other
1960	44.0	23.2	15.9	12.6	4.2
1970	46.9	17.1	23.0	8.1	4.9
1980	47.2	12.5	30.5	4.7	5.1
1990	45.2	9.1	36.8	3.4	5.4
2000	49.6	10.2	32.2	3.4	4.5
2004	43.0	10.1	39.0	3.7	4.2
2005	43.0	12.9	36.9	3.4	3.8
2006	43.4	14.7	34.8	3.1	4.1
2007	45.3	14.4	33.9	2.5	3.9
2008 (est)	48.4	13.7	36.1	2.7	−0.9
2009 (est)	46.6	12.6	35.2	2.6	3.1
2010 (est)	48.4	11.6	34.3	2.1	3.8

SOURCE: Budget of the United States Government, Fiscal Year 2009, Historical Tables, http://origin.www.gpoaccess.gov/usbudget/fy09/pdf/hist.pdf (accessed 7/15/09).

of an income tax is to raise revenue, each tax has a different impact on the economy, and the government can plan for that impact.

After passing major tax cuts in 2001, President Bush proposed and Congress passed a sweeping new round of cuts in 2003. Bush's plan was intended to promote investment by reducing taxes on most stock dividends, to spur business activity by offering tax breaks to small businesses, and to stimulate the economy by reducing the tax rates for all taxpayers. In 2006, Congress extended the rate reductions on dividends and capital gains, a move that estimates showed would cost the treasury $70 billion over five years. The Bush administration tax cuts were criticized on several grounds. Many Democrats argued that the tax cuts were simply a giveaway to the wealthy and to corporations, who had grown even wealthier relative to ordinary Americans in recent years (see "Analyzing the Evidence" on page 394). There has been concern that the tax cuts are responsible for the large federal deficits: the federal budget moved from running surpluses in 2000 to steep deficits only four years later (Figure 13.1).

FIGURE 13.1 U.S. BUDGET DEFICITS AND SURPLUSES, 1962–2009*

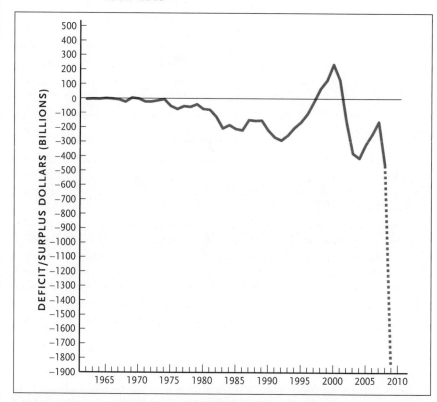

*Estimate

SOURCE: Budget of the United States Government, Fiscal Year 2009, Historical Tables, http://origin .www.gpoaccess.gov/usbudget/fy09/pdf/hist.pdf (accessed 7/15/09).

CHAPTER 13   INTRODUCTION TO PUBLIC POLICY

A tax is called **progressive** if the rate of taxation goes up with each higher income bracket. The decision to make the income tax progressive was one of the most important policy choices Congress made. A tax is called **regressive** if people in lower income brackets pay a higher proportion of their income in taxes than people in higher income brackets. For example, a sales tax is deemed regressive because everybody pays at the same rate, so that the proportion of total income paid in taxes goes down as the total income goes up (assuming, as is generally the case, that as total income goes up, the amount spent on taxable purchases increases at a lower rate).

The administration of fiscal policy occurs primarily in the Treasury Department. In addition to collecting income, corporate, and other taxes, the Treasury also manages the enormous national debt—$12 trillion in 2009. (The national debt was a mere $710 billion in 1980.)[5] Debt is not simply something the country owes; it is something a country has to manage and administer. The debt is also a fiscal instrument in the hands of the federal government that can be used—through manipulation of interest rates and through the buying and selling of government bonds—to slow down or to speed up the activity of the entire national economy, as well as to defend the value of the dollar in international trade.

Spending and Budgeting.   The federal government's power to spend is one of the most important tools of economic policy. Decisions about how much to spend affect the overall health of the economy. They also affect aspects of American life, from the distribution of income through the availability of different modes of transportation to the level of education in society. It is not surprising that the fight for control over spending is one of the most contentious in Washington, as interest groups and politicians strive to determine the priorities and appropriate levels. Decisions about spending are made as part of the annual budget process. During the 1990s, when the federal **budget deficit** became a major political issue and parties were deeply split on spending, the budget process became the focal point of the entire policy-making process. Though the budget deficit disappeared in the late 1990s. However, during the Bush era, the costs of the wars in Iraq and Afghanistan produced new deficits, which are bound to increase as the Obama administration's ambitious social spending programs are implemented.

The president and Congress have each created institutions to assert control over the budget process. The OMB, in the Executive Office of the President, is responsible for preparing the president's budget. This budget contains the president's spending priorities and the estimated costs of the president's policy proposals. It is viewed as the starting point for the annual debate over the budget. When different parties control the presidency and Congress, the president's budget may have little influence on the budget that is ultimately adopted. Members of the president's own party may also have different priorities.

---

[5] U.S. Department of the Treasury, "The Debt to the Penny and Who Holds It," www.treasurydirect.gov/ NP/BPDLogin?application=np (accessed 7/15/09). About 60 percent of the debt is held by the public, corporations, foreign governments, and other creditors. About 40 percent of the debt consists of "intragovernmental holdings." These are funds borrowed by the Treasury from other governmental agencies, in particular the Social Security and Medicare trust funds, which serve as a major source of funding for the federal government's current expenditures.

Congress has its own budget institutions. It created the Congressional Budget Office in 1974 so that it could have reliable information about the costs and economic impact of the policies it considers. At the same time, Congress set up a budget process designed to establish spending priorities and consider individual expenditures in light of the entire budget. A key element of the process is the annual budget resolution, which designates broad targets for spending. By estimating the costs of policy proposals, Congress hoped to control spending and reduce deficits. When the congressional budget process proved unable to hold down deficits in the 1980s, Congress instituted stricter measures to control spending, including *spending caps* that limit spending on some types of programs.

A very large and growing proportion of the annual federal budget takes the form of **mandatory spending**, expenditures that are, in the words of the OMB, "relatively uncontrollable." Interest payments on the national debt, for example, are determined by the size of the national debt. Legislation has mandated payment rates for such programs as retirement under Social Security, retirement for federal employees, unemployment assistance, Medicare, and farm price supports (Figure 13.2). These payments increase with the cost of living; they increase as the average age of the population goes up; they increase as national and world agricultural surpluses go up. In 1970, 38.6 percent of the total federal budget was made up of these **uncontrollables**; in 1975, 52.5 percent fell into that category; and by 2001, around 64.7 percent was in the uncontrollable category. This means that the national government now has very little **discretionary spending** with which to counteract fluctuations in the business cycle.

This has a profound political implication. With mandatory or relatively uncontrollable spending on the rise, there is less scope for the exercise of discretion. If a budget has to be cut and categories of mandatory spending are taken off the table, then the cuts will fall disproportionately on what remains. With the pain of cutting "available" programs, the prospects for distributing the cuts in a manner acceptable to all interested parties grow dim. Thus the politics will be more intense and dirtier; groups will be more highly mobilized and energized—they will be at one another's throats; Congress and the president will be eyeball to eyeball as they seek to protect their different constituencies; and political partisans will not be in the mood to compromise.[6]

Government spending as a fiscal policy works fairly well when deliberate deficit spending is used to stop a recession and speed up the recovery period. But it does not work very well in fighting inflation because elected politicians are politically unable to make the drastic expenditure cuts necessary to balance the budget, much less to produce a budgetary surplus.

---

[6] Of course, it should be underscored that "relatively uncontrollable" is itself a policy decision made by the president and Congress. It is not carved in granite; it can be undone. To undo some things, such as not making a promised payment on the national debt, would have horrible consequences in credit markets. A modest across-the-board reduction in outlays for hospital assistance under Medicare, on the other hand, though painful (literally and figuratively), might nevertheless be accommodated (with hospitals and patients sharing the burden in various ways—for example, by deferring elective procedures or delaying a salary increase). That is, things that are alleged to be off the table can be put right back on the table.

mandatory spending Federal spending that is made up of "uncontrollables."

uncontrollables Budgetary items that are beyond the control of budgetary committees and can be controlled only by substantive legislative action in Congress. Some uncontrollables, such as the interest on the debt, are beyond the power of Congress because the terms of payments are set in contracts.

discretionary spending Federal spending on programs that are controlled through the regular budget process.

FIGURE 13.2 UNCONTROLLABLES AS A PERCENTAGE OF THE TOTAL FEDERAL BUDGET

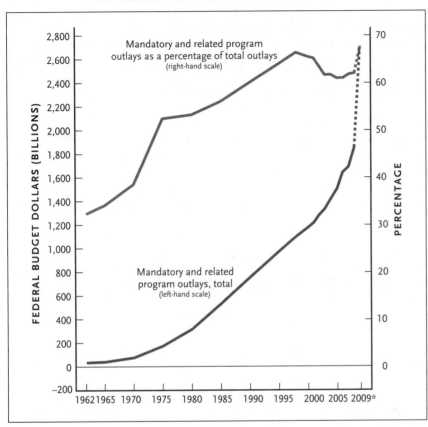

*Data for 2009 are estimates.

SOURCE: Office of Management and Budget, http://origin.www.gpoaccess.gov/usbudget/fy09/hist.html (accessed 5/20/09).

THE WELFARE SYSTEM AS FISCAL AND SOCIAL POLICY

Government involvement in the relief of poverty and dependency was insignificant until the twentieth century because of Americans' antipathy to government and because of their confidence that all of the deserving poor could be cared for by private efforts alone. This traditional approach crumbled in 1929 in the wake of the Great Depression, when some misfortune befell nearly everyone. Americans finally confronted the fact that poverty and dependency could be the result of imperfections of the economic system itself, rather than a result of individual irresponsibility. Americans held to their distinction between the deserving and undeserving poor but significantly altered these standards regarding who was deserving and who was not. And once the idea of an imperfect system was established, a large-scale public

The Income Gap

Examined carefully, data often raise more questions than they answer. When viewing a table or figure, especially in the context of policy debates, it is usually prudent to make a list of the questions raised by the data presented rather than simply accepting the interpretation offered by the analyst presenting the data. Take, for example, the so-called income gap that has become a major issue in contemporary American politics. As indicated by the table below, in the last several years the difference or "gap" between the share of America's income going to the richest and poorest segments of the population has been increasing. Many Democrats blame Republican tax cuts for making the rich richer and the poor poorer and assert that major changes in tax policy are needed to restore a measure of equality to American society.

THE PROPORTION OF MONEY INCOME GOING TO EACH FIFTH OF THE POPULATION

Family Income Bracket	1929 (%)	1934 (%)	1944 (%)	1950 (%)	1960 (%)	1970 (%)	1980 (%)	1990 (%)	2006 (%)
Lowest fifth	5.4	5.9	4.9	4.5	4.8	4.1	4.3	3.9	3.4
Second fifth	10.1	11.5	10.9	12.0	12.2	10.8	10.3	9.6	8.6
Third fifth	14.4	15.5	16.2	17.4	17.8	17.4	16.9	15.9	14.5
Fourth fifth	18.8	20.4	22.2	23.5	24.0	24.5	24.9	24.0	22.9
Highest fifth	51.3	49.7	45.8	42.6	41.3	43.3	43.7	46.6	50.5
Gap between lowest and highest fifths	45.9	43.8	40.9	38.1	36.5	39.2	39.4	42.7	47.1

Note: Figures are not strictly comparable because of difference in calculating procedures.

Source: Data for 1929–50, Allan Rosenbaum, "State Government, Political Power, and Public Policy: The Case of Illinois" (Ph.D. diss., University of Chicago, 1974), chaps. 10–11, used by permission; for 1960–2006, *Statistical Abstract of the U.S.*, 2009, Table 675.

These data may indicate an emergent social problem in the United States, but at least two questions must be answered before we can draw any meaningful conclusions from them and before we can make policy recommendations. First, the data deal with differences among income groups but they do not show the absolute income of any group. It is possible that all income groups are better off today than they were in prior years. If everyone is better off, perhaps we do not want to change our tax policies, even if they tend to increase income inequality. This possibility is at least partially borne out by census data: Between 1980 and 2004, the average incomes of every income group increased—though the incomes of the wealthiest Americans increased more sharply than those of any others.

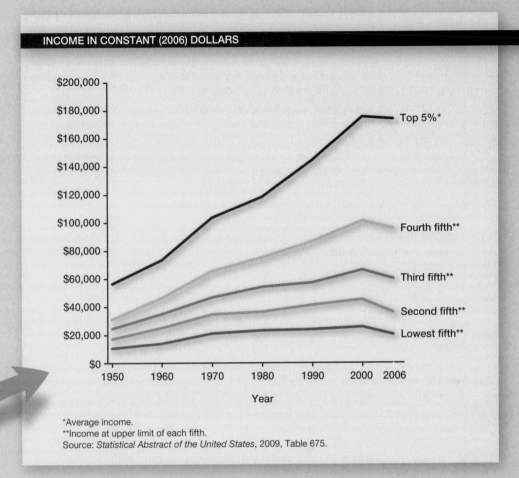

INCOME IN CONSTANT (2006) DOLLARS

Top 5%*

Fourth fifth**

Third fifth**

Second fifth**

Lowest fifth**

Year

*Average income.
**Income at upper limit of each fifth.
Source: *Statistical Abstract of the United States*, 2009, Table 675.

A second consideration is that the data showing a growing income gap deal with aggregates, not individuals. We cannot know from the data presented whether families are generally locked into a particular income quartile or are likely to move from year to year. If the latter, then the apparent increase in inequality shown in the first table is at least mitigated by social mobility. In recent years, for example, the percentage of black families in the lowest income group has decreased more sharply than the percentage of white families in that group. At the same time, the percentage of black families in the highest income group has increased more substantially than their white counterparts, suggesting that there is social mobility across the income groups.[1] Thus, in considering the income gap, we may want to consider whether policies designed to reduce inequality might interfere with social mobility.

[1]*Statistical Abstract of the United States*, 2007, Table 676.

approach became practical not only to alleviate poverty but also to redistribute wealth and to manipulate economy activity through fiscal policy.

The architects of the original Social Security system in the 1930s were probably well aware that a large welfare system can be good *fiscal* policy. When the economy is declining and more people are losing their jobs or are retiring early, welfare payments go up automatically, thus maintaining consumer demand and making the "downside" of the business cycle shorter and shallower. Conversely, during periods of full employment or high levels of government spending, when inflationary pressures can mount, welfare taxes take an extra bite out of consumer dollars, tending to damp inflation, flattening the "upside" of the economy.

However, the authors of Social Security were more aware of the *social* policy significance of the welfare system. They recognized that a large proportion of the unemployment, dependency, and misery of the 1930s was due to the imperfections of a large, industrial society and occurred through no fault of the victims of these imperfections. They also recognized that opportunities to achieve security, let alone prosperity, were unevenly distributed in our society. This helps explain how the original Social Security laws came to be called—both by supporters and by critics—"the welfare state." The 1935 Social Security Act provided for two separate categories of *welfare—contributory* and *noncontributory.* Table 13.2 outlines the key programs in each of these categories.

Social Security

contributory program A social program financed in whole or in part by taxation or other mandatory contributions by its present or future recipients. The most important example is Social Security, which is financed by a payroll tax.

Social Security A contributory welfare program into which working Americans contribute a percentage of their wages and from which they receive cash benefits after retirement.

Contributory programs are financed by taxation in a way that can be called "forced savings." These programs are what most people have in mind when they refer to **Social Security** or social insurance. Under the original old-age insurance program, the employer and the employee were each required to pay equal amounts, which in 1937 were set at 1 percent of the first $3,000 of wages, to be deducted from the paycheck of each employee and matched by the same amount from the employer. This percentage has increased over the years; the total contribution is now 9.1 percent subdivided as follows: 6.20 percent on the first $106,800 of income for the Social Security benefits and an additional 2.9 percent on all earnings for Medicare.[7]

Social Security is a rather conservative approach to welfare. In effect, the Federal Insurance Contributions Act (FICA) tax, as Social Security is formally known, sends a message that people cannot be trusted to save voluntarily to take care of their retirement needs. But in another sense, it is quite radical. Social Security is not real insurance: Workers' contributions do not accumulate in a personal account as an annuity does. Consequently, contributors do not receive benefits in proportion to their contributions, and this means that there is a redistribution of wealth. In brief, contributory Social Security mildly redistributes wealth from higher- to lower-income people, and it significantly redistributes wealth from younger workers to older retirees. Since 1972, Social Security benefits and costs have been ad-

---

[7] The figures cited are for 2009. Although on paper the employer is taxed, this is all part of "forced savings," because in reality the employer's contribution is nothing more than a mandatory wage supplement that the employee never sees or touches before it goes into the trust fund held exclusively for the contributory programs.

TABLE 13.2 PUBLIC WELFARE PROGRAMS

	Year Enacted	Federal Outlays in 2008 (in billions of dollars)	Federal Outlays (2009 estimate in billions of dollars)	Federal Outlays (2010 estimate in billions of dollars)
Contributory				
Old-Age and Survivors Insurance; Disability Insurance (Social Security)	1935	617	652	690
Medicare	1965	403	413	427
Unemployment compensation	1935	37	43	41
Noncontributory				
Medicaid	1965	204	216	230
Food Stamps	1964	39	40	41
Supplemental Security Income	1974	38	40	42
National School Lunch Program (listed as Child Nutrition and Special Milk Programs)	1946	14	15	15
Temporary Assistance for Needy Families (TANF, listed as Family Support Payments to States)	1996	21	21	21

SOURCE: Office of Management and Budget, *Budget of the U.S. Government, Fiscal Year 2008, Historical Tables* (Washington, D.C.: Government Printing Office, 2007), Table 11.3, pp. 205–229.

justed through **indexing**, whereby benefits paid out under contributory programs are modified annually by cost-of-living adjustments (COLAs) based on changes in the consumer price index, so that benefits increase automatically as the cost of living rises. And to pay for these automatic adjustments, Social Security taxes (contributions) also increased. These changes made Social Security, in the words of one observer, "a politically ideal program. It bridged partisan conflict by providing liberal benefits under conservative financial auspices."[8] In other words, conservatives

indexing Periodic adjustments of welfare payments, wages, or taxes, tied to the cost of living.

---

[8] Edward J. Harpham, "Fiscal Crisis and the Politics of Social Security Reform," in *The Attack on the Welfare State*, Anthony Champagne and Edward J. Harpham, eds. (Prospect Heights, Ill.: Waveland Press, 1984), p. 13.

could more readily yield to the demands of the well-organized and expanding constituency of elderly voters if benefit increases were guaranteed and automatic, and liberals could cement conservative support by agreeing to finance the expanded benefits through increases in the regressive Social Security tax rather than through general revenues from the more progressive income tax.

The Politics of Reforming Social Security.   In 2007, nearly 50 million Americans received almost $525 billion in Social Security benefits, distributed to 42 million retirees and dependents or survivors and 8 million disabled people—up by more than 2 million since 2003.[9] For more than half of all American workers, Social Security is their only pension plan. And if there were no Social Security, half of all senior citizens would be living below the poverty line. No wonder Social Security is called the untouchable "third rail" of American politics.

Social Security has had its moments of potential crisis, but the only real crisis was in the late 1970s, triggered by the earlier decision to index benefits to the cost of living. The historic (for America) inflation of the 1970s caused the crisis, and it was readily "fixed" by increasing the payroll tax and the level of earnings (the cap) to which the tax applied. But a more fundamental reform would have to come as the ratio between contributing workers and retirees declined, from a comfortable sixteen contributors to one retiree downward toward three contributors to one retiree. With the record-breaking retirement of the baby boomers to begin around 2010, the ratio of contributors to workers will drop toward two to one. Fear is therefore growing in all circles that contributions today will not pay for the retirements of tomorrow. Until recently, the system has run a surplus. But the low ratio of contributors to retirees coupled with projected higher life expectancies could bankrupt the system. That is, without reform.

Reforms have been proposed but tossed aside. One of the best ideas—and certainly the earliest, going back to the 1940s, when the system was just beginning to take hold—was to safeguard the reserve (the trust fund) by having the Treasury invest the contributions in *private* securities, earning interest and at the same time keeping the reserve safely away from politics and government. One of the elder statesmen of that time retorted, "Why, that would be socialism!" A more recent reform, on which Al Gore staked his 2000 presidential campaign, was simply to respect the trust fund by keeping it in interest-bearing government securities but in a "locked box," unavailable to serve as a hidden part of the national debt. Gore's position was ridiculed.

Social Security got its boost to the top of the domestic policy agenda from President George W. Bush, not during his first term but after his reelection in 2004. And he pushed reform all the more intensely because of his awareness that 2005 might be his only chance to succeed—because AARP was campaigning to make 2006 an election year that would frighten a large number of Republican representatives in whose districts there were a significant number of retired persons, who are any election's most likely voters. As the *Economist* put it, "If [Social Security is] the third rail

---

[9] See www.socialsecurity.gov.

of American politics, the AARP generates much of the lethal current."[10] That threat called for equal intensity in return from Bush. The president began with a warning that unless something drastic is done now, the system will be paying out more than it takes in by 2018 and will certainly end up in bankruptcy by the 2040s. This stark warning appeared to have the same objective as his proclamation in 2003 of Iraq's imminent nuclear capacity—galvanizing the country to action through fear. That projection of Social Security doom, especially in his February 2005 State of the Union address, was followed by a cross-country campaign blitz, mainly in the "red states." He was showing his willingness to "spend the political capital" that he claimed to have earned by his reelection.

Bush's campaign contained no new and startling changes in Social Security itself. The radical part of his reform was his commitment to "the ownership society," which has no bearing whatsoever on the operating parts of the Social Security system. The ownership society is, instead, an effort to alter the principle of Social Security itself, which is governmentally guaranteed security. The ownership society was Bush's name for the proposal to permit employees to voluntarily divert up to about one third of their payroll tax into an individual private account (a maximum of about $1,000 per year).

Those who opposed the Bush reform argued first that the private account would outperform the government's account only during a sustained bull market and could yield a punishing reduction in the value of the annuity if retirement should come during a bad market. Opponents also argued that the government would have to go into stupendously greater debt to make up for the money diverted from the contributions into the private accounts.

Medicare

The biggest single expansion in contributory programs since 1935 was the establishment in 1965 of **Medicare**, which provides substantial medical services to elderly persons who are already eligible to receive old-age, survivors', and disability insurance under the original Social Security system. Medicare provides hospital insurance but allows beneficiaries to choose whether or not to participate in a government-assisted insurance program to cover doctors' fees. A major role is guaranteed to the private health-care industry by essentially limiting Medicare to a financing system. Program recipients purchase all their health services in the free market. The government's involvement is primarily payment for these services. As a result, there is little government control over the quality of the services provided and the fees that health-care providers charge.

Like Social Security, Medicare is not means tested. The benefits are available to all former workers and their spouses over the age of sixty-five—over 40 million people today—whether they are poor or not. Spending on Medicare has proved difficult to control in recent years, in part because of the growing numbers of people eligible for the programs but also because of rising health-care costs. Health-care expenditures,

Medicare National health insurance for the elderly and for the disabled.

---

[10] "The AARP—Still the Biggest Bruiser?" *Economist*, February 5, 2005, p. 26.

especially the cost of prescription drugs, have risen much more sharply than inflation in recent years.

Between the 1970s and the 1990s, there was mounting concern among policy makers about the rising costs of Medicare, and cost containment was a constant theme. The start of the Medicare prescription-drug benefit debate in the mid-1990s, stemming from the exorbitant medication costs being borne by people with Medicare, coupled with worries about the impending retirement of the baby-boom generation, led to the birth of a full-fledged movement to "overhaul" Medicare. Proponents of this effort propagated the idea that the Medicare program needed to be "saved," claiming Medicare was out-of-date and on the brink of bankruptcy.

In 2003, Congress enacted a major reform of the Medicare program, which has provided health care to seniors since 1964. Most notably, Congress added a prescription drug benefit to the package of health benefits for the elderly. The high cost of prescription drugs is an issue of growing concern to millions of older Americans.

Public Assistance Programs

noncontributory programs Social programs that provide assistance to people based on demonstrated need rather than any contribution they have made.

Aid to Families with Dependent Children (AFDC) Federal funds, administered by the states, for children living with persons or relatives who fall below state standards of need. Abolished in 1996 and replaced with TANF.

Temporary Assistance to Needy Families (TANF) A policy by which states are given block grants by the federal government in order to create their own programs for public assistance.

means testing Procedure by which potential beneficiaries of a public assistance program establish their eligibility by demonstrating a genuine need for the assistance.

Medicaid A federally financed, state-operated program providing medical services to low-income people.

Programs to which beneficiaries do not have to contribute—**noncontributory programs**—are also known as public assistance programs, or, derisively, as welfare. Until 1996, the most important noncontributory program was **Aid to Families with Dependent Children** (**AFDC**, originally called Aid to Dependent Children, or ADC), which was founded in 1935 by the original Social Security Act. In 1996, Congress abolished AFDC and replaced it with the **Temporary Assistance to Needy Families** (**TANF**) block grant. Eligibility for public assistance is determined by **means testing**, a procedure that requires applicants to show a financial need for assistance. Between 1935 and 1965, the government created programs to provide housing assistance, school lunches, and food stamps to other needy Americans.

Like contributory programs, the noncontributory public assistance programs also made their most significant advances in the 1960s and 1970s. The largest single category of expansion was the establishment in 1965 of **Medicaid**, a program that provides extended medical services to all low-income persons who have already established eligibility through means testing under AFDC or TANF. Noncontributory programs underwent another major transformation in the 1970s in the level of benefits they provide. Besides being means tested, noncontributory programs are federal rather than national; grants-in-aid are provided by the national government to the states as incentives to establish the programs (see Chapter 3). Thus, from the beginning there were considerable disparities in benefits from state to state. The national government sought to rectify the disparities in levels of old-age benefits in 1974 by creating the **Supplemental Security Income (SSI)** program to augment benefits for the aged, the blind, and the disabled. SSI provides uniform minimum benefits across the entire nation and includes mandatory COLAs. States are allowed to be more generous if they wish, but no state is permitted to provide benefits below the minimum level set by the national government. As a result, twenty-five states increased their own SSI benefits to the mandated level.

The TANF program is also administered by the states and, as with the old-age benefits just discussed, benefit levels vary widely from state to state (see Figure 13.3). For example, although the median national "standard of need" for

FIGURE 13.3 VARIATIONS IN STATE SPENDING ON TANF BENEFITS

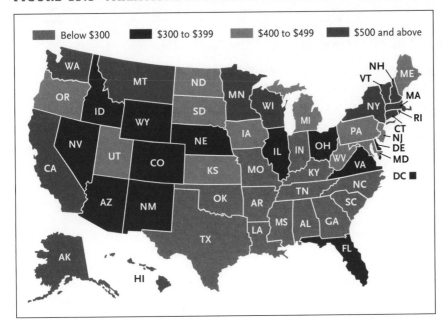

SOURCE: U.S. House of Representatives, Ways and Means Committee, *2003 Green Book*, waysandmeans.house.gov/media/pdf/greenbook2003/section7.pdf (accessed 7/15/09).

a family of three was $1,306 per month (55 percent of the poverty-line income) in 2004, the states' monthly TANF benefits varied from $170 in Mississippi to $923 in Alaska.[11] Even the most generous TANF payments are well below the federal poverty line. In 2008, the poverty level for a family of three included an income of less than $17,600, or $1,466 a month.

The number of people receiving AFDC benefits expanded in the 1970s, in part because new welfare programs had been established in the mid-1960s: Medicaid (discussed earlier) and **Food Stamps**, which are coupons that can be exchanged for food at most grocery stores. These programs provide what are called **in-kind benefits**—noncash goods and services that would otherwise have to be paid for in cash by the beneficiary. In addition to simply adding on the cost of medical services and food to the level of benefits given to AFDC recipients, the possibility of receiving Medicaid benefits provided an incentive for poor Americans to establish their eligibility for AFDC, which would also establish their eligibility to receive Medicaid. At the same time, the government significantly expanded its publicity efforts to encourage the dependent unemployed to establish their eligibility for these various programs.

Another more complex reason for the growth of AFDC in the 1970s was that it became more difficult for the government to terminate people's AFDC benefits for lack of eligibility. In the 1970 case of *Goldberg v. Kelly*, the Supreme Court held that

Supplemental Security Income (SSI) A program providing a minimum monthly income to people who pass a "means test" and who are sixty-five or older, blind, or disabled. Financed from general revenues rather than from Social Security contributions.

Food Stamps Coupons that can be exchanged for food at most grocery stores; the largest in-kind benefits program.

in-kind benefits Goods and services provided to needy individuals and families by the federal government.

---

[11] U.S. House of Representatives, Ways and Means Committee, *2003 Green Book*, http://waysandmeans .house.gov/media/pdf/greenbook2003/section7.pdf (accessed 7/15/09).

The Welfare State as Fiscal and Social Policy

Fiscal policy—When the economy is declining and more and more people have less money to spend, welfare payments increase, which helps maintain consumer spending, thus shortening the "downside" of the business cycle. On the other hand, if inflation is threatening, then welfare taxes absorb some consumer dollars, having a (desired) damping effect on an economy that is growing too quickly.

Social policy—Contributory programs were established in recognition of the fact that not all people have the means to establish financial security, that is, to save for the future. These programs are financed by taxation and can be considered "forced savings." Noncontributory programs provide assistance to those who cannot provide for themselves.

entitlement Eligibility for benefits by virtue of a category of benefits defined by legislation.

the financial benefits of AFDC could not be revoked without due process—that is, a hearing at which evidence is presented, and so on.[12] This ruling inaugurated the concept of the **entitlement**, a class of government benefits with a status similar to that of property (which, according to the Fourteenth Amendment, cannot be taken from people "without due process of law"). *Goldberg v. Kelly* did not provide that the beneficiary had a "right" to government benefits; it provided that once a person's eligibility for AFDC was established, and as long as the program was still in effect, that person could not be denied benefits without due process. The decision left open the possibility that Congress could terminate the program and its benefits by passing a piece of legislation. If the welfare benefit were truly a property right, Congress would have no authority to deny it by a mere majority vote.

Thus the establishment of in-kind benefit programs and the legal obstacles involved in terminating benefits contributed to the growth of the welfare state. But it is important to note that real federal spending on AFDC itself did not rise after the mid-1970s. Unlike Social Security, AFDC was not indexed to inflation; without cost of living adjustments, the value of AFDC benefits fell by more than one-third. Moreover, the largest noncontributory welfare program, Medicaid (as shown by Table 13.2), actually devotes less than one-third of its expenditures to poor families; the rest goes to the disabled and the elderly in nursing homes.[13] Together, these programs have significantly increased the security of the poor and the vulnerable and must be included in a genuine assessment of the redistributive influence and the cost of the welfare system today.

Welfare Reform

During the 1992 presidential campaign, Bill Clinton promised to "end welfare as we know it," but not until the approach of the 1996 presidential campaign was the Personal Responsibility and Work Opportunity Act (PRA) signed into law.

---

[12] *Goldberg v. Kelly*, 397 U.S. 254 (1970).

[13] See U.S. House of Representatives, Committee on Ways and Means, *Where Your Money Goes: The 1994–95 Green Book* (Washington, D.C.: Brassey's, 1994), pp. 325, 802.

The new law replaced the sixty-one-year-old program of AFDC and its education–work training program, known as JOBS, with block grants to the states over a five-year period for Temporary Assistance to Needy Families (TANF). The Act not only imposed the five-year time limit on the TANF benefits but also required work after two years of benefits. It also required community service after two months of benefits, unless the state administrators agree to an exemption of the rule. Many additional requirements for eligibility were spelled out in the law. And the states are under severe obligation to impose all these requirements lest they lose their TANF federal grants.

Since this new welfare law was enacted, the number of families receiving assistance has dropped by 58 percent.[14] Some observers take this as a sign that welfare reform is working; indeed, former welfare recipients have been more successful at finding and keeping jobs than many critics of the new law predicted.

Other additional evidence suggests more caution in declaring welfare reform a success. Early studies show that welfare recipients are not paid enough to pull their families out of poverty and that child care and transportation continue to cause many problems for people seeking to leave welfare.[15] Moreover, welfare reform was implemented in a time of record low unemployment levels. As unemployment rose in 2009, welfare recipients had enormous difficulty finding jobs. These concerns suggest that the 1996 law may not mark the end of welfare reform but may be a prelude to a round of future reforms.

IMPLEMENTING PUBLIC POLICIES: THE TECHNIQUES OF CONTROL

Up to this point, our introduction to public policy has focused on the substance and goals of policies, particularly economic policies. But underlying each substantive policy issue and each policy goal are means and methods for satisfying the substantive demands and for implementing the goals. These are called *techniques of control*. Techniques of control are to policy makers roughly what tools are to a carpenter. There are a limited number of techniques; there is a logic or an orderliness to each of them; and an accumulation of experience helps us know if a certain technique is likely to work. There is no unanimous agreement on technique, just as carpenters will disagree about the best tool for a task. But we offer here a workable elementary handbook of techniques that will be useful for analyzing all policies.

The "In Brief" box on page 404 lists important techniques of control available to policy makers. They are grouped into three categories—promotional, regulatory, and redistributive techniques. In this section, the specifics of each will be discussed and explained. Each category of policy is associated with a different kind of politics.

---

[14] *1998 Green Book*, Overview of Entitlement Programs, http://aspe.hhs.gov/98gb/intro.htm (accessed 7/15/09).

[15] See National Conference of State Legislatures, "Tracking Recipients after They Leave Welfare," www.ncsl.org/statefed/welfare/followup.htm (accessed June 1998).

Techniques of Public Control

Types of Techniques	Techniques	Definitions and Examples
Promotional techniques	Subsidies and grants of cash, land, etc.	"Patronage" is the promotion of private activity through what recipients consider benefits (Example: During the nineteenth century, the government encouraged westward settlement by granting land to those who went west.)
	Contract	Agreement with individuals or firms in the private sector to purchase goods or services
	License	Unconditional permission to do something that is otherwise illegal (franchise, permit)
Regulatory techniques	Criminal penalties	Heavy fines or imprisonment; loss of citizenship
	Civil penalties	Less onerous fines, probation, exposure, restitution
	Administrative regulation	Setting interest rates, maintaining standards of health, investigating and publicizing wrongdoing
	Subsidies, contracting, and licensing	Regulatory techniques when certain conditions are attached (Example: The government refuses to award a contract to a firm that shows no evidence of affirmative action in hiring.)
	Regulatory taxation	Taxes that keep consumption or production down (liquor, gas, cigarette taxes)
	Expropriation	"Eminent domain"—the power to take private property for public use
Redistributive techniques	Fiscal use of taxes	Altering the distribution of money by changing taxes or tax rules
	Fiscal use of budgeting	Deficit spending to pump money into the economy when it needs a boost; creating a budget surplus through taxes to discourage consumption in inflationary times
	Fiscal use of credit and interest (monetary techniques)	Changing interest rates to affect both demand for money and consumption. When rates are low, it is easy to borrow and thus invest and consume

In other words, since these techniques are different ways of using government, each type is likely to develop a distinctive pattern of power.

Promotional Techniques

Promotional techniques are the carrots of public policy. Their purpose is to encourage people to do something they might not otherwise do, or to get people to do more of what they are already doing. Sometimes the purpose is merely to compensate people for something done in the past. As the "In Brief" box demonstrates, promotional techniques can be classified into at least three separate types—subsidies, contracts, and licenses.

Subsidies. **Subsidies** are simply government grants of cash, goods, services, or land. Although subsidies are often denounced as "giveaways," they have played a fundamental role in the history of government in the United States. As we discussed in Chapter 3, subsidies were the dominant form of public policy of the national government throughout the nineteenth century. They continue to be an important category of public policy at all levels of government. The first planning document ever written for the national government, Alexander Hamilton's *Report on Manufactures,* was based almost entirely on Hamilton's assumption that American industry could be encouraged by federal subsidies and that these were not only desirable but constitutional.

The thrust of Hamilton's plan was not lost on later policy makers. Subsidies in the form of land grants were given to farmers and to railroad companies to encourage western settlement. Substantial cash subsidies have traditionally been given to commercial shipbuilders to help build the commercial fleet and to guarantee the use of the ships as military personnel carriers in time of war.

Subsidies have always been a technique favored by politicians because subsidies can be treated as "benefits" that can be doled out in response to many demands that might otherwise produce profound conflict. Subsidies can, in other words, be used to buy off the opposition.

So widespread is the use of the subsidy technique in government that it takes encyclopedias to keep track of them all. Indeed, for a number of years, one company published an annual *Encyclopedia of U.S. Government Benefits,* a thousand-page guide to benefits

> for every American—from all walks of life . . . [R]ight now, there are thousands of other American Taxpayers who are missing out on valuable Government Services, simply because they do not know about them. . . . Start your own business. . . . Take an extra vacation. . . . Here are all the opportunities your tax dollars have made possible.[16]

---

[16] Roy A. Grisham and Paul McConaughty, eds., *Encyclopedia of U.S. Government Benefits* (Union City, N.J.: William H. Wise, 1972). The quote is taken from the dust jacket. A comparable guide published by the *New York Times* is called *Federal Aid for Cities and Towns* (New York: Quadranble Books, 1972). It contains 1,312 pages of federal government benefits that cities and towns, rather than individuals, can apply for.

promotional technique A technique of control that encourages people to do something they might not otherwise do, or to continue an action or behavior. Three types of promotional techniques are subsidies, contracts, and licenses.

subsidy A government grant of cash or other valuable commodities, such as land, to an individual or organization; used to promote activities desired by the government, to reward political support, or to buy off political opposition.

Another secret of the popularity of subsidies is that those who receive the benefits do not perceive the controls inherent in them. In the first place, most of the resources available for subsidies come from taxation. (During the nineteenth century, there was a lot of public land to distribute, but that is no longer the case.) Second, the effect of any subsidy has to be measured in terms of what people *would be doing* if the subsidy had not been available. For example, many thousands of people settled in lands west of the Mississippi only because land subsidies were available. Hundreds of research laboratories exist in universities and corporations only because certain types of research subsidies from the government are available. And finally, once subsidies exist, the threat of their removal becomes a very significant technique of control.

Contracting.   Like any corporation, a government agency must purchase goods and services by contract. The law requires open bidding for a substantial proportion of these contracts because government contracts are extremely valuable to businesses in the private sector and because the opportunities for abuse are great. But contracting is more than a method of buying goods and services. Contracting is also an important technique of policy because government agencies are often authorized to use their **contracting power** as a means of encouraging corporations to improve themselves, as a means of helping to build up whole sectors of the economy, and as a means of encouraging certain desirable goals or behavior, such as equal employment opportunity.

contracting power The power of government to set conditions on companies seeking to sell goods or services to government agencies.

For example, the infant airline industry of the 1930s was nurtured by the national government's lucrative contracts to carry airmail. A more recent example is the use of contracting to encourage industries, universities, and others to engage in research and development.

The power of contracting was of great significance for administrations such as those of Reagan and Bush because of their commitment to "privatization." When a presidential administration wants to turn over as much government as possible to the private sector, it may seek to terminate a government program and leave the activity to private companies to pick up. That would be true privatization. But in most instances, true privatization is neither sought nor achieved. Instead, the government program is transferred to a private company to provide the service *under a contract with the government,* paid for by the government, and supervised by a government agency. In this case, *privatization* is only a euphemism. Government by contract has been around for a long time and has always been seen by business as a major source of economic opportunity.

license Permission to engage in some activity that is otherwise illegal, such as hunting or practicing medicine.

Licensing.   A **license** is a privilege granted by a government to do something that it otherwise considers to be illegal. For example, state laws make practicing medicine or driving a taxi illegal without a license. The states then create a board of doctors and a "hack bureau" to grant licenses for the practice of medicine or for the operation of a cab to all persons who have met the particular qualifications specified in the statute or by the agency.

Like subsidies and contracting, licensing has two sides. One is the giveaway side, making the license a desirable object of patronage. The other side of licensing is the control or regulatory side.

Regulatory Techniques. If promotional techniques are the carrots of public policy, **regulatory techniques** are the sticks. Regulation comes in several forms, but all regulatory techniques share a common trait—direct government control of conduct. The conduct—such as drunk driving or false advertising—may be regulated because people feel it is harmful or threatens to be. Or the conduct—such as prostitution, gambling, or drinking—may be regulated because people think it's just plain immoral, whether it's harming anybody or not. Because there are many forms of regulation, we subdivide them here: (1) police regulation, through civil and criminal penalties, (2) administration regulation, and (3) regulatory taxation.

Police Regulation. "Police regulation" is not a technical term, but we use it for this category because these techniques come closest to the traditional exercise of **police power.** After a person's arrest and conviction, these techniques are administered by courts and, where necessary, penal institutions. They are regulatory techniques.

    Civil penalties usually are fines or some other form of material restitution (such as public service) as a sanction for violating civil laws or such common-law principles as negligence. Civil penalties can range from a $5 fine for a parking violation to a heavier penalty for late payment of income taxes to much more onerous penalties for violating antitrust laws against unfair competition or environmental protection laws against pollution. *Criminal penalties* usually refer to imprisonment but can also involve heavy fines and the loss of certain civil rights and liberties, such as the right to vote or freedom of speech.

Administrative Regulation. Police regulation addresses conduct considered immoral. In order to eliminate such conduct, strict laws have been passed and severe sanctions enacted. But what about conduct that is not considered morally wrong but has harmful consequences? There is, for example, nothing morally wrong with radio or television broadcasting. But broadcasting on a particular frequency or channel is regulated by government because there would be virtual chaos if everybody could broadcast on any frequency at any time.

    This kind of conduct is thought of less as *policed* conduct and more as *regulated* conduct. When conduct is said to be regulated, the purpose is rarely to eliminate the conduct but rather to influence it toward more appropriate channels, toward more appropriate locations, or toward certain qualified types of persons, all for the purpose of minimizing injuries or inconveniences. This type of regulated conduct is sometimes called **administrative regulation** because the controls are given over to administrative agencies rather than to the police. Each regulatory agency in the executive branch has extensive powers to keep a sector of the economy under surveillance and also has powers to make rules dealing with the behavior of individual companies and people. But these administrative agencies have fewer powers of punishment than the police and the courts have, and the administrative agencies generally rely on the courts to issue orders enforcing the rules and decisions made by the agencies.

    Sometimes a government will adopt administrative regulation if an economic activity is considered so important that it is not to be entrusted to competition among several companies in the private sector. This is the rationale for the

regulatory technique A technique that government uses to control the conduct of the people.

police power Power reserved to the state to regulate the health, safety, and morals of its citizens.

administrative regulation Rules made by regulatory agencies and commissions.

regulation of local or regional power companies. A single company, traditionally called a *utility*, is given an exclusive license (or franchise) to offer these services, but since the one company is made a legal monopoly and is protected from competition by other companies, the government gives an administrative agency the power to regulate the quality of the services rendered, the rates charged for those services, and the margin of profit that the company is permitted to make.

At other times, administrative regulation is the chosen technique because the legislature decides that the economy needs protection from itself—that is, it may set up a regulatory agency to protect companies from destructive or predatory competition, on the assumption that economic competition is not always its own solution. This is the rationale behind the Federal Trade Commission, which has the responsibility of watching over such practices as price discrimination or pooling agreements between companies when their purpose is to eliminate competitors.

Subsidies, licensing, and contracting are listed twice in the "In Brief" box on page 404 because although these techniques can be used strictly as promotional policies, they can also be used as techniques of administrative regulation. It all depends on whether the law sets serious conditions on eligibility for the subsidy, license, or contract. To put it another way, the government can use the threat of losing a valuable subsidy, license, or contract as a sanction to improve compliance with the goals of regulation. For example, the threat of removal of the subsidies called "federal aid to education" has had a very significant influence on the willingness of schools to cooperate in the desegregation of their student bodies and faculties. For another example, social welfare subsidies (benefits) can be lowered to encourage or force people to take low-paying jobs, or they can be increased to placate people when they engage in political protest.[17]

Like subsidies and licensing, government contracting can be an entirely different kind of technique of control when the contract or its denial is used as a reward or punishment to gain obedience in a regulatory program. For example, presidents Kennedy and Johnson initiated the widespread use of executive orders, administered by the Office of Federal Contract Compliance in the Department of Labor, to prohibit racial discrimination by firms receiving government contracts.[18] Several federal statutes also prohibit discriminatory practices by contractors. The value of these contracts to many private corporations was so great that they were quite willing to alter if not eliminate racial discrimination in employment practices if that was the only way to qualify to bid for government contracts. Today it is common to see on employment advertisements the statement "We are an equal opportunity employer."

Regulatory Taxation.   Taxation is generally understood to be a fiscal technique, and it will be discussed as such below. But in many instances, the primary purpose

---

[17] For an evaluation of the policy of withholding subsidies to carry out desegregation laws, see Gary Orfield, *Must We Bus?* (Washington, D.C.: Brookings Institution, 1978). For an evaluation of the use of subsidies to encourage work or to calm political unrest, see Frances Fox Piven and Richard Cloward, *Regulating the Poor: The Functions of Public Welfare* (New York: Random House, 1971).

[18] For an evaluation of Kennedy's use of this kind of executive power, see Carl M. Brauer, *John F. Kennedy and the Second Reconstruction* (New York: Columbia University Press, 1977), especially chap. 3.

of the tax is not to raise revenue but to discourage or eliminate an activity altogether by making it too expensive for most people. For example, since the end of Prohibition, although there has been no penalty for the production or sale of alcoholic beverages, the alcohol industry has not been free from regulation. First, all alcoholic beverages have to be licensed, allowing only those companies that are *bonded* to put their product on the market. Federal and state taxes on alcohol are also made disproportionately high, on the theory that, in addition to the revenue gained, less alcohol will be consumed.

We may be seeing a great deal more regulation by taxation in the future for at least the following reasons. First, it is a kind of hidden regulation, acceptable to people who in principle are against regulation. Second, it permits a certain amount of choice. For example, a heavy tax on gasoline or on smokestack and chemical industries (called an "effluent tax") will encourage drivers and these companies to regulate their own activities by permitting them to decide how much pollution they can afford. Third, advocates of regulatory taxation believe it to be more efficient than other forms of regulation, requiring less bureaucracy and less supervision.

Expropriation. Expropriation—seizing private property for a public use—is a widely used technique of control in the United States, especially in land-use regulation. Almost all public works, from highways to parks to government office buildings, involve the forceful taking of some private property in order to assemble sufficient land and the correct distribution of land for the necessary construction. The vast Interstate Highway Program required expropriation of thousands of narrow strips of private land. "Urban redevelopment" projects often require city governments to use the powers of seizure in the service of private developers, who actually build the urban projects on land that would be far too expensive if purchased on the open market. Private utilities that supply electricity and gas to individual subscribers are given powers to take private property whenever a new facility or a right-of-way is needed.

We generally call the power to expropriate eminent domain.[19] The Fifth Amendment to the U.S. Constitution surrounds this expropriation power with important safeguards against abuse, so that government agencies in the United States are not permitted to use that power except through a strict due process, and they must offer "fair market value" for the land sought. Another form of expropriation is forcing individuals to work for a public purpose—for example, drafting people for service in the armed forces.

Redistributive Techniques

Redistributive techniques are usually of two types—fiscal and monetary—but they have a common purpose: to control people by manipulating the entire economy rather than by regulating people directly. As observed earlier, regulatory techniques

---

[19] For an evaluation of the politics of eminent domain, see Theodore Lowi, Benjamin Ginsberg, et al., *Poliscide* (New York: Macmillan, 1976 and 1990), especially chaps. 11 and 12, written by Julia and Thomas Vitullo-Martin.

focus on individual conduct. The regulatory rule may be written to apply to the whole economy: "Walking on the grass is not permitted," or "Membership in a union may not be used to deny employment, nor may a worker be fired for promoting union membership." Nevertheless, the regulation focuses on individual strollers who might walk on the grass or individual employers who discriminate against a trade-union member. In contrast, techniques are redistributive if they seek to control conduct more indirectly by altering the conditions of conduct or manipulating the environment of conduct.

Fiscal Techniques.   Fiscal techniques of control are the government's taxing and spending powers. Personal and corporate income taxes, which raise most government revenues, are the most prominent examples. Although the manifest purpose of taxes is to raise revenue, each type of tax has a different impact on the economy, and government can plan for that impact. For example, although the main reason given for increasing the Social Security tax (which is an income tax) under President Carter was to keep Social Security solvent, a big reason for it in the minds of many legislators was that it would reduce inflation by shrinking the amount of money people could spend on goods and services.

Likewise, President Clinton's commitment in his 1992 campaign to a "middle-class tax cut" was motivated by the goal of encouraging economic growth through increased consumption. Soon after the election, on learning that the deficit was far larger than had earlier been reported, he had to break his promise of such a tax cut. Nevertheless, the idea of a middle-class tax cut is still an example of a fiscal policy aimed at increased consumption, because of the theory that people in middle-income brackets will tend to spend a high proportion of unexpected earnings or windfalls, rather than saving or investing them.[20]

Monetary Techniques.   Monetary techniques also seek to influence conduct by manipulating the entire economy through the supply or availability of money. The Federal Reserve Board (the Fed) can adopt what is called a "hard money policy" by increasing the interest rate it charges member banks (called the discount rate). Another monetary policy is to increase or decrease the reserve requirement, which sets the actual proportion of deposited money that a bank must keep "on demand" as it makes all the rest of the deposits available as new loans. A third important technique used by the Fed is open-market operations—the buying and selling of Treasury securities to absorb excess dollars or to release more dollars into the economy.

Spending Power as Fiscal Policy.   Perhaps the most important redistributive technique of all is the most familiar one—the **"spending power,"** which is a combination of subsidies and contracts. These techniques can be used for policy goals far beyond the goods and services bought and the individual conduct regulated.

spending power A combination of subsidies and contracts that the government can use to redistribute income.

---

[20] For a fascinating behind-the-scenes look at how and why President Clinton abandoned his campaign commitment to tax cuts and economic stimulus, and instead accepted the fiscal conservatism advocated by the Federal Reserve and its chair, Alan Greenspan, see Bob Woodward, *The Agenda: Inside the Clinton White House* (New York: Simon & Schuster, 1994).

One of the most important examples of the national government's use of purchasing power as a fiscal or redistributive technique is found in another of the everyday activities of the Federal Reserve Board. As mentioned above, the Fed goes into the "open market" to buy and sell government bonds in order to increase or decrease the amount of money in circulation. By doing so, the Fed can raise or lower the prices paid for goods and the interest rate paid on loans.

CHAPTER REVIEW

Madison set the tone for this chapter in *The Federalist*, No. 51, in three sentences of prose that have more the character of poetry:

> Justice is the end of government.
> It is the end of civil society.
> It ever has been and ever will be
>   pursued
>   Until it be obtained,
> Or until liberty be lost in the pursuit.

Our economic system is the most productive ever developed, but it is not perfect—and many policies have been adopted over the years to deal with its imperfections. Policy is the purposive and deliberate aspect of government in action. But if a policy is to come anywhere near obtaining its stated goal (clean air, stable prices, equal employment opportunity), it must be backed up by some kind of sanction—the ability to reward or punish—coupled with some ability to administer or implement those sanctions. These "techniques of control" were presented in three categories—promotional techniques, regulatory techniques, and redistributive techniques. These techniques are found in the multitude of actual policies adopted by legislatures and implemented by administrative agencies. Good policy analysis consists largely of identifying the techniques of control and choosing the policies that seek to manipulate "the economy as a system."

Promotional techniques are thought to be the carrots of public policy. Government subsidies, government contracts, and licensing are examples of incentives available to government to get people to do things they might not otherwise do, or to do more of what they are already doing. The first part of this chapter examined how promotional techniques are used to promote and maintain the national market economy.

Regulatory techniques seek to control conduct by imposing restrictions and obligations directly on individuals. Although many people complain about regulatory policies, the purpose of most such policies is to benefit the economy by imposing restrictions on companies thought to be engaging in activities harmful to the economy. For example, antitrust policies are intended to benefit economic competition by restricting monopolistic practices. Less popular regulatory policies seek to protect the consumer even if the regulation is an intervention in the economy that reduces competition or efficiency. Laws requiring companies to reduce air and water pollution, laws keeping new drugs off the market, and laws requiring the full labeling of the contents of foods and drugs are examples of such regulatory policies.

Redistributive techniques fall into two groups: fiscal and monetary policies. The government uses redistributive techniques to influence the entire economy, largely in a capitalistic direction. Currency, banks, and credit are heavily shaped by national monetary policies. Taxation, the most important fiscal policy, exists for far more than raising revenue. Taxation is a redistributive policy that can be either progressive (with higher taxes for upper than for lower incomes) or regressive (applying one rate to all and therefore taking a higher percentage tax from the lowest brackets). Various exemptions, deductions, and investment credits are written into taxes to encourage desired behavior, such as more investment or more saving versus more consumption.

The capitalist system is the most productive type of economy on earth, but it is not perfect. Poverty amid plenty continues. Many policies have emerged to deal with these imperfections. A part of this chapter discussed the welfare state and gave an account of how Americans came to recognize extremes of poverty and dependency and how Congress then attempted to reduce these extremes with policies that moderately redistribute resources.

Welfare state policies are subdivided into several categories. First there are the contributory programs. Virtually all employed persons are required to contribute a portion of their wages into welfare trust funds, and later on, when they retire or are disabled, they have a right, or entitlement, to draw on those contributions. Another category of welfare is composed of noncontributory programs, also called public assistance. These programs provide benefits for people who can demonstrate need by passing a means test. Assistance from contributory and noncontributory programs can involve either cash benefits or in-kind benefits.

FOR FURTHER READING

Barth, James, Gerard Caprio, and Ross Levine. *Rethinking Bank Regulation*. New York: Cambridge University Press, 2005.

Beland, Daniel. *Social Security: History and Politics from the New Deal to the Privatization Debate*. Lawrence: University Press of Kansas, 2007.

Ehrenreich, Barbara. *Nickel and Dimed: On (Not) Getting By in America*. New York: Holt, 2001.

Epsing-Andersen, Gøsta. *Why We Need a New Welfare State*. New York: Oxford University Press, 2002.

Farrier, Jasmine. *Passing the Buck: Congress, the Budget, and Deficits*. Lexington: University Press of Kentucky, 2004.

Gilbert, Neil. *Transformation of the Welfare State*. New York: Oxford University Press, 2004.

Hacker, Jacob. *The Divided Welfare State: The Battle over Public and Private Social Benefits in the United States*. New York: Cambridge University Press, 2002.

Ingham, Geoffrey. *The Nature of Money*. New York: Polity, 2004.

Keith, Robert, and Allen Schick. *The Federal Budget Process*. New York: Nova, 2003.

McCarty, Nolan, Keith Poole, and Howard Rosenthal. *Polarized America: The Dance of Unequal Riches*. Cambridge, Mass.: MIT Press, 2006.

Meyers, Annette. *Evolution of United States Budgeting*. New York: Praeger, 2002.

Murray, Charles. *In Our Hands: A Plan to Remake the Welfare State*. Washington, D.C.: American Enterprise Institute Press, 2006.

Sachs, Jeffrey. *The End of Poverty: Economic Possibilities for Our Time*. New York: Penguin, 2006.

Shipler, David. *The Working Poor*. New York: Vintage, 2005.

Skocpol, Theda. *The Missing Middle: Working Families and the Future of American Social Policy*. New York: Norton, 2000.

Stern, Gary, and Ron Feldman. *Too Big to Fail: The Hazards of Bank Bailouts*. Washington, D.C.: Brookings Institution, 2004.

Stiglitz, Joseph. *Making Globalization Work*. New York: Norton, 2006.

Trattner, Walter. *From Poor Law to Welfare State*. 6th ed. New York: Free Press, 1998.

Weir, Margaret, ed. *The Social Divide: Political Parties and the Future of Activist Government*. Washington, D.C.: Brookings Institution, 1998.

Wells, Donald. *The Federal Reserve System*. Jefferson, N.C.: McFarland, 2004.

Wilson, Graham. *Business and Politics*. Washington, D.C.: Congressional Quarterly Press, 2003.

○ reader selection

Additional study and review materials are available online at wwnorton.com/studyspace/

14

Foreign Policy and Democracy

HOW DOES FOREIGN POLICY WORK?

The term foreign policy refers to the programs and policies that determine America's relations with other nations and foreign entities. Foreign policy includes diplomacy, military and security policy, international human rights policies, and various forms of economic policy, such as trade policy and international energy policy. Of course, foreign policy and domestic policy are not completely separate categories but are closely interwined. Take security policy, for example. Defending the nation requires the design and manufacture of tens of billions of dollars worth of military hardware. The manufacture and procurement of this military equipment involves a host of economic policies, and paying for it shapes America's fiscal policies.

At first glance, the basic contours of the foreign-policy arena seem similar to those of America's other policy domains. The nation's chief foreign-policy makers are the president, Congress, and the bureaucracy. Just as in the cases of economic and social policy, battles over foreign policy often erupt between and within these institutions as competing politicians and a variety of organized groups and rival political forces pursue their own version of the national interest or their own more narrow purposes, which they seek to present as the national interest. In many instances, the outcome of these battles among competing forces depends on the relative power of the institutions they control. Institutions affect foreign as well as domestic policy outcomes. In the foreign-policy arena, the institutional powers of the presidency give presidents and their allies an advantage over political forces based in Congress, although Congress is not without institutional resources of its own through which to influence the conduct of foreign policy. Moreover, like domestic-policy matters, foreign-policy issues often figure prominently in public debate and national election campaigns as competing forces seek to mobilize popular support for their positions or at least to castigate the opposition for the putative shortcomings of its policies.

Despite these similarities, the foreign- and domestic-policy arenas differ in at least three important ways. The first is history. History always matters, but history and historical memory play a larger role in the foreign-policy realm than in most areas of domestic policy. Foreign policy, as we shall see, is guided by historical events, experiences, and commitments. Debates over foreign policy tend to be strongly affected by competing historical perceptions. For example, those who argue in favor of confronting Iran, North Korea, and other potentially hostile powers often refer to the disastrous consequences of pre–World War II efforts by Britain and France to "appease" Nazi Germany. On the other hand, those who favor withdrawing American forces from Iraq, a process that began in 2009, cite the parallels to America's failed efforts in Vietnam. Each group's view of the present is strongly shaped by its understanding of the past.

Second, in the foreign-policy arena, questions of the national interest figure more prominently than in most domestic-policy debates. To be sure, advocates of competing social and economic policies argue that their preferred programs promote the interests of the nation as a whole. Yet such pronouncements are usually taken with a grain of salt, and we are usually prepared to forgive advocates whose preferred economic or social policies turn out to serve discrete constituencies rather than the entire nation. In the realm of foreign policy, though, the public interest looms larger. In a world where entities ranging from rival nation-states to shadowy terrorist goups present genuine threats to the security of the entire nation, advocates of particular foreign policies are more likely than their domestic counterparts to be asked to demonstrate that the policies they espouse serve broad national interests. In the realm of foreign policy, unlike, say, the arena of health-care reform, advocates can and do accuse one another of threatening the nation's security and demonstrating outright disloyalty.

Finally, the foreign-policy arena is affected by America's historic wariness of foreign commitments and the difficulties of making and justifying what are often cold, harsh, calculating foreign-policy decisions in a democratic context. Ever since George Washington, in his Farewell Address, warned the American people "to have . . . as little political connection as possible" to foreign nations and to "steer clear of permanent alliances," Americans have been distrustful of foreign policy. Despite this distrust, the United States has been forced to pursue its national interests in the world, even when this has meant fighting a war. As a result of its foreign entanglements, the United States emerged as a world power, but not without maintaining some misgivings about foreign policy.

THE GOALS OF FOREIGN POLICY

Although U.S. foreign policy has a number of purposes, three main goals stand out. These are security, prosperity, and the creation of a better world. These goals are, of course, closely intertwined and can never be pursued fully in isolation from each other.

Security

To many Americans, the chief purpose of the nation's foreign policy is protection of America's security in an often hostile world. Traditionally, the United States has been concerned about threats that might emanate from other nations, such as Nazi Germany during the 1940s and then Soviet Russia until the Soviet Union's collapse in the late 1980s. Today, American security policy is concerned not only with the actions of other nations but also with the activities of terrorist groups and other hostile **non-state actors**.[1] To protect the nation's security from foreign threats, the United States has built an enormous military apparatus and a complex array of intelligence-gathering institutions, such as the Central Intelligence Agency (CIA), charged with evaluating and anticipating challenges from abroad.[2]

Security is, of course, a broad term. Policy makers must be concerned with Americans' physical security. The 9/11 terrorist attacks killed and injured thousands of Americans; the government constantly fears that new attacks could be even more catastrophic. As Figure 14.1 shows, U.S. military spending has in-

non-state actor
A group other than a nation-state that attempts to play a role in the international system. Terrorist groups are one type of non-state actor.

[1] Rupert Smith, *The Utility of Force: The Art of War in the Modern World* (New York: Vintage, 2008).

[2] D. Robert Worley, *Shaping U.S. Military Forces: Revolution or Relevance in a Post–Cold War World* (Westport, Conn.: Praeger Security International, 2006).

FIGURE 14.1 U.S. MILITARY EXPENDITURE SINCE 2001

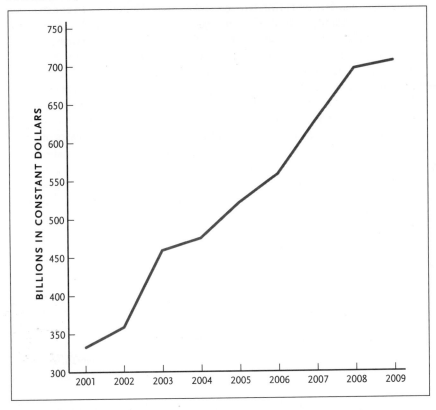

NOTE: Figure includes Department of Defense spending, Department of Energy's nuclear weapons program, the costs of the wars in Iraq and Afghanistan, and DoD-related spending by other agencies.

SOURCE: Center for Arms Control and Non-Proliferation, www.armscontrolcenter.org/policy/securityspending/articles/defense_spending_since_2001/index.html (accessed 7/16/09).

creased dramatically since 2001. Policy makers must also be concerned with such matters as the security of America's food supplies, transportation infrastructure, and energy supplies. Many of our efforts in the Middle East, for example, are aimed at ensuring continuing American access to vital oil fields. In recent years, cyberspace has become a new security concern. The nation's dependence on computers means that the government must be alert to efforts by hostile governments, groups, or even individual "hackers" to damage computer networks. Some thinkers also believe that the spread of democracy to other countries is a key component in promoting security (see "Analyzing the Evidence" on page 440).

Economic Prosperity

A second major goal of U.S. foreign policy is promoting American prosperity. America's international economic policies are intended to expand employment opportunities in the United States, to maintain access to foreign energy supplies at a reasonable cost, to promote foreign investment in the United States, and to lower the prices Americans pay for goods and services.

Among the most visible and important elements of U.S. international economic policy is trade policy. The promotion and advertising of American goods and services abroad is a long-standing goal of U.S. trade policy, and it is one of the major obligations of the Department of Commerce. Yet modern trade policy involves a complex arrangement of treaties, tariffs, and other mechanisms of policy formation. For example, the United States has a long-standing policy of granting **most favored nation status** to certain countries—that is, the United States offers to another country the same tariff rate it already gives to its most favored trading partner, in return for trade (and sometimes other) concessions. In 1998, to avoid any suggestion that "most favored nation" implied some special relationship with an undemocratic country (China, for example), President Clinton changed the term from "most favored nation" to "normal trade relations."[3]

The most important international organization for promoting free trade is the **World Trade Organization (WTO)**, which officially came into being in 1995. The WTO grew out of the **General Agreement on Tariffs and Trade (GATT)**. Following World War II, GATT had brought together a wide range of nations for regular negotiations designed to reduce barriers to trade. Such barriers, many believed, had contributed to the breakdown of the world economy in the 1930s and had helped to cause World War II. The WTO has 153 members worldwide; decisions about trade are made by the Ministerial Conference, which meets every two years. Similar policy goals are pursued in regional arrangements, such as the **North American Free Trade Agreement (NAFTA)**, a trade treaty among the United States, Canada, and Mexico.

For over a half century, the United States has led the world in supporting free trade as the best route to growth and prosperity. Yet the American government, too, has sought to protect domestic industry when it is politically necessary. Subsidies, as we have seen, have long boosted American agriculture, artificially lowering the price of American products on world markets. The U.S. trade deficit remains significant (see Figure 14.2), and job growth in the United States had been low for several years. Analysts predicted that many of the 2.8 million manufacturing jobs lost in the recession of the early 2000s would never return to the United States.

International Humanitarian Policies

A third goal of American policy is to make the world a better place for all its inhabitants. The main forms of policy that address this goal are international environmental policy, international human rights policy, and international peacekeeping. The United States also contributes to international organizations such

most favored nation status An agreement to offer a trading partner the lowest tariff rate offered to other trading partners.

World Trade Organization (WTO) The international trade agency promoting free trade that grew out of the General Agreement on Tariffs and Trade.

General Agreement on Tariffs and Trade (GATT) The international trade organization, in existence from 1947 to 1995, that set many of the rules governing international trade.

North American Free Trade Agreement (NAFTA) A trade treaty among the United States, Canada, and Mexico to lower and eliminate tariffs among the three countries.

---

[3]This was done quietly in an amendment to the Internal Revenue Service Reform Act (PL 105-206), June 22, 1998. But it was not accomplished easily. See Bob Gravely, "Normal Trade with China Wins Approval," *Congressional Quarterly Weekly Report*, July 25, 1998; and Richard Dunham, "MFN by any other name is . . . NTR?," Business Week online news flash, June 19, 1997.

FIGURE 14.2 U.S. INTERNATIONAL TRADE IN GOODS AND SERVICES

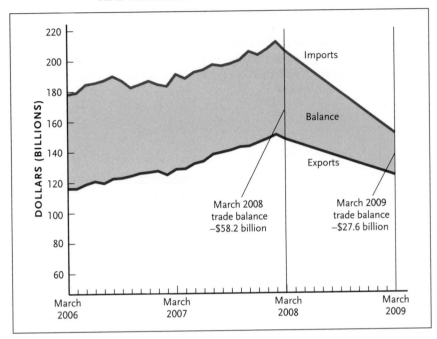

SOURCE: U.S. Census Bureau, www.census.gov/indicator/www/ustrade.html (accessed 5/20/09).

as the World Health Organization that work for global health and against hunger. These policies are often seen as secondary to the other goals of American foreign policy, forced to give way if they interfere with security or foreign economic policy. Moreover, although the United States spends billions annually on security policy and hundreds of millions on trade policy, it spends relatively little on environmental, human rights, and peacekeeping efforts. Some critics charge that America has the wrong priorities, spending far more to make war than to protect human rights and the global environment. Nevertheless, a number of important American foreign policy efforts are, at least in part, designed to make the world a better place.

WHO MAKES AND SHAPES FOREIGN POLICY?

The President

Although many foreign policy decisions can be made without the president's approval, these decisions must be made and implemented in the name of the president. This is not simply a matter of American preference. It is in the nature of international relations that all foreign policies must originate with the president as head of state. The terrorist attacks of September 11, 2001, accentuated the president's role and place in foreign policy immensely. Congress's first action after the attacks was to approve virtually unanimously in both the House and Senate an authorization for the president to use "all necessary and appropriate force," coupled with a $40 billion emergency appropriation bill for home defense and reconstruction. Significant as this was, however, it only emphasized what was already true—that the president is America's head of state and the epicenter of foreign policy (see Table 14.1).

TABLE 14.1 PRESIDENTIAL AND CONGRESSIONAL POWERS AND ROLES IN FOREIGN POLICY

Power	Constitutional Provision		Informal Roles	
	President	Congress	President	Congress
War power	Acts as commander in chief	Declares war, provides for the "common defense"	Makes preemptive military commitments, threatens war, makes secret agreements	Refuses to appropriate funds, investigates and exposes, threatens to impeach
Treaty power	Negotiates treaties	Ratifies treaties (by two-thirds vote in Senate)	Makes executive agreements	Issues resolutions condemning the refusal to appropriate funds
Appointment power	Selects and nominates ambassadors	Approves appointment of ambassadors (by majority vote in Senate)	Makes recess appointments	Issues resolutions condemning appointments, rejects later appointments
Foreign commerce power	Negotiates treaties	Regulates foreign commerce	Makes executive agreements, requests foreign aid	Cuts or reduces aid
Recognition power	Receives ambassadors	Has no explicit powers	Makes friendly visits, conducts negotiations	Makes symbolic visits, issues resolutions

The Bureaucracy

The major foreign policy players in the bureaucracy are the secretaries of the departments of state, defense, and the treasury; the Joint Chiefs of Staff (JCOS), especially the chair of the JCOS; and the director of the Central Intelligence Agency (CIA). A separate unit in the bureaucracy comprising these people and a few others is the National Security Council (NSC), whose main purpose is to iron out the differences among the key players and to integrate their positions in order to confirm or reinforce a decision the president wants to make in foreign policy or military policy. The secretary of commerce has also become an increasingly important foreign-policy maker, with the rise and spread of economic globalization.

To this group another has been added: the Department of Homeland Security. The department has four main divisions: Border and Transportation Security; Emergency Preparedness and Response; Chemical, Biological, Radiological, and Nuclear Countermeasures; and Information Analysis and Infrastructure Protection.

Coordinating the diverse missions of a single agency is a challenge; coordinating the efforts of multiple agencies is especially problematic. The National Security Council and now the Department of Homeland Security attempt to keep the various players on the same page. But will these agencies—each with its own authority, interests, and priorities—follow the same protocol?

In addition to top cabinet-level officials, key lower-level staff members have policy-making influence as strong as that of the Cabinet secretaries. Some may occasionally exceed Cabinet influence. These include the two or three specialized national security advisors in the White House, the staff of the NSC (headed by the national security advisor), and a few other career bureaucrats in the departments of state and defense whose influence varies according to their specialty and to the foreign policy issue at hand.

Congress

In foreign policy, Congress has to be subdivided into three parts. The first part is the Senate. For most of American history, the Senate was the only important congressional foreign policy player because of its constitutional role in reviewing and approving treaties. The treaty power is still the primary entrée of the Senate into foreign-policy making. But since World War II and the continual involvement of the United States in international security and foreign aid, Congress as a whole has become a major foreign-policy maker because most modern foreign policies require financing, which requires approval from both the House of Representatives and the Senate. Congress has also become increasingly involved in foreign-policy making because of the increasing use by the president of **executive agreements** to conduct foreign policy. Executive agreements have the force of treaties but do not require prior approval by the Senate. They can, however, be revoked by action of both chambers of Congress.

The third group of congressional players comprise the foreign-policy and military policy committees: in the Senate these are the Foreign Relations Committee

executive agreement Agreement between the president and another country, which has the force of a treaty but does not require the Senate's "advice and consent."

and the Armed Services Committee; in the House, these are the International Affairs Committee and the Armed Services Committee. Usually, a few members of these committees who have spent years specializing in foreign affairs become trusted members of the foreign-policy establishment and are actually makers rather than mere shapers of foreign policy. In fact, several members of Congress have left to become key foreign-affairs Cabinet members.[4]

Interest Groups

Far and away the most important category of nonofficial player is the interest group—that is, the interest groups to whom one or more foreign-policy issues are of long-standing and vital relevance. The type of interest group with the reputation for the most influence is the economic interest group. Yet the heft of the myths about these groups' influence far outweighs the reality. The influence of organized economic interest groups in foreign policy varies enormously from issue to issue and year to year. Most of these groups are *single-issue* groups and are therefore most active when their particular issue is on the agenda. On many of the broader and more sustained policy issues, such as the North American Free Trade Agreement (NAFTA) or the general question of American involvement in international trade, the larger interest groups find it difficult to maintain tight enough control of their many members to speak with a single voice. The most systematic study of international trade policies and their interest groups concluded that the leaders of these large, economic interest groups spend more time maintaining consensus among their members than lobbying Congress or pressuring major players in the executive branch.[5] The economic interest groups more successful in influencing foreign policy are the narrower, single-issue groups such as the tobacco industry, which over the years has successfully kept American foreign policy from putting heavy restrictions on international trade in and advertising of tobacco products. Likewise, the computer hardware and software industries have successfully hardened the American attitude toward Chinese piracy of intellectual property rights.

Another type of interest group with a well-founded reputation for influence in foreign policy is made up of people with strong attachments and identifications to their country of origin. The interest group with the reputation for greatest influence is Jewish Americans, some of whom maintain family and emotional ties to Israel that may make them particularly concerned with U.S. policies toward Israel. Similarly, some Americans of Irish heritage, despite having resided in the United States for two, three, or four generations, still maintain vigilance about American policies toward Ireland and Northern Ireland. Many other ethnic and national interest groups wield similar influence over American foreign policy.

A third type of interest group, one with a reputation that has been growing in the past two decades, is the human rights interest group. Such groups are made

---

[4] For example, under President Clinton, Senator Lloyd Bentsen and Representative Les Aspin left Congress to become the secretaries of the treasury and defense, respectively.

[5] Raymond A. Bauer, Ithiel de Sola Pool, and Lewis Anthony Dexter, *American Business and Public Policy: The Politics of Foreign Trade*, 2nd ed. (Chicago: Aldine-Atherton, 1972).

up of people who, instead of having self-serving economic or ethnic interests in foreign policy, are genuinely concerned for the welfare and treatment of people throughout the world—particularly those who suffer under harsh political regimes. A relatively small but often quite influential example is Amnesty International, whose exposés of human rights abuses have altered the practices of many regimes around the world. In recent years, the Christian right has also been a vocal advocate for the human rights of Christians who are persecuted in other parts of the world, most notably in China, for their religious beliefs. For example, the Christian Coalition joined groups such as Amnesty International in lobbying Congress to cut trade with countries that permit attacks against religious believers.

A related type of group with a fast-growing influence is the ecological or environmental group, sometimes called the "greens." Groups of this nature often depend more on demonstrations than on the usual forms and strategies of influence in Washington—lobbying and using electoral politics, for example. Demonstrations in strategically located areas can have significant influence on American foreign policy. Recent important examples were the demonstrations against the World Trade Organization (WTO) and its authority to impose limits and restrictions on sovereign nations, even in the United States, such as the 1999 protests in Seattle, Washington, and the 2005 protest in Hong Kong.

The Media

The most important element of the policy influence of the media is the speed and scale with which the media can spread political communications. In that factor alone, the media's influence is growing. More news reaches more people faster, and people's reaction times are therefore shorter than ever before. When we combine this ability to communicate faster with the "feedback" medium of public opinion polling, it becomes clear how the media have become so influential—they enable the American people to reach the president and the other official makers of foreign policy.[6]

Putting It Together

What can we say about who really makes American foreign policy? First, except for the president, the influence of players and shapers varies from case to case—this is a good reason to look with some care at each example of foreign policy in this chapter. Second, since the one constant influence is the centrality of the president in foreign-policy making, it is best to evaluate other actors and factors as they interact with the president.[7] Third, the reason influence varies from case to case is that each case arises under different conditions and with vastly different constraints: for issues that arise and are resolved quickly, the opportunity for influence is limited. Fourth, foreign-policy experts will usually disagree about the level of influence any player or type of player has on policy making.

But just to get started, let's make a few tentative generalizations and then put them to the test with the substance and experience reported in the remainder of this chapter. First, when an important foreign-policy decision has to be made under conditions of crisis—where "time is of the essence"—the influence of the presidency is at its strongest. Second, under those time constraints, access to the decision-making process is limited almost exclusively to the narrowest definition of the "foreign-policy establishment." The arena for participation is tiny; any discussion at all is limited to the officially and constitutionally designated players. To put this another way, in a crisis, the foreign-policy establishment works as it is supposed to.[8] As time becomes less restricted, even when the decision to be made is of great importance, the arena of participation expands to include more government players and more nonofficial, informal players—the most concerned interest groups and the most important journalists. In other words, the arena becomes more pluralistic, and therefore less distinguishable from the politics of domestic policy making. Third, because there are so many other countries with power and interests on any given issue, there are severe limits on the choices the United States can make.

---

[6] For further discussion of the vulnerability of modern presidents to the people through the media, see Theodore Lowi, *The Personal President: Power Invested, Promise Unfulfilled* (Ithaca, N.Y.: Cornell University Press, 1985); Jeffrey K. Tulis, *The Rhetorical Presidency* (Princeton, N.J.: Princeton University Press, 1987); Samuel Kernell, *Going Public: New Strategies of Presidential Leadership* (Washington, D.C.: Congressional Quarterly Press, 1986); Richard Rose, *The Postmodern President: The White House Meets the World* (Chatham, N.J.: Chatham House, 1988); and George C. Edwards, *The Public Presidency: The Pursuit of Popular Support* (New York: St. Martin's, 1983).

[7] A very good brief outline of the centrality of the president in foreign policy will be found in Paul E. Peterson, "The President's Dominance in Foreign Policy Making," *Political Science Quarterly* 109, no. 2 (Summer 1994): 215, 234.

[8] One confirmation of this will be found in Theodore Lowi, *The End of Liberalism*, 2nd ed. (New York: Norton, 1979), pp. 127–30; another will be found in Stephen Krasner, "Are Bureaucracies Important?" *Foreign Policy* 7 (Summer 1972): 159–79. However, it should be added that Krasner was writing his article in disagreement with Graham T. Allison, "Conceptual Models and the Cuban Missile Crisis," *American Political Science Review* 63, no. 3 (September 1969): 689–718.

As one author concludes, in foreign affairs, "policy takes precedence over politics."[9] Thus, even though foreign-policy making in noncrisis situations may more closely resemble the pluralistic politics of domestic policy making, foreign-policy making is still a narrower arena with few participants.

THE VALUES OF AMERICAN FOREIGN POLICY

When President George Washington was preparing to leave office in 1796, he crafted with great care, and with the help of Alexander Hamilton and James Madison, a farewell address that is one of the most memorable documents in American history. In it, one of Washington's greater concerns was to warn the nation against foreign influence:

> History and experience prove that foreign influence is one of the most baneful foes of republican government. . . . The great rule of conduct for us in regard to foreign nations is, in extending our commercial relations to have with them as little political connection as possible. So far as we have already formed engagements let them be fulfilled with perfect good faith. Here let us stop. . . . There can be no greater error than to expect or calculate upon real favors from nation to nation. . . . Trust to temporary alliances for extraordinary emergencies, [but in all other instances] steer clear of permanent alliances with any portion of the foreign world. . . . Such an attachment of a small or weak toward a great and powerful nation dooms the former to be the satellite of the latter.[10]

With the exception of a few leaders such as Thomas Jefferson and Thomas Paine, who were eager to take sides with the French against all others, Washington was probably expressing sentiments shared by most Americans. In fact, during most of the nineteenth century, American foreign policy was to a large extent no foreign policy. But Americans were never isolationist, if isolationism means the refusal to have any associations with the outside world. Americans were eager for trade and for treaties and contracts facilitating trade. Americans were also expansionists, but their vision of expansionism was limited to the North American continent.

Three familiar historical factors help explain why Washington's sentiments became the tradition and the source of American foreign-policy values. The first was the deep antistatist ideology shared by most Americans during the nineteenth century and into the twentieth century. Although we witness widespread antistatism today in the form of calls for tax cuts, deregulation, privatization, and other efforts to "get the government off our backs," such sentiments were far more intense

---

[9] Peterson, "The President's Dominance in Foreign Policy Making," p. 232.

[10] A full version of the text of the farewell address, along with a discussion of the contribution to it made by Hamilton and Madison, will be found in Daniel J. Boorstin, ed., *An American Primer* (Chicago: University of Chicago Press, 1966), 1: 192–210. This editing is by Richard B. Morris.

in the past, when many Americans opposed foreign entanglements, a professional military, and secret diplomacy. The second factor was federalism. The third was the position of the United States in the world as a **client state** (a state that has the capacity to carry out its own foreign policy most of the time but still depends on the interests of one or more of the major powers). Most nineteenth-century Americans recognized that if the United States became entangled in foreign affairs, national power would naturally grow at the expense of the states, and so would the presidency at the expense of Congress. Why? Because foreign policy meant having a professional diplomatic corps, professional armed forces with a general staff—and secrets. This meant professionalism, elitism, and remoteness from citizens. Being a client state gave America the luxury of being able to keep its foreign policy to a minimum. Moreover, maintaining American sovereignty was in the interest of the European powers, because it prevented any one of them from gaining an advantage over the others in the Western Hemisphere.

client state
A nation-state dependent on a more powerful nation-state but still with enough power and resources to conduct its own foreign policy up to a point.

Legacies of the Traditional System

Two identifiable legacies flowed from the long tradition based on antistatism, federalism, and client status. One is the intermingling of domestic and foreign policy institutions. The second is unilateralism—America's willingness to go it alone. Each of these reveals a great deal about the values behind today's conduct of foreign policy.

Intermingling of Domestic and Foreign Policy.   Because the major European powers once policed the world, American political leaders could treat foreign policy as a mere extension of domestic policy. The **tariff** is the best example. A tax on one category of imported goods as a favor to interests in one section of the country would cause friction elsewhere in the country. But the demands of those adversely affected could be met without compromising the original tariff by adding a tariff to still other goods that would placate those who were complaining about the original tariff. In this manner, Congress was continually adding and adjusting tariffs on more and more classes of commodities.

tariff A tax placed on imported goods.

    An important aspect of the treatment of foreign affairs as an extension of domestic policy was amateurism. Unlike many other countries, Americans refused to develop a tradition of a separate foreign service composed of professional people who spent much of their adult lives in foreign countries, learning foreign languages, absorbing foreign cultures, and developing a sympathy for foreign points of view. Instead, Americans have tended to be highly suspicious of any American diplomat or entrepreneur who spoke sympathetically of any such foreign viewpoints.[11] No systematic progress was made to create a professional diplomatic corps until after the passage of the Foreign Service Act of 1946.

Unilateralism.   Unilateralism, not isolationism, was the American posture toward the world until the middle of the twentieth century. Isolationism means to

---

[11] E. E. Schattschneider, *Politics, Pressures, and the Tariff* (Englewood Cliffs, N.J.: Prentice-Hall, 1935).

try to cut off contacts with the outside, to be a self-sufficient fortress. America was never isolationist; it preferred **unilateralism,** or "going it alone." Americans have always been more likely to rally around the president in support of direct action rather than sustained, diplomatic involvement.

The Great Leap to World Power

The traditional era of U.S. foreign policy came to an end with World War I for several important reasons. First, the "balance of power" system[12] that had kept the major European powers from world war for a hundred years had collapsed.[13] In fact, the great powers themselves had collapsed internally. The most devastating of all wars up to that time had ruined their economies, their empires, and, in most cases, their political systems. Second, the United States was no longer a client state but in fact one of the great powers. Third, as we saw in earlier chapters, the United States was soon to shed its traditional domestic system of federalism with its national government of almost pure promotional policy. Thus, virtually all the conditions that contributed to the traditional system of American foreign policy had disappeared. Yet there was no discernible change in America's approach to foreign policy in the period between World War I and World War II. After World War I, as one foreign-policy analyst put it, "the United States withdrew once more into its insularity. Since America was unwilling to use its power, that power, for purposes of foreign policy, did not really exist."[14]

The great leap in foreign policy was finally made thirty years after conditions demanded it and only after another world war. Following World War II, pressure for a new tradition came into direct conflict with the old. The new tradition required foreign entanglements; the old tradition feared them deeply. The new tradition required diplomacy; the old distrusted it. The new tradition required acceptance of antagonistic political systems; the old embraced democracy and was aloof from all else.

The values of the new tradition were all apparent during the **Cold War.** Instead of unilateralism, the United States pursued **multilateralism,** entering into treaties with other nations to achieve its foreign policy goals. The most notable of these treaties is the one that formed the **North Atlantic Treaty Organization (NATO)** in 1949, which allied the United States, Canada, and most of Western Europe. With its NATO allies, the United States practiced a two-pronged policy in dealing with its rival, the Soviet Union: **containment** and **deterrence.** Fearing that the Soviet Union was bent on world domination, the United States fought wars in Korea and Vietnam to "contain" Soviet power. And in order to deter a direct attack against itself or

---

[12] "Balance of power" was the primary foreign policy role played by the major European powers during the nineteenth century. It is a role available to the United States in contemporary foreign affairs, a role occasionally adopted but not on a world scale. This is the third of the four roles identified and discussed later in this chapter.

[13] The best analysis of what he calls the "100 years' peace" will be found in Karl Polanyi, *The Great Transformation* (New York: Rinehart, 1944; Beacon paperback ed., 1957), pp. 5ff.

[14] John G. Stoessinger, *Crusaders and Pragmatists: Movers of Modern American Foreign Policy* (New York: Norton, 1985), pp. 21, 34.

unilateralism A foreign policy that seeks to avoid international alliances, entanglements, and permanent commitments in favor of independence, neutrality, and freedom of action.

Cold War The period of struggle between the United States and the former Soviet Union between the late 1940s and 1990.

multilateralism A foreign policy that seeks to encourage the involvement of several nation-states in coordinated action, usually in relation to a common adversary, with terms and conditions usually specified in a multicountry treaty, such as NATO.

North Atlantic Treaty Organization (NATO) A treaty organization comprising the United States, Canada, and most of Western Europe, formed in 1949 to counter the perceived threat from the Soviet Union.

containment The policy used by the United States during the Cold War to restrict the expansion of communism and limit the influence of the Soviet Union.

deterrence The development and maintenance of military strength as a means of discouraging attack.

its NATO allies, the United States developed a multibillion-dollar nuclear arsenal capable of destroying the Soviet Union many times over.

An arms race between the United States and the Soviet Union was extremely difficult if not impossible to resist because there was no way for either side to know when it had enough deterrent power to continue preventing aggression by the other side. The Cold War ended abruptly in 1989 after the Soviet Union had spent itself into oblivion and allowed its empire to collapse. Many observers called the end of the Cold War a victory for democracy. But more important, it was a victory for capitalism over communism, a vindication of the free market as the best way to produce the greatest wealth of nations. Furthering capitalism has long been one of the values guiding American foreign policy. This might be truer at the beginning of the twenty-first century than at any time before.

THE INSTRUMENTS OF MODERN AMERICAN FOREIGN POLICY

Any government has at hand certain instruments, or tools, to use in implementing its foreign policy. An instrument is neutral, capable of serving many goals. There have been many instruments of American foreign policy, and we can deal here only with those instruments we deem to be most important in the modern epoch: diplomacy, the United Nations, the international monetary structure, economic aid, collective security, and military deterrence. Each of these instruments will be evaluated in this section for its utility in the conduct of American foreign policy, and each will be assessed in light of the history and development of American values.

Diplomacy

We begin this treatment of instruments with diplomacy because it is the instrument to which all other instruments should be subordinated, although they seldom are. **Diplomacy** is the representation of a government to other foreign governments. Its purpose is to promote national values or interests by peaceful means. According to Hans Morgenthau, "a diplomacy that ends in war has failed in its primary objective."[15]

The first effort to create a modern diplomatic service in the United States was made through the Rogers Act of 1924, which established the initial framework for a professional foreign-service staff. But it took World War II and the Foreign Service Act of 1946 to forge the foreign service into a fully professional diplomatic corps.

Diplomacy, by its very nature, is overshadowed by spectacular international events, dramatic initiatives, and meetings among heads of state or their direct

diplomacy The representation of a government to other foreign governments.

---

[15] Hans Morgenthau, *Politics among Nations*, 2nd ed. (New York: Knopf, 1956), p. 505.

personal representatives. The traditional American distrust of diplomacy continues today, albeit in weaker form. Impatience with or downright distrust of diplomacy has been built into not only all the other instruments of foreign policy but also the modern presidential system itself.[16] So much personal responsibility has been heaped on the presidency that it is difficult for presidents to entrust any of their authority or responsibility in foreign policy to professional diplomats in the State Department and other bureaucracies.

Distrust of diplomacy has also produced a tendency among all recent presidents to turn frequently to military and civilian personnel outside the State Department to take on a special diplomatic role as direct personal representatives of the president. As discouraging as it is to those who have dedicated their careers to foreign service to have personal appointees chosen over their heads, it is probably even more discouraging when they are displaced from a foreign-policy issue as soon as relations with the country they are posted to begin to heat up. When a special personal representative is sent abroad to represent the president, that envoy holds a status higher than that of the local ambassador, and the embassy becomes the envoy's temporary residence and base of operation. Despite the impressive professionalization of the American foreign service—with advanced training, competitive exams, language requirements, and career commitment—the practice of displacing career ambassadors with political appointees and with special personal presidential representatives continues. For instance, when President Clinton in 1998 sought to boost the peace process in Northern Ireland, he called on the former senator George Mitchell. Mitchell received almost unanimous praise for his skill and patience in chairing the Northern Ireland peace talks. The caliber of his work in Northern Ireland led to Senator Mitchell's becoming involved in another of the world's apparently unsolvable conflicts, that between the Israelis and the Palestinians.

Despite the United States' track record of distrust of diplomacy, immediately following the terrorist attacks of September 11, 2001, questions arose about how we could go after terrorist networks without the active cooperation of dozens of governments. Getting access to terrorists in various countries, plus putting together and keeping together the worldwide alliance of governments to fight terrorism, was a diplomatic, not a military, chore. In calls to more than eighty nations, the former secretary of state Colin Powell helped to extract dozens of pledges that would have been more difficult to get months later, when sympathy for America began to wane. In short, global unity and success in fighting terrorism required constant diplomatic efforts, not only by Powell, but also by other leading players, including President Bush himself.

In 2008, both parties' presidential candidates criticized the Bush administration for having failed to use diplomacy to secure greater international support for the Iraq war. Both promised to revitalize American diplomacy. President Obama appointed Hillary Clinton as his secretary of state in part to underline the importance

---

[16] See Theodore Lowi, *The Personal President: Power Invested, Promise Unfulfilled* (Ithaca, N.Y.: Cornell University Press, 1985), pp. 167–69.

he attached to diplomacy by appointing such a prominent figure as America's chief diplomat.

The significance of diplomacy and its vulnerability to politics may be better appreciated as we proceed to the other instruments. Diplomacy was an instrument more or less imposed on Americans as the prevailing method of dealing among nation-states in the nineteenth century. The other instruments to be identified and assessed below are instruments that Americans self-consciously crafted for themselves to take care of their own chosen place in the world affairs of the second half of the twentieth century and beyond. They therefore better reflect American culture and values than diplomacy does.

The United Nations

United Nations (UN) An organization of nations founded in 1945 to be a channel for negotiation and a means of settling international disputes peaceably. The UN has had frequent successes in providing a forum for negotiation and on some occasions a means of preventing international conflicts from spreading. On a number of occasions, the UN has been a convenient cover for U.S. foreign-policy goals.

The utility of the **United Nations (UN)** to the United States as an instrument of foreign policy can be too easily underestimated, because the United Nations is a very large and unwieldy institution with few powers and no armed forces to implement its rules and resolutions. Its supreme body is the UN General Assembly, comprising one representative of each of the 192 member states; each member representative has one vote, regardless of the size of the country. Important issues require a two-thirds majority vote, and the annual session of the General Assembly runs only from September to December (although it can call extra sessions). It has little organization that can make it an effective decision-making body, with only six standing committees, few tight rules of procedure, and no political parties to provide priorities and discipline. Its defenders are quick to add that although it lacks armed forces, it relies on the power of world opinion, and this is not to be taken lightly. The powers of the United Nations devolve mainly to its "executive committee," the UN Security Council, which alone has the real power to make decisions and rulings that member states are obligated by the UN Charter to implement. The Security Council may be called into session at any time, and each member (or a designated alternate) must be present at UN Headquarters in New York at all times. It is composed of fifteen members: five are permanent (the victors of World War II), and ten are elected by the General Assembly for two-year, nonrepeatable terms. The five permanent members are China, France, Russia, the United Kingdom, and the United States. Each of the fifteen members has only one vote, and a nine-vote majority of the fifteen is required on all substantive matters. But each of the five permanent members also has a negative vote, a veto, and one veto is sufficient to reject any substantive proposal.

The UN can be as a useful forum for international discussions and an instrument for multilateral action. Most peacekeeping efforts to which the United States contributes, for example, are undertaken under UN auspices.

The International Monetary Structure

Fear of a repeat of the economic devastation that followed World War I brought the United States together with its allies (except the USSR) to Bretton Woods, New Hampshire, in 1944 to create a new international economic structure for the postwar world. The result was two institutions: the International Bank for Reconstruction and Development (commonly called the World Bank) and the International Monetary Fund.

The World Bank was set up to finance long-term capital. Leading nations took on the obligation of contributing funds to enable the World Bank to make loans to capital-hungry countries. (The U.S. quota has been about one-third of the total.)

The **International Monetary Fund (IMF)** was set up to provide for the short-term flow of money. After the war, the dollar, instead of gold, was the chief means by which the currency of one country would be "changed into" currency of another country for purposes of making international transactions. To permit debtor countries with no international balances to make purchases and investments, the IMF was set up to lend dollars or other appropriate currencies to needy member countries to help them overcome temporary trade deficits. For many years after World War II, the IMF, along with U.S. foreign aid, in effect constituted the only international medium of exchange.

International Monetary Fund (IMF) An institution established in 1944 at Bretton Woods, New Hampshire, to provide loans to needy member countries and to facilitate international monetary exchange.

During the 1990s, the IMF returned to a position of enhanced importance through its efforts to reform some of the largest debtor nations and formerly communist countries, to bring them more fully into the global capitalist economy. For example, in the early 1990s, Russia and thirteen other former Soviet republics were invited to join the IMF and the World Bank with the expectation of receiving $10.5 billion from these two agencies, primarily for a currency-stabilization fund. Each republic was to get a permanent IMF representative, and the IMF increased its staff by at least 10 percent to provide the expertise necessary to cope with the problems of these emerging capitalist economies.[17]

The IMF, with $93 billion, has more money to lend poor countries than do the United States, Europe, or Japan (the three leading IMF shareholders) individually. It makes its policy decisions in ways that are generally consonant with the interests of the leading shareholders.[18] Two weeks after September 11, 2001, the IMF approved a $135 million loan to economically troubled Pakistan, a key player in the war against the Taliban government of Afghanistan because of its strategic location. Turkey, also because of its strategic location in the Middle East, was likewise put back in the IMF pipeline.[19] The future of the IMF, the World Bank, and all other private sources of international investment will depend in part on extension of more credit to the Third World and other developing countries, because credit means investment and productivity. But the future may depend even more on reducing the debt that is already there from previous extensions of credit.

[17] "IMF: Sleeve-Rolling Time," *Economist*, May 2, 1992, pp. 98–99.

[18] James Dao and Patrick E. Tyler, "U.S. Says Military Strikes Are Just a Part of Big Plan," *The Alliance*, September 27, 2001; and Joseph Kahn, "A Nation Challenged: Global Dollars," *New York Times*, September 20, 2001, p. B1.

[19] Turkey was desperate for help to extricate its economy from its worst recession since 1945. The Afghanistan crisis was going to hurt Turkey all the more; its strategic location helped its case with IMF. "Official Says Turkey Is Advancing in Drive for I.M.F. Financing," *New York Times*, October 6, 2001, p. A7.

Economic Aid and Sanctions

Every year, the United States provides nearly $30 billion in economic assistance to other nations. Some aid has a humanitarian purpose, such as helping to provide health care, shelter for refugees, or famine relief. A good deal of American aid, however, is designed to promote American security interests or economic concerns. For example, the United States provides military assistance to a number of its allies in the form of advanced weapons or loans to help them purchase advanced weapons. Such loans generally stipulate that the recipient must purchase the designated weapons from American firms. In this way, the United States hopes to bolster its security and economic interests with one grant. The two largest recipients of American military assistance are Israel and Egypt, American allies that fought two wars against one another. The United States believes that its military assistance allows both to feel sufficiently secure to remain at peace with one another.

Aid is an economic carrot. Sanctions are an economic stick. Economic sanctions that the United States employs against other nations include trade embargoes, bans on investment, and efforts to prevent the World Bank or other international institutions from extending credit to a nation against which the United States has a grievance. Sanctions are most often employed when the United States seeks to weaken what it considers a hostile regime or when it is attempting to compel some particular action by another regime. Thus, for example, in order to weaken the Castro government, the United States has long prohibited American firms from doing business with Cuba, though President Obama has called for a relaxation of current trade and travel restrictions. In recent years, the United States has maintained economic sanctions against Iran and North Korea in an effort to prevent those nations from pursuing nuclear weapons programs.

Unilateral sanctions by the United States usually have little effect, since the target can usually trade elsewhere, sometimes even with foreign affiliates of U.S. firms. If, however, the United States is able to convince its allies to cooperate, sanctions have a better chance of success. International sanctions applied to Libya, for example, played a role in the regime's decision to enter into negotiations with the United States over Libyan responsibility for a number of terrorist attacks.

Collective Security

In 1947, most Americans hoped that the United States could meet its world obligations through the United Nations and economic structures alone. But most foreign-policy makers recognized that was a vain hope even as they were permitting and encouraging Americans to believe it. They had anticipated the need for military entanglements at the time of drafting the original UN Charter by insisting on language that recognized the right of all nations to provide for their mutual defense independent of the United Nations. And almost immediately after enactment of the Marshall Plan, designed to promote European economic recovery, the White House and a parade of State and Defense Department officials followed up with an urgent request to the Senate to ratify, and to both houses of Congress to finance, mutual defense alliances.

At first quite reluctant to approve treaties providing for national security alliances, the Senate ultimately agreed with the executive branch. The first collective security agreement was the Rio Treaty (ratified by the Senate in September 1947), which created the Organization of American States (OAS). This was the model treaty, anticipating all succeeding collective-security treaties by providing that an armed attack against any of its members "shall be considered as an attack against all the American States," including the United States. A more significant break with U.S. tradition against peacetime entanglements came with the North Atlantic Treaty (signed in April 1949), which created the North Atlantic Treaty Organization (NATO). ANZUS, a treaty tying Australia and New Zealand to the United States, was signed in September 1951. Three years later, the Southeast Asia Treaty created the Southeast Asia Treaty Organization (SEATO).

In addition to these multilateral treaties, the United States entered into a number of **bilateral treaties**—treaties between two countries. As one author has observed, the United States has been a *producer* of security, whereas most of its allies have been *consumers* of security.[20]

bilateral treaty
A treaty made between two nations.

This pattern has continued in the post–Cold War era, and its best illustration is in the Persian Gulf War. The United States provided the initiative, the leadership, and most of the armed forces, even though its allies were obliged to reimburse over 90 percent of the cost.

It is difficult to evaluate collective security and its treaties, because the purpose of collective security as an instrument of foreign policy is prevention, and success of this kind has to be measured in terms of what did *not* happen. Critics have argued that U.S. collective-security treaties posed a threat of encirclement to the Soviet Union, forcing it to ensure its own collective security, particularly the Warsaw Pact.[21] Nevertheless, no one can deny the counterargument that more than sixty years have passed without a world war.

In 1998, the expansion of NATO took its first steps toward former Warsaw Pact members, extending membership to Poland, Hungary, and the Czech Republic. Most of Washington embraced this expansion as the true and fitting end of the Cold War, and the U.S. Senate echoed this with a resounding 80-to-19 vote to induct these three former Soviet satellites into NATO. The expansion was also welcomed among European member nations, which quickly approved the move, hailing it as the final closing of the book on Yalta, the 1945 treaty that divided Europe into Western and Soviet spheres of influence after the defeat of Germany. Expanded membership seems to have made NATO less threatening and more acceptable to Russia. Russia became a partner when the NATO-Russia Council was formed in 2002. Finally, although the expanded NATO membership (now twenty-eight countries) reduces the threat to Russia, it also reduces the utility of

---

[20] George Quester, *The Continuing Problem of International Politics* (Hinsdale, Ill.: Dryden Press, 1974), p. 229.

[21] The Warsaw Pact was signed in 1955 by the Soviet Union, the German Democratic Republic (East Germany), Poland, Hungary, Czechoslovakia, Romania, Bulgaria, and Albania. Albania later dropped out. The Warsaw Pact was terminated in 1991.

NATO as a military alliance. The September 11 attack on the United States was the first time in its fifty-plus-year history that Article 5 of the North Atlantic Treaty had to be invoked; it provides that an attack on one country is an attack on all the member countries. In fighting the war on terror, the Bush administration recognized that no matter how preponderant American power was, some aspects of its foreign policy could not be achieved without multilateral cooperation. On the other hand, the United States did not want to be constrained by its alliances. The global coalition initially forged after September 11 numbered over 170 countries. Not all joined the war effort in Afghanistan, but most if not all provided some form of support for some aspect of the war on terrorism, such as economic sanctions and intelligence. The war in Iraq, however, put the "coalition of the willing" to a test. The Bush administration was determined not to make its decision to go to war subject to the UN or NATO or any other international organization. The breadth of the United States' coalition was deemed secondary to its being nonconstraining. As a result, other than the British government, no major power supported the United States' actions.

Military Force

The most visible instrument of foreign policy is, of course, military force. The United States has built the world's most imposing military, with army, navy, marine and air force units stationed in virtually every corner of the globe. The United States spends nearly as much on military might as the rest of the world combined (Figure 14.3). The famous Prussian military strategist Carl von Clausewitz called war "politics by other means." By this he meant that nations use force not simply to demonstrate their capacity for violence. Rather, force or the threat of force is a tool nations must sometimes use to achieve their foreign-policy goals. Military force may be needed to protect a nation's security interests and economic concerns. Ironically, force may also be needed to achieve humanitarian goals. For example, without international military protection, the Africans who have taken refuge in Darfur camps would be at the mercy of the violent Sudanese regime.

Though force is sometimes necessary, military force is generally seen as a last resort and avoided if possible because of a number of problems commonly associated with its use. First, the use of military force is extremely costly in both human and financial terms. In the past fifty years, tens of thousands of Americans have been killed and hundreds of billions of dollars spent in America's military operations. Before they employ military force to achieve national goals, policy makers must be certain that achieving these goals is essential and that other means are unlikely to succeed.

Second, the use of military force is inherently fraught with risk. However carefully policy makers and generals plan for military operations, results can seldom be fully anticipated. Variables ranging from the weather to unexpected weapons and tactics deployed by opponents may upset the most careful calculations and turn military operations into costly disasters. Maneuvers that were expected to be quick and decisive may turn into long, drawn-out, expensive struggles. For example, American policy makers expected to defeat the Iraqi army quickly and easily

FIGURE 14.3 MILITARY SPENDING, 2008

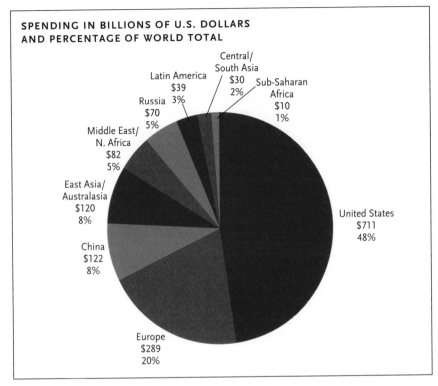

SPENDING IN BILLIONS OF U.S. DOLLARS
AND PERCENTAGE OF WORLD TOTAL

Central/
South Asia
$30
2%

Sub-Saharan
Africa
$10
1%

Latin America
$39
3%

Russia
$70
5%

Middle East/
N. Africa
$82
5%

East Asia/
Australasia
$120
8%

China
$122
8%

United States
$711
48%

Europe
$289
20%

NOTE: 2008 total military spending: $1.473 trillion

SOURCE: Center for Arms Control and Non-Proliferation, www.armscontrolcenter.org/policy/securityspending/articles/fy09_dod_request_global/ (accessed 7/16/09).

in 2003—and they did. Policy makers did not anticipate, however, that American forces would still be struggling years later to defeat the insurgency that arose in the war's aftermath.

Finally, in a democracy, any government that chooses to address policy problems through military means is almost certain to encounter political difficulties. Generally speaking, the American public will support relatively short and decisive military engagements. If, however, a conflict drags on, producing casualties and expenses with no clear outcome, the public loses patience, and opposition politicians point to the government's lies and ineptitude. Korea, Vietnam, and Iraq are all examples of protracted conflicts whose domestic political repercussions brought down the governments that decided military force was needed.

Thus, military force remains a major foreign policy tool, and the United States currently possesses a more powerful and effective set of military forces than any other nation. Nevertheless, even for the United States, the use of military force is fraught with risk and is not to be undertaken lightly.

Arbitration

The final foreign-policy tool we will consider is dispute arbitration. Arbitration means referring an international disagreement to a neutral third party for resolution. Arbitration is sometimes seen as a form of "soft power" as distinguished from military force, economic sanctions, and other coercive foreign-policy instruments. The United States will occasionally turn to international tribunals to resolve disputes with other countries. For example, in February 2008, the U.S. government asked the International Court of Justice to resolve a long-standing dispute with Italy over American property confiscated by the Italian government more than forty years ago. To take another example, in 1981 the United States and Iran established an arbitral tribunal to deal with claims arising from Iran's seizure of the U.S. embassy in Tehran in 1979.

More important, the United States relies heavily on the work of arbitral panels to maintain the flow of international trade on which America's economy depends. American firms would be reluctant to do business abroad if they could not be certain that their property and contractual rights would be honored by other nations. Arbitration helps produce that certainty. Almost every international contract contains an arbitration clause requiring that disputes between the parties will be resolved not by foreign governments, but by impartial arbitral panels accepted by both sides. By the terms of the New York Convention, virtually every nation in the world has agreed to accept and enforce arbitral verdicts. The United States has incorporated the terms of the New York Convention into federal law, and U.S. courts vigorously enforce arbitral judgements. The United States may not be happy with the outcome of every arbitral proceeding, but the arbitral system is essential to America's economic interests.

AMERICA'S ROLE IN THE WORLD

When policy makers choose courses of action and select the policy instruments they will employ, they do not begin with a blank slate. Presidents and other policy makers are generally guided by some overall vision of America's national interest and the nation's place in the world. Some recent presidents, Jimmy Carter for example, have seen America as a great power in decline, compelled to act cautiously on the world stage. Others, such as Ronald Reagan, have seen America as a rising power—"It's morning in America" was Reagan's slogan—capable of undertaking bold and decisive foreign policy moves.

In general terms, it is possible to identify four distinct visions of America's world role that, at various times, have guided recent presidents. These are:

The Napoleonic Role. The **Napoleonic role** takes its name from the role played by postrevolutionary France under Napoleon. The French at that time felt not only that their new democratic system of government was the best on earth but also that France would not be safe until democracy was adopted universally. If this meant intervention in the internal affairs of France's neighbors, and if that meant warlike reactions, then so be it. President Woodrow Wilson expressed a similar viewpoint

Napoleonic role Strategy pursued by a powerful nation to prevent aggressive actions against itself by improving the internal state of affairs of a particular country, even if this means encouraging revolution in that country.

The Roles Nations Play

Napoleonic role—A country feels that in order to safeguard its form of government (for example, democracy), it must ensure (by force if necessary) that other countries adopt the same form of government.

Holy Alliance role—Using every political instrument available to keep existing governments in power, whatever form those governments may take; keeping peace is more important than promoting one particular form of government.

Balance-of-power role—Major powers play off each other so that no one power or combination of powers can impose conditions on others.

Economic expansionist role—Being primarily concerned with what other countries have to buy or to sell and with their dependability in honoring contracts, regardless of their form of government.

when he supported the U.S. declaration of war in 1917 with his argument that "the world must be made safe for democracy." Obviously any powerful nation can adopt such a position as a rationalization for intervening at its convenience in the internal affairs of another country. But it can also be sincerely espoused, and in the United States it has from time to time enjoyed broad popular consensus. The United States played the Napoleonic role recently in ousting the Philippine dictator Ferdinand Marcos (February 1986), the Panamanian leader Manuel Noriega (December 1989), the Sandinista government of Nicaragua (February 1990), the military rulers of Haiti (September 1994), and the Iraqi dictator Saddam Hussein (April 2003).

The Holy Alliance Role. The concept of the **Holy Alliance role** emerged out of the defeat of Napoleon and the agreement by the leaders of Great Britain, Russia, Austria, and Prussia to preserve the social order against *all* revolution, including democratic revolution, at whatever cost. (Post–Napoleonic France also joined it.) The Holy Alliance made use of every kind of political instrument available— including political suppression, espionage, sabotage, and outright military intervention—to keep existing governments in power. The Holy Alliance role is comparable to the Napoleonic role in that each operates on the assumption that intervention in the internal affairs of other countries is justified for the maintenance of peace. But Napoleonic intervention is motivated by fear of dictatorship, and it can accept and even encourage revolution. In contrast, Holy Alliance intervention is antagonistic to any form of political change, even when this means supporting an existing dictatorship.[22] Because the Holy Alliance role became more important after the Cold War ended, illustrations of this role will be given later in the chapter.

Holy Alliance role
A strategy pursued by a superpower to prevent any change in the existing distribution of power among nation-states, even if this requires intervention into the internal affairs of another country in order to keep a ruler from being overthrown.

---

[22] For a thorough and instructive exposition of the original Holy Alliance Pattern, see Paul M. Kennedy, *The Rise and Fall of the Great Powers: Economic Change and Military Conflict from 1500 to 2000* (New York: Random House, 1987), pp. 159–60. And for a comparison of the Holy Alliance role with the balance-of-power role, to be discussed next, see Polanyi, *The Great Transformation*, pp. 5–11 and 259–62.

The Balance-of-Power Role. The **balance-of-power role** is basically an effort by the major powers to play off each other so that no great power or combination of great and lesser powers can impose conditions on others. The most relevant example of the use of this strategy is found in the nineteenth century, especially the latter half. The feature of the balance-of-power role that is most distinct from the two previously identified roles is that this role accepts the political system of each country, asking no questions except whether the country will join an alliance and will use its resources to ensure that each country will respect the borders and interests of all the others.[23]

The Economic Expansionist Role. The **economic expansionist role**, also called the capitalist role, shares with the balance-of-power role the attitude that the political system or ideology of a country is irrelevant; the only question is whether a country has anything to buy or sell and whether its entrepreneurs, corporations, and government agencies will honor their contracts. Governments and their armies are occasionally drawn into economic expansionist relationships in order to establish, reopen, or expand trade relationships, and to keep the lines of commerce open. But the role is political, too. The point can be made that the economic expansionist role was the role consistently played by the United States in Latin and Central America, until the Cold War (perhaps in the 1960s and beyond) pushed us toward the Holy Alliance role with most of those countries.

Economic expansion does not happen spontaneously, however. In the past, economic expansion owed a great deal to military backing, because contracts do not enforce themselves, trade deficits are not paid automatically, and new regimes do not always honor the commitments made by regimes they replace. The only way to expand economic relationships is through diplomacy.

The Choice of Roles for America Today

These four roles should not be literally translated into models that heads of state or foreign-policy establishments consciously adopt. They are the names of patterns of policy conduct that have prevailed during certain important points in history. These labels were actually used by key participants during those points in history or by historians to capture and evaluate the patterns of conduct. In our time, they remain useful descriptions of patterns that enable us to compare an important pattern of conduct today with real moments in the past. The sequence of these roles in post–World War II history is not precisely the same as the sequence in historical time. They do, however, capture the highlights of our own epoch, and the comparisons do give us a better basis for evaluation.

A new alliance with a new purpose was struck in response to the terrorist attacks of September 11, 2001. Such a great-power alliance for international order has not been seen since the mid-nineteenth century, when the threat came from middle-class revolutionaries rather than religious fanatics. But even though the

---

[23] Felix Gilbert et al., *The Norton History of Modern Europe* (New York: Norton, 1971), pp. 1222–24.

enemies are different, the goals and strategies are about the same. All countries in the West are vulnerable because Al Qaeda and its associated groups are opposed to the West. All capitalist and developing countries are susceptible because terrorism is intensely anticapitalist. And all moderate Arab regimes are vulnerable because they are seen by Al Qaeda as traitors and as collaborators with the West. All of these vulnerable nation-states need each other to deprive terrorists of the turf they need for safe havens, headquarters, training, and communication, not to mention financing. Even though the war against the Taliban regime was conducted almost entirely by the United States, there was no hope for a sustained campaign without the substantial cooperation and participation of many other countries. Pakistan was most vital, and its participation came at the risk of undermining its own regime. Russia and several other former Soviet republics on the northern border of Afghanistan were vital as well. The NATO nations were contractually an important part of the alliance, if only because the NATO charter was built on a solemn promise that an attack on any member was tantamount to an attack on all members.

Yet once the Afghan phase of the war on world terrorism began quieting down, the United States confronted a new challenge: the resurgence of Iraq and the possibility—which turned out to be unfounded—that the weapons of mass destruction that Saddam had once possessed would be used against the United States or one of its allies. President Bush's response, the Bush Doctrine, was a significant departure from the Holy Alliance model and a move toward a Napoleonic role. The tenets of the doctrine allowed the United States to (1) take preemptive action against a hostile state without waiting for an attack on us, (2) eliminate permanently the threat of WMDs, (3) eliminate the regime itself, and (4) remain as an occupying power in Iraq long enough to rebuild the country into a modern democratic state.

Although the Holy Alliance role continues to be the principal role among the four historically and conventionally defined roles, it is not the only one that America plays, and more to the point, it is never played exactly the same way in every case. Even in Afghanistan, the alliance to defeat the Taliban and contain terrorism was accompanied by a genuine, albeit secondary version of the Napoleonic role. The Bush and Obama administrations seemed determined to both rebuild the Afghan economy along capitalist lines and to move the Afghan regime toward some form of democratization. But in the short run at least, the United States quickly settled for an imposed national leader presiding over a domestic coalition of mutually distrustful warlords, with only the barest hint of any kind of democratic process. That is the underlying Holy Alliance at work. The Obama administration is just as committed as its predecessors to a balance-of-power role in the perennial Middle East hot spot, the Israel-Palestine conflict. The United States has succeeded in keeping the neighboring Arab countries from forming their own anti-Israel (and therefore anti-United States) alliance. (Keeping antagonistic alliances from forming is an essential feature of the balance-of-power role: Like spokes on a wheel, all the countries are kept dependent on the United States at the hub while separated from each other.) But the use of terrorism by the Palestinians has prevented the United States from playing the balance-of-power role of "honest broker."

No foreign-policy role—however the roles are categorized—can ever relieve the United States of the need for sustained diplomacy. In fact, diplomacy has become

The Democratic Peace and Foreign Policy

In 1795, the philosopher Immanuel Kant proposed the idea that representative governments were far less likely than other types of regimes to initiate wars. Hence, if representative governments replaced monarchies and other autocracies throughout the world, the result would be "perpetual peace." Today, Kant's idea is called democratic peace theory and has considerable support among scholars, commentators, and government officials.

Immanuel Kant

This idea has significant implications for foreign policy. For example, the Bush administration argued that transforming Iraq into a democracy would help to promote peace in the Middle East. And many policy makers believe that by helping China develop a more open and responsive government, the United States can increase the likelihood of peace with that nation.

Proponents of democratic peace theory assert that democracies seldom, if ever, fight one another. Many argue that democracies are usually reluctant to attack nondemocracies, as well. The core logic of democratic peace theory is that ordinary citizens bear the burdens of war and are usually not eager to send their children to fight unless it is absolutely necessary. Thus, to the extent that governments answer to ordinary citizens, they will be constrained from going to war. Critics of the theory point out that even in democracies, wars are often initially popular, though citizens may eventually become disenchanted with the bloodshed. Many scholars have attempted to collect data on the involvement of democracies in wars.

The table on the following page is a fairly comprehensive list of military conflicts involving democratic regimes. Whether these data support or call into question democratic peace theory depends on how the information is assessed. Relatively few conflicts have pitted one democracy against another. Yet, on many occasions, democracies have launched attacks against other nations. Does this mean that if all the world's regimes were democracies there would be no more wars, or could there be other factors at work? For example, the contemporary democracies might be members of the same trade and military alliances and these alliances, rather than their democratic constitutions, could keep them at peace with one another.

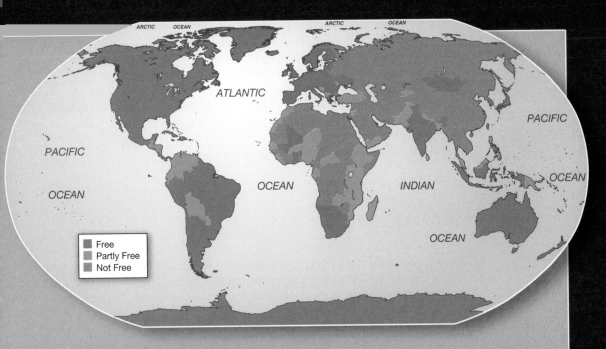

Free
Partly Free
Not Free

Freedom House ranks 89 countries in the worlds as "free" electoral democracies and 58 countries as "partly free" electoral democracies*, yet many of these countries have been involved in wars at some point since adopting democratic regimes.

MILITARY CONFLICTS INVOLVING DEMOCRATIC REGIMES

American Revolutionary War	1775–1783	World War II	1939–1945
War of 1812	1812–1815	Continuation War	1941–1944
Mexican-American War	1846–1848	Indo-Pakistani War of 1947	1947–1948
Sonderbund War	1847	1948 Arab-Israeli War	1947–1949
French Second Republic vs. Roman Republic (19th century)	1849	Cod Wars	1958–1976
		Operation Power Pack	1965
Ecuadorian-Colombian War	1863	Six-Day War	1967
War of the Pacific	1879–1884	Turkish invasion of Cyprus	1974
First Boer War	1880–1881	Paquisha War	1981
Spanish-American War	1898	Yugoslav Wars	1991–1999
Philippine-American War	1899–1913	Cenepa War	1995
Second Boer War	1899–1902	Eritrean-Ethiopian War	1998–2000
World War I	1914–1918	Kargil War	1999
Irish War of Independence	1919–1921	2006 Lebanon War	2006
Polish-Lithuanian War	1920		

*Source: Freedom House, Map of Freedom in the World, 2009 Edition, www.freedomhouse.org.

all the more important because despotic regimes eventually fail and, in their failure, create instability. Since September 11, it has also become clear that failing regimes can become breeding grounds for world terrorism. This is not to argue that war is never justifiable or that peace can always be achieved through discussions among professional diplomats. It is only to argue that there are limits to any role a country chooses to play and that failure will come faster and will be more serious if the choice of the role is not made with patience, deliberation, rationality, and, most important, a knowledge of and sensitivity to history.

CHAPTER REVIEW

This chapter began by looking at the general goals of American foreign policy: security, economic goals, and humanitarian goals. Although all three are important, security and economic goals have tended to take precedence over humanitarian goals.

The second section of this chapter looked at the players in foreign policy: the makers and the shapers. The influence of institutions and groups historically has varied from case to case, with the important exception of the president. Since the president is central to all foreign policy, it is best to assess how other actors interact with the president. In most instances, this interaction involves only the narrowest element of the foreign policy establishment. The American people have an opportunity to influence foreign policy, but primarily through Congress or interest groups.

The next section, on values, traced the history of American values that had a particular relevance to American perspectives on the outside world. We found that the American fear of a big government applied to foreign as well as domestic governmental powers. The Founders and the active public of the Founding period all recognized that foreign policy was special, that the national government had special powers in its dealings with foreigners, and that presidential supremacy was justified in the conduct of foreign affairs. The only way to avoid the big national government and presidential supremacy was to avoid the foreign entanglements that made foreign policy, diplomacy, secrecy, and presidential discretion necessary. Americans held on to their "antistatist" tradition until World War II, long after world conditions cried out for American involvement. And even as it became involved in world affairs, the United States held on tightly to the legacies of one hundred fifty years of tradition: the intermingling of domestic- and foreign-policy institutions and unilateralism, the tendency to "go it alone" when confronted with foreign conflicts.

We then looked at the instruments—that is, the tools—of American foreign policy. These are the basic statutes and the institutions by which foreign policy has been conducted since World War II: diplomacy, the United Nations, the international monetary structure, economic aid, collective security, and military deterrence. Although Republicans and Democrats look at the world somewhat differently, and although each president has tried to impose a distinctive flavor on foreign policy, they have all made use of these basic instruments, and that has given foreign policies a certain continuity. When Congress created these instruments after World War II, the old tradition was still so strong that it moved Congress to try to create instruments that would do their international work with a minimum of diplomacy—a minimum of human involvement. This is what we called power without diplomacy.

The next section concentrated on the role or roles the president and Congress have sought to play in the world. To help simplify the tremendous variety of tactics and strategies that foreign-policy leaders can select, we narrowed the field down to four categories of roles nations play, suggesting that there is a certain amount of consistency and stability in the conduct of a nation-state in its dealings with other nation-states. These were labeled according to actual roles that diplomatic historians have identified in the history of major Western nation-states: the Napoleonic, Holy Alliance, balance-of-power, and economic expansionist roles. We also attempted to identify and assess the role of the United States in the post–Cold War era, essentially the Holy Alliance role. But whatever its advantages may be, the Holy Alliance approach will never allow the United States to conduct foreign policy without diplomacy. America is tied inextricably to the perils and ambiguities of international relationships, and diplomacy is still the monarch of all available instruments of foreign policy.

FOR FURTHER READING

Bacevich, Andrew. *The New American Militarism: How Americans Are Seduced by War*. New York: Oxford University Press, 2006.

———. *The Limits of Power: The End of American Exceptionalism*. New York: Metropolitan Books, 2008.

Berman, Paul. *Terror and Liberalism*. New York: Norton, 2004.

Daalder, Ivo H., and James M. Lindsay. *America Unbound—The Bush Revolution in Foreign Policy*. Washington, D.C.: Brookings Institution Press, 2003.

Fisk, Robert. *The Great War for Civilisation: The Conquest of the Middle East*. New York: Knopf, 2005.

Gaddis, John L. *The Cold War. A New History*. New York: Penguin, 2005.

Hook, Stephen, and John Spanier. *American Foreign Policy since World War II*. Washington, D.C.: Congressional Quarterly Press, 2006.

Jentleson, Bruce. *American Foreign Policy—The Dynamics of Choice in the Twenty-First Century*. 2nd ed. New York: Norton, 2004.

Johnson, Chalmers. *The Sorrows of Empire*. New York: Holt, 2004.

Kagan, Robert. *Dangerous Nation*. New York: Knopf, 2006.

Kennan, George F. *Around the Cragged Hill: A Personal and Political Philosophy*. New York: Norton, 1993.

Mandelbaum, Michael. *The Case for Goliath: How America Acts as the World's Government in the Twenty-First Century*. Washington, D.C.: Public Affairs Press, 2005.

Mann, James. *Rise of the Vulcans.* New York: Penguin, 2004.

Mayer, Jane. *The Dark Side: The Inside Story of How the War on Terror Turned into a War on American Identity.* New York: Doubleday, 2008.

Reid, T. R. *The United States of Europe—The New Superpower and the End of American Supremacy.* New York: Penguin, 2004.

U.S. Congress. *Report of the Congressional Committees Investigating the Iran-Contra Affair.* Washington, D.C.: Government Printing Office, 1987.

reader selection Yoo, John. *The Powers of War and Peace.* Chicago: University of Chicago Press, 2005.

 Additional study and review materials are available online at wwnorton.com/studyspace/

Appendix

The Declaration of Independence

In Congress, July 4, 1776

The Unanimous Declaration of the Thirteen United States of America

When in the course of human events, it becomes necessary for one people to dissolve the political bands which have connected them with another, and to assume among the Powers of the earth, the separate and equal station to which the Laws of Nature and of Nature's God entitle them, a decent respect to the opinions of mankind requires that they should declare the causes which impel them to the separation.

We hold these truths to be self-evident, that all men are created equal, that they are endowed by their Creator with certain unalienable rights, that among these are Life, Liberty, and the pursuit of Happiness. That to secure these rights, Governments are instituted among Men, deriving their just powers from the consent of the governed. That whenever any Form of Government becomes destructive of these ends, it is the Right of the People to alter or to abolish it, and to institute new Government, laying its foundation on such principles and organizing its powers in such form, as to them shall seem most likely to effect their Safety and Happiness. Prudence, indeed, will dictate that Governments long established should not be changed for light and transient causes; and accordingly all experience hath shown, that mankind are more disposed to suffer, while evils are sufferable, than to right themselves by abolishing the forms to which they are accustomed. But when a long train of abuses and usurpations, pursuing invariably the same Object evinces a design to reduce them under absolute Despotism, it is their right, it is their duty, to throw off such Government, and to provide new Guards for their future security.— Such has been the patient sufferance of these Colonies; and such is now the necessity which constrains them to alter their former Systems of Government. The history of the present King of Great Britain is a history of repeated injuries and usurpations, all having in direct object the establishment of an absolute Tyranny over these States. To prove this, let Facts be submitted to a candid world.

He has refused his Assent to Laws, the most wholesome and necessary for the public good.

He has forbidden his Governors to pass Laws of immediate and pressing importance, unless suspended in their operation till his Assent should be obtained; and when so suspended, he has utterly neglected to attend to them.

He has refused to pass other Laws for the accommodation of large districts of people, unless those people would relinquish the right of Representation in the Legislature, a right inestimable to them and formidable to tyrants only.

He has called together legislative bodies at places unusual, uncomfortable, and distant from the depository of their public Records, for the sole purpose of fatiguing them into compliance with his measures.

He has dissolved Representative Houses repeatedly, for opposing with manly firmness his invasions on the rights of the people.

He has refused for a long time, after such dissolutions, to cause others to be elected; whereby the Legislative powers, incapable of Annihilation, have returned to the People at large for their exercise; the State remaining in the mean time exposed to all dangers of invasion from without, and convulsions within.

He has endeavored to prevent the population of these States; for that purpose obstructing the Laws of Naturalization of Foreigners; refusing to pass others to encourage their migrations hither, and raising the conditions of new Appropriations of Lands.

He has obstructed the Administration of Justice, by refusing his Assent to Laws for establishing Judiciary powers.

He has made Judges dependent on his Will alone, for the tenure of their offices, and the amount and payment of their salaries.

He has erected a multitude of New Offices, and sent hither swarms of Officers to harass our People, and eat out their substance.

He has kept among us, in times of peace, Standing Armies without the Consent of our legislature.

He has affected to render the Military independent of and superior to the Civil Power.

He has combined with others to subject us to a jurisdiction foreign to our constitution, and unacknowledged by our laws; giving his Assent to their Acts of pretended Legislation:

For quartering large bodies of armed troops among us:

For protecting them, by a mock Trial, from Punishment for any Murders which they should commit on the Inhabitants of these States:

For cutting off our Trade with all parts of the world:

For imposing taxes on us without our Consent:

For depriving us in many cases, of the benefits of Trial by jury:

For transporting us beyond Seas to be tried for pretended offences:

For abolishing the free System of English Laws in a neighboring Province, establishing therein an Arbitrary government, and enlarging its Boundaries so as to render it at once an example and fit instrument for introducing the same absolute rule into these Colonies:

For taking away our Charters, abolishing our most valuable Laws, and altering fundamentally the Forms of our Governments:

For suspending our own Legislatures, and declaring themselves invested with Power to legislate for us in all cases whatsoever.

He has abdicated Government here, by declaring us out of his Protection and waging War against us.

He has plundered our seas, ravaged our Coasts, burnt our towns, and destroyed the lives of our people.

He is at this time transporting large armies of foreign mercenaries to compleat the works of death, desolation, and tyranny, already begun with circumstances of Cruelty & perfidy scarcely paralleled in the most barbarous ages, and totally unworthy the Head of a civilized nation.

He has constrained our fellow Citizens taken Captive on the high Seas to bear Arms against their Country, to become the executioners of their friends and Brethren, or to fall themselves by their Hands.

He has excited domestic insurrections amongst us, and has endeavored to bring on the inhabitants of our frontiers, the merciless Indian Savages, whose known rule of warfare, is an undistinguished destruction of all ages, sexes, and conditions.

In every stage of these Oppressions We have Petitioned for Redress in the most humble terms: Our repeated Petitions have been answered only by repeated injury. A Prince, whose character is thus marked by every act which may define a Tyrant, is unfit to be the ruler of a free people.

Nor have We been wanting in attention to our British brethren. We have warned them from time to time of attempts by their legislature to extend an unwarrantable jurisdiction over us. We have reminded them of the circumstances of our emigration and settlement here. We have appealed to their native justice and magnanimity, and we have conjured them by the ties of our common kindred to disavow these usurpations, which would inevitably interrupt our connections and correspondence. They too must have been deaf to the voice of justice and of consanguinity. We must, therefore, acquiesce in the necessity, which denounces our Separation, and hold them, as we hold the rest of mankind, Enemies in War, in Peace Friends.

WE, THEREFORE, the Representatives of the UNITED STATES OF AMERICA, in General Congress, Assembled, appealing to the Supreme Judge of the world for the rectitude of our intentions, do, in the Name, and by Authority of the good People of these Colonies, solemnly publish and declare, That these United Colonies are, and of Right ought to be FREE AND INDEPENDENT STATES; that they are Absolved from all Allegiance to the British Crown, and that all political connection between them and the State of Great Britain, is and ought to be totally dissolved; and that as Free and Independent States, they have full Power to levy War, conclude Peace, contract Alliances, establish Commerce, and to do all other Acts and Things which Independent States may of right do. And for the support of this Declaration, with a firm reliance on the Protection of Divine Providence, we mutually pledge to each other our Lives, our Fortunes, and our sacred Honor.

The foregoing Declaration was, by order of Congress, engrossed, and signed by the following members:

John Hancock

NEW HAMPSHIRE
Josiah Bartlett
William Whipple
Matthew Thornton

MASSACHUSETTS BAY
Samuel Adams
John Adams
Robert Treat Paine
Elbridge Gerry

RHODE ISLAND
Stephen Hopkins
William Ellery

CONNECTICUT
Roger Sherman
Samuel Huntington
William Williams
Oliver Wolcott

DELAWARE
Caesar Rodney
George Read
Thomas M'Kean

MARYLAND
Samuel Chase
William Paca
Thomas Stone
*Charles Carroll, of
Carrollton*

VIRGINIA
George Wyth
Richard Henry Lee
Thomas Jefferson
Benjamin Harrison
Thomas Nelson, Jr.
Francis Lightfoot Lee
Carter Braxton

NEW YORK
William Floyd
Philip Livingston
Francis Lewis
Lewis Morris

NEW JERSEY
Richard Stockton
John Witherspoon
Francis Hopkinson
John Hart
Abraham Clark

PENNSYLVANIA
Robert Morris
Benjamin Rush
Benjamin Franklin
John Morton
George Clymer
James Smith
George Taylor
James Wilson
George Ross

NORTH CAROLINA
William Hooper
Joseph Hewes
John Penn

SOUTH CAROLINA
Edward Rutledge
Thomas Heyward, Jr.
Thomas Lynch, Jr.
Arthur Middleton

GEORGIA
Button Gwinnett
Lyman Hall
George Walton

Resolved, That copies of the Declaration be sent to the several assemblies, conventions, and committees, or councils of safety, and to the several commanding officers of the continental troops; that it be proclaimed in each of the United States, at the head of the army.

The Constitution of the United States of America

Annotated with references to the Federalist Papers

[PREAMBLE]

We the People of the United States, in Order to form a more perfect Union, establish Justice, insure domestic Tranquility, provide for the common defence, promote the general Welfare, and secure the Blessings of Liberty to ourselves and our Posterity, do ordain and establish this Constitution for the United States of America.

ARTICLE I

Section 1
[LEGISLATIVE POWERS]

All legislative Powers herein granted shall be vested in a Congress of the United States, which shall consist of a Senate and House of Representatives.

Section 2
[HOUSE OF REPRESENTATIVES, HOW CONSTITUTED, POWER OF IMPEACHMENT]

The House of Representatives shall be composed of Members chosen every second Year by the People of the several States, and the Electors in each State shall have the Qualifications requisite for Electors of the most numerous Branch of the State Legislature.

No Person shall be a Representative who shall not have attained to the Age of twenty-five Years, and been seven Years a Citizen of the United States, and who shall not, when elected, be an inhabitant of that State in which he shall be chosen.

Representatives and *direct Taxes*[1] shall be apportioned among the several States which may be included within this Union, according to their respective Numbers, *which shall be determined by adding to the whole Number of free Persons, including those bound to Service for a Term of Years*, and excluding Indians not taxed, *three-fifths of all other Persons.*[2] The actual Enumeration shall be made within three Years after the first Meeting of the Congress of the United States, and within every subsequent Term of ten Years, in such Manner as they shall by Law direct. The Number of Representatives shall not exceed one for every thirty Thousand, but each State shall have at Least one Representative; *and until such enumeration shall be made, the State*

55–56 ★ (Madison)

---

[1]Modified by Sixteenth Amendment.

[2]Modified by Fourteenth Amendment.

of New Hampshire shall be entitled to chuse three, Massachusetts eight, Rhode-Island and Providence Plantations one, Connecticut five, New-York six, New Jersey four, Pennsylvania eight, Delaware one, Maryland six, Virginia ten, North Carolina five, South Carolina five, and Georgia three.[3]

When vacancies happen in the Representation from any State, the Executive Authority thereof shall issue Writs of Election to fill such Vacancies.

The House of Representatives shall chuse their Speaker and other Officers; and shall have the sole Power of Impeachment.

Section 3

[THE SENATE, HOW CONSTITUTED, IMPEACHMENT TRIALS]

The Senate of the United States shall be composed of two Senators from each State, *chosen by the Legislature thereof,*[4] for six Years; and each Senator shall have one Vote.

Immediately after they shall be assembled in Consequence of the first Election, they shall be divided as equally as may be into three Classes. The Seats of the Senators of the first Class shall be vacated at the Expiration of the second Year, of the second Class at the Expiration of the fourth Year, and of the third Class at the Expiration of the sixth Year, so that one third may be chosen every second Year: *and if vacancies happen by Resignation, or otherwise, during the Recess of the Legislature of any State, the Executive thereof may make temporary Appointments until the next Meeting of the Legislature, which shall then fill such Vacancies.*[5]

No person shall be a Senator who shall not have attained to the Age of thirty Years, and been nine Years a Citizen of the United States, and who shall not, when elected, be an Inhabitant of that State for which he shall be chosen.

The Vice-President of the United States shall be President of the Senate, but shall have no Vote, unless they be equally divided.

The Senate shall chuse their other Officers, and also a President pro tempore, in the Absence of the Vice-President, or when he shall exercise the Office of President of the United States.

The Senate shall have the sole Power to try all Impeachments. When sitting for that Purpose, they shall be on Oath or Affirmation. When the President of the United States is tried, the Chief Justice shall preside: And no Person shall be convicted without the Concurrence of two-thirds of the Members present.

Judgment in Cases of Impeachment shall not extend further than to removal from Office, and disqualification to hold and enjoy any Office of honor, Trust or Profit under the United States: but the Party convicted shall nevertheless be liable and subject to Indictment, Trial, Judgment and Punishment, according to Law.

Section 4

[ELECTION OF SENATORS AND REPRESENTATIVES]

The Times, Places and Manner of holding Elections for Senators and Representatives, shall be prescribed in each State by the Legislature thereof; but the

---

[3]Temporary provision.

[4]Modified by Seventeenth Amendment.

[5]Modified by Seventeenth Amendment.

Margin notes:

79 ★ (Hamilton)

39,45 ★ (Madison)
60 ★ (Hamilton)
62–63 ★ (Madiran)
59 ★ (Hamilton)
68 ★ (Hamilton)

62 ★ (Hamilton)

39 ★ (Madison)
65–67, 79 ★ (Hamilton)
65 ★ (Hamilton)

84 ★ (Hamilton)

59–61 ★ (Hamilton)

Congress may at any time by Law make or alter such Regulations, except as to the Places of chusing Senators.

The Congress shall assemble at least once in every Year, and such Meeting shall be on the first Monday in December, unless they shall by Law appoint a different Day.[6]

Section 5
[QUORUM, JOURNALS, MEETINGS, ADJOURNMENTS]

Each House shall be the Judge of the Elections, Returns and Qualifications of its own Members, and a Majority of each shall constitute a Quorum to do Business; but a smaller Number may adjourn from day to day, and may be authorized to compel the Attendance of absent Members, in such Manner, and under the Penalties as each House may provide.

Each House may determine the Rules of its Proceedings, punish its Members for disorderly Behavior, and, with the Concurrence of two-thirds, expel a Member.

Each House shall keep a Journal of its Proceedings, and from time to time publish the same, excepting such Parts as may in their Judgment require Secrecy; and the Yeas and Nays of the Members of either House on any questions shall, at the Desire of one-fifth of the present, be entered on the Journal.

Neither House, during the Session of Congress, shall, without the Consent of the other, adjourn for more than three days, nor to any other Place than that in which the two Houses shall be sitting.

Section 6
[COMPENSATION, PRIVILEGES, DISABILITIES]

The Senators and Representatives shall receive a Compensation for their Services, to be ascertained by Law, and paid out of the Treasury of the United States. They shall in all Cases, except Treason, Felony and Breach of the Peace, be privileged from Arrest during their Attendance at the Session of their respective Houses, and in going to and returning from the same; and for any Speech or Debate in either House, they shall not be questioned in any other Place.

No Senator or Representative shall, during the time for which he was elected, be appointed to any civil Office under the authority of the United States, which shall have been created, or the Emoluments whereof shall have been encreased during such time; and no Person holding any Office under the United States, shall be a Member of either House during his Continuance in Office.

55 ★ (Madison)
76 ★ (Hamilton)

Section 7
[PROCEDURE IN PASSING BILLS AND RESOLUTIONS]

All Bills for raising Revenue shall originate in the House of Representatives; but the Senate may propose or concur with Amendments as on other Bills.

Every Bill which shall have passed the House of Representatives and the Senate, shall, before it become a Law, be presented to the President of the United States; if he approve he shall sign it, but if not he shall return it, with his Objections

66 ★ (Hamilton)

69, 73 ★ (Hamilton)

---

[6]Modified by Twentieth Amendment.

to that House in which it shall have originated, who shall enter the Objections at large on their Journal, and proceed to reconsider it. If after such Reconsideration two-thirds of that House shall agree to pass the Bill, it shall be sent, together with the Objections, to the other House, by which it shall likewise be reconsidered, and if approved by two-thirds of that House it shall become a Law. But in all such Cases the Votes of both Houses shall be determined by Yeas and Nays, and the Names of the Persons voting for and against the Bill shall be entered on the Journal of each House respectively. If any Bill shall not be returned by the President within ten Days (Sundays excepted) after it shall have been presented to him, the Same shall be a Law, in like Manner as if he had signed it, unless the Congress by their Adjournment prevent its Return, in which Case it shall not be a Law.

69, 73 ★ (Hamilton)

Every Order, Resolution, or Vote to which the Concurrence of the Senate and House of Representatives may be necessary (except on a question of Adjournment) shall be presented to the President of the United States; and before the Same shall take Effect, shall be approved by him, or being disapproved by him, shall be re-passed by two-thirds of the Senate and House of Representatives, according to the Rules and Limitations prescribed in the Case of a Bill.

Section 8
[POWERS OF CONGRESS]

The Congress shall have Power

30–36 ★ (Hamilton)
41 ★ (Madison)
56 ★ (Madison)
42, 45, 41 ★
(Madison)

To lay and collect Taxes, Duties, Imposts and Excises, to pay the Debts and provide for the common Defence and general Welfare of the United States; but all Duties, Imposts and excises shall be uniform throughout the United States;

To borrow Money on the Credit of the United States;

To regulate Commerce with foreign Nations, and among the several States, and with the Indian Tribes;

32 ★ (Hamilton)
42 ★ (Madison)
42 ★ (Madison)

To establish an uniform Rule of Naturalization, and uniform Laws on the subject of Bankruptcies throughout the United States;

To coin Money, regulate the Value thereof, and of foreign Coin, and fix the Standard of Weights and Measures;

42 ★ (Madison)

To provide for the Punishment of counterfeiting the Securities and current Coin of the United States;

42 ★ (Madison)
43 ★ (Madison)

To establish Post Offices and post Roads;

To promote the Progress of Science and useful Arts, by securing for limited Times to Authors and Inventors the exclusive Right to their respective Writings and Discoveries;

81 ★ (Hamilton)
42 ★ (Madison)

To constitute Tribunals inferior to the supreme Court;

To define and Punish Piracies and Felonies committed on the high Seas, and Offences against the Law of Nations;

41 ★ (Madison)

To declare War, grant Letters of Marque and Reprisal, and make Rules concerning Captures on Land and Water;

23, 24, 26★
(Hamilton)
41 ★ (Madison)

To raise and support Armies, but no Appropriation of Money to that Use shall be for a longer Term than two Years;

To provide and maintain a Navy;

To make Rules for the Government and Regulation of the land and naval forces;

To provide for calling for the Militia to execute the Laws of the Union, suppress Insurrections and repel Invasions; 29 ★ (Hamilton)

To provide for organizing, arming, and disciplining, the Militia, and for governing such Part of them as may be employed in the Service of the United States, reserving to the States respectively, the Appointment of the Officers, and the Authority of training the Militia according to the discipline prescribed by Congress; 29 ★ (Hamilton) 56 ★ (Madison) 32 ★ (Hamilton)

To exercise exclusive Legislation in all Cases whatsoever, over such District (not exceeding ten Miles square) as may, by Cession of particular States, and the Acceptance of Congress, become the Seat of the Government of the United States, and to exercise like Authority over all Places purchased by the Consent of the Legislature of the State in which the Same shall be, for the Erection of Forts, Magazines, Arsenals, dock-Yards, and other needful Buildings;—And 43 ★ (Madison) 43 ★ (Madison)

To make all Laws which shall be necessary and proper for carrying into Execution the foregoing Powers, and all other Powers vested by this Constitution in the Government of the United States, or in any Department or Officer thereof. 29, 33 ★ (Hamilton) 44 ★ (Madison)

Section 9
[SOME RESTRICTIONS ON FEDERAL POWER]

The Migration or Importation of such Persons as any of the States now existing shall think proper to admit, shall not be prohibited by the Congress prior to the Year one thousand eight hundred and eight, but a Tax or Duty may be imposed on such Importation, not exceeding ten dollars for each Person.[7] 42 ★ (Madison)

The privilege of the Writ of *Habeas Corpus* shall not be suspended, unless when in Cases of Rebellion or Invasion the public Safety may require it. 83, 84 ★ (Hamilton)

No Bill of Attainder or ex post facto Law shall be passed. 84 ★ (Hamilton)

No Capitation, or other direct, Tax shall be laid, unless in Proportion to the Census or Enumeration herein before directed to be taken.[8]

No Tax or Duty shall be laid on Articles exported from any State.

No Preference shall be given by any Regulation of Commerce or Revenue to the Ports of one State over those of another; nor shall vessels bound to, or from, one State, be obliged to enter, clear, or pay Duties in another. 32 ★ (Hamilton)

No Money shall be drawn from the Treasury, but in Consequence of Appropriations made by Law; and a regular Statement and Account of the Receipts and Expenditures of all public Money shall be published from time to time.

No Title of Nobility shall be granted by the United States: And no Person holding any Office of Profit or Trust under them, shall, without the Consent of the Congress, accept of any present, Emolument, Office or Title, of any kind whatever, from any King, Prince, or foreign State. 39 ★ (Hamilton) 84 ★ (Hamilton)

Section 10
[RESTRICTIONS UPON POWERS OF STATES]

No State shall enter into any Treaty, Alliance, or Confederation; grant Letters of Marque and Reprisal; coin Money; emit Bills of Credit; make any Thing but gold and silver Coin a Tender in Payment of Debts; pass any Bill of Attainder, ex 33 ★ (Hamilton) 44 ★ (Madison)

---

[7]Temporary provision.

[8]Modified by Sixteenth Amendment.

post facto Law, or Law impairing the Obligation of Contracts, or grant any Title of Nobility.

No State shall, without the Consent of the Congress, lay any Imposts or Duties on Imports or Exports, except what may be absolutely necessary for executing its inspection Laws: and the net Produce of all Duties and Imposts, laid by any State on Imports or Exports, shall be for the Use of the Treasury of the United States; and all such Laws shall be subject to the Revision and Control of the Congress.

No State shall, without the Consent of Congress, lay any Duty of Tonnage, keep Troops, or Ships of War in time of Peace, enter into any Agreement or Compact with another State, or with a foreign Power, or engage in War, unless actually invaded, or in such imminent Danger as will not admit of Delay.

ARTICLE II

Section 1
[EXECUTIVE POWER, ELECTION, QUALIFICATIONS OF THE PRESIDENT]

The executive Power shall be vested in a President of the United States of America. *He shall hold his Office during the Term of four years and, together with the Vice-President, chosen for the same Term, be elected, as follows:*[9]

Each State shall appoint, in such Manner as the Legislature thereof may direct, a Number of Electors, equal to the whole Number of Senators and Representatives to which the State may be entitled in the Congress: but no Senator or Representative, or Person holding an Office of Trust or Profit under the United States, shall be appointed an Elector.

The electors shall meet in their respective States, and vote by ballot for two Persons, of whom one at least shall not be an Inhabitant of the same State with themselves. And they shall make a List of all the Persons voted for, and of the Number of Votes for each; which List they shall sign and certify, and transmit sealed to the Seat of the Government of the United States, directed to the President of the Senate. The President of the Senate shall, in the Presence of the Senate and House of Representatives, open all the Certificates, and the Votes shall then be counted. The Person having the greatest Number of Votes shall be the President, if such Number be a Majority of the whole Number of Electors appointed; and if there be more than one who have such Majority and have an equal Number of Votes, then the House of Representatives shall immediately chuse by Ballot one of them for President; and if no person have a Majority, then from the five highest on the List the said House shall in like Manner chuse the President. But in chusing the President, the Votes shall be taken by States, the Representation from each State having one Vote; A quorum for this Purpose shall consist of a Member or Members from two-thirds of the States, and a Majority of all the States shall be necessary to a Choice. In every Case, after the Choice of the President, the person having the greatest Number of Votes of the Electors shall be the Vice-President. But if there should remain two or more who have equal vote, the Senate shall chuse from them by Ballot the Vice-President.[10]

---

[9]Number of terms limited to two by Twenty-second Amendment.

[10]Modified by Twelfth and Twentieth Amendments.

32 ★ (Hamilton)
44 ★ (Madison)

39 ★ (Madison)
70, 71, 84 ★ (Hamilton)
69, 71 ★ (Hamilton)
39, 45 ★ (Madison)
68, 77 ★ (Hamilton)

66 ★ (Hamilton)

The Congress may determine the Time of chusing the Electors, and the Day on which they shall give their Votes; which Day shall be the same throughout the United States.

64 ★ (Jay)

No Person except a natural born Citizen, or a Citizen of the United States, at the time of the Adoption of this Constitution, shall be eligible to the Office of President; neither shall any Person be eligible to that Office who shall not have attained to the Age of thirty-five Years, and been fourteen Years a Resident within the United States.

In Case of the Removal of the President from Office, or his Death, Resignation, or Inability to discharge the Powers and Duties of the said Office, the same shall devolve on the Vice-President, and the Congress may by Law provide for the Case of Removal, Death, Resignation, or Inability, both of the President and Vice-president, declaring what Officer shall then act as President, and such Officer shall act accordingly, until the Disability be removed, or a President shall be elected.

The President shall, at stated Times, receive for his Services, a Compensation, which shall neither be encreased nor diminished during the Period for which he shall have been elected, and he shall not receive within that Period any other Emolument from the United States, or any of them.

73, 79 ★ (Hamilton)

Before he enter on the Execution of his Office, he shall take the following Oath or Affirmation:—"I do solemnly swear (or affirm) that I will faithfully execute the Office of President of the United States, and will to the best of my Ability, preserve, protect and defend the Constitution of the United States."

Section 2
[POWERS OF THE PRESIDENT]

The President shall be Commander in Chief of the Army and Navy of the United States, and of the Militia of the several States, when called into the actual Service of the United States; he may require the Opinion, in writing, of the principal Officer in each of the executive Departments, upon any Subject relating to the Duties of their respective Offices, and he shall have Power to grant Reprieves and Pardons for Offences against the United States, except in Cases of Impeachment.

69, 74 ★ (Hamilton)
74 ★ (Hamilton)

69 ★ (Hamilton)
74 ★ (Hamilton)
42 ★ (Madison)

He shall have Power, by and with the Advice and Consent of the Senate, to make Treaties, provided two-thirds of the Senators present concur; and he shall nominate, and by and with the Advice and Consent of the Senate, shall appoint Ambassadors, other public Ministers and Consuls, Judges of the Supreme Court, and all other Officers of the United States, whose Appointments are not herein otherwise provided for, and which shall be established by Law: but the Congress may by Law vest the Appointment of such inferior Officers, as they think proper, in the President alone, in the Courts of Law, or in the Heads of Departments.

64 ★ (Jay)
66 ★ (Hamilton)
42 ★ (Madiaon)
66, 69, 76, 77 ★
(Hamilton)

The President shall have Power to fill up all Vacancies that may happen during the Recess of the Senate, by granting Commissions which shall expire at the End of their next Session.

67, 76 ★ (Hamilton)

Section 3
[POWERS AND DUTIES OF THE PRESIDENT]

He shall from time to time give to the Congress Information of the State of the Union, and recommend to their Consideration such Measures as he shall

77 ★ (Hamilton)
69, 77 ★ (Hamilton)

judge necessary and expedient; he may, on extraordinary Occasions, convene both Houses, or either of them, and in Case of Disagreement between them, with Respect to the Time of Adjournment, he may adjourn them to such Time as he shall think proper; he shall receive Ambassadors and other public Ministers; he shall take Care that the Laws be faithfully executed, and shall Commission all the Officers of the United States.

Section 4
[IMPEACHMENT]

The President, Vice-President and all civil Officers of the United States shall be removed from Office on Impeachment for, and Conviction of, Treason, Bribery, or other high Crimes and Misdemeanors.

ARTICLE III

Section 1
[JUDICIAL POWER, TENURE OF OFFICE]

The judicial Power of the United States, shall be vested in one supreme Court, and in such inferior Courts as the Congress may from time to time ordain and establish. The Judges, both of the supreme and inferior Courts, shall hold their Offices during good Behavior, and shall, at stated Times, receive for their Services, a Compensation, which shall not be diminished during their Continuance in Office.

Section 2
[JURISDICTION]

The judicial Power shall extend to all Cases, in Law and Equity, arising under this Constitution, the Laws of the United States, and Treaties made, or which shall be made, under their Authority;—to all Cases affecting Ambassadors, other public Ministers and Consuls;—to all Cases of admiralty and maritime Jurisdiction;—to Controversies to which the United States shall be a party;—to Controversies between two or more States;—*between a State and Citizens of another State;*— between Citizens of different States,—between Citizens of the same State claiming Lands under Grants of different States, *and between a State,* or the Citizens thereof, *and foreign States, Citizens or Subjects.*[11]

In all Cases affecting Ambassadors, other public Ministers and Consuls, and those in which a State shall be Party, the supreme Court shall have original Jurisdiction. In all the other Cases before mentioned, the supreme Court shall have appellate Jurisdiction, both as to Law and Fact, with such Exceptions, and under such Regulations as Congress shall make.

The Trial of all Crimes, except in Cases of Impeachment, shall be by Jury; and such Trial shall be held in the State where the said Crimes shall have been committed; but when not committed within any State, the Trial shall be at such Place or Places as the Congress may by Law have directed.

---

[11]Modified by Eleventh Amendment.

Section 3
[TREASON, PROOF, AND PUNISHMENT]

Treason against the United States, shall consist only in levying War against them, or in adhering to their Enemies, giving them Aid and Comfort. No Person shall be convicted of Treason unless on the Testimony of two Witnesses to the same overt Act, or on Confession in open Court.

43 ★ (Madison)
84 ★ (Hamilton)

The Congress shall have Power to declare the Punishment of Treason, but no Attainder of Treason shall work Corruption of Blood, or Forfeiture except during the Life of the Person attained.

43 ★ (Madison)
84 ★ (Hamilton)

ARTICLE IV

Section 1
[FAITH AND CREDIT AMONG STATES]

Full Faith and Credit shall be given in each State to the public Acts, Records, and judicial Proceedings of every other State. And the Congress may by general Laws prescribe the Manner in which such Acts, Records and Proceedings shall be proved, and the Effect thereof.

42 ★ (Madison)

Section 2
[PRIVILEGES AND IMMUNITIES, FUGITIVES]

The Citizens of each State shall be entitled to all Privileges and Immunities of Citizens in the several States.

80★ (Hamilton)

A person charged in any State with Treason, Felony or other Crime, who shall flee from Justice, and be found in another State, shall on Demand of the executive Authority of the State from which he fled, be delivered up to be removed to the State having Jurisdiction of the Crime.

No person held to Service or Labour in one State, under the Laws thereof, escaping into another, shall, in Consequence of any Law or Regulation therein, be discharged from such Service or Labour, but shall be delivered up on Claim of the Party to whom such Service or Labour may be due. [12]

Section 3
[ADMISSION OF NEW STATES]

New States may be admitted by the Congress into this Union; but no new State shall be formed or erected within the Jurisdiction of any other State; nor any State be formed by the Junction of two or more States, or Parts of States, without the Consent of the Legislatures of the States concerned as well as of the Congress.

43 ★ (Madison)

The Congress shall have Power to dispose of and make all needful Rules and Regulations respecting the Territory or other Property belonging to the United States; and nothing in this Constitution shall be so construed as to Prejudice any Claims of the United States, or of any particular State.

43 ★ (Madison)

---

[12]Repealed by the Thirteenth Amendment.

Section 4
[GUARANTEE OF REPUBLICAN GOVERNMENT]

39, 43 ★ (Madison)

The United States shall guarantee to every State in this Union a Republican Form of Government, and shall protect each of them against Invasion; and on Application of the Legislature, or of the Executive (when the Legislature cannot be convened) against domestic Violence.

ARTICLE V
[AMENDMENT OF THE CONSTITUTION]

39, 43 ★ (Madison)
85★ (Hamilton)

The Congress, whenever two-thirds of both Houses shall deem it necessary, shall propose Amendments to this Constitution, or, on the Application of the Legislatures of two-thirds of the several States, shall call a Convention for proposing Amendments, which, in either Case, shall be valid to all Intents and Purposes, as Part of this Constitution, when ratified by the Legislatures of three-fourths of the several States, or by Conventions in three-fourths thereof, as the one or the other Mode of Ratification may be proposed by the Congress; *Provided that no Amendment which may be made prior to the Year One thousand eight hundred and eight shall in any Manner affect the first and fourth Clauses in the Ninth Section of the first Article;* [13] and that no State, without its Consent, shall be deprived of its equal Suffrage in the Senate.

ARTICLE VI
[DEBTS, SUPREMACY, OATH]

43 ★ (Madison)

All Debts contracted and Engagements entered into, before the Adoption of this Constitution, shall be as valid against the United States under this Constitution, as under the Confederation.

27, 33 ★ (Hamilton)
39, 44

This Constitution, and the Laws of the United States which shall be made in Pursuance thereof; and all Treaties made, or which shall be made, under the Authority of the United States, shall be the supreme Law of the Land; and the Judges in every State shall be bound thereby, any Thing in the Constitution or Laws of any State to the Contrary notwithstanding.

27 ★ (hamilton)
44

The Senators and Representatives before mentioned, and the Members of the several State Legislatures, and all executive and judicial Officers, both of the United States and of the several States, shall be bound by Oath or Affirmation, to support this Constitution; but no religious Test shall be required as a Qualification to any Office or public Trust under the United States.

ARTICLE VII
[RATIFICATION AND ESTABLISHMENT]

39, 40, 43 ★
(Madison)

The Ratification of the Conventions of nine States, shall be sufficient for the Establishment of this Constitution between the States so ratifying the Same. [14]

---

[13] Temporary provision.

[14] The Constitution was submitted on September 17, 1787, by the Constitutional Convention, was ratified by the conventions of several states at various dates up to May 29, 1790, and became effective on March 4, 1789.

Done in Convention by the Unanimous Consent of the States present the Seventeenth Day of September in the Year of our Lord one thousand seven hundred and Eighty seven and of the Independence of the United States of America the Twelfth. In Witness whereof We have hereunto subscribed our Names,

G:⁰ WASHINGTON—
Presidt, and Deputy
from Virginia

New Hampshire	JOHN LANGDON	Maryland	JAMES MCHENRY
	NICHOLAS GILMAN		DAN OF ST. THOS. JENIFER
Massachusetts	NATHANIEL GORHAM		DANL CARROLL
	RUFUS KING		
		Virginia	JOHN BLAIR—
Connecticut	WM SAML JOHNSON		JAMES MADISON JR.
	ROGER SHERMAN		
		North Carolina	WM BLOUNT
New York	ALEXANDER HAMILTON		RICHD DOBBS SPAIGHT
			HU WILLIAMSON
New Jersey	WIL: LIVINGSTON		
	DAVID BREARLY	South Carolina	J. RUTLEDGE
	WM PATERSON		CHARLES COTESWORTH
	JONA: DAYTON		PLNCKNEY
			PIERCE BUTLER
Pennsylvania	B FRANKLIN		
	THOMAS MIFFLIN	Georgia	WILLIAM FEW
	ROBT MORRIS		ABR BALDWIN
	GEO. CLYMER		
	THOS. FITZSIMONS		
	JARED INGERSOLL		
	JAMES WILSON		
	GOUV MORRIS		
Delaware	GEO READ		
	GUNNING BEDFOR JUN		
	JOHN DICKINSON		
	RICHARD BASSETT		
	JACO: BROOM		

Amendments to the Constitution

Proposed by Congress and Ratified by the Legislatures of the Several States, Pursuant to Article V of the Original Constitution

Amendments I–X, known as the Bill of Rights, were proposed by Congress on September 25, 1789, and ratified on December 15, 1791. *The Federalist Papers* comments, mainly in opposition to a Bill of Rights, can be found in number 84 (Hamilton).

AMENDMENT I
[FREEDOM OF RELIGION, OF SPEECH, AND OF THE PRESS]

Congress shall make no law respecting an establishment of religion, or prohibiting the free exercise thereof; or abridging the freedom of speech, or of the press; or the right of the people peaceably to assemble, and to petition the Government for a redress of grievances.

AMENDMENT II
[RIGHT TO KEEP AND BEAR ARMS]

A well regulated Militia, being necessary to the security of a free State, the right of the people to keep and bear Arms, shall not be infringed.

AMENDMENT III
[QUARTERING OF SOLDIERS]

No Soldier shall, in time of peace be quartered in any house, without the consent of the Owner, nor in time of war, but in a manner to be prescribed by law.

AMENDMENT IV
[SECURITY FROM UNWARRANTABLE SEARCH AND SEIZURE]

The right of the people to be secure in their persons, houses, papers, and effects, against unreasonable searches and seizures, shall not be violated, and no Warrants shall issue, but upon probable cause, supported by Oath or affirmation, and particularly describing the place to be searched, and the persons or things to be seized.

AMENDMENT V
[RIGHTS OF ACCUSED PERSONS IN CRIMINAL PROCEEDINGS]

No person shall be held to answer for a capital, or otherwise infamous crime, unless on a presentment or indictment of a Grand Jury, except in cases arising in the land or naval forces, or in the Militia, when in actual service in time of War or in public danger; nor shall any person be subject for the same offence to be twice put in jeopardy of life or limb; nor shall be compelled in any Criminal Case to be a witness against himself, nor be deprived of life, liberty, or property, without due process of law; nor shall private property be taken for public use, without just compensation.

AMENDMENT VI
[RIGHT TO SPEEDY TRIAL, WITNESSES, ETC.]

In all criminal prosecutions, the accused shall enjoy the right to a speedy and public trial, by an impartial jury of the State and district wherein the crime shall have been committed, which district shall have been previously ascertained by law, and to be informed of the nature and cause of the accusation; to be confronted with the witnesses against him; to have compulsory process for obtaining Witnesses in his favor, and to have the Assistance of Counsel for his defence.

AMENDMENT VII
[TRIAL BY JURY IN CIVIL CASES]

In suits at common law, where the value in controversy shall exceed twenty dollars, the right of trial by jury shall be preserved, and no fact tried by a jury shall be otherwise re-examined in any Court of the United States, than according to the rules of the common law.

AMENDMENT VIII
[BAILS, FINES, PUNISHMENTS]

Excessive bail shall not be required, nor excessive fines imposed, nor cruel and unusual punishments inflicted.

AMENDMENT IX
[RESERVATION OF RIGHTS OF PEOPLE]

The enumeration in the Constitution, of certain rights, shall not be construed to deny or disparage others retained by the people.

AMENDMENT X
[POWERS RESERVED TO STATES OR PEOPLE]

The powers not delegated to the United States by the Constitution, nor prohibited by it to the States, are reserved to the States respectively, or to the people.

AMENDMENT XI
[Proposed by Congress on March 4, 1794; declared ratified on January 8, 1798.]

[RESTRICTION OF JUDICIAL POWER]

The Judicial power of the United States shall not be construed to extend to any suit in law or equity, commenced or prosecuted against one of the United States by Citizens of another State, or by Citizens or Subjects of any Foreign State.

AMENDMENT XII

[Proposed by Congress on December 9, 1803; declared ratified on September 25, 1804.]

[ELECTION OF PRESIDENT AND VICE-PRESIDENT]

The Electors shall meet in their respective states, and vote by ballot for President and Vice-President, one of whom, at least, shall not be an inhabitant of the same state with themselves; they shall name in their ballots the person voted for as President, and in distinct ballots the person voted for as Vice-President, and they shall make distinct lists of all persons voted for as President, and of all persons voted for as Vice-President, and of the number of votes for each, which lists they shall sign and certify, and transmit sealed to the seat of the government of the United States, directed to the President of the Senate;—The President of the Senate shall, in presence of the Senate and House of Representatives, open all the certificates and the votes shall then be counted;—The person having the greatest number of votes for President, shall be the President, if such number be a majority of the whole number of Electors appointed; and if no person have such majority, then from the persons having the highest numbers not exceeding three on the list of those voted for as President, the House of Representatives shall choose immediately, by ballot, the President. But in choosing the President, the votes shall be taken by states, the representation from each state having one vote; a quorum for this purpose shall consist of a member or members from two-thirds of the states, and a majority of all states shall be necessary to a choice. And if the House of Representatives shall not choose a President whenever the right of choice shall devolve upon them, before the fourth day of March next following, then the Vice-President, shall act as President, as in the case of the death or other constitutional disability of the President. The person having the greatest number of votes as Vice-President, shall be the Vice-President, if such a number be a majority of the whole number of Electors appointed, and if no person have a majority, then from the two highest numbers on the list, the Senate shall choose the Vice-President; a quorum for the purpose shall consist of two-thirds of the whole number of Senators, and a majority of the whole number shall be necessary to a choice. But no person constitutionally ineligible to the office of President shall be eligible to that of Vice-President of the United States.

AMENDMENT XIII

[Proposed by Congress on January 31, 1865; declared ratified on December 18, 1865.]

Section 1

[ABOLITION OF SLAVERY]

Neither slavery nor involuntary servitude, except as a punishment for crime whereof the party shall have been duly convicted, shall exist within the United States, or any place subject to their jurisdiction.

Section 2
[POWER TO ENFORCE THIS ARTICLE]

Congress shall have power to enforce this article by appropriate legislation.

AMENDMENT XIV
[Proposed by Congress on June 13, 1866; declared ratified on July 28, 1868.]

Section 1
[CITIZENSHIP RIGHTS NOT TO BE ABRIDGED BY STATES]

All persons born or naturalized in the United States, and subject to the jurisdiction thereof, are citizens of the United States and of the State wherein they reside. No state shall make or enforce any law which shall abridge the privileges or immunities of citizens of the United States; nor shall any State deprive any person of life, liberty, or property, without due process of law; nor deny to any person within its jurisdiction the equal protection of the laws.

Section 2
[APPORTIONMENT OF REPRESENTATIVES IN CONGRESS]

Representatives shall be apportioned among the several States according to their respective numbers, counting the whole number of persons in each State, excluding Indians not taxed. But when the right to vote at any election for the choice of electors for President and Vice-President of the United States, Representatives in Congress, the Executive and Judicial officers of a State, or the members of the Legislature thereof, is denied to any of the male inhabitants of such State, being twenty-one years of age, and citizens of the United States, or in any way abridged, except for participation in rebellion, or other crime, the basis of representation therein shall be reduced in the proportion which the number of such male citizens shall bear to the whole number of male citizens twenty-one years of age in such State.

Section 3
[PERSONS DISQUALIFIED FROM HOLDING OFFICE]

No person shall be a Senator or Representative in Congress, or elector of President and Vice-President, or hold any office, civil or military, under the United States, or under any State, who, having previously taken an oath, as a member of Congress, or as an officer of the United States, or as a member of any State legislature, or as an executive or judicial officer of any State, to support the Constitution of the United States, shall have engaged in insurrection or rebellion against the same, or given aid or comfort to the enemies thereof. But Congress may by a vote of two-thirds of each House, remove such disability.

Section 4
[WHAT PUBLIC DEBTS ARE VALID]

The validity of the public debt of the United States, authorized by law, including debts incurred for payment of pensions and bounties for services in suppressing insurrection or rebellion, shall not be questioned. But neither the United States nor any State shall assume or pay any debt or obligation incurred in aid of insurrection or rebellion against the United States, or any claim for the loss or emancipation of any slave; but all such debts, obligations and claims shall be held illegal and void.

Section 5
[POWER TO ENFORCE THIS ARTICLE]

The Congress shall have power to enforce, by appropriate legislation, the provisions of this article.

AMENDMENT XV
[Proposed by Congress on February 26, 1869; declared ratified on March 30, 1870.]

Section 1
[NEGRO SUFFRAGE]

The right of citizens of the United States to vote shall not be denied or abridged by the United States or by any State on account of race, color, or previous condition of servitude.

Section 2
[POWER TO ENFORCE THIS ARTICLE]

The Congress shall have power to enforce this article by appropriate legislation.

AMENDMENT XVI
[Proposed by Congress on July 12, 1909; declared ratified on February 25, 1913.]

[AUTHORIZING INCOME TAXES]

The Congress shall have power to lay and collect taxes on incomes, from whatever source derived, without apportionment among the several States, and without regard to any census or enumeration.

AMENDMENT XVII
[Proposed by Congress on May 13, 1912; declared ratified on May 31, 1913.]

[POPULAR ELECTION OF SENATORS]

The Senate of the United States shall be composed of two Senators from each State, elected by the people thereof, for six years; and each Senator shall have one vote. The electors in each State shall have the qualifications requisite for electors of the most numerous branch of the State Legislature.

When vacancies happen in the representation of any State in the Senate, the executive authority of such State shall issue writs of election to fill such vacancies: Provided, That the Legislature of any State may empower the executive thereof to make temporary appointment until the people fill the vacancies by election as the Legislature may direct.

This amendment shall not be so construed as to affect the election or term of any Senator chosen before it becomes valid as part of the Constitution.

AMENDMENT XVIII

[Proposed by Congress December 18, 1917; declared ratified on January 29, 1919.]

Section 1

[NATIONAL LIQUOR PROHIBITION]

After one year from the ratification of this article the manufacture, sale, or transportation of intoxicating liquors within, the importation thereof into, or the exportation thereof from the United States and all territory subject to the jurisdiction thereof for beverage purposes is hereby prohibited.

Section 2

[POWER TO ENFORCE THIS ARTICLE]

The Congress and the several states shall have concurrent power to enforce this article by appropriate legislation.

Section 3

[RATIFICATION WITHIN SEVEN YEARS]

This article shall be inoperative unless it shall have been ratified as an amendment to the Constitution by the legislatures of the several states, as provided in the Constitution, within seven years from the date of the submission hereof to the states by the Congress.[15]

AMENDMENT XIX

[Proposed by Congress on June 4, 1919; declared ratified on August 26, 1920.]

[WOMAN SUFFRAGE]

The right of the citizens of the United States to vote shall not be denied or abridged by the United States or by any state on account of sex.

Congress shall have power to enforce this article by appropriate legislation.

AMENDMENT XX

[Proposed by Congress on March 2, 1932; declared ratified on February 6, 1933.]

Section 1

[TERMS OF OFFICE]

The terms of the President and Vice-President shall end at noon on the 20th day of January, and the terms of the Senators and Representatives at noon on the 3rd day of January, of the years in which such terms would have ended if this article had not been ratified; and the terms of their successors shall then begin.

---

[15] Repealed by the Twenty-first Amendment.

Section 2

[TIME OF CONVENING CONGRESS]

The Congress shall assemble at least once in every year, and such meeting shall begin at noon on the 3rd day of January, unless they shall by law appoint a different day.

Section 3

[DEATH OF PRESIDENT-ELECT]

If, at the time fixed for the beginning of the term of the President, the President-elect shall have died, the Vice-President-elect shall become President. If a President shall not have been chosen before the time fixed for the beginning of his term, or if the President-elect shall have failed to qualify, then the Vice-President-elect shall act as President until a President shall have qualified; and the Congress may by law provide for the case wherein neither a President-elect nor a Vice-President-elect shall have qualified, declaring who shall then act as President, or the manner in which one who is to act shall be selected, and such person shall act accordingly until a President or Vice President shall have qualified.

Section 4

[ELECTION OF THE PRESIDENT]

The Congress may by law provide for the case of the death of any of the persons from whom the House of Representatives may choose a President whenever the right of choice shall have devolved upon them, and for the case of the death of any of the persons from whom the Senate may choose a Vice-President whenever the right of choice shall have devolved upon them.

Section 5

[AMENDMENT TAKES EFFECT]

Sections 1 and 2 shall take effect on the 15th day of October following ratification of this article.

Section 6

[RATIFICATION WITHIN SEVEN YEARS]

This article shall be inoperative unless it shall have been ratified as an amendment to the Constitution by the legislatures of three-fourths of the several States within seven years from the date of its submission.

AMENDMENT XXI

[Proposed by Congress on February 20, 1933; declared ratified on December 5, 1933.]

Section 1

[NATIONAL LIQUOR PROHIBITION REPEALED]

The eighteenth article of amendment to the Constitution of the United States is hereby repealed.

Section 2
[TRANSPORTATION OF LIQUOR INTO "DRY" STATES]

The transportation or importation into any State, Territory, or Possession of the United States for delivery or use therein of intoxicating liquors, in violation of the laws thereof, is hereby prohibited.

Section 3
[RATIFICATION WITHIN SEVEN YEARS]

This article shall be inoperative unless it shall have been ratified as an amendment to the Constitution by conventions in the several States, as provided in the Constitution, within seven years from the date of the submission hereof to the States by the Congress.

AMENDMENT XXII
[Proposed by Congress on March 21, 1947; declared ratified on February 26, 1951.]

Section 1
[TENURE OF PRESIDENT LIMITED]

No person shall be elected to the office of President more than twice, and no person who has held the office of President or acted as President for more than two years of a term to which some other person was elected President shall be elected to the Office of the President more than once. But this Article shall not apply to any person holding the office of President when this Article was proposed by the Congress, and shall not prevent any person who may be holding the office of President, or acting as President, during the term within which this Article becomes operative from holding the office of President or acting as President during the remainder of such term.

Section 2
[RATIFICATION WITHIN SEVEN YEARS]

This Article shall be inoperative unless it shall have been ratified as an amendment to the Constitution by the legislatures of three-fourths of the several states within seven years from the date of its submission to the States by the Congress.

AMENDMENT XXIII
[Proposed by Congress on June 21, 1960; declared ratified on March 29, 1961.]

Section 1
[ELECTORAL COLLEGE VOTES FOR THE DISTRICT OF COLUMBIA]

The District constituting the seat of Government of the United States shall appoint in such manner as the Congress may direct:

A number of electors of President and Vice-President equal to the whole number of Senators and Representatives in Congress to which the District would be entitled if it were a State, but in no event more than the least populous State; they shall be in addition to those appointed by the States, but they shall be considered, for the purposes of the election of President and Vice-President, to be electors appointed by a State; and they shall meet in the District and perform such duties as provided by the twelfth article of amendment.

Section 2
[POWER TO ENFORCE THIS ARTICLE]

The Congress shall have power to enforce this article by appropriate legislation.

AMENDMENT XXIV
[Proposed by Congress on August 27, 1963; declared ratified on January 23, 1964.]

Section 1
[ANTI-POLL TAX]

The right of citizens of the United States to vote in any primary or other election for President or Vice-President, for electors for President or Vice-President, or for Senator or Representative of Congress, shall not be denied or abridged by the United States or any State by reasons of failure to pay any poll tax or other tax.

Section 2
[POWER TO ENFORCE THIS ARTICLE]

The Congress shall have power to enforce this article by appropriate legislation.

AMENDMENT XXV
[Proposed by Congress on July 7, 1965; declared ratified on February 10, 1967.]

Section 1
[VICE-PRESIDENT TO BECOME PRESIDENT]

In case of the removal of the President from office or his death or resignation, the Vice-President shall become President.

Section 2
[CHOICE OF A NEW VICE-PRESIDENT]

Whenever there is a vacancy in the office of the Vice-President, the President shall nominate a Vice-President who shall take the office upon confirmation by a majority vote of both houses of Congress.

Section 3
[PRESIDENT MAY DECLARE OWN DISABILITY]

Whenever the President transmits to the President pro tempore of the Senate and the Speaker of the House of Representatives his written declaration that he is unable to discharge the powers and duties of his office, and until he transmits to them a written declaration to the contrary, such powers and duties shall be discharged by the Vice-President as Acting President.

Section 4
[ALTERNATE PROCEDURES TO DECLARE AND TO END PRESIDENTIAL DISABILITY]

Whenever the Vice-President and a majority of either the principal officers of the executive departments, or of such other body as Congress may by law provide, transmit to the President pro tempore of the Senate and the Speaker of the House of Representatives their written declaration that the President is unable to discharge the powers and duties of his office, the Vice-President shall immediately assume the powers and duties of the office as Acting President.

Thereafter, when the President transmits to the President pro tempore of the Senate and the Speaker of the House of Representatives his written declaration that no inability exists, he shall resume the powers and duties of his office unless the Vice-President and a majority of either the principal officers of the executive departments, or of such other body as Congress may by law provide, transmit within four days to the President pro tempore of the Senate and the Speaker of the House of Representatives their written declaration that the President is unable to discharge the powers and duties of his office. Thereupon Congress shall decide the issue, assembling within 48 hours for that purpose if not in session. If the Congress, within 21 days after receipt of the latter written declaration, or, if Congress is not in session, within 21 days after Congress is required to assemble, determines by two-thirds vote of both houses that the President is unable to discharge the powers and duties of his office, the Vice-President shall continue to discharge the same as Acting President; otherwise, the President shall resume the powers and duties of his office.

AMENDMENT XXVI
[Proposed by Congress on March 23, 1971; declared ratified on June 30, 1971.]

Section 1
[EIGHTEEN-YEAR-OLD VOTE]

The right of citizens of the United States, who are eighteen years of age or older, to vote shall not be denied or abridged by the United States or by any State on account of age.

Section 2
[POWER TO ENFORCE THIS ARTICLE]

The Congress shall have power to enforce this article by appropriate legislation.

AMENDMENT XXVII
[Proposed by Congress on September 25, 1789; ratified on May 7, 1992.]

No law varying the compensation for the services of the Senators and Representatives shall take effect until an election of Representatives shall have intervened.

The Federalist Papers

NO. 10: MADISON

Among the numerous advantages promised by a well-constructed Union, none deserves to be more accurately developed than its tendency to break and control the violence of faction. The friend of popular governments never finds himself so much alarmed for their character and fate as when he contemplates their propensity to this dangerous vice. He will not fail, therefore, to set a due value on any plan which, without violating the principles to which he is attached, provides a proper cure for it. The instability, injustice, and confusion introduced into the public councils have, in truth, been the mortal diseases under which popular governments have everywhere perished, as they continue to be the favorite and fruitful topics from which the adversaries to liberty derive their most specious declamations. The valuable improvements made by the American constitutions on the popular models, both ancient and modern, cannot certainly be too much admired; but it would be an unwarrantable partiality to contend that they have as effectually obviated the danger on this side, as was wished and expected. Complaints are everywhere heard from our most considerate and virtuous citizens, equally the friends of public and private faith and of public and personal liberty, that our governments are too unstable, that the public good is disregarded in the conflicts of rival parties, and that measures are too often decided, not I according to the rules of justice and the rights of the minor party, but by the superior force of an interested and overbearing majority. However anxiously we may wish that these complaints had no foundation, the evidence of known facts will not permit us to deny that they are in some degree true. It will be found, indeed, on a candid review of our situation, that some of the distresses under which we labor have been erroneously charged on the operation of our governments; but it will be found, at the same time, that other causes will not alone account for many of our heaviest misfortunes; and, particularly, for that prevailing and increasing distrust of public engagements and alarm for private rights which are echoed from one end of the continent to the other. These must be chiefly, if not wholly, effects of the unsteadiness and injustice with which a factious spirit has tainted our public administration.

By a faction I understand a number of citizens, whether amounting to a majority or minority of the whole, who are united and actuated by some common impulse of passion, or of interest, adverse to the rights of other citizens, or to the permanent and aggregate interests of the community.

There are two methods of curing the mischiefs of faction: the one, by removing its causes; the other, by controlling its effects.

There are again two methods of removing the causes of faction: the one, by destroying the liberty which is essential to its existence; the other, by giving to every citizen the same opinions, the same passions, and the same interests.

It could never be more truly said than of the first remedy that it was worse than the disease. Liberty is to faction what air is to fire, an aliment without which it instantly expires. But it could not be a less folly to abolish liberty, which is essential to political life, because it nourishes faction than it would be to wish the annihilation of air, which is essential to animal life, because it imparts to fire its destructive agency.

The second expedient is as impracticable as the first would be unwise. As long as the reason of man continues fallible, and he is at liberty to exercise it, different opinions will be formed. As long as the connection subsists between his reason and his self-love, his opinions and his passions will have a reciprocal influence on each other; and the former will be objects to which the latter will attach themselves. The diversity in the faculties of men, from which the rights of property originate, is not less an insuperable obstacle to a uniformity of interests. The protection of these faculties is the first object of government. From the protection of different and unequal faculties of acquiring property, the possession of different degrees and kinds of property immediately results; and from the influence of these on the sentiments and views of the respective proprietors ensues a division of the society into different interests and parties.

The latent causes of faction are thus sown in the nature of man; and we see them everywhere brought into different degrees of activity, according to the different circumstances of civil society. A zeal for different opinions concerning religion, concerning government, and many other points, as well of speculation as of practice; an attachment to different leaders ambitiously contending for pre-eminence and power; or to persons of other descriptions whose fortunes have been interesting to the human passions, have, in turn, divided mankind into parties, inflamed them with mutual animosity, and rendered them much more disposed to vex and oppress each other than to co-operate for their common good. So strong is this propensity of mankind to fall into mutual animosities that where no substantial occasion presents itself the most frivolous and fanciful distinctions have been sufficient to kindle their unfriendly passions and excite their most violent conflicts. But the most common and durable source of factions has been the various and unequal distribution of property. Those who hold and those who are without property have ever formed distinct interests in society. Those who are creditors, and those who are debtors, fall under a like discrimination. A landed interest, a manufacturing interest, a mercantile interest, a moneyed interest, with many lesser interests, grow up of necessity in civilized nations, and divide them into different classes, actuated by different sentiments and views. The regulation of these various and interfering interests forms the principal task of modern legislation and involves the spirit of party and faction in the necessary and ordinary operations of government.

No man is allowed to be judge in his own cause, because his interest would certainly bias his judgment and, not improbably, corrupt his integrity. With equal, nay with greater reason, a body of men are unfit to be both judges and parties at the same time; yet what are many of the most important acts of legislation but so many judicial determinations, not indeed concerning the rights of single persons, but concerning the rights of large bodies of citizens? And what are the different classes of legislators but advocates and parties to the causes which they determine? Is a law proposed concerning private debts? It is a question to which the creditors are parties on one side and the debtors on the other. Justice ought to hold the balance between them. Yet the parties are, and must be, themselves the judges; and the most numerous party, or in other words, the most powerful faction must be expected to prevail. Shall domestic manufacturers be encouraged, and in what degree, by restrictions on foreign manufacturers? are questions which would be differently decided by the landed and the manufacturing classes, and probably by neither with a sole regard to justice and the public good. The apportionment of taxes on the various descriptions of property is an act which seems to require the most exact impartiality; yet there is, perhaps, no legislative act in which greater opportunity and temptation are given to a predominant party to trample on the rules of justice. Every shilling with which they overburden the inferior number is a shilling saved to their own pockets.

It is in vain to say that enlightened statesmen will be able to adjust these clashing interests and render them all subservient to the public good. Enlightened statesmen will not always be at the helm. Nor, in many cases, can such an adjustment be made at all without taking into view indirect and remote considerations, which will rarely prevail over the immediate interest which one party may find in disregarding the rights of another or the good of the whole.

The inference to which we are brought is that the *causes* of faction cannot be removed and that relief is only to be sought in the means of controlling its *effects*.

If a faction consists of less than a majority, relief is supplied by the republican principle, which enables the majority to defeat its sinister views by regular vote. It may clog the administration, it may convulse the society; but it will be unable to execute and mask its violence under the forms of the Constitution. When a majority is included in a faction, the form of popular government, on the other hand, enables it to sacrifice to its ruling passion or interest both the public good and the rights of other citizens. To secure the public good and private rights against the danger of such a faction, and at the same time to preserve the spirit and the form of popular government, is then the great object to which our inquiries are directed. Let me add that it is the great desideratum by which alone this form of government can be rescued from the opprobrium under which it has so long labored and be recommended to the esteem and adoption of mankind.

By what means is this object attainable? Evidently by one of two only. Either the existence of the same passion or interest in a majority at the same time must be prevented, or the majority, having such coexistent passion or interest, must be rendered, by their number and local situation, unable to concert and carry into effect schemes of oppression. If the impulse and the opportunity be suffered to coincide, we well know that neither moral nor religious motives can be relied on as an adequate control. They are not found to be such on the injustice and violence of individuals, and lose their efficacy in proportion to the number combined together, that is, in proportion as their efficacy becomes needful.

From this view of the subject it may be concluded that a pure democracy, by which I mean a society consisting of a small number of citizens, who assemble and administer the government in person, can admit of no cure for the mischiefs of faction. A common passion or interest will, in almost every case, be felt by a majority of the whole; a communication and concert results from the form of government itself; and there is nothing to check the inducements to sacrifice the weaker party or an obnoxious individual. Hence it is that such democracies have ever been spectacles of turbulence and contention; have ever been found incompatible with personal security or the rights of property; and have in general been as short in their lives as they have been violent in their deaths. Theoretic politicians, who have patronized this species of government, have erroneously supposed that by reducing mankind to a perfect equality in their political rights, they would at the same time be perfectly equalized and assimilated in their possessions, their opinions, and their passions.

A republic, by which I mean a government in which the scheme of representation takes place, opens a different prospect and promises the cure for which we are seeking. Let us examine the points in which it varies from pure democracy, and we shall comprehend both the nature of the cure and the efficacy which it must derive from the Union.

The two great points of difference between a democracy and a republic are: first, the delegation of the government, in the latter, to a small number of citizens elected by the rest; secondly, the greater number of citizens and greater sphere of country over which the latter may be extended.

The effect of the first difference is, on the one hand, to refine and enlarge the public views by passing them through the medium of a chosen body of citizens, whose wisdom may best discern the true interest of their country and whose patriotism and love of justice will be least likely to sacrifice it to temporary or partial considerations. Under such a regulation it may well happen that the public voice, pronounced by the representatives of the people, will be more consonant to the public good than if pronounced by the people themselves, convened for the purpose. On the other hand, the effect may be inverted. Men of factious tempers, of local prejudices, or of sinister designs, may, by intrigue, by corruption, or by other means, first obtain the suffrages, and then betray the interests of the people. The question resulting is, whether small or extensive republics are most favorable to the election of proper guardians of the public weal; and it is clearly decided in favor of the latter by two obvious considerations.

In the first place it is to be remarked that however small the republic may be the representatives must be raised to a certain number in order to guard against the cabals of a few; and that however large it may be they must be limited to a certain number in order to guard against the confusion of a multitude. Hence, the number of representatives in the two cases not being in proportion to that of the constituents, and being proportionally greatest in the small republic, it follows that if the proportion of fit characters be not less in the large than in the small republic, the former will present a greater option, and consequently a greater probability of a fit choice.

In the next place, as each representative will be chosen by a greater number of citizens in the large than in the small republic, it will be more difficult for unworthy candidates to practise with success the vicious arts by which elections are too often carried; and the suffrages of the people being more free, will be more likely to center on men who possess the most attractive merit and the most diffusive and established characters.

It must be confessed that in this, as in most other cases, there is a mean, on both sides of which inconveniencies will be found to lie. By enlarging too much the number of electors, you render the representative too little acquainted with all their local circumstances and lesser interests; as by reducing it too much, you render him unduly attached to these, and too little fit to comprehend and pursue great and national objects. The federal Constitution forms a happy combination in this respect; the great and aggregate interests being referred to the national, the local and particular to the State legislatures.

The other point of difference is the greater number of citizens and extent of territory which may be brought within the compass of republican than of democratic government; and it is this circumstance principally which renders factious combinations less to be dreaded in the former than in the latter. The smaller the society, the fewer probably will be the distinct parties and interests composing it; the fewer the distinct parties and interests, the more frequently will a majority be found of the same party; and the smaller the number of individuals composing a majority, and the smaller the compass within which they are placed, the more easily will they concert and execute their plans of oppression. Extend the sphere and you take in a greater variety of parties and interests; you make it less probable that a majority of the whole will have a common motive to invade the rights of other citizens; or if such a common motive exists, it will be more difficult for all who feel it to discover their own strength and to act in unison with each other. Besides other impediments, it may be remarked that, where there is a consciousness of unjust or dishonorable purposes, communication is always checked by distrust in proportion to the number whose concurrence is necessary.

Hence, it clearly appears that the same advantage which a republic has over a democracy in controlling the effects of faction is enjoyed by a large over a small republic—is enjoyed by the Union over the States composing it. Does this advantage consist in the substitution of representatives whose enlightened views and virtuous sentiments render them superior to local prejudices and to schemes of injustice? It will not be denied that the representation of the Union will be most likely to possess these requisite endowments. Does it consist in the greater security afforded by a greater variety of parties, against the event of any one party being able to outnumber and oppress the rest? In an equal degree does the increased variety of parties comprised within the Union increase this security? Does it, in fine, consist in the greater obstacles opposed to the concert and accomplishment of the secret wishes of an unjust and interested majority? Here again the extent of the Union gives it the most palpable advantage.

The influence of factious leaders may kindle a flame within their particular States but will be unable to spread a general conflagration through the other States. A religious sect may degenerate into a political faction in a part of the Confederacy; but the variety of sects dispersed over the entire face of it must secure the national councils against any danger from that source. A rage for paper money, for an abolition of debts, for an equal division of property, or for any other improper or wicked project, will be less apt to pervade the whole body of the Union than a particular member of it, in the same proportion as such a malady is more likely to taint a particular county or district than an entire State.

In the extent and proper structure of the Union, therefore, we behold a republican remedy for the diseases most incident to republican government. And according to the degree of pleasure and pride we feel in being republicans ought to be our zeal in cherishing the spirit and supporting the character of federalist.

PUBLIUS

NO. 51: MADISON

To what expedient, then, shall we finally resort, for maintaining in practice the necessary partition of power among the several departments as laid down in the Constitution? The only answer that can be given is that as all these exterior provisions are found to be inadequate the defect must be supplied, by so contriving the interior structure of the government as that its several constituent parts may, by their mutual relations, be the means of keeping each other in their proper places. Without presuming to undertake a full development of this important idea I will hazard a few general observations which may perhaps place it in a clearer light, and enable us to form a more correct judgment of the principles and structure of the government planned by the convention.

In order to lay a due foundation for that separate and distinct exercise of the different powers of government, which to a certain extent is admitted on all hands to be essential to the preservation of liberty, it is evident that each department should have a will of its own; and consequently should be so constituted that the members of each should have as little agency as possible in the appointment of the members of the others. Were this principle rigorously adhered to, it would require that all the appointments for the supreme executive, legislative, and judiciary magistracies should be drawn from the same fountain of authority, the people, through channels having no communication whatever with one another. Perhaps such a plan of constructing the several departments would be less difficult in practice than it may in contemplation appear. Some difficulties, however, and some additional expense would attend the execution of it. Some deviations, therefore, from the principle must be admitted. In the constitution of the judiciary department in particular, it might be inexpedient to insist rigorously on the principle: first, because peculiar qualifications being essential in the members, the primary consideration ought to be to select that mode of choice which best secures these qualifications; second, because the permanent tenure by which the appointments are held in that department must soon destroy all sense of dependence on the authority conferring them.

It is equally evident that the members of each department should be as little dependent as possible on those of the others for the emoluments annexed to their offices. Were the executive magistrate, or the judges, not independent of the legislature in this particular, their independence in every other would be merely nominal.

But the great security against a gradual concentration of the several powers in the same department consists in giving to those who administer each department the necessary constitutional means and personal motives to resist encroachments of the others. The provision for defense must in this, as in all other cases, be made commensurate to the danger of attack. Ambition must be made to counteract ambition. The interest of the man must be connected with the constitutional rights of the place. It may be a reflection on human nature that such devices should be necessary to control the abuses of government. But what is government itself but the greatest of all reflections on human nature? If men were angels, no government would be necessary. If angels were to govern men, neither external nor internal controls on government would be necessary. In framing a government which is to be administered by men over men, the great difficulty lies in this: you must first enable the government to control the governed; and in the next place oblige it to control itself. A dependence on the people is, no doubt, the primary control on the government; but experience has taught mankind the necessity of auxiliary precautions.

This policy of supplying, by opposite and rival interests, the defect of better motives, might be traced through the whole system of human affairs, private as well as public. We see it particularly displayed in all the subordinate distributions of power, where the constant aim is to divide and arrange the several offices in such a manner as that each may be a check on the other—that the private interest of every individual may be a sentinel over the public rights. These inventions of prudence cannot be less requisite in the distribution of the supreme powers of the State.

But it is not possible to give to each department an equal power of self-defense. In republican government, the legislative authority necessarily predominates. The remedy for this inconveniency is to divide the legislature into different branches; and to render them, by different modes of election and different principles of action, as little connected with each other as the nature of their common functions and their common dependence on the society will admit. It may even be necessary to guard against dangerous encroachments by still further precautions. As the weight of the legislative authority requires that it should be thus divided, the weakness of the executive may require, on the other hand, that it should be fortified. An absolute negative on the legislature appears, at first view, to be the natural defense with which the executive magistrate should be armed. But perhaps it would be neither altogether safe nor alone sufficient. On ordinary occasions it might not be exerted with the requisite firmness, and on extraordinary occasions it might be perfidiously abused. May not this defect of an absolute negative be supplied by some qualified connection between this weaker branch of the stronger department, by which the latter may be led to support the constitutional rights of the former, without being too much detached from the rights of its own department?

If the principles on which these observations are founded be just, as I persuade myself they are, and they be applied as a criterion to the several State constitutions, and to the federal Constitution, it will be found that if the latter does not perfectly correspond with them, the former are infinitely less able to bear such a test.

There are, moreover, two considerations particularly applicable to the federal system of America, which place that system in a very interesting point of view.

First. In a single republic, all the power surrendered by the people is submitted to the administration of a single government; and the usurpations are guarded against by a division of the government into distinct and separate departments. In the compound republic of America, the power surrendered by the people is first divided between two distinct governments, and then the portion allotted to each subdivided among distinct and separate departments. Hence a double security arises to the rights of the people. The different governments will control each other, at the same time that each will be controlled by itself.

Second. It is of great importance in a republic not only to guard the society against the oppression of its rulers, but to guard one part of the society against the injustice of the other part. Different interests necessarily exist in different classes of citizens. If a majority be united by a common interest, the rights of the minority will be insecure. There are but two methods of providing against this evil: the one by creating a will in the community independent of the majority—that is, of the society itself; the other, by comprehending in the society so many separate descriptions of citizens as will render an unjust combination of a majority of the whole very improbable, if not impracticable. The first method prevails in all governments possessing an hereditary or self-appointed authority. This, at best, is but a precarious security; because a power independent of the society may as well espouse the unjust views of the major as the rightful interests of the minor party, and may possibly be turned against both parties. The second method will be exemplified in the federal republic of the United States. Whilst all authority in it will be derived from and dependent on the society, the society itself will be broken into so many parts, interests and classes of citizens, that the rights of individuals, or of the minority, will be in little danger from interested combinations of the majority. In a free government the security for civil rights must be the same as that for religious rights. It consists in the one case in the multiplicity of interests, and in the other in the multiplicity of sects. The degree of security in both cases will depend on the number of interests and sects; and this may be presumed to depend on the extent of country and number of people comprehended under the same government. This view of the subject must particularly recommend a proper federal system to all the sincere and considerate friends of republican government, since it shows that in exact proportion as the territory of the Union may be formed into more circumscribed Confederacies, or States, oppressive combinations of a majority will be facilitated; the best security, under the republican forms, for the rights of every class of citizen, will be diminished; and consequently the stability and independence of some member of the government, the only other security, must be proportionally increased. Justice is the end of government. It is the end of civil society. It ever has been and ever will be pursued until it be obtained, or until liberty be lost in the pursuit. In a society under the forms of which the stronger faction can readily unite and oppress the weaker, anarchy may as truly be said to reign as in a state of nature, where the weaker individual is not secured against the violence of the stronger; and as, in the latter state, even the stronger individuals are prompted, by the uncertainty of their condition, to submit to a government which may protect the weak as well as themselves; so, in the former state, will the more powerful factions or parties be gradually induced, by a like motive, to wish for a government which will protect all parties, the weaker as well as the more powerful. It can be little doubted that if the State of Rhode Island was separated from the Confederacy and left to itself, the insecurity of rights under the popular form of government within such narrow limits would be displayed by such reiterated oppressions of factious majorities that some power altogether independent of the people would soon be called for by the voice of the very factions whose misrule had proved the necessity of it. In the extended republic of the United States, and among the great variety of interests, parties, and sects which it embraces, a coalition of a majority of the whole society could seldom take place on any other principles than those of justice and the general good; whilst there being thus less danger to a minor from the will of a major party, there must be less pretext, also, to provide for the security of the former, by introducing into the government a will not dependent on the latter, or, in other words, a will independent of the society itself. It is no less certain than it is important, notwithstanding the contrary opinions which have been entertained, that the larger the society, provided it lie within a practicable sphere, the more duly capable it will be of self-government. And happily for the *republican cause*, the practicable sphere may be carried to a very great extent by a judicious modification and mixture of the *federal principle*.

PUBLIUS

Glossary

administrative legislation Rules made by **regulatory agencies** and commissions.

administrative regulation Rules made by **regulatory agencies** and commissions.

affirmative action A policy or program designed to redress historic injustices against specified groups by actively promoting equal access to educational and employment opportunities.

agents of socialization Social institutions, including families and schools, that help to shape individuals' basic political **beliefs** and **values.**

agency representation The type of representation by which representatives are held accountable to their constituents if they fail to represent them properly.

agenda setting The power of the media to bring public attention to particular issues and problems.

Aid to Families with Dependent Children (AFDC) Federal funds, administered by the states, for children living with persons or relatives who fall below state standards of need. Abolished

in 1996 and replaced with **Temporary Assistance to Needy Families (TANF).**

amicus curiae Literally, "friend of the court"; individuals or groups who are not parties to a lawsuit but seek to assist the court in reaching a decision by presenting an additional briefs.

Antifederalists Those who favored strong state governments and a weak national government and who were opponents of the constitution proposed at the American Constitutional Convention of 1787.

antitrust policy Government regulation of large businesses that have established monopolies.

appropriations The amounts of money approved by Congress in statutes (bills) that each unit or agency of government can spend.

Articles of Confederation America's first written constitution. Adopted by the Continental Congress in 1777, the Articles of Confederation and Perpetual Union was the formal basis for

America's national **government** until 1789, when it was superseded by the Constitution.

Australian ballot An electoral format that presents the names of all the candidates for any given office on the same ballot. Introduced at the turn of the twentieth century, the Australian ballot replaced the partisan ballot and facilitated split-ticket voting.

authoritarian government A system of rule in which the **government** recognizes no formal limits but may, nevertheless, be restrained by the power of other social institutions.

autocracy A form of **government** in which a single individual—a monarch or dictator—rules.

balance-of-power role The strategy whereby many countries form alliances with one or more other countries in order to counterbalance the behavior of other, more powerful, nation-states.

bicameralism Division of a legislative assembly into two houses, chambers, or branches.

bilateral treaty A treaty made between two nations.

Bill of Rights The first ten amendments to the U.S. Constitution, ratified in 1791. They ensure certain rights and liberties to the people.

block grant A federal grant-in-aid that allow states considerable discretion in how the funds should be spent.

brief A written document in which attorneys explain why a court should rule in favor of their client.

budget deficit The amount by which **government** spending exceeds government revenue in a fiscal year.

bureaucracy The complex structure of offices, tasks, rules, and principles of organization that are employed by all large-scale institutions to coordinate the work of their personnel.

bureaucratic drift The oft-observed phenomenon of bureaucratic implementation that produces policy more to the liking of the **bureaucracy** than to the original intention of the legislation that created it, but without triggering a political reaction from elected officials.

Cabinet The secretaries, or chief administrators, of the major departments of the federal **government.** Cabinet secretaries are appointed by the president with the consent of the Senate.

casework An effort by members of Congress to gain the trust and support of constituents by providing personal service. One important type of casework consists of helping constituents obtain favorable treatment from the federal **bureaucracy.**

categorical grant-in-aid A grant by Congress to states and localities, given with the condition that expenditures be limited to a problem or group specified by the national government.

caucus (political) A normally closed meeting of a political or legislative group to select candidates, plan strategy, or make decisions regarding legislative matters.

checks and balances Mechanisms through which each branch of **government** is able to participate in and influence the activities of the other branches.

chief justice Justice on the **Supreme Court** who presides over the Court's public sessions.

civil law A system of jurisprudence, including private law and governmental actions, to settle disputes that do not involve criminal penalties.

civil liberties Areas of personal freedom with which governments are constrained from interfering.

civil rights Legal or moral claims that citizens are entitled to make on the government to protect them from the illegal actions of other citizens and government agencies.

class action suit A lawsuit in which large numbers of persons with common interests join together under a representative party to bring or defend a lawsuit, such as hundreds of workers together suing a company.

clientele agency Department or bureau of **government** whose mission is to promote, serve, or represent a particular interest.

client state A nation-state dependent upon a more powerful nation-state but still with enough power and resources to conduct its own foreign policy up to a point.

closed primary A primary election in which voters can participate in the nomination of candidates, but only of the party in which they are enrolled for a period of time prior to primary day. Contrast with **open primary**.

closed rule Provision by the House Rules Committee limiting or prohibiting the introduction of amendments during debate.

cloture Rule allowing a supermajority of the members in a legislative body to set a time limit on debate over a given bill.

coercion Forcing a person to do something by threats or pressure.

Cold War The period of struggle between the United States and the former Soviet Union between the late 1940s and 1990.

collective goods Benefits, sought by groups, that are broadly available and cannot be denied to nonmembers.

commander in chief The position of the president as commander of the national military and the state national guard units (when they are called into service).

commerce clause Article I, Section 8, of the Constitution delegates to Congress the power "to regulate Commerce with foreign Nations, and among the several States, and with the Indian Tribes. . . ." The Supreme Court interpreted this clause in favor of national power over the economy.

concurrent powers Authority possessed by *both state* and national **governments,** such as the power to levy taxes.

conference committee A joint committee created to work out a compromise on House and Senate versions of a piece of legislation.

conservative Today this term refers to one who generally supports the social and economic status quo and is suspicious of efforts to introduce new political formulae and economic arrangements. Conservatives believe that a large and powerful **government** poses a threat to citizens' freedom.

constituency Members of the district from which an official is elected.

constitutional government A system of rule in which formal and effective limits are placed on the powers of the **government**.

containment The policy used by the United States during the cold war to restrict the expansion of communism and limit the influence of the Soviet Union.

contracting power The power of **government** to set conditions on companies seeking to sell goods or services to government agencies.

contributory programs Social programs financed in whole or in part by taxation or other mandatory contributions by their present or future recipients. The most important example is **Social Security**, which is financed by a payroll tax.

cooperative federalism A type of **federalism** existing since the New Deal era, in which **grants-in-aid** have been used strategically to encourage states and localities (without commanding them) to pursue nationally defined goals. Also known as intergovernmental cooperation.

court of appeals A court that hears the appeals of trial court decisions.

criminal law The branch of law that deals with disputes or actions involving criminal penalties (as opposed to civil law). It regulates the conduct of individuals, defines crimes, and provides punishment for criminal acts.

de facto segregation Racial segregation that is not a direct result of law or **government** policy but is, instead, a reflection of residential patterns, income distributions, or other social factors.

defendant The individual or organization against whom a complaint is brought in criminal or civil cases.

de jure segregation Racial segregation that is a direct result of law or official policy.

delegate A representative who votes according to the preferences of his or her constituency.

delegated powers Constitutional powers that are assigned to one governmental agency but are exercised by another agency with the express permission of the first.

democracy A system of rule that permits citizens to play a significant part in the governmental process, usually through the election of key public officials.

deregulation A policy of reducing or eliminating regulatory restraints in the conduct of individuals or private institutions.

deterrence The development and maintenance of military strength as a means of discouraging attack.

devolution A policy to remove a program from one level of government by delegating it or passing it down to a lower level of government, such as from the national government to the states.

diplomacy The representation of a government to other foreign governments.

discount rate The interest rate charged by the **Federal Reserve** when commercial banks borrow in order to expand their lending operations; an effective tool of monetary policy.

discretionary spending Federal spending on programs that are controlled through the regular budget process.

dissenting opinion Decision written by a justice in the minority in a particular case, in which the justice wishes to express his or her reasoning in the case.

distributive tendency The tendency of Congress to spread the benefits of a bill over a wide range of members' districts.

divided government The condition in American **government** in which one party controls the presidency while the opposing party controls one or both houses of Congress.

dual federalism The system of **government** that prevailed in the United States from 1789 to 1937 in which most fundamental governmental powers were shared between the federal and state government with the state exercising the most important powers. Compare with **cooperative federalism.**

due process To proceed according to law and with adequate protection for individual rights.

economic-expansionist role The strategy often pursued by capitalist countries to adopt foreign policies that will maximize the success of domestic corporations in their dealings with other countries.

electoral realignment The point in history when a new party supplants the ruling party, becoming in turn the dominant political force. In the United States, this has tended to occur roughly every thirty years.

eminent domain The right of the **government** to take private property for public use, with reasonable compensation rewarded for the property.

entitlement Eligibility for benefits by virtue of a category of benefits defined by legislation.

equal protection clause A clause in the Fourteenth Amendment that requires that states provide citizens "equal protection of the laws." This clause has served as the basis for the **civil rights** of African Americans, women, and other groups.

equal time rule The requirement that broadcasters provide candidates for the same political office an equal opportunity to communicate their messages to the public.

establishment clause The First Amendment clause that says, "Congress shall make no law respecting an establishment of religion." This law means that a wall of separation exists between church and state.

exclusionary rule The ability of the court to exclude evidence obtained in violation of the Fourth Amendment.

executive agreement Agreement between the president and another country, which has the force of a treaty but does not require the Senate's "advice and consent."

executive order A rule or regulation issued by the president that has the effect and formal status of legislation.

executive privilege The claim that confidential communications between a president and close advisers should not be revealed without the consent of the president.

expressed power The notion that the Constitution grants to the federal government only those powers specifically named in its text. E.g. Those powers granted to Congress under Article 1, Section 8 of the Constitution, or specific powers granted to the president under Article II, Sections 2 and 3 of the Constitution.

expropriation Confiscation of property with or without compensation.

fairness doctrine An FCC requirement that broadcasters who air programs on controversial issues provide time for opposing views.

federal funds rate The interest rate on loans between banks that the Federal Reserve Board influences by affecting the supply of money available.

federalism System of **government** in which power is divided by a constitution between a central government and regional governments.

Federalists Those who favored a strong national government and supported the constitution proposed at the American Constitutional Convention of 1787.

Federal Reserve System (the Fed) Consisting of twelve Federal Reserve Banks, an agency that facilitates exchanges of cash, checks, and credit; it regulates member banks; and it uses monetary policies to fight inflation and deflation.

fighting words Speech that directly incites damaging conduct.

filibuster A tactic used by members of the Senate to prevent action on legislation they oppose by continuously holding the floor and speaking until the majority backs down. Once given the floor, senators have unlimited time to speak, and it requires a vote of three fifths of the Senate to end a filibuster.

fiscal policy The government's use of taxing, monetary, and spending powers to manipulate the economy.

Food Stamps Coupons that can be exchanged for food at most grocery stores; the largest in-kind benefits program.

formula grant A grant-in-aid in which a formula is used to determine the amount of federal funds a state or local **government** will receive.

free riders Those who enjoy the benefits of **collective goods** but did not participate in acquiring them. See also **public good.**

full faith and credit clause Article IV, Section I, of the Constitution provides that each state must accord the same respect to the laws and judicial decisions of other states that it accords to its own.

gender gap A distinctive pattern of voting behavior reflecting the differences in views between women and men.

General Agreement on Tariffs and Trade (GATT) The international trade organization, in existence from 1947 to 1995, that set many of the rules governing international trade.

gerrymandering Apportionment of voters in districts in such a way as to give unfair advantage to one political party.

going public A strategy that attempts to mobilize the widest and most favorable climate of opinion.

government Institutions and procedures through which a territory and its people are ruled.

grand jury A jury that determines whether sufficient evidence is available to justify a trial. Grand juries do not rule on the accused's guilt or innocence.

grant-in-aid A general term for funds given by Congress to state and local **governments.** See also **categorical grants-in-aid.**

grassroots lobbying A lobbying campaign in which a group mobilizes its membership to contact government officials in support of the group's position.

Great Compromise Agreement reached at the Constitutional Convention of 1787 that gave each state an equal number of senators regardless of its population, but linked representation in the House of Representatives to population.

habeas corpus A court order demanding that an individual in custody be brought into court and shown the cause for detention. *Habeas corpus* is guaranteed by the Constitution and can only be suspended only in cases of rebellion or invasion.

Holy Alliance role A strategy pursued by a superpower to prevent any change in the existing distribution of power among nation-states, even if this requires intervention into the internal affairs of another country in order to keep a ruler from being overthrown.

home rule Power delegated by the state to a local unit of **government** to manage its own affairs.

impeachment To charge a governmental official (president or otherwise) with "Treason, Bribery, or other high Crimes and Misdemeanors" and bring him or her before Congress to determine guilt.

implementation The efforts of departments and agencies to translate laws into specific bureaucratic routines.

implied powers Powers derived from the **necessary and proper clause** of Article I, Section 8, of the Constitution. Such powers are not specifically **expressed** but are implied through the expansive interpretation of **delegated powers.**

incumbency Holding a political office for which one is running.

indexing Periodic adjustments of welfare payments, wages, or taxes, tied to the cost of living.

informational benefits Special newsletters, periodicals, training programs, conferences, and other information provided to members of groups to entice others to join.

inherent powers Powers claimed by a president that are not expressed in the Constitution, but are inferred from it.

initiative The process that allows citizens to propose new laws and submit them for approval by the state's voters.

in-kind benefits Goods and services provided to needy individuals and families by the federal **government.** The largest in-kind federal welfare program is **Food Stamps.**

institutions The rules and procedures that guide political behavior.

interest group A group of people organized around a shared belief or mutual concern who try to influence the government to make policies promoting their belief or concern.

intermediate scrutiny The test used by the Supreme Court in gender discrimination cases. Intermediate scrutiny places the burden of proof partially on the government and partially on the challengers to show that the law in question is constitutional.

International Monetary Fund (IMF) An institution established in 1944 at Bretton Woods, New Hampshire, to provide loans to needy member countries and to facilitate international monetary exchange.

issue voting Electoral choice based on issue preferences rather than partisanship, personality, or other factors.

judicial activism Proclivity of a court to select cases because of their importance to society rather than adhere to strict legal standards of jurisdiction.

judicial restraint Judicial deference to the views of legislatures and adherence to strict jurisdictional standards.

judicial review Power of the courts to declare actions of the legislative and executive branches invalid or unconstitutional. **The Supreme Court** asserted this power in *Marbury v. Madison* (1803).

jurisdiction The authority of a court to consider a case initially. Distinguished from appellate jurisdiction, which is the authority to hear appeals from a lower court's decision.

legislative initiative The president's inherent power to bring a legislative agenda before Congress.

legislative supremacy The preeminence of Congress among the three branches of government, as established by the Constitution.

Lemon test Rule articulated in *Lemon v. Kurtzman* according to which governmental action in respect to religion is permissible if it is secular in purpose, does not lead to "excessive entanglement" with religion, and neither promotes nor inhibits the practice of religion.

libel A written statement made in "reckless disregard of the truth" and considered damaging to a victim because it is "malicious, scandalous, and defamatory."

liberal A liberal today generally supports political and social reform; extensive governmental intervention in the economy; the expansion of federal social services; more vigorous efforts on behalf of the poor, minorities, and women; and greater concern for consumers and the environment.

license Permission to engage in some activity that is otherwise illegal, such as hunting or practicing medicine.

line-item veto Power that allows a governor (or the president) to strike out specific provisions (lines) of bills that the legislature passes. Without a line-item veto, the governor (or president) must accept or reject an entire bill. The line-item veto is no longer in effect for the president.

lobbying Strategy by which organized interests seek to influence the passage of legislation by exerting direct pressure on members of the legislature; this term is derived from having to wait in the lobbies just outside the floor of the legislature, where outsiders are not permitted.

logrolling A legislative practice wherein reciprocal agreements are made between legislators, usually in voting for or against a bill. In contrast to bargaining, parties to logrolling have nothing in common but their desire to exchange support.

majority leader The elected leader of the party holding a majority of the seats in the House of Representatives or the Senate. In the House, the majority leader is subordinate in the party hierarchy to the Speaker.

majority party The party that holds the majority of legislative seats in either the House or the Senate.

majority rule Type of electoral system in which, to win a seat in the parliament or other representative body, a candidate must receive a majority of all the votes cast in the relevant district.

mandatory spending Federal spending that is made up of **"uncontrollables."**

Marshall Plan The U.S. European Recovery Plan, in which over $34 billion was spent for relief, reconstruction, and economic recovery of Western Europe after World War II.

material benefits Special goods, services, or money provided to members of groups to entice others to join.

means testing Procedure by which potential beneficiaries of a public assistance program establish their eligibility by demonstrating a genuine need for the assistance.

Medicaid A federally financed state-operated program providing medical services to low-income people.

Medicare National health insurance for the elderly and the disabled.

minority leader The elected leader of the party holding less than a majority of the seats in the House or Senate.

Miranda rule Principles developed by the **Supreme Court** in *Miranda v. Arizona* (1966) requiring those under arrest be informed of their legal rights, including right to counsel, prior to police interrogation.

monetary policy Effort to regulate the economy through manipulation of the supply of money and credit. America's most powerful institution in the area of monetary policy is the Federal Reserve Board.

mootness A criterion used by courts to screen cases that no longer require resolution.

most favored nation status An agreement to offer a trading partner the lowest tariff rate offered to other trading partners.

Motor Voter bill A legislative act passed in 1993 that requires all states to allow voters to register by mail when they renew their drivers' licenses and provides for the placement of voter registration forms in motor vehicle, public assistance, and military recruitment offices.

multilateralism A foreign policy that seeks to encourage the involvement of several nation-states in coordinated action, usually in relation to a common adversary, with terms and conditions usually specified in a multicountry treaty, such as NATO.

multiple-member district An electorate that selects all candidates at large from the whole district; each voter is given the number of votes equivalent to the number of seats to be filled.

Napoleonic role Strategy pursued by a powerful nation to prevent aggressive actions against itself by improving the internal state of affairs of a particular country, even if this means encouraging revolution in that country.

National Security Council (NSC) A presidential foreign policy advisory council composed of the president; the vice president; the secretaries of state, defense, and the treasury; the attorney general; and other officials invited by the president. The NSC has a staff of foreign policy specialists.

nation-state A political entity consisting of a people with some common cultural experience (nation), who also share a common political authority (state), recognized by other sovereignties (nation-states).

necessary and proper clause Article I, Section 8, of the Constitution, which enumerates the powers of Congress and provides Congress with the authority to make all laws "necessary and proper" to carry them out; also referred to as the "elastic clause."

New Jersey Plan A framework for the Constitution, introduced by William Paterson, which called for equal representation in the national legislature regardless of a state's population.

nomination The process through which political parties select their candidate for election to public office.

noncontributory programs Social programs that provide assistance to people based on demonstrated need rather than any contribution they have made. Also known as *public assistance programs*.

non-state actor A group other than a nation-state that attempts to play a role in the international system. Terrorist groups are one type of non-state actor.

North American Free Trade Agreement (NAFTA) A trade treaty among the United States, Canada, and Mexico to lower and eliminate tariffs among the three countries.

North Atlantic Treaty Organization (NATO) A treaty organization comprising the United States, Canada, and most of Western Europe, formed in 1948 to counter the perceived threat from the Soviet Union.

oligarchy A form of **government** in which a small group—landowners, military officers, or wealthy merchants—controls most of the governing decisions.

open-market operations The buying and selling of **government** securities to help finance government operations and to loosen or tighten the total amount of credit circulating in the economy.

open primary A primary election in which the voter can wait until the day of the primary to choose which party to enroll in to select candidates for the general election. Contrast with **closed primary**.

open rule Provision by the House Rules Committee that permits floor debate and the addition of amendments to a bill.

opinion The written explanation of the **Supreme Court's** decision in a particular case.

oral argument Oral presentations to a court made by attorneys for both sides in a dispute.

oversight The effort by Congress, through hearings, investigations, and other techniques, to exercise control over the activities of executive agencies.

party caucus (party conference) A normally closed meeting of a political or legislative group to select candidates, plan strategy, or make decisions regarding legislative matters.

party identification An individual voter's psychological ties to one party or another.

party vote A roll-call vote in the House or Senate in which at least 50 percent of the members of one party take a particular position and are opposed by at least 50 percent of the members of the other party. Party votes are rare today although they were fairly common in the nineteenth century.

patronage The resources available to higher officials, usually opportunities to make partisan appointments to offices and to confer grants, licenses, or special favors to supporters.

permanent campaign Description of presidential politics in which all presidential actions are taken with reelection in mind.

plaintiff The individual or organization who brings a complaint in court.

pluralism The theory that all interests are and should be free to compete for influence in the **government**. The outcome of this competition is balance and compromise.

plurality rule Type of electoral system in which, to win a seat in the parliament or other representative body, a candidate need only receive the most votes in an election, not necessarily a majority of votes cast.

pocket veto A presidential veto of legislation wherein the president takes no formal action on a bill. If Congress adjourns within ten days of passing a bill, and the president does not sign it, the bill is considered to be vetoed.

police power Power reserved to the state to regulate the health, safety, and morals of its citizens.

political action committee (PAC) A private group that raises and distributes funds for use in election campaigns.

political party An organized group that attempts to influence the government by electing its members to important government offices.

political socialization The induction of individuals into the political culture; learning the underlying **beliefs and values** upon which the political system is based.

politics The conflicts and struggles over the leadership, structure, and policies of government.

poll tax A state-imposed tax on voters as a prerequisite for registration. Poll taxes were rendered unconstitutional in national elections by the Twenty-fourth Amendment, and in state elections by the Supreme Court in 1966.

pork-barrel legislation Appropriations made by legislative bodies for local projects that are often not needed but are created so that local representatives can win reelection their home district.

precedent A prior case whose principles are used by judges as the bases for their decisions in a present case.

principal-agent relationship The relationship between a principal and his or her agent; this relationship may be affected by the fact that each is motivated by their own self-interest.

prior restraint An effort by a government agency to block the publication of material it deems libelous or harmful in some other way; censorship. In the United States, the courts forbid prior restraint except under the most extraordinary circumstances.

privatization Removing all or part of a program from the public sector to the private sector.

privileges and Immunities clause Provision from Article IV, Section 2, of the Constitution that a state cannot discriminate against someone from another state or give its own residents special privileges.

progressive taxation Taxation that hits the upper income brackets more heavily.

project grant A grant program in which state and local governments submit proposals to federal agencies and for which funding is provided on a competitive basis.

promotional technique A technique of control mat encourages people to do something they might not otherwise do, or to continue an action or behavior; Three types of promotional techniques are **subsidies**, contracts, and **licenses.**

proportional representation A multiple-member district system that awards seats based on the percentage of the vote won by each candidate. By contrast, the "winner-take-all" system of elections awards the seat to the one candidate who wins the most votes.

prospective voting Voting based on the imagined future performance of a candidate.

public good A good that (1) may be enjoyed by anyone if it is provided and (2) may not be denied to anyone once it has been provided. See also free riding.

public law Cases in private law, civil law, or criminal law in which one party to the dispute argues that a license is unfair, a law is inequitable or unconstitutional, or an agency has acted unfairly, violated a procedure, or gone beyond its jurisdiction.

public opinion Citizens' attitudes about political issues, personalities, institutions, and events.

public opinion polls Scientific instruments for measuring public opinion.

public policy A law, rule, statute, or edict that expresses the **government's** goals and provides for rewards and punishments to promote their attainment.

purposive benefits Selective benefits of group membership that emphasize the purpose and accomplishments of the group.

push polling A polling technique m which the questions are designed to shape the respondent's opinion.

recall Procedure to allow voters an opportunity to remove state officials from office before their terms expire.

referendum The practice of referring a measure proposed by a legislature to the vote of the electorate for approval or rejection,

regressive taxation Taxation that hits the lower income brackets more heavily.

regulated federalism A form of **federalism** in which Congress imposes legislation on the states and localities requiring them to meet national standards.

regulatory agency Department, bureau, or independent agency whose primary mission is to impose limits, restrictions, or other obligations on the conduct of individuals or companies in the private sector.

regulatory technique A technique the government uses to control the conduct of the people.

representative democracy A system of government that provides the populace with the opportunity to make the government responsive to its views through the selection of representatives who, in turn, play a significant role in governmental decision making.

reserved powers Powers, derived from the Tenth Amendment of the Constitution, that are not specifically delegated to the national government or denied to the states.

reserve requirement The amount of liquid assets and ready cash that the **Federal Reserve** requires banks to hold to meet depositors' demands for their money.

retrospective voting Voting based on the past performance of a candidate.

right to privacy The right to be let alone, which has been interpreted by the Supreme Court to entail free access to birth control and abortions.

right of rebuttal An FCC regulation giving individuals the right to have the opportunity to respond to personal attacks made on a radio or TV broadcast.

roll-call vote A vote in which each legislator's yes or no vote is recorded as the clerk calls the names of the members alphabetically.

senatorial courtesy The practice whereby the president, before formally nominating a person for a federal judgeship, will seek approval of the nomination from the senators who represent the candidate's own state.

seniority Priority or status ranking given to an individual on the basis of length of continuous service in a committee in Congress.

"separate but equal" rule Doctrine that public accommodations could be segregated by race but still be equal.

separation of powers The division of governmental power among several institutions that must cooperate in decision making.

signing statement An announcement made by the president when signing bills into law, often presenting the president's interpretation of the law.

single-member district An electorate that is allowed to elect only one representative from each district; the normal method of representation in the United States.

slander An oral statement made in "reckless disregard of the truth" and considered damaging to a victim because it is "malicious, scandalous, and defamatory."

social benefits Selective benefits of a group membership that emphasize friendship, networking, and consciousness raising.

Social Security A contributory welfare program into which working Americans contribute a percentage of their wages and from which they receive cash benefits after retirement.

solicitor general The top government lawyer in all cases before the appellate courts where the government is a party.

Speaker of the House The chief presiding officer of the House of Representatives. The Speaker is elected at the beginning of every Congress on a straight party vote. The Speaker is the most important party and House leader and can influence the legislative agenda, the fate of individual pieces of legislation, and members' positions within the House.

speech plus Speech accompanied by activities such as sit-ins, picketing, and demonstrations. Protection of this form of speech under the First Amendment is conditional, and restrictions imposed by state or local authorities are acceptable if properly balanced by considerations of public order.

spending power A combination of **subsidies** and contracts that the government can use to redistribute income.

standing The right of an individual or organization to initiate a court case.

standing committee A permanent committee with the power to propose and write legislation that covers a particular subject such as finance or appropriations.

stare decisis Literally "let the decision stand." A previous decision by a court applies as a precedent in similar cases until that decision is overruled.

state sovereign immunity A legal doctrine that holds that states cannot be sued for violating an act of Congress.

states' rights The principle that states should oppose increasing authority of the national government. This view was most popular before the Civil War.

strict scrutiny Higher standard of judicial protection for speech cases and other civil liberties and civil rights cases, in which the burden of proof shifts from the complainant to the government.

subsidy A government grant of cash or other valuable commodities, such as land, to individuals or organizations; used to promote activities desired by the government, reward political support, or buy off political opposition.

Supplemental Security Income (SSI) A program providing a minimum monthly income to people who pass a "means test" and who are sixty-five or older, blind, or disabled. Financed from general revenues rather than Social Security contributions.

supremacy clause Article VI of the Constitution, which states that all laws passed by the national government and all treaties are the supreme laws of the land and superior to all laws adopted by any state or any subdivision.

supreme court The highest court in a particular state or in the United States. This court primarily serves an appellate function.

tariff A tax placed on imported goods.

Temporary Assistance to Needy Families (TANF) A policy by which states are given block grants by the federal government in order to create their own programs for public assistance. See **Aid to Families with Dependent Children (AFDC)**.

third party A party that organizes to compete against the two major American political parties.

Three-fifths Compromise Agreement reached at the Constitutional Convention of 1787 that stipulated that for purposes of the apportionment of congressional seats, every slave would be counted as three-fifths of a person.

totalitarian government A system of rule in which the government recognizes no formal limits on its power and seeks to absorb or eliminate other social institutions that might challenge it.

trial court The first court to hear a criminal or civil case.

trustee A representative who votes based on what he or she thinks is best for his or her constituency.

uncontrollables Budgetary items that are beyond the control of budgetary committees and can be controlled only by substantive legislative action in Congress. Some uncontrollables such as interest on the debt, are beyond the power of Congress because the terms of payments are set in contracts.

unfunded mandates Regulations or conditions for receiving grants that impose costs on state and local governments for which they are not reimbursed by the federal government.

unilateralism A foreign policy that seeks to avoid international alliances, entanglements, and permanent commitments in favor of independence, neutrality, and freedom of action.

United Nations (UN) The organization of nations founded in 1945, mainly to serve as a channel for negotiation and a means of settling international disputes peacefully. It has had frequent successes in providing a forum for negotiation and on some occasions a means of preventing international conflicts from spreading. On a number of occasions, the UN has been a convenient cover for U.S. foreign-policy goals.

veto The president's constitutional power to turn down acts of Congress. A presidential veto may be overridden by a two-thirds vote of each house of Congress.

Virginia Plan A framework for the Constitution, introduced by Edmund Randolph, which called for representation in the national legislature based upon the population of each state.

War Powers Resolution A resolution of Congress that the president can send troops into action only by authorization of Congress or if American troops are already under attack or serious threat.

whip system Primarily a communications network in each house of Congress, whips take polls of the membership in order to learn their intentions on specific legislative issues and to assist the majority and minority leaders in various tasks.

World Trade Organization (WTO) The international trade agency promoting free trade that grew out of the General Agreements on Tariffs and Trade.

writ of *certiorari* A decision of at least four of the nine Supreme Court justices to review a decision of a lower court; from the Latin "to make more certain."

Index